Cornes and Lupton's Design Liability in the Construction Industry

Fifth edition

Sarah Lupton
MA DipArch LLM FCIArb CArb RIBA
Professor, Welsh School of Architecture, Cardiff University
Partner, Lupton Stellakis

WILEY Blackwell

This edition first published 2013

© 2013 Sarah Lupton and DL Cornes

Registered office:
John Wiley & Sons, Ltd, The Atrium, Southern Gate, Chichester, West Sussex, PO19 8SQ, UK

Editorial offices:
9600 Garsington Road, Oxford, OX4 2DQ, UK
The Atrium, Southern Gate, Chichester, West Sussex, PO19 8SQ, UK
2121 State Avenue, Ames, Iowa 50014-8300, USA

For details of our global editorial offices, for customer services and for information about how to apply for permission to reuse the copyright material in this book, please see our website at www.wiley.com/wiley-blackwell.

Library of Congress Cataloging-in-Publication Data
Lupton, Sarah.
  Cornes and Lupton's design liability in the construction industry / Sarah Lupton. – 5th ed.
    p. cm.
  Includes bibliographical references and index.
  ISBN 978-1-4443-3006-9 (hard cover : alk. paper)
  1. Architects–Malpractice–Great Britain. 2. Engineers–Malpractice–Great Britain.
  3. Construction contracts–Great Britain. I. Cornes, David L. Design liability in the construction industry. II. Title. III. Title: Design liability in the construction industry.
  KD2978.C67 2012
  346.4203'6–dc23
                         2011035005

A catalogue record for this book is available from the British Library.

Wiley also publishes its books in a variety of electronic formats. Some content that appears in print may not be available in electronic books.

Cover design by Workhaus

Set in 10/12.5 pt Minion by Toppan Best-set Premedia Limited
Printed and bound in Malaysia by Vivar Printing Sdn Bhd

[1 2013]

Contents

Acknowledgements

The author would like to express her gratitude to David Cornes for his enthusiastic agreement to the author's proposal for this new edition.

She is also grateful to the following people for their extremely helpful advice and, in many cases, for reading and commenting on draft sections of this book: Jerry Abeles of Arent Fox LLP, Tim Browne of Blainey North, Jeff Cooke of Allen Jack + Cottier, Ksenia Bruk of Salens, Professor Monika Chao-Duivis, director of the Dutch Institute of Construction Law and professor of construction law at the Technical University of Delft, Ashley Howlett of Jones Day, Professor Giovanni Iudica and Roberto Panetta of the Università Bocconi di Milano, Joachim Jobi and Alexandra Nicklas of the Federal Chamber of German Architects (*Bundesarchitektenkammer*), Benoît Kohl, Professor of the University of Liège and attorney of the Brussels Bar, David Lasfargue and Ekaterina Vilenskaya of GIDE, Luciano Lazzari of Studio Architetti Zelco Lazzari, Marlena Lubas of Arup Legal Group, Alasdair Niven and Melinda Parisotti of the Wren Insurance Association Ltd, Dr Jay Palmos of the British University in Dubai, Michel Process of Université Catholique de Louvain, UCL LOCI, Philip Ridgway of aaPGR – Prat Gigou Ridgway Architects, Sam Ross-Gower of RB-Architectes, Eric Teo of Al Tamimi & Company, and Katja Timmermann of Capita Symonds.

She would also like to thank her partner, Manos Stellakis, for his support and encouragement throughout the writing of this book.

Preface

This book examines the nature and extent of the liability of a designer in the construction industry, from the perspective of the consultant providing design services, and of the contractor engaged to design and construct. In doing so it explores how the courts and legislators have dealt with the processes and products of design, and the problems that have resulted when mistakes are made.

A recurring theme of the book is that of interfaces, as these are frequently areas of difficulty. For example there are often technical problems at the interfaces between different elements of a building, particularly if the design or construction of these is split between different tender packages. Where several consultants are involved, it can sometimes be difficult to determine where the role of one ends and another begins. Another grey area can arise in the consultant–contractor relationship when trying to determine the extent of the responsibility of one to point out the design errors of the other. Legally, also there are overlaps, including definitional (what is considered 'design' and what 'workmanship'); and between areas of the law, i.e. contract and tort (e.g. where parallel duties in tort may arise) or tort and statutory law (e.g. the Defective Premises Act 1972).

To set the scene, the book first looks at the industry context, including the role of the designer, who may currently be a professional architect or engineer, or a general contractor, or a specialist company designing, supplying and installing components or systems (simple product liability is covered briefly, but a detailed discussion is beyond the scope of this work). The book then sets out the basic legal framework, i.e. liability under statute, under contract and under tort. It then examines the differing levels of liability normally implied for a consultant or a contractor, i.e. that of negligence, and 'fitness for purpose'.

The core of the work discusses liability issues that might arise at different stages in the procurement process, including briefing (e.g. how relevant is the client's level of expertise) detailed design; special or innovative design; inspection; and the duty to review the design during construction. It also considers particular issues that arise in relation to contractual networks, examining the potential for tortious liability between team members, the use of warranties, and the implications of collaborative working and BIM.

Having mapped out the liability in these varying situations, the book then looks more closely at measures for limiting liability, for example through caps and net contribution clauses. It examines the more commonly used standard forms of contract, appointment and warranty and contract, to determine how these affect the nature and extent of the parties' obligations, particularly to what extent they seek to limit liability. There is also a chapter on PI insurance and its role in protecting the designer and its clients.

Finally, the book closes with two chapters outlining briefly the comparative position in key EU countries, and in selected jurisdictions outside the EU.

This is the fifth edition of the book of the same title by David Cornes. The fourth edition was published in 1994. There have been significant changes since then in all areas of the law relating to design liability, particularly in the law of tort. The full effects of *Murphy v Brentwood District Council* (1991) had at that time not yet been established, and in fact the last 18 years has witnessed many significant developments in the law of tort. In contract law there have been developments in the areas of letters of intent and contract formation, and there have been several new editions of key standard form contracts, for example 1998, 2005 and 2011 editions of JCT forms, the publication of NEC3 and PPC2000, and of a new suite of FIDIC forms.

The new edition draws to a certain extent on earlier editions, particularly on the very clear and authoritative sections introducing the fundamental principles of the law, for example of contract, tort, statute and insurance, which have been retained largely as they were in the fourth edition. However the majority of the book has been extensively re-written. The sections on dispute resolution have been removed, and some new sections have been added, including the chapters on liability in the EU and on other jurisdictions. Apart from the fourth edition, the sources of information used have been wide-ranging, including primary sources such as case law and legislation and secondary sources such as authoritative texts, research work and reports (all of which are referenced). With respect to case law, the emphasis has been in using cases that relate directly to the construction industry and design disputes, although others are also referred to where they are of fundamental legal importance. The material for the EU and other jurisdictions was drawn primarily from research studies, and cross checked by the author wherever possible with professionals working in the relevant country.

Sarah Lupton

Chapter 1
The Industry Context

This work explores the nature and extent of liability for design. Modern construction is a complex process, with many parties contributing to the design of buildings, including consultants, contractors and specialist manufacturers. When problems occur, questions arise as to who made the relevant decisions, whether they are liable for any resulting losses, and if so, to whom?

Many things will determine who is liable. The procurement route selected and the skills of those involved might provide an overall indication of the intended distribution of liability, but are by no means determinative. The next step is to examine the contract documents agreed between the parties. Often these will purport to precisely describe design duties, but sometimes will be unclear or incomplete.

External factors will also play a part. Legislation can affect the contractual provisions, operating to imply terms into an agreement, or to render terms void. It can also create a separate duty to third parties outside the contract. Designers can also become liable in tort to third parties. Consultants may therefore find themselves liable in ways they did not anticipate.

A simple model of design liability might be that the party that makes a design decision will bear liability if the decision is wrong. However, that simple model does not always arise. First, the parties might agree a different system, for example under a partnering or collaborative arrangement they might agree to share the risk of errors. Second, one party may be liable for the decisions of another, even when they thought they had delegated those decisions, for example a consultant will normally be liable for sub-consultants, and may be liable for design delegated to a specialist sub-contractor.

Therefore, even in simple procurement arrangements, the distribution of design liability can become quite difficult to pin down, and in modern complex procurement systems with many participating in the design process, the network of responsibility can become extremely intricate.

1.1 What is design?

In the author's view the answer to this question is very simple: any decision that affects the final form or composition of the building is a design decision. This covers a wide

Cornes and Lupton's Design Liability in the Construction Industry, Fifth Edition. Sarah Lupton.
© 2013 Sarah Lupton and DL Cornes. Published 2013 by Blackwell Publishing Ltd.

spectrum, from strategic space planning choices down to the smallest level of detail, such as the choice of fixings, adhesives, size of pipes and type of circuit breaker. As Sir Hugh Casson once put it, 'to design is to decide'.[1] A similar approach can be seen in this definition: 'Design is . . . the coming-into-being of an object which could be other than it is'[2] and in *Hudson's Building and Engineering Contracts*: '. . . the essential element of the function of design is choice'.[3] A more complex definition along the same lines was developed by the Design Council in relation to engineering education:

> Conceptual design involves identifying needs or requirements, weighing up and analysing possible solutions (including those that are already known) and coming to a properly thought out decision as to which design or designs will be most promising. The next, and equally important, phase is to reduce the concept to a practical scheme design that will show whether a useful product is likely to emerge. The detailed design must then be completed. This may mean that a set of detailed drawings, specifications and other documents have to be produced so that manufacturing and quality targets, together with satisfactory service in the field, can be achieved. The designer's task is not finished until it has been shown that the product can be manufactured, tested and maintained to cost targets, and that it performs properly at all points in the specified performance envelope, even when it is made from components at the extremes of the tolerances and degraded by reasonable wear.[4]

In practice an alternative approach is sometimes taken, for example some would say that smaller levels of detail are 'not really design', but something else, perhaps 'workmanship', and the term 'workmanship' is commonly used to refer to finer details of construction.[5] Often such details are worked out not by the consultant who is considered the primary 'designer' of a building, but often by manufacturers or craftsmen, through a process of preparing shop drawings. This approach is described in *Building Contract Disputes: Practice and Precedents*:[6]

> In the normal case of traditional contracts (i.e., where the design is not the responsibility of the contractor but that of the employer's architect) then much importance can be attached to the question of whether a defect is a design defect or a defect of workmanship. It is impossible to lay down hard and fast rules as to whether any particular defect will be one or another, for the choice between a flat roof and a pitched roof will be a matter of design, but the choice between a screw and a nail may well be a matter of workmanship. As a rule of thumb, the

---

[1] Sir Hugh Casson, Romanes Lecture delivered in Oxford, 12 November 1979, *The Guardian*, Saturday 24 November 1979.

[2] D. Fleming, 'Design Talk: Constructing the Object in Studio Conversations', *Design Issues*, 13(2), (1998), 41–62. The author thanks Dr Rachael Luck of Reading University for supplying this definition.

[3] (12th edn, 2010), para. 3–085.

[4] Design Council Committee on the Current Education of Engineering Designers in Britain, *Engineering Design Education* (London: The Design Council, 1976), para. 1.2.

[5] Atkins Chambers, *Hudson's Building and Engineering Contracts*, 12th edn (London: Sweet & Maxwell, 2010), para. 3–084.

[6] Robert Fenwick Elliot and Jeremy Glover, *Building Contract Disputes: Practice and Precedents* (London: Sweet & Maxwell, subscription series), para. 1–142.

shape, dimensions, choice of material and other matters apparent from the drawings are generally regarded as design matters and the things left over for the good sense of the contractor are generally regarded as matters of workmanship.

Another means by which smaller decisions are left to the contractor is through the use of performance specifications. As indicated in the Design Council definition, the result of the design process is usually communicated through detailed drawings, specifications and other documents. There are two types of specification, a prescriptive and a performance specification, and the distinction is significant. The former involves the precise and complete description of the materials and arrangement of these, whereas the latter specifies the performance required, together with provisions as to testing, assumed usage and maintenance, and leaves the means of achieving it up to the supplier or contractor. Therefore, when something is specified by performance, an element of design is always left to be completed.[7]

What people mean when they refer to 'design' can therefore vary. In practice this can sometimes cause confusion between parties, especially when agreeing the extent of respective parties' duties. It would only be critical with respect to liability if a court was to use its definition of design to assign liability, for example if a court were to start by deciding who is responsible for design, and then look at the error in question and decide if it constitutes design. If, on the other hand, the court simply analyses the contractual framework to determine who was responsible for that particular decision, then whether or not it is considered 'design' is a moot point.

The borderline between design and 'workmanship', the effect of any delegation of a detailed design decision, and the court's approach to these issues are recurring themes in this book. For clarity, the simple 'to design is to decide' definition is adopted throughout this book, and 'workmanship' is taken to be the *manner* in which the work is carried out, not *what* that work comprises, unless stated otherwise in the context of a particular discussion.

1.2 Procurement routes

Below is a brief outline of alternative procurement routes, included in order to highlight where in the process the design activity will occur. For a full explanation of the various advantages and problems, readers should consult one of the texts listed in the Bibliography.[8]

1.2.1 Traditional

'Traditional' procurement, as the name suggests, is the oldest formalised system for undertaking a building project, and is still the most commonly used system in the UK

---

[7] See Sarah Lupton, 'Performance Specification: the legal implications', *The International Construction Law Review* 13(1), (1996), 28–55, and Sarah Lupton and Manos Stellakis *Performance Specification: a guide to its preparation and use*, (London: RIBA Publications, 2000).

[8] e.g. Sarah Lupton et al., *Which Contract?*, 5th edn (London: RIBA Publishing, 2012).

(together with 'traditional plus design' as described below, accounting for around 76% of projects in 2010, and 41% of the total value).[9] In fact standard form construction contracts reflecting the traditional route can be traced back to the late nineteenth century. In traditional procurement it is assumed that the main role of the contractor is to carry out and complete the work, and that the design will be prepared by consultants engaged separately by the client. It is normally assumed that, subject to any express provisions to the contrary, the contractor has no obligation as to design, although in some circumstances a limited design obligation may arise. Usually a standard form traditional contract is administered by an independent contract administrator appointed by the client. A single stage tender procedure is normally adopted with full, detailed design information issued to the tendering firms, although an alternative two-stage tender process is sometimes used. Here the first tender is on limited design information, and the successful tenderer is then involved in the design finalisation, advising on its buildability and cost implications.

1.2.2 Traditional plus design

It is increasingly common within the context of traditional procurement, where the contractor is to carry out and complete the work, for the contractor to have limited obligations as to the design of discrete parts or aspects of the project. In fact it is rarely the case, at least in the UK, that the entire project, including the finest levels of detail and specialist systems such as structural glazing and heating, are designed entirely by the employer's directly engaged consultants. The contract can still be considered 'traditional' in the sense that the contractor's 'design' obligation is limited to an identifiable part or aspect of a project that is primarily designed by others. As above, the terms are usually administered by an independent contract administrator appointed by the client.

Frequently responsibility for the part to be designed will be delegated to a specialist company (common examples are cladding, glazing systems, tanking, and mechanical and/or electrical service systems). Less frequently the design of the discrete part will be sub-contracted to a consultant. In either case, the selection of the specialist sub-contractor or consultant can be left entirely to the contractor, and the contractor will retain responsibility for that design. However often the client will seek to retain a degree of control over that choice, either by requiring the contractor to engage a particular firm, or by limiting the choice to specific companies, or by being involved in the contractor's selection process and having the right to approve or reject the contractor's proposed company. For any of these options, the firm undertaking the design will usually be asked to enter into a collateral warranty with the employer. These contractual arrangements often give rise to complex issues regarding liability for any design errors that subsequently become apparent.

---

[9]RICS and Davis Langdon, *Contracts in Use; a Survey of Building Contracts in Use During 2010* (London: RICS, 2012).

1.2.3 Design-build

Design-build procurement emerged in the 1960s, largely in an attempt to speed up the production of new housing after the Second World War, but also with the aim of including the contractor's expertise in buildability in the design process. It is now the most common method of procurement for larger projects, accounting for around 39% of the value of projects undertaken in 2010.[10] In design-build procurement the contractor is required to carry out and to complete the work and in addition to design or to complete the design for the project. There is usually no independent contract administrator, although there is frequently a named employer's agent.

In many cases, although a design-build procurement route is adopted, the project will have been partly designed by a consultant appointed by the client before the contractor is approached. The design-build contractor may then be required either to take over responsibility for the entire design (as if it had been the designer from the start), or (a more limited obligation) to complete the partially finished design and to be liable for the design of only the completed part. In such cases establishing the cut-off point and the split of design responsibility between client and contractor must be handled carefully. As with traditional procurement, a two stage tender process is sometimes used. In design-build, this allows a period for the consultants to work with the contractor in developing the design proposals, prior to the contract being finalised. During this period the contractor may be appointed separately for advice and design services.

The role of the design consultant is to act throughout the project for one party, ie for the client or the contractor.[11] An alternative is for the consultant to swap from the employer to the contractor at the time the main design-build contract is let to the contractor, a process which is often (and sometimes inaccurately) termed 'novation'.

In a true novation (also called novation *ab initio*), the contract between employer and consultant is replaced by a contract on identical terms between the architect and the contractor. A simpler (although less accurate) way of describing the process is that the contractor will replace the employer as client under the original appointment. The contractor accepts all the obligations and liabilities that had formerly been the employer's under the appointment, and the consultant's prior and future obligations/liabilities are now owed to the contractor. A deed of variation to the appointment is required to reflect this change, which should include any necessary or preferred alterations. All three parties enter into a novation agreement. In reality, a novation of a consultant's services is rarely a true novation in this sense, as the services undertaken for the contractor are usually different to those undertaken for the employer. A novation *ab initio* may occur in other circumstances when, for example, a funder steps in and runs a project on behalf of an insolvent contractor.

An alternative arrangement, also often referred to as novation, but sometimes termed 'consultant switch', is for the original appointment with the employer as client to be

---

[10] ibid.

[11] Where two separate design firms are engaged, one by the employer and one by the contractor, this is sometimes termed 'bridging', especially in the US, see Justin Sweet and Marc M. Schneier, *Legal Aspects of Architecture, Engineering and the Construction Process* (Stamford: Cengage Learning, 2009).

brought to an end and a new appointment entered into between the consultant and the contractor. An agreement between all three parties is necessary to permit this change.[12] The consultant will normally remain liable to the employer for any breach of duty under the earlier appointment with the employer, but will not be liable to the employer for any default in services performed for the contractor (unless a consultant–employer warranty is entered into, which is often the case).[13]

1.2.4 Management methods

Management procurement is a more recent development, at least within the UK, dating from around the 1980s. In this system the contractor is appointed on a fee basis for managing the carrying out and completion of the work; the actual construction work is divided into 'packages' to be undertaken by specialist 'works' or 'trade' contractors. In the variant termed 'management contracting' the contractor enters into contracts on a rolling programme basis with successive trade contractors. In the other variant, 'construction management', the client enters into contracts with the specialist companies, the management contractor acting purely as an advisor to the client, arranging for the tendering of the packages and coordinating the specialist companies' work.

So far as design responsibility is concerned, this can lie entirely with the client's directly appointed design consultants, in the same way it would with traditional procurement. Each separate trade contractor is supplied with all information it needs to construct its section, and carries no design liability. More usually at least some of the packages are let on a design-build basis, with the trade contractor responsible for design and construction of its part. Usually the interfaces between packages are critical to the success of the project, particularly when packages are designed by different parties.

1.2.5 'Turnkey' contracting

There are several variants of design and build, whereby in addition to the contractor designing and constructing the project, the contractor takes on further responsibilities, for example running and maintaining the installation.

The term 'turnkey' contracting is often used where the contractor designs and builds the project, usually for a fixed price. The project is fully equipped, commissioned and handed over ready to operate. The system can also be termed Engineering, Procurement and Construction (EPC). In some cases the contractor can also provide financing and/ or land procurement services.[14] In a turnkey arrangement the owner provides a brief that describes the required outputs, including detailed performance specifications for the completed facility. Turnkey arrangements are typically used in large international engineering, power or process plant construction projects. A further variant is Build

---

[12]The CIC publish a Novation Agreement (CIC/NovAgr) for use in this situation.
[13]For a more detailed explanation see Construction Industry Council, Liability Briefing: *Novation of Consultants' Appointments on Design and Build* (London: CIC, 2008).
[14]Lawrence Bennett, *The Management of Construction: A Project Life Cycle Approach* (Oxford: Butterworth-Heinemann, 2003).

Operate Transfer (BOT) or Build Own Operate Transfer (BOOT; the terms are used synonymously), where the supplier will finance, design, build, operate, manage and maintain the facility, and then transfer it to the client (normally a government) following a concession period where the costs are recovered through, for example, levying a toll. As with turnkey contracting this is often used for utility projects, and also for transport and infrastructure projects such as major bridges and tunnels.

In the UK the Private Finance Initiative (PFI) is a particularly significant variant of these systems. Introduced by the Conservative Government in 1992, it is a means of transferring the risks associated with public service projects to the private sector in part or in full.[15] PFI is a form of public–private partnership (PPP) whereby a public infrastructure project is initially funded with private capital. In PFI a legal entity, known as a 'special purpose vehicle' (SPV), takes on the obligation for maintenance and, possibly, operation as well as design and construction of the facility. In PFI the costs are recouped from the public body during the operation period. In other types of PPP, the cost will be recouped from the users.

1.2.6 Partnering

Partnering was first used by the US Army Corps of Engineers in the late 1980s and was first applied in the UK in the North Sea oil and gas industries in the early 1990s.[16] Shortly afterwards the UK Government commissioned Sir Michael Latham to review the construction industry's procurement routes and contracts, and to propose solutions to problems the industry was facing. The resulting report[17] criticised the fragmented nature of the industry, finding the normal procurement routes inefficient and fostering an adversarial culture. It called for a more integrated and collaborative approach, and advocated the use of partnering. This influential report was swiftly followed by further initiatives and reports, including '*Partnering in the Team*'[18] and '*Trusting the Team: the Best Practice Guide to Partnering in Construction*'.[19] In 1998 the new concept of partnering was given further support by the government-sponsored Egan report.[20]

The partnering approach focuses on cooperative (rather than adversarial) working, to achieve common aims. It has been defined as:

> a management approach used by two or more organisations to achieve specific business objectives by maximising the effectiveness of each participant's resources. It requires that the parties work together in an open and trusting relationship based on mutual objectives, an agreed method of problem resolution and an active search for continuous measurable improvements.[21]

---

[15] House of Commons, *The Private Finance Initiative (PFI); Research Paper 01/117* (London: House of Commons, 2001).

[16] Chris Skeggs, 'Project partnering in the international construction industry', *International Construction Law Review*, 20(4) (2003), 456–82.

[17] Sir Michael Latham, *Constructing the Team* (London: HMSO, 1994).

[18] Construction Industry Board, *Partnering in the Team* (London: HMSO, 1996).

[19] John Bennett and Sarah Jayes, *Trusting the Team* (Reading: Centre for Strategic Studies in Construction, The University of Reading, with the partnering task force of the Reading Construction Forum, 1995).

[20] Sir John Egan, *Rethinking Construction: Report of the Construction Task Force* (London: HMSO, 1998).

[21] ibid., *Trusting the Team*, p. 2.

In theory, therefore, partnering can be used along with any of the above forms of procurement. There are two principle ways of doing this: the first is for all parties to agree to a simple 'mission statement', which sets out the parties' intention to work in a cooperative manner, in good faith, to achieve mutual goals. The second is to incorporate mechanisms for shared risks and rewards, linked to defined targets (e.g. that any cost savings below the target cost will be shared between the parties). In design terms, the collaborative working will often involve all parties contributing their expertise to the design process, including the contractor and specialist sub-contractors. The pain/gain mechanism may be linked to a quality objective such as a 'minimal defects' target or the measurement of the building's performance in use.

Although it was initially envisaged that the partnering team would be retained over several projects, the approach is often used on single contracts, termed 'single project partnering'. Since 2000 dedicated standard forms of contract have been published to cover this procurement method (e.g. see PPC2000 and the JCT Constructing Excellence). As partnering has received government approval, it has been used on many public projects, including those under the Private Finance Initiative.

1.2.7 Prime contracting

Prime contracting is a process that was advocated in the UK in the late 1990s as one of the three preferred government methods of procurement (along with design-build and PFI),[22] and is still used for a significant number of projects, particularly by the Ministry of Defence. It is often used with partnering, and the MOD has defined the prime contractor as responsible for 'the management and delivery of a project using a system of incentivisation and collaborative working to integrate the activities of the Supply Chain members to achieve a project that is on time, within budget and is in accordance with the specified outputs and it is fit purpose'.[23] Typically the prime contractor is required to design and construct the facility to meet stated purposes and to maintain it for up to seven years after completion to prove the design as constructed meets the stated performance requirements and operating costs.

1.2.8 Integrated project delivery and BIM

A recent development to emerge in the US is that of Integrated Project Delivery (IPD). This was first defined by the American Institute of Architects (AIA) in 2007 as 'a project delivery approach that integrates people, systems, business structures and practices into a process that collaboratively harnesses the talents and insights of all participants to reduce waste and optimise efficiency through all phases of design, fabrication and

---

[22] Issaka Ndekugri and Pauline Corbett, *Supply Chain Integration in Construction by Prime Contracting: Some Research Issues*, COBRA 2004 conference proceedings (London: RICS, 2004).
[23] ibid.

construction'.[24] Like partnering, it can be used with a variety of contractual structures, but it advocates the appointment of the whole team at an early stage, and the use of synchronised contracts, incentives and risk sharing. Standard form contracts drafted for use with IPD include the American Institute of Architects (AIA) A295 and C195 families of forms and ConsensusDocs 300, developed by a pan-industry group including contractor and sub-contractor organisations.

IPD is in turn is closely linked with developments in computer technology, such as Building Information Modelling (BIM). BIM has been defined as 'a model-based technology linked with a database of project information'[25] or, more fully as:

> a digital representation of physical and functional characteristics of a facility. As such it serves as a shared knowledge resource for information about a facility forming a reliable basis for decisions during its lifecycle from inception onward. A basic premise of BIM is collaboration by different stakeholders at different phases of the life cycle of a facility to insert, extract, update or modify information in the BIM to support and reflect the roles of that stakeholder. The BIM is a shared digital representation founded on open standards for interoperability.[26]

Although BIM is often referred to as if it were a procurement method in itself, it is essentially a digital tool that might be used in any context.[27] However, as reflected in the above definition, it is generally considered that to be used effectively it requires close collaboration between the parties. Similarly, although IPD is possible using traditional IT systems[28] these are seen not to be conducive to collaborative working, for example the AIA maintains 'Building Information Modelling . . . is essential to efficiently achieve the collaboration required for Integrated Project Delivery'.[29] Collaborative procurement methods and BIM are therefore seen as interdependent. BIM can be used at various levels:

0. *Unmanaged* CAD probably 2D, with paper (or electronic paper) as the most likely data exchange mechanism.
1. *Managed CAD in 2D or 3D format* using BS1192:2007 with a collaboration tool providing a common data environment, possibly some standard data structures and formats. Commercial data managed by standalone finance and cost management packages with no integration.
2. *Managed 3D* environment held in separate discipline 'BIM' tools with attached data. Commercial data managed by an ERP. Integration on the basis of proprietary

---

[24]American Institute of Architects California Council, *Integrated Project Delivery: A Working Definition*, v2, updated 13 June 2007 (California: McGraw-Hill, 2007), p. 1.

[25]American Institute of Architects California Council, *Integrated Project Delivery: A Guide* (California: McGraw-Hill, 2007), p. 10.

[26]National Building Information Model Standard (NBIMS) committee, cited ibid., p. 53.

[27]BIM Working Group, *BIM: Management for Value, Cost and Carbon Improvement*. A report for the Government Construction Client Group (London: March 2011).

[28]American Institute of Architects California Council, *Integrated Project Delivery: A Working Definition*, v2, updated 13 June 2007 (California: McGraw-Hill, 2007), p. 1.

[29]ibid.

interfaces or bespoke middleware could be regarded as 'pBIM' (proprietary). The approach may utilise 4D program data and 5D cost elements as well as feed operational systems.

3. *Fully open process and data integration* enabled by 'web services' compliant with the emerging IFC/IFD standards, managed by a collaborative model server. Could be regarded as iBIM or integrated BIM potentially employing concurrent engineering processes.[30]

BIM is widely used in the US, where two protocols were published in 2008 to allow its use with standard form contracts: the AIA E202 – 2008 BIM Protocol Exhibit and the ConsensusDOCS 301: BIM Addendum. It has also been adopted in other countries, for example BIM has been compulsory on public projects in Finland and Denmark since 2007.[31]

The UK government has confirmed its commitment to the adoption of BIM in its 2011 Construction Strategy, which stated that the government 'will require fully collaborative 3D BIM (with all project and asset information, documentation and data being electronic) as a minimum by 2016'.[32] BIM has already been used on high-profile projects in the UK (e.g. St Bartholomew's Hospital, Heathrow Express and Heathrow Terminal Five) and has been adopted by many larger practices within the UK, one recent survey indicating that 31% professionals are using BIM.[33] A BIM Protocol has recently been published by the Construction Industry Council (February 2013), and several of the more widely used standard forms of contract now include references to the use of BIM.

The use of IPD and BIM with its closely integrated development of the design on a common digital model, often accessed by all parties through an intranet system, is an interesting development that may raise particular problems when it comes to allocating and identifying design responsibility (see section 10.6).

1.3 The construction professions: who are the designers?

1.3.1 Architect

An 'architect' is one who possesses, with due regard to aesthetic as well as practical considerations, adequate skill and knowledge to enable him (i) to originate, (ii) design and plan, (iii) to arrange for and supervise the erection of such building or other works calling for skill in design and planning as he might in the course of his business, reasonably be asked to carry out or in respect of which he offers his services as a specialist.[34]

Architects are recognised throughout the world as the profession with the key role in the design of buildings. Depending on jurisdiction, the actual role, function and legal

---

[30] Building Information Modelling (BIM) Working Group, *BIM: Management for Value, Cost and Carbon Improvement*. A report for the Government Construction Client Group (London: March 2011).
[31] Martin Roberts, *BIM: Legal and Contractual Implications*, slides of presentation (London: RICS, 2012).
[32] The Cabinet Office, *Government Construction Strategy* (London: HMSO, 2011) p. 14.
[33] National Building Specification, *National BIM Report 2012* (London: RIBA Enterprises, 2012).
[34] *R v Architects Registration Tribunal, ex parte Jagger* [1945] 2 ER 131.

status of an architect varies considerably, as does their influence and significance within the construction industry. In the UK, the title 'architect' is protected by statute, in that only those who are registered with the Architects Registration Board (ARB) may use it.[35] In fact in the UK architecture is the only construction profession that has a protected title and is subject to statutory regulation. However there is no protection of function, as there is no requirement under the law to engage an architect (or other design professional) for any stage of the building design or construction process. This is not the case in other countries, where function but not title may be protected, and in some jurisdictions neither, or both, may be protected by that national legal system.

1.3.1.1 ARB and Registration

There are currently around 33,500 registered architects, of which about 21% are women.[36] ARB is established through the Architects Act 1997, which replaced the former larger Architects Registration Council of the UK (ARCUK) and repealed the Architects (Registration) Act 1931. The Board comprises seven members elected by persons on the register and eight persons appointed by the Privy Council in consultation with the Secretary of State. ARB is entirely funded through the subscriptions of the registered architects.

The primary role of ARB is consumer protection, in other words to ensure that those practicing under the title 'architect' are competent to do so. The competence levels are established through setting standards of entry onto the register, and through the requirement to comply with ARB's Code, which in turn refers to standards of conduct and practice.[37]

Persons are eligible for registration if they hold such qualifications and have gained such experience as ARB may prescribe, or if they have an equivalent standard of competence. For UK nationals this normally means that they must pass recognised Parts 1, 2 and 3 qualifications.[38] ARB prescribes these qualifications using published Criteria (agreed jointly with the RIBA) which set out required learning outcomes. In addition, applicants for registration are required to complete a minimum period of two years' professional experience which complies with rules agreed jointly with the RIBA.

In addition to the Board, the Architects Act 1997 makes provision for a statutory Professional Conduct Committee (PCC) which is responsible for disciplinary matters. This also comprises registered and appointed members, and it is notable that the majority on both the Board and the PCC lies with non-registered persons (i.e. outside the architectural profession). If a complaint is referred to the PCC it will consider all the evidence, including any alleged breach of the Code, and may dismiss the complaint, or implement a fine, a reprimand or suspend or remove the person from the register.

---

[35] Architects Act 1997, s. 20: 'A person shall not practise or carry on business under any name, style or title containing the word "architect" unless he is a person registered under this Act'.

[36] Figures from the ARB Annual Report 2012.

[37] The Code can be viewed on the ARB website at www.arb.org.uk.

[38] A list of these is available on the ARB website: www.arb.org.uk.

The ARB Code is primarily concerned with the protection of the interests of the public and relations between architects and their clients. It consists of an Introduction, 12 Standards and Guidance which are intended to be read together (although sections B and C of the Guidance do not form part of the Code). A section of the Code that is particularly relevant to design competence would be Standard 2:

Standard 2 Competence:

1. You are expected to be competent to carry out the professional work you undertake to do, and if you engage others to do that work you should ensure that they are competent and adequately supervised.
2. You are expected to make appropriate arrangements for your professional work in the event of incapacity, death, absence from, or inability to, work.
3. You are expected to ensure that the necessary communication skills and local knowledge are available to you to discharge your responsibilities.
4. You are expected to keep your knowledge and skills relevant to your professional work up to date and be aware of the content of any guidelines issued by the Board from time to time.

ARB publishes additional guidance on maintaining competence to practise as required under this Standard. The Code applies to all architects whatever the form of practice or business they choose to adopt. Employer architects and employee architects are equally bound to respect and observe the Code obligations. UK registered architects are still subject to the ARB Code when they practise abroad, and only if it can be shown that compliance would be inconsistent with local law and customs will any relaxation be possible.

1.3.1.2 RIBA

The largest professional body for architects, and the only one with exclusively architect membership, is the Royal Institute of British Architects (RIBA). The RIBA was founded in 1834 and currently has over 28,000 chartered members.[39] The RIBA is established by Royal Charter, and is a registered charity. Membership is voluntary, and the organisation is funded through the subscription of its members, the commercial activities of its various companies, and to a certain extent through bequeath.

The RIBA Council, a body of 60 members elected by ballot to ensure national and regional representation, is presided over by the President. This is an honorary office, and the Charter allows for 'such other Honorary Officers to be elected as the Byelaws prescribe'. At present these include Vice Presidents, an Honorary Secretary, and an Honorary Treasurer. The RIBA has recently set up a governing Board, responsible for directing the overall business of the RIBA. It operates under the overall authority and policy of the elected Council, and co-ordinates the operations of the subsidiary companies.

---

[39] Figure from RIBA online directory of members.

The RIBA Supplemental Charter 1971, in paragraph 2.1, states that 'the objects of the Royal Institute are the advancement of Architecture and the promotion of the acquirement of the knowledge of the Arts and Sciences connected therewith'. Ever since the original Charter, primacy has been given to the advancement of architecture, not to the advancement of architects. The RIBA therefore plays a key role in setting and upholding design standards, both generally and in the requirements for competence of its members. Currently RIBA efforts to advance the cause of architecture are expressed in many ways, for example through seeking to influence government and public opinion, providing support services for practitioners, and by striving to improve the status and competence of architects through continuing professional education and research.

As with ARB, two key mechanisms for achieving competence are through setting standards for entry, and through disciplining those who fail to display an acceptable level of competence as required by the RIBA Code.[40] Through its Code, its admission standards, appointing documents, and range of other publications, the Institute is able to assure the public of the standards of integrity and competence of its members.

The RIBA sets standards for entry through validating qualification, using the jointly held Criteria referred to above. The RIBA takes a keen interest in the way that architecture is handled in school curricula, and closely monitors the way that architecture is taught in higher education. It reviews courses and examinations in Schools of Architecture on a quinquennial basis, including through a visit to the school.

The most recent version of the RIBA Code of Professional Conduct came into effect in January 2005. The 2005 Code comprises an introduction, a statement of the Royal Institute's values, three principles of professional conduct, and brief notes that explain how the principles can be upheld. A series of nine related Guidance Notes are published separately. The RIBA website explains that these guidance notes are intended 'to provide both advice and information on best practice and to act as a support and aide to members in their professional work. They distinguish between conduct and practice which is obligatory and that which is only advisable or preferable. This distinction will be taken into account when a formal complaint of professional misconduct is made against a member.'

Inevitably the RIBA Code of Professional Conduct and Standard of Professional Performance has much in common with the ARB Code of Conduct although there are some differences. In particular, the RIBA Code's provisions covering the behaviour of members to each other has no equivalent in the ARB Code.

The Values are stated as follows:

Honesty, integrity and competency, as well as concern for others and for the environment, are the foundations of the Royal Institute's three principles of professional conduct set out below. All members of the Royal Institute are required to comply.

---

[40] The Code can be viewed at the RIBA website www.architecture.com.

The Code has three principles based on integrity, competence and relationships with others as follows:

Principle 1: Integrity. Members shall act with honesty and integrity at all times.

Principle 2: Competence. In the performance of their work Members shall act competently, conscientiously and responsibly. Members must be able to provide the knowledge, the ability and the financial and technical resources appropriate for their work.

Principle 3: Relationships. Members shall respect the relevant rights and interests of others.

In relation to Principle 2 – Competence, the Code states:

2.1 Members are expected to apply high standards of skill, knowledge and care in all their work. They must also apply their informed and impartial judgment in reaching any decisions, which may require members having to balance differing and sometimes opposing demands (e.g. the stakeholders' interests with the community's and the project's capital costs with its overall performance).

2.2 Members should realistically appraise their ability to undertake and achieve any proposed work. They should also make their clients aware of the likelihood of achieving the client's requirements and aspirations. If members feel they are unable to comply with this, they should not quote for, or accept, the work.

2.3 Members should ensure that their terms of appointment, the scope of their work and the essential project requirements are clear and recorded in writing. They should explain to their clients the implications of any conditions of engagement and how their fees are to be calculated and charged. Members should maintain appropriate records throughout their engagement.

2.4 Members should keep their clients informed of the progress of a project and of the key decisions made on the client's behalf.

2.5 Members are expected to use their best endeavours to meet the client's agreed time, cost and quality requirements for the project.

The RIBA requires all chartered practicing members to undertake CPD (RIBA Byelaw 2.8(a)). Guidance Note 6 explains what is required, and the RIBA's own CPD scheme can be found on the RIBA website.

1.3.1.3 ACA

The Association of Consultant Architects (ACA) is an organisation comprising members who are in private practice. All members are registered architects, and can form any size of or type of practice. It is run by a Council elected from its national membership. Like the RIBA, the organisation organises conferences and seminars, and acts as a political voice and lobbying body. It does not play a formal role in education, nor does it have its own Code of Conduct.

As a result of general dissatisfaction with the 1980 JCT Standard Form of Building Contract, in 1982 the organisation published its own 'ACA Form of Building Agreement', together with a form of sub-contract. This was supplemented in 2000 by a new standard form, the Project Partnering Contract (PPC 2000), which has grown to a suite of three forms. The ACA also publishes its own Standard Form of Appointment. In 1996 it launched an ACA Professional Indemnity Insurance scheme, together with Towergate Professional Indemnity Ltd.

1.3.2 Engineers

The engineers that have the closest involvement with the design and procurement of buildings are structural and mechanical services engineers. Professional engineers in the UK are not held as highly in the public esteem as they are in other EU countries and elsewhere. Neither the title nor the function are protected by law, whereas in other countries either or both may be regulated, and 'engineer' is often used as a title to the surname in the same way that 'doctor' is used in the UK. In Italy, for example the title is limited to people who both hold an engineering degree and have passed a professional qualification examination. In Portugal, professional engineer titles and accredited engineering degrees are regulated and certified.

In the UK the Engineering Council holds a national register of 235,000 Chartered Engineers (CEng), Incorporated Engineers (IEng), Engineering Technicians (EngTech) and Information and Communications Technology Technicians (ICTTech). However this is a voluntary organisation (not statutory). To join, members must already be members of another engineering institution, such as the Institute of Civil Engineers.

There are strict controls over entry to the major UK engineering institutions. The first institutions to be formed were the three institutions of civil, mechanical and electrical engineers (ICE, IMechE and IEE). There are now many more, of which the most likely to be encountered in the context of building construction are the Institute of Structural Engineers (IStructE) and the Chartered Institute of Building Services Engineers (CIBSE). Each of these has its own admission and membership requirements, for example, the Institute of Civil Engineers (the ICE) has various levels of membership. To become a Chartered Engineer requires accredited BEng (Hons) or BSc (Hons) or a MEng, to have completed an ICE approved training scheme (professional experience), and to pass a professional assessment. Becoming a Chartered Structural Engineer similarly involves holding an Institution-accredited MEng degree or the equivalent, successfully complete an IPD training programme, and passing a Professional Review Interview and a seven-hour Chartered Membership Exam. All members of both institutions are bound by rules of professional conduct, and disciplinary regulations are contained in the byelaws. All members are required to undertake CPD.

The Association for Consultancy and Engineering (ACE) exists to promote the advancement of the profession of those engineers who practise as consulting engineers. The ACE does not deal with educational standards or qualifications. It used to require its members to be Fellows of one of the institutes above but in 1993 the membership was changed to firms rather than individuals. The ACE has its own rules for professional conduct dealing with a great many aspects of a professional engineer's practice, including competence, limiting liability and insurance. The ACE also publishes terms of engagement which are widely used by consultant engineers.

1.3.3 Surveyors

As with engineers, there is a wide range of different types of surveyor. The most commonly encountered in UK construction projects is the quantity surveyor, although this profession is unusual in most other countries, where the role is performed by architects or engineers. There are also building surveyors, who in the UK may design buildings and perform many of the functions of an architect. They are more likely to be employed to prepare reports and give advice regarding property, especially in connection with refurbishment and repair, and to organise and supervise this work. They frequently act as expert witnesses regarding building defects.

The Royal Institute of Chartered Surveyors (RICS) is the leading professional institute for surveyors, with over 100,000 members. It is organised into a series of professional groups which include building surveying, building control, project management, quantity surveying and construction, facilities management, and property valuation. All RICS members must abide by a code of core ethical values. As with the above institutions, membership requires academic qualifications, practical experience and a final assessment. The RICS is very active in the industry and in research, organising conferences and publishing useful papers and reports, many of which are available on its comprehensive website.

1.3.4 General and specialist contractors

It is now common for contractors to take responsibility for design. Frequently the task of designing is delegated to a firm of consultants of one of the above disciplines, although sometimes the firm will engage in-house designers. For many specialist aspects of design, such as mechanical services or cladding panels, either the client or the contractor will engage a specialist company to design, manufacture and install.

There is no requirement for contracting firms to join any particular organisation, but there are many trade associations and representative bodies. Prominent among these are the UK Contractors Group (UKCG) and the Construction Alliance. The UKCG, which was formed in 2009, represents over 30 major contractors that undertake work in the UK. It supports several Codes, namely the UKCG Competition Law code of conduct, the UKCG Health and Safety Charter and the UKCG Anti-Bribery code of conduct. The Construction Alliance was founded in 2010, and comprises trade bodies such as the Civil Engineering Contractors Association (CECA), the Scottish Building Federation (SBF), the National Federation of Builders (NFB) and the Federation of Master Builders (FMB). Specialist contractors are represented primarily by the National Specialist Contractors Council and Specialist Engineering Contractors Group.

The Chartered Institute of Building (CIOB) was established in 1980. Its members must have construction-related qualifications and experience, and are drawn from a wide range of professional disciplines working within building and construction including construction managers and consultants as well as specialists in regulation, research and education. All members are required to abide by a code of conduct. The CIOB offers training and qualifications in a range of skills such as site supervision and site management, but not in any design-related activities.

1.3.5 Construction Industry Council (CIC)

The CIC is a membership body with representatives from many sectors of the industry, mainly professional institutions and business associations (although there are also research institutions and some individual honorary affiliate members). Its wide membership enables it to act as a forum for debate, to collate and disseminate industry views on issues of importance, and to liaise with other pan-industry bodies and with government. It publishes a range of documents including a consultant's appointment, several warranties, a novation agreement, and a series of Risk Management Briefings. It has recently published a BIM Protocol and related PII advice, enabled through funding from the Department for Business, Innovation and Skills.

Chapter 2
Liability under Contract

The designer can become liable for a design error under the law of contract, or tort, or, in some instances, under statute (as a criminal liability, and to those who have statutory rights). All three liabilities can coexist for the same error, but the starting point in assessing any liability is normally to examine the terms of any contract entered into by the designer. This section sets out the broad parameters of relevant contract law. Tort law and statute are dealt with in subsequent chapters.

An examination of the contract between parties is the first step in establishing the nature and extent of any liability for design. In the case of design consultants, this would be the terms of engagement with their clients, whereas with contractors it would be the building contract. Normally contractual obligations are owed only to the client commissioning the design services, although collateral warranties, assignment, and the Contracts (Rights of Third Parties) Act 1999 may create liabilities to other parties (people other than the client) as well. In the UK there have traditionally been few legislative controls over the terms parties may agree (under the principle termed 'freedom to contract'). This is in contrast to many other EU countries, where the obligations that may be agreed between parties are often highly regulated under the country's Civil Code, so that the Code will be a primary reference in determining these obligations (see Chapters 17 and 18). In the UK the agreed terms will be the main determining factor, and these vary considerably from project to project. There are, of course, widely used standard form contracts published by a variety of private and public institutions, but the range has increased rapidly over recent years. In addition (and perhaps unfortunately), parties in the UK are often asked to enter into contracts on non-standard or amended terms.[1] It is notable that in a recent move to reduce inefficiency and waste in construction procurement, the government has stated its intention to 'move towards using only standard forms of contract with minimal amendment for all new central government procurement activity',[2] however it will take time before this move has a significant effect on the industry.

Given the variety of possible terms that might be agreed, it is important to understand the principles that apply to interpreting contracts. It is therefore useful to set out

---

[1] See Construction Industry Council, *Benefits of Standardised Consultancy Contracts* (London: CIC, 2011).
[2] The Cabinet Office, *Government Construction Strategy* (London: HMSO, 2011).

Cornes and Lupton's Design Liability in the Construction Industry, Fifth Edition. Sarah Lupton.
© 2013 Sarah Lupton and DL Cornes. Published 2013 by Blackwell Publishing Ltd.

some of these key rules as derived from common law and legislation. In the UK, much of this law of contract derives from decisions of the courts rather than legislation, i.e. it depends on legal precedent, although there are a few key statutes that affect construction contracts. These rules govern the formation and discharge of a contract, the issue of a breach of contract and the damages that may be claimed. To a certain extent they will also control the content of contracts, implying terms into them where the parties have not dealt with a matter, limiting to what extent the parties may exclude liability for certain issues, and in some cases requiring specific clauses in all contracts of a particular type.

2.1 Formation of a contract

A contract comes into being where one person makes an offer, the offer is accepted and there is consideration for the promise made in the offer; or in other circumstances where, although no specific offer and acceptance can be identified, the court is satisfied that the parties have assumed contractual obligations to one another.

A contract for design work does not have to be in writing to be enforceable (although some contracts, e.g. hire purchase contracts, are required to be in writing). It follows that a contract can be created orally, such contracts being known as parol contracts. Sometimes a contract can be formed which is partly oral and partly in writing. For example, a designer might write to the employer saying: 'I am writing to confirm the agreement reached at our meeting today for us to carry out the design work that was discussed at the meeting, payment for which will be made on our scale of fees.' In such a case, there is consideration by way of the promise to pay on the scale of fees and the promise to undertake the design. There is also agreement as to the work that is to be carried out even though it is not described in the letter; it would be necessary in any proceedings for evidence to be given as to what the design work was. Clearly, there is scope for misunderstanding and uncertainty in such arrangements.

All text books and guidance notes advise that contracts should be fully set out in writing, and the Codes of Conduct of professional institutes normally require consultant designers to ensure that the terms of engagement are in writing.[3] However it is surprising how often work is undertaken where the exact terms are not in writing, or are uncertain and still under negotiation, and where formal contract documents have not been executed. Many disputes about design liability therefore often begin with a dispute about the contract: whether it exists, and what its terms are. These matters have to be established before there can be any real examination of the exact extent of the designer's obligations.

In establishing whether a contract has come into existence, the courts will look for three key elements:

[3] See, e.g. Standard 4.4 of the ARB *Architects Code: Standards of Conduct and Practice* (London: Architects Registration Board, 2010).

- intention to create legal relations
- consideration
- agreement.

The first two are not usually in doubt in the context of construction contracts. 'Intention to create legal relations' means what it says, i.e. there must have been an intention to form a binding agreement. Arguments regarding this requirement usually only arise with very informal arrangements, for example when friends get together to purchase lottery tickets. 'Consideration' means something given in exchange. The courts in England and Wales will not normally enforce a unilateral promise, unless there was something promised in exchange. The consideration does not have to be money (for example it could be a promise to do something or not do something), and it does not have to be a fair price, but it must be of some value.

Often, however, it can be difficult to establish whether agreement has been reached, and this is often a matter of dispute in itself. The courts analyse 'agreement' in terms of 'offer' and 'acceptance'. Agreement is reached when an unconditional offer is unconditionally accepted. In the context of professional services, if the professional submits a firm fee proposal to the client to carry out services, and this is accepted, then a contract will normally have been formed. In a contract to carry out works, the offer will usually be in the form of a tender to carry out specified work for a proposed sum.

As noted above, contracts can be oral, written, or partly oral and partly in writing. In an oral contract there must be clear evidence of words used at the time of contract formation that were intended by the parties to have legal effect as the terms of their contract, and in practice such evidence is often hard to establish. Contracts in writing can be in any format, for example an exchange of letters or emails between the parties. If the client accepts the terms of a written offer without qualification, a contract is formed. The acceptance can be oral, in writing, or by behaviour.[4] If the response contains a qualification (e.g. a request for a fee reduction), this is not an acceptance, but a counter offer, which the other party may accept in writing, or be deemed to have accepted by conduct.[5]

Once an offer is accepted, the next step is normally to record the contract in a set of formally executed contract documents. These documents should ideally be prepared as soon as agreement is reached, and before work is started. Failure to execute the documents does not necessarily mean that no contract is in existence, but can often lead to avoidable arguments about what was agreed.

2.1.1 Problems with contract formation

What can tend to happen in practice is that work can begin (including consultancy services, or construction works) at a point where, although some aspects of the contract

---

[4]For an example of acceptance by conduct, see *ERDC Group Ltd v Brunel University* [2006] BLR 255.
[5]For a full discussion of contract formation see Atkins Chambers, *Hudson's Building and Engineering Contracts*, 12th edn (London: Sweet & Maxwell, 2010), Section 1.2.

have been agreed, negotiations are still underway on some of the terms. In these cases it can be very difficult to work out whether agreement has, in fact, been reached. One party will then bring a claim seeking to rely on an alleged contract, and the other will deny its existence. Normally a court will endeavour to 'find' a contract amongst the correspondence and other evidence, particularly if the work in question is nearing completion, and where the parties have acted as if there was an agreement between them. A key aspect it will examine is whether all the 'essential' terms have been agreed.[6] These have been described as being (a) scope of work and the price (b) the contract terms (c) the start and finish dates.[7] However what is essential will also depend on the context, including whether the parties themselves have treated a matter as being essential.

Aspects of contract formation that seem to cause particular problems in practice are the use of 'letters of intent' and what is often termed the 'battle of the forms'.

2.1.1.1 *Letters of intent*

Letters of intent can take many forms. Those that simply express a hope or desire to enter into a contract at some point in the future are unlikely to be of binding effect. Agreements to negotiate are not recognised as binding and not enforced by the courts.[8] Often, though, the letter attempts to do more than that. In *Tesco Stores Ltd v Costain Construction Ltd*[9] work began on the basis of a 'letter of intent' and no formal contract was ever entered into. In this case the court decided that a contract had been formed by Costain countersigning and returning to Tesco the letter, which contained all the essential terms, and constituted the only document incorporated into the contract. HH Justice Ramsey helpfully explained what the courts understand by a letter of intent:

> It is part of the folklore of the construction industry that there exists a mythical beast, '*the Letter of Intent*', the legal effect of which, if it is acted upon, is that it entitles a contractor to payment for what he does, but does not expose him to any risk because it imposes no contractual obligations upon him. As Robert Goff J pointed out in the passage quoted in the preceding paragraph, in fact the legal effect of a letter of intent depends upon the true construction of the communications between the parties and the effect, if any, of their actions pursuant to those communications;[10]
>
> . . . It has become increasingly common in recent years in the construction industry for a form of 'letter of intent' to be employed which, while it does indeed contain a request to a contractor to commence the execution of works, also seeks to circumscribe the remuneration to which he will be entitled in respect of work done pursuant to the request in the event that no contract is concluded. Typically the 'letter of intent' will seek to provide that the remunera-

---

[6] *Courtney & Fairbairn Ltd v Tolaini Bros* (1975) 2 BLR 100 (CA).
[7] *Cunningham & others v Collett & Farmer* [2006] EWHC 1771 (TCC) HHJ Peter Coulson QC, at para. 90.
[8] *Multiplex Constructions (UK) Ltd v Cleveland Bridge UK Ltd* [2006] EWHC 1341 (TCC) is an example of this principle being applied.
[9] [2003] EWHC 1487 (TCC).
[10] ibid., para. 160.

tion of the contractor will not include any element of profit in addition to out of pocket expenses incurred in doing the relevant work or that the remuneration payable will be ascertained by someone like a quantity surveyor employed by the person making the request for work to be done. It is also likely to request that the addressee indicates his agreement to the terms set out in the 'letter of intent'. The natural interpretation of a 'letter of intent' of the sort now under consideration is that it is an offer to engage the addressee to commence the execution of work which it is anticipated will, in due course, be the subject of a more formal or detailed contract, but upon terms that, unless and until the more formal or detailed contract is made, the requesting party reserves the right to withdraw the request and its only obligation in respect of the making of payment for work done before the more formal or detailed contract is made is that spelled out in the 'letter of intent'. If an offer in those terms is accepted either expressly, as, for example, it could be by countersigning and returning a copy of the 'letter of intent' to indicate agreement to its terms, or by conduct in acting upon the request contained in the letter, it would seem that a binding contract was thereby made, albeit one of simple content.[11]

A letter of intent *can* therefore result in a binding contract, separate to the envisaged final contract, and based on the terms it contains or refers to[12]; however whether one is actually concluded will depend on the sequence of events and the wording of the letter itself. An example of the difficulties that may arise can be seen in the case of *Haden Young Ltd v Laing O'Rourke Midlands Ltd*.[13]

This concerned a sub-contract between Haden Young, a mechanical and electrical sub-contractor, and the main contractor Laing O'Rourke, which was never signed. In this case the price, scope and quality of the work to be carried out had been agreed, but other terms were not. Amongst other things, the sub-contractor wished to cap its liability for consequential losses to £1.5 million under both the sub-contract and related collateral warranties. The work was carried out and following practical completion, Haden Young claimed there was no contract between the parties, because all the essential terms were not agreed and it was therefore entitled to payment on a *quantum meruit* basis. Laing O'Rourke disagreed, arguing that the parties had agreed all the essential terms. The court agreed with Haden Young: what constituted an essential term for a particular contract was a matter for the parties themselves to decide. In this case, the limit of liability for consequential losses in the sub-contract and collateral warranty had been regarded as critical by the parties, and as no agreement had been reached on these terms, no contract had been concluded.

In extreme cases consultants may be found liable for failing to arrange for formal contracts. This occurred in *Trustees of Ampleforth Abbey Trust v Turner & Townsend Project Management Ltd*[14] where a project of the value of approximately £5 million was let on a series of letters of intent, with the result that the employer was unable to claim any liquidated damages for the extensive delays. Although the court was clear that there

---

[11] ibid., para. 162.

[12] For a further example of where a letter of intent did result in a contract see *Durabella v Jarvis & Sons* (2001) 83 Con LR 145.

[13] [2008] EWHC 1016 (TCC).

[14] [2012] EWHC 2137 (TCC).

was no absolute obligation to ensure that a formal contract was executed, in this case the Judge decided that TTPM had failed to take the steps that could reasonably be expected of a competent project manager for the purpose of finalising the contract, and was therefore negligent and in breach of its terms of engagement. He stated:

> The execution of a contract is to be seen not as a mere aspiration but rather as fundamental. It is the contract that defines the rights, duties and remedies of the parties and that regulates their relationships. Standard-form contracts, such as the JCT contracts, are precise, detailed and structured documents; their elaborate nature reflects the complexities of the projects to which they relate and attempts to address the many and varied problems that can arise both during the execution of the works and afterwards. By contrast, letters of intent such as those used in the present case are contracts of a skeletal nature; they pave the way for the formal contract, once executed, to apply retrospectively to the works they have covered, but they expressly negative the application of most of the provisions of the formal contract until it has been executed. They do not protect, and are not intended to protect, the employer's interests in the same manner as would the formal contract; that is why their 'classic' use is for restricted purposes.[15]

Where a 'letter of intent' or other correspondence is stated to be 'subject to contract' this will generally mean that the parties intend there to be no binding agreement until the contract is formally executed.[16] The case of *RTS Flexible Systems Ltd v Molkerei Alois Müller GmbH & Co*[17] is an example of the court making an exception to this principle. Here as above, work began under a letter of intent before contract terms were finalised. The claimant (RTS) supplied quotations for automated equipment to the defendant dairy manufacturer (Müller). Müller issued a letter of intent, confirming its wish to proceed with the project 'as set out in the offer', subject to finalisation of price and completion date. The letter provided for the whole agreed contract price and was not limited to the letter of intent period. It envisaged that the contract terms would be based on Müller's amended form of contract (MF/1) to be executed within four weeks of the date of the letter of intent. Work started, but negotiations continued and the letter of intent was extended for three months. A final draft contract was produced, setting out all the essential terms, but stating that the contract would not become effective until the parties had executed and exchanged the formal documents. This never took place, but the Technology and Construction Court (TCC) held that, after the lapse of the letter of intent, the parties had reached full agreement on the obligations relating to the work, and a contract was formed. Müller appealed and the Court of Appeal (CA) held that MF/1 could not become operative until signed and thus no contract had been concluded after the letter of intent lapsed. RTS then appealed, and the Supreme Court upheld the appeal, stating that all the essential terms were agreed, despite the draft written contract's provisions regarding execution. It should be noted that many commentators saw this as an unusual case, decided on its own particular facts. The Court itself emphasised that a court will not lightly find that a party has waived reliance on a 'subject to contract' term:

---

[15] ibid, Judge Keyser, para. 97.
[16] *Bennett (Electrical) Services Ltd v Inviron Ltd* [2007] EWHC 49 (QB).
[17] [2010] BLR 337 (SC).

... in a case where a contract is being negotiated subject to contract and work begins before the formal contract is executed, it cannot be said that there will always or even usually be a contract on the terms that were agreed subject to contract. That would be too simplistic and dogmatic an approach. The court should not impose binding contracts on the parties which they have not reached. All will depend upon the circumstances ...[18]

Lord Clarke stated that the moral of the case was 'to agree first and to start work later'.[19]

2.1.1.2 Disagreement over terms: 'battle of the forms'

It can quite often happen that during negotiations both parties send each other their standard printed terms, which conflict, and the conflicts are not noticed or resolved before work commences. *GHSP Inc v AB Electronic Ltd*[20] is an example of this type of disagreement, in which some useful principles of construction were outlined.

The claimant was a Michigan company that designed and manufactured electro-mechanical controls systems for motor vehicles. It placed orders with the defendant, an English company that manufactured industrial position sensors, for the manufacture of three-track pedal sensors. Unfortunately one batch of sensors was defective, and the claimant suffered substantial losses as a result.

The claimant argued that when it placed its order it clearly referred to its own standard terms as applying and that as the covering email had said 'use this email as your authorisation to proceed' the claimant had accepted these terms by its subsequent conduct, i.e. in delivering the ordered goods. The defendant on the other hand said that it did not accept the claimant's purchase order until it sent an 'acknowledgment of order' (AO), which expressly incorporated and referred to its own conditions (which significantly reduced its liability for losses). As the claimant had not immediately responded to or rejected the AO, and had accepted the subsequent deliveries, the contract was formed on these conditions. The Court decided that the contract did not include either set of standard terms because the parties had not reached agreement on their precise wording and there was no conduct that could be interpreted as accepting the other's terms. It helpfully summarised some of the key principles from previous cases where there is a 'battle of the forms', for example, it stated:

> In a case of 'Battle of the Forms', as in any other case of construction of contract, the test is objective (*RTS Flexible Systems Ltd v Molkerei Alois Müller GmbH & Co KG* [2010] 1 WLR 753), subject to the Court's entitlement and obligation to take into account the factual matrix; and ordinary principles of offer and acceptance and of certainty and sufficiency of terms apply as to when and how a contract (and what contract) is made.[21]

---

[18] ibid., paras 47 and 56.
[19] ibid., para.1.
[20] [2010] EWHC 1828 (Comm).
[21] ibid., para. 10.

It also confirmed that in most cases a contract is formed once the last set of terms is sent and received without the recipient objecting, and that one party can be found to have accepted the other party's terms by its conduct, provided that it is clear, looking at it objectively, that it intended to accept those terms. Where parties have not agreed which set of standard terms applies, there may be a contract, but one which incorporates neither party's conditions.[22]

2.2 Terms of the contract

2.2.1 Express terms

Even when it can be established with certainty that a contract has come into existence, there can often be arguments over what exactly has been agreed. Generally speaking, parties are bound by the terms of the contract that they have expressly set out. In practice there may be difficulties in establishing exactly what these terms are: they may be scattered amongst several documents, they may be ambiguous or contradictory, or they may be silent on some aspect of the matter under dispute. The process of piecing together and interpreting the terms of a contract is governed by a distinct area of law. Some of the more important rules are:[23]

- words should be given their ordinary literal meaning (one party is unlikely to be able to persuade a court that it intended an obscure or unusual meaning of a word or phrase). An 'objective bystander' test is used, so that the ordinary meaning would be preferred over an obscure one. However the context is important, particularly when trade or technical terms are considered, the 'meaning of words is a matter of dictionaries and grammars; the meaning of the document is what the parties using those words against the relevant background would reasonably have been understood to mean'.[24]
- where there is ambiguity or a conflict, generally a court will determine, on an objective basis, what it considers were the true intentions of the parties. For example, specially agreed terms will normally prevail over standard printed terms, as these are more likely to represent the parties' intentions. However this would not apply to some standard forms (e.g. JCT SBC11) as they contain a clause which states that the printed terms prevail
- the contract is usually construed most strongly against the party who drew it up (termed the *contra proferentem* rule). It is generally considered, however,[25] that this rule would not apply to JCT standard forms as they are negotiated, rather than drawn up by one party.[26] It may nevertheless apply to other contract documents such as a

---

[22] ibid., paras 11–13.
[23] Some of the rules are usefully set out by Lord Hoffmann in *Investors Compensation Scheme Ltd v West Bromwich Building Society* [1998] 1 All ER 98 at 114–115.
[24] ibid. at 115.
[25] Atkins Chambers, *Hudson's Building and Engineering Contracts*, 12th edn (London: Sweet & Maxwell, 2010), p. 41.
[26] ibid.

form of appointment, unless the terms in question had been specifically negotiated, and may also apply to any form that has been amended in significant respects

- generally speaking, evidence of previous negotiations is not admissible to contradict the express terms of the contract, although the document may be interpreted against the background knowledge available to a reasonable person at the time of contracting, including the 'matrix of fact'. Evidence of the factual background may also be used in relation to implied terms (see below).

Courts have recently taken a more flexible and pragmatic approach to the interpretation of contracts, focusing on determining the presumed intention of the parties, and using other legal rules regarding interpretation as a fallback where necessary. For example, it has been noted that:

the rejection of literalism when it conflicts with commercial commonsense is now seen as a regular feature of the House of Lords in construing commercial agreements[27]

And in *Chartbrook Ltd v Persimmon Homes Ltd* Lord Hoffman stated:

the meaning which the parties would reasonably be taken to have intended could be given effect despite the fact that it was not, according to conventional usage, an 'available' meaning of the words or syntax which they had used. . . .[28]

In the *Chartbrook* case, however, the House of Lords confirmed the rule that evidence of previous negotiations is inadmissible, and that the interpretation must remain objective (i.e. the parties' actual intentions are irrelevant).

2.2.2 Implied terms

In addition to the interpretative rules outlined above, there are several mechanisms whereby terms, which the parties have not expressly set out, may be implied into a contract.

A term can be implied 'in fact' or 'in law'. Terms are implied *in fact* to give effect to the presumed but unexpressed intentions of the parties and will not be implied if they would contradict the express terms. They are implied on the basis of the particular circumstances of that contract and normally must survive a 'test of necessity'; in other words, that without the implication the contract would be so unbusiness like that no sensible person would ever have agreed to it. The courts have not always applied the test with this degree of stringency, and will sometimes imply a term on the basis that it appears the parties intended it.

In addition, the courts' approach to the range of circumstances that can be looked at, sometimes referred to as the 'factual matrix', has varied considerably from a broad

---

[27] *Internet Broadcasting Corporation Ltd. v Mar LLC* [2009] EWHC 844 (Ch), para. 27.
[28] [2009] AC 1101 (HL), para. 37.

approach taking into account a wide variety of surrounding circumstances, to a very narrow one which confines itself to the 'four corners' of the contract documents. In practice it would be unwise to rely on a term being implied on the basis of the surrounding circumstances. In summary:

> ... for a term to be implied, the following conditions (which may overlap) must be satisfied: (1) it must be reasonable and equitable; (2) it must be necessary to give business efficacy to the contract, so that no terms will be implied if the contract is effective without it; (3) it must be so obvious that 'it goes without saying'; (4) it must be capable of close expression; (5) it must not contradict any express terms of the contract.[29]

Terms are implied *in law* where either a) they are always implied into that type of contract as a matter of legal incidence or b) through the operation of statute. In neither case is the term based on the presumed intention of the parties. The fact that a term contradicts the express terms of a contract will not necessarily prevent its being implied. An example of terms implied as a necessary incidence are certain obligations that would always be implied into contracts between landlord and tenant.

2.2.3 Terms implied by statute

There are a number of Acts that operate to imply terms into contracts. The most significant of these statutes in relation to design liability are the Sale of Goods Act 1979, the Supply of Goods and Services Act 1982 (both amended by the Sale and Supply of Goods Act 1994). Both of these Acts operate to protect the 'buyer', and derive from principles of law relating to consumer protection. The first is a development from the 1893 Act of the same name, and the second largely codified what was the position at common law. A basic outline of their provisions is given below, and their relationship to the level of design liability is discussed in Chapters 6 and 7.

2.2.3.1 Sale of Goods Act 1979

This statute implies terms into contracts for the sale of goods regarding title (s. 12), correspondence with description (s. 13) quality and fitness for purpose (s. 14) and sale by sample (s. 15). Section 14 states that:

(2)   Where the seller sells goods in the course of a business, there is an implied term that the goods supplied under the contract are of satisfactory quality.

(2A)   For the purposes of this Act, goods are of satisfactory quality if they meet the standard that a reasonable person would regard as satisfactory, taking account of any description of the goods, the price (if relevant) and all the other relevant circumstances.

---

[29] Lord Simon in *BP Refinery (Westernport) Pty Ltd v Shire of Hastings* (1978) 52 ALJR 20 at 26 (PC).

(2B) For the purposes of this Act, the quality of goods includes their state and condition and the following (among others) are in appropriate cases aspects of the quality of goods—
  (a) fitness for all the purposes for which goods of the kind in question are commonly supplied,
  (b) appearance and finish,
  (c) freedom from minor defects,
  (d) safety, and
  (e) durability.

The term 'satisfactory quality' was introduced by the amending Act in 1994, and replaces the older term 'merchantable quality'. The new definition clarifies what is meant by 'satisfactory quality', and in particular includes the concept that it should be fit for *all* the purposes for which goods of the kind in question are normally used. In addition, section 14(3) of the Sale of Goods Act states that:

(3) Where the seller sells goods in the course of a business and the buyer, expressly or by implication, makes known –
  (a) to the seller, or
  (b) where the purchase price or part of it is payable by instalments and the goods were previously sold by a credit-broker to the seller, to that credit-broker,
  any particular purpose for which the goods are being bought, there is an implied [term] that the goods supplied under the contract are reasonably fit for that purpose, whether or not that is a purpose for which such goods are commonly supplied, except where the circumstances show that the buyer does not rely, or that it is unreasonable for him to rely, on the skill or judgment of the seller or credit-broker.

In short, if the seller makes known the particular purpose for which goods are being bought, then the goods should be reasonably fit for that purpose, with the important exception where buyers do not rely, or where it would be unreasonable for buyers to rely, on the skill or judgement of the seller. What would be considered 'fit for purpose' would depend on the context, but would probably include the factors listed above in section 2B, for example consideration of safety, durability and performance.

The above Act of course applies only to contracts for the sale of goods, and most contracts that of relevance to this book will be either for services only (i.e. a professional consultant, or a contractor who executes work but without supplying materials), or a contract for work and materials. These all fall under the Supply of Goods and Services Act 1982.

2.2.3.2 Supply of Goods and Services Act 1982

This statute covers contracts for work and materials, contracts for the hire of goods, and contracts for services. Parts of the Act apply to the transfer of property in goods and these contracts are defined as ones under which one person transfers or agrees to transfer to another the property in goods, excluding excepted contracts. The exceptions do not include or extend to construction contracts and the provisions in the Act as to supply of goods therefore apply to construction works and design and build. There are provisions in relation to the selection, quality or the like of the goods. Section 3 provides that there will be an implied condition that the goods will correspond with the description where there is a contract for the transfer of goods by which the transferor transfers or agrees to transfer the property and the goods by description (ss. 3(1) and (2)).

Where there is a contract for the transfer of property in goods and the transferor transfers the property and the goods in the course of a business, then there is to be implied a condition that the goods supplied are of satisfactory quality (s. 4, subss. (1) and (2)). 'Satisfactory quality' is defined as per the Sale of Goods Act section 14 (2A) quoted above. That condition will not be implied where defects are specifically drawn to the transferee's attention before the contract was made or the transferee examined the goods before the contract was made as regards defects which that examination ought to have revealed (s. 4(3)).

As to fitness for the purpose, the Act provides that where the property in the goods is transferred in the course of business and the transferee makes known to the transferor a particular purpose for which the goods are being acquired, then there will be an implied condition that the goods are reasonably fit for that purpose, whether or not that is a purpose for which the goods are commonly supplied (s. 4, subss. (4) and (5)). However, as with contracts for the sale of goods, no implied condition that the goods are reasonably fit for their purpose will be made where the transferee does not rely, or it would be unreasonable for him to rely, on the skill and judgement of the transferor.

This position substantially puts in statutory form the existing common law position in building contracts; where the architect or employer selects particular materials and instructs the contractor to use them, they will not be relying on the contractor's skill and care and a condition that those goods will be fit for their purpose will not usually be implied in the building contract. The classic case that decided this point was *Young and Marten and McManus Childs*.[30]

In this case a contractor supplied tiles for roofs for a housing scheme from a supplier named by the employer. McManus Childs were the main contractors for a housing and Young & Marten were a firm of roofing sub-contractors. At a meeting before commencement of the works, McManus Childs suggested that certain roof tiles, called 'Somerset 13', should be used. Young & Marten agreed to the suggestion, and through its sub-sub-contractor obtained the required tiles from the manufacturer. Although on delivery they appeared to be sound, they later developed faults. The case proceeded to the House of Lords, and the key question for decision was whether the roofing sub-contractor should be held liable for the losses caused by the defective tiles. The sub-contractor, Young & Marten, had purchased the specified tiles in the ordinary course of business and fixed them in the required manner. No criticism was made of the quality of its work, or of the fact that it accepted the materials. The House of Lords decided that the sub-contractor impliedly warranted that the materials used would be of 'merchantable quality'. However as the tiles to be used were chosen by McManus

---

[30] [1969] 1 AC 454.

Childs, it had not placed reliance upon the sub-contractor in specifying this particular tile. Accordingly, the implied term as to fitness for purpose of the tile was excluded. However the House of Lords held that even if there was no reliance on the skill of the sub-contractor in the selection of the materials, that would not prevent the contract being subject to an implied term that the material supplied must be of merchantable quality.

The definition of a contract for supply of services in the Supply of Goods and Services Act 1982 is a contract 'under which a person ('the supplier') agrees to carry out a service'. This is so whether or not goods are also transferred or to be transferred under the contract (s. 12, subss. (1) and (3)). The effect of these provisions is therefore that the sections relating to supply of services will apply to architects, engineers, designers in general, contractors, and specialist sub-contractors.

The Act provides that, where a person acting in the course of a business supplies a service, there is to be an implied term that the services will be carried out with reasonable skill and care (s. 13). A consultant or contractor undertaking a design service would therefore be required to undertake it with reasonable skill and care, as would a contractor undertaking construction work. That particular implication by statute is the same as that to be implied at common law.[31]

Where there is already an express term in the contract as to carrying out the service with reasonable skill and care, that term will not negative the term to be implied by the Act unless inconsistent with it (s.16(2)). Furthermore, the contents of the Act do not prejudice any rule of law which imposes on the supplier of the service a duty which is stricter than that of reasonable skill and care (s.16(3)a). It therefore follows, for example, that where a design and build contractor is operating under a contract which impliedly or expressly imposes on the contractor an obligation that the design will be fit for its purpose, it will not be able to argue that this stricter duty is cut down by the implied term of the Act. The same applies to architects and engineers.

There are also terms to be implied by the Act providing that, where no time is fixed for the completion of the service, the obligation will be to complete the service within a reasonable time, and where the consideration for the service has not been fixed, the supplier will be paid a reasonable sum. The Act provides that what is a reasonable time and what is a reasonable sum are to be questions of fact (ss. 14 and 15).

As to whether the rights, duties and liabilities which arise by reason of the provisions of the Act can be negatived or varied, the Act provides that in respect of suppliers' goods and suppliers' services they can be negatived or varied by:

- express agreement
- course of dealing between the parties, or
- such usage as binds both parties to the contract.

Such exclusion of liability is expressly made to be subject to the Unfair Contract Terms Act 1977 (ss. 11(1) and 16(1)), discussed below.

---

[31] See e.g. *Lanphier v Phipos* (1838) 8 C & P 475 and *Duncan v Blundell* (1820) 3 Stark 6.

The Sale of Goods Act 1979 and Supply of Goods and Services Act 1982 (together with the restrictions on the right to exclude liability) are key consumer protection mechanisms in the context of construction, in that they set a base level standard of quality, namely that materials supplied should be of satisfactory quality and fit for their intended purpose, and that work will be carried out with skill and care. This principle has been extended through case law so that in contracts for work and materials, it will also normally be implied that the resulting component or building will also be fit for its intended purpose, unless it is clear that the buyer is not relying on the supplier's skill and judgment, or the terms of the contract exclude this reliance. The 'fit for purpose' obligation is discussed in more detail in Chapter 7.

A further Act that implies terms into construction contracts is the Housing Grants, Construction and Regeneration Act 1996 (as amended by the Local Democracy, Economic Development and Construction Act 2009) which requires all construction contracts falling within the definition of that Act contain certain provisions (the right to stage payments; the right to notice of the amount to be paid; the right to suspend work for non-payment; the right to take any dispute arising out of the contract to adjudication). However, although of great significance to the construction industry, as that Act is solely concerned with payment and dispute resolution it is outside the scope of this book.

2.3 Exemption clauses

More important for the purposes of this book is the scope for excluding liability under statute for quality and fitness for purpose. These limitations are contained mainly in two significant pieces of legislation, the Unfair Contract Terms Act 1977, and the Unfair Terms in Consumer Contracts Regulations 1994.

2.3.1 Unfair Contract Terms Act 1977

The Unfair Contract Terms Act 1977 (UCTA) applies to both business-to-consumer, and business-to-business contracts. It applies only to exclusion and limitation of liability clauses (and indemnity clauses in consumer contracts), including terms excluding certain liabilities in tort. It has the effect of rendering various exclusion clauses void. These include: any clauses excluding liability for death or personal injury resulting from negligence;[32] any attempt to exclude liability for Sale of Goods Act 1979, section 12 obligations (terms as to title) and the equivalent under the Supply of Goods and Services Act 1982;[33] and any attempt to exclude liability for Sale of Goods Act 1979, sections 13, 14 or 15 obligations (terms as to correspondence with description, quality and fitness for purpose, and sale by sample) and the equivalent under the Supply of

---

[32] s. 2(1).
[33] ss. 6(1) and 7(3A).

Goods and Services Act 1982, where they are operating against any person dealing as consumer. It also renders certain other exclusion clauses void in so far as they fail to satisfy a test of reasonableness. Examples are clauses excluding liability for negligence other than liability for death or personal injury,[34] which applies to all contracts, and liability for breach of sections 13, 14 and 15 obligations in contracts which do not involve a consumer.[35]

The term 'consumer' in 'dealing as a consumer' is defined in section 12(1) as a person who does not make the contract 'in the course of a business nor holds himself out as doing so'. In a construction context this would cover homeowners, etc., but might also cover a company or business, provided it is not acting in a business capacity, for example if it was commissioning work for the personal benefit of a director (a company that purchased a car for the personal use of a director has been considered to be acting as consumer as defined under the Act).[36]

The term 'reasonableness' is defined in section 11, and Schedule 2 to the 1977 Act gives guidance as to the test on reasonableness. This sets out a list of factors which must be considered and balanced in the light of all circumstances known at the time of contracting. The list includes: the strength of the bargaining position between the parties; whether the customer could have contracted with another party on different terms, whether the customer should have known of the term, and whether the goods were made to the specific requirements of the customer.

2.3.2 Unfair Terms in Consumer Contracts Regulations 1999

The Unfair Terms in Consumer Contracts Regulations 1999 were introduced to protect consumers against unfair standard terms in contracts that they make with sellers or suppliers. They are also designed to protect consumers from terms that reduce their statutory or common law rights and from terms that seek to impose an unfair burden on the consumer. Unlike UCTA they only apply to terms in contracts between a seller of goods or supplier of goods and services and a consumer. A consumer is defined as a 'natural person' who, in making a contract, is acting 'for purposes which are outside his trade, business or profession' (s. 3(1)), which unlike UCTA, would exclude businesses. An 'unfair term' is defined in regulation 5, and would include any term which has not been individually negotiated (this would generally include all standard forms) and which causes a significant imbalance in the parties' rights to the detriment of the consumer. The regulations state that any such term will not be binding on the consumer. Under regulation 6, terms which relate to the main subject-matter of the contract are not subject to the regulations, provided they are written in plain intelligible language, however any terms which are not clear will be interpreted '*contra proferentum*'. An indicative list of unfair terms is given in Schedule 2 and includes any term 'giving

---

[34] ss. 2(2).
[35] ss. 6(3) and 7(3).
[36] *R & B Customs Brokers v United Dominions Trust* [1988] 1 WLR 321 (CA).

the seller or supplier the right to determine whether the goods or services supplied are in conformity with the contract'[37] and also any term 'excluding or hindering the consumer's right to take legal action . . . particularly by requiring the consumer to take the dispute exclusively to arbitration . . . '.[38] It is important, therefore, if contracting with a consumer to ensure that any terms which could be seen as limiting the consumer's rights have been explained and discussed, in order that they can be considered to have been individually negotiated.

2.4 Privity of contract

The doctrine of privity in broad terms limits the right to bring an action for breach of contract to those who are parties to that contract, one of the results being that where a contract between two people purports to confer a benefit on a third, the third person cannot invoke the law to claim that benefit. There are some common law exceptions, but these are not relevant to the subject of this book. The doctrine began to receive some criticism, both from legal commentators and from the courts, in that it could in certain circumstances result in an unfair outcome for the third party. The voices of criticism became louder as a result of the reduction in scope for bringing a claim in tort following *Murphy v Brentwood District Council* (see Chapter 3). Partly as a result of this, the Contracts (Rights of Third Parties) Act was passed and came into effect in 1999. One of the stated objectives of the Act was that 'subsequent purchasers or tenants of buildings can be given rights to enforce an architect's or building contractor's contractual obligations without the cost, complexity and inconvenience of a large number of separate contracts'.[39]

2.4.1 Contracts (Rights of Third Parties) Act 1999

In broad terms, this Act created rights for a person not party to a contract to bring an action for breach of a contract, where that contract expressly gave a benefit, or purported to give a benefit to that person. The Act however allows parties to a contract to exclude its provisions and it is common to routinely exclude the Act from construction contracts and consultants' appointments. More recently, though, attitudes have changed and some standard form contract publishing bodies have incorporated provisions to take advantage of the statutory right. For example the 2003 JCT Major Projects Form was the first standard form of building contract to include a schedule of third party rights for funders, purchasers and tenants (later carried into the 2011 editions of the larger JCT forms).

---

[37] Schedule 2, para. 1(m).
[38] Schedule 2, para. 1(q).
[39] Law Commission report No. 242 (1996) *Privity of Contract: Contracts for the Benefit of Third Parties,* para. 1.2.

The Act provides that for the purpose of enforcing any term, the third party has the remedies that it would have had, had it been a party to the contract (although the Act makes it clear that the third party rights holder does not thereby become a party to the contract). Any restrictions or exclusions within the contract will, however, apply, as the third party can only enforce a term, subject to any other relevant contractual provisions. Contractual benefits resulting from the operation of the Act can be assigned in the same way as other contractual rights.

Developers and others now often use the Act as an alternative to warranties. The advantages are perceived as a reduction in the amount of documentation required, and consequential savings in cost and time. On the other hand, many third parties prefer to stipulate precisely their own terms and rights of action. A significant number of clauses are required to ensure that these rights are precisely defined in the main contract (rather than relying on a general right), and the person wishing to rely on the rights would of course want a copy of the relevant sections of the form, so some of the time/cost savings may be less than originally envisaged. Warranties are therefore still commonly requested.

2.5 Assignment

In a construction context, it often happens that the party who procures the building project decides to sell it on to a third party, and in many cases this may happen even before the construction work is complete. The person purchasing the property may wish to be able to bring an action against the contractor or consultant should defects later develop. One method of attempting to achieve this is by the person who procures the project assigning the contract to the third party (others are through the use of the Contracts (Rights of Third Parties) Act, or collateral warranties, see above and section 10.4).

Strictly speaking, it is the 'benefit' in the contract which is assigned. In law a party to a contract (the assignor) may assign the rights arising from the contract (the *benefit*) to a third party (the assignee) if it wishes, although it may not assign its obligations (the *burden*) without the agreement of the other party to the contract. For example in a contract to sell a car, the buyer may assign the right to receive the car (the benefit) but not the obligation to pay for it, and the car-dealer may assign the right to be paid, but not the obligation to supply the car. The law relating to assignment is complex, and the following is a brief outline only.[40]

An assignment is a unilateral act, not a contract, and therefore does not depend on there being any consideration.[41] Section 136 of the Law of Property Act 1925 lays down the formalities needed for a 'legal' assignment. These are as follows:

---

[40] This outline is based in part on Construction Industry Council, *Liability Briefing: Assignment* (Unpublished: CIC, 2008: in turn based on text by Tony Blackler).

[41] Note that the law of Scotland differs in this respect as Scottish contract law does not recognise the concept of 'consideration' and unilateral contracts are possible.

(i)   The assignment must be 'absolute', in writing and signed by the assignor personally.
(ii) It must relate to a debt or other 'legal thing in action'. (This would include the benefits arising under a contract or the right to sue for its breach).
(iii) Notice in writing must be given to the debtor.

There are also 'equitable' assignments, which may arise where the assignor attempts to assignee the rights, but the above formalities are not observed. Under an equitable assignment, the assignee may not later bring an action in its own name, it would need to join the assignor. There are also restrictions on what may be assigned.

It should be noted that once the assignment occurs, the assignor ceases to have an interest and can no longer make a claim. The requirement for the assignment to be 'absolute' means that it cannot be made subject to conditions, or be for a part only of a debt or thing in action, or by way of security rather than an outright transfer. The combined effect is that an owner/developer cannot retain any partial rights to bring an action, nor can it make a legal assignment of rights of action to several different purchasers or tenants. The assignment must be complete and to one party only.

Obviously developers and clients are likely to be keen to retain the option of assigning the right to bring claims to a subsequent owner, but conversely the designer or contractor is more likely to want to restrict or preclude this right. For this reason most standard forms contain a restriction or prohibition on assignment. The effectiveness of such clauses was confirmed in the *Linden Gardens* and *St Martins*[42] cases, which were heard together in the House of Lords in 1993. Also, it should be noted that there are restrictions on what damages may be claimed following an assignment. The assignee, though it sues for its own losses, will not be allowed to make a more extensive claim than the assignor himself could have made. However it will be able to claim for losses that it suffers following the assignment, even though at the time of the assignment no breach of contract had been established. The issue of damages following an assignment is discussed at section 11.4.

---

[42] *Linden Gardens Trust Ltd v Lenesta Sludge Disposals Ltd; St Martins Property Corporation Ltd v Sir Robert McAlpine & Sons Ltd* (1993) 63 BLR 1 (HL), see section 11.4.

Chapter 3
Liability under Tort: Part 1

The law of tort is the most complex area of the law that affects designers. A designer's contractual obligations can be determined initially through examining the contract terms themselves. Those arising under statute are determined primarily through the appropriate instrument (in both cases of course an examination of case law may also be required). However with tort there is no equivalent point of reference, the answers exist solely in case law. This means that it is more difficult to set out the law with certainty, and it is more subject to change. In fact there have been rapid changes and reversals over the last few decades, as discussed below.

There are several torts, and broadly they are all concerned with a wrongdoing between individuals, i.e. one party causing another harm. Not all instances of wrongdoing will fall under an area of tort, as this would prove too wide-reaching. Instead, what is or is not a tort, and the boundaries of what types of behaviours will give rise to a cause of action, have grown, shrunk and been consistently re-defined over the years.

Several torts are of direct relevance to designers, for example trespass, nuisance, public nuisance, but in practical terms claims in relation to design-related errors are most likely to be brought in the tort of negligence. Negligence in relation to design liability concerns a duty to take care when providing a design service that others (not just those with whom there is a contractual relationship) do not suffer harm as a result. Questions that any professional might ask are:

- Who can be liable?
- To whom might I be liable?
- What types of activity can give rise to negligence claims?
- How careful do I need to be?
- What sorts of outcomes (consequences) do I have to consider?

The answers to these questions, which might be summarised as the range of situations in which the tort may arise, has changed significantly over the years. The tort of negligence of course concerns not just designers (and in fact specific examples of designers being found liable are few and appeared relatively recently) so an examination of tort must begin with a broader consideration encompassing many fields of activity, before any conclusions can be reached with respect to design.

Cornes and Lupton's Design Liability in the Construction Industry, Fifth Edition. Sarah Lupton.
© 2013 Sarah Lupton and DL Cornes. Published 2013 by Blackwell Publishing Ltd.

In order to explain why the 'state of play' with respect to any design duty is difficult to state with certainty, it is necessary to look at the differing approaches taken to similar situations by courts, particularly in the last decade or so, and in order to understand these recent cases it is necessary to set out some of the 'building block' cases that established the key principles underlying the tort of negligence, still being refined today.

This chapter covers 'early' developments in the tort of negligence, up till what is generally considered a turning point in the case of *Murphy v Brentwood* in 1992 (the point at which the last edition of this book was published). There have been significant developments since that date, which are examined in the next Chapter.

3.1 Definition of a tort

The law of tort is separate and distinct from the law of contract. A breach of contract arises from the failure to perform an obligation undertaken by a party to a contract. Liability in tort arises independently of contract. Every book on tort begins by explaining how difficult it is to define a tort. It is a fact that a definition covering every aspect is extremely difficult. A simple, and rather simplistic definition is that a tort is any act or omission that infringes an obligation imposed by the law which gives the injured party the right to bring an action for damages.

A simple example of a tortious liability is that arising in cases of car accidents where there is no contractual arrangement between the parties; a liability arises on the part of the party at fault to make good the damages to the innocent party. Designers can, therefore, have a liability to make good damage to persons who are not parties to their design contracts.

3.2 Liability and parties in tort

It is beyond the scope of this book to consider those who could possibly be parties to an action in tort. However, the most common parties are likely to be companies and partnerships, as well as individuals. Insofar as companies are concerned, they can sue for all torts committed against them. There are, of course, some torts that cannot be committed against companies by reason of the fact that they are artificial legal entities. For example, a company cannot be assaulted.

All the partners of a firm are liable for any tort committed by a partner who committed the tort in the ordinary course of the firm's business or with the express or implied authority of the co-partners. This liability arises on the basis of vicarious liability (see below) because each partner is the agent of his or her co-partners.

3.3 Vicarious liability

A person who commits a tort is liable for the damage caused. Another person can also be liable in respect of the same tort even though he or she did not commit it. This can arise, for example, where an employee commits a tort in the course of employment; the employer will be liable for the tort of the employee. This is known as vicarious liability.

In considering vicarious liability lawyers normally use the terminology of 'masters' and 'servants'. Thus masters are liable for the tort of servants not only when they authorise it or ratify it, but also when the tort is committed in the course of a servant's employment. This raises two important issues: who is a 'servant' and what is the meaning of 'course of employment'?

People are 'servants' in circumstances where their employers have the right to control the work they do and the way in which they do it.[1] The test is whether there is a right of control and not whether control was in fact exercised in the particular case. It follows that where people are employed to carry out design work by a partnership or by a company, the partnership or company will be responsible for the torts of their employed designers provided the tort was committed in the course of the employee's employment.

The position of an employee or servant must be distinguished carefully from the position of an independent contractor. The term 'independent contractor' in a legal context means a person whose work is not under the control of the person for whom it is carried out. The employer of an independent contractor will not normally be liable for the torts of that contractor. An example can be seen in the case of *Rowe v Herman*,[2] where a homeowner engaged a contractor to construct a garage, and the contractor left an obstruction in the highway which a passer by tripped over and was injured. The Court of Appeal held that the employer was not liable. There are some exceptions to the rule that an employer is not liable for the tort of an independent contractor, which generally relate to extra hazardous work or to cases of nuisance or damage to neighbouring land. For example, a homeowner was found liable when builders he engaged caused damage to the adjoining property through faulty workmanship at the junction between the roof and the party wall.[3] However these exceptions are restricted in scope and are not likely to be of great importance when considering design liability.

It follows that, subject to the terms of any contract that may be relevant, if a designer delegates work to another party, the designer will be liable for that party's tort if he or she has the right to control the work and the way in which it is done (master and servant) but will not be liable where there is no right of control (independent contractor).

A resident engineer who is employed by, and whose salary is paid by, the building owner is a servant and not an independent contractor.[4] 'In the course of employment' means within the scope of those categories of work which the employee was employed to carry out. It follows that where a designer is employed to carry out design and is negligent in that work, then provided an action can be brought in tort, the employer, as

---

[1] *Hewitt v Bonvin* [1940] 1 KB 762; *Mersey Docks and Harbour Board v Coggins & Griffith (Liverpool) Ltd* [1947] AC 1; *Biffa Waste Services Ltd v Maschinefabrak Ernst Hese GmBH* [2009] BLR 1 (CA).
[2] (1997) 58 Con LR 33 (CA).
[3] *Alcock v Wraith* (1982) 58 BLR 16; *Biffa Waste Services Ltd v Maschinefabrak Ernst Hese GmBH* [2009] BLR 1 (CA).
[4] *Morran v Swinton and Pendlebury Borough Council* [1965] 1 WLR 576.

well as the employee, will be liable in respect of that negligence. An injured party in such circumstances can elect to sue the employer or the employee, or both. In cases where the employer's contract with the innocent party has a clause excluding or limiting the employer's liability, provided there is a cause of action in tort, there is nothing to prevent the injured party suing the employee, who normally cannot rely upon the exclusion clause in his employer's contract, as she or he is not a party to that contract.[5]

Furthermore it has been held by the House of Lords in *Lister v Romford Ice and Cold Storage Co Ltd*[6] that employees have a duty to perform their work with reasonable skill and care, and that if any employee, by their negligence, causes the employer to be vicariously liable for a tort, the employee will be liable to the employer for breach of contract. The basis of this finding was that the House of Lords held that a term is to be implied into the contract of employment that an employee will indemnify his or her employer in respect of the employer's loss that arises from the employee's negligence. In the *Lister* case, a lorry driver employed by a company negligently reversed a lorry into his father who was also employed by the same company. The company's insurers paid damages to the father and then sued the lorry driver to recover what they had paid to the father. The court held that they could recover damages by reason of a breach by the lorry driver of his duty to perform his work with reasonable skill and care.

In such a case, the damages awarded against the employee are likely to be the full amount of the employer's loss. Where the employer is insured there will be nothing to prevent the insurance company from making use of its rights of subrogation, bringing an action against the employee to recover the sums that it has paid (but see section 16.3.4). Nor is there anything in law or practice which prevents an employer, who has suffered loss as the result of the conduct of an employee, for recovering its loss from the employee.[7]

3.4 Negligence

The tort of negligence is concerned with breach of duty to take care. This duty arises independently of any contractual relationship. In order to succeed in an action for negligence a claimant must prove that the:

- the defendant owed the claimant a legal duty of care, and
- the defendant was in breach of that duty, and
- the claimant has suffered damage as a result of the breach.

Whether there is or is not a duty of care in a particular case is a question of law. The courts now have a long series of cases to guide them in deciding whether there is a duty of care.

---

[5] *Adler v Dixon* [1955] 1 QB 158: the effect of exclusion clauses is considered further at Chapter 10.
[6] [1957] AC 555 (HL).
[7] *Janata Bank v Ahmed* (1981) IRLR 457.

3.4.1 Existence of a duty of care

In 1932 the celebrated case of *Donoghue (or McAlister) v Stevenson*[8] reached the courts. A young lady was bought a bottle of ginger beer by a friend. She had drunk some of the ginger beer, which was in an opaque bottle, before she discovered that there was a decomposing snail within the bottle. It was alleged she became ill as a result. There was no question in this case of the friend bringing an action in contract under the then Sale of Goods Act (1893) against the retailer from whom the ginger beer had been purchased because the friend had not suffered any damage. The plaintiff could not sue the retailer because she had no contract with him.

The House of Lords was asked whether she had a cause of action against the manufacturer. The question was stated by Lord Atkin in these terms:

> The question is whether the manufacturer of an article of drink sold by him to a distributor, in circumstances which prevent the distributor or ultimate purchaser or consumer from discovering by inspection by any defect, is under any legal duty to the ultimate purchaser or consumer to take reasonable care that the article is free from defect likely to cause injury to health.[9]

The House held that a manufacturer that sold products in such a form that they were likely to reach the ultimate consumer in the state in which they left the manufacturer, with no possibility of intermediate action, owed a duty to the consumer to take reasonable care to prevent injury. In order to understand what a radical departure and important step this was for the development of the law of the England and indeed the UK, it is only necessary to look at the dissenting judgment of Lord Buckmaster in that case:

> There can be no special duty attaching to the manufacture of food apart from that implied by contract or imposed by statute. If such a duty exists, it seems to me it must cover the construction of every article, and I cannot see any reason why it should not apply to the construction of a house. If one step than why not 50? If a house be, as it sometimes is, negligently built and in consequence of that negligence the ceiling falls and injures the occupier or anyone else, no action against the builder exists according to English law, although I believe such a right did exist according to the laws of Babylon.[10]

Lord Buckmaster's view did not prevail, and the majority reached a different conclusion. Lord Atkin formulated a principle so as to test whether a duty of care exists, which in summary runs like this: there must be personal injury or there must be damage to the injured party's property, other than the product itself and there must have been no reasonable possibility of intermediate examination which would have enabled the injured party to realise the possibility of harm before it occurred. Or in Lord Atkin's own words:

---

[8] [1932] AC 562 (HL).
[9] ibid., at 578–9.
[10] ibid., at 577–8.

There must be, and is, some general conception of relations giving rise to a duty of care, of which the particular cases found in the books are but instances. . . . The rule that you are to love your neighbour becomes in law you must not injure your neighbour; and the lawyer's question: 'Who is my neighbour?' receives a restricted reply. You must take reasonable care to avoid acts or omissions which you can reasonably foresee would be likely to injure your neighbour. Who, then, in law, is my neighbour? The answer seems to be – persons who are so closely and directly affected by my act that I ought reasonably to have them in contemplation as being so affected when I am directing my mind to the acts or omissions that are called in question . . . a manufacturer of products, which he sells in such a form as to show that he intends them to reach the ultimate consumer in the form in which they left him with no reasonable possibility of intermediate examination, and with knowledge that the absence of reasonable care in the preparation or putting up of products will result in an injury to the consumer's life or property, owes a duty to the consumer to take that reasonable care.[11]

He further developed this test into a concept of 'proximity':

. . . a duty to take due care did arise when the person or property of one was in such proximity to the person or property of another that, if due care was not taken, damage might be done by the one to the other . . . proximity . . . extend[s] to such close and direct relations that the act complained of directly affects the person whom the person alleged to be bound to take care would know would be directly affected by his careless act. . . . That this is the sense in which nearness of 'proximity' was intended by Lord Esher is obvious from his own illustration in *Heaven v Pender* (11 QBD 503, at 510) of the application of his doctrine to the sale of goods. 'This . . . rule includes the case of goods, etc., supplied to be used immediately by a particular person or persons, or one of a class of persons, where it would be obvious to the person supplying, if he thought, that the goods would in all probability be used at once by such persons before a reasonable opportunity for discovering any defect which might exist, and where the thing supplied would be of such a nature that a neglect of ordinary care or skill as to its conditions or manner of supplying it would probably cause danger to the person or property of the person for whose use it was supplied, and who was about to use it. It would exclude a case in which the goods are supplied under circumstances in which it would be a chance by whom they would be used or whether they would be used or not, or whether they would be used before there would probably be means of observing any defect, or where the goods would be of such a nature that a want of care or skill as to their condition or the manner of supplying them would not probably produce danger of injury to person or property.' This is obviously . . . to call attention to the proximate relationship, which may be too remote where inspection even of the person using, certainly of an intermediate person, may reasonably be interposed. With this necessary qualification of proximate relationship . . . I think the judgment of Lord Esher expresses the Law of England.[12]

Following *Donohue v Stevenson* the law of tort remained fairly static until in the 1960s, the 1970s and the early 1980s it began to develop at a fast pace with the categories of negligence and the persons and parties capable of being liable greatly extended by

---

[11] ibid., at 580.
[12] ibid., at 581.

the courts. There was then a massive retrenchment by the courts in these fields, culminating in the case of *Murphy v Brentwood* in 1992, which has in followed more recently by something of a counter-revolution. In order to understand these developments, it is necessary to trace some of the history of the law following the *Donoghue* case. Although concerning a customer and a manufacturer, *Donoghue v Stevenson* established a broad principle of responsibility which is still referred to by judges 80 years later.

3.5 Historical perspective

3.5.1 1932–1964

It took from *Donoghue* until 1964 to extend the principles of *Donoghue* to statements that are given negligently (as opposed to acts or omissions). This was in the case of *Hedley Byrne v Heller & Partners Ltd*.[13] Advertising agents, Hedley Byrne, needed a reference from a banker as to the credit-worthiness of a potential customer. They approached their bankers who sought the advice of merchant bankers who in turn reported to Hedley Byrne. The report, which was headed 'without responsibility', said that the potential customer was good for ordinary business arrangements. Hedley Byrne proceeded with their contract, and by reason of the customer not being good for ordinary business arrangements, lost a considerable amount of money. They sued the merchant bankers. The merchant bankers escaped liability by reason of having expressed their report to be 'without responsibility' but the House of Lords held that professionals are liable for statements made negligently in circumstances where they know that those statements are going to be acted on, and they were acted on.

Two key features of this case are that the liability attached to a negligent statement, not an act or omission, and that the merchant bankers were held liable for causing economic loss that was not related to any physical injury to a person, or damage to their property (often termed 'pure economic loss). This was therefore a dramatic expansion of the possible range of circumstances in which a person might be liable in tort. The principle, i.e. that a person might be liable for pure economic loss for negligent statements, is often referred to as the *Hedley Byrne* principle. It formed the basis of what became known as the 'assumption of responsibility' test for ascertaining whether a duty arose. This required:

> . . . a negligent misrepresentation by the defendant, or some other form of active intervention, advice or conduct amounting to a representation, made in circumstances where, while there was no contract as such between plaintiff and defendant, there was nevertheless a 'special relationship' involving a high degree of proximity, including in particular reliance by the representee and an inferred assumption of responsibility by the representor, and where financial damage, if the defendant representation was inaccurate and acted upon, would clearly result for the plaintiff.[14]

---

[13] [1964] AC 465 (HL).
[14] As summarised in *Hudson's Building and Civil Engineering Contracts* 2010, at p. 109.

Key elements are: the advice (which could be in the form of a document) should be given deliberately;[15] the advice should relate to the particular expertise of the giver, and the close nature of the relationship, which should be 'equivalent to contract'.[16] However the mere existence of such a relationship would not create a positive duty to act (this has only been found in special non-construction relationships such as doctor–patient).

This important decision was clearly of great potential significance for designers, as it could lead, for example, to liability for statements given to a contractor at pre-tender stage as to the design, or nature of the sub-soil, or the possibility of constructing the works in a certain order, and so on. Likewise the designer could incur liability to the building owner, sub-contractors, suppliers, and others involved in the construction process that might rely on design advice. Key cases that have later developed this strand of the law of negligence are discussed in Chapter 4.

3.5.2 1972–1978

The next major extension of Lord Atkin's test is to be found in a case in 1972, *Dutton v Bognor Regis Urban District Council*[17] (now overruled by *Murphy*). In Bognor Regis there was a rubbish tip which had been filled in. In 1958 a builder bought land in the area which included the filled rubbish tip and developed the site as a housing estate. One of the houses that he built was sold to Mr Clark. He only lived there a short while and then sold the house to Mrs Dutton. In due course, the walls and ceilings cracked, the staircase slipped, and the doors and window would not close: the damage was caused by inadequate foundations. Mrs Dutton sued the builder and the local authority. She, of course, had no contractual relationship with either. Before the hearing, the action with the builder was settled. It was held by the Court of Appeal (in relation to the action against the local authority) that the council, through its building inspector, owed a duty of care to Mrs Dutton to ensure that the inspection of the foundations to the house was properly carried out and that the foundations were adequate and the council was liable to Mrs Dutton for the damage caused by the breach of duty of its building inspector in failing to carry out a proper inspection of the foundations.

Lord Denning said in his judgment that the case was entirely novel because no such claim had ever been made before against a council or its surveyor for negligence in inspecting the foundations. The application of the test of Lord Atkin to the facts in the *Dutton* case is best seen in the following extract from the judgment:

> . . . the foundations of a house are in a class by themselves. Once covered up they will not be seen again until the damage appears. The inspector must know this or, at any rate, he ought to know it. Applying the test laid down by Lord Atkin in *Donoghue and Stevenson* I should have thought that the inspector ought to have had subsequent purchasers in mind when he

---

[15] [1964] AC 463, Lord Morris at 496–7.
[16] ibid., Lord Devlin at 528–9.
[17] [1972] 1 QB 373.

was inspecting the foundations – he ought to have realised that, if he was negligent, he might suffer damage.[18]

The *Dutton* case not only had great implications for local authorities; the previously existing law was radically changed also in respect of builders who developed their own land. Until that time, the seller of a house owed no duties to the purchaser of the house or to a visitor on the premises.[19] This was known as the 'let the buyer beware' principle, or '*caveat emptor*'. Builder–developers thought they were in the same position prior to the *Dutton* case. The Court of Appeal held that where the seller is also the builder, it would be liable for negligence in constructing a house in a defective manner. The *Dutton* case was followed on this point in many subsequent cases before finally being overruled in *Murphy*, discussed below. It is interesting to note that the basis for the later destruction of these developments is to be found in the judgment of Lord Justice Stamp which, although expressing no concluded opinion, took a rather different approach:

> I may be liable to one who purchases in the market a bottle of ginger beer which I have carelessly manufactured and which is dangerous and causes injury to persons or property; but it is not the law that I am liable to him for the loss he suffers because what is found inside the bottle and for which he has paid money is not ginger beer but water. I do not warrant, except to an immediate purchaser, and then by the contract and not in tort, that the thing I manufacture is reasonably fit for purpose. The submission is, I think, a formidable one and in my view raises the most difficult point for decision in this case. Nor can I see any valid distinction between the case of a builder who carelessly builds a house which, though not a source of danger to personal property, nevertheless, owing to a concealed defect in its foundations, starts to settle and crack and become valueless, and the case of a manufacturer who carelessly manufactures an article which, thought not a source of danger to its owner or to his other property, nevertheless owing to hidden defects quickly disintegrates. To hold that either the builder or the manufacturer was liable except in contract would be to open up a new field of liability the extent of which could not, I think, be logically controlled and since it is not in my judgement necessary to do so for the purposes of this case, I do not more particularly because of the absence of the builder express an opinion whether the builder has a higher or lower duty than the manufacturer.[20]

3.6 Anns v Merton London Borough Council *(1978)*

In 1978 the position altered again with *Anns v Merton Borough Council*.[21] In this case, the lessees of flats claimed against the local authority in negligence in relation to the local authority's powers of inspection under the by-laws in that, it was said, they had allowed contractors to build foundations in breach of the by-laws, with resulting damage to the flats. Lord Wilberforce, in a passage of crystal clarity, which later became

---

[18] [1972] 1 QB 373, at 47.
[19] *Otto v Bolton and Norris* [1936] 2 KB 46; *Bottomly v Bannister* [1952] 1 KB 458 (CA).
[20] [1972] 1 QB 373, at 414–15.
[21] [1978] AC 728 (HL).

the excuse for a far-reaching and dramatic expansion of the circumstances in which a duty of care might be held to exist, said the following:

> Through the trilogy of cases in this house, *Donoghue and Stevenson, Hedley Byrne v Heller* and *Dorset Yacht*, the position has now been reached that in order to establish that a duty of care arises in a particular situation, it is not necessary to bring the facts of that situation within those of previous situations in which a duty of care has been held to exist. Rather the question has to be approached in two stages. First one has to ask whether, as between the alleged wrongdoer and the person who has suffered damage there is sufficient relationship of proximity or neigh-bourhood such that, in the reasonable contemplation of the former, carelessness on his part may be likely to cause damage to the latter – in which case a prima facie duty of care arises. Secondly, if the first question is answered affirmatively, it is necessary to consider whether there are any considerations which ought to negative, or to reduce or limit the scope of the duty or class of person to whom it is owed or the damages to which a breach of it may give rise.[22]

This passage became known as the 'two-stage test'. Legal commentators frequently refer to two alternative approaches taken by the courts to the development of the law of tort. The first is an 'incremental' approach, whereby the law develops through analogy to earlier cases of similar facts – this still allows for gradual change over time. The second is a more principled approach, whereby the court will seize an opportunity to review the law in a specific area, and set out broad principles for its future application. *Anns* and the two-stage test are an example of the latter.

In *Anns*, the House of Lords was concerned with a claim against a local authority in an action to which a builder was not a party. However they felt obliged, as they had in *Dutton*, to consider the position of the builder, if it had been sued, on the basis that it would be unreasonable to impose liability on the council if the builder, whose primary fault it was, was immune from liability. Lord Wilberforce, having considered *caveat emptor* (buyer beware) and other similar propositions said:

> I am unable to understand why this principle or proposition should prevent recovery in a suitable case by a person, who has subsequently acquired the house, upon the principle of *Donoghue v Stevenson*: the same rule should apply to all careless acts of a builder: whether he happens to own the land or not. I agree generally with the conclusions of Lord Denning MRon this point in *Dutton v Bognor Regis Urban District* Council [1972] 1 QB 373, at 392–4. In the alternative, since it is the duty of the builder (owner or not) to comply with the by-laws, I would be of the opinion that an action could be brought against him, in effect, for breach of statutory duty by any person for whose benefit or protection the by-law was made. So I do not think there is any basis here for arguing from a supposed immunity of the builder to immunity of the council.[23]

The *Anns* decision was of fundamental importance at the time for many reasons. First, there appeared to be a clear acceptance of the principles set out in *Dutton*, namely

---

[22] ibid., at 751–2.

[23] ibid., at 760. Note that 'breach of statutory duty' was later stated not to create a right of action in tort, see Chapter 5.

that a contractor may be liable for negligence in building a house to a party with whom it is not in contract, not only in respect of physical injury but also in respect of damage to the property itself. Second, *Anns* appeared to place the main emphasis for establishing a duty of care on the foreseeability of harm rather than giving emphasis to proximity and/or neighbourhood. Third, the judges tended to perceive the policy restrictions (the second part of the two-stage test) as restrictions that should only be applied in fairly exceptional circumstances. Fourth, and very importantly, lawyers and judges in particular had at last a test which they could apply with a measure of ease to almost any factual background in order to establish whether or not a duty of care existed.

In *Batty v Metropolitan Realisation Ltd*[24] a development company and a builder had inspected land on the side of a valley. There was nothing on the land forming the site to show it unsuitable for building; however, on the other side of the valley and on an adjoining lane, there were signs that a soil investigation was necessary. One of the plots of land on which a builder built a house was on a plateau above a steep slope. Three years after the house had been sold there was a severe landslip below the house, damaging the garden but not the house. The developer provided a contractual warranty to the new owners to build the house 'in an efficient and workmanlike manner and with proper materials and so as to be fit for habitation'. The court at first instance held that the builder was liable to the purchasers in negligence, however it found that the developer did not owe any obligation in tort, in addition to the developer's liability in contract. The builders appealed and the Court of Appeal upheld the finding against them. Although the house itself was undamaged by the landslip, the Court treated it as 'doomed' and as falling within the 'present and imminent danger' test in *Anns*. However the Court of Appeal held that the Judge had been wrong to decide that the developer could not owe a duty in tort in parallel with its contractual duty to the owners. Megaw LJ stated 'In my judgement the plaintiffs were entitled here to have judgment entered in their favour on the basis of tortious liability as well as on the basis of breach of contract, assuming that the plaintiffs had established a breach by the first defendant of their common law duty of care owed to the plaintiffs.'[25] Although the decision affecting the builders was later overruled in *D & F Estates*, that regarding the developers was not.

3.7 Junior Books *(1983)*

The development and extension of the law of tort during the period up to 1988 probably reached its climax in the House of Lords in *Junior Books Ltd v Veitchi Co. Ltd*.[26] In that case, on appeal from Scotland, specialist flooring subcontractors had laid a floor to the employer's factory and it was said by the employer that the floor was defective. The employer, who was not in contract with the subcontractor, brought an action in delict, which is substantially the same cause of action in Scotland as negligence in

---

[24] [1978] 2 All ER 445.
[25] ibid., at 453.
[26] *Junior Books v Veitchi* [1983] 1 AC 520.

England. There was no allegation by the employer in this action that there was a present or imminent danger to the occupier.

Notwithstanding the potential difficulties, the employer succeeded in its argument that the sub-contractor owed it a duty of care in negligence and that the sub-contractor was in breach of that duty. It was said in this case that there was a close commercial relationship between the employer and the sub-contractor. Lord Brandon, the dissenting judge, did however draw attention to the fact that *Donoghue* was based on a danger of personal injury or damage to the plaintiff's property other than the product itself.

3.8 1985–1988: the retreat

At the time of the *Junior Books* decision in 1983, many people in the construction industry and the professions were beginning to think that the floodgates were now fully open and that almost anything they did was capable of creating a liability to someone. The first major step on the road of retrenchment came with governors of the *Peabody Donation Fund v Sir Lindsay Parkinson & Co. Ltd.*[27] This case concerned drains that had to be reconstructed when they were found to be unsatisfactory. In discussing the issue as to whether the local authority owed a duty in tort to Peabody, Lord Keith of Kinkel said:

> The true question in each case is whether the particular defendant owed the particular plaintiff a duty of care having the scope contended for, and whether he was in breach of that duty with consequent loss to the plaintiffs. A relationship of proximity in Lord Atkins' sense must exist before any duty of care can arise, but the scope of the duty must depend upon all the circumstances of the case.[28]

He also said the following on Lord Wilberforce's judgment (the so-called 'two-stage test'): 'There has been a tendency in some recent cases to treat these passages as being in themselves of definitive character. This is a temptation that should be resisted.'[29]

This tentative step down the route of retreat from *Anns* was followed in the case of *Leigh and Sullivan Ltd v Aliakmon Shipping Co. Ltd ('The Aliakmon')*[30] where Lord Brandon made the following comment in relation to Lord Wilberforce's test in *Anns*:

> The first observation which I would make is that the passage does not provide, and cannot in my view have been intended by Lord Wilberforce to provide, a universally applicable test of the existence and scope of a duty of care in the law of negligence.[31]

In the same case, Lord Brandon drew the court's attention to Lord Keith's comment in the *Peabody* case above and then went on:

---

[27] [1985] AC 210 (HL).
[28] ibid., at 240.
[29] ibid., at 240.
[30] [1986] AC 785 (HL).
[31] ibid., at 815.

The second observation which I would make is that Lord Wilberforce was dealing, as is clear from what he said, with the approach to the questions of the existence and scope of a duty of care in a novel type of factual situation which was not analogous to any factual situation in which the existence of such duty had already been held to exist. He was not, as I understood the passage, suggesting that the same approach should be adopted to the existence of a duty of care in a factual situation in which a duty of care had repeatedly been held not to exist.[32]

In *Curran & Another v Northern Ireland Co-ownership Housing Association Ltd & Others*,[33] it was held that the Northern Ireland Housing executive, which had exercised its statutory power to pay an improvement grant for the building of an extension to a house, but had no power of control over the building operation, did not owe a duty of care to future owners of the house to see that the extension had been properly constructed. In this case, it was said that *Anns* represented the high watermark of a trend in the development of the law of negligence towards the elevation of the 'neighbourhood' principle into one of general application from which a duty of care might always be derived unless there were clear countervailing considerations to exclude it. It is important to note that Lord Bridge referred in this case, with approval, to a case in the High Court of Australia where that court specifically refused to adopt the two-stage *Anns* approach.

These three cases, *Peabody*, *The Aliakmon* and *Curran*, have often been referred to as the 'Retreat from *Anns*' but the retreat continued. In the case of *Yuen Kun-Yeu v Attorney General of Hong Kong*,[34] the two-stage test of Lord Wilberforce in *Anns* was put to rest by Lord Keith of Kinkel in these words (although *Anns* was not then overruled):

Their Lordships venture to think that the two-stage test formulated by Lord Wilberforce for determining the existence of a duty of care in negligence has been elevated to a degree of importance greater than it merits, and greater perhaps than its author intended. Further the expression of the first stage of the test carries with it a risk of mis-interpretation. As Gibbs CJ pointed out in *Sutherland Shire Council v Heyman* 59 ALJR 564, 570 there are two possible views of what Lord Wilberforce meant. The first view, favoured in a number of cases mentioned by Gibbs CJ, is that he meant to test the sufficiency of proximity simply by the reasonable contemplation of likely harm. The second view, favoured by Gibbs CJ himself, is that Lord Wilberforce meant the expression 'proximity or neighbourhood' to be a composite one, importing the whole concept of necessary relationship between plaintiff and dependant described by Lord Atkin in *Donoghue v Stevenson* [1932] AC 562, at 580. In their Lordship's opinion, the second view is the correct one. As Lord Wilberforce himself observed in *McLoughlin v O'Brien*[1983] 1 AC 410, at 420,it is clear that foreseeability does not of itself, and automatically, lead to a duty of care. There are many other statements to the same effect. The truth is that the trilogy of cases referred to by Lord Wilberforce each demonstrate particular sets of circumstances, differing in character, which were adjudged to have the effect of bringing into being a relationship apt to give rise to a duty of care. *Foreseeability of harm is a necessary ingredient of such a relationship but it is not the only one.* Otherwise there would be liability in

---

[32]ibid., at 815.
[33][1987] AC 718.
[34][1988] AC 175.

negligence on the part of one who sees another about to walk over a cliff with his head in the air and forebears to shout a warning.[35]

In *Simaan General Contracting Co. v Pilkington Glass Ltd*[36] it was held that a supplier of glass units for a new building who had no contractual relationship with the main contractor, and had not assumed responsibility to that contractor, was not liable in tort for foreseeable economic loss caused by defects in the units where there was no physical damage to the units, and the contractor had no proprietary or possessory interest in the property. In this Court of Appeal case, many of the authorities referred to above were discussed. In particular, some emphasis was laid by Lord Justice Bingham on words of Lord Keith in *Peabody*:

> So in determining whether or not a duty of care of particular scope was incumbent upon a defendant, it was material to take into consideration whether it was just and reasonable that it should be so.[37]

3.9 D & F Estates Ltd v Church Commissioners for England *(1988)*

In *D & F Estates Ltd & Others v Church Commissioners for England and Others*,[38] judgment was given in the House of Lords in 1988. The case concerned defective plastering carried out by sub-contractors to a main contractor. The non-occupying leaseholder, which was a company, claimed against the main contractor (with whom it did not at any time have a contract) in respect of costs of repair to plastering actually carried out, future repair costs and loss of rent. The case was heard by five judges, Lord Bridge, delivering the main speech; Lord Oliver delivering a shorter concurring speech; and the remainder agreeing with Lord Bridge and Lord Oliver. Accordingly, this decision is not a majority decision and no substantial dissent between the judges appears in the report of the case.

The non-occupying leaseholder claimants had no option but to bring its case in tort against the main contractor for the simple reason that it had no contract with them. It was not an easy case to frame in tort for the reason that a contractor has no liability in law for the torts of its independent contractors (namely the sub-contract plasterers). Accordingly, the case could not be put on the simple basis that the contractor owed the same duty of care to the claimants as did the plastering sub-contractors had they been sued. The duty was put by the claimants as a duty to adequately supervise the work of the plasterers. As a matter of fact, it was found that the plasterers had failed to follow the plaster manufacturers' instructions. The judge at first instance concluded that the contractors were in breach of their duty to provide adequate and proper supervision of the plastering work and that they were liable in negligence to the claimants for that breach of their duty. The House of Lords found differently on this point and their

---

[35] ibid. at 191; emphasis added.
[36] [1988] QB 758 (CA).
[37] ibid., at 773.
[38] [1989] AC 177.

reasons are of fundamental importance in the area of negligence liability in the construction industry.

Lord Bridge, having reconsidered many of the previous cases touched on above, took the view that it was more profitable to examine the issues in this case from first principles on the basis that the authorities '. . . speak with such an uncertain voice that, no matter how searching the analysis to which they are subject, they yield no clear and conclusive answer.'[39] He went onto quote from Lord Brandon's judgement in *Junior Books*:

> It is, however, of fundamental importance to observe that the duty of care laid down in *Donoghue v Stevenson* was based on the existence of a danger of physical injury to persons or their property. This is clear from the observations made by Lord Atkin at pages 581–82 with regard to the statements of law of Brett MR in *Heaven v Pender* (1883) 11 QBD 503, at 509. It has, further, until the present case, never been doubted so far as I know that the relevant property for the purpose of the wider principle on which the decision in *Donoghue v Stevenson* was based was property other than the very property which gave rise to the danger of physical damage concerned.[40]

Lord Bridge then turned to the second part of the two-stage test put forward by Lord Wilberforce in *Anns*, namely the question as to whether there are any considerations which ought to limit the scope of the duty which exists. He said:

> To that second question, I would answer that there are two important considerations which ought to limit the scope of the duty of care which it is common ground was owed by the appellants to the respondents on the assumed facts of the present case. The first consideration is that, in *Donoghue v Stevenson* itself and in all the numerous cases in which the principle of that decision has been applied to different but analogous factual situations, it has always been either stated expressly, or taken for granted, that an essential ingredient in the cause of action relied on was the existence of danger, or the threat of danger of physical damage to persons or their property, excluding for this purpose the very piece of property from the defective condition of which such danger, or threat of danger, arises. To dispense with that essential ingredient in a cause of action of the kind concerned in the present case would, in my view, involve a radical departure from long-established authority.[41]

Lord Bridge regarded the above passages as receiving powerful support from the unanimous decision of the Supreme Court of the United States of America in *East River Steamship Corporation v Transamerica Delaval Inc.*[42] which he regarded in turn as undermining the earlier American authorities relied on in the New Zealand case of *Bowen v Paramount Buildings (Hamilton) Ltd.*[43] Lord Bridge makes the following important statement:

> If the hidden defect in the chattel is the cause of personal injury or of damage to property other than the chattel itself, the manufacturer is liable. But if the hidden defect is discovered before

---

[39] ibid., para. 25.
[40] [1989] AC 177, para. 26, citing [1983] AC 520, *per* Lord Brandon at 549.
[41] [1989] AC 177, para. 27, citing [1983] AC 520, *per* Lord Brandon at 551–2.
[42] (1986)106 S Ct 2295 (US Supreme Court).
[43] [1977] 1 NZLR 394 (CA).

any such damage is caused, there is no longer any room for the application of the *Donoghue v Stevenson* principle. The chattel is now defective in quality, but is no longer dangerous. It may be valueless or it may be capable of economic repair. In either case the economic loss is recoverable in contract by a buyer or hirer of the chattel entitled to the benefit of a relevant warranty of quality, but is not recoverable in tort by a remote buyer or hirer of the chattel.[44]

Lord Bridge then considered whether or not the issues may be different in a complex building project where the whole project is an entire series of separate pieces brought together. Taking the example of a garden wall, as a simple structure, he came to the clear view that there is no reason in principle why an action should lie in tort against the builder for the cost of either repairing or demolishing a damaged garden wall in circumstances where no personal injury had occurred and there was no damage to property other than the wall itself. He went on to say:

> However, I can see that it may well be arguable that in the case of complex structures, as indeed possibly in the case of complex chattels, one element of the structure should be regarded for the purpose of the application of the principles under discussion as distinct from another element, so that damage to one part of the structure caused by a hidden defect in another part may qualify to be treated as damage to 'other property', and whether the argument should prevail may depend upon the circumstances of the case. It would be unwise and unnecessary for the purpose of deciding the present appeal to attempt to offer authoritative solutions to these problems in the abstract. I should wish to hear fuller argument before reaching any conclusion as to how far the decision in the New Zealand Court of Appeal in *Bowen v Paramount Builders (Hamilton) Limited* should be followed as a matter of English law. I do not regard *Anns* as resolving that issue.[45]

On this basis, it was easy for the House of Lords in *D & F* to come to the view that the plaster, being the damaged thing itself, had not caused damage to persons or property (other than a *de minimis* cost of cleaning of carpets of £50) and that the non-occupying leaseholder was not entitled, therefore, to succeed against the contractor.

Clearly, the House of Lords had great difficulty in trying to reconcile its decision in *D & F* with its previous decision in *Anns*. In truth, such a reconciliation was not possible and it became inevitable that someone, sometime, would mount a concerted attack on *Anns* in the House of Lords. The final assault on *Anns* was not long in coming: 1990 saw the decision in *Murphy v Brentwood District Council*.

3.10 Murphy v Brentwood District Council[46] *(1990)*

The decision in *Murphy* was given in July of 1990. The case was a claim by homeowners against a local authority for negligent inspection of foundations (i.e. a similar factual

---

[44] [1989] AC 177 para. 31.
[45] ibid., para. 34.
[46] [1990] 2 All ER 908; 50 BLR 1 (HL); note on the same day as the decision in *Murphy*, the HL concluded the case of *Department of the Environment v Thomas Bates* [1991] 1 AC 499, inevitably reaching the same result.

context to *Anns*). It had been very widely known that *Anns* was under attack in the argument before the House of Lords. Their Lordships carefully reviewed in their speeches the law of negligence as it had developed since 1932 and gave consideration to cases from the Commonwealth as well as America. They had also to look again at *Anns* and *D & F*. In particular, Lord Keith expressly approved a passage from an Australian case in which the High Court of Australia had refused to follow *Anns*: *Sutherland Shire Council v Heyman*.[47] In that case, the Australian court had decided that the proper approach to the extension of the duty of care in novel situations was an incremental one. Lord Keith went on to say:

> In my opinion, there can be no doubt that *Anns* has for long been widely regarded as an unsatisfactory decision. In relation to the scope of the duty owed by a local authority it proceeded upon what must, with due respect to its source, be regarded as a somewhat superficial examination of principle and there has been extreme difficulty, highlighted most recently in the speeches in *D & F Estates*, in ascertaining upon exactly what basis of principle it did proceed. I think it must now be recognised it did not proceed on any basis of principle at all, but constituted a remarkable example of judicial legislation. It has engendered a vast spate of litigation, and each of the cases in the field which have reached this House has been distinguished. Others have been distinguished in the Court of Appeal. The result has been to keep the effect of the decision within reasonable bounds, but that has been achieved only by applying strictly the words of Lord Wilberforce and by refusing to accept the logical implications of the decision itself. These logical implications show that the case properly considered had potentiality for collision with long-established principles regarding liability and the tort of negligence for economic loss. There can be no doubt that to depart from the decision would establish a degree of certainty in this field of law which it has done a remarkable amount to upset.[48]

Lord Keith then pointed out that *Anns* had stood as law for 13 years and that the House of Lords should be cautious in overturning its own previous decisions but he nonetheless went on to overrule *Anns* in a robust manner:

> My Lords, I would hold that *Anns* was wrongly decided as regards the scope of any private law duty of care resting upon local authorities in relation to their function of taking steps to secure compliance with building by-laws or regulations and should be departed from. It follows that *Dutton v Bognor Regis Urban District Council* should be overruled as should all cases subsequent to *Anns* which were decided in reliance on it.[49]

It is not difficult to see that this was a landmark decision of enormous importance in the field of professional liability and other fields. However, the manner of the overruling of *Anns* left considerable doubt as to which cases, precisely, had also been overruled.

---

[47] (1985) 60 ALR 1; 157 CLR 424 (Australia).
[48] [1990] 2 All ER 908, at 923.
[49] ibid., at 924.

3.11 Tests for establishing a duty of care in respect of economic loss

Around the same time as *Murphy* the House of Lords re-considered the tests for establishing a tortious duty of care to avoid economic loss. In *Smith v Eric Bush*[50] surveyors
acting for a mortgage company were found liable to a purchaser when their valuation
of a house was carried out negligently. The advice was not given directly to the claimant,
but in the form of a report to the mortgage company, on which the purchaser relied.
The House of Lords found that a duty of care existed, even though there was no relationship 'akin to contract', Lord Jauncey stating 'I prefer to approach the matter by
asking whether the facts disclose that the appellants in inspecting and reporting must,
but for the disclaimers, by reason of the proximate relationship between them, be
deemed to have assumed responsibility towards Mrs Smith as well as to the building
society who instructed them.'[51]

The idea that to satisfy the 'proximity test' did not require actual contact between the
advisor and the claimant, but could be 'deemed' to exist by the court, obviously widened
the scope for liability in tort.

Shortly after, the case of *Caparo Industries Plc v Dickman* was concerned with whether
it was reasonably foreseeable that shareholders and potential investors might rely on an
auditor's report when dealing in the shares of the company. It was found that there was
no such duty owed by auditors to that class of persons. In reaching this finding, the
House of Lords acknowledged the need to develop limits to the categories of situation
where negligence may arise: 'Thus the postulate of a simple duty to avoid any harm
that is, with hindsight, reasonably capable of being foreseen becomes untenable without
the imposition of some intelligible limits to keep the law of negligence within the
bounds of common sense and practicality'.[52] It suggested a 'threefold' test[53] for the
establishment of a duty, which in summary required the court to address:

> . . . whether loss to the claimant was a reasonably foreseeable consequence of what the defend-
> ant did or failed to do; whether the relationship between the parties was one of sufficient
> proximity; and whether in all the circumstances it is fair, just and reasonable to impose a duty
> of care on the defendant towards the claimant.[54]

It also recommended taking an 'incremental approach' to the development of this
area of the law,[55] and cited with approval (as had the court in *Murphy*) Brennan J's
remarks in the High Court of Australia in *Sutherland Shire Council v Heyman*:

> It is preferable, in my view, that the law should develop novel categories of negligence incre-
> mentally and by analogy with established categories, rather than by a massive extension of a

---

[50] [1990] 1 AC 831

[51] at 871.

[52] [1990] 1 All ER 568, Lord Oliver at 585.

[53] [1990] 1 All ER 568 at 585;[1990] 2 AC 605, Lord Bridge at 617, Lord Oliver, at 632.

[54] As summarised in *Bank of Credit & Commerce International (Overseas) Ltd & others v Price Waterhouse (A
Firm) & another* [1998] EWCA Civ 236.

[55] [1990] 2 AC 605, *per* Lord Bridge at 618.

prima facie duty of care restrained only by indefinable considerations which ought to negative, or to reduce or limit the scope of the duty or the class of person to whom it is owed.[56]

The overruling of *Anns* and the development of a more restrictive approach to the finding of new categories of situation where liability in tort might arise together set the scene for further refinement over the following two decades.

3.12 Contract and tort concurrently?

What is the position where there is a contract but there is also, prima facie, a duty of care owed in tort? Is it possible to bring proceedings both in contract and tort?

This issue is important because of the difference between tort and contract in limitation and damages. A cause of action in contract is barred six years after the cause of action accrues (12 if a deed or under seal). In tort, the date on which the claim will be barred is also six years from the date on which the cause of action accrues. However the accrual of the cause of action in tort is usually later than in contract. Further, if the Latent Damage Act 1986 applies only to claims in negligence as a tort, then there is another difference with contract because such tort claims can be brought for up to three years from the 'date of knowledge' (see Chapter 11). It follows that in tort, claims are likely to be statute-barred at a later date than contractual claims. It is also important because in tort a designer may have available a defence not available in contract: i.e. the delegation of work to an independent contractor.

There have, historically, been a great number of cases where liability has been held, and in many cases assumed, to arise both in contract and tort concurrently. For example, in *Donoghue v Stevenson*, Lord Macmillan, in a passage which must be *obiter dicta* but highly persuasive nevertheless, said:

> The fact that there is a contractual relationship between the parties which may give rise to an action for breach of contract does not exclude the co-existence of a right of action founded on negligence as between the same parties, independently of the contract, though arising out of the relationship in fact brought about by the contract. Of this the best illustration is the right of the injured railway passenger to sue the railway company either for breach of the contract of safe carriage or for negligence in carrying him.[57]

On the face of it, therefore, there would appear to be no reason why actions in tort should not be brought where there is a tortious duty, even in cases where there is a contract.

However case law has not always been consistent on this point. In the early case of *Bagot v Stevens Scanlan & Co.*[58] an employer of a firm of architects sought damages

---

[56] (1985) 60 ALR 1 at 43–4.
[57] [1932] All ER 1 at 24.
[58] [1964] 3 ALL ER 577.

for breach of contract and for the tort of negligence in relation to the inspection of foundations and drainage works. The court held that duties owed arose only in contract and not in tort:

> It seems to me that, in this case, the relationship which created the duty on the part of the architects towards their clients to exercise reasonable skill and care arose out of the contract and not otherwise. The complaint that is made against them is of a failure to do the very thing which they contracted to do. That was the relationship which gave rise to the duty which was broken. It was a contractual relationship, a contractual duty, and any action brought for failure to comply with that duty is, in my view, an action founded on contract. It is also, in my view, an action founded on contract alone.[59]

Lord Denning MR in *Esso Petroleum Co. Ltd v Mardon*[60] had to consider whether there was tortious liability in respect of pre-contract negotiations in circumstances where a contract was ultimately entered into. It had been argued in the case that the fact that there was a contract excluded any tortious liability. In referring to the *Bagot* case, Lord Denning suggested that the decision was in conflict with decisions of higher authority to which that court was not referred in coming to its decision, and he quoted passages from two old House of Lords' cases:

> . . . wherever there is a contract, and something to be done in the course of the employment which is the subject of that contract, if there is breach of duty in the course of that employment, the plaintiff may either recover in tort or in contract . . .[61]
>   . . . the solicitor contracts with his client to be skilful and careful. For failure to perform his obligation he may be made liable at law in contract or even in tort, for negligence in breach of a duty imposed on him. . . .[62]

Lord Denning went on to conclude that a professional person could be liable for negligent misrepresentation in a situation where the representations led to the formation of a contract, stating:

> It seems to me that *Hedley Byrne & Co. Ltd v. Heller & Partners Ltd* [1964] AC 465, properly understood, covers this particular proposition: if a man, who has or professes to have special knowledge or skill, makes a representation by virtue thereof to another – be it advice, information or opinion – with the intention of inducing him to enter into a contract with him, he is under a duty to use reasonable care to see that the representation is correct, and that the advice, information or opinion is reliable. If he negligently gives unsound advice or misleading information or expresses an erroneous opinion, and thereby induces the other side to enter into a contract with him, he is liable in damages.[63]

---

[59] ibid., Diplock LJ, at 581.
[60] [1976] QB 801.
[61] *Boorman v Brown* (1842) 3 QB 511, at 525–6.
[62] *Nocton v Lord Ashburton* [1914] A.C. 932, at 956.
[63] [1976] QB 801, at 820.

Shortly after this case, in *Batty v Metropolitan Realisations Ltd*[64] the Court of Appeal found that a developer was liable in tort to homeowners to whom it had provided a contractual warranty. The Court of Appeal again doubted the *Bagot* decision, on the basis of Lord Denning's comments in the *EssoMardon* case, but did not overrule it.

Those criticisms were such that in another case in 1978, *Midland Bank Trust Co. Ltd v Hett, Stubbs and Kemp*,[65] a Judge, sitting alone, felt able to satisfy himself that he was not bound by the *Bagot* decision, and held that a solicitor could be liable to his client for negligence either in contract or in tort. He said of the argument in *Bagot*, that the cause of action there was necessarily in contract alone because the architects in that case had failed to do the very thing which they contracted to do:

> Well, so they had, but the form of the breach cannot affect the nature of the duty, nor does an obligation imposed by law become an obligation different in quality simply because the obligee agrees to accept money for its performance ... The case of a layman consulting a solicitor for advice seems to me to be as typical a case as one could find of the sort of relationship in which the duty of care described in the *Hedley Byrne* case exists; and if I am free to do so in the instant case, I would, therefore, hold that the relationship of solicitor and client gave rise to a duty on the defendants under the general law to exercise that care and skill on which they must have known perfectly well that their client relied.[66]

Subsequent to this the courts showed a general openness to the possibility that a professional person might be liable in tort to their client, irrespective of the existence of a contract between them. This ultimately led to the case of *Henderson v Merrett*, discussed in the next chapter, where this liability was confirmed, but the trend began much earlier. For example, in *Pirelli General Cable Works Ltd v Oscar Faber & Partners*[67] the court proceeded on the basis that a firm of engineers could be liable to its client in tort for negligently approving the design of a chimney which later cracked (although in that case limitation prevented a finding of liability). In *Cynat Products Ltd v Landbuild (Investments and Property) Ltd*[68] both contractor and designer were found to have a parallel liability in tort. In *Lancashire and Cheshire Baptist Churches Incorporated v Howard and Seddon Partnership*[69] Howard and Seddon were architects for a church sanctuary completed in 1980. It was alleged that there was condensation and inadequate ventilation. The claim in contract was out of time for limitation purposes and the action proceeded on the claim in tort. The Judge had no difficulty in holding that the architect owed duties in tort.

However there were exceptions to this general trend. For example, in *Tai Hing Cotton Mill Ltd v Liu Chong Hing Bank Ltd* the House of Lords refused to accept that a parallel duty in tort could be more extensive than that undertaken in a contract,

---

[64] (1977) 7 BLR 1. (CA), see section 3.6.
[65] [1978] 3 All ER 571.
[66] ibid., at 595.
[67] (1983) 21 BLR 99.
[68] [1984] 3 All ER 163.
[69] (1993) 65 BLR 21.

stating: 'Their Lordships do not believe that there is anything to the advantage of the law's development in searching for a liability in tort where the parties are in a contractual relationship. This is particularly so in a commercial relationship'.[70] In *Greater Nottingham Co-operative Society v Cementation Piling and Foundations Ltd*[71] the court refused to find nominated sub-contractors liable in tort to the employer for defective piling. The court bore in mind that the parties had an actual opportunity to define their relationship by means of a contract and took it; and that 'the general contractual structure as between [the employer], the main contractor and Cementation provided a channel of claim which was open to [the employer]'. It therefore found that although a concurrent liability could in principle exist, it could not be more extensive than that defined in the warranty. The effect of the contractual context and the presence of disclaimers are discussed further in Chapter 10.

3.13 Summary of the position in 1994

The previous edition of this book summarised the position (with reservations as to the strong likelihood of subsequent change) as follows:

(1) Where defects are discovered before they cause either personal injury or damage to property other than to the 'thing itself', damages are not recoverable. Those damages (even if they are, e.g. the cost of rectification of defects) are to be categorised as economic loss.

(2) Economic loss cannot generally be recovered in tort in building cases except where:
   (a) the cause of action falls within the principles of *Hedley Byrne*, for example, negligent advice. The extent to which 'design' is '*advice*' for this purpose is likely to be explored in future cases.
   (b) the 'complex structure' argument can be used. This does not appear to be a promising area for potential claimants.
   (c) personal injuries arise.

(3) Local authorities are not likely to be liable if they perform their building control responsibilities negligently.

(4) The Defective Premises Act 1972 provides a statutory remedy in the case of dwellings.

(5) There will usually be concurrent rights against a designer in contract and tort. The existence of the contract provides the necessary proximity for the tortious claim. The existence of the contract may be relevant in deciding the nature and extent of the tortious duty. However, it may also be that the tortious duty cannot be any more extensive than the contractual duty.

---

[70] [1985] 2 All ER 947 at 957, [1986] AC 80 at 107.
[71] (1988) 17 Con LR 43; 41 BLR 43.

Chapter 4
Liability under Tort: Part 2 (Post-*Murphy*)

There have been significant developments in the law of tort post-*Murphy*. These are mainly in the area of liability for 'pure' economic loss caused by negligent actions, in particular the liability of a contractor for the provisions of defective construction work. Put simply, *Murphy* was followed by something of a 'counter-revolution' to the perceived restrictions it established. But the counter-revolution was not wholeheartedly accepted, and the recent case of *Robinson v Jones*[1] can be seen as a retreat from that position back to a *Murphy*-alignment. These developments are outlined below; the effect of the contractual context on tortious liability is discussed further in Chapter 10. Before analysing these complications the chapter begins with a review of the more settled area of liability for physical injury and damage to property.

4.1 Liability for physical injury and damage to other property

As confirmed in the cases of *D & F Estates*[2] and *Murphy*,[3] it remains the position that a contractor or consultant may be liable for negligently causing physical injury, or damage to property other than to the works they are being contracted to complete. As stated in *Anns v Merton London Borough Council*: 'If there was at one time a supposed rule that the doctrine of *Donoghue v Stevenson* did not apply to realty, there is no doubt that under modern authority a builder of defective premises may be liable in negligence to persons who thereby suffer injury.'[4] A further example can be seen in *Target v Torfaen Borough Council*[5] where landlords were held liable for the negligent design of an external stairway to a house. The stair was poorly lit and the handrail inadequate, and as a result the claimant fell and was injured.

Liability for damage to 'other property' has been considered in a number of cases. For example, in *Nitrigin Eireann Teoranta v Inco Alloys Ltd*[6] when pipes supplied by a

---

[1] [2011] 3 BLR 206 (CA).
[2] [1989] AC 177, see also *Rimmer v Liverpool City Council* [1984] 2 WLR 426 (CA).
[3] (1990) 50 BLR 1 (HL).
[4] [1978] AC 728 (HL); Lord Wilberforce at 758.
[5] [1992] 3 All ER 27 (CA).
[6] [1992] 1 WLR 498.

Cornes and Lupton's Design Liability in the Construction Industry, Fifth Edition. Sarah Lupton.
© 2013 Sarah Lupton and DL Cornes. Published 2013 by Blackwell Publishing Ltd.

specialist pipe manufacturer exploded due to cracking, and damaged other areas of the plant in which they were installed, this was considered 'other property' and the cost of repair was recovered by the building owner. A more recent example concerning a contractor is *Barclays Bank Plc v Fairclough Building Ltd*.[7] Here a specialist working on one part of a building (the roof) negligently caused asbestos fibres to infiltrate other parts of the building, and the Judge considered that there was liability for causing damage to 'other property'. Similarly, in *London Waste Ltd v Amec Civil Engineering Ltd*,[8] where newly-installed faulty cables caused damage to electrical equipment, the damage was recoverable. It is considered likely that this principle would extend to situations where a contractor working on a flat causes damage to other flats in the same block.[9]

However where the work is carried out to a whole building, the courts are likely to treat it as one unit, rather than to consider parts as 'other property'. For example, in *Bellefield Computer Services v E Turner & Sons Ltd*[10] the defendant contractor, E Turner & Sons Ltd had built a dairy building in 1981, and had sub-contracted some of the design to Horace D Watkins, a firm of architects. In 1989 the original owners of the dairy sold it to the claimant Bellefield Computers Ltd, who used it for storing goods. A fire broke out in 1995 in the storage area and spread to the rest of the building, causing extensive damage to the building and its contents, and losses to Bellefield. Bellefield brought a claim against the contractor. It was accepted at the first trial that the spread of the fire was attributable to the contractor's failure to construct a compartment wall and/or fire lining in accordance with good building practice (the wall was not sufficiently high and did not form a proper fire enclosure to the storage area). As a preliminary issue the court was asked to decide whether the contractor owed a duty of care in respect of the damage caused. The court found that the claimant was entitled to recover loss caused by fire damage to contents, but not to the building itself. The claimant appealed, and the Court of Appeal agreed with the lower court. It refused to accept the argument that the fact that one side of building was used for a different purpose to the other, made it 'other property'.

Clearly claimants would benefit from persuading a court that damage was in fact to 'other property', as their ability to establish that a defendant owed any duty in tort may depend on this. The dividing line between what constitutes damage to the work itself, and damage to 'other property' is, however, often far from clear and has led to the development of an area of the law termed the 'complex structure' theory.

4.2 The 'complex structure' theory after Murphy

In *D & F Estates*, Lord Bridge had raised the possibility that one element of a structure could be regarded as distinct from the other elements, so that damage to one part of the structure caused by a hidden defect in another part could qualify as damage to

---

[7] (1994) 10 ConLJ 48, (1993) CILL 848, reversed at CA, but not on this point.
[8] (1997) 83 Build LR 136.
[9] Stephen Furst and Vivien Ramsey (eds), *Keating on Construction Contracts*, 9th edn (London: Sweet & Maxwell, 2012), p. 239 para. 7–008, citing *Lindenberg v Canning* (1992) 62 BLR 117.
[10] [2000] BLR 97 (CA).

'other property'.[11] This raised the possibility of using this so-called 'complex structure' theory to pursue cases in tort that might otherwise have been hopeless.[12] The theory was revisited by the House of Lords in *Murphy* where Lord Bridge said:

> A critical distinction must be drawn here between some part of a complex structure which is said to be a 'danger' only because it does not perform its proper function in sustaining the other parts and some distinct item incorporated in the structure which positively malfunctions so as to inflict positive damage on the structure in which it is incorporated. Thus, if a defective central heating boiler explodes and damages a house or a defective electrical installation mal-functions and sets the house on fire, I see no reason to doubt that the owner of the house, if he can prove that the damage was due to the negligence of the boiler manufacturer in the one case or the electrical contractor in the other, can recover damages in tort on *Donoghue v Stevenson* principles. But the position of the law is entirely different where, by reason of the inadequacy of the foundations of the building to support the weight of the superstructure, differential settlement and consequential cracking appears. Here, once the first cracks appear, the structure as a whole is seen to be defective and the nature of the defect is known. Even if, contrary to my view, the initial damage could be regarded as damage to other property caused by a latent defect, once the defect is known, the situation of the building owner is analogous to that of the car owner who discovers that the car has faulty brakes. He may have a house which, until repairs are effected, is unfit for habitation, but the building no longer represents a source of danger and as it deteriorates will only damage itself.[13]

In the same case Lord Keith of Kinkel said this:

> I think that it would be unrealistic to take this view as regards a building the whole of which had been erected and equipped by the same contractor. In that situation, the whole package provided by the contractor would, in my opinion, fall to be regarded as one unit rendered unsound as such by a defect in the particular part. On the other hand, where, for example, the electric wiring had been installed by a sub-contractor and due to a defect caused by lack of care a fire occurred which destroyed the building, it might not be stretching ordinary princi-ples too far to hold the electrical sub-contractor liable for the damage.[14]

It can be seen that there are fairly close parallels in the speeches of Lord Keith and Lord Bridge as to the principles involved. However, Lord Jauncey said that the only context in which the complex structure theory might operate would be:

> . . . where one integral component of the structure was built by a separate contractor and where a defect in such a component had caused damage to other parts of the structure, e.g. a steel frame erected by a specialist contractor which failed to give adequate support to floor or walls. Defects in such ancillary equipment as central heating boilers or electrical installations

---

[11] [1989] AC 177 (HL), para. 34.

[12] see e.g. *Hoskisson & another v Donald Moody Ltd* (1989) 46 BLR 81 where it was suggested that a firm of engineers could be liable in tort to a homeowner with whom it had no contract on a complex structure basis – the foundations it designed had caused damage to the rest of the house.

[13] [1991] 1 AC 398 at 478–9 (or [1990] 2 All ER 990, at 926).

[14] [1991] 1 AC 398 at 478–9 at p. 470.

would be subject to the normal *Donoghue v Stevenson* principles if such defects gave rise to damage to other parts of the building.[15]

These speeches taken together raise as many questions as they answer. It is unfortunate that the law in this important area should have been left as such by the House of Lords in a case where opportunity could have been taken to establish clear precedent: Lords Keith and Bridge appear to associate the complex structure theory with catastrophic failure, explosions and fires. They also appear to say that a building is otherwise to be regarded as 'one unit' (Lord Keith) and that foundations and superstructure are indivisible (Lord Bridge). That might be regarded as the majority decision of the House of Lords. On the other hand, a steel frame erected by a specialist sub-contractor is divisible from the floors and walls (Lord Jauncey). It is difficult, if not impossible, to justify an apparent distinction between, on the one hand, structure and foundations being indivisible and, on the other hand, steel structure and walls and floors being separable albeit on the assumption that the steel frame work, was sub-contracted.

Clearly, the complex structure theory was not overruled by *Murphy*. It was the situation of an exploding catastrophic failure in a pipe, damaging other parts of the plant, that had led to liability for that damage in *Nitrigin Eireann Teoranta v Inca Alloys*[16] mentioned above. In this case the faulty pipes had been supplied by a separately engaged specialist pipe manufacturer and therefore fell squarely under the situation defined above by Lord Jauncey.

The complex structure theory was applied shortly after in 1994 in the case of *Jacobs v Morton & Partners*,[17] where negligently constructed underpinning caused damage to a house. Four years later, however, in *Tunnel Refineries Ltd v Donkin & Co Ltd*[18] the theory was considered but not applied. In this case Tunnel Refineries contracted with Donkin to provide two eight-ton compressors, which included fans provided by sub-contractor, Alsthom. The fans were defective and wrecked the compressors. The court found that the fans and the compressors constituted one item, and the complex structure theory could not be used. It followed *Warner v Basildon Development Corporation*[19] where the Court of Appeal held that the subsequent purchaser of a house could not rely upon any theory of complex structures in suing a builder in tort for negligently constructing the foundations. Subsequent cases such as *Bellefield*, outlined above, also refused to apply the theory, with Schiemann LJ commenting:

> . . . the whole of the dairy was built at the same time by the builders, marketed as a unit, bought as a unit to be used as a unit and was used as a unit. I have no doubt that any holding either that (1) the rooms on one side of the wall should be treated for present purposes as constituting a different building from the rooms on the other side of the wall, or that (2) the wall should be treated as constituting a different building from the rooms on one side of it, would be a thoroughly undesirable approach to the issues before us.[20]

---

[15] ibid., at 497.
[16] (1991) 60 BLR 65.
[17] (1994) 72 Build LR 92.
[18] [1998] CILL 1392.
[19] (1991) 7 Const LJ 146, 156.
[20] [2000] BLR 97, at para. 22.

Similarly, in *Payne v Setchell* Judge Humphrey Lloyd concluded that 'not only is the "complex structure" exception no longer tenable but it is also clear that in approaching the question of "another part of the property" it is necessary to avoid any artificiality and to be realistic'.[21] He refused to accept that part of a continuous foundation slab running under one property should be treated as separate to that part running under the adjoining property.

The case of *Linklaters Business Services v Sir Robert Mc Alpine Ltd*[22] required a re-examination of the 'complex structure' theory as it applies to sub-contractors. The claimant (Linklaters), appointed a developer to undertake extensive refurbishment works to their premises at 1 Silk Street, London. The developer engaged Sir Robert McAlpine Ltd who in turn engaged a specialist mechanical and electrical engineering subcontractor, How Engineering Services (HES). HES then entered into a further sub-contract with Southern Insulation Ltd (Southern) to supply and install thermal insulation to the vertical chilled water pipework. The work was completed in 1996, and in October 2009, Linklaters commenced proceedings against the main contractor and HES with respect to a leak found in 2006 in one of the vertical chilled water pipes. The leak had caused extensive rust or corrosion due to a failure to properly apply the thermal insulation and vapour barrier to the pipework. HES in turn commenced proceedings against Southern, who applied to strike out the claim on the basis that it was clear law that it did not owe a duty of care in tort. One of the key issues was 'whether one must classify the insulated steel pipework as one "thing" or, in the context that the pipework was part of an installation in an overall building, whether it is to be considered simply as an indivisible part of the whole building'.[23] The Judge declined to strike out the claim, stating that he was 'nowhere near confident enough' that this was an appropriate case for strike out. A material factor in his decision was that this is an area of developing jurisprudence. However when the case went to full trial in 2010, he decided that Southern had not been in breach of any duty of care. Furthermore, after analysing the position in *D & F Estates* and *Murphy* he concluded:

> I have formed the view that the insulated chilled water pipework was essentially one 'thing' for the purposes of tort. One would simply never have chilled water pipework without insulation because the chilled water would not remain chilled and it would corrode. The insulation is a key component but a component nonetheless. It would follow that no cause of action arises in tort as between Southern and Linklaters.[24]

Although the complex theory did not work in this situation, the Judge did not dismiss it entirely, and appeared to accept that it may apply in situations where a distinct element of a structure causes damage to another part. However until this question is given further judicial consideration it has to be regarded as unresolved.

---

[21] [2002] BLR 489, at para. 39.
[22] [2010] EWHC 1145 (TCC); [2010] EWHC 2931 (TCC).
[23] [2010] EWHC 1145 (TCC), at para. 25.
[24] [2010] EWHC 2931 (TCC), at para. 119.

4.3 What if a defect is patent?

Generally a designer would be unlikely to be held liable to a future owner or occupier if they were to purchase or take occupation of a property where the defects in question were self-evident, i.e. they were patent, rather than latent. What if the defects are patent but the owner has not in fact seen them?

Baxall Securities Ltd v Sheard Walshaw Partnership[25] explored the question of whether and to what extent the fact that the defect could have been spotted would have on the designer's liability. The case concerned errors in the design of a roof drainage system of a warehouse, which resulted in floods that damaged the stored contents. The architect for the project was Sheard Walshaw Partnership, who had been engaged by the developer Beresford Property Investments to design light industrial units for a site in Greater Manchester. Baxall was the tenant of one of the units. Prior to taking up the lease Baxall had engaged a surveyor to undertake a survey, which had detected damp but not its cause. After moving in there were two very heavy rainstorms, which caused two successive floods due to problems with the roof drainage system. The judge at first instance found that the architects were negligent in failing to specify sufficiently precise design requirements. He also found that if the claimant had been warned of the absence of overflows 'the floods would not have occurred'. He decided that the architects were not liable for damage caused by the first flood, as the inspection ought to have revealed the problem, however he found them liable for the second. The Court of Appeal concluded that the architects were not liable for the damage from either of the floods. It stated:

> Actual knowledge of the defect, or alternatively a reasonable opportunity for inspection that would unearth the defect, will usually negative the duty of care or at least break the chain of causation unless (as is not suggested in the present case) it is reasonable for the claimant not to remove the danger posed by the defect and to run the risk of injury: see *Targett v Torfaen BC* [1992] 3 All ER 27 at 37, *per* Nicholls V-C.[26]

Pearson Education Ltd v The Charter Partnership Ltd[27] is of significance in that it examined and expressed doubts over both the 'negative the duty of care' and the 'causation'[28] arguments in *Baxall*. The facts are remarkably similar to those in *Baxall*, in that it concerned the negligent design of a valley gutter. Pearson Education Ltd was the lessee of a warehouse, which it used to store books. The architects were the Charter Partnership Ltd, which had overall responsibility for the design and specification of the warehouse including the design of the rainwater system.

As with *Baxall*, there were two floods. In this case, following the first flood in 1994, there was an investigation including a survey by the insurer's engineers. The nature of the defect became apparent to the owner's loss adjusters, however the loss adjuster did not inform the lessee. The lease was then transferred to the claimant in 2000, however

---

[25] [2002] BLR 100 (CA) (at First Instance [2001] BLR 36 (TCC)).
[26] ibid., David Steel J, at para. 54.
[27] [2006] PNLR 14 CA (at First Instance [2005] EWHC 2021 (TCC)).
[28] Causation is explained in section 11.1.1.

Pearson did not arrange for a survey to be carried out before purchasing the lease. The court decided that such a survey would have disclosed the inadequacy. A second flood, eight years after the first, caused over £2,000,000 of damage to books stored in the warehouse by the claimant.

The judge at first instance decided that the ingress occurred because the system was inadequate to deal with foreseeable rainfall intensity. The defendant architects nevertheless contended that they were only potentially liable in respect of the defective guttering so long as that defect remained latent, and that therefore after the first flood they could no longer be held liable. They relied upon the previous decision in *Baxall*. However the Judge (HHJ Thornton QC) held the architects liable at first instance and the Court of Appeal upheld this decision. It distinguished *Baxall* on the basis of differences in the facts, but it was clear it was not satisfied by the reasoning in that case, finding it not to be 'wholly satisfactory'. In respect of whether the fact that a defect was 'patent' could negative a duty of care it stated:

> ... if an architect who has the primary responsibility for producing a safe design produces a defective design, it is not obviously fair, just and reasonable that he should be absolved from any liability in tort in respect of its consequences on the ground that another professional could reasonably be expected to discover his shortcoming.[29]

It also implied, by its approval of criticism made in *Hudsons*,[30] that the *Baxall* 'patent defect defence' should only apply where a defect is so obvious no reasonably competent professional could have failed to identify it. It would seem unlikely, therefore, that a designer would be able to rely on this defence, except in unusual circumstances.

4.4 Liability for economic loss

The case of *Murphy v Brentwood* left many areas of the law of negligence up for debate, and these have been explored through case law during the last 20 years.

A key area to be resolved after *Murphy* was the tension between *Hedley Byrne* liability for economic loss through negligent advice, and the clear statement in *Murphy v Brentwood* regarding the position of a contractor with regard to these losses when caused by a negligent act. *Murphy v Brentwood* had expressly preserved the position regarding *Hedley Byrne* type of liability, which was founded on the assumption of responsibility by the giver of the advice, and on the close relationship between the parties.

However in a complex construction procurement context, the distinction between these types of liability may be far from clear. Where does design fit in this scenario, is it 'advice' or an act? What happens in the case where a contractor undertakes design and/or provides advice in relation to a project it constructs? Does it make a difference

---

[29] [2002] BLR 100 (CA) Lord Phillips of Worth Matravers, CJ at para. 32.
[30] Mr Duncan Wallace QC: First Supplement to the 11th edn, *Hudson's Building and Engineering Contracts*, at para. 1.314; and in (2003) 119 LQR at 19.

if the advice is part of the services contracted for, or volunteered outside of the contract (a true *Hedley Byrne* situation)?

A 1995 case of fundamental importance was the House of Lords' decision in *Henderson v Merrett Syndicates Ltd*[31] and in particular the speeches of Lord Goff. Like *Hedley Byrne* this case concerned financial advice. Lloyd's of London is organised into syndicates which act as a market offering both insurance services and investment opportunities. Each syndicate shares the risk of underwriting insurance policies, with each investor having unlimited liability, and the business of the syndicate is managed by underwriting agents. In some cases where an investor (known as a 'name') became a member of a syndicate, the name's underwriting agent would enter into a sub-agency agreement under which it appointed a managing agent as its sub-agent to act as such in relation to the name. In such a case the name was known as an indirect name. In 1992 the extensive damage resulting from Hurricane Andrew led to exceptional losses for insurers, and investors were required to cover their share of the losses. They claimed against the underwriting agents for negligent mismanagement of the investment fund. (Mr Henderson was one of the investors, and Merrett Syndicates Ltd was one of the underwriting agents.)

It was accepted that the underwriting agents had a duty to exercise due care and skill in their activities, but the question at issue was whether the underwriting agents could be held liable to what were essentially indirect investors with whom they had not formed any contract. The underwriting agents argued that the question of liability on their part with respect to the syndicates' investors should be governed by the terms of the contracts between the parties and not by the law of tort. The court however found that the agents had a duty of care to avoid causing economic loss.

Although it related to financial services, the judgment was more widely expressed to suggest that it could include other types of service. Lord Goff held that the principle underlying *Hedley Byrne* was an assumption of responsibility by the person providing information or services to the claimant together with reliance by the claimant. (Amongst other cases[32] he relied on *Batty v Metropolitan Property Realisations Ltd*,[33] which found that there could be a parallel tortious duty to that in contract, a finding not over-ruled by *Murphy v Brentwood*.) Lord Goff stated:

> We can see that it rests upon a relationship between the parties, which may be general or specific to the particular transaction, and which may or may not be contractual in nature. All of their Lordships spoke in terms of one party having assumed or undertaken a responsibility towards the other . . . though *Hedley Byrne* was concerned with the provision of information and advice, the example given by Lord Devlin of the relationship between solicitor and client, and his and Lord Morris's statements of principle, show that the principle extends beyond the provision of information and advice to include the performance of other services . . . The concept provides its own explanation as to why there is no problem in cases of this kind about liability for pure economic loss; for if a person assumes responsibility to another in respect of

---

[31] [1995] 2 AC 145.
[32] E.g. *Caparo Industries Plc v Dickman* [1990] 2 AC 605.
[33] (1977) 7 BLR 1 (CA), see section 3.6.

certain services there is no reason why he should not be liable in damages for that other in respect of economic loss which flows from the negligent performance of those services. It follows that, once the case is identified as falling within the *Hedley Byrne* principle, there should be no need to embark upon further enquiry whether it is 'fair, just and reasonable' to impose liability for economic loss – a point which is, I consider, of some importance in this present case.[34]

He subsequently added:

I do not find it objectionable that the claimant may be entitled to take advantage of the remedy which is most advantageous to him, subject only to ascertaining whether the tortious duty is so inconsistent with the applicable contract that, in accordance with ordinary principle, the parties must be taken to have agreed that the tortious remedy is to be limited or excluded. . . .

Henderson v Merrett was of great significance to the issue of liability for pure economic loss without injury to person or property, for two principle reasons: it extended the principle established in *Hedley Byrne v Heller* from the making of negligent misstatements to negligent performance of services; and in addition it established that the performance of services can create a tortious duty concurrently with contractual obligations. It therefore brought together principles established in *Hedley Byrne* and in *Batty*. The House of Lords also accepted that in some circumstances the existence of a contractual relationship may in itself be sufficient to justify an 'assumption of responsibility' in pure economic loss cases, but only where there is an express or implied obligation to exercise reasonable skill and care.

4.5 *Application of the tests following* Henderson v Merrett

In *Henderson* the House of Lords reached its decision by using the 'assumption of responsibility' test, rather than applying the three-stage test developed in *Caparo v Dickman* (see section 3.11). It found that there was sufficient proximity between the parties despite the lack of direct contact, stating 'the relationship between name and managing agent appears to provide a classic example of the type of relationship to which the principle in *Hedley Byrne* applies.'[35] The defendants were taken to have assumed responsibility to the claimant to guard against the type of loss for which damages were claimed.

The tests were further considered in subsequent cases. In *Merret v Babb*[36] the Court of Appeal, following *Smith v Eric Bush*,[37] found a surveyor engaged by a mortgage company liable to a home purchaser, although he had never met the claimants. The Court stated 'the law recognises that in those circumstances there is a duty of

---

[34] [1994] 3 All ER 506 at 520–1.
[35] ibid.
[36] [2001] BLR 483.
[37] [1990] 1 AC 831 (HL).

care without the need to find any direct overt dealings between the valuer and the purchaser.'[38]

In *Customs & Excise Commissioners v Barclays Bank plc*[39] the House of Lords took the opportunity to thoroughly review the alternative approaches. Three were identified:

- the 'assumption of responsibility' test (as established in *Hedley Byrne*, see section 3.5.1)
- the threefold test, and
- the incremental approach (both as recognised in *Caparo*, see section 3.11).

Some useful comments were made on the application of these tests. Their Lordships confirmed that there are cases 'in which one party can accurately be said to have assumed responsibility for what is said or done to another, the paradigm situation being a relationship having all the indicia of contract save consideration'. *Hedley Byrne* fell into this category. They pointed out that if there is proof of an assumption of responsibility, assessed on an objective basis, there is no need to look further as to whether it might be fair, just or reasonable to impose a duty.[40] Conversely, although proof of actual assumption may be a sufficient condition to establish a duty, it may not always be necessary; where there is no proof then the threefold test may be appropriate. The threefold test could be applied in novel situations, but is not straightforward. The incremental test is 'of little value as a test in itself' but may be used in conjunction with another test.[41]

Generally in a construction context the emphasis has been on the assumption of responsibility' test,[42] objectively applied. By 'objective' the courts mean that the actual intention is not relevant, it is whether, considering the circumstances of the event, an objective bystander would conclude that responsibility was assumed. As noted in *Customs & Excise*, 'the more notional the assumption of responsibility becomes, the less difference there is between this test and the threefold test' i.e. the party is 'taken to have assumed responsibility' in situations where the courts think this would be reasonable.

Examples of the developing law in this area are discussed below and in Chapter 10. However, it has to be said that although the tests provide general guidelines, they have developed over time, and have not always been applied consistently. It is therefore difficult to be precise about exactly which situations are likely to give rise to a duty, especially to third parties.

---

[38] [2001] BLR 483 (CA).

[39] [2007] 1 AC 181.

[40] *Henderson v Merrett Syndicates Ltd* [1995] 2 AC 145 (HL).

[41] [2007] 1 AC 181 (HL), Lord Bingham, at 189–92.

[42] see Stephen Furst and Vivien Ramsey (eds.), *Keating on Construction Contracts* (London: Sweet & Maxwell, 2012), 7–002.

4.6 *Contractors' liability for pure economic loss*

There then followed a sequence of cases which at the time of writing culminated in a Court of Appeal decision in *Robinson v P E Jones (Contractors) Ltd*[43] where the court addressed the core question 'can a builder in principle and without more, owe a duty of care in tort to his client, concurrent with his duty in contract, in respect of economic loss?' The sequence leading up to this case was helpfully summarised by Lord Justice Jackson in that case as follows:

> The question whether building contractors owe concurrent duties of care in tort to protect their employers against economic loss has been discussed in a number of first instance decisions of Official Referees and TCC Judges. In *Storey v Charles Church Developments plc* [1995] 73 Con LR 1 Judge Hicks QC, sitting as Official Referee, held that there was such a duty. In *Payne v John Setchell Ltd* [2002] BLR 489 Judge Humphrey Lloyd QC considered that there was not: see para. 30. In *Tesco Stores Ltd v Costain Construction Limited* [2003] EWHC 1487 (TCC) Judge Seymour QC considered that there was such a duty: see para. 230. In *Mirant-Asia Pacific Limited v OAPIL* [2004] EWHC 1750 (TCC) Judge Toulmin CMG QC held that engineers owed concurrent duties of care in contract and tort to protect their clients against economic loss. However, he indicated that contractors might be in a different category: see paras 395–7.[44]

Although not all of those cases dealt with contractors in a parallel contract situation, they nevertheless made useful comments on the above dichotomy. As *Robinson v Jones* may well not be the end of the matter, it is worth examining the cited examples in sequence, and then looking at the post-*Robinson v Jones* position of contractors and consultants.

The first case in the above quoted sequence was *Storey v Charles Church Developments Ltd*.[45] Charles Church, a contractor, designed and built a house for Mr and Mrs Storey, who subsequently claimed for the cost of underpinning required to rectify structural problems. These problems were caused by an error in the design of the foundations, but it was accepted that the loss was economic. As it had taken some time for the damage to appear, the claim was statute-barred and the case was brought on the basis of a concurrent duty of care in tort. HHJ Hicks QC applied *Henderson v Merrett* and found that by contracting with the claimant the contractor assumed responsibility to exercise reasonable skill and care in design and the owner had relied upon it to do so, therefore the *Hedley Byrne* principle applied, and the claimant could recover for economic loss. He concluded that such a duty was not affected by the fact that the designer in the case was also the builder; he therefore saw no reason to make a distinction between a professional or a design-build company. However he emphasised that the finding was based on the fact that is was a design error, not a construction fault, and that he considered

---

[43] [2011] 3 BLR 206 (CA).
[44] ibid., at para. 52.
[45] (1995) 73 Con LR 1.

Henderson extended to design services. He indicated that in his view 'a line must be drawn somewhere if builders are not to be concurrently liable in tort for all their contractual obligations, including workmanship as well as design, and including those which amount to warranties as well as those which can be expressed in terms of a duty of care'.[46] But he did not express any view as to exactly where it should be drawn.

The next significant case in the sequence is that of *Payne v Setchell*[47] (although it is worth noting that in *Bellefield Computer Services v E Turner & Sons Ltd*[48] a contractor was assumed to have a parallel duty). *Payne v Setchell* considered the liability of an engineer for economic losses resulting from negligent design and advice, but in doing so also commented on the position of a contractor. The case concerned two pairs of cottages, on two sites. Mr Wright engaged the structural engineers John Setchell Ltd to advise on the viability of extending an existing cottage on a site owned by his wife. This first engagement was to investigate the site and provide advice in the form of a report, which recommended that rather than extending the existing cottage, it should be demolished and a new structure erected on a reinforced concrete raft foundation. Mr Wright accepted the advice and in 1988 appointed John Setchell Ltd to design foundations for two new cottages (Nos 1 and 2) on the site and to inspect the works, and engaged Mr Samual Payne (Payne) to construct the cottages. The foundations were inspected, and Mr Setchell wrote to Mr Wright stating 'I hereby certify that the construction has been satisfactorily carried out to our design'.

Mr Wright's wife then bought the neighbouring site, and in 1990 transferred ownership to Mr Wright, who engaged Mr Payne to build two further cottages (Nos 3 and 4). During construction Mr Setchell certified the foundations of these cottages. On completion of the work, Mr Payne was paid by the transfer of one cottage (No. 3), leaving Mr Wright with No. 4. Mr Payne's son Gary bought No. 3 from Payne, using the August 1990 letter (Setchell's certification of the foundations) to obtain a mortgage. Mrs Wright fell in arrears with her mortgages for Nos 1 and 2 and these were re-possessed in 1992, following which Mr Payne bought No. 1 and his daughter bought No. 2. In 1997 cottage No. 4 developed cracks, Mr Wright started an action which was settled. In October 1999 a structural survey was undertaken which reported that Nos 1 and 2 had tilted, and on 29 December 1999 Mr Payne and his daughter started a further action.

To summarise, during the project Mr Setchell had prepared an initial report, designed the foundations, inspected the works and had issued two certificates, the first in October 1988 for cottages Nos 1 and 2 on the first site, for Mr Wright, the second in August 1990 for cottages Nos 3 and 4 on the second site, for Mr Payne. Because of limitation problems, the action was brought in tort, and various preliminary issues were raised. Essentially these concerned whether the engineers owed any duty in tort to Mr Payne or his daughter not to cause them economic loss. The Judge decided that the engineers had a duty to the claimants to avoid causing them loss or damage but that the duty was limited to avoiding causing physical injury or loss and damage to other property,

---

[46] ibid., at para. 29.
[47] [2002] BLR 489 (TCC).
[48] [2000] BLR 96 (CA), Schieman LJ at para. 17.

and did not extend to avoiding economic loss. The engineers did however owe a duty of care to third party purchasers of the cottages to avoid causing economic loss due to negligent statements made in the 'letter certificates'. In reaching this conclusion he reviewed previous case law and formed conclusions with more wide-reaching implications:

> In my judgment *Murphy* and *DOE v Bates*[49] establish that, as a matter of policy, any person undertaking work or services in the course of a construction process is ordinarily liable only for physical injury or for property damage other than to the building itself but is not liable for other losses – i.e. economic loss. If any liability for such economic loss is to arise it must be for other reasons, e.g. as a result of advice or statements made upon which reliance is placed in circumstances which create a relationship where there is in law to be an assumption of the responsibility for loss – i.e. within the principle of *Hedley Byrne v Heller* . . . In my judgment a designer is not liable in negligence to the client or to a subsequent purchaser for the cost of putting right a flaw in a design that the designer has produced that has not caused physical injury or damage, just as a contractor is not liable.[50]

Two subsequent cases criticised the above comments. The first was *Tesco Stores Ltd v Costain Construction Ltd.*[51] Tesco engaged Costain to design and build a supermarket, on a letter of intent in which the usual terms regarding skill and care were implied. Costain sub-contracted the design to a firm of architects, including the design of the fire-stopping. When a fire broke out the lack of fire-stops meant that damage was more extensive than it would otherwise have been. Tesco brought an action where it claimed that Costain was in breach of the contract by which it had agreed to design and construct the store, and that it was negligent, owing a duty of care which mirrored its contractual obligations. Amongst other things Costain argued that as it did not design the Redditch store itself, it did not owe any duty in respect of design or the fitness for purpose of the same, and that in any event it did not owe a duty of care in respect of damage to the property itself and/or economic loss. The court found that 'the duty of care owed by Costain to Tesco was to execute any building or design work which Costain in fact carried out itself with the care and skill to be expected of a reasonably competent building contractor so as not to cause damage to person or property or economic loss' but that a party to a contract did not owe a duty of care in tort for work it had not undertaken itself. The court concluded that 'anyone who undertakes by contract to perform a service for another upon terms, express or implied, that the service will be performed with reasonable skill and care, owes a duty of care to like effect to the other contracting party or parties which extends to not causing economic loss'. In commenting on *Payne v Setchell* the Judge held that:

> I differ from the analysis of Judge Lloyd with great hesitation, but I have to say that it does not seem to me that *Murphy v Brentwood District Council* and the other authorities to which

---

[49] [1991] 1 AC 499.
[50] [2002] BLR 489, at para. 30. See also paras 33 and 34 for summary on engineer's duty.
[51] [2003] CILL 2062 (TCC).

he referred do establish the proposition that a builder never owes a duty of care which extends to not causing economic loss, only that he does not do so in the absence of 'a special relationship' . . . If the position now is, as I consider that it is, that anyone who undertakes by contract to perform a service for another upon terms, express or implied, that the service will be performed with reasonable skill and care, owes a duty of care to like effect to the other contracting party or parties which extends to not causing economic loss, there seems to be no logical justification for making an exception in the case of a builder or the designer of a building. My reading of the authorities does not require or permit the making of such exception. I draw comfort in my analysis from the observation of Schiemann LJ in *Bellefield No. 1* that in his view the builder in that case did owe a duty of care to the original owner in respect of damage to the building itself.'[52]

The second case that declined to follow the reasoning in *Payne v Setchell* was *Mirant Asia-Pacific Construction (Hong Kong) v Ove Arup and Partners International (No. 2)*.[53] On the facts, Ove Arup was in breach of its duty to ensure the suitability of the design of foundations, including confirmation of the design assumptions. HHJ Toulmin distinguished *Murphy v Bentwood* on the basis that this did not concern the duty of professionals, and held that *Henderson* principles applied in the case of an engineer's concurrent duty of care to his client in respect of economic losses referable to design errors. After reviewing the speeches of Lord Goff, he concluded that:

Applying an objective test and bearing in mind the questions raised by Sir Brian Neill in both the cited judgments, I conclude that in relation to CEPAS, Arup assumed a responsibility for economic loss following the reasoning derived from Lord Goff's judgment. In so far as I need to do so I respectfully disagree with the judgment of HH Judge Lloyd QC in *Payne v Setchell* where he places a designer in the same position as a contractor. It seems to me that where the designer performs services of a professional or quasi-professional nature it is in the same position as bankers, solicitors, surveyors, valuers and accountants. . . . Arup assumed responsibility to CEPAS for design services and there is no reason why it should not be liable in damages for any economic loss which flows from the negligent performance of such services. . . . It is not part of the reasoning of my finding, but in relation to the distinction between builder and designer it is right to note that a builder warrants that its works will be fit for the purpose, see *Young and Marten v McManus Childs* [1968] 9 BLR 7 whereas a professional advisor warrants only that he will exercise reasonable care and skill.[54]

Unlike *Payne v Setchell*, the court here took a different approach to the position of a contractor as to that of a professional.

Robinson v P E Jones (Contractors) Ltd[55] tied together some of the above threads in that it considered the issue of whether a builder can owe a duty of care for economic loss where there is a parallel contract with the claimants. Mr Robinson entered into a contract with a building company (Jones) whereby Jones agreed to build and sell to Mr

---

[52] ibid., at para. 230.
[53] [2004] 97 Con LR 1 (TCC).
[54] Paras 395–7.
[55] [2011] 3 BLR 206 (CA).

Robinson a new house on a plot in Prestbury, Cheshire. Mr Robinson wished to have gas fires in the lounge and in the family room, so the contractor constructed chimney flues in both rooms. Mr Robinson arranged directly with British Gas for the supply and installation of the gas fires. Over 12 years later, the fire in the lounge failed a service test by British Gas. The test checked that the gas fire was effectively drawing combustion products from the room in which it was located, and it was noted by the service engineer that the gas fire had a 'poor flue run'. The fires were disconnected and a subsequent report by a surveyor concluded that the flues had not been constructed in accordance with good building practice or with the applicable Building Regulations. The Technology and Construction Court was asked to decide as a preliminary issue:

> Whether or not a builder who contracts with his client to undertake building works can, in principle and without more, owe his client a duty of care in tort, concurrent with his duty in contract, to undertake the works with reasonable care and skill so as to prevent his client from incurring the cost of putting right defects in the works. Put more succinctly, can a builder owe a duty of care in tort to his client, concurrent with his duty in contract, in respect of economic loss?[56]

The defence accepted that, following the decision of the House of Lords in *Henderson v Merrett Syndicates*,[57] it was possible for a party to be held to have assumed responsibility to another party for the provision of information or services so as to found a duty of care in tort not to cause economic loss, but argued that the duty required something more than the existence of a contractual relationship, and that there was nothing more in this case. It also argued that *Tesco Stores v Costain & Others*,[58] where the judge held that the defendant builder did owe a concurrent duty of care in tort to the claimant employer, was wrongly decided and should not be followed. HHJ Stephen Davies examined *Murphy v Brentwood*, and concluded:

> It appears that the speeches are all directed to the position where there is no contractual relationship between the builder and the owner . . . it is clear from the speech of Lord Bridge, in particular those passages at pp. 475D–F, 479B–C, 480F–G and 481D, that nothing in his judgment was intended to exclude a duty of care to guard against economic loss arising where there was a special relationship of proximity, as in *Hedley Byrne v Heller* . . . It follows that I do not agree with the submission of Mr Budworth that *Murphy v Brentwood* is binding authority to the effect that a builder who contracts with the claimant to build a house can not be held to owe a duty of care to owners or occupiers of property constructed by the builder save in relation to defects which cause either personal injury or physical damage to real property other than the property itself.[59]

This conclusion was supported by his analysis of earlier cases, in particular *Batty v Metropolitan Property Realisations Ltd*[60] of which he said:

---

[56] [2010] EWHC 102 (TCC), HHJ Stephen Davies at para. 6.
[57] [1995] 2 AC 145.
[58] [2003] EWHC 1487 (TCC).
[59] [2010] EWHC 102 (TCC) at paras 22–3.
[60] (1977) 7 BLR 1 (CA), see section 3.6.

Batty stands as a decision of the Court of Appeal, which has not been overruled or doubted on this point, to the effect that a developer who enters into a contractual warranty with a purchaser to build a house in an efficient and workmanlike manner can also owe the purchaser a duty of care in tort under the principle in *Hedley Byrne v Heller*.[61]

He also reviewed *Henderson v Merrett* and took the analysis one step further, concluding that not only could a party owe a parallel duty in tort, but that the contractual relationship itself may be enough to create such a duty, stating:

> In my judgement it is clear from the speech of Lord Goff that the existence of a contractual relationship, where there is an express or implied obligation to exercise reasonable care and skill, may in itself be sufficient to justify an assumption of responsibility and concomitant reliance, and that this principle is capable of applying to all cases involving the provision of services, not just the provision of professional services by professional men.[62]

The key distinction was not between a contract for professional services and one for undertaking construction work, but whether the contract required the contractor to use skill and care (as opposed to providing something fit for purpose). He found 'powerful support' in the case of *Barclays Bank Plc v Fairclough Building Ltd*.[63] In that case specialist sub-sub-contractors were found liable in tort to sub-contractors, when roof cleaning work that they had undertaken caused the sub-contractors economic loss (due to amounts paid to the main contractor). The Court of Appeal had reached its conclusion after a thorough examination of the authorities, including *Murphy* and *Henderson v Merrett*, and stated that the sub-contractor had 'a concurrent duty in tort to avoid causing economic loss by failing to exercise the care and skill of a competent contractor'. It had emphasised the specialist nature of the task, with Beldam LJ stating:

> A skilled contractor undertaking maintenance work to a building assumes a responsibility which invites reliance no less than the financial or other professional adviser does in undertaking his work. The nature of the responsibility is the same although it will differ in extent.[64]

In conclusion HHJ Stephen Davies relied on *Storey v Charles Church Developments Ltd*[65] in support of his view that this duty could be owed by a contractor as well as by a professional. The Judge therefore decided that the contractor could owe a duty to its client to avoid causing it economic loss. However in this particular case, the contract contained provisions which successfully excluded the contractor's liability in tort (the sales agreement expressly excluded any liability for defects in the house other than as provided by an NHBC agreement).

---

[61] [2010] EWHC 102 (TCC), at para. 20.
[62] [2010] EWHC 102 (TCC), ibid., para. 35, referring to [1995] 2 AC 145, at 193B.
[63] (1995) 44 Con LR 35.
[64] ibid., at para. 47.
[65] (1995) 73 Con LR 1.

The decision was appealed, and although the Court of Appeal dismissed the appeal, it did not agree with the lower court's reasoning regarding the relationship between contract and tort, and the possibility of parallel tortious duties. It stated:

> Absent any assumption of responsibility, there do not spring up between the parties duties of care co-extensive with their contractual obligations. The law of tort imposes a different and more limited duty upon the manufacturer or builder. That more limited duty is to take reasonable care to protect the client against suffering personal injury or damage to other property. The law of tort imposes this duty, not only towards the first person to acquire the chattel or the building, but also towards others who foreseeably own or use it.[66]

The Court therefore concluded firmly that a contractual obligation to use skill and care was not sufficient to establish a tortious duty. It then examined whether a *Hedley Byrne* type relationship nevertheless existed in this situation, so as to give rise to a duty of care:

> It is perhaps understandable that professional persons are taken to assume responsibility for economic loss to their clients. Typically, they give advice, prepare reports, draw up accounts, produce plans and so forth. They expect their clients and possibly others to act in reliance upon their work product, often with financial or economic consequences.
>
> When one moves beyond the realm of professional retainers, it by no means follows that every contracting party assumes responsibilities (in the *Hedley Byrne* sense) to the other parties co-extensive with the contractual obligations. Such an analysis would be nonsensical. Contractual and tortious duties have different origins and different functions. Contractual obligations spring from the consent of the parties and the common law principle that contracts should be enforced. Tortuous duties are imposed by law, as a matter of policy, in specific situations. Sometimes a particular set of facts may give rise to identical contractual and tortious duties, but self-evidently that is not always the case.[67]

It then considered the application of this reasoning to the facts of the case and concluded:

> In the present case I see nothing to suggest that the defendant 'assumed responsibility' to the claimant in the *Hedley Byrne* sense. The parties entered into a normal contract whereby the defendant would complete the construction of a house for the claimant to an agreed specification and the claimant would pay the purchase price. The defendant's warranties of quality were set out and the claimant's remedies in the event of breach of warranty were also set out. The parties were not in a professional relationship whereby, for example, the claimant was paying the defendant to give advice or to prepare reports or plans upon which the claimant would act.[68]

---

[66] [2011] 3 BLR 206 (CA) Jackson LJ, at para. 68.
[67] ibid., at paras 75 and 76.
[68] ibid., at para. 83.

It seems clear that, following the above case, a contractor is unlikely to be found to be under a duty to protect its employer from 'pure' economic losses due to its negligence, solely on the basis that there is a contract between the parties. It should be noted, however, that in *Robinson v Jones* the Court of Appeal emphasised that this was a contract to build and sell (although the principle would also apply to a builder who was not a vendor),[69] distinguishing it from a 'professional' contract to provide a service or advice. However the precise basis for this distinction is not clear. The Court did not comment on *Barclays Bank Plc v Fairclough Building Ltd*, so left unanswered the question as to whether or not a contract for construction services, even if of a specialist nature, would normally be in the same category as a professional contract.[70] It also did not explore whether the fault in the flue was one of workmanship or design, but treated the contract as a single package, and furthermore did not discuss whether it accepted Judge Hick's distinction in *Storey v Charles Church Developments* between a contractor's tortious duties for construction work and for design services. It therefore left open some scope for a duty to arise in other circumstances, for example where the contractor provides design advice only, or undertakes to design and construct. At the time of writing there have been no further decisions on this point, the current position being reflected in these comments from *Broster v Galliard Docklands Ltd*:

> There would, on the pleaded case, be a cause of action in contract as between Galliard and ECL but the cause of action in tort would, in the light of the recent Court of Appeal decision in *Robinson v P E Jones (Contractors) Ltd* 2011 EWCA Civ 9, be limited at most to a complaint not of bad workmanship (failing to put in straps specified in the design) but of bad design (failing to specify straps in the design).[71]

What about the contractor's liability to third parties? *Murphy v Brentwood* was understood to severely restrict the scope and likelihood for such a duty being found, and none of the cases above (and indeed any subsequent cases) found a contractor liable to third parties for pure economic loss. This general principle has been frequently re-affirmed, for example in *Linklaters Business Services v Sir Robert McAlpine Ltd* where the court stated that 'cases such as *Murphy*, *D & F Estates* and *Bellefield* . . . were primarily concerned with whether the overall builder of the whole building owes a duty of care to owners or occupiers of that building with whom it has not been in contract. It is well-established law in such a case that the builder's duty of care, at least generally if not invariably, does not extend to damage to the building itself'.[72] Nevertheless, although this would undoubtedly apply to normal contracts for work and materials there remains a possibility, as discussed above, that a *Hedley Byrne* type of duty might arise in special circumstances, for example where a contractor provides advice on design matters.

---

[69] Stanley Burnton LJ, at para. 92.
[70] Note that *Barclays Bank Plc v Fairclough Building Ltd* had been criticised by the *Building Law Report* editors at 76 BLR 4, and by other commentators.
[71] [2011] EWHC 1722 (TCC).
[72] [2010] EWHC 1145 (TCC), Akenhead J, at para. 25.

4.7 *Consultants' liability for pure economic loss*

Following *Henderson v Merrett* there was a sequence of cases where consultants have been found to have a parallel duty to their client to avoid causing them economic loss. It is obvious that the consultant/client relationship is likely to establish the kind of close proximity, and the expectation of reliance on advice, on which the *Hedley Byrne* principle is based, and it would be a natural progression to extend this to cover design services. As outlined above, the *Hedley Byrne* principle was extended in *Henderson v Merrett* to cover a wider range of circumstances than the provision of financial or other advice, to include other services, and other professions: 'As a matter of principle, it is difficult to see why concurrent remedies in tort and contract, if available against the medical profession, should not also be available against members of other professions, whatever form the relevant damage may take'.[73]

Even prior to *Henderson v Merrett*, there had been cases, for example *Pirelli General Cable Works Ltd v Oscar Faber & Partners*[74] (approved in *Murphy v Brentwood*), where such a duty had been found. Similarly, in the cases of *Wessex Regional Health Authority v HLM Design*,[75] an architect was found liable to his client in tort for negligent certification, and the issuing of an extension of time. In *Conway v Crowe Kelsey & Partner*[76] architects were also found liable for economic loss.

The 1993 case of *Lancashire and Cheshire Baptist Churches Incorporated v Howard and Seddon Partnership*[77] should also be noted. The architects Howard and Seddon were appointed through the Manpower Services Commission, to design a sanctuary for a church. The architects in turn engaged the workforce, and were effectively acting as main contractor, on a design-build basis. It was alleged that there was condensation and inadequate ventilation. The claim in contract was out of time for limitation purposes and the action proceeded on the claim in tort. The Judge had no difficulty in holding that the architect owed parallel duties in tort to avoid causing their clients economic loss.[78] However, although in principle liable, he decided that in this case there had been no assumption of responsibility stating:'I find as a fact that when submitting designs the defendants did not make any express statement about the technical qualities of the proposed building . . . it would, in my judgement, be artificial to treat the submission of drawings and designs by an architect to his client as some form of implied statement as to the technical adequacy of the proposed building'.[79] This distinction between statements or advice and drawings and designs has however not generally been followed in later cases and is thought to be incorrect.[80] Depending on the circumstances a consultant could be taken to have assumed responsibility to their client even where no express statement is made about the design.

---

[73] [1995] 2 AC 145, Lord Goff.
[74] (1983) 21 BLR 99 (HL), see 3.11 and 12.3.2.
[75] (1995) 71 BLR 32 (TCC).
[76] (1994) 39 ConLR 1.
[77] [1993] 3 All ER 467.
[78] ibid., at 474.
[79] ibid., at 477.
[80] Stephen Furst and Vivien Ramsey (eds), *Keating on Construction Contracts*, 9th edn (London: Sweet & Maxwell, 2012), 7–035, fn 206.

Following *Henderson* and *Merrett*, further cases appeared. In *Holt v Payne Skillington and De Groot Collis*[81] solicitors were found liable in tort to their clients in respect of advice given regarding the purchase of a property. More recently, in *Bellefield Computer Services v E. Turner & Sons Ltd (No. 2)*[82] the court accepted, following *Henderson*, that the architects owed concurrent duties in tort, inlcuding for design services, to the builder by whom they were employed. Of course in *Payne v Setchell* the court found that *neither* the designer nor the contractor had a concurrent duty in negligence to avoid causing the client 'pure' economic loss. However, as noted above,the court in *Mirant Asia Pacific Construction (Hong Kong) Ltd v Ove Arup & Partners (No 2)*[83] disagreed with the approach in Payne and the engineers were held liable in tort to their clients for losses caused by negligent inspection and verification of design assumptions. As summarised in *Robinson v Jones*:

> *Henderson* is now taken as the leading authority on concurrent liability in professional negligence. In my view, the conceptual basis upon which the concurrent liability of professional persons in tort to their clients now rests is assumption of responsibility. That is, for example, the underlying rationale of the engineers' liability to their clients in *Pirelli*. It is also the basis of the duty of care owed by the architects to their client in *Bellefield (No. 2)*. It is also the basis of the engineers' tortious liability to their clients in *Mirant-Asia*. See para. 395: 'Arup assumed a responsibility for economic loss.'[84]

The position now seems quite clear, in that a consultant would normally owe a duty in tort to its client to avoid causing the client economic loss (assuming there are no express limiting clauses in the contract). At first sight this may appear to be unfairly penalising consultants as opposed to contractors, i.e. making exactly the kind of distinction based on 'the now outmoded concept of status' that was criticised by Lord Goff in *Henderson v Merret*.[85] As noted above, the basis for the distinction as set out in *Robinson v Jones* is unclear. However, the difference has been explained as merely reflecting the usual relationship between professionals and their client, where the professional is more likely than a contractor to assume this responsibility,[86] in which case there is nothing to prevent there being exceptions either way round.

The position is less clear regarding liability outside of a parallel duty in contract. Generally speaking, courts are reluctant to find that a consultant would have a duty to third parties to avoid economic loss, except where a clear *Hedley Byrne* situation arises. For example, whereas in *Tesco Stores Ltd v the Norman Hitchcox Partnership Ltd*[87] the court found the architects liable to Tesco for damage to other property, it stated: 'In my

---

[81] (1995) 77 BLR 51.

[82] [2003] Lloyd's Rep PN 53 (CA).

[83] [2006} 1 BLR 187, see also *Riyad Bank v AHLI United Bank (UK) Plc* [2006] EWCA Civ 780 where a bank was held liable for failing to take reasonable care to protect investors against economic loss.

[84] [2011] 3 BLR 206 (CA), Jackson LJ, at para. 74.

[85] [1995] 2 AC 145, at 185–7; note also *Payne v Setchell* at para. 29, where it was concluded that there was nothing in the speeches in *Murphy* and *DOE v Bates* that justified 'a distinction being made between the "designer" and the "builder", nor is there any operational, practical or social reason to do so'.

[86] Stephen Furst and Vivien Ramsey (eds), *Keating on Construction Contracts*, 9th edn (London: Sweet & Maxwell, 2012), 7–024, citing *Robinson v Jones* [2011] 3 BLR 206 (CA), para. 75.

[87] (1997) 56 Con LR 42.

view, however, the decisions in *D & F Estates v Church Commissioners* and *Murphy v Brentwood DC* preclude Tesco from recovering any loss caused to them as a result of physical damage to the structure of the supermarket as opposed to the damage caused to stock and equipment.'[88]

In *Machin v Adams*,[89] a claim was brought by a purchaser against a firm of architects who wrote a letter to their client indicating that works to an extension had been satisfactorily carried out, with two weeks left to complete the project. The architects were aware that the owner would pass on the letter to a purchaser. However the architects were also under the impression that they would return to site for further inspections, and to issue further certificates, and were not aware the purchaser would make a decision on the basis of the letter alone. The court found that in these circumstances there was no assumption of responsibility, and the architects were not liable. More recently, in *Architype Projects Ltd v Dewhurst Macfarlane & Partners*[90] the court refused to find an engineer sub-consultant liable to the client for economic losses due to design errors, on the basis that the parties had 'structured their relationship in such a way that it is inconsistent with any such assumption of responsibility'.[91]

In *Technotrade Ltd v Larkstore Ltd*,[92] the developer of a site claimed against an engineer (Technotrade) which had negligently prepared a soil report. The developer had purchased the site from another developer, who had engaged Technotrade to undertake a survey and prepare the report. Following the purchase the second developer acquired and relied on the report, but unfortunately during construction a landslip occurred, and the project required extensive stabilisation works. It brought its claim in tort on *Hedley Byrne* principles, but the Judge at first instance held that 'an inference of proximity to a class of developers was not warranted or fair'.[93] Technotrade did not know at the time of its report that the development would be carried out by another party, to whom its report would be passed, nor that its report would be 'recycled' to satisfy further planning permission conditions. The court therefore found that the engineer did not owe the second developer a duty (although it did owe the house owners a duty in respect of the physical damage to the houses, which meant that the developer could claim contribution towards its own liability to the house owners, see 11.3).

4.8 Summary of the position in 2013

This is an unsettled area of the law, which in practical terms, for the purposes of designers, is difficult to set down as a clear set of precise guiding rules. For example, there is no hard and fast matrix of the situations where a duty of care to avoid economic loss may arise. It would be, in fact, very difficult to classify such situations with precision,

---

[88] ibid., HHJ Esyr Lewis at 170.
[89] [1997] 84 BLR 79 (CA).
[90] [2004] 96 Con LR 3 (TCC).
[91] ibid., HH Judge John Toulmin, at paras 69 and 70, see also section 10.2.1.
[92] [2006] BLR 345.
[93] ibid., at para. 56.

not least because the procurement routes and relationships between parties are becoming even more varied and complex.

It is nevertheless possible to tentatively summarise the general position at the time of writing as follows:

(a) those providing design services, whether as consultant or as a design and build contractor, owe a duty to take care to avoid injury to others caused by negligent design;[94]

(b) consultants and design-build contractors also owe such a duty to prevent damage to property, other than the works themselves (e.g. goods stored in the building, but not damage to the element that was the result of the design);[95]

(c) with respect to damage to 'other property', the complex structure theory is unlikely to succeed, but remains open to argument;[96]

(d) any duty to third parties will normally be founded on the concepts of proximity and reliance;[97]

(e) it is unlikely that the courts would make any distinction between 'design' and 'advice'; although there may still be a distinction between 'construction', a 'design and build' service and a 'design only';[98]

(f) consultants are likely to owe a parallel duty to their clients to avoid economic loss caused by negligent design;[99]

(g) a contractor who designs and constructs a house (or constructs to another's design) and sells it to a client is unlikely to owe a parallel duty to avoid economic loss;[100] although where a contractor is an expert providing design services, the existence of a duty remains an open question;

(h) a consultant (or contractor) providing design services is unlikely to owe duties to a third party to avoid economic loss, unless it is possible to establish a close relationship and reliance, e.g. if the consultant/contractor gives advice to that third party direct, and it is clear at the time the design/advice is given, that the third party intends to rely on it.[101] Tortious liability between parties working closely together as a team is discussed in Chapter 10.

---

[94] *Rimmer v Liverpool City Council* [1984] 2 WLR 426; *Murphy v Brentwood District Council* (1990) 50 BLR 1 (HL); *Targett v Torfaen Borough Council* [1992] 3 All ER 27 (CA).

[95] *Baxall Securities Ltd v Sheard Walshaw Partnership* (2002) BLR 100 (CA); *Bellefield Computer Services v E Turner & Sons Ltd (No 2)* [2003] Lloyd's Rep PN 53 (CA).

[96] *Murphy v Brentwood District Council* (1990) 50 BLR 1 (HL); *Linklaters Business Services v Sir Robert McAlpine Ltd* [2010] EWHC 1145 (TCC).

[97] *Henderson v Merrett Syndicates Ltd* [1995] 2 AC 145; *Customs & Excise Commissioners v Barclays Bank* [2007] 1 AC 181 (HL).

[98] *Batty v Metropolitan Property Realisations Ltd* (1977) 7 BLR 1; *Henderson v Merrett Syndicates Ltd* [1995] 2 AC 145 (HL).

[99] *Henderson v Merrett Syndicates Ltd* [1995] 2 AC 145 (HL); *Mirant Asia-Pacific Construction (Hong Kong) v Ove Arup and Partners International (No. 2)* (2006) 1 BLR 187 (TCC).

[100] *Payne v John Setchell Ltd* [2002] BLR 489; *Robinson v P E Jones (Contractors) Ltd* [2011] 3 BLR 206 (CA).

[101] *Murphy v Brentwood District Council* (1990) 50 BLR 1 (HL); *Tesco Stores Ltd v The Norman Hitchcox Partnership Ltd* (1997) 56 Con LR 42; *Payne v John Setchell Ltd* [2002] BLR 489; *Tesco Stores Ltd v Costain Construction Ltd* [2003] EWHC 1487; *Robinson v P E Jones (Contractors) Ltd* [2011] 3 BLR 206 (CA).

Chapter 5
Liability under Statute

There are several scenarios in which a breach of a statutory requirement may result in some form of liability for a designer. The first, as is obvious, is that a designer should normally be working within the requirements of any relevant statute or regulation relating to development control or the built form. A client would expect any appointed designer, whether a consultant or design-build contractor, to be aware of, understand and comply with such legislation. Breach of a regulation would therefore be evidence that a designer had failed to act with the necessary level of skill and care. A second scenario is where legislation places a direct obligation on designers, breach of which could result in criminal prosecution or civil liability.

A third possible scenario, i.e. where breach of a regulation would form a tort in its own right distinct from that of negligence, appears to have been rejected by the courts. In *Worlock v Saws and Rushmoor Borough Council*[1] when the case was before Mr Justice Wool, His Lordship held that contractors were not liable to an owner for breach of duty imposed by Building Regulations on the basis that it would be wrong to regard those Regulations as giving rise to a statutory duty creating an absolute liability. This case went on appeal to the Court of Appeal. The appeals were dismissed but the rulings of the Court of Appeal are consistent with the view that the duty was not an absolute duty independent of fault.

In *Taylor Woodrow Construction (Midlands) Ltd v Charcon Structures Ltd and Others*,[2] where there had been reference to *Worlock* (at first instance), the Court of Appeal did not have to, and did not, decide the issue but Lord Justice Waller said that whether or not a breach of the Regulations in that case gave rise to an action for damages without proof of negligence is 'to say the least, doubtful'. In *Perry v Tendring District Council*,[3] Judge Newey QC found that breach of the Building Regulations did not *per se* give rise to a liability in damages. Lord Oliver, in *Murphy v Brentwood*, said that 'there is nothing in the terms or purpose of the statutory provisions which supports the creation of a private right of action for breach of statutory duty'.[4] Against the background of such a

---

[1](1983) 22 BLR 66 (CA).
[2](1983) 7 Con LR 1 (CA).
[3](1984) 30 BLR 118.
[4](1990) 50 BLR 1, at para. 97.

Cornes and Lupton's Design Liability in the Construction Industry, Fifth Edition. Sarah Lupton.
© 2013 Sarah Lupton and DL Cornes. Published 2013 by Blackwell Publishing Ltd.

statement in a House of Lords' decision, it is unlikely that, unless the legislation specifically states otherwise, breach of that legislation would automatically give rise to a tort.

5.1 Defective Premises Act 1972

The Defective Premises Act 1972 (DPA) imposes duties on those undertaking work in connection with dwellings, and creates a civil right of action for persons that is separate and additional to any right they might have to bring a claim in contract or tort. The key duty is set out in section 1(1):

1 Duty to build dwellings properly

(1) A person taking on work for or in connection with the provision of a dwelling (whether the dwelling is provided by the erection or by the conversion or enlargement of a building) owes a duty—
  (a) if the dwelling is provided to the order of any person, to that person; and
  (b) without prejudice to paragraph (a) above, to every person who acquires an interest (whether legal or equitable) in the dwelling;

to see that the work which he takes on is done in a workmanlike or, as the case may be, professional manner, with proper materials and so that as regards that work the dwelling will be fit for habitation when completed.

The duty is a far-reaching and significant in several respects. It applies to a wide range of professionals, contractors, sub-contractors and possibly suppliers of pre-fabricated elements. The 'work' would include design, construction, and inspection relating to new-build and conversion or improvement work that creates a new dwelling, but would not apply to repair work[5] or to alterations. The restriction to new dwellings was confirmed in the recent case of *Jenson v Faux*.[6] Here the owners had undertaken extensive alterations to a house, including remodelling of the loft, first floor and ground floor, plus the excavation of a new basement, but were unable to persuade the Court of Appeal that this constituted a 'new' dwelling (the Court of Appeal relied on two cases, *Jacobs v Morton*[7] and an unreported CA case[8]). The Court did acknowledge, however, that there may be situations where works to an existing building are so extensive that they justify the conclusion that a new dwelling has been created, but it would seem that such instances are likely to be very rare.

The DPA would apply to a contractual arrangement for work, but also to one where the work is provided as a favour, or where parties were undertaking work themselves on their own property. The phrase 'to see that' means that a professional who arranged for others to undertake work would be liable, so that for example an architect would

---

[5] *Jacobs v Morton & Partners* (1994) 72 BLR 92.
[6] [2011] EWCA Civ 423 (CA).
[7] (1994) 72 BLR 92.
[8] *Saigol v Cranley Mansions*, unreported, 6 July 1995 (CA).

be liable for any sub-let work. The duty is owed not only to the person for whom the work is carried out, but also to anyone who acquires an interest in the dwelling, which would include for example subsequent owners and tenants.

Although the duty applies only to the provision of dwellings, including dwellings that are created by conversion, and does not apply to other categories of construction, no definition of 'dwellings' is given in the Act and it could therefore arguably be stretched to cover blocks of flats, and possibly projects involving nursing or care homes, prisons and hotels. The courts have generally applied a wide definition, for example in *Uratemp Ventures Ltd v Collins*[9] the word 'dwelling' was defined as the place where a person lives or resides 'and makes one's home', which in that case was considered to include residing in a hotel. Lord Irvine stated:

> A single room, as part of a house, may be a dwelling-house; and on this appeal there is no issue of shared accommodation or facilities. The key issue is: whether the room which Mr Collins occupied, in the Viscount Hotel, Prince of Wales Terrace, Kensington, when proceedings were brought, could in law qualify as a 'dwelling' only if cooking facilities were there available. Unless constrained to the contrary by authority, I would impose no such restrictive interpretation.[10]

In *Catlin Estates Ltd, Mr Stephen Catlin v Carter Jonas*[11] the court further considered the issue of what constituted a 'dwelling' under the Act. Catlin Estates Ltd engaged Carter Jonas, a firm of building surveyors, to design and then manage the construction contract for a hunting lodge on an exposed site in the North-East. The second claimant relied upon section 1 of the DPA but the defendant argued that the lodge was not a dwelling within the terms of the Act, and that in any event it was fit for habitation. The Judge decided that the lodge was a dwelling although it was used for business, stating:

> In relation to the claim that the Lodge is not a dwelling I conclude that a dwelling house is a building used or capable of being used as a dwelling house, not being a building which is used predominantly for commercial and industrial purposes. I have concluded that the claim that the building would have been used as a conference centre was misconceived not least because the covenant imposed by the vendors, Northumbrian Water, was designed to ensure that the building was not used predominantly for commercial purposes. I set out my reasons in detail later. There I conclude that it is a dwelling house, being a building which is used or capable of being used as a dwelling house, and that it is not used predominantly for commercial or industrial purposes. The evidence is that Mr Catlin uses it for his family and when entertaining business associates.[12]

Looking at the duty in more detail, questions arise from the rather complex wording of section 1 'to see that the work which he takes on is done in a workmanlike or, as

---

[9] [2001] UKHL 43 (HL).
[10] ibid., para. 2.
[11] [2005] EWHC 2315 (TCC).
[12] ibid., para. 296.

the case may be, professional manner, with proper materials *and so that* as regards that work the dwelling will be fit for habitation when completed'. What exactly is the nature of the duty? For example; are there two separate duties: to see that the work is done professionally, and to see that the dwelling is fit for habitation? If the answer is 'yes' this would mean that any unprofessional work could incur a liability, even if the resulting dwelling were fit for habitation. The courts have, however, not taken this approach.

An early case was *Alexander & Another v Mercouris*[13] where the Court of Appeal considered *when* the duty arose, rather than its extent, but made some observations that are relevant and although *obiter* were relied on in subsequent cases. For example, Lord Justice Buckley stated:

> It seems to me clear upon the language of s. 1(1) that the duty is intended to arise when a person takes on the work. The word 'owes' is used in the present tense and the duty is not to ensure that the work has been done in a proper and workmanlike manner with proper materials so that the dwelling is fit for habitation when completed, but to see that the work is done in a proper and workmanlike manner with proper materials so that the work will be fit for habitation when completed. The duty is one to be performed during the carrying on of the work. The reference to the dwelling being fit for habitation indicates the intended consequence of the proper performance of the duty and provides a measure of the standard of the requisite work and materials. It is not, I think, part of the duty itself.[14]

Lord Justice Buckley added 'the concluding words of the section do not state the duty but the measure of the duty imposed by the earlier words, that is to say, to do the work in a workmanlike, or as the case may be, professional manner and to do it with proper materials, so that the result may be produced that the dwelling will be fit for habitation when completed'.

Subsequently the case *Miles (Charles Thompson) v Clive Alexander & Partners*[15] dealt specifically with the question, that is:

(1) Is it sufficient to prove merely that the defect arose out of a failure by the other party to carry out their work in a professional manner or with proper materials; or

(2) is it also necessary to prove that the defect rendered the dwelling unfit for habitation when completed?

The Official Referee decided that the duty imposed by section 1(1) is limited to the kind of defect in the work done and the materials used whether by a builder or a professional, such as an architect or engineer, which makes the dwelling unfit for habitation on completion. He said that it was not enough to prove that the defects arose solely from a failure on the part of a party to carry out their work in a professional manner and with proper materials, it must also be shown that the defect renders the dwelling unfit. Commentators have questioned whether this is correct, and whether the Law

---

[13] [1979] 1 WLR 1279.
[14] Buckley LJ, at 1274.
[15] (1992) 59 BLR 77.

Commission had intended that the obligations in the Act should be disjunctive and not conjunctive,[16] but the conjunctive approach has been followed in subsequent cases.

A third question is whether the duty is intended to be a strict one. In other words, supposing the work was carried out with due skill and care, but as a result of a design error the dwelling was not fit for habitation, would the designer nevertheless be liable?

The answer is that the duty generally interpreted as being a strict one. This can be seen in leading commentaries, such as *Keating on Building Contracts* where it states firmly: 'It is thought that all persons coming within the section are under a strict duty to fulfill its requirements, and it would not be a defence to show that the work was done with proper care'.[17] A similar comment was made in In *Murphy v Brentwood District Council* where Lord Bridge stated:

> By section 1 of the Defective Premises Act 1972 Parliament has in fact imposed upon builders and others undertaking work in the provision of dwellings the obligations of a transmissible warranty of quality of their work and of the fitness for habitation of the completed dwelling.[18]

In a claim against a designer, it would still be necessary to show that the designer failed to do the work in a 'professional manner', but only in order to demonstrate causation, i.e. that the professional made an error which at least in part caused the unfitness. It would not be necessary to show that the designer's performance had fallen below the normal standards of skill and care. An example of this approach can be seen in *Bole v Huntsbuild*, discussed below, where evidence was led to demonstrate that errors had been made by the architect, but not that the architect had fallen below normal standards. In practice the distinction may not be as significant as it seems. In reality, if a professional's design error has resulted in problems serious enough to result in the building being unfit for habitation, it is more than likely that the professional will have been negligent, and a defence that due skill and care was used is therefore unlikely to succeed.

Other cases have examined the question of what is meant by 'unfit for habitation'. In *Andrews v Schooling*[19] the Court of Appeal was concerned with penetrating damp in a cellar of a house converted into flats by the third defendant developers. Relying on *Alexander & Another v Mercouris* (see above) the Court found that a dwelling could be unfit for habitation even though the problem was not manifest; for example, a missing damp course could render it unfit, even thought the damp was not yet apparent. It also held that section 1(1) of the DPA imposed a liability not only for misfeasance but also for non-feasance, i.e. that the section applies to a failure to carry out necessary work as well as to carrying it out badly.

---

[16] Law Commission Working Paper No. 40: *Civil Liability of Vendors and Lessees for Defective Premises.*
[17] Stephen Furst and Vivien Ramsey (eds), *Keating on Construction Contracts*, 9th edn (London: Sweet & Maxwell, 2012), p. 572 para. 16-002.
[18] [1991] 1 AC 398 (HL), at 422.
[19] (1991) 53 BLR 73.

In *Bayoumi v Protim Services*[20] the court again considered the issue of inadequate damp-proofing, and confirmed it was sufficient to render a property unfit for habitation. It also confirmed that in order to succeed the plaintiff does not have to prove that the defendants' breach of duty was the only cause of the building being unfit.

The case of *Bole v Huntsbuild*[21] further considered the meaning of 'unfit for habitation'. The claimants, Mr and Mrs Bole, bought a new house, which had been constructed by the first defendant, Huntsbuild Ltd (Huntsbuild). Before starting work on the house, Huntsbuild had asked the second defendant engineers, Richard Money Associates (RMA) for its advice on the new foundations. RMA undertook a site investigation, and provided a report and recommendations regarding the depth of foundations, in particular in relation to retained and newly planted trees. Unfortunately the recommendations and, in particular, the design of the foundations, did not specify the precise depths of foundations, or take into account trees which had been removed from the site (a willow tree, removed from within the planned footprint of the house, and a row of conifer trees). The RMA recommendations were therefore in breach of NHBC Standards Chapter 4.2 'Building near trees'.

Following completion the house developed cracking. Mr and Mrs Bole sued Huntsbuild for breach of contract and breach of section 1 of the DPA. They also sued RMA for breach of section 1. The trial Judge (HHJ Toulmin CMG QC) found that the house suffered cracking because of heave, which had occurred because of the foundations, which were inadequate because they did not take account of the removed trees. The Judge then analysed the evidence of the cracking and its impact on Mr and Mrs Bole and said:

> In all the circumstances, applying the test of whether the house was unfit for habitation in the sense of being unsuitable for its purpose, I have no hesitation in finding that the house, as built, was unfit for habitation under section 1 of the DPA in that it was built with unstable foundations which resulted in movement and cracking and other defects caused by heave.[22]

Both the architect and the contractor were found liable. The court emphasised that a decision regarding 'fitness for habitation' was one on the facts in each case. In reaching his conclusion the Judge considered the Law Commission Report '*Civil Liability of Vendors and Lessees for Defective Premises*'[23] which led directly to the DPA, and the previous authorities on the DPA. He also noted section 604(1) of the Housing Act 1985, which provides a definition of 'fit for habitation'. This incorporates a checklist of the kind of defects which might be sufficiently fundamental, including not only structural matters but also lighting, drainage, sanitation and water supply. The court gave the following guidance, which was subsequently approved by the Court of Appeal:[24]

> On the basis of the authorities, it is not necessary, as contended for by the second defendant [RMA], that a finding that the premises are in imminent danger of collapse is a necessary

---

[20] [1996] 1 WLR 785.
[21] (2009) 124 Con LR 1.
[22] ibid., para. 179.
[23] Law Com No. 40.
[24] ibid., paras 37 and 38.

precursor to making a finding under the DPA that a dwelling house in unfit for human habitation. I conclude on the authorities that I must construe the Act with the following considerations in mind:

i) The finding of unfitness for habitation when built is a matter of fact in each case.

ii) Unfitness for habitation extends to what Lord Bridge described as 'defects of quality' rendering the dwelling unsuitable for its purpose as well as to 'dangerous defects'.

iii) Unfitness for habitation relates to defects rendering the dwelling dangerous or unsuitable for its purpose and not to minor defects.

iv) Such a defect in one part of the dwelling may render the dwelling unsuitable for its purpose and therefore unfit for habitation as a dwelling house even if the defect does not apply to other parts of the dwelling. This is also the case under the Housing Act – see *Summers v Salford Corporation*.[25]

v) The Act will apply to such defects even if the effects of the defect were not evident at the time when the dwelling was completed.

vi) In considering whether or not a dwelling is unfit for habitation as built one must consider the effect of the defects as a whole.

Subsequently in *Harrison & Ors v Shepherd Homes Ltd & Ors*[26] the court considered the principles set out above in *Bole v Huntsbuild*. In this case it found that even though cracking was not serious, so as to render the property incapable of occupation, the defendant was nevertheless in breach of the Act, stating 'any significant defects in foundations are properly matters which could be said to give rise to a lack of fitness for habitation'.[27]

There are some situations when the duty would not arise. Section 1 of the Act (as amended) states:

(2) A person who takes on any such work for another on terms that he is to do it in accordance with instructions given by or on behalf of that other shall, to the extent to which he does it properly in accordance with those instructions, be treated for the purposes of this section as discharging the duty imposed on him by subsection (1) above except where he owes a duty to that other to warn him of any defects in the instructions and fails to discharge that duty.

(3) a person shall not be treated for the purposes of subsection (2) above as having been given instructions for the doing of work merely because he has agreed to the work being done in a specified manner, with specified materials, or to a specified design.

This section therefore would provide a defence to a contractor who was following a design and prescriptive specification provided by others. A contractor who had offered a possible design to a client, following which the client instructed it to proceed on the basis of that design, would not, however, be exempt.

There is an exception to the imposition of the duty, where 'an approved scheme' is in operation in respect to the dwelling. There the Act provides that no action can be brought

---

[25] [1943] AC 283.
[26] [2011] EWHC 1811 (TCC).
[27] ibid., at para. 164.

in respect of the duty in section 1 of the DPA (see s. 2(1)). The NHBC Schemes of 1973, 1975 and 1977 were approved under the DPA, section 2, but the last scheme came to an end in 1979. Subsequent schemes including the current BuildMark Scheme have not been approved, so the remedies under both the DPA and the Scheme are available.

Finally, it is important to note that any clauses in an agreement that attempt to restrict or exclude any liability under the Act would be void under the DPA, section 6(3).

Under section 1(5) the date on which the cause accrues is the date when the dwelling is complete, not the date when the damage appears. The effect of this is that the limitation period is less than it would be for a claim in tort, but might (in the case of a professional who designs but then withdraws from the project) be more than would be the case under its terms of engagement. However if further work is done by the same person to remedy the defect, the cause of action will start when the work is finished.[28] Finally, it should be noted that a claim for breach of statutory duty under the DPA 1972 is not an 'action for damages for negligence' within the meaning of section 14A of the Limitation Act 1980[29] (see Chapter 12).

5.2 *Building Act 1984*

The Building Regulations 2010 were made under the Building Act 1984. The Act does not place any specific duties on designers, but contravention of the Act by a contractor (including a developer or design-build contractor) or a client could result in a prosecution.

The Act sets out broad performance requirements for the finished building, and procedural requirements to be followed if work is proposed. The Building Regulations require that all work is carried out in accordance with Schedule 1, which sets out detailed technical requirements, again essentially performance-based. Regulation 8 states that nothing need be done other than work necessary to secure reasonable standards of health and safety for persons in or around buildings, but there are important exceptions to this, namely Parts E, L and M, which relate to passage of sound, conservation of fuel and power, and disabled access.

The Regulations refer to Approved Documents, which set out methods for meeting the Regulations, with a separate Approved Document for every part of Schedule 1 to the Regulations. Under section 35 of the Building Act 1984 any contravention of the Building Regulations is an offence. Contravention of the Approved Documents would not be, as it is open to the designer to demonstrate that the Regulations have been met in some other way.

Generally if the offence is a procedural one, an action will be brought against the contractor undertaking the work. The authority would have the right to take enforcement action stopping the work. If the work as constructed does not comply with requirements, under section 36 the local authority can issue an enforcement notice requiring the work to be re-done (termed a 'section 36 notice'). There are rights of appeal against such a notice, with the opportunity to prepare and submit an expert report to demonstrate that the work does in fact comply. The section 36 notice may be

---

[28] *Alderson v Beetham Organisation* [2003] BLR 217 (CA).
[29] *Payne v John Setchell Ltd* [2002] BLR 489.

issued to the owner. (A 'self-build' designer should therefore note that it could be subject to prosecution or an enforcement notice).

Clearly if the design is in contravention, the owner/client is likely to bring an action against the designer, and the contravention would be evidence of failure to use reasonable skill and care. A breach of Building Regulations is also a matter that would be taken seriously by a professional disciplinary body, particularly if the architect was aware (or should have been aware) that the design did not comply, and the error affected the safety of occupants. For example, in April 2011 an architect was found guilty by the ARB Professional Conduct Committee of both unacceptable professional conduct and serious professional incompetence, for certifying work that she knew to be in contravention of the Regulations.[30] Although the architect argued that the building inspector had orally approved the contravention, and had accepted the use of moveable furniture as a means of access to a fire escape window, the PCC found this acceptance to be unlikely and there was no written evidence of it. In unusual cases such as this it would be essential for the designer to ensure there was a written confirmation.

5.2.1 Section 38 of the Building Act 1984

In addition to the above, the Building Act 1984 has a section dealing with civil liability for breach of the Building Regulations. Although this has never been brought into force, it is far-reaching enough to be worth noting. Section 38 provides that:

(a) breach of a duty imposed by building regulations, so far as it causes damage, is actionable, except in so far as the regulations provide otherwise, and,

(b) as regards such a duty, building regulations may provide for a prescribed defence to be available in an action for breach of that duty brought by virtue of this sub-section.

The effect of the section would be to provide that certain Building Regulations will be actionable as a breach of duty and that there may be prescribed defences in the regulations. This section could be of great importance to designers in relation to any liability they may incur under the Building Regulations. Indeed, the wording of the section itself could cause some difficulty in respect of the date from which the limitation period is said to run: the liability is subject to the words 'so far as it causes damage' so it will almost certainly be argued that these words mean that the cause of action does not arise, and hence the period of limitation does not begin to run, until the damage has occurred. However, no use can be made of this section until secondary legislation is passed to bring it into operation.

5.3 Health and safety

The Health and Safety at Work etc. Act 1974, and Regulations made under it, have established a large part of the modern framework for health and safety on construction projects. Designers tend to assume that such matters are only the responsibility of the

---

[30] PCC case reports are published for a limited period on the ARB website: www.arb.org.uk.

employer and the contractor. That is an erroneous assumption. For example, designers have duties under sections 2 and 3 of the Act. Section 3 requires that employers and the self-employed conduct their undertakings in a way such as to ensure that persons *not in their employment* are not exposed to risks to their health and safety.

5.3.1 Construction (Design and Management) (CDM) Regulations 2007

The Construction (Design and Management) (CDM) Regulations 2007, which were passed under the above Act, replaced earlier legislation[31] that had implemented the EU Temporary or Mobile Construction Sites Directive (1992/57/EEC). The Regulations are also supported by the Approved Code of Practice (ACoP) that aims to clarify the key requirements and provides guidance.

The key objective of the CDM Regulation is to reduce the risk to health and safety of those who construct and undertake maintenance work on a building. (The health and safety of occupants is dealt with under a raft of other legislation, the majority passed under the Health and Safety at Work etc. Act 1974).

The key duty holders are the Client, the CDM Coordinator, the Principal Contractor and the Designer. The Client's duties do not relate to design, other than to allow adequate resources for the project, and to appoint competent persons for the other roles, so that budget constraints would not be an acceptable excuse for a project that was unsafe.

The CDM Co-ordinator's duties are to:

- advise and assist the Client
- co-ordinate design work
- identify, extract and provide H&S information as required by those that require it
- liaise with the Principal Contractor in relation to design changes
- prepare the H&S File and pass that File onto the client at the end of the construction phase.

The designer must ensure so far as is reasonably practicable that persons engaged in constructing the design (or subsequently maintaining, cleaning or redecorating it) are not exposed to risks (reg. 13). The designer must give adequate information about any aspects of the design or materials which might affect health and safety of operatives and must cooperate with the planning supervisor. This Regulation applies to all projects, even those exempt from the other regulations.

Designers have a duty to:

1. Make sure that they are competent and adequately resourced to address the health and safety issues likely to be involved in the design.
2. Check that clients are aware of their duties.

---

[31] Construction (Design and Management) Regulations 1994 and Construction (Health, Safety and Welfare) Regulations 1996.

3. When carrying out design work, avoid foreseeable risks to those involved in the construction and future use of the structure. In doing so, they should eliminate hazards (so far as is reasonably practicable, taking account of other design considerations) and reduce risk associated with those hazards which remain.
4. Provide adequate information about any significant risks associated with the design.
5. Co-ordinate their work with that of others in order to improve the way in which risks are managed and controlled.

It should be noted that it is not necessary to be formally appointed to attract 'designer' duties under CDM 2007. The fact that individuals are designing something (even in the preliminary stages) means that they must have regard to foreseeable hazard elimination and risk reduction.

CDM does not create a separate civil liability, but of course, as with planning, building regulations, fire safety regulations and all other key technical requirements stipulated by law, breach of such a regulation would be a factor in a claim under contract or tort. Breach of health and safety legislation can also give rise to prosecution, and this applies also to designers. In a much publicised decision[32] an architects practice was fined £120,000 and ordered to pay costs of £60,000 after it pleaded guilty to breaching regulations 13 and 14, of the Construction (Design and Management) Regulations 1994. An operative of a sub-contractor was carrying out snagging works on air conditioning plant, which was built on a platform accessed by a ladder at the edge of a flat roof. The roof only had a low parapet, which failed to prevent the worker from falling nine metres to the ground, resulting in his death. A key issue was that the original design had not included an air-conditioning unit on the roof, the unit was moved there later following a design amendment. The design risk assessment had been undertaken in 2003 and was not reviewed following the design change in 2004. The court agreed that the architects were best placed to address the risk of falls from height and the judge commented that, as designers, they had failed to provide a 'safe environment' for the deceased.

5.4 Copyright

The matter of copyright is of great importance to designers. It is an area of law designed to protect the designer's rights in ideas and creativity from exploitation by others. It can give rise to an element of security for fees: making a licence for use of the copyright by the developer conditional on the payment of the designer's fees. What follows is an outline only, for fuller coverage readers should consult one of the texts listed in the Bibliography.

Owning copyright in a work is essentially the right to make copies and to prevent others from doing so. An aspect that frequently causes confusion in practice is that there is no copyright in ideas, only in the manner of their expression. Therefore the essential idea or concept underlying a design does not tend to attract copyright, this is limited to the drawings, reports, and constructed details, elements or entire erected buildings.

---

[32] 30 January 2010, HSE Release No. 739/SWW/09.

Another issue is that even if the designer does own the copyright, this may not prevent the employer from altering the design and building something similar but significantly different, either on the same site (in place of the agreed design) or on a different site. Also, although the designer may retain the copyright, this would not supersede express or implied obligations of privacy, for example it would not give the designer the right to copy and distribute or otherwise publish a confidential report.

5.4.1 Copyright, Designs and Patents Act 1988

The key legislation governing copyright is the Copyright, Designs and Patents Act 1988, and Regulations made under that Act. Copyright covers artistic works, literary works, computer software and other matters of less relevance to construction such as music compositions, dramatic works, broadcast recordings etc.

Under the Act copyright arises automatically in original artistic works provided the author is a 'qualifying person' or if the work was first published in the United Kingdom or a country to which the Act has application by reason of a Statutory Instrument. There is no need for the work to be registered, or to carry a copyright mark.

Works of architecture are defined as 'artistic works' under section 4 of the Act:

> (1) in this Part 'artistic work' means—
>> (a) a graphic work, photograph, sculpture or collage, irrespective of artistic quality,
>> (b) a work of architecture being building or a model of a building, or
>>   a work of artistic craftsmanship.
> (2) In this Part—
>>   'building' includes any fixed structure, and a part of a building or fixed structure;
>>   'graphic work' includes—
>> (a) any painting, drawing, diagram, map chart or plan, and
>> (b) any engraving, etching, lithograph, woodcut or similar work . . .

As already indicated, the 'work' can therefore be the building itself, or a drawing or model, but not the design idea. An example of this can be seen in the case of *Gareth Pearce v Ove Arup Partnership Ltd and Rem Koolhaas*.[33] Gareth Pearce believed that features of his final year design project for a town hall in the Docklands, undertaken at the Architectural Association School in London, had been copied in the design of Kunsthal Museum in Rotterdam. It was held that although Kunsthal had similar features to Pearce's design, it was independently designed and there was no infringement.[34]

For the work to be 'original' probably means nothing more than the artistic work is not copied; there is no need for subjective originality.[35] It is accepted, for example, that an artistic work can draw inspiration from another source; all that is needed to

---

[33] [2001] EWHC Ch 455.
[34] For a further example see the leading case of *Designers Guild Ltd v Russell Williams (Textiles) Ltd* [2001] FSR 113.
[35] *University of London Press Ltd v University Tutorial Press Ltd* [1916] 2 Ch 601.

demonstrate originality is some alteration or new development of the idea.[36] There is also no need for architectural or artistic merit in the design.

The incorporation of standard components will not of itself prevent a design being original for this purpose[37] and neither will any constraints to the design imposed by the site or context.[38] In a New Zealand case, skill was said to be a necessary ingredient.[39] Although there is no authority on the point, it is likely that 'publication' will include the public exhibition of scheme designs during or after an architectural competition. Under section 175 of the Act, construction of the building does act as 'publication' for the purposes of the Act.

The period of copyright created by the Act for literary and artistic works is 70 years from the end of the year in which the designer dies, and vests in the author who is the person who creates the design (s. 9 of the Act, as amended by the Copyright and Rights in Performance Regulations 1995).

Under section 16 of the Act, an infringement occurs where whole or a substantial part of the building is copied without permission, or with the copying of plans. The copying of plans in brochures, such as estate agents particulars, is not an infringement if it is for the purpose of sale or letting of the building (s. 63). An architect who is engaged to design an extension to an existing building, which was designed by another architect will infringe the first architect's copyright if the extension is in substantially the same style.[40] To prove infringement the designer must show that copyright existed in the work and is vested in the designer, that the infringement reproduces a substantial part of the work in material particulars, and that is was copied form the designer's work. Constructing a building from drawings can constitute an infringement.[41] Also, copying a building by constructing another identical to it will also be an infringement. *Meikle v Maufe*[42] is the key case concerning this, where the department store Heals in Tottenham Court Road in London constructed an extension. It engaged architects Maufe who reproduced features which appeared in the original northern section in the new southern section, in order to maintain consistency along the street frontage. In determining whether there has been an infringement, the court will undertake an objective visual comparison, examining similarities and differences, and assess the number of features and parts that are objectively similar (i.e. it is not a global comparison, but an incremental one). If these are sufficient to suggest that they may be the result of copying rather than coincidence, the burden will then pass to the defendant to show that this was not the case.[43]

The remedies for an infringement are damages and/or an account of profits and/or, possibly, an injunction. Prior to the present Act (1988), injunction was not available as

---

[36] *Designers Guild Ltd v Russell Williams (Textiles) Ltd* [2001] FSR 113.

[37] *Hay and Hay Construction v Sloan* (1957) 12 DLR (2d) 397 (Ont HC, Canada).

[38] *Kaffka v Mountain Side Developments Ltd* (1982) 62 CPR (2d) 157 (BC SC) (British Columbia).

[39] *Beazley Homes Ltd v Arrowsmith* [1978] 1 NZLR 394 (NZ).

[40] *Chabot v Davies* [1936] 3 All ER 221.

[41] ibid.

[42] *Meikle v Maufe* [1941] 3 All ER 144.

[43] *Designers Guild Ltd v Russell Williams (Textiles) Ltd* [2001] FSR 113.

a remedy under section 17(4) of the predecessor Act of 1956. And on usual principles, an injunction will not be granted if damages are an adequate remedy.[44] The Act also provides for a remedy where the copyright owner refuses to grant a licence on reasonable terms, known as a 'Licence of right' procedure. Architects also have the right (as individuals, not as companies) to be identified on buildings they have designed provided they follow the procedure in the Act in relation to asserting those 'moral rights' (see s. 78 on assertion formalities). Another moral right created by the Act enables architects to have their name removed from a building if the work is being exploited in a derogatory manner: for example, if the building has been altered by another architect in a derogatory manner.

5.4.2 Copyright under SA10

Most of the standard conditions of engagement contain provisions as to copyright, as do most collateral warranties.

For example, the RIBA Standard Agreement 2010 (SA10) contains this:

> 6.1 The Architect shall own all intellectual property rights including the copyright in the original work produced in the performance of the Services and generally asserts the Architect's moral rights to be identified as the author of such work.

That provision, which is typical of those included in consultant's standard forms, should be sufficient to prevent an argument that the building owner or the contractor, not the architect, is the 'author' of the design for copyright purposes. Such a proposition is, in any event, supported by authority[45] and by the current statute which says that the creator of the work owns copyright as opposed to the commissioner (as was the case pre-1988), as long as the building in question was built after 1 August 1989 (s. 11). It should be noted, however, that employees of an architects' practice will not own the copyright of work they carry out whilst in employment, this would be owned by their employers.

Further provisions of SA10 deal with other aspects of copyright:

> 6.3 The Client shall have a licence to copy and use drawings, documents and all other such work produced by or on behalf of the Architect in performing the Services, hereinafter called the 'Material'.
>
> The Material may be used for the construction of the project and for the operation, maintenance, repair, restatement, alteration, proportion, leasing and/or sale of the Project. The Material may not be used for reproduction of the design for any part of any extension to the Project, and/or for any other project except on payment of a licence fee specified in this Agreement or subsequently agreed.

---

[44] *American Cyanamid Co. v Ethicon Ltd* (No 1) [1975] AC 396.
[45] *Meikle v Maufe* [1941] 3 All ER 144.

Copying or use of the Material by an Other Person providing services to the Project shall be deemed to be permitted under a sub-licence granted by the Client, whether such Material was issued by the Client or on the Client's behalf.

The architect shall not be liable if the Material is modified other by or with the consent of the Architect or used for any purpose other than the purposes for which it was prepared.

It is to be noted that these provisions set out reasonably clearly the position on copyright in various typical situations and that there is a linking of copyright and fees so as to give architects some element of security for their fees.

Chapter 6
Liability for Professional Negligence

The phrase 'professional negligence' is used in a generic sense to cover all situations in law where a professional person is being pursued for some act or omission, irrespective of the precise nature of the legal right being cited. This rather imprecise language can lead to confusion. 'Negligence' can, for example, refer to breach of an obligation (either express or implied) in contract to use reasonable skill and care, or to a claim in the tort of negligence. It may also be used in relation to breach of statutory duty such as the duty set up by the Defective Premises Act 1972. Although when considering a claim it is important in the law to be very precise as to the nature of the case being made, there are some general points that can be made regarding the duty to exercise reasonable skill and care, which are considered below.

6.1 Reasonable skill and care

There will usually be a contract arising out of the relationship between designer and employer. This contract can take many forms including an agreement by word of mouth, or a simple written agreement such as an exchange of letters, or the more detailed ACE or RIBA conditions of engagement. The terms of such a contract may consist of express and implied terms. Standard forms of appointment normally contain an express obligation to exercise reasonable skill and care (see Chapter 15), and if none were included such an obligation would normally be implied. This is broadly the same liability as might arise under a tortious obligation, or in some cases might be required by statute.

A person holding themselves out as being a designer, whether or not they possess qualifications, impliedly warrants that they are reasonably competent to carry out the task. Indeed, 'the failure to afford the requisite skill which has been expressly or impliedly promised is a breach of legal duty'.[1] 'Every person who enters into a learned profession undertakes to bring to the exercise of it a reasonable degree of care and skill[2]'.

---

[1] *Harmer v Cornelius* (1858) 28 LJCP 85.
[2] *Lanphier v Phipos* (1838) 8 C & P 475, at 478.

Cornes and Lupton's Design Liability in the Construction Industry, Fifth Edition. Sarah Lupton.
© 2013 Sarah Lupton and DL Cornes. Published 2013 by Blackwell Publishing Ltd.

It is not difficult to see that a designer who proves in the event not to have the necessary skill may be liable for any damage caused to the employer; but in order that an
employer may establish that the designer has liability it must show that there has been
a breach of duty by the designer that has caused the damage. In order to establish that
there has been a breach of duty, it must be shown that the designer was negligent.
'Negligence' in this sense (i.e. in a contractual context) is analogous to the standard of
care in the law of negligence (i.e. tort).

In the ordinary case of negligence, outside the field of professional negligence, the
test that is applied in order to decide whether there has been a breach of duty amounting to negligence was set out in 1856 in *Blyth v Birmingham Water Works Co*:[3]

> Negligence is the omission to do something which a reasonable man, guided upon those
> considerations which ordinarily regulate the conduct of human affairs, would do, or doing
> something which a prudent and reasonable man would not do.

6.1.1 Reasonable skill and care: the test

This leaves open the difficulty of defining the reasonable man. Lawyers were known in
long-gone days to refer to the 'ordinary man on the Clapham omnibus' in relation to
duties. It was this view that was said to be the test of the standards expected of professional designers who exercise every day special skills of which the ordinary man is
usually ignorant. The courts have therefore evolved a special way of looking at the
professional man's obligations. In a leading medical negligence case, *Bolam v Friem
Hospital Management Committee,* it was put this way by Mr Justice McNair:

> How do you test whether this act or failure is negligence? In an ordinary case it is generally
> said that you judge that by the action of the man in the street. He is the ordinary man. In one
> case it has been said that you judge it by the conduct of the man on the top of a Clapham
> omnibus. He is the ordinary man. But where you get a situation which involves the use of
> some special skill or competence, then the test whether there has been negligence or not is not
> the test of the man on top of the Clapham omnibus, because he has not got this special skill.
> A man need not possess the highest expert skill at the risk of being found negligent. It is well-
> established law that it is sufficient if he exercised the ordinary skill of an ordinary competent
> man exercising that particular art.[4]

This speech was approved in *Whitehouse v Jordan,*[5] and in *Greaves v Baynham Meikle*[6]
a construction case in the Court of Appeal. This test is to be applied to all professions
requiring special skill, knowledge and experience.[7]

---

[3](1856) 11 Ex 781.
[4][1957] 1 WLR 582, at 586.
[5][1981] 1 WLR 246.
[6][1975] 1 WLR 1095.
[7]*Gold v Haringey Health Authority* [1988] QB 481.

6.2 Application of the test to designers

The exact level of skill and care that ought to have been applied in a particular case will of course be decided by the court. It should be understood that 'reasonable skill and care' is not an all-embracing obligation in the sense of describing all the designer's obligations but rather a convenient framework against which to assess particular and precise points.

As it is a question of fact rather than one of law, a court would not be bound by a decision regarding similar circumstances made by another court. Nevertheless it is useful to look at how the level is assessed in practice, and at some illustrative examples.

In deciding whether there is negligence, it is necessary to look at what an ordinary competent designer exercising the particular skill would do and to compare that with the actions of the person against whom the negligence is alleged. One way that this can be done in practice is to seek the views of other designers as to the action that was taken by the designer whose actions have been questioned. The court will therefore usually hear evidence from expert witnesses. These are professionals who practice in the same field, and who are engaged by the parties or occasionally appointed by the court, and whose role is to inform the court on an impartial basis, rather than to act as advocates for their appointing party. Those 'expert' witnesses give evidence of opinion about relevant current standards in the industry, and whether, in their view, there is or is not a body of reasonable competent professionals who would have acted similarly in the same circumstances. The role of the experts is intended to be a neutral one, i.e. to inform the court about current practice and acceptable standards in the industry, it is not to argue a case for the party they are representing. Part 35 of the Civil Procedure Rules 1998 sets out the expert's role and states:

(1) It is the duty of experts to help the court on matters within their expertise.
(2) This duty overrides any obligation to the person from whom experts have received instructions or by whom they are paid.[8]

Also, their role is not to base their evidence on what they would have done, but on what would generally be good practice by a member of that profession (for useful discussions see *Royal Brompton Hospital v Hammond (No 7)*[9] and *J D Williams & Co Ltd v Michael Hyde and Associates Ltd*[10]).

Normally the experts are drawn from the same profession as the designer whose services are at issue. It is common sense to do this, and the courts have normally expressed a preference for the use of like disciplines, for example in *Sansom v Metcalf Hambleton & Co*,[11] where it was held by the Court of Appeal that a structural engineer was not competent to give evidence on the professional standards of a building surveyor, Butler-Sloss LJ stated:

---

[8] CPR 35.3.
[9] (2001) 76 Con LR 148.
[10] [2001] PNLR 233 CA.
[11] [1998] 2 EGLR 103.

In my judgment, it is clear . . . that a court should be slow to find a professionally qualified man guilty of a breach of his duty of skill and care towards a client (or third party) without evidence from those within the same profession as to the standard expected on the facts of the case and the failure of the professionally qualified man to measure up to that standard. It is not an absolute rule but, unless it is an obvious case, in the absence of the relevant expert evidence the claim will not be proved.[12]

The Court relied on *Worboys v Acme Investments*,[13] a case which failed partly because of the lack of expert evidence adduced. The Building Law Report commentators, in summarizing the views of Sachs LJ, concluded:

except in the plainest cases a party who accuses a professional man of negligence must call evidence as to what constitutes lack of care in the circumstances of the case . . . the evidence should normally come from someone who is of equal experience or standing to the professional man in question, although evidence from a person who is acquainted with the standards may also suffice.[14]

This view was developed in the case of *Pantell Associates Ltd v Corporate City Developments Number Two Ltd*[15] which concerned a claim of professional negligence against a firm of quantity surveyors. Mr Justice Coulson emphasised the importance of basing such claims on appropriate written expert evidence:

. . . it is standard practice that, where an allegation of professional negligence is to be pleaded, that allegation must be supported (in writing) by a relevant professional with the necessary expertise. That is a matter of common sense: how can it be asserted that act X was something that an ordinary professional would and should not have done, if no professional in the same field had expressed such a view? CPR Part 35 would be unworkable if an allegation of professional negligence did not have, at its root, a statement of expert opinion to that effect.

However professional qualifications may not always be necessary. In *James Longley and Co Ltd v South West Regional Health Authority*[16] the court stated 'An expert may be qualified by skill and experience, as well as by professional qualifications'.[17]

6.3 *Examples of failure to take care*

What exact level of knowledge and skill is generated by applying the test? Guidance was given in the case of *Eckersley & Others v Binnie & Partners & Others*,[18] which concerned

---

[12] ibid., at 156.
[13] (1969) 4 BLR 133.
[14] ibid., at 134.
[15] [2010] EWHC 3189 (TCC), see also for a further example *Cooperative Group Ltd v John Alien Associates Ltd* [2010] EWHC 2300 (TCC).
[16] (1983) 25 BLR 56.
[17] ibid., Lloyd J at p. 62.
[18] (1988) 18 Con LR 1 (CA).

the design of a water tunnel and valve housings on a link between the Rivers Lune and Wyre. An accumulation of methane gas infiltrated from the tunnel into a pumping house causing an explosion and the death of 16 people visiting the site. The legal representatives of the visitors claimed damages in negligence against the engineers responsible for the design of the link. The engineers argued that their pre-design investigations were sufficient in the light of contemporary knowledge and that methane was not present during construction. It was held that applying the standard of the ordinary competent and skilled professional, the engineers should reasonably have foreseen the presence of some, although not necessarily a dangerous, quantity of methane and should therefore have reviewed their ventilation design in the light of experience during construction. Lord Justice Bingham said:

> a professional man should command the corpus of knowledge which forms part of the professional equipment of the ordinary member of his profession. He should not lag behind other ordinarily assiduous and intelligent members of his profession in knowledge of new advances, discoveries and developments in his field. He should have such awareness as an ordinarily competent practitioner would have of the deficiencies in his knowledge and the limitations on his skill. He should be alert to the hazards and risks inherent in any professional task he undertakes to the extent that other ordinarily competent members of the profession would be alert. He must bring to any professional task he undertakes no less expertise, skill and care than other ordinarily competent members of his profession would bring, but need bring no more. The standard is that of the reasonable average. The law does not require of a professional man that he be a paragon, combining the qualities of polymath and prophet.[19]

The Australian case, *Voli v Inglewood Shire Council,*[20] is of some help with respect to architects:

> An architect undertaking any work in the way of his profession accepts the ordinary liabilities of any man who follows a skilled calling. He is bound to exercise due care, skill and diligence. He is not required to have an extraordinary degree of skill or the highest professional attainments. But he must bring to the task he undertakes the competence and skill that is usual among architects practising their profession. And he must use due care. If he fails in these matters and the person who employed him thereby suffers damage, he is liable to that person. The liability can be said to arise either from a breach of his contract or in tort.[21]

It follows that in the usual case, provided designers can show that they acted in accordance with the usual practice of the profession, then they will normally escape liability for problems arising (the unusual situation where the designer undertakes a strict obligation is examined in Chapter 7). The same principles would apply where there were several accepted but differing practices within the profession and the designer acted in accordance with one of those practices.

---

[19] ibid., at 80, approved in *J D Willliams & Co Ltd v Michael Hyde & Associates Ltd* [2001] BLR 99 (CA).
[20] (1963) ALR 657.
[21] ibid., Mr Justice Windeyer at 661.

This last point is by analogy with the finding in the *Bolam* case, which was concerned partly with the question as to the scope for genuine difference of opinion in the medical profession in relation to different methods of treatment adopted by different doctors. The adoption by a doctor of one, out of several, methods of treatment does not imply negligence, provided that his belief is based on reasonable grounds. It will not necessarily be sufficient to establish negligence for the claimant to show that there was a body of competent professional opinion that considered the decision had been wrong, if there was also a body of professional opinion, equally competent, that supported the decision as having been reasonable in the circumstances.[22] This is sometimes referred to as the 'responsible body' test.[23]

An example can be seen in an unusual case where the claim was that engineers had over-designed a structure, thereby causing unnecessary costs to the employers. *London Underground Ltd v Kenchington Ford*[24] concerned the alleged over-design at Canning Town station on the Jubilee Line extension. The engineers were required to work to a specification that stipulated a 120-year design life for the superstructure, and a 400-year life for the substructure. LUL then claimed that the structure was over-designed, contending that a reasonably competent engineer would have designed a thinner, cheaper, slab for the concourse. The judge however accepted strong evidence that the engineers' design would have been approved of by a reasonable body of competent professional engineers, and the claim therefore failed (in this case there had been prolonged discussion of the design with the design team, including of the technical, cost and construction aspects).

The question sometimes arises whether the general practice of the profession is the right practice and whether in those circumstances a designer could escape liability by saying that he or she merely did what everyone else in the profession was doing. This point has been considered both in relation to solicitors' duties and doctors' duties. A firm of solicitors has been held negligent for failing to make a commons registration search in a conveyancing transaction and their defence that they made all the searches that solicitors usually make was rejected by the court.[25]

Sidaway v Governors of Bethlem Royal Hospital[26] concerned amongst other things the extent of a surgeon's duty to inform a patient of risks in such a way that the patient is fully informed and therefore able to give full consent based on a proper understanding of the risks. Although there were clearly policy decisions in this case which was in any event a medical negligence case, and which may not be appropriate in the average building negligence problem, it is clear that it is open to the court to reject expert evidence as to the practice of a profession, at least in certain circumstances. In the Court of Appeal, Sir John Donaldson MR had suggested that:

---

[22] *Maynard v West Midlands Area Health Authority* [1984] 1 WLR 634 (HL); see also *Nye Saunders and Partners v Bristow* (1987) 37 BLR 92 (CA) for its application to architects.

[23] Atkins Chambers. *Hudson's Building and Engineering Contracts,* 12th edn (London: Sweet & Maxwell, 2010, para. 2-051.

[24] (1998) 63 Con LR.

[25] *G & K Ladenbau (UK) Ltd v Crawley & de Reya* [1978] 1 WLR 266.

[26] [1984] QB 493 (CA).

In an appropriate case, a judge would be entitled to reject a unanimous medical view if he was satisfied that it was manifestly wrong and that the doctors must have been mis-directing themselves as to their duty in law.[27]

He went on to say that he thought his view could be best expressed in this way:

The duty is fulfilled if the doctor acts in accordance with a practice rightly accepted as proper by a body of skilled and experienced medical men.[28]

This point was considered again in the House of Lords where Lord Templeman said:

In the case of a general danger, the court must decide whether the information afforded to the patient was sufficient to alert the patient to the possibility of serious harm of the kind in fact suffered. If the practice of the medical profession is to make express mention of a particular kind of danger, the court will have no difficulty in coming to a conclusion that the doctor ought to have referred expressly to this danger as a special danger unless the doctor can give reasons to justify the form or absence of warning adopted by him. Where the practice of the medical profession is divided or does not include express mention, it will be for the court to determine whether the harm suffered is an example of a general danger inherent in the nature of the operation and if so whether the explanation afforded to the patient was sufficient to alert the patient to the general dangers of which the harm suffered is an example.[29]

These cases indicate that in an appropriate case a court may have the right to reject expert evidence where that evidence is of a general practice in a profession which is not a 'rightful practice'.

Sometimes, also, the error will be seen to have been one of failure to use common sense, rather than failure to comply with currently accepted standards, as in *J D Williams & Co Ltd v Michael Hyde and Associates Ltd*.[30] In this case Michael Hyde was engaged by JD Williams, a mail order company with large stocks of clothing, to provide services as architect and engineers on a project to convert two derelict mills in Oldham into storage facilities for materials.

In developing the design and specification of the heating systems Michael Hyde contacted British Gas, who suggested that a direct-fired gas system would be an economical and flexible solution. The British Gas quotation contained a disclaimer which said 'British Gas plc will not be liable for any discolouration effect on material resulting from direct gas fired heating'. The 'discolouration effect' referred to the phenomenon of phenolic yellowing, whereby the exhaust products from direct gas fire heating, by raising nitrous oxide levels, can cause discolouration of materials including textiles, foam and packaging.

Hyde telephoned the British Gas representative for an explanation, and was told that there had been problems in relation to foam caused by an older type of direct gas-fired heating system. The implication was that it would not apply to the current situation,

---

[27] ibid., at 513-14.
[28] ibid., at 514.
[29] [1985] AC 871, at 903.
[30] [2001] BLR 99 (CA).

although the supplier did not withdraw the disclaimer. Hyde accepted the assurance and made no further enquiries, but unfortunately once the warehouses were in use, there were significant problems of discolouration of stored fabrics.

At the first trial, Hyde was found to be negligent, as the disclaimer by British Gas ought to have investigated further despite the fact that the proposed system complied with British Standards. The court decided that on the balance of probabilities, if further investigation had been carried out, the problem would have been identified and avoided. The Court of Appeal overturned the decision. Although it could not interfere with the finding of negligence (as this was a finding of fact), in relation to causation it did not agree that, on the balance of probabilities, further investigation would necessarily have revealed the nature of the problem.

In reaching its conclusions, the Court of Appeal considered how the first instance judge had dealt with the conflicting expert evidence. The Lord Justices' views differed. Lord Justice Wade felt that the matter was one of common sense, and the Bolan test did not apply. Lord Justice Sedley confirmed that a professional person must not fall below a proper standard but distinguished two situations: the Bolan test applied where 'the neglect is said to lie in the conscious choice of available courses', but may not be appropriate where the matter is one of 'oversight'. However the court agreed that the judge in this case did not err in setting aside the experts' view and reaching his own view on whether there had been negligence.

From a practical point of view it is useful to note that in some circumstances it may not be enough simply to comply with British Standards, nor to accept the assurance of a sales representative. The fact that a body of professionals would have done the same thing in similar circumstances may not be sufficient to demonstrate that enough care was taken. Further examples of what might be considered an acceptable level of skill and care are examined in Chapter 8.

6.4 Special skills

The emphasis above is on the 'ordinary skilled man'. Where designers hold themselves out as having special skills, the question as to what the appropriate test for negligence is will arise. This has been considered in two cases, one in construction and one in medicine.

The test, approved in the House of Lords, is that set out in *Bolam*, which is the ordinary skill of an ordinary competent man exercising that particular art. In *Wimpey Construction UK Ltd v Poole*[31] the court had to consider what the effect of that test was in circumstances where a professional man held himself out as having especially high skills and had been retained on that basis. It was held that you judge that professional man by the standards of an ordinary skilled man exercising and professing to have the special professional skill. The court rejected the view that the test should be that of a man exercising or professing to have especially high professional skills. If such a man had as a matter of fact a higher degree of knowledge of awareness and acted in a way

---

[31] (1984) 27 BLR 58.

which, in the light of that actual knowledge, produced damage which he ought reasonably to have foreseen, then he would be liable in negligence; that would be so even though the ordinary skilled man would not have had that knowledge. In *Ashcroft v Mersey Regional Health Authority*[32] a medical negligence case, it was said that the more skilled a person is, the more is the care which is to be expected of him; but that 'it is preferable in my judgment to concentrate on and to apply the test which has long been established in the law and to avoid all commentary and gloss'.[33]

A contrasting example can be found in *Gloucestershire Health Authority v Torpy*.[34] This case concerned the liability of engineers for the selection of waste incinerators for hospital authorities. Before they were awarded the commission the engineers Torpy had claimed 'extensive experience – both technical and historical . . . of incinerator and waste handling technology'. It was argued that they should not be judged as ordinary competent engineers, but as specialists. The judge disagreed, stating:

> to claim extensive experience in a field does not make a practitioner a specialist. A general practitioner doctor may claim extensive experience in delivering babies, but that would not make him a specialist obstetrician even if he also claimed he was uniquely qualified to deal with a particular delivery in particular circumstances; such a person would remain a general practitioner even though he claimed he was a very good general practitioner in a particular field (see *Wimpey Construction UK Ltd v D V Poole* . . .). There is a considerable difference between saying 'I have extensive experience in field X' and saying 'I am a specialist in field X'.[35]

6.5 'State of the art' defence

It will usually be the case that the courts will judge the standard against which negligence will be assessed by reference to the state of the art of that design at the time when the design was carried out. Most cases will proceed on that basis. In other words, the standards to apply to the alleged negligent design will be the professional standards of the time at which it was designed and not any later standards which may be different or higher.[36] This has become known as the 'state of the art defence' to a claim for professional negligence.

A designer is only expected to design in conformity with the accepted standards of the time. These standards will be established by reference to Codes of Practice, National Standards and relevant authoritative published information or widely accepted guidance information. Often the designer will plead that the matter was one which an architect at that time could not have been expected to know. However there are situations where the 'state of the art' defence will be inappropriate or will not apply.

---

[32] [1983] 2 All ER 245.
[33] ibid., Kilner Brown J, at 247.
[34] (1997) 55 Con LR 124.
[35] ibid., at 145–6.
[36] *Wimpey Construction (UK) Ltd v Poole* (1985) 27 BLR 58; *Kensington and Chelsea and Westminster AHA v Adams Holden & Partners & Another* (1984) 31 BLR 57.

One is already mentioned above, i.e. that the court might take the view that the practice of the profession at the time that the design was carried out was not a 'rightful practice.'[37] Another area, discussed at Section 8.4.2, is where a design is novel or at the frontiers of knowledge, where the court may take the view that it would be foolhardy even to try to construct such a structure, so the fact that is was designed to available current knowledge and standards is not enough of a defence. As the court said in *IBA v EMI and BICC* 'the law requires even pioneers to be prudent'.[38]

---

[37] *Sidaway v Board of Governors of the Bethlem Royal Hospital and the Maudsley Hospital* [1985] AC 871 (HL).
[38] (1980) 14 BLR 1, Lord Edmund Davies at 28.

Chapter 7
'Fitness for Purpose' Liability

The preceding chapter discussed the nature of the duty normally implied into a contract for services, i.e. that the service provider must undertake the agreed tasks with a reasonable level of skill and care. This would normally apply to consultants undertaking design under a contract for services only.

When a contractor undertakes to design and construct a building for a client,[1] the implied obligation is often stated to be to deliver something 'fit for purpose'. The distinction between the use of reasonable skill and care and an obligation as to 'fitness for purpose' is important. A consultant will, of course, endeavor to design something that meets the client's requirements. However if the design fails to achieve this, the consultant will not necessarily be liable: the client still has to prove there was negligence. When a contractor designs a building, the result should normally meet any requirements made known by the client (unless the contract sets out a different level of liability). If it does not, the contractor will be in breach of contract regardless of how much care was taken in the design. A 'fitness for purpose' obligation is in fact a shorthand way of describing a strict obligation in the context of design. The effect of such an obligation was neatly summarised in *George Fischer Holdings Ltd v Multi Design Consultants Ltd* as follows:

> If, as I have found, MDC warranted the sufficiency and operational performance of the project works then distinctions between design, workmanship and supervision fall away, as do issues of care and skill . . . negligence in any of those respects is not a necessary condition of liability if an alleged defect exists and affects the sufficiency or performance of the works.[2]

As this is clearly of major significance to contractors, it is important to examine the basis for the implication.

7.1 Contractors' obligations

7.1.1 Obligation as to materials

Where there is a contract for sale of goods, the Sale of Goods Act 1979 implies a condition that the goods shall be of satisfactory quality and be reasonably fit for any purpose

---

[1] As opposed to a contract for sale of a completed property, where there would be no such implied terms.
[2] (1998) 61 Con LR 85 at para. 95.

Cornes and Lupton's Design Liability in the Construction Industry, Fifth Edition. Sarah Lupton.
© 2013 Sarah Lupton and DL Cornes. Published 2013 by Blackwell Publishing Ltd.

made known to the seller by the buyer, unless the buyer is not relying on the seller's skill and judgement.

The purpose needs to be clear. *J Murphy & Sons Ltd v Johnston Precast Ltd*[3] concerned a contract to manufacture and supply glass reinforced plastic pipes for a water main. The pipes were bedded in concrete foam. After they were laid, the pipes cracked causing extensive damage. It was discovered that the cracks had formed at a point where there was a large void in the foam, and that the presence of the void had caused the problem. The court found that the supplier was not liable for failing to provide something fit for purpose, as at the time the contract was formed it had not been told that the pipes would be used with foam concrete, therefore it was clear that the buyer was not relying on the seller's skill and judgement.

However, in some circumstances a court may decide that the purpose has 'impliedly' been made known. For example, in *BSS Group Plc v Makers (UK) Ltd*[4] an order was placed for valves for a plumbing system in a public house. Although the order did not specify the type of valves, the supplier had regularly supplied other parts for the project, and the order made it clear which project they were for. The valves turned out to be incompatible with the other components, and the suppliers were held liable for failing to supply valves that were fit for purpose.

In *Lowe v W. Machell Joinery Ltd*[5] a joinery company fabricated and supplied a timber spiral staircase for a barn conversion, with a balustrade that had been selected from a catalogue by the clients. The stair did not comply with building regulations as the spindles were too far apart, and the client rejected it. The Court of Appeal found that the staircase 'had to be fit for the purpose of being installed in a building to be used as a residence'. The client was entitled to reject it, even though it matched the balustrade selected. It was clear that the client was relying on the joinery firm's skill and judgement (no professional consultants were involved).[6] It is likely, however, that in a commercial situation a buyer may have been obliged to accept the stair.

The Supply of Goods and Services Act 1982 requires that any goods supplied under a contract for work and materials, shall also be of satisfactory quality and reasonably fit for any purpose made known (the Acts are outlined in Chapter 2). Selecting materials for use in construction works is clearly an aspect of design, and the effect of the 1982 Act is therefore to imply terms that such decisions shall be taken not just with skill and care, but so that a result is achieved. This can be exemplified by case law preceding and following the enactment of the Supply of Goods and Services Act 1982 (that Act codified what was already considered to be an accepted legal principle).

For example, in *G. H. Myers & Co v Brent Cross Service Co*[7] the Court of Appeal considered a contract for work and labour and the supply of materials. The case concerned the repair of a motor vehicle. The relevant principle was stated by Du Parcq J in the following terms:

---

[3] [2008] EWHC 3104 (TCC).
[4] [2011] EWCA Civ 809.
[5] [2011] BLR 5901 (CA).
[6] Note however that the *Building Law Report* editors have suggested that the stair ought to have been the client's risk.
[7] [1934] 1 KB 46.

But it would not be true to say that wherever you find a contract to do work and supply materials it necessarily follows, even apart from special conditions, that the person supplying the materials is liable if some of them are defective by reason of latent defect. That depends upon the terms of the contract, and I think that the true view is that a person contracting to do work and supply materials warrants that the materials which he uses will be of good quality and reasonably fit for the purpose for which he is using them, unless the circumstances of the contract are such as to exclude any such warranty.[8]

This decision of Du Parcq J was approved and followed by the House of Lords in *Young & Marten Ltd v McManus Childs Ltd*[9] (see 2.2.3.2). and by the High Court of Australia in *Helicopter Sales (Australia) Pty Ltd v Rotor-Work Pty Ltd*.[10] In other words, the position of a builder supplying materials as part of its work under the building contract, will usually be much the same as it would be if the Sale of Goods Act 1979 applied to the transaction, provided the employer relied on the skill and judgement of the contractor.

7.1.2 Obligation as to workmanship

The term 'workmanship' usually refers to the way work is carried out, i.e. its physical execution. Generally a contractor will be obliged to carry out work with a reasonable level of skill and care, as required under the Supply of Goods and Services Act 1982.[11] Sometimes, however, 'workmanship' can refer to decisions regarding detailing, for example the fixings to be used to attach a cladding panel. Strictly speaking, these are matters of design, not workmanship, as they relate to *what* the final structure will be, not the manner or sequence of its erection. In that sense, it is suggested that if the contractor makes such decisions, it will be obliged to ensure the detailed design results in something suitable, in the same way that it would be for larger scale design, as discussed below.

7.1.3 Design and construction of a house

Where a contractor is employed to build a house, there is a term implied by law that the contractor will do the work in a good and workmanlike manner and that the house will be reasonably fit for human habitation on completion. In other words, a contractor's duty in such circumstances is not limited to using reasonable skill and care; it is obliged to ensure that the finished work is reasonably fit for the purpose of human habitation. The basis for this was set up in early cases of *Miller v Cannon Hill Estates Ltd*[12] which concerned new-build suburban houses that on completion were found to have serious defects, including leaks. Swift J held that the builder was obliged to complete the buildings to a good and workmanlike standard. This was followed in *Perry v*

---

[8] ibid., at 55.
[9] [1969] 1 AC 454.
[10] [1974] HCA 72.
[11] Which in turn embodies common law principles, see e.g., *Duncan v Blundell* (1820) 3 Stark 6.
[12] [1931] 2 KB 113.

Sharon Development Co. Ltd[13] which again involved suburban houses with leaks, defective plaster, and incomplete services installations. The Court of Appeal held that there was an implied term that the houses when complete would be ready for occupation. The implication was further confirmed in *Hancock v B.W. Brazier (Anerley) Ltd*[14] and *Test Valley Borough Council v GLC*.[15] The common law principle is now embodied in the Defective Premises Act 1972 (see Chapter 5).

7.1.4 Design and construction of other buildings

The fitness for purpose of a complete structure was considered (although not finally decided) in 1980 in a House of Lords' case, *Independent Broadcasting Authority v EMI Electronics Ltd and BICC Construction Ltd*.[16] The case is of such importance that the facts and findings are worth setting out in some detail.

On 19 March 1969, a 1250-foot high television mast at Elmley Moor in Yorkshire collapsed. The owner of the mast, IBA, had engaged EMI to design and construct the mast, and EMI had in turn sub-let the design to BICC. IBA sued EMI, as main contractors and BICC, their sub-contractors, for damages. IBA alleged breach of the contract (which was in the form of the Model Conditions of the IMechE/IEE for home contracts with erection) and negligence against EMI, and negligence, breach of warranty and negligent misstatement against BICC. The judge who originally heard the case had determined that the reason for the failure was the fracture of a flange at 1027 feet above ground level and that this failure had been caused primarily by vortex shedding (induced by wind) and to a lesser extent by the asymmetric loading of ice on the mast. The House of Lords held that:

(1) BICC had been negligent in the design of the mast
(2) a statement in a letter from BICC to IBA that 'We are all well satisfied that the structures will not oscillate dangerously' was, in the state of BICC's then knowledge, a negligent misstatement
(3) that assurance had no contractual effect
(4) EMI were under contractual liability to IBA for the design of the mast; at its least, that responsibility extended to responsibility for a negligent design; and since the design was negligent it was unnecessary further to consider the full extent of that responsibility.

The House of Lords, because of its findings on other issues, did not decide whether there was to be a term implied in law that the television mast should be fit for its purpose. This is because Their Lordships found that EMI had a contractual responsibility for the design of the mast and that at the very least that responsibility must have extended to seeing that the design would not be carried out negligently. They found

---

[13] [1937] 4 All ER 390 (CA).
[14] [1966] 2 All ER 901.
[15] (1979) 13 BLR 63.
[16] (1980) 14 BLR 1.

that the design had been carried out negligently so it follows that it was not necessary for them to consider the fitness for purpose issue. However, there are some comments in that case that are highly relevant. Viscount Dilhorne, for example, said:

> In the circumstances it was not necessary to consider whether EMI had by their contract undertaken to supply a mast reasonably fit for the purpose for which they knew it was intended and whether BICC had by their contract with EMI undertaken a similar obligation but had that been argued, I would myself have been surprised if it had been concluded that they had not done so.[17]

Lord Fraser in the *IBA* case considered the *Young and Marten* case in relation to materials and said that he thought the same principle should be applied in this case in respect of the complete structure, including its design; he appears to have adopted this argument on the basis that the implication of a warranty as to fitness for purpose would be reasonable in most cases because the main contractor, liable to the employer for defective material, would generally have a right of redress against the person from whom he bought the material. In other words, there should be a chain of responsibility. Lord Fraser said:

> In the present case, it is accepted by BICC that if EMI are liable in damages to IBA for the design of the mast, then BICC will be liable in turn to EMI. Accordingly, the principle that was applied in *Young and Marten Limited* in respect of materials ought in my opinion to be applied here in respect of the complete structure, including its design. Although EMI had no specialist knowledge of mast design, and although IBA knew that and did not rely on their skill to any extent for the design, I can see nothing unreasonable in holding that EMI are responsible to IBA for the design seeing that they can in turn recover from BICC who did the actual designing.[18]

Lord Scarman in the same case referred to *Samuels v Davis*[19] in which the Court of Appeal had held that where a dentist agrees to make false teeth for a patient for a fee, then there will be an implied term in the contract that the false teeth will be reasonably fit for their intended purpose. He approved the distinction made in *Samuels v Davis* between a dentist's obligation to use reasonable care in taking out a tooth and the entirely different case where false teeth are to be designed and supplied.[20]

Lord Scarman, therefore, formed the view that in the absence of any term negativing the obligation, a person 'who contracts to design an article for the purpose made known to him undertakes that the design is reasonably fit for the purpose. Such a design obligation is consistent with the statutory law regulating the sale of goods.'[21]

The Supreme Court of Ireland had previously considered but decided against the implication of a term as to fitness for purpose of a sub-contractor's design into a main contractor's contract in *Norta Wallpapers (Ireland) v Sisk & Sons (Dublin)*.[22] The employer contracted with a contractor to build a factory and specified that the roof

---

[17] ibid., at 26.
[18] ibid., at 45.
[19] [1943] KB 526.
[20] (1980) 14 BLR 1 at 48.
[21] ibid., at 48.
[22] (1978) 14 BLR 49.

was to be supplied and erected by a particular sub-contractor who manufactured and supplied superstructures. The sub-contractor under the sub-contract indemnified the contractor against any liability which might arise under the main contract as a result of the sub-contractor's breach of the sub-contract. After completion, the roof leaked and was unsuitable for its purpose. An arbitrator found that the problem was 85 per cent due to the defective design of roof lights.

It was held on appeal that there is normally implied in a building contract a term making the contractor liable to the employer for any loss suffered as a result of the sub-contractor's goods, materials or installations not being fit for their intended purpose, but that such an implied term cannot be held to exist unless it comes within the presumed intention of the parties and should not be read into the contract unless it would be reasonable to do so. The court concluded that as the employer was relying on its engineers, and not the contractor, to check the design, no such term could be implied in relation to the fitness of the roof's design.[23]

At first sight, the *IBA* case appears to be inconsistent with the *Norta* case, although both are similar on their facts. Lord Fraser in the *IBA* case explained the apparent inconsistency by pointing out that before the main contract in the *Norta* case was agreed, Norta had already approved the sub-contractor's design, specification and price. Thus, Sisk were given no option but to use the sub-contractor, its design and its price. In the *IBA* case, EMI had no option but to appoint BICC but they were not bound to accept any particular design at any particular price. So it is possible to argue that there is no inconsistency between the *IBA* and the *Norta* cases.

The key case to establish the liability of a contractor for providing a building that is 'fit for purpose', is that of *Viking Grain Storage v T H White Installations Ltd*.[24] Viking Grain entered into a contract with White to design and erect a grain drying and storage installation with the capacity to handle 10,000 tons of grain. The site was in Grantham, Lincolnshire. Viking had commissioned a site report based on one borehole, and subsequently White commissioned further site investigations, all of which stated that the boreholes were dry, although expressed reservations that the absence of water might be due to impermeability rather than a low water table. Following installation there were numerous problems, including with the steel superstructure, cladding and insulation, and with seepage of water into the various parts of the structure below ground.

Viking commenced proceedings against the contractor claiming that, because of defects, the grain store was unfit for its intended use. It argued that terms should be implied to the effect that the contractor would use materials of good quality and reasonably fit for their purpose, and that the completed works should be reasonably fit for their intended purpose. The contractor claimed that its obligation was limited to the use of reasonable skill and care in carrying out the design.

Judge John Davies QC decided that Viking did not have any other specialist advice or assistance and had been relying entirely on the expertise of the contractor for the design. He then remarked:

---

[23] A similar result was achieved a year earlier in *John Mowlem & Co. Ltd v British Insulated Callendars Pension Trust Ltd* (1977) 3 Con LR 64, where the court refused to imply a design obligation into a contract let on JCT63, and more recently in *Sinclair v Woods of Winchester Ltd (No. 2)* (2006) 109 Con LR 14.
[24] (1985) 33 BLR 103.

. . . whilst in the ordinary case of the sale of an article other than under its trade or patent name, if the purpose is known to the seller so as to show reliance on his skill and judgement, a warranty of fitness will be implied irrespective of whether he is the manufacturer. Does the analogy hold good in the case of a supplier of a multi-partite installation like this one, where a variety of different parts of the entity are the subject of specialist sub-contractors?[25]

He examined the terms of the contract, and could find no contrary indication that a term should be implied. He did not consider that there was any merit in breaking down the obligations of a contractor under a design and build contract (i.e. a strict liability to provide suitable materials, but the lesser obligation to use skill and care in the design). The specification of the functional parts of the installation as a whole and the conditions of the ground were integral and interdependent part of the whole. He stated:

In the absence of any contrary indication that I can find in the contract, I turn therefore to the positive question: should a term of reasonable fitness for purpose be implied, or is it that in matters of the design, specification and supervision of the works, White's obligation is, as they contend, limited to the exercise of reasonable care and skill? It is worthy of note that they admit an implied obligation, unqualified by negligence, to use materials of good quality and that they also admitted during the hearing the further obligation that those materials should be reasonably fit for the purpose 'subject to the terms of the contract'. I confess at the outset that I find it difficult to comprehend why an entire contract to build an installation should need to be broken into so many pieces with differing criteria of liability. The virtue of an implied term of fitness for purpose is that it prescribes a relatively simple and certain standard of liability based on the 'reasonable' fitness of the finished product, irrespective of considerations of fault and of whether its unfitness derived from the quality of work or materials or design. In my view, such a term is to be implied in this case . . . I find it impossible to distinguish between the reliance placed by Viking on White with regard to the quality of the materials and their design, the design and specification of the functional parts as a whole, and the condition of the ground, All these things were integral and interdependent parts of the whole . . . .[26]

and

The suggestion that matters of design should be regarded as involving no higher duty than that of reasonable care was put forward and rejected in *IBA v EMI* (1978) 11 BLR 38, where the judgment was delivered by Roskill LJ, where the Court of Appeal could see no good reason for importing into a contract of this nature a different obligation in relation to design from that which plainly exists in relation to materials. To find otherwise in this particular case, when Viking clearly relied, in all aspects, including design, on the skill and judgement of White to produce an end result would, in my view, be to destroy the whole basis of the bargain. The obligations to design a product fit for its purpose is already tempered by the fact that only 'reasonable' fitness is demanded; to add to that a requirement of proof of lack of due care seems to emasculate, and magnify the uncertainty of, the obligation to such an extent as would be neither acceptable nor realistic in a commercial transaction.[27]

There are several useful points to note about this case. First, the obligation is only to provide something reasonably fit for its purpose. The tempering by the term

---

[25] ibid., at 113.
[26] ibid., at 117.
[27] ibid., at 118.

'reasonable' means that there could be situations where the result of the design fell short in some way, but the contractor may still be found to have fulfilled its duty. In the Australian case of *Barton v Stiff*[28] a contractor was engaged to construct a house in Wodonga, and a clause in the contract stated:

> 11.5 The Builder warrants that if the work consists of the erection or construction of a home, or is work intended to renovate, alter, extend, improve or repair a home to a stage suitable for occupation, the home will be suitable for occupation at the time the work is completed.
>
> 11.6 If the Contract states the particular purpose for which the work is required, or the result which the Owners wishes the work to achieve, so as to show that the Owner relies on the Builder's skill and judgement, the Builder warrants that the work and any material used in carrying out the work will be reasonably fit for that purpose or will be of such a nature and quality that they might reasonably be expected to achieve that result.

When constructing the house the contractor used bricks below the DPM level that were not resistant to the salty groundwater. However soil reports provided at that time had not revealed these unusual conditions, and there was no means by which the contractor could have foreseen them. Justice Hargrave considered *IBM v BICC* and *Viking*, and concluded:

> If [it] is not the case [that the reasoning in *IBM* is applicable], it would be tantamount to finding that the contract provided for the builders to be insurers of the house. The parties could not have intended this. I hold that the warranties of fitness for purpose in this case required the builders to provide materials, and a completed house, which would be proof against any groundwater conditions likely to be encountered at the land.[29]

The Judge explained clearly that this did not mean 'that the warranty of fitness for purpose is not absolute. It means that the absolute warranty of fitness for purpose relates to the purpose as properly identified'.[30] This would be important, for example, when issues such as durability and life-span are considered, where reasonable levels of usage and maintenance would be assumed (if not stipulated in the contract).

Secondly, it should be noted that in *Viking* the contract documents did include design documents and a specification prepared by the contractor White. These proved to be inadequate, but the contractor's obligation was seen to be wider that simply to provide a building according to the incorporated design and specification, i.e. to provide something that worked (similarly in *Basildon District Council v J E Lesser (Properties) Ltd*[31] the contractor's design was incorporated in the contract, yet a 'fit for habitation' obligation was implied). This can be contrasted with the earlier case of *Lynch v Thorne*.[32] Here a builder sold a house in the course of erection, and the contract of sale included plans and a specification which it had prepared. These showed an external wall of 9" brick, which later suffered from damp penetration and was found to be inadequate. The court decided that although the contractor would normally be under an implied duty to design a structure that was weatherproof, in this case the express terms displaced the implication.

---

[28] [2006] VSC 307.
[29] ibid., para. 39.
[30] ibid., para. 37.
[31] (1987) 8 Con LR 89.
[32] [1956] 1 All ER 744.

Finally, it is also interesting to note the Judge's clear understanding and sensible approach in *Viking* to matters of scale and the interrelatedness of parts. The employer approached the contractor with a requirement for a building to fulfil a well-defined purpose, and it would be of little use to the owner if the separate materials were of good quality, or even if separate parts were well designed and worked, if the building as a whole did not fulfil the required function. The Judge therefore had little difficulty in implying this overall obligation. Although the term was implied on the facts, one would expect a similar implication to arise in most design and build contracts, where the purpose was made clear by e.g., a brief or performance specification, and the express terms did not state anything to the contrary. Examples of such an implication can be seen in more recent cases such as *Tesco Stores Ltd v Costain Construction Ltd*[33] discussed below.

The courts appear to have a little more difficulty with implying a fit for purpose obligation with respect to a system. In the recent case of *Trebor Bassett Holdings Ltd v ADT Fire and Security Plc*,[34] ADT was engaged to design and install a fire protection system in a popcorn factory. The system failed, causing a fire in a hopper to spread and destroy the entire premises. It was common ground that the fire suppression system did not automatically discharge CO_2 into the hopper as, had it been properly designed to deal with a deep-seated fire of the type which had occurred, it would have done. However the court at first instance found that ADT was not liable for providing a system that was fit for purpose (and the Court of Appeal agreed). Instead its obligation was limited to designing it with reasonable skill and care. Several reasons were stated, including that 'it is not a natural or accurate use of language in this context to regard "the system" as simply "goods" attracting without more the well-known statutory incidents of quality and fitness for purpose . . . Once it is accepted, as I do, that "the system" cannot be equated with or is not be regarded as without more "goods", those implied terms have no relevance'.[35] It was also found that the purpose had not been sufficiently made clear, i.e., although a fire suppression system had been requested, the description of the risks it had to meet was not sufficiently precise. Both reasons seem inconsistent with the above cases, i.e. a system is arguably the same as a complex component, and the purpose was obvious from the circumstances. However it should be borne in mind that the factory owner had also been negligent (the court had found it 75% responsible). A 'fit for purpose' finding would have meant that this contributory negligence could not have been applied, a fact which may have influenced the decision.

7.2 *Reliance and partial reliance*

As noted above, the strict obligation to supply materials, components and parts of or entire buildings 'fit for purpose' would not be implied in cases where the buyer was not relying on the seller's skill and judgement. Whether or not there has been reliance in

---

[33] [2003] EWHC 1487 (TCC).
[34] [2012] EWCA Civ 1158 (CA).
[35] ibid., para. 49.

any particular circumstances is therefore a crucial question, as the contractor's liability may depend on it. The existence of 'reliance' in any particular case is a question of fact, and any finding is not binding on subsequent courts, but it is nevertheless interesting to examine the range of circumstances in which reliance has or has not be found.

In the case of selection of a material, providing a detailed prescriptive specification which leaves no choice to the contractor would normally be sufficient to displace the implied warranty. A case exemplifying this is *Bowmer & Kirkland Ltd v Wilson Bowden Properties Ltd.*[36] This concerned the construction of two, two-storey office buildings, the original contract value of which was approximately £2.8 million, but which following construction suffered defects that cost around £1 million to repair. The employer argued that there should be implied into the contract a series of terms which included that the builder would use materials of good quality and which were fit for their intended purposes, and that the builder would carry out and complete the works so that the works, when completed, would be fit for their intended purposes. There had, however, been architects engaged on the project who had prepared detailed plans and specifications. Judge Bowsher, relying on *Lynch v Thorn*,[37] decided that none of these terms were to be implied into the contract; to the extent that materials, products and workmanship are fully specified, the builder has performed its contract if it does what is specified.

In *Viking Grain* above, the reliance was clear: the client had engaged the contractor to design and supply the grain store, had not supplied the contractor with a design or specification, and had taken no advice from other sources. In *Bowmer & Kirkland* it was clear there was no reliance. Frequently the position is not so clear-cut.

In *Cammell Laird & Co v Manganese Bronze and Brass Co*[38] the defendants agreed to construct two propellers for two ships for the plaintiff. These were to be made according to certain specifications laid down by the plaintiffs, but certain matters, in particular, the thickness of the blades, were left to the defendants. One of the propellers proved to be useless owing to defects in matters not laid down in the specifications, and the manufacturers were held liable. As explained by Lord Warrington:

> Here there was a substantial area outside the specification which was not covered by its directions and was therefore necessarily left to the skill and judgement of the seller. Without attempting to express an opinion on the actual cause of the trouble, I think it is clear that it arose from some defect in the seller's area. Four propellers were made, each in accordance with the specification. Two were noisy, two were not.[39]

In considering what was required to demonstrate reliance Lord Wright said:

> But the more difficult question remains whether the particular purpose for which the goods were required was not merely made known, as I think it was, by the appellants to the respondents, but was made known so as to show that the appellants as buyers relied on the seller's skill

---

[36] (1996) 80 BLR 131.
[37] [1956] 1 All ER 744. See Section 7.1.
[38] [1934] AC 402.
[39] ibid., at 414.

and judgement. Such a reliance must be affirmatively shown; the buyer must bring home to the mind of the seller that he is relying on him in such a way that the seller can be taken to have contracted on that footing. The reliance is to be the basis of a contractual obligation . . . In some cases the matter may be very simple: the purpose for which a hot water bottle is required is easily determined and equally easy is it to determine the extent of reliance on the seller.[40]

He added:

But, in my opinion, there is no general rule that where a maker agrees to make a machine of a description which it is in the course of his business to supply, in accordance with a design or specification given him by the buyer, s. 14(1) must necessarily be excluded.

Similarly, in *Lynch v Thorne*[41] Parker LJ stated:

'Th[at] contract was, at any rate, partly a contract for work and labour. The plaintiff clearly desired the house for habitation, and to some extent relied on the skill and judgement of the defendant, who was a builder of houses. Those facts must be taken to have been known by the defendant. In those circumstances I think that prima facie there is an implied condition that the house, when built, shall be fit for human habitation. I say 'prima facie' because, of course, the express terms of the contract may be such as to show that they are wholly or partly inconsistent with any such implied condition. If they are wholly inconsistent, that will quite clearly negative any reliance which, otherwise, it could be said the buyer placed on the skill and judgement of the seller. If, on the other hand, the express terms are only partly inconsistent, there will be room for the implied condition to operate in the area not covered by the express condition.[42]

Cammell Laird was approved in *Hancock v Brazier (Anerley) Ltd.*[43] That case concerned a contract of sale of land on which the vendor builders agreed to construct a house 'in a proper and workmanlike manner . . . in accordance with the plan and specification supplied to the purchaser.' The plan specified for a concrete floor which was to be laid over 'hardcore', although the type was not specified. A few years later the floors and walls cracked. The cracking was caused by the effect of sodium sulphate in the hardcore used by them on the concrete slab, which caused, in the presence of water, a chemical reaction between the hardcore and the concrete. This chemical reaction caused the floor to break up. There was no criticism of the skill and care used in its selection, as the builders were unaware, and had no reason to be aware, of the presence of the sodium sulphate, so the question was whether they were nevertheless under a strict obligation to provide a suitable material. Diplock LJ (sitting at first instance) considered a number of authorities, including *Cammell Laird* and *Lynch v Thorn*, and concluded that the vendor, in addition to the express warranty to construct the house in a proper and workmanlike manner, impliedly warranted that 'the house should be

---

[40] ibid., 423-4.
[41] [1956] 1 All ER 744.
[42] ibid., at 750.
[43] [1966] 2 All ER 1.

built of materials suitable and fit and proper for the purpose'. When the express and implied warranties were taken together, an alternative way of stating them was that the house was warranted to be 'habitable and fit for humans to live in'. Since there had been no definite specification concerning the hardcore to be used, as there had been with regard to the brickwork in *Lynch v Thorne*, there was room for an implied condition that the hardcore should be fit, proper and suitable and that the defendants were in breach of that condition. He stated that:

> . . . it cannot have been intended by the parties that any old hardcore, anything which could be described as hardcore, however unsuitable for the purpose, could properly be used in performance of this contract . . . It seems to me that since there was no definite specification of the hardcore to be used, as there was with regard to the material to be used in that part of *Lynch v Thorne* which came to the Court of Appeal, there is, in the words of Parker LJ ([1956] 1 All ER at p. 750), 'room for the implied condition that the materials shall be fit, proper and suitable for the purpose to operate in the area of the hardcore', and I would read this clause as containing a contractual warranty on the part of the builders that the hardcore used for the purpose of being put under the site concrete of the floors should be fit, proper and suitable for that purpose.[44]

The case went to appeal, where the decision was upheld.[45] Lord Denning MR stated:

> . . . when a purchaser buys a house from a builder who contracts to build it, there is a threefold implication: that the builder will do his work in a good and workmanlike manner; that he will supply good and proper materials; and that it will be reasonably fit for human habitation. Sometimes this implication, or some part of it, may be excluded by an express provision . . . The question in this case is whether the threefold implication is excluded by clause 9. I think not. For this simple reason: clause 9 deals only with workmanship. It does not deal with materials. The quality of the materials is left to be implied. And the necessary implication is that they should be good and suitable for the work. I am quite clear that it is implied in the contract that the hardcore must be good and proper hardcore, in the same way as the bricks must be good and proper bricks. I know the builders were not at fault themselves. But nevertheless this is a contract: it was their responsibility to see that good and proper hardcore was put in. As it was not put in, they are in breach of their contract.[46]

In all the above cases the contract was based on plans and a specification, but to the extent that the design was incomplete (in that it did not finally decide all matters necessary) the court had no difficulty in implying an obligation that the contractor was responsible for the design decisions that it did, in fact, make.

The courts, however, are less ready to do this where there is an architect and/or other consultants involved in preparing the design, particularly where their involvement continues through the project. For example, in the Canadian case of *Sunnyside Nursing*

---

[44] ibid., at 8.

[45] [1966] 1 WLR 1317.

[46] ibid., at 1323: see also *Ashington Piggeries Ltd v Christopher Hill Ltd* [1972] AC 441.

Home v Builders Contract Management Ltd & Others[47] the employer invited tenders from contractors who were asked to suggest a proposed structural system. The employer had previously invited architects and engineers to prepare tender documents and after acceptance of the tender the architects completed the plans and specifications based on the system for the structure designated by the successful tenderer, Builders Contract Management Ltd (BCM). The work proceeded in the way envisaged save that there were design (and workmanship) defects in the works and an issue inevitably arose as to whether BCM had a design responsibility. It was held in this case that the employer did not rely entirely, or at all, on the experience, judgement or skill of BCM in the design and that in general, a contractor is unlikely to have a design obligation where the employer engages an architect and/or an engineer.

It is interesting to contrast *Hancock v Brazier* with the later case of *Rotherham MBC v Frank Haslam Milan and M. J. Gleeson)*,[48] also a Court of Appeal case. Rotherham MBC entered into a contract to build a new office block. The contract (JCT63) involved the laying of fill on the site and the contractor, Gleeson, was given a detailed specification as to the material of the fill: '. . . hardcore shall be graded or uncrushed gravel, rock fill, crushed concrete or slag or natural sand or a combination of any of these.' The clause omitted to state the types of slag that could be used and the unweathered steel slag selected by the contractor proved to be expansive, causing cracking in the concrete ground floor slab (around £700,000 worth of damage). The Court of Appeal, overturning the decision of the Official Referee at first instance, found the contractor was not liable for the damage caused by the heave.

The Court emphasised, among other things, that the fact that the employer had engaged a contract administrator to write the specification showed the employer did not intend to rely on the skill and expertise of the contractor in selecting the hardcore. It also noted that neither the specifier nor the contractor were aware that there was more than one type of slag. If it had not been for these special circumstances, however, the Court stated that it would have found the contractor strictly liable for providing a slag that was fit for the purpose for which it was to be used. It should be noted that Rotherham was concerned with an omission within the design information, and that the Court of Appeal made it clear that it was not the express terms of JCT63 that prevented the contractor assuming design liability, but the surrounding circumstances.

Although the author has doubted the reasoning in *Rotherham*[49] the finding that there was, in fact, no actual intention to rely on the builder's skill and care in that case has been supported by other commentators.[50]

More recently, in *Tesco Stores Ltd v Costain Construction Ltd*, the court considered the terms to be implied into a design-build contract formed on a letter of intent.[51] There the Judge stated that:

---

[47] (1986) 2 Const LJ 240.
[48] (1996) 78 BLR 1 (CA).
[49] See Sarah Lupton, 'Rotherham M B C v Frank Haslam Milan: a question of policy', *The International Construction Law Review*, 14(2), (1997), 234–244.
[50] see Atkins Chambers *Hudson's Building and Engineering Contracts*, 11th edn, p. 472.
[51] [2003] EWHC 1487 (TCC).

It may be appropriate to imply into a construction contract a term that the structure to be erected will, when complete, be reasonably fit for its intended purpose, but that will only be so if and insofar as the structure is to be designed by the contractor . . .

Thus the answer to Issue 2(iv) is that there were implied terms of the contract which I have found that Costain would perform any construction work which it undertook under the contract in a good and workmanlike manner and, insofar as any design decision in relation to the Store was made by Costain, the element designed would be reasonably fit for its intended purpose.[52]

This therefore reflects the approach taken in *Cammell Laird* and *Hancock v Brazier*; i.e. to the extent that the contractor undertook any design, it was required to provide something fit for purpose.

As highlighted in the introduction, whether or not it can be objectively construed that the client intended to rely on the skill and judgement of the contractor, such as to a result in an implied obligation that the result will be fit for purpose, will always be a question of fact in each case. It is worth noting that in the Sale of Goods Act 1979 the relevant wording places the onus on the supplier to prove that the reliance was *not* placed on it, rather than on the purchaser to show that it relied on the seller. Lord Wright's comment above that 'Such a reliance must be affirmatively shown' is therefore, at least in theory, no longer the case. However cases such as *Sunnyside Nursing Home* and *Rotherham* show that where consultants have been engaged to design a project, the burden of showing that reliance was not intended may not be that difficult to discharge.

7.3 Consultants and strict liability

As already discussed, the normal obligation, whether under contract or tort, imposed on a consultant providing design services only, is to use reasonable skill and care, and in fact by far the majority of claims against consultants would be brought on the basis of a breach of this duty (see Chapter 6). But can there ever arise situations where there is an obligation to see that the design is fit for its purpose? More precisely, would the liability of a consultant ever be strict?

The implied term as to reasonable skill and care under the Supply of Goods and Services Act 1982 does not prejudice any rule of law which imposes a duty stricter than that of reasonable skill and care (s. 16(3)(a)); so that Act does not of itself prevent the implication of a fitness for purpose term. Therefore it may be possible to imply a strict obligation on the facts of the case. For example, in *CFW Architects (A Firm) v Cowlin Construction Ltd*[53] it was held that there was an implied term in an architect's appointment to a contractor under a design-build procurement arrangement that drawings would be delivered according to an agreed programme (as opposed to using a reasonable level of skill and care to meet that programme).

The issue of a strict liability in relation to design arose in the case of *Greaves (Contractors) Ltd v Baynham Meikle & Partners*.[54] The case concerned a design and build

---

[52]ibid., paras 180 and 181.
[53](2006) Con LR 116.
[54](1975) 4 BLR 56.

contract. Contractors by a contract agreed to design and construct a warehouse and office for a company that intended to use the warehouse for storage of barrels of oil. The contractor engaged structural engineers to design the structure of the warehouse and in the course of giving instructions to those structural engineers, the contractor told them that the first and upper floors of the warehouse would have to take the weight of fork-lift trucks carrying heavy barrels of oil. The warehouse, which was built following the structural engineers' design, was brought into use and the floors began to crack. It was found at the trial that the cracks were the result of vibration of the forklift trucks. The Court of Appeal held that there was a term to be implied in the designer's contract that they should design a warehouse fit for the purpose for which it was required, namely reasonably fit for the use of forklift trucks carrying barrels of oil. As the structural engineers had not produced such a design, they were liable to the contractor for the cost of the remedial works required by the building owner. In the alternative, if there was no such term to be implied, the structural engineers were in breach of their duty to use reasonable skill and care because they knew or ought to have known that the purpose of the floors was to carry forklift trucks laden with barrels of oil.

Lord Denning in his judgment in the *Greaves* case drew the distinction between a term which is to be implied *by law* and a term which is to be implied *in fact* (see Chapter 2). The decision in the *Greaves* case was based on a term that was found to have been implied in fact and does not therefore give rise to any general assumption that there is to be implied into a designer's contract a term that the design will be fit for its purpose. Lord Denning put it this way:

> The law does not usually imply a warranty that he will achieve the desired result but only a term that he will use reasonable skill and care. The surgeon does not warrant that he will cure the patient. Nor does the solicitor warrant that he will win the case. But, when a dentist agrees to make a set of false teeth for a patient, there is an implied warranty that they will fit his gums, see *Samuels v Davis* [1943] 1 KB 526.
>
> What then is the position when an architect or an engineer is employed to design a house or a bridge? Is he under an implied warranty that, if the work is carried out to his design, it will be reasonably fit for the purpose or is he only under a duty to use reasonable skill and care? This question may require to be answered some day as a matter of law. But, in the present case I do not think we need answer it. For the evidence shows that both parties were of one mind on the matter. Their common intention was that the engineer should design a warehouse which would be fit for the purpose for which it was required. That common intention gives rise to a term implied *in fact*.[55]

By way of emphasis, Lord Justice Browne in the same case said that the decision in the case laid down no general principle as to the obligations and liabilities of professional men; it was a case that depended on the special facts and circumstances that had arisen.

The *dicta* of Lord Denning in *Greaves* were considered in *George Hawkins v Chrysler (UK) Ltd and Burne Associates*[56] in the Court of Appeal. The claimant was an employee

---

[55] ibid., at 61.
[56] (1986) 38 BLR 36.

of Chrysler who slipped and fell in a shower room after using the shower. He sued Chrysler and Burne, who had designed and supervised the shower installation, in respect of his injuries, and Chrysler also sued Burne. Chrysler settled the action with Hawkins, but continued against Burne. Chrysler alleged:

(1) that it was an implied term of the contract that Burne would use reasonable care and skill in selecting the material to be used for the floor of the showers; and
(2) there was an implied warranty that the material used for the floor would be fit for use in a wet shower room.

The Court of Appeal applied the *dicta* of Lord Denning in *Greaves* regarding the implication of a warranty of fitness. They decided that in this case there was nothing to give rise to the inference of any warranty other than to take reasonable care: further that such a warranty would only be implied where it was necessary to give business efficacy to the contract. The Court of Appeal therefore found that no warranty was to be implied beyond that of reasonable skill and care and that whilst there may be anomalies between the positions of contractors and subcontractors in this respect (i.e. fitness for purpose), as opposed to professional people, in the absence of special circumstances it was not open to the court to extend the responsibilities of professionals beyond the duty to exercise reasonable care and skill in accordance with the usual standards of their profession.

The above approach is reflected in more recent judgments, for example in *Payne v John Setchell*[57] HH Judge Humphrey Lloyd stated:

> a professional person . . . does not normally undertake obligations of an absolute nature but only undertakes to exercise reasonable professional skill and care in performance of the relevant service or in the production of the product.[58]

Nevertheless there may still be exceptions to this general rule. In *Platform Funding Ltd v Bank of Scotland Plc*,[59] where a surveyor valued the wrong property, it was held that the surveyor was in breach of an implied strict obligation (with Sir Anthony Clarke MR dissenting). The obligation was implied on the basis of it being the presumed intentions of the parties, the court relying on *Greaves v Baynham Meikle*. The Court however agreed that, in principle, 'it requires special facts or clear language to impose an obligation stricter than that of reasonable care'.[60]

A strict obligation has also been implied in a design build procurement context where the architect and the engineer are engaged by the contractor, rather than the employer. In *Consultants Group International v John Worman Ltd*,[61] a decision of Judge John Davies QC, Official Referee, there were preliminary issues before the court and it was held that there was an express term in the contract between the contractor (Worman)

---

[57] [2002] PNLR 7.
[58] ibid., para. 20.
[59] [2008] EWCA Civ 930 (CA).
[60] ibid., at para. 69.
[61] (1985) 9 Con LR 46.

and the employer, that the building would be fit for its intended purpose (an abbatoir) and comply with EEC standards so as to qualify for the appropriate grant aid. It was further held that the design obligations of the consultants were co-extensive with those of the contractors and, on its true construction, it was a term of the agreement between the contractor and the consultant that the works would be so designed by the consultant that the completed project would be fit for the purpose defined in the contract between the contractor and the employer. A further interesting point decided in this case is that the consultants were held liable to indemnify the contractors in respect of the design of specialist equipment to be supplied by nominated suppliers which was defective.

A similar situation arose relatively recently in the case of *Associated British Ports v Hydro Soil Services NV.*[62] Associated British Ports entered into a contract on an amended ICE standard form with Hydro Soil Services for strengthening works to a steel sheet pile quay wall prior to dredging. The contract stated that 'The works shall be designed to be fit for the purpose as described within the Design Parameters and Requirements Employer's Requirements.'[63] Hydro Soil sub-contracted the design work to a firm of engineers. During the works the sheet piles were damaged and Associated British Ports brought a claim against Hydro Soil, alleging breach of contract on the basis that the works were not fit for purpose. Hydro Soil brought the designers into the proceedings, claiming that any unfitness for purpose of the works was caused by or contributed to by breach of the design contract. The engineers' terms of engagement stated 'The Designer declares to be acquainted with and to accept the terms and conditions of the main contract, insofar as these are related to the works to be carried out by the Designer' and also that 'The assignment entrusted to the designer, comprising the works as described in the present Article[s] 2.1 to 2.3, constitutes for the account of the designer a duty to achieve a given result . . . .'[64] Therefore the designers had to concede that they owed the same obligation to Hydro Soil in relation to fitness for purpose as Hydro Soil owed to the employer under the main contract.

Conflicting or ambiguous clauses in a consultant's terms of engagement may also impose fitness for purpose obligations. In *Costain v Charles Haswell & Partners*[65] the consultant's terms contained the following:

> The Consultant warrants that:
> 7.1 . . .
> 7.2 In the provision of the Services the Consultant shall exercise all reasonable professional skill, care and diligence.
> 7.3 . . .
> 7.4 Any part of the works designed pursuant to this Agreement if constructed in accordance with such design, shall meet the requirements described in the Specification or reasonably to be inferred from the Tender Documents or the Contract or the written requirements of Costain and designed in accordance with good up-to-date engineering practice and with

---

[62] [2006] EWHC 1187.
[63] ibid., para. 187.
[64] ibid., para. 314.
[65] (2010) 128 Con LR 154 (TCC).

all applicable laws, by laws, codes or mandatory regulations and in all respects with the requirements of the Contract.

One of the issues before the court was whether clause 7.4 constituted a strict obligation on the designer to comply with the specification, etc, or whether it was qualified by clause 7.2, so that the designer was only obliged to use reasonable skill and care to design the project to meet those requirements. The court decided that the former interpretation was correct:

> It seems to me quite plain that Clause 7.4 is adding something different to Clause 7.2, otherwise it would not need to be there. In my view, Clause 7.2 is a general provision relating to all the services provided by the Consultant as a professional man. That would include his services of preparation, supervision, advising, testing and preparation of supporting documentation. By contrast, Clause 7.4 is limited to one particular part of the Consultant's obligations, *vis.* the design of the permanent works. Clause 7.4 only imposes an obligation on Haswell in relation to any part of the works which are constructed in accordance with the design produced by Haswell. This is a limited, albeit highly important, part of the general services to be provided by Haswell. I can see no reason why this critical activity should not be singled out in the Contract for special treatment.[66]

It also added that:

> . . . it is perfectly normal, in any given case, for such a professional man to give express warranties which impose strict liability or a performance obligation such as that the finished building will be reasonably fit for a specified purpose. There is nothing in principle wrong or unusual in finding such provisions in professional engagements and subject to the arguments to the contrary raised on behalf of Haswell, I consider that Clause 7.4 fits into this category.[67]

Clearly consultants should be careful not to include any terms that might suggest that the design will be fit for purpose, or meet any specific requirements, even in an appointment where there is a general obligation to use reasonable skill and care, such as clause 7.2 above. The combined effect would be difficult to predict with certainty.

The cases set out above indicate that although the English courts are unlikely to find that an obligation should be implied as to fitness for purpose in a professional designer's contract, it is possible that such duty could arise due to the particular circumstances of the case, or to expressly agreed terms.

7.4 Contractor's duty to warn

The concept of a 'duty to warn' has been applied in the case of consultants and contractors and refers to a duty that is over and above the normal express or implied duties

---

[66] ibid., Richard Fernyhough QC at para. 53.
[67] ibid., at para. 55.

that arise under contract. It has manifested itself as an implied obligation under a contract and (less frequently) as a tortious duty. It generally refers to advising on another party's apparent failure to fulfil its obligations, either to that party or to a third party. This section examines the contractor's duty to warn of errors in the design (the consultant's duty to advise on its own errors is considered in section 8.8).

7.4.1 Origins of the duty

It is an aspect of a contractor's general competence that it should undertake work thoughtfully. An early case to consider this was *Duncan v Blundell* where a builder was engaged to install a stove in a shop, together with a flue pipe under the floor, and the plan failed entirely. Bailey J decided that the builder was not entitled to any remuneration, and said:

> Where a person is employed in a work of skill, the employer buys both his labour and his judgement; he ought not to undertake the work if he cannot succeed, and he should know whether it will or not; of course it is otherwise if the party employing him chose to supersede the workman's judgment by using his own.[68]

A duty to warn is essentially an aspect of this obligation to exercise judgement. In the early Canadian case of *Brunswick Construction Ltd v Nowlan*[69] an owner employed an experienced contractor to erect a house in accordance with plans prepared by an engineer. The engineer was not involved in supervising the works. The contractor built the house as required by the plans, whereupon dry rot developed in the roof because of lack of ventilation. Despite the fact that the plans had shown no requirement for ventilation, the Supreme Court held that the contractor had acted in breach of contract. Ritchie J, with whom the majority of the court agreed, said:

> In my opinion a contractor of this experience should recognise the defects in the plans which were so obvious to the architect subsequently employed by [the owner] and knowing of the reliance which was being placed upon it, I think the [Contractor] was under duty to warn [the owner] of the danger inherent in executing the plans . . . .[70]

The issue also arose in *Equitable Debenture Assets Corporation Ltd v William Moss Group Ltd & Others*[71] where the judge, relying on *Blundell* and *Brunswick*, held that Moss, a large and experienced builders' firm, having formed the view that part of the architect's design would not work, had a duty to immediately pass this concern to the architect; and that there was, therefore, an implied term in the building contract to warn of design defects. The Official Referee in this case found that this duty was both

---

[68] (1820) 3 Stark 6.
[69] (1975) 21 BLR 27, Canada.
[70] ibid., at 34.
[71] (1984) 2 Con LR 1.

an implied term in contract and a duty in tort. This duty arose, notwithstanding the fact that Moss had no design obligation in the building contract.

Shortly after, in *Victoria University of Manchester v Hugh Wilson & Lewis Womersley (A Firm) and Pochin (Contractors) Ltd*,[72] the same Judge who heard the *Equitable Debenture* case, Judge John Newey QC, Official Referee, decided that the contractors owed a duty to warn the architects, as agents of the University, of defects in the design of the architect which it believed to exist, as soon as it came to believe that they existed. The case arose out of problems with the failure of ceramic tiles to adhere to the external walls of two new complexes built for the University. The contract between the contractor and the employer was on the JCT63 form. The allegations in negligence had been abandoned against the contractor so the Judge's finding in this case was limited to contract. In the ruling His Lordship said:

> The University alleged that a duty to warn was to be implied. The contractor did not admit the allegation, but the matter was not argued at length because in *Equitable Debenture Assets Corporation Limited v William Moss & Others* (1984) 2 Con LR 1 I had decided that such a term could be implied.
>
> My conclusion in *EDAC* was based upon *Duncan v Blundel* (1820) 3 Stark 6, Bayley J, and *Brunswick Construction Limited v Nowlan* (1974) 21 BLR 27 (Supreme Court of Canada), both construction cases, and on the application of *The Moorcock* [1889] 14 PD 64 (CA), *Reigate v Union Manufacturing Co.* [1918] 1 KB 592 (CA) and *Liverpool City Council v Irwin* [1977] AC 239 (House of Lords), which deal with implication of terms.
>
> In this case I think that a term was to be implied in each contract requiring the contractors to warn the architects as the University's agents, of defects in design, which they believed to exist. Belief that there were defects required more than mere doubt as to the correctness of the design, but less than actual knowledge of errors.[73]

7.4.2 Development of the duty

In a later case in 1988, considerable doubt was cast on the existence and/or the scope of a duty to warn. In *University Court of the University of Glasgow v W. Whitfield and John Laing Construction Ltd*[74] Judge Peter Bowsher QC, Official Referee, reviewed many of the authorities referred to above, but he did so in the context of the development of the law of tort and the retrenchment that had taken place in the preceding years. This case, in fact, raised the possibility of two different categories of duty to warn. First, the duty considered above, namely a duty on the part of the contractor, owed to the employer, to warn the employer or the employer's architect as agent of errors in the design (which would allow for an order for contribution against the contractor). Secondly, a duty of care by the contractor to the architect to inform the architect of defects in the design of which it knew or ought to have known.

---

[72] (1984) 2 Con LR 43.
[73] (1984) 2 Con LR 43 at 77.
[74] (1988) 42 BLR 66.

As to the first type of duty alleged, namely to the employer or to the architect of the employer as agent, the Judge found that where there was a detailed contract as here (JCT 1963, 1971 Revision with Scottish appendix), there was no room for the implication of a duty to warn about possible defects in design: it was said that this followed from *Tai Hing Cotton Mill Ltd v Liu Chong Hing Bank Ltd*.[75] As to the duty being put as a duty in tort, it was said that there was a clear contractual duty governing the relationship between the parties in relation to the damage arising out of the defective building, and counsel for the contractor suggested that whilst there might conceivably be a concurrent duty in tort, it was limited to a duty of care to avoid acts or omissions which are liable to cause damage to persons or to some property other than the defective building under construction. In the Judge's view, that submission was well-founded on the then current state of the law, referring to *Simaan General Contracting Co. v Pilkington Glass Ltd*.[76] That finding is consistent with *D & F* and *Murphy*, which came later. It followed from this that there was no duty to warn the employer of design defects.

As to the architect's allegation that the contractor owed a duty to the architect, again, having reviewed the recent cases and also concluding that the architect was not relying on the contractor for design advice, the court came to the view that no such duty was owed. It therefore followed that the architect in this case was not entitled to any contribution whatsoever from the contractor.

The decision in the *University of Glasgow* case therefore distinguished the decisions in *Equitable Debenture Assets Corporation Ltd v William Moss Group Ltd* and *Victoria University of Manchester*. In commenting on developments in tort law the Judge in *University of Glasgow* said:

> The decisions in *EDAC v Moss* and *Victoria University of Manchester* could stand with more recent decisions if they were read as cases where there was a special relationship between the parties, but not otherwise, and bearing in mind the difficulties in analyzing the meaning of the words 'special relationship' and 'reliance' demonstrated by Robert Goff LJ in *Muirhead v Industrial Tank Limited* [1986] 1 QB 507 at 527H.[77]

Shortly after, in *Oxford University Press v John Stedman Design Group*,[78] HH Judge Esyr Lewis QC preferred the analysis in *University of Glasgow v W. Whitfield*.[79] The Judge said that in *Equitable Debenture*, reference had been made to *Duncan v Blundell*, but he noted that the proviso stated in that case was important, namely that the employer could not be said to 'buy' the builders judgement if the employer 'chose to supersede the workman's judgment by using his own'.[80] In this case Oxford University Press had relied on the architects so it could not be said they had relied on the contractors. He

---

[75] [1986] AC 80.
[76] (1988) 40 BLR 28.
[77] (1988) 42 BLR 66, HHJ Peter Bowsher QC at 83.
[78] (1990) 34 Con LR 1.
[79] (1988) 42 BLR 66.
[80] (1820) 3 Stark 6.

could therefore see no basis for finding on the part of the contractor a duty, in tort, to warn of design defects, unless they might give rise to danger to the safety of persons or damage to some property other than that which was the subject of the defect. There was also a detailed building contract and he could see no basis for the implication of a term in contract either. He pointed out that it would give rise to difficulties in practice if a contractor had to warn his employer about matters of design where that employer had engaged an architect to be responsible for that design.

A potentially massive extension of the duty to warn was overturned in the Court of Appeal in *T. E. Eckersley & Others v Binnie and Partners, Edmund Nuttall Ltd and the North West Water Authority*.[81] This case concerned the explosion at the Abbeystead pumping station in the spring of 1984 due to the presence of methane gas. Nuttalls were the main contractors and Binnie were the engineers. After the project was constructed, and the contractor had left site, but before it was fully operational some residents were invited to visit for a demonstration of the pump. Unfortunately the explosion occurred, causing death and serious injury to the visitors.

The Judge, at first instance, decided that although it had no design obligation, if Nuttalls had used a proper system of testing for methane during construction there was a possibility that they would have discovered the seepage of methane; if they had, they would have warned the engineer who would have redesigned the pumping chamber in such a way as to avoid the danger of methane being pushed into it, with the consequent risk of explosion. It was a tortuous route to a duty to warn. The judge found the contractors 15% responsible for the explosion, with Binnie 55% and the Water Authority 30% responsible.

The Court of Appeal, however, reversed the decision in relation to Nuttals and the Water Authority (finding the engineers 100% responsible). It decided that the purpose of testing during construction was to ensure, for the benefit of the workforce, that the concentration of methane was such that there would be no explosion. There was nothing in the relationship between Binnie and Nuttalls to put Nuttalls on notice that testing had to be continued upon their ceasing to occupy the site. Nuttalls was never requested by Binnie to test for the safety of the permanent works and it was therefore found that there was no duty on Nuttalls as had been found by the Judge at first instance.

In 1992, *Edward Lindenberg v Joe Canning Jerome Contracting Ltd*[82] was heard by Judge Newey QC, the same Judge who heard *Equitable Debenture* and *Victoria University of Manchester*. Edward Lindenberg engaged the contractor for work to a block of flats. During the construction loadbearing walls were demolished in the basements, which caused damage to the flat above. The contractor had been given surveyor's drawings which had shown the walls as non-loadbearing. The contractor was held liable to make a contribution to the cost of the remedial works resulting from the demolition of load-bearing walls. The damages that the plaintiff would have been entitled to were reduced by 75% due to its contributory negligence in supplying the defective drawings, and the contractor was liable for the remaining 25%. The Judge commented:

---

[81] (1988) 18 Con LR 1 (CA)

[82] (1992) 62 BLR 147.

Mr Canning should I think have proceeded with the very greatest caution. At the very least, he should have raised with [Mr Lindenberg's surveyor] doubts as to his plan and asked whether [he] was sure the 9 inch walls were not loadbearing. Even if [he] had given assurances, Mr Canning would, I think, have been prudent to have put in temporary propping, but in the absence of such an assurance, he should undoubtedly have done so. Instead, without taking any precautions whatsoever, Mr Canning proceeded to demolish the walls. I think he behaved with much less care than was to be expected of the ordinary competent builder and that he therefore acted in breach of contract.[83]

In the course of his judgment the Judge referred to *Equitable Debenture Assets Corporation v William Moss* but it is apparent that he preferred (although he did not express the preference in this case) to put the point as breach of an implied term that the contractor would exercise the care to be expected of an ordinary competent builder, rather than a tortious duty.

In *Plant Construction v Clive Adams Associates and JMH Construction Services Ltd*[84] Ford Motor Company engaged Plant on a JCT WCD contract to design and construct two pits for engine mount rigs at Ford's research and engineering centre in Essex. Part of the work included underpinning an existing column and in the course of the work temporary support was required to the column and the floor above. JMH was sub-contracted to carry out this concrete work.

Ford's own engineer gave instructions regarding the temporary supports, which comprised four Acrow props. JMH and Plant's engineers, Clive Adams Associates, felt the props to be inadequate and discussed this on site. The support was installed as instructed and failed, so that a large part of a concrete floor slab collapsed. Plant settled with Ford, and brought a claim against JMH and Clive Adams (who settled).

The court found that the temporary works were obviously dangerous and the sub-contractor had realised this. The sub-contractor was held liable, despite the fact that the client's engineer had instructed it to proceed with the design. The court decided its duties included warning of any aspect of the design that it knew to be unsafe, and considered that the sub-contractor, knowing of the danger, should have made a more vigorous protest (this was an implied contractual duty, not a tortious one). The extent of the sub-contractor's liability was reduced by 80% to take account of the contractor's contributory negligence in not recognising the potential danger.[85] The court did not go so far as to reach a view on whether the duty would extend to warn of unsafe aspects the sub-contractor ought to have known about, or design errors that were not unsafe. It avoided making general rules and instead suggested that each case had to be viewed on its merits, with several factors affecting the final decision including: the terms of the contract, the experience and level of expertise of the contractor, the reliance placed by the employer upon the contractor's specialist knowledge, and the relationship between the contractor and the employer.

---

[83] ibid., at 161.
[84] [2000] BLR 158 (CA).
[85] see also the supplementary judgment on causation, [2000] EWHC Technology 119 (31st March, 2000).

In *Aurum Investments Ltd v Avonforce Ltd (In Liquidation)*[86] an underpinning sub-contractor was held not to be liable under the duty to warn principle when part of excavation works collapsed. The sub-contractors were required to underpin the flank wall of property adjacent to that where the main building work was to be carried out. After the underpinning was complete and the sub-contractor had left site, the main contractor excavated the basement of the main property, but provided no temporary lateral support for the underpinned flank wall, thus causing the collapse. The contractor argued that the sub-contractor should have warned it of the need to provide support during the excavation of the basement. The court dismissed this argument. Where the main contractor could adopt several methods of construction, the sub-contractor cannot be held liable for not informing the contractor of potential dangers in one particular method, as it would not know which one would be adopted. The judge felt that the fact that the client was advised by an independent professional person was relevant to the question of whether there is a duty to warn should be implied, as there was therefore no reason to suppose an unsafe method would be used. The position could be different where the sub-contractor knows the method by which the contractor will carry out the work; in that situation it would be under a duty to warn. The court showed a restrictive approach to the implication of a duty: 'It is clear from Plant that the law is moving with caution in this area . . . a court should not hold a contractor to be under a duty to warn his client unless it is reasonable to do so'.[87]

More recently, *J Murphy & Sons Ltd v Johnston Precast Ltd*[88] usefully illustrated that a 'duty to warn' may be implied into a contract in situations where a 'fitness for purpose' obligation is rejected by the court. Murphy was engaged by Thames Water to design and undertake refurbishment works to the mains water system in Holland Park, London. Murphy in turn engaged Johnston Precast to manufacture and supply a length of glass reinforced pipe. The pipe was laid by Murphy in a tunnel and surrounded by foam concrete. Four years later, the pipe burst causing extensive damage in the surrounding area. A void was found in the foam concrete around the top of the pipe and the point of failure was in the middle of that void. Due to alkaline attack the pipe that area had been unable to withstand the pressure required by the contract.

The court found that there was no implied term in the contract with Johnston that the pipe should be suitable for these particular conditions, because when the contract had been made Murphy had not identified that the pipe was to be surrounded by foam concrete. It nevertheless found that it was an implied term of the contract that if Johnston knew or should have known that the pipe might not be suitable for use in foam concrete it was obliged to warn Murphy.[89] However there was no reason why Johnston should have suspected that the pipe could not be used with foam concrete, therefore Johnston was not in breach of the implied term.

---

[86] [2001] CILL 1729.
[87] ibid., Mr Justice Dyson at para. 18.
[88] [2008] EWHC 3024 (TCC).
[89] it relied on many of the above cases, see ibid., para. 129.

7.4.3 Current position

The current position appears to be that contractors may be under an implied contractual duty to point out errors in the design of which they actually become aware. The implication is more likely to arise in situations where there are no detailed contract terms, and the employer is not advised by an independent consultant, and would almost certainly arise in any situation where health and safety are at risk. The duty to warn could extend to situations where the contractor is not actually aware of the design error, but where a competent contractor would have been aware.

Chapter 8
Duties in Detail

8.1 General duties of a designer

The particular obligations that a designer undertakes will primarily be governed by the arrangements between designer and employer, which will normally be set out in detailed terms of appointment. It may be that the designer is engaged for a limited function, say, to obtain planning permission only. It may be that the employer only requires a feasibility study in order to decide whether it should proceed with the construction work. It is, therefore necessary in any particular circumstances to look at precisely what obligations the designer has undertaken.

Where there is any doubt as to the obligations undertaken by the designer, perhaps because the services are described in general or vague terms, it would be necessary to call members of the same profession to give evidence as to what a reasonably competent member of their profession would do in the circumstances that has given rise to the dispute. It follows that it is impossible to give a detailed and accurate list of the duties that would fit every possible case. Judge Stabb QC made some observations as to the general duties of an architect in the case of *Sutcliffe v Chippendale and Edmondson*[1] which subsequently went to the Court of Appeal (but not on this point):

> It can be said that when a person engages an architect in relation to the building of a house, he is entitled to expect that the architect will perform his duties in such a manner as to safeguard his interest and that he will do all that is reasonably within his power to ensure that work is properly and expeditiously carried out, so as to achieve the end result as contemplated by the contract. In particular the building owner is entitled to expect his architect so to administer the contract and supervise the work, as to ensure as far as is reasonably possible, that the quality of the work matches up to the standard contemplated.[2]

Hudson's Building and Engineering Contracts[3] emphasises that there are many different roles that professionals can play, and the duties will be defined in the appointment. However it suggests that where this is stated as merely a general obligation to 'carry the

---

[1] (1971) 18 BLR 157.
[2] ibid., at 162.
[3] 12th edn 2010, Sweet and Maxwell.

Cornes and Lupton's Design Liability in the Construction Industry, Fifth Edition. Sarah Lupton.
© 2013 Sarah Lupton and DL Cornes. Published 2013 by Blackwell Publishing Ltd.

project through to completion', it is possible to list the duties that would normally be assumed. *Hudson's* list of duties as they are generally carried out in the United Kingdom (and excluding those matters not related to design and supervision of the construction of that design) is as follows:

(a)　To advise and consult with the employer (not as a lawyer) as to any limitation which may exist as to the use of the land to be built on, either (*inter alia*) by planning legislation, restrictive covenants, or the rights of adjoining owners or the public over the land, or by statutes and by-laws affecting the works to be executed.

(b)　To examine the site, sub-soil and surroundings.

(c)　To consult with and advise the employer as to the design, extent and cost of the proposed work.

(d)　To prepare preliminary sketch plans and an outline or approximate specification, having regard to all the conditions known to exist and to submit them to the employer for approval, with an estimate of the probable cost, if requested.

(e)　To elaborate and, if necessary, modify or amend the sketch plans, and then, if so instructed, to prepare drawings and a more detailed specification of the work to be carried out as a first step in the preparation of contract documents.

(f)　To consult with and advise the employer as to the form of contract to be used (including whether or not to use bills of quantities) and as to the necessity or otherwise of employing a quantity surveyor (engineers usually do not employ an independent quantity surveyor) to prepare bills and carry out the usual valuation services during the currency of the contract.

(g)　To bring the contract documents to their final state before inviting tenders, with or without the assistance of quantity surveyors and structural engineers, including the obtaining of detailed quotations from and arrangement of delivery dates with any nominated sub-contractors or suppliers whose work may have to be ready or available at an early stage of the main contractor's work.[4]

Apart from authorities such as *Hudson's*, there are other points of reference for establishing the scope of duties that might be assumed if not specifically described. The RIBA Plan of Work sets outs the tasks to be performed at various defined work stages. It exists in two versions, an outline plan,[5] which forms the basis for the forms of appointment, and a full plan,[6] which covers the services to be provided by all of the project team. Many standard forms of appointment for consultants also contain detailed schedules of services (a good example is the CIC Scope of Services).[7] Practical texts such as the *Architect's Job Book*[8] and other project management and design guides will outline the tasks that are normally performed in a design activity. Any or of all of these

---

[4] For the full list see *Hudson's Building and Engineering Contracts*, 12th edn, at p. 225.
[5] Downloadable free from www.architecture.com; note that at the time of writing this is under review.
[6] Phillips, R, *Plan of Work: Multi-Disciplinary Services* (London: RIBA Publishing, 2008). Note the Plan was revised in 2013, but still sets out services to be performed.
[7] CIC 2007, RIBA Publishing.
[8] Reid S (ed) (2008) *Architect's Job Book*, 8th edn (London: RIBA Publishing, 2008).

might be referred to in a dispute about what ought to have been done by a particular consultant.

The following sections examine some of the normal duties and obligations of design professionals, and explore what might be expected of them, including areas where problems often arise. In all cases, of course, what might be expected would be governed by not only any agreed terms, but also the particular circumstances of the case.

8.2 Appraisal and site investigation

All projects, whether new-build or alterations to an existing building, will require a thorough site appraisal, which will normally comprise a visual inspection, detailed technical investigations, and a study of the various statutory and legal restrictions that may affect any proposed development.

8.2.1 Site investigation?

It is hard to imagine that a designer would design a project without visiting the site; and at this visit the designer will look for all the things that are readily apparent on the site which may affect the design. It will be possible to see whether there are buildings adjacent to the site that give rise to problems relating to party walls or rights of light. There may be footpaths which would cause the designer to make enquiries as to the possibility of the existence of rights of way. It is also essential to know the exact area of the site and the location of all the boundaries to some degree of accuracy and this may itself require a survey to be carried out to produce a plan and a grid of levels of the site. It probably will not assist designers to say they relied on information produced by the Ordnance Survey[9] (or Google Earth) or that they relied on information provided by the employer.[10]

8.2.1.1 Ground conditions

The designer will also need to ascertain the nature and load bearing capacity of the soil underneath ground level. Most professional conditions of engagement refer to soil 'investigations' and it is the usual practice for a company specialising in soil mechanics to take cores, by drilling, and to produce from the cores a section drawing showing the strata at various depths and to test the cores in order to produce the information that engineers need to determine the appropriate foundations for the site. This may not be needed if the designer is already familiar with the site, but is the usual way to proceed. An example can be seen in the case of *Eames London Estates v North*

---

[9] *Columbus v Clowes* [1903] 1 KB 244.
[10] *Moneypenny v Hartland* (1826) 2 C & P 378.

Hertfordshire District Council.[11] There a factory with a pre-cast concrete frame was designed by an architect and erected by sub-contractors specialising in this kind of work. The architect had not inspected the site but had given the subcontractor a building inspector's report specifying the soil-bearing capacity of the land. The excavation contractors had been concerned about the soil conditions they found following excavating of the pad foundations, and raised the question with the architect of how deep the excavation should be, but the plans were not varied. Having initially discussed the matter with the building inspector, the architect appeared to assume the foundations were a matter to be agreed between the inspector and the sub-contractor. After hearing expert evidence the court decided that the architect's approach to the site investigation was negligent:

> I consider it normal practice for an architect to draw his client's attention to the need for ground conditions to be investigated. Also, that the client be advised of the possible need to carry out a detailed site investigation, if the architect was uncertain in any way of the type and bearing capacity of the ground.[12]

If a claim is brought against a designer, it will not help to argue that the designer agreed the bearing capacity of the ground with the local authority's building inspector or district surveyor, at least where no soil investigation has been carried out. In the *Eames* case, the architect agreed with the building inspector that three-quarters of a ton per square foot bearing capacity was the load that the local authority wanted for this particular site. The whole of the site of the building was on made-up ground and in part of the site there had been an old railway embankment, which was well consolidated being more than 100 years old. The architect did not obtain boreholes or advise that boreholes should be taken or that specialist engineering advice be obtained. Although the site was filled, the 25-inch Ordnance Survey map showed that a railway crossed only part of the site. Evidence was given at the trial that a proper investigation would have indicated that simple shallow foundations would be bound to lead to serious, uneven and continuing settlement. It was held that the architect could not shed responsibility by ascertaining what the local authority would accept; specifying three quarters of a ton per square foot indicated that the architect appreciated the inferior nature of the ground and ought to have been aware that further investigation or specialist design was required. The architect was held to have been negligent, both in relying on the inspector, and in not taking account of the query raised by 'some practical men on the spot' who though it might be necessary to take the foundations down to virgin soil.

Furthermore, any warning that further investigations are needed should normally be given to the client (unless some other communication route has been specifically agreed). Structural engineers engaged by an architect who warned the architect of the need for further soil reports and the risk of proceeding without such reports were held

---

[11] (1980) 18 BLR 50.
[12] ibid., at 70.

liable in tort to the employer for failing to give that warning to the employer, notwith-standing the fact that there was no contract between the engineer and the employer.[13]

Does the designer have to look beyond the employer's land when examining the site, for example should there be an investigation of neighbouring land? This point arose in *Batty v Metropolitan Property Realisations Ltd*[14] (since overruled but not on the following aspect); the developer and the builder had inspected the site but they had not inspected adjoining land, or land on the other side of the valley, where there were signs that a detailed inspection by experts might have revealed the possibility of a landslip on the site. The court held that the builder's duty was not limited to defects that could be observed on the land owned by the builder in circumstances where a careful and competent builder would have observed defects on adjoining land or where he would not have built until there had been a further site investigation or an expert's report on the condition of the subsoil. Although the case is relevant to a builder's duty when examining a site before building on it, certain conclusions can be drawn in respect of designer's responsibility. Designers should, therefore, ensure that they not only examine the site but also look for problems on neighbouring land and obtain a soil investigation or an expert's report in circumstances where a competent designer would do so.

8.2.1.2 Trees

The designer should also consider the effect of trees on the site; it has been commonly accepted as 'state of the art' knowledge since about 1971 that the felling of trees, for the purposes of a development, can result in substantial heave of clay subsoil. This is because the trees, before they were felled, absorbed moisture from the clay, which moisture is taken up again by the soil when the trees have gone. This issue arose in *Balcomb v Wards Construction (Medway) Ltd*,[15] where engineers who failed to make enquiries as to whether there had been trees on the site were held liable to their client, the builder, in contract for failing to exercise professional skill and care:

> I find the conclusion inescapable that in 1971, a competent engineer encountering London clay, as in this case, would have made enquiries whether there had been trees on the site and, finding that there had been, would have caused moisture content and plastic limit tests to be carried out. Had that course been taken it is not disputed, and there can be no doubt that [the designer] would have advised, that the proposed foundations were inadequate.

A later example concerning trees is *Kaliszewska v John Clague & Partners*.[16] Here a bungalow was built on an orchard site, from which trees had to be removed prior to construction. The Judge, having found that the defendant's design did not comply with the Building Regulations and the current code of practice CP 101:1963 said:

---

[13] *District of Surrey v Carroll-Hatch and Associates Ltd* (1979) 10 DLR (3d) 218, Canada.
[14] (1977) 7 BLR 1.
[15] (1981) 259 EG 765.
[16] (1984) Con LR 62.

I am sure the truth simply was that the defendant did not pay any or sufficient regard to the trees on this particular site. He said as much in the course of his evidence: 'I did not think that the trees were a problem, that is why I did not take them seriously. I do not think I considered the trees large enough to be of any concern.' He was patently in error. This had nothing to do with local practice. If, which I doubt, he made any allowance for the trees as opposed to the sloping site, either in going deeper than usual or in using reinforcement, there was no attempt to deal with the problem in a methodical way and to bring to his aid the current knowledge available to him. In using his judgement he was, as [the plaintiff's expert] so neatly said, acting by guess and by God. This was not good enough for this site, as he should have been aware, and his design inevitably failed.[17]

8.2.2 Public and private rights

It is the designer's duty to find out from the employer whether there are any restrictions on the use to which the site may be put. This could arise, for example, by way of a restrictive covenant in the sale of the land to the employer which could involve a limitation as to the type of building that could be erected and the nature of the materials that may be used in its construction. Or there may be easements affecting the land, such as the right of adjoining owners to carry wires over the land or drainage or other services underneath the land. It is for this reason that the designer should specifically ask the employer about the existence of any such restrictions or easements. Additionally, the designer should, when examining the site, carefully have regard to any evidence of such rights that are apparent on visual inspection.

A question as to rights relating to light affecting adjoining owners may also arise and it is essential that the designer should not design in such a way that those rights are affected because by so doing this will put the employer at risk of an action by the adjoining owner. This may be an action for damages or an action for a mandatory injunction requiring the employer to pull down that part of the building that infringes the rights.[18] Infringement of such rights is, of course, a matter of expert evidence and where such evidence cannot establish on the balance of probabilities that the neighbour's rights are in fact infringed, then the designer may escape liability.[19]

An action for trespass can be brought by an adjoining owner without the need to prove any damage, in other words trespass is actionable *per se*. Designers are, therefore, at risk of an action should their design necessitate a trespass. This could arise if a means of escape in case of fire from the roof of a building involves those escaping from the fire passing over an adjoining owner's roof without that owner's consent. Where a designer is in the position that the design must necessarily involve a trespass, then the designer should immediately draw the problem to the employer's attention so that either the design can be varied or the employer can seek the necessary consents.

---

[17] ibid., at 77.
[18] *HKRUK II (CHC) Ltd v Heaney* [2010] EWHC 2245 (Ch).
[19] *Armitage v Palmer* (1960) 175 EG 315.

Designers must comply with the building lines set down by local authorities and, in particular, will be liable if they do not, by the exercise of reasonable care and diligence, prevent the encroachment of a building under construction over the street line.[20]

A case in relation to damage, both actual and prospective, to adjoining property by construction work provides a useful summary of both the law in relation to rights of support and the liability of designers in such circumstances. In *Midland Bank plc v Bardgrove Property Services Ltd*[21] Midland Bank was lessee and occupier of premises next to land which was developed by Bardgrove Property Services Ltd. Its contractor was John Willmott. Marshall Botting Associates were structural engineers retained to advise Bardgrove and/or Willmott on and design temporary works of shoring to the boundary with Midland's property. Structural Design Partnership was retained by Bardgrove to advise on and design the temporary and permanent works in connection with the excavation. The Midland Bank asserted that the work on the adjoining site had caused damage to its property (subsidence, broken roadway and unsafe gas pipe) and this meant that it had to carry out its own works, including the construction of a sheet piled retaining wall on its own land to restore its stability. However, the sheet piling was put in to deal with future stability issues, not the previous damage. The cost was about £318,000 including professional fees.

Midland Bank brought proceedings in negligence against all the other parties. In addition, it claimed against Bardgrove and Willmott for interference with a natural right of support. At first instance Judge Thayne-Forbes QC decided that Bardgrove did not owe a duty of care because it was entitled to carry out excavation on its own land. He decided that mere loss of stability was not sufficient to constitute the actual damage that is required to give rise to an actionable claim for wrongful interference with a natural right of support to the land. He also decided that the other defendants, including the designers, could not owe a wider duty to Midland than Bardgrove. As there was no special relationship and the claim was for economic loss, the claim in negligence failed (note the Court of Appeal was concerned only with the duty of Bardgrove and Willmott, where it upheld the lower court's decision).

8.2.3 Development controls

A designer would normally be responsible for considering all development controls, and ought to take account of all relevant guidance on these, for example all relevant environmental legislation, planning policy documents and guidance, historic building controls, Building Regulations, Codes of Practice, etc.[22] In *Townsend (Builders) Ltd v*

---

[20] *Siegel v Swartz* (1943) OWN 532 (Canada).

[21] (1993) 60 BLR 1 (CA).

[22] It should be noted that failure to comply with regulations may also be a breach of a professional Code of Conduct, e.g. in 2012 the ARB PCC found an architect guilty of serious professional incompetence when a project was constructed without Building Control approval.

Cinema News and Property Management Ltd[23] an architect was found liable to his client (and to the contractor) when, following a project to alter and renovate a property, it was found the premises did not comply with a local by-law (a wc opened directly off a bedroom). A more recent example is *McGlinn, Ian v Waltham Contractors Ltd*[24] where the architect was found liable for (amongst other things) designing two stone balustrades that did not conform to the Jersey building bye-laws. The court made this finding even though the balustrades had been designed to the client's specific requirements: he had instructed that they should be lower than the regulation height to prevent them interrupting his view of the sea.

However, although breach of statutory requirements is evidence that there was negligence, it may not always be sufficient. In *BL Holdings v Robert J Wood & Partners*[25] an architect put in a planning application for an office block on behalf of experienced office developers. At that time such developments required an office development permit (OPD). These were very difficult to obtain, but were not required for developments under 10,000 square feet. Relevant government circulars indicated that ancillary areas such as car parking and flats would have to be included in any calculation of area. Despite this, when the architect met the local planning officers he was told that it was their policy to disregard such areas. The architect therefore submitted a proposal which exceeded the permitted 10,000 square feet in relation to these ancillary areas. The proposal received planning permission, but the ODP restriction was later enforced so that the building could not be used as offices. The Court of Appeal held that it was not negligent of the architect to believe that the characterisation of the areas and hence the exact calculation was a matter of opinion, or that the planning authority had a discretion in the matter. It is useful to note that the architect had kept the client fully informed throughout the process of application, and that the client was experienced. It might be that in other cases, if these conditions did not apply, the architect might be in breach of its duty of care to the client in not advising them to follow the government guidance strictly, or to take expert legal advice.

Where other consultants are engaged for their expertise in legislative matters, it would normally be reasonable for a designer to rely on their advice, except if they make an error which is so obvious that any competent designer ought to have noticed it (see *Fitzroy Robinson v Mentmore Towers*[26]).

8.2.4 Appraisal and relevance of client's expertise

As a general rule the courts are unlikely to accept, as a valid reason for taking a particular course of action, the proposition that the designer relied on the client's input or expertise. Generally speaking it will be for the designer to explain matters clearly to the client, and to check all information provided.

---

[23] (1958) 20 BLR 118.
[24] (2007) 111 Con LR 1 (CA).
[25] (1979) 12 BLR 1 (CA).
[26] [2009] BLR 505.

In *Worboys v Acme Developments*[27] an architect was found not negligent when houses were designed without ground floor toilets as the need for them was obvious to the informed (developer) client. However it was made clear by the court that the fact that an employer has approved a design is not by itself a defence. Similarly, in *Stormont Main Working Mens Club v J Roscoe Milne Partnership*[28] an architect was asked to design an extension to the working men's club. The club brought a claim against the architect because the positioning of pillars meant that the space around the snooker table was less than that needed for international competitions. The claim failed because the court found the club had not intended the extension to be used for international competition snooker, and the brief had not set out this requirement. However the judge noted that had there been any doubt as to what the brief required, the architect should have sought clarification.

Any explanation or warning to the client must be very clear if it is to be effective in discharging the designer's normal obligation. *Six Continents Retail Ltd v Carford Catering Ltd*[29] concerned a claim against the project manager Carford Catering Equipment Ltd, who had been retained to design and install kitchen equipment at a Harvester restaurant. In March 1997 there was a fire at the restaurant, which began behind a gas fire chicken rotisserie fixed to a tile clad timber stud partition wall. The owners (Six Continents) had specified the kitchen equipment they wanted and identified the supplier, and following delivery the project manager arranged for the rotisserie to be hung on wall brackets which were fixed to a wall designed by the architect. There were problems with the installations when some tiles detached from the wall, and two months before the fire the equipment supplier inspected the rotisserie and wrote to the project managers:

> The spit roast unit is mounted on a partition wall (not solid) and 3 tiles between and just above the 2 wall brackets had come away from the wall – we do not know whether this was due to a) deflection of the wall due to the weight of the unit – or b) heat effect from the burners. If it was heat we recommend fitting a stainless sheet at the back of the unit to prevent a fire risk. Note – We did not replace these tiles.

The project manager then wrote to a project manager at the owner's construction department, stating:

> Please find enclosed a copy of the engineer's report after a recent service call at the above house on the spit roaster. Could you please advise us what action, if any, you wish us/the builders to take.

The owners took no action following the letter, nor did they reply. The Court of Appeal held that the project manager could not discharge its duty by notifying the owners that a risk of fire had arisen, when this risk arose from the project manager's

---

[27] (1969) 4 BLR 136.
[28] (1989) 13 Con LR 127.
[29] [2003] EWCA Civ 1790.

own want of care. It also commented that the warning given by the project manager was insufficient:

> I find it very difficult to see how the giving of such a warning ought to transpose the burden of avoiding that very outcome from the respondents, who owed a duty in effect to prevent it, to the appellants who were the beneficiaries of that duty . . . But in any event I do not consider that the letter was a warning – certainly not a sufficient warning – that there was a risk of fire happening as this fire happened. The wording of the letter did not in terms amount to a warning at all. Indeed the expression 'please advise us what action, if any, you wish us/the builders to take' suggesting that action was optional rather than necessary, is all but inconsistent with the notion of a warning; and the enclosed fax is, to say the least, indefinite as to fire risk. To constitute a proper warning the respondents must have drawn attention – in terms, or at least very plainly – to the fact that the unit was fixed directly on to a combustible surface.[30]

This is an interesting example of the fact of a client's apparent condoning of a dangerous detail not discharging the designer from his or her professional responsibilities.

A second case involving a fire, *Sahib Foods Ltd v Paskin Kyriakides Sands (A Firm)*[31] also concerned the significance of the client's expertise in determining the designer's liability. This case concerned a food factory in Brent Road, Southall, which prepared chilled and frozen food for supermarkets, including Waitrose and Sainsburys. The first claimants (Sahib) operated the factory as leaseholders. The factory was refurbished in 1995, and architects Paskin Kyriakides Sands were engaged in relation to the work. There were no written terms of business of any kind, however the architects admitted that they regarded Sahib as the client and provided drawings to Sahib to ensure that Sahib's requirements were met, and the Judge decided that there was a contract between them (although he also noted that the architects would have owed similar duties in tort).

The fire started as a result of the negligence of employees of Sahib. The claimants alleged that the extensive and disastrous spread of the fire was due to the negligence of the architects. One area of the factory was designed as a fire resistant enclosure; this was a section that contained two continuous deep fat fryers, 7 metres long and 2 metres high, through which food passed through on a conveyor belt system, and which was attended by operatives from the outside at each end. The room was enclosed with sandwich panels ('Flameguard') filled with non-combustible mineral wool (as required by Sahib). The fire in fact started outside the enclosure, in a room called the 'veg prep cook area'. In that room were three Bratt Pans, one of which was gas heated. This was used to fry food, and on the day the fire started had been used to caramelise onions. The pan was used inappropriately (too much oil was used), and due to various errors on the part of Sahib it caught fire. This area was clad in combustible steel EPS sandwich panels, and the fire spread rapidly and destroyed most of the factory, although nobody was hurt. By contrast the fire enclosure was largely undamaged. The expert witnesses in the action agreed that if the veg prep area had been similarly protected with a one-

---

[30] ibid., Lord Justice Laws, at paras 22–3.
[31] (2003) 93 Con LR 1.

hour fire enclosure then despite the concurrence of a number of negligent acts and omissions on the part of the claimants, the factory would not have burnt down.

The Judge decided that the defendants owed a duty to perform their services with reasonable skill and care, referring to *Wimpey Construction UK Ltd v Poole*[32] for guidance as to the level required. The architects argued that they were not liable as Sahib had all the information that was available to the architects, and therefore also knew of the risk. His Honour Judge Bowsher QC held that this provided no defence:

> A competent architect does not present a design that he knows to be deficient in an important respect and then discuss with the client whether the deficiency should be removed. Still less does he present such a design and say, 'I did not need to tell the client about that deficiency because the client already knew that such a feature was not required'. Take a simple example. An architect designs a house as a residence for a client who happens to be a surveyor and forgets to require a damp-proof course under a parapet wall. If after construction the client complains, it is no answer for the architect to say 'well you knew about the need for the damp proof course as well as I did'. The architect is employed to use his own skill and judgement. There is no duty on the client who happens to have a particular skill to examine the architect's designs and tell the architect where he has gone wrong. If I, as a lawyer, go to a solicitor for advice and pay him for it, I do not see why I should be criticised if I fail to do that solicitor's work all over again and check whether he has got it right.[33]

The Judge also did not accept as a defence that the damage was the fault of Sahib, due to its misuse of equipment:

> If equipment were only slightly misused in the manner suggested by him, there would be no fires and no need to design buildings against the risk of fire. But we all know that there are fires, particularly in cooking areas. That is why, in this cooking area, there was provision for a fire alarm, a fire blanket, and a fire extinguisher. Moreover, the architect could have seen by inspection that there was a naked gas flame under one of the bratt pans, and that deep fat frying did take place. If, as is alleged, he made a risk assessment, he could have discovered that normal procedure in the factory meant that if the gas was not turned off at the end of the day, the pan would be left unattended with the gas turned on with fat being supposedly left to cool until the cleaners came on duty at 10 pm.[34]

By contrast *J Sainsbury plc v Broadway Malyan*[35] is an example where client control over the design reduced the liability of the designers. Architects Broadway Malyan and structural engineers Ernest Green were engaged by Sainsburys to design a store in Chichester. In December 1993 the supermarket was destroyed by a fire started in the stores area, and had to be demolished. Sainsburys brought an action against Broadway Malyan, who accepted that its design had failed to provide sufficient fire protection. A settlement was reached with Sainsburys, but the architects continued with third party

---

[32] (1984) 27 BLR 58, see section 6.4.
[33] (2003) 93 Con LR 1, para. 41.
[34] ibid., para. 56.
[35] (1999) 61 Con LR 31.

proceedings against Ernest Green, in which it was necessary for the Judge to consider the apportionment of responsibility, including any proportion that Sainsburys should have borne. Broadway Malyan argued that Sainsburys shared some responsibility for the problem as it had exercised a tight degree of control over the design. The original design had been prepared by in-house architects for Sainsburys, but they had been too busy to complete the project and Broadway Malyan had been engaged from about stage D onwards. It was agreed at trial that Sainsburys had exerted a degree of control, and that every drawing which Broadway Malyan produced had to be submitted to the in-house architects and engineers' department for comment. The court decided that the employer's claim should be reduced by 20% for contributory negligence,[36] since the department should have spotted errors in one of the architects' drawings.

The different results in the above cases can perhaps be explained by the relative knowledge of the clients, together with the degree of control exerted. In *Sahib Foods* the clients were not experts in design or regulations, despite being aware of the risk of fire. Similarly, in *McGlinn v Waltham Contractors Ltd* (see section 8.2.3), although the client was told that the lower balustrade would breach regulations, the onus was on the designer to make the consequences crystal clear, and not to simply acquiesce. In *Sainsbury's* above, the drawings were commented on by design professionals, therefore it seems reasonable that they should share some of the responsibility for the error.

Nevertheless, designers should be slow to assume that having the most expert clients will in any way reduce their required level of skill and care. As noted in *London Underground Ltd v Kenchington Ford* (the case concerning over-design of a slab, see section 6.3):

> The plaintiffs were well informed, technically discriminating and interventionist in the design development of the concourse slab. That is not to say however that LUL's responsible monitoring of, and intervention in the design process in any way relieved the defendants of their design obligations under the contract or where appropriate modified their duty of care.[37]

8.3 Budget issues

Almost all projects are subject to significant cost constraints, and a designer would normally be expected to prepare a design that accords with the client's budget.[38] If designers do not produce a design capable of being constructed within the client's budget, they are not necessarily precluded from obtaining a proper fee for their services; the test will be whether the architect, having genuinely exercised reasonable skill and care, produced a design which was capable of being constructed within or approximating to the specified cost. And if the employer brings evidence that the design was incapable of being so constructed within the cost, that evidence is admissible but will not be conclusive.[39] It is often exceedingly difficult in practice to show what the damage

---

[36] See section 11.3.
[37] (1998) 61 Con LR 1, at 7.
[38] *Moneypenny v Hartland* (1826) 2 C & P 378; 31 RR 672.
[39] *Nemer v Whitford* (1982) 31 SASR 475.

is that the designer's client has suffered in such circumstances: clients will usually have received a benefit from the services (e.g. an increase in value of their property due to receipt of planning permission, or completion of the building works) and in many cases will be unable to show that they have suffered a loss and, if they have suffered no loss, will be unable to prove negligence. But each case of this kind has to be considered on its own particular facts.

Whether or not an architect who fails to warn of the risks of inflation on a building contract is negligent was considered by the Court of Appeal in *Nye Saunders and Partners v Alan E. Bristow*.[40] There the architects as plaintiffs started proceedings for unpaid fees amounting to £15,581.59. The defendant employer defended the claim on the basis that the architects had failed in their duty to take due care in providing a reliable approximate estimate in 1974 and that they had failed to draw the employer's attention to the fact that since inflation would increase the cost, the total cost of the project would rise to a figure beyond the amount which the employer had said was at his disposal for the purposes of the building works. In detail, the employer had told the architects that he had about £1 million to spend on the work. Before the planning application had been granted, the employer asked the architects to provide a written estimate of the cost of the works; the architects brought in a quantity surveyor and thereafter they wrote to the employer setting out a schedule of costs totalling some £238,000 but they did not show any figure covering to inflation, nor did they include any sum at all for contingencies. After the architects had been engaged, and planning permission granted, an up-to-date estimate was provided amounting to some £440,000 which included for the first time a figure for the likely increase in costs over the estimated 18-month contract period. The employer abandoned the project and terminated the architects' engagement. The architects' claim for fees failed in the Court of First Instance, and on appeal. The Court of Appeal found that the cause of the massive increase in cost which led the employer to cancel the project was inflation, and in respect of that element of cost, he had not been warned. It commented that, although it may have been prudent for the architects to consult a quantity surveyor, they could not thereby avoid responsibility for not drawing to the attention of the employer the fact that inflation had not been taken into account.

It often happens that the employer becomes increasingly concerned during the progress of a project with escalating costs. In order to try to prevent the project losing its viability, the employer may request or even insist on the designer reducing the quality of the works by both omissions and variations. Where these changes are likely to lead to a result that is unsatisfactory, then the designer's duty is to tell the employer in clear language of the likely outcome of the instructions. That warning by the designer may be sufficient to discharge the designer from further liability. This is often required specifically in standard terms of appointment, for example the RIBA Standard Agreement 2010 states:

> The Architect shall keep the Client informed of progress in the performance of the Services and of any issue that may affect the Brief, the Construction Cost, the Timetable, or the quality of the Project.' (cl. 2.2).

---

[40] (1987) 37 BLR 92 (CA).

However, where the employer insists upon changes that would result in a defective construction or a breach of the law, for example of the Building Regulations, then the position is much more difficult. On the one hand, the designer is obliged to have regard to the employer's wishes; and on the other hand the designer has a duty to use reasonable skill and care and to comply with the general law. It may well be that, if designers cannot discharge their duty to use reasonable skill and care by giving a warning that carrying out the employer's wishes would produce a defective building (particularly where this could involve breach of statutory requirements), they may have no alternative but to resign. Of course such a course of action should not be undertaken lightly because an employer could treat that resignation as a repudiation of the contract. Where a serious matter of this sort arises, designers would be well advised to seek legal advice.

An early example of the normal approach is seen in the case of *City of Brantford v Kemp & Wallace-Carruthers Ltd*[41] where the Court of Appeal stated:

> it was [the engineer's] duty to inform either the city or Kemp ... of the risk involved in his plan, as well as the superior safety of the alternative, and the difference in cost. It would then have been the responsibility of the city to take the risk if it so decided ....[42]

Where there are these alternative solutions, then the designer would be well advised to discuss them with the employer so that the employer is in a position to understand and to make any commercial decisions that should be made in the light of the risks that have been ascertained. The responsibility should be on the employer; a designer would make these decisions for an employer at her or his peril. A designer designing a cheaper method of construction involving risk, without discussing the alternative of a more expensive safe scheme, will be liable in negligence if the design fails.

A more recent example of client input can be seen in *Pride Valley Foods Ltd v Hall & Partners (Contract Management) Ltd*[43] (upheld by the Court of Appeal). In this case polystyrene panels, which had good food safety properties but were highly combustible, were used to line walls and ceilings at a pitta and naan bread-making factory. A fire occurred in an oven flue, which spread and destroyed the whole factory. The defendant project managers maintained that they had warned the client orally of the risks of using these less expensive panels. The Court did not accept this evidence. It found that the consultants should have warned the clients that the use of EPS panels represented a much greater risk to safety to the building than available alternatives, and that competent consultants would have given the advice in writing.[44] However the designer would not be liable if it could be shown that the client would have ignored the advice if properly given.

In any event the designer would always be expected to include all the information necessary for a complete project. It is usually said that the design must be comprehensive, and it should include everything necessary in order that the works may be properly completed. For example, in *Wilkes v Thingoe RDC*[45] the design for a housing scheme

---

[41] (1960) 23 DLR (2d) 640 (Ont. 1 960 CA) Canada.
[42] ibid., at 652.
[43] (2001) 76 Con LR 1
[44] ibid., para. 178.
[45] (1984) 164 EG 86.

omitted sufficient cookers and toilets for the number of houses. The architects were under extreme pressure to meet the local authority's cost yardsticks, but the court found them negligent. If they had explained the position to their client, it would have made the savings elsewhere.

8.4 Design development

8.4.1 Detailed design and technical information

The amount of information and level of detail to be supplied by a designer to the contractor will of course depend on the circumstances in every case, including the terms of appointment, the procurement and contractual context, and the involvement of other specialists. No general rules can be stated. As pointed out, in *Bellefield Computer Services v E Turner & Sons Ltd (No 2)*:[46]

> The detailed duties of an architect in relation to his design function depend upon the application of the general principles above stated to the particular facts of the case, including any special terms agreed. The precise ambit of such duties will usually depend upon expert evidence from members of the profession as to what a competent, experienced architect would do in the circumstances.[47]

In traditional procurement full information would normally be expected. In *Plymouth and South West Co-operative Society Ltd v Architecture Structure and Management Ltd*[48] a project was let on a JCT Standard Building Contract with approximate quantities, 1998 edition, following a two stage tender process. Little progress had been made in finalising the design during the tender period, and a very substantial part of the contract sum was provisional and related to work which was not detailed save 'in a very rudimentary form'. The architects were found liable for failing to warn their client of the risks in proceeding in this way.

In a design-build procurement route the level of detail required would normally be less. *Bellefield*, a design-build project, was notable in that there were no written terms of appointment. The architects were engaged by the contractor to supply information, which was described as being 'on demand'. The claim concerned inadequate fire stopping, which had allowed fire to spread from one part of a dairy to another, causing extensive damage to goods.[49] The trial Judge decided the architects were not under a duty to design the detailed fire requirements as no drawing of the detail in question had been asked for. The Court of Appeal did not agree with this aspect of the decision. This was partly due to ambiguous statements given by the architects in their witness statements, and the fact that drawings had clearly been provided from time to time that had not been asked for. However the appeal court moved out of the particular facts of the case to make some more general statements:

---

[46] [2003] Lloyds Rep PN 53.
[47] ibid., Lord Justice Potter, para. 48.
[48] [2006] CILL 2366 (TCC).
[49] [2003] Lloyds Rep PN 53, Lord Justice Potter, para. 48.

In this respect, the somewhat informal or, at any rate, ill-defined nature of the relationship between Watkins and Turner, their previous experience in working together and Turner's apparent acceptance of the Contract Drawings (as subsequently amended) as sufficient for the purposes of constructing the compartment wall and providing a fire barrier, combined to produce a somewhat 'grey' area so far as the necessity for a detail of the fire lining was concerned.

In seeking to illuminate that grey area, I approach the matter upon the following basis. It is reasonable to expect that in a matter which affects the design safety of a building, whenever the architect has reason to suppose that the achievement of a detail of construction which is not illustrated upon the contractual drawings but which is necessary should be effected in a particular manner or to a particular standard, may present problems of interpretation and solution to the contractor or sub-contractor who is to effect the work concerned, there is an obligation upon the architect, before the work is done, to clarify with the contractor or sub-contractor his design intention and/or the solution to be employed. This will usually be best achieved by the supply of a detailed drawing. However, depending upon the nature of the detail or technique required, and the skill and understanding of the contractor or sub-contractor, it may be sufficient to resolve the matter by written instructions, by express approval of the contractors' or sub-contractors' proposed solution, or in direct discussions which render the matter clear.[50]

The above passage is important in that it introduces a presumption that, in the absence of express terms to the contrary, the onus is on the architect to anticipate what might be needed, especially where it affects design safety.

The first instance Judge had made an alternative finding in that if he did decide that providing the details was part of the architects' duty, they had provided enough information. He examined all the drawings very carefully, and described them in detail in the judgment. In particular he decided that 'As it happens, Drawing 11C also provided Turner with a clear and sufficient specification for the construction of the compartment walls, floors and adjacent fire lining in order to achieve the required fire rating.'[51] The Court of Appeal accepted that Drawing 11C together with subsequent discussions had sufficiently conveyed the design intention[52] and the decision was upheld.

In reaching his decision, Lord Justice May made some interesting comments on the 'borderlines of responsibility':

The extent of an architect's responsibility for the detailed working out of construction details for which he has provided an underlying design again depends on the express and implied terms of his engagement and its interrelation with the responsibility of others. The scope of any such responsibility depends on the facts of each case. There is a blurred borderline between architectural design and the construction details needed to put it into effect. Borderlines of responsibility cannot be defined in the abstract. A carpenter's choice of a particular nail or screw is in a sense a design choice, yet very often the choice is left to the carpenter and the responsibility for making it merges with the carpenter's workmanship obligations. In many circumstance, the scope of an architect's responsibility extends to providing drawings or specifications which give full construction details. But responsibility for some such details may rest with other consultants, e.g. structural engineers, or with specialist contractors or subcon-

---

[50] ibid., paras 58 and 59.
[51] ibid., para. 30, citing para. 61 of first instance judgment by Judge Thayne Forbes.
[52] ibid., paras 62 and 63.

tractors, depending on the terms of their respective contracts and their interrelationship. As with the carpenter choosing an appropriate nail, specialist details may be left to specialist subcontractors who sometimes make detailed 'design' decisions without expecting or needing drawings or specifications telling them what to do. In appropriate circumstances, this would not amount to delegation by the architect of part of his own responsibility. Rather that element of composite design responsibility did not rest with him in the first place.[53]

The above statements of Lord Justice May are made in the context of design-build procurement, where delegation of detailed design may be appropriate. In practice, if a designer leaves detailed matters to be decided by others, unless this is clarified in the appointment documents, confusion can arise regarding liability for any resulting mistakes (see Chapter 9 for a full discussion of delegation of design duties).

It should also be noted that in contrast to *Bellefield* there have been many cases where consultants have been found liable for failing to provide enough detailed information, despite the involvement of other specialists. For example, *Baxall Securities Ltd v Sheard Walshaw Partnership*[54] concerned the design of a roof drainage system of a warehouse, which flooded and damaged the stored contents. It was agreed that by the experts that the architects ought to have known of British Standard for Drainage of Roofs and Paved Areas, BS6367:1983, and to have therefore been aware that for the situation in that case (a valley gutter using a symphonic drainage system) that a design rate 150 mm of rainfall per hour should have been used. The Judge at first instance found that the architects were negligent in failing to specify a design requirement for the drains, and in particular to specify a requirement for rainfall intensity of 150 mm per hour. The Judge considered that an ordinarily experienced architect ought to have consulted the relevant BS and specified the parameters within which the sub-contractor should design:

> Mr Woodward also said, and I accept, that there was a fundamental deficiency in the design information given by the defendants. To enable the potential tenderers for the roof drainage to carry out their technical design, they ought to have been given information of the design requirement for the rate of rainfall. That requirement was not given. The tenderers provided their own design requirement and left to their own devices, would have been tempted to put in the lowest and cheapest requirement. Mr Woodward gave it as his opinion, with which I agree, that any shortfall in the capacity of the gutters to dispose of short duration rainfall appropriate to the location of the building would be as a direct result of the failure of the architect to incorporate the necessary information within the specification requirement.[55]

The Court of Appeal upheld this finding, rejecting an argument that the design flow rate could take into account the capacity the overflow system.[56] The architects were therefore found liable for the damage to the stored goods. Similarly in *Try Build Ltd v Invicta Leisure Tennis Ltd*,[57] engineers Buro Happold were found liable for failing to specify the edge strip to be used in a roofing material. The court commented:

---

[53] ibid., para. 76.
[54] [2001] BLR 36; [2002] BLR 100 (CA).
[55] [2001] BLR 36, at para. 81
[56] [2002] BLR 100 (CA) at para. 38.
[57] (1997) 71 ConLR 140.

The thickness of the edge tape was at least as important as the thickness of the foil of the main body of the cushions. It seems a very strange proceeding to specify such an important detail by implication only. I cannot see that the thickness of the foil was specified by implication. Clauses 8.7 and 8.8 were concerned with strength, not thickness. I hold that BH did *not* specify the thickness of the edge material and that they ought to have done so… .[58]

The above two cases provide an interesting contrast. In *Baxall*, it appears that the court considered that the provision of a performance specification (i.e. design rainfall rate) would have discharged the architect's duties. In *Invicta*, the engineers provided a performance requirement for strength, but were criticised by the court for failing to specify one for water-tightness, including the wind and rainfall conditions the joint should have withstood.[59] However the court concluded that the engineers should also have specified the strip thickness – i.e. although it is not stated specifically, it appears that in this even a detailed performance specification for the strip would not have been enough. The difference in approach may be accounted for by the contractual background, as in *Baxall* the parties had agreed that the specialist roofing company was to complete the detailed design, whereas in *Invicta*, although a specialist roofing company was engaged, the engineers' appointment nevertheless required them to provide drawings of the joint details. In addition, *Invicta* concerned a novel type of construction, where the designers might be expected to pay particular attention to the detailed design.

To avoid any uncertainty as to the extent of the consultant's duties, the best solution is of course to agree in the terms of appointment (or failing that, to clarify in writing at an early stage) exactly what level of detail is to be covered. This is obviously closely linked to the right of the consultant to delegate responsibility to others, and the amount of detail to be provided by the contractor. It would be unwise to assume that the contractor will be responsible for providing any detailed design aspects that are not fully developed, unless the contract documents have made this clear.

8.4.2 Innovative and risky design

Where an ordinary and routine piece of design fails in practice, this may provide evidence of the designer's negligence, although it will in practice usually be necessary to call expert evidence. What is the position where designers are operating at the frontiers of knowledge where there is no fund of knowledge or codes of practice upon which they can rely?

There is a very old case, *Turner v Garland and Christopher*,[60] which indicates that failure by a designer to succeed with a new method, of which he had professed no expertise, was not negligence. A designer was employed to prepare plans and superintend the erection of model lodging houses for an employer who instructed him to put in new patent concrete roofing, which was much cheaper than lead or slate. The con-

---

[58] ibid., para. 84.
[59] ibid., para. 74.
[60] (1853) *Hudson's Building Contracts*, 4th edn, vol. 2, p. l.

crete roofing proved a failure and had to be removed and replaced. The employer brought an action for negligence against the designer. The Judge told the jury that although failure in an ordinary building was evidence of want of competent skill, yet if out of the ordinary course of things a designer is employed in some novel thing in which he has no experience and which has not the test of experience, failure may be consistent with skill.

That case was decided over 150 years ago and conditions in the construction industry and the law have changed out of all recognition since then. It is probable that the result of that case would be different if it were to be heard today.

Brickfield Properties v Newton[61] is an example of a later case where experimental design was considered, and interestingly the court emphasised the need to look at the design even where the claim related only to inspection, and that the inspection duty would also include a duty to re-check the design:

> The design has inevitably to be closely examined even if the only claim relates to superintendence, and all the more so if the designs are, as is alleged here, experimental or such as need amplification as the construction progresses.[62]

This aspect of design was touched upon in the case of *IBA v EMI and BICC*.[63] In that case a 1250-foot high television mast collapsed, and it was accepted that the design of such a cylindrical mast was 'both at and beyond the frontier of professional knowledge' at that time. It was also accepted that although subsequent to the collapse of the mast, the reasons for the collapse were known to designers, such knowledge was not available at the time of the design. It was therefore agreed that it could not have been negligent to design the mast without having regard to the factors that did cause the collapse. One of these factors was asymmetric loading caused by ice on the stays. A code of practice was followed which purported to enable subcontractors of BICC to design a 1250-foot aerial mast to withstand pressures caused by 80mph winds. The code applied to lattice masts where high winds were assumed to blow off accumulations of ice. However, with the cylindrical mast proposed by BICC, there was a possibility that it might begin to oscillate dangerously even at low wind speeds at a time when any ice would not have fallen off. Lord Edmund Davies held that the very fact that BICC's design was a 'venture into the unknown' created a clear duty to identify and think through potential problems and not merely rely on a code of practice. It had been assumed in the design that such excessive deposits of ice would crack and fall away in fluctuating winds. Viscount Dilhorne said of that assumption, in his judgment in the House of Lords:

> Was it right to make such an assumption with regard to a design which was at and beyond the frontiers of professional knowledge? I see no justification for doing so. BICC's experience with lattice masts, where vortex shedding was no problem, may have led them to believe that ice would be shaken off the stay ropes in strong winds but when they knew that the critical

---

[61] [1971] 1 WLR 862.
[62] ibid., at 873, E–F *per* Sachs LJ.
[63] (1980) 14 BLR 1 (HL).

wind speeds were so low, they should surely have considered whether at such wind speeds the ice would crack and fall from the stays. No consideration was, it appears, given to asymmetric icing on the stays then I am at a loss to understand why it would have been assumed that the ice loading would be symmetric; [the designer] was asked in cross-examination whether it was not obvious that there might be additive stresses caused by vortex shedding and ice loading. He said it was not obvious because it had never been considered.[64]

Lord Edmund Davies summarised his views as follows:

> What is embraced by the duty to exercise reasonable care must always depend on the circumstances of each case. They may call for particular precautions: *Readhead v Midland Railway Co* (1869). The graver the foreseeable consequences of failure to take care, the greater the necessity for special circumspection: *Paris v Stepney Borough Council* (1951). Those who engage in operations inherently dangerous must take precautions which are not required of persons engaged in the ordinary routine of daily life: *Glasgow Corporation v Muir* (1953). The project may be alluring. But the risks of injury to those engaged in it, or to others, or to both, may be so manifest and substantial and their elimination may be so difficult to ensure with reasonable certainty that the only proper course is to abandon the project altogether. Learned Counsel for BICC appeared to regard such a defeatist outcome as unthinkable. Yet circumstances can and have at times arisen in which it is plain commonsense and any other decision foolhardy. The law requires even pioneers to be prudent.[65]

It is clear that the Judges in this case did not regard the fact that there was no precedent for a design of such a tall cylindrical mast as being any reason for excusing the designers when the mast collapsed. Indeed, the Court took the view that the designer needs to take added precautions in order to discharge the duty of reasonable skill and care in the circumstances of a novel design. In particular, it emphasised that following a code of practice may not be enough; Lord Fraser said that he had 'reached the firm conclusion that BICC failed in their duty of care when they applied the code of practice that had been found appropriate'.

This principle, that the designer must take special precautions in relation to innovative design, has been reiterated in more recent cases. For example, in *Try Build Ltd v Invicta Leisure Tennis Ltd*,[66] the court placed emphasis on the novelty of the proposed roof design in deciding not only that the foil thickness should have been specified by the engineers, but also that an exact performance specification should have been given in relation to the 'water-tightness' of the roof, and that appropriate tests should have been required.[67]

When considering developing an innovative design, it would be sensible for consultants to explain the risks to their clients. In *Victoria University of Manchester v Hugh Wilson* it was stated:

---

[64] ibid., at 20.
[65] (1980) 14 BLR 1 (HL) at 29.
[66] (1997) 71 Con LR 140.
[67] ibid., paras 77 and 88.

For architects to use untried, or relatively untried materials or techniques cannot in itself be wrong, as otherwise the construction industry can never make any progress. I think however, that architects who are venturing into the untried or little tried would be wise to warn their clients specifically of what they are doing and to obtain their express approval.[68]

It is therefore clear that not only will the novelty of a design not be an excuse for any defects, but that when undertaking a novel design the designer should take special precautions.

8.5 *Commenting on/approving others' designs*

In modern procurement, drawings and other documents and are often circulated to designers for comment or approval. As a general rule, any comments or approval will not lessen the responsibility of the author for any errors contained, and frequently standard form construction contracts will make this clear (e.g. the JCT Contractor's Design Submission Procedure, cl. 8.3). What is often less clear is the position of those making the comments or giving the approval, will they take on some liability for any errors that are missed? If they are to any degree responsible the client may pursue both parties (i.e. author and commentator), and may be entitled to recover all losses from either.

Generally a consultant whose duties include checking the drawings of others will be liable to use a reasonable level of skill and care in so doing, unless the appointment itself sets out any limitations on this duty, but much will depend on the circumstances, for example the purpose of the checking or approval process.

In *Try Build v Invicta Leisure Tennis*,[69] in addition to the claims of negligent design and specification of the edge strip (see above), there were also claims regarding approval of shop drawings. In their appointment terms engineers Buro Happold (BH) were responsible for 'Examining shop details for general dimensions and adequacies of members and connections', and by an addendum BH agreed to 'undertake the additional duties of checking the material and fabrication of the components of the Vector foil roofing system during production and upon delivery to site, and . . . to issue a formal certificate of our inspection in the form appended hereto'. The inspection certificate was duly issued, and stated 'we have reviewed the shop drawings and the materials proposed by Vector and have visually inspected the foil roof components in the sample assembly at the Vector factory in Bremen and were satisfied that the components as proposed were in accordance with the said specification and suitable for incorporation in the roof system.'[70]

BH was found negligent with respect to the certificate, and the Judge was very critical of BH's performance, stating 'There is, however, absolutely no doubt that the certificate

---

[68] 2 Con LR 43, HHJ Newey QC at 74.
[69] (1997) 71 ConLR 140.
[70] ibid., para. 61.

was false in important respects and ought not to have been given'.[71] He also did not accept an argument that the appointment did not require BH to inspect the drawings regarding water-tightnesss – this was 'too obvious to state.'[72]

George Fischer Holdings Ltd v Multi Design Consultants Ltd and Davis Langdon & Everest,[73] concerned defects in the roof of a new warehousing complex. The design was largely undertaken by Multi Design Consultants, with Davis Langdon & Everest (DLE) taking on the role of quantity surveyors and employer's representative. Under their terms of appointment, DLE had a duty to:

> . . . carry out an appraisal of the design drawings and documentation available and as provided by the design and build contractor and to highlight any aspects of the design proposals which he considers to be unsatisfactory, which might be seen as presenting potential problems at a later stage . . . .[74]

The roof had been designed to have a very low pitch of 1.5 degrees, and the cladding material to have lap joints. The court found DLE jointly liable with Multi Design Consultants with respect to the design, due to its failure to query the proposals put forward. Interestingly, the court commented:

> There was some dispute as to whether Mr Gardiner of DLE, who dealt with such matters, actually saw the material drawings, but I do not find it necessary to resolve that dispute, since it was undoubtedly DLE's duty to obtain and approve all working drawings.[75]

A further case of interest is *London Underground Ltd v Kenchington Ford*.[76] This case has already been discussed with respect to the alleged over-design of a concourse slab at Canning Town station on the Jubilee Line extension (for which the engineers Kenchington Ford were found not to be negligent, see section 6.3). However, there was another aspect to the claim, which concerned the design of a diaphragm wall. One of the services listed under the engineers' appointment was 'the correction of any errors, ambiguities or omissions arising and answering requests for clarification on design matters from Mowlem.'[77]

The wall was in fact designed by Cementation-Bachy (CB), a subcontractor to the main contractor Mowlem. The engineers had provided CB with drawings that had correctly shown the loadings to be taken account of in CB's detailed design. Although the drawings were clear, CB misinterpreted them and queried whether the loadings were to be added together, and the engineers incorrectly confirmed that they were. This resulted in a duplication of loadings, which the engineers failed to notice in the drawings submitted by CB for approval. As a result, the diaphragm wall panels were designed

---

[71] ibid., para. 92.
[72] ibid., para. 54.
[73] (1998) 61 Con LR 85.
[74] ibid., at para. 91.
[75] ibid., at para. 135.
[76] [1999] 63 Con LR1.
[77] ibid., at 36.

3.5 m too deep. The court determined that 'a careful engineer should have checked and had he done so should have picked up the error'[78] and found the engineers liable for the cost of the over dig, materials and additional work paid by LUL to Mowlem.[79]

Adopting a 'no comment' approach is also unlikely to relieve the consultant from liability. In *Baxall v Sheard Walshaw Partnership*,[80] a firm of architects had overall responsibility for the design of a roof, with the detailed design prepared by the specialist roof designer. The sub-contractor issued drawings and explanatory notes indicating that a design rainfall rate of 75 mm per hour had been used, which it transpired did not comply with the relevant British Standard. The architects admitted that they had neither approved nor disapproved the sub-contractor's design rate, and the court found them liable for failing to specify the correct rate themselves.

All the above cases therefore take a fairly stringent approach to the interpretation of a duty to review another party's design proposals. However there have, of course, been cases where the consultants have been held not liable when drawings approved by them have contained errors. In *Acme Investments v York Structural Steel*[81] a specialist contractor was engaged to build the structural steel frame and roof deck of a shopping mall. The contractor submitted drawings for approval by the architect. Although the architect approved them, the design did not comply in some respects with the relevant Building Code, and the steel frame deflected excessively in certain snow loading conditions. The court held that the architect's approval did not relieve the contractor from its duty to design the steel structure to comply with the Codes. The architect's responsibility was limited to ascertaining that the part designed by the contractor coordinated with the architect's design of the envelope.

A similar approach was taken in more recent case of *Cooperative Group Ltd v John Allen Associates Ltd*.[82] John Allen Associates (JAA) were engineers for the design of a supermarket, and while designing the floor slab they contacted Keller, a geotechnical contractor, who recommended that a technique called vibro compacting was used. Eventually another specialist firm was engaged for this work (Pennine). The floor settled causing significant problems, and among other things the Cooperative Group claimed that JAA had failed to carry out adequate checks on calculations provided by Pennine. The engineers were appointed under the under the ACE Conditions to provide 'Normal Services', and there was nothing in the appointment requiring JAA to carry out any services or duties beyond these. The Judge summarised the issue as follows:

> The central question is how far that checking should have gone. Should it have been a full check of the geotechnical design or was it limited to checking that the input data was correct, that the output data satisfied the required specification and that the arithmetic was correct?[83]

---

[78] ibid., at 37.

[79] It is interesting to note that although the engineers were found liable for the sum of £66,650 they succeeded in a counterclaim for their fees in the amount of £348,808.

[80] (2002) BLR 100 (CA).

[81] (1974) 4 SARL 223, SA.

[82] [2010] EWHC 2300 (TCC).

[83] ibid., para. 280.

The court decided that the duty of JAA was to check those matters which were within the skill and knowledge of an ordinary competent consulting structural and civil engineer, which in this case meant the more limited option described in the extract above. Checking the detailed geotechnical design within those calculations 'were not the type of matters which ordinary competent civil and structural engineers would have checked'.[84] The engineers were found not liable.

In *J Sainsbury plc v Broadway Malyan (A Firm) (Ernest Green Partnership Ltd, Third Party)*[85] Sainsburys engaged architects, Broadway Malyan (BM), and structural engineers Ernest Green Partnership (EMP) in connection with the construction of its 262nd store in Chichester. The supermarket was destroyed by a fire started in the stores area, and had to be demolished. Sainsburys brought an action against the architects, claiming that the fire had spread to the sales area through a compartment wall because Broadway Malyan had failed in its design to provide sufficient fire protection (the compartment wall as the top part of the compartment wall had only about a half hour fire resistance instead of two hours). Broadway Malyan accepted that it was negligent and reached a settlement with Sainsburys. It brought third party proceedings against Ernest Green that the latter was also liable to Sainsburys, as it had negligently failed to comment on Broadway Malyan's drawing showing the design for the protection of the structural steel work forming part of the wall, or to advise it that the proposal was inadequate. The architects had set out the details of the dry construction wall on their drawing 3133/A3/6 and sent it to the engineers under cover of a letter which stated:

> Following discussion with yourselves, we have re-detailed the means of fire stopping the top of the wall to the back of the Sales Area along Grid K. We enclose a copy of Drawing No. 3133/A3/6 for comment. This shows a patent metal framed panel system in Supalux board, supported from the lattice truss on Grid K by means of continuous angle and tee sections bolted to the top and bottom members of the lattice. Where cross-lattices occur, the panels are cut around the steel members and fire stopped with mineral wool.

The drawing described the Supalux as being '2hr fire resisting 6mm Supalux board', however at the trial it was accepted that it was a bad detail as it did not provide 2-hour fire resistance to the lattice girder (among other things the cladding was to one side only, with the girder exposed on the store side). EGP made no comment on the drawing and did not advise BM of the need for fire protection. EGP considered it only in relation to structural implications of the change, a witness for EGP stating 'I certainly would not have looked at the detail from the point of view of fireproofing. I merely saw that there was no longer any high level blockwork and therefore no further stability problems.' He did accept that if an architect were to send him a drawing showing steelwork which required fire protection but which did not provide it then it would be foolish not to comment on it. The Judge, HHJ Humphrey LLoyd QC, agreed with the arguments put forward by EGP, stating:

---

[84] ibid., para. 283.
[85] (1999) 61 Con LR 31.

In my judgement it was not incumbent on EGP to look again at the architect's proposals to see whether the girder now required different treatment under the Building Regulations and it was not in breach of its duties to Sainsburys in not doing so . . . EGP had hitherto not been required to consider the wall except in terms of loading and stability. I have no doubt that a request for comment would ordinarily be read as inviting comment on the dry construction of the wall. As such no comment was needed. If BM was concerned also with fire protection it ought to have specifically said so. I accept Mr Hotchkiss' evidence as to what an architect ought to have done: if an architect wanted an engineer to revisit the structural adequacy of a beam he would have 'to list the specifics that I was wanting him to address himself to' and that the letter of 30 October 1984 was quite inadequate for that purpose.[86]

He added:

It is also in my view significant both that the drawing was not sent 'for approval' and that BM did not pursue EGP for an answer on the point which it is now said was the reason why the drawing was submitted, namely that EGP should have commented on the architect's detail for fire protection. The lack of pursuit in itself suggests that the request was not looking for approval.[87]

The Judge therefore decided that the engineers did not have a duty to consider the fire protection measures and were not negligent in their review of the drawing.

Although it is difficult to draw general conclusions, it is clear from the above that whether the matter is within the ordinary competence of a member of that profession is an important factor in deciding whether or not a duty to comment existed. If there is a duty, then a reasonably vigilant inspection is required. It is more likely that the consultant would be found liable if there is an express duty to check, but even if the consultant's duties are more generally expressed, the duty may be implied, especially where they have overall responsibility for that aspect of the design. It would therefore be wise to specify the extent of the checking duties, and their purpose, for example is it to check for dimensional coordination only, or does it also include checking underlying assumptions or calculations? When sending a drawing or document for comment, it is sensible to be clear what aspects are to be checked.

8.6 Inspection and certification

8.6.1 General considerations

It is commonplace for an employer who finds that it has defective construction to bring proceedings against both the contractor and the designer. The reason for this is twofold. First, it can be extremely difficult in practice to distinguish between damage caused by defective workmanship, for which the contractor will be liable, and damage caused by

---

[86] ibid., para. 2.25.
[87] ibid., para. 2.27.

defective design, for which the designer will be liable. By bringing proceedings against both the designer and the contractor, the employer will hope to avoid falling between two stools. Secondly, where there is defective workmanship, then there is, on the face of it, the possibility of an allegation that the designer was negligent in carrying out duties as to supervision or inspection of the contractor's work.

In any particular case, it is necessary to look at the conditions of engagement of the designer and the contract between the contractor and the employer as well as the general law. The reason for this is that the conditions of engagement may set out particular obligations, and the construction contract may give guidance as to the obligations that the designer undertakes in respect of the contractor's work.

In the past, such documents would often refer to 'supervision', whereas now they are more likely to refer to 'inspection'. Sometimes the terms are used interchangeably, for example in *Brown and Brown v Gilbert-Scott and Payne*[88] the court commented that 'the use of the word "supervision" does not enlarge his duty in any way'. However 'inspection' is generally thought to be a lesser obligation. For example, in the case of *Consarc Design Ltd v Hutch Investments Ltd*,[89] architects Consarc were engaged on the RIBA Standard Form of Appointment 1992 in relation to a project to convert a summerhouse into a residence for a Sheikh. The work included the laying of a limestone floor on an existing concrete slab. The floor once laid had serious defects and had to be re-laid at a cost of £110,988.05. The architects brought a claim for their fees, and Hutch Investment brought a counterclaim, which included an allegation of failure to inspect. SFA 92 required at K08 that DLE '[a]t intervals appropriate to the stage of construction visit the Works to inspect the progress and quality of the Works and to determine that they are being executed generally in accordance with the Contract documents'. His Honour Judge Bowsher decided that the architects had not been negligent in their inspections. He commented:

> The standard form contracts on this topic have varied. The older forms of contract required the architect to 'supervise'. The more recent contracts, including the contract in this case, require the architect to 'visit the Works to inspect the progress and quality of the Works'. It seems to me that inspection is a lesser responsibility than supervision ... Even where the architect's duty requires supervision, it is difficult to define the limits of the duty or to say when the architect has failed in his duty ... What is absolutely clear is that the architect does not guarantee that his inspection will reveal or prevent all defective work.[90]

This was followed in *McGlinn v Waltham Contractors Ltd*[91] where the court commented that the change from supervision to inspection represented 'a potentially important reduction in the scope of an architect's services'.[92] Despite this change, earlier cases concerning supervision are still significant, partly because the court's findings on some aspects are equally relevant to inspection, and also because a duty to supervise

---

[88] (1992) 35 Con LR 120.
[89] [2002] 84 Con LR 36 at 60, para. 91.
[90] ibid., paras 88–91.
[91] [2007] 111 Con LR 1.
[92] ibid., Peter Coulson J, at 216.

may occasionally be undertaken by a consultant, either intentionally, or perhaps implied when the terms of appointment are silent on the matter.

The following sections explore issues relating to supervision and inspection, concluding with a discussion of *McGlinn*, which usefully summarises the current understanding of many aspects of this area of law.

8.6.2 The basis of liability

There will not usually be a claim for negligent inspection unless there is also defective workmanship or materials, because in the absence of the latter, there will not usually be any damage that would make it worthwhile to pursue allegation of negligent inspection. Where there is defective workmanship, the contractor will be liable in damages, usually for the costs of repair. What therefore, is the position where there is defective workmanship for which the employer has a cause of action against the contractor, and there is also negligent inspection? Does the employer have an additional cause of action against the designer for negligent inspection?

It is quite clear that the employer has a cause of action against both the contractor and the designer. Against the contractor, there will be a claim for breach of contract at the very least, and against the designer there will be a cause action for breach of duty in negligently failing to prevent, or detect and have corrected, the defective work. The claim is most likely to arise where the designer has authorised payment for the defective work and may encompass both negligent inspection, and negligent over-certification.[93]

The causes of action against the contractor and the consultant are separate and distinct: the employer can choose which to pursue or may pursue both causes of action. Judge Fay QC, Official Referee, in *Hutchinson v Harris*[94] (which subsequently went to the Court of Appeal, but not on this point), put it this way:

> Where the duty of a contracting party is to supervise the work of another contracting party, it seems to me that there is a direct causal connect between the supervisor's negligent failure to prevent negligent work and damage represented by their negligent work. No doubt the builder is also liable. It is a case of concurrent breaches of contract producing the same damage. In my judgment the plaintiff has an action against both, although she cannot obtain damages twice over.[95]

A similar point arose in *London Borough of Merton v Lowe and Pickford*[96] where it was argued by the defendant architects that they should not be held liable by reason of the fact that although the self-same damage could have been recovered in tort from a solvent sub-contractor; the building owner had chosen not to do so. The Court of Appeal rejected that argument and held the architects liable.

---

[93] see e.g. *Sutcliffe v Thackrah* [1974] AC 727.
[94] (1979) 10 BLR 19.
[95] ibid., p. 22.
[96] (1981) 18 BLR 130.

In such a case, where there is liability for the same damage on the part of both defendants, and whether or not that liability is in tort or contract, the court has power to apportion liability between the parties under the Civil Liability (Contribution) Act 1978 (see Section 11.3.2). In *Townsend v Stone Toms & Partners*[97] it was held that, where a claimant sues designers and contractors as co-defendants, and the action against the contractors is settled by the claimant accepting a sum of money paid into court by the contractors, the action can proceed against the designer where there is a separate cause of action, but that no one should recover more in damages than the loss suffered. The burden is on the wrongdoer to show that the claimant has already received compensation. In this case, the Judge had taken the view that part of the contractor's payment was for losses attributable to both defendants and the Judge had only awarded a further small sum against the architects. The Court of Appeal did not disagree with the Judge's assessment. The courts, in apportioning liability between such co-defendants must determine what contribution is just and equitable, having due regard to the extent of each defendant's liability for damage.

The courts tend to the view 'that the blameworthiness of the policeman who fails to detect the crime is less than that of the criminal himself.'[98] However, there are circumstances that can arise where designers can find themselves in a position where they have to meet the full amount of the employer's claim. This position could arise where the contractor is unable to meet its liabilities because of lack of funds; it is well known that construction is a risky business and there is a higher rate of company insolvency in this sector than in most others.

Designers can also find themselves in the position of meeting the whole of the employer's claim in circumstances where they have deprived the employer of the right to bring an action against the contractor in respect of its defective workmanship. Although many interim payment certificates are 'on account', so that if defective work is discovered after it is certified, the situation can be remedied by the following certificate, this is not always the case. Under earlier versions of the 1963 edition of the JCT Contract (subsequently altered), clause 30(7) provided that a final certificate should be 'conclusive evidence in any proceedings . . . that the works have been properly carried out and completed in accordance with the terms of this contract . . . .'. Subject to some exceptions which were expressly set out in the contract, the employer would be deprived of any right of action against the contractor in respect of defective workmanship once that certificate was issued. One of the exceptions was in relation to any defect which reasonable inspection during the carrying out of the works or before the issue of the final certificate would not have disclosed. It followed that, where the architect failed to discover a defect which reasonable inspection would have disclosed, or the architect knew of a defect and issued the final certificate, the employer's right of action against the contractor would be extinguished, but the employer would be likely to have a cause of action against the architect. In *London Borough of Merton v Lowe and Pickford*,[99] a

---

[97] (1984) 27 BLR 26 (CA).
[98] *per* Judge Edgar Fay QC in *Eames London Estates Ltd & Others v North Herefordshire District Council & Others* (1980) 18 BLR 50.
[99] (1981) 18 BLR 130.

case on the 1963 edition of the JCT Contract, architects were held liable in respect of defective workmanship by a contractor's nominated sub-contractors in circumstances where they knew of the defective workmanship at the time that they issued the final certificate.

The construction contract may also provide that the works shall be executed as set out in the specification and to the reasonable satisfaction of the designer. Such a clause will impose two obligations: to execute the works in the manner set out in the specification and also to execute them to the reasonable satisfaction of the designer.[100] The dangers to an employer in having wording which imports conclusiveness into certificates of an architect or engineer is amply demonstrated by the case *Ata Ul Haq v The City Council of Nairobi.*[101] Ata Ul Haq was contractor engaged to build 17 blocks on a housing estate for the City of Nairobi. Amongst other things the contract between the parties contained the following terms:

> **7(iv)** When the Works have been completely executed according to the provisions of the Contract and to the satisfaction of the Engineer, the date of such completion shall be certified by him, and such date shall be the date of commencement of such period of maintenance as may be provided by the Contract.

It was held by the Privy Council that the whole scheme of the contract demonstrated that a certificate issued under clause 7(iv) was intended to be conclusive 'as to the sufficiency of the work in all respects' and thereby terminated the contractor's liability, subject only the maintenance period provisions. A similar conclusion was drawn in *Colbart Ltd v H Kumar,*[102] *Crown Estate Commissioners v John Mowlem*[103] and *London Borough of Barking & Dagenham v Terrapin.*[104] All these decisions were on the particular facts and on the particular contract involved, and many current standard forms produce a different outcome.[105] Nevertheless, any consultant undertaking a certification role should check what the effect of any certificate would be, clearly if it is conclusive that the consequences of it being issued negligently will be far more serious for the client.

8.6.3 Nature of the duty

A designer will not be liable for negligent inspection if he or she fails to discover every single defect in a contractor's work. The question in every case is whether the designer exhibited the degree of skill that an ordinary competent designer would exhibit in the same circumstances. It follows that the duty may vary according to the circumstances

---

[100] *National Coal Board v William Neill & Son* (1984) 26 BLR 81.
[101] (1962) 28 BLR 76 (PC).
[102] (1992) 59 BLR 89.
[103] (1994) 70 BLR 1 (CA).
[104] [2000] BLR 479.
[105] It should be noted that the JCT has amended the relevant wording in its contracts, so that the certificates are only conclusive as specifically stated in the relevant clause, see section 14.3.1.

and laying down rigid guidelines as to what is appropriate in general is impossible. A useful indication of the way in which a court approaches the problem was given by Lord Upjohn in the case of *East Ham Corporation v Bernard Sunley & Sons Ltd*:[106]

> As is well known, the architect is not permanently on the site but appears at intervals, it may be of a week or a fortnight, and he has, of course, to inspect the progress of the works. When he arrives on the site there may be many very important matters with which he has to deal: the work may be getting behindhand through labour troubles; some of the suppliers of materials or the subcontractors may be lagging; there may be physical trouble on the site itself, such as, for example, finding an unexpected amount of underground water. All these are matters which may call for important decisions by the architect. He may, in such circumstances, think that he knows the builders sufficiently well and can rely upon them to carry out a good job; that it is more important that he should deal with urgent matters on site than he should make a minute inspection on site to see that the builder is complying with the specification laid down by him ... it by no means follows that, in failing to discover a defect which a reasonable examination would have disclosed, in fact the architect was necessarily thereby in breach of duty to the building owner so as to be liable in an action for negligence. It may well be that the omission of the architect to find the defect was due to no more than an error of judgment, or was a deliberately calculated risk which, in all the circumstances of the case was reasonable and proper.[107]

It is evident from that speech, and other cases, that the courts do not take a rigid view of the designer's duty to supervise or inspect: it must be reasonable in all the circumstances. However, it has been held that extent and frequency of inspections must enable the architect to be in a position to properly certify that the construction work has been carried out in accordance with the contract.[108]

8.6.4 Competence of the contractor

The relationship between the degree of supervision to be expected of an architect and the competence of the contractor was considered in a case heard by Judge Stabb QC, *Sutcliffe v Chippendale and Edmondson*.[109] This case subsequently went to the Court of Appeal when it became known as *Sutcliffe v Thackrah*[110] but the statements of the Judge on this aspect of the dispute were not involved in the appeal.

> ... the building owner is entitled to expect his architect so to administer the contract and supervise the work, [so] as to ensure, as far as is reasonably possible, that the quality of the work matches up to the standard contemplated ....
>
> I think that the degree of supervision required must be governed to some extent by his confidence in the contractor. If and when something occurs which should indicate to [the

---

[106] [1965] 3 All ER 619.
[107] ibid., Lord Upjohn at 636.
[108] *Jameson v Simon* (1899) 1 F (Ct of Session) 1211.
[109] (1971) 18 BLR 149.
[110] 4 BLR 16 (HL).

architect] a lack of competence in the contractor, then, in the interests of the employer, the standard of his supervision should be higher. No-one suggests that the architect is required to tell a contractor how his work is to be done, nor is the architect responsible for the manner in which the contractor does the work. What his supervisory duty does require of him is to follow the progress of the work and to take steps to see that those works comply with the general requirements of the contract in specification and quality. If he should fail to exercise his professional care and skill in this respect, he would be liable to his employer for any damage attributed to that failure.[111]

In *Brown and Brown v Gilbert-Scott and Payne*[112] an Official Referee had to deal with the issue of a duty to 'supervise' an inexperienced builder. Tenders had been sought for the construction of a conservatory but they were all over budget and that was how the inexperienced builder came to be appointed. Extensive and expensive remedial works were required. The court found that an inexperienced builder required more supervision than a more experienced one would have done, and that the architect's duty was to give that supervision even though he had to travel a long distance and was working on a low profit. It was said that the architect should have been present at crucial stages such as the laying of the damp proof membrane.

8.6.5 Contractor's method of working

In very general terms, the duty is to see that the contractor constructs the work in accordance with the contractual obligation of the contractor to the employer. It must be emphasised that the designer's duty as to inspection is normally owed to the employer and not to the contractor: the designer's duty of care does not extend to how the contractor carries out its work. An early example is *Clayton v Woodman & Son (Builders) Ltd.*[113] An architect refused to vary contract works which involved alterations to an existing building, but was held not liable to one of the contractor's workmen when a part of the building fell on him. Pearson LJ said:

> [The architect's] function is to make sure that in the end, when the work has been completed, the owner will have a building properly constructed in accordance with the contract and plans and specifications and drawings and any supplementary instructions which the architect may have given. The architect does not undertake . . . to advise the builders as to what safety precautions should be taken or, in particular, as to how he should carry out his building operations.[114]

A similar view was expressed in *Sutcliffe v Thackrah*[115] and in *Oldschool v Gleeson (Construction) Ltd*:[116]

---

[111] (1971) 18 BLR 149 at 162.
[112] (1992) 35 Con LR 120.
[113] (1962) 4 BLR 65 (CA).
[114] ibid., at 77.
[115] 4 BLR 16 (HL).
[116] (1976) 4 BLR 103.

Not only has he no duty to instruct the builder how to do the work, or what safety precautions to take, but he has no right to do so; nor is he under any duty to the builder to detect faults during the progress of the work. The architect, in that respect, may be in breach of his duty to his client, the building owner, but this does not excuse the builder for faulty work.[117]

However there are exceptions to this general rule. A designer could, for example, be liable in tort for causing injury through negligent inspection. In *Oldschool* the court found that an architect may be obliged to a builder if unsafe methods are being adopted.[118] In *Clay v Crump*,[119] an architect was found liable to a workman when a wall collapsed and injured the workman, and killed several others (the liability was shared with the contractors). The architect had allowed the wall to remain standing although the drawings had indicated it should be demolished. The architect accepted the demolition contractor's assurance that the wall was safe, and did not inspect it himself.

In an Australian case, *Florida Hotels Pty v Mayo*[120] where the circumstances were unusual, architects were held liable in respect of injured workmen. The architects were engaged to supervise the execution of construction work and did not see reinforcement that had been wrongly fixed before the concrete was placed in the formwork. When the formwork was removed several workmen were injured by the collapse of the reinforced concrete. There was no contractor, the employer having employed workmen direct. It was held that:

(1) the architects were in breach of duty in failing to supervise;
(2) the architects must have had in their contemplation when carrying out their supervising duties that the employer would suffer loss in the event that workmen were injured; and,
(3) the architects were liable to the employer in respect of the damages paid by the employer to injured workmen.

Hart Investments v Fidler (No 2)[121] arose after part of the front and side façades of a building in Muswell Hill collapsed. The scheme was one to develop two terraced properties, and, as is often the case, the planning authority required the façades to be retained, even though a large part of the building was entirely re-built. A new double basement was also excavated, but the contractor did not install adequate temporary shoring as shown on the method statement drawings. The engineer was found liable to the client (in contract and tort) for failing to take any action when he observed that the temporary works that had been designed by the contractor were in a dangerous state. The Judge stated:

In my judgement if an engineer employed by an owner in respect of permanent works observes a state of temporary works which is dangerous and causing immediate peril to the permanent

[117] ibid., HHJ Stabb QC, at 131.
[118] ibid., at 124.
[119] (1963) 4 BLR 80 (CA).
[120] (1965) 113 CLR 588 (Australia: High Court).
[121] (2007) 112 Con LR 33.

works in respect of which he is employed, he is obliged to take such steps as are open to him to obviate that danger. It seems to me that that follows, partly as a matter of common sense, but also because the engineer is, after all, instructed in relation to the permanent works as a whole. It would appear strange if he is under a duty to take such steps as he can to see that they survive for say, the next 25 years, or whatever the design life for the building is, but is not obliged to take any steps to warn of an immediate danger to those works caused by an imperilling act by the contractor.[122]

The above cases represent an extreme position because of their unusual facts, in that they all involved a serious risk to health and safety. Under normal circumstances it is doubtful whether a court would ever find that a designer was responsible for working methods. However it would seem sensible for a consultant to raise any significant concerns with the contractor (in addition to any duties they might have with respect to CDM).

8.6.6 Delegation of supervision duties

It is commonplace on modern construction projects for supervision work to be carried out by clerks of works or resident engineers or inspectors. Various aspects of the supervision process may be handled by these people and their positions and authority are sometimes set out in the construction contract. The question arises as to whether the delegation of these duties relieves the designer of any part of his or her liability. In order to answer this question, it is necessary to look at the two ways in which delegation takes place because the legal consequences are different.

8.6.6.1 *Employees of the designer*

It is not unusual in civil engineering contracts for the resident engineer to be an employee of the engineer although it is very much less common for the clerk of the works to be an employee of the architect. In any event, the position where a designer delegates to an employee some or all of the supervisory duties is reasonably straightforward. The designer will remain liable for the acts and omissions of the employee, both under the law of contract, and under the law of tort on the principle of vicarious liability. The designer cannot escape liability even in circumstances where the employee acted for his or her own benefit such as, for example, taking a bribe or turning a blind eye.[123] Where the designer has instructed the employee as to the way in which the supervision should be carried out, the designer will not escape liability if the employee ignores those instructions.[124] However, the overriding principle still applies that the designer will not necessarily be held liable for failing to inspect every aspect of the construction process or failing to detect every minor piece of poor workmanship.

---

[122] ibid., Mr Recorder Roger Stewart QC, at para. 22.
[123] *Lloyd v Grace, Smith & Co.* [1912] AC 716.
[124] *London County Council v Cattermoles (Garages) Ltd* [1953] 1 WLR 997.

8.6.6.2 *Employees of the employer*

It is common for the clerk of the works and, sometimes, the resident engineer to be an employee of the employer rather than of the designer, although the latter may have a say in the selection of an appropriate person, and in the terms and conditions of engagement. In such circumstances, it has been held that consultants cannot delegate matters of importance so as to divest themselves of responsibility but can delegate matters of minor importance.

In the case of *Leicester Board of Guardians v Trollope*[125] architects were engaged to design and to supervise the construction of new buildings for a hospital in Leicestershire. Extensive dry rot in the floors was discovered four years after the work was completed. It was found that the cause of the dry rot was that the timber joists had been supported on pegs driven into the ground, through which moisture could pass, before laying of concrete, instead of joists being placed on previously laid concrete. The architects denied that it was their duty to supervise the laying of the concrete, saying that was the duty of the clerk of works. The court found that the duty of a clerk of works was to supervise the details of the work; the work complained of here was not such a detail and the architects were liable.

In the *Leicester Guardians* case expert evidence had been given to the court that an architect's duty was to supervise the general scheme and that the clerk of works' duty was to see that the details of construction were properly carried out. The court adopted that evidence and the trial Judge said:

> The defence is that this dry rot was the fault of the clerk of the works. That is so in one sense. It clearly was the duty of the clerk of the works to attend to the laying of concrete in accordance with the design, but does that relieve the defendant? To my mind there is little difficulty in deciding the point. The position of the architect and of the clerk of the works was made quite clear. The details were to be supervised by the clerk of the works. The architect could not be at the works all the time, and it was for that reason that the clerk of the works was employed to protect the building owner . . . If the architect had taken steps to see that the first block was all right, and had then told the clerk of the works that the work in the others was to be carried out in the same way, I would have been inclined to hold that the architect had done his duty; but in fact he did nothing to see that the design was complied with. In my view, this was not a matter of detail which could be left to the clerk of the works. It may have been natural to leave it to him, but in my judgment it was an omission to do that which it was his duty to do . . . .[126]

Further support for the view that only minor matters can be delegated, so as to relieve the designer of responsibility, is to be found in the even older case of *Lee v Bateman*.[127] There, the architects were engaged in relation to the restoration of the kitchen wing of a mansion house after a fire. The architects left it to the clerk of works, who was employed by the employer, to decide whether new beams were required. It was held

---

[125] (1911) 75 JP 197.
[126] ibid., Mr Justice Chalmell.
[127] *The Times*, 31 October 1893 (unreported).

that, although the architects were not liable for the negligence of the clerk of works, the question as to whether new beams were required or not was one that the architects should have answered and not the clerk of works.

It may be that the clerk of works or resident engineer appointed by the employer is incompetent. However, such incompetence will not usually provide a defence to a claim against the designer for breach of a duty to supervise, at least in circumstances where the designer relied on the clerk of works or engineer, knowing that they were incompetent or unreliable.[128] It follows from these cases that the designers will usually be liable for breach of duty in supervision if they:

(1) purport to delegate a matter which they should not have delegated but rather should have seen to personally;[129]
(2) purport to delegate where they should have given instructions as to how the supervision was to be carried out, but failed to give such instructions;[130]
(3) rely on an unreliable clerk of works or resident engineer when they know that that clerk of works or resident engineer is unreliable.[131]

A further and important point arises in relation to the effect of the negligence of a clerk of works employed by the employer on any claim that the employer may make in relation to defects against a contractor. This point was considered in *Kensington and Chelsea and Westminster Area Health Authority v Wettern Composites and Adams, Holden and Pearson.*[132] In this case, the court found that the clerk of works had been negligent in his supervision and inspection duties. He was employed by the employer but was under the control and direction of the architect, a very common approach to the appointment of a clerk of the works. Judge David Smout QC, Official Referee, said that:

> The clerk of works by the very nature of his occupation carries out his duties at the premises of the building owner and for the protection and interests of the building owner. In those circumstances, it would need strong evidence indeed to displace the inference that the clerk of works was acting otherwise than as the servant of the building owner. There is no such evidence in this case. In my view the plaintiffs are vicariously liable for the negligence of the clerk of works.[133]

It followed from this that the burden of proof rested on the employer plaintiffs to shift the *prima facie* responsibility for the negligence of the servant employed and paid by them, and the Judge applied *Mersey Docks and Harbour Board v Coggins and Griffiths (Liverpool) Ltd.*[134] The Judge then went on to reduce the damages recoverable from the

---

[128] *Saunders v Broadstairs Local Board* (1890) Hudson's Building Contracts 4th edn, 1914, vol. 2, p. 164.
[129] *Leicester Board of Guardians v Trollope* (1911) 75 JP 197; *Lee v Bateman* The Times, 31 October 1893.
[130] *Leicester Board of Guardians v Trollope* (1911) 75 JP 197.
[131] ibid.
[132] (1985) 1 Con LR 114.
[133] ibid., at 139.
[134] [1947] AC 1.

architect defendants by 20 per cent in respect of this negligence by the plaintiffs'
employee, the clerk of works. The Judge put it this way:

> I have reached the conclusion that the clerk of works' negligence whilst more than minimal
> is very much less than that of the architects. If I may adapt the military terminology: it was
> the negligence of the chief petty officer as compared with that of the captain of the ship. I
> assess responsibility as to the clerk of works at 20% and as to the architects at 80% by reason
> of the vicarious liability of the plaintiff [employer] I make a finding of contributory negligence
> of 20%.[135]

8.6.7 Certification: Quality not quantity

One of the purposes of supervision and inspection is to enable the consultant to give
proper certificates both as to interim and final payment.[136] For example, the JCT SBC11
contract requires the architect to state the sum due on an interim certificate (cl. 4.10.1)
and the main ingredient of the value on that certificate is 'the total value of the work
properly executed' by the contractor (cl. 4.16.1.1). The phrase 'properly executed'
should be noted, i.e. non-compliant or defective work should not be included in the
valuation. If a quantity surveyor prepares the valuation, the onus is on the architect to
inform the quantity surveyor of any relevant problems with the work. An example can
be seen in *Sutcliffe v Chippendale and Edmondson*[137] where the court stated:

> . . . I readily accept that any prolonged or detailed inspection or measurement at interim stage
> is impracticable, and not to be expected. On the other hand… the issuing of certificates is to
> continuing process, leaving each time a limited amount of work to be inspected and I should
> have thought that more than a glance round was to be expected. Furthermore, since everyone
> agreed that the quality of the work was always the responsibility of the architect and never
> that of the quantity surveyor and since work properly executed is the work for which a progress
> payment is being recommended, I think that the architect is in duty bound to notify the
> quantity surveyor in advance of any work which he, the architect, classifies as not properly
> executed.[138]

A recent example of this can be seen in *Dhamija v Sunningdale Joineries Ltd,
Lewandowski Willcox Ltd, McBains Cooper Consulting Ltd*.[139] The claimants brought an
action arising out of alleged defects in the design and construction of their home; the
action was brought against the building contractor, the architect, and the quantity
surveyor (McBains). There had been no written or oral contract with the quantity
surveyors, so the terms of their engagement were those that would be implied. The

---

[135] (1985) 1 Con LR 114, at 139.
[136] *Jameson v Simon* (1899) 1 F (Ct of Session) 1211.
[137] ibid.
[138] *Sutcliffe v Chippendale and Edmondson* (1971) 18 BLR 149, at 166.
[139] [2010] EWHC 2396 (TCC).

claimants argued that there was an implied term that the quantity surveyors would only value work that had been properly executed by the contractor and was not obviously defective.

Coulson J held that the quantity surveyor's contract of retainer included an implied term that the quantity surveyor should act with the reasonable skill and care of quantity surveyors of ordinary competence and experience when valuing the works properly executed for the purposes of interim certificates. The term was implied in order to give the contract business efficacy. However, the Judge held that the QS would not owe an implied duty to exclude the value of defective works from valuations, however obvious the defects. This was the exclusive responsibility of the architect appointed under the contract. Further, the QS owed no implied duty to report the existence of defects to the architect.

8.6.8 The nature and frequency of inspections

Judge Bowsher QC, Official Referee, had to deal with the issue of what constitutes adequate supervision in *Corfield v Grant & Others*.[140] This case arose, as do so many others, from an architect suing for his fees. The client counterclaimed for damages for breach of contract, including damages for failure adequately to supervise. It is on this point alone that the case is reported. The judge said:

> What is adequate by way of supervision and other work is not in the end to be tested by the number of hours worked on site or elsewhere, but by asking whether it was enough. At some stages of some jobs exclusive attention may be required to the job in question (either in the office or on site): at other stages of the same jobs, or during most of the duration of other jobs, it will be quite sufficient to give attention to the job only from time to time. The proof of the pudding was in the eating. Was the attention given enough for this particular job?[141]

He went on to discuss the facts of this case against that statement and in particular the large amount of work facing the architect on this job in a relatively short space of time. Then, he said:

> Plainly one man could not do all these things at once. He needed at least one, skilled and experienced assistant. One of the complaints, which I find justified is that the [architect] did not have a skilled and experienced assistant. For this job, he used [an assistant] who had previously had only a few months experience in training in an architect's office . . . an expert witness on behalf of the [architect], described the job as a 'controlled muddle', meaning to refer to the need to do everything at once. For my part, I would not go so far as to refer to it as an uncontrolled muddle, but it was inadequately controlled muddle and in that regard the [architect] was in continuous breach of contract.[142]

---

[140] (1992) 29 Con LR 58; 59 BLR 102.
[141] ibid., at 119.
[142] ibid., at 120.

Where there is an obligation to supervise, therefore, being too busy on other aspects of the project or not having enough staff of appropriate experience for the project will not constitute any sort of defence to an allegation of negligent supervision.

The question of 'how much is enough' arose again a few years later. The case of *George Fischer Holdings Ltd v Multi Design Consultants Ltd and Davis Langdon & Everest*,[143] concerned defects in the roof of a new warehousing complex. The design was largely undertaken by Multi Design Consultants, with Davis Langdon & Everest (DLE) taking on the role of quantity surveyors and employer's representative. Included in DLE's appointment was a requirement to 'make visits to the site sufficient to monitor the Contractor's workmanship and progress; to check on the use of materials, to check on the works conformity to the Specifications and drawings and to report generally on the progress and quality of the works having regard to the terms of the Contract between the Employer and the Contractor'. The roof had been designed to have a very low pitch of 1.5 degrees, and the cladding material to have lap joints. The court decided that although the pitch was at the lower limits of what was acceptable, if detailed properly, it would nevertheless have been watertight. However the use of laps could and ought to have been avoided, as 'to make every lap joint perfectly is difficult and expensive and unlikely to be achieved by the ordinary standards of workmanship and ordinary levels of supervision which suffice in less extreme conditions'. The Judge in addition found DLE to be negligent, stating:

> DLE made no visits to the roof whatever during the period when the panels were being laid and the lap joints formed, so they were undeniably in gross breach of duty. Mr Gardiner's only excuse for that omission was that access was not safe. That is obviously no answer; he was entitled to require the contractor to provide safe access . . . the formation of the joints was so obviously crucial that even if the overall frequency of visits was not increased special attention should have been paid to ensuring that they fully covered this aspect. But . . . since this whole discussion predicates the acceptance by DLE of the very risky and inadvisable inclusion of lap joints in such shallow slopes, it was incumbent upon them to exercise the closest and most rigorous inspection and supervision of the process. The last point also disposes of the suggestion that workmen will 'put on a show' either they cannot do that all the time, or if they do that achieves the object anyway. Moreover it is any event part of the necessary skill of a competent inspecting officer to detect and make allowances for such behaviour.[144]

These comments were approved by the court in *Ian McGlinn v Waltham Contractors Ltd & Others*.[145] This case concerned a house in Jersey called '*Maison d'Or*' that was designed and built for the claimant, Mr McGlinn. The house took three years to build, but after it was substantially complete, it sat empty for the next three years whilst defects were investigated. It was completely demolished in 2005 having never been lived in, and was not rebuilt. Mr McGlinn brought an action against the various consultants, includ-

---

[143] (1998) 61 Con LR 85.
[144] ibid., at paras 136–137.
[145] (2007) 111 Con LR 1 (CA).

ing the architects, and the contractor, claiming that *Maison d'Or* was so badly designed, and so badly built, that he was entitled to demolish it and start again. The contractor however had gone into administration and played no part in the hearing.

The architect's terms of appointment were disputed, but the court concluded that these were on the RIBA Standard Form of Appointment 1982 edition, as amended 1990, and included a duty to make periodic inspections of the works. After examining the various authorities[146] Peter Coulson QC, LJ usefully summarised the principles relating to inspection as follows:

a) The frequency and duration of inspections should be tailored to the nature of the works going on at site from time to time: see *Corfield v Grant* and para. 8-240 of Jackson & Powell. Thus it seems to me that it is not enough for the inspecting professional religiously to carry out an inspection of the work either before or after the fortnightly or monthly site meetings, and not otherwise. The dates of such site meetings may well have been arranged some time in advance, without any reference to the particular elements of work being progressed on site at the time. Moreover, if inspections are confined to the fortnightly or monthly site meetings, the contractor will know that, at all other times, his work will effectively remain safe from inspection.

b) Depending on the importance of the particular element or stage of the works, the inspecting professional can instruct the contractor not to cover up the relevant elements of the work until they have been inspected: see *Florida Hotels Pty Ltd v Mayo* (1965) 113 CLR 588 and para. 8-241 of Jackson & Powell. However, it seems to me that such a situation would be unlikely to arise in most cases because, if the inspecting officer is carrying out inspections which are tailored to the nature of the works proceeding on site at any particular time, he will have timed his inspections in such a manner as to avoid affecting the progress of those works.

c) The mere fact that defective work is carried out and covered up between inspections will not, therefore, automatically amount to a defence to an alleged failure on the part of the architect to carry out proper inspections; that will depend on a variety of matters, including the inspecting officer's reasonable contemplation of what was being carried out on site at the time, the importance of the element of work in question, and the confidence that the architect may have in the contractor's overall competence: see *Sutcliffe v Chippendale* and para. 8-242 of Jackson & Powell.

d) If the element of the work is important because it is going to be repeated throughout one significant part of the building, such as the construction of a proprietary product or the achievement of a particular standard of finish to one element of the work common to every room, then the inspecting professional should ensure that he has seen that element of the work in the early course of construction/assembly so as to form a view as to the contractor's ability to carry out that particular task: see *George Fischer*.

e) However, even then, reasonable examination of the works does not require the inspector to go into every matter in detail; indeed, it is almost inevitable that some defects will escape his notice: see *East Ham Corporation v Bernard Sunley* [1966] AC 406 and para. 8-239 of Jackson & Powell.

---

[146] In addition to those listed in the quoted passage the Judge had also considered *Consarc Design Ltd v Hutch Investments Ltd* [2002] 83 Con LR 36.

f) It can sometimes be the case that an employer with a claim for bad workmanship against a contractor makes the same claim automatically against the inspecting officer, on the assumption that, if there is a defect, then the inspector must have been negligent or in breach of contract for missing the defect during construction. That seems to me to be a misconceived approach. The architect does not guarantee that his inspection will reveal or prevent all defective work: see *Corfield v Grant*. It is not appropriate to judge an architect's performance by the result achieved: see para. 8-238 of Jackson & Powell.[147]

The advice above, as it was given in the context of an appointment that referred to 'periodic inspections', is both useful and of considerable significance to architects and others who have undertaken to provide this service. In particular, consultants should note that inspections should be arranged according to progress, and not merely to coincide with the periodic site meetings, and the importance of 'ensuring' that a timely inspection is made of any element of work or detail which will be repeated.

8.7 Duty to review the design

Once a design is complete, a question may arise as to whether the designer has any duty to re-visit and check the decisions made. When a claim is brought against a designer some years after the services were undertaken the claimant may argue, for example, that not only was the design flawed, but that the consultant was negligent in failing to subsequently check that design. This is often raised in the hope that, although it may be too late to bring a claim regarding the first breach, the limitation period may not yet have expired for the second.

As a general rule, once a professional's duties are discharged, he or she is not under a continuing obligation to re-visit their activities and search for errors. As explained in *Midland Bank Trust Co. Ltd v Hett, Stubbs & Kemp*, 'It is not seriously arguable that a solicitor who or whose firm has acted negligently comes under a continuing duty to take care to remind himself of the negligence of which, *ex hypothesi*, he is unaware.'[148]

Nevertheless, in the context of construction, reference is often made to a 'continuing duty' to check the design. An early case establishing this duty is that of *Brickfield Properties v Newton*[149] where it was stated:

> Where there are found in completed buildings serious defects of the type here under review the facts relating to design, execution and superintendence are inextricably entangled until such time as the court succeeds in elucidating the position through evidence. The design has inevitably to be closely examined even if the only claim relates to superintendence, and all the more so if the designs are, as is alleged here, experimental or such as need amplification as the

---

[147] (2007) 111 Con LR 1, at 7, para. 218.
[148] [1979] Ch 384, Oliver J, at 403C.
[149] [1971] 1 WLR 862.

construction progresses. The architect is under a continuing duty to check that his design will work in practice and to correct any errors which may emerge. It savours of the ridiculous for the architect to be able to say, as it was here suggested that he could say: 'True, my design was faulty but, of course, I saw to it that the contractors followed it faithfully' and be enabled on that ground to succeed in the action.[150]

The above passage refers to a 'continuing duty'; subsequent case law has shed light on what precisely is the nature and extent of this obligation.

8.7.1 The nature of the duty

Brickfield was followed in *London Borough of Merton v Lowe & Pickford*,[151] which concerned the application of the product Pyrok (a proprietary plaster top coat specified by the architects) to the walls and ceilings of a swimming pool. Practical completion was certified and the architects inspected at the end of the rectification period and found cracks in ceilings in nine rooms. Investigations had by then shown that the problem might be due to the base layers being a much weaker mix than the Pyrok (who had by now revealed the specification for this mix). The architects asked the deputy pool manager to keep an eye on the problem. They did not carry out any other further investigation. A final certificate was issued in May 1973, following which further cracks appeared. The pool was closed to the public as it was determined to be unsafe, and the whole ceiling was taken down and replaced.

The Judge at first instance (Judge Stabb QC) found that the architects were negligent in not realising at a much earlier stage what the problem might be, in checking the design in 1967 when the first cracks appeared, and in instigating appropriate investigations. They were also negligent in issuing the final certificate. He commented on the point at which the duty might appear:

I consider that the architect was responsible for the design and that that responsibility was a continuing one in the sense that, if he subsequently discovered that what he may initially have been justified in assuming was an adequate design was in fact a defective design, his responsibility remains.

And concluded:

I am now satisfied that the architect's duty of design is a continuing one, and it seems to me that the subsequent discovery of a defect in the design, initially and unjustifiably thought to have been suitable, reactivated or revived the architect's duty in relation to design and imposed upon them the duty to take such steps as were necessary to correct the result of that initially defective design.[152]

---

[150] ibid., at 973 E–F, *per* Sachs LJ.
[151] (1981) 18 BLR 130.
[152] ibid., quoted in BLR commentary at 130.

This decision was upheld in the Court of Appeal, where Eveleigh LJ stated:

> I accept that it is by no means going to follow that if one patch of a ceiling in one room is defective the ceilings in the whole house, as it were, are also going to be faulty; but when you have it in nine different rooms and it reveals the standard of workmanship of the people engaged in those nine rooms, and when those people are the same people who are responsible for the other large room – in other words, the pool in this case – to my mind there is evidence on which to suspect that the fault is not an isolated one but may run throughout the building.[153]

The decision in *Brickfield* was also followed in *Equitable Debenture Assets Corporation Ltd v William Moss Group Ltd*[154] where there were ongoing problems during construction of leaking patent glazing. Judge Newey, QC, held that an architect's obligation in respect of the design was not a once and for all obligation performed when a complete set of working drawings was concluded. The architects had both the right and the duty to check their initial design as work proceeded and to correct it if it was necessary.

In both the above cases serious problems occurred which would give the designer cause for concern. Neither therefore needed to address the question as to whether the duty to review required a 'trigger' event, or whether it was ongoing on all projects, although Judge Stabb's reference to the duty being 'reactivated or revived' suggested a trigger is needed.

The case of *New Islington and Hackney Housing Association Ltd v Pollard Thomas Edwards Ltd*,[155] has largely settled this question. Pollard Thomas Edwards (PTE) were appointed as architects in 1990 under the RIBA standard conditions of engagement to design and supervise the construction of six properties in London N5. PTE were to provide the 'Normal Services', which included: 'Making periodic visits to the site . . . issuing certificates and . . . Accepting the building on behalf of the client'. The construction work was let under two building contracts, both on the JCT IFC84 Standard Form. PTE certified practical completion in January and March 1992 under the two contracts, followed by certificates of making good defects, and final certificates in February 1993 and January 1994.

After practical completion, but before the final certificates, tenants complained about the noise levels in the blocks of flats, and in December 1992 the Association wrote to PTE asking it for details of the design and specification for soundproofing insulation and whether it complied with the Building Regulations. The architects set out the specification, and stated the information 'was part of the Full Plan Building Regulations approval received and was subject to the normal site inspections carried out by the District Surveyor.' PTE however did not investigate the complaint or review its design, and failed to discover that it had made an error and that the design did not in fact comply with the regulations.

---

[153] ibid., at 141.
[154] (1984) 2 Con LR 1.
[155] [2001] 1 BLR 74.

The Housing Association brought an action against the architects regarding the soundproofing of all six buildings, which it claimed to be inadequate in that it failed to meet the standards prescribed by the Building Regulations. PTE denied liability, and also argued that the claim was time-barred. The judgment dealt only with the limitation issues, but in doing so had to consider the extent of the duty to review.

The Housing Association argued that the architect was under a duty to review the design until the end of its retainer, i.e. the issue of final certificates. The Judge acknowledged that 'The express terms do not include the duty of keeping the design under review, still less do they include the duty of reviewing the design after practical completion and the handing over of the building'[156] but noted the certification duties of the architect following practical completion.

He then conducted a review of earlier cases and confirmed that, although it is necessary to look at the circumstances of each engagement, a designer who also supervises or inspects work will generally be obliged to review that design up until that design has been included in the work.[157] However he held that the architect is not under a duty specifically to review that design following its incorporation, unless something occurs to make it necessary, or at least prudent, for a reasonably competent architect to do so. He outlined some possible circumstances as follows:

> For example, a specific duty might arise if, before completion, the inadequacy of the foundations causes the building to show signs of distress; or if the architect reads an article which shows that the materials that he has specified for the foundations are not fit for their purpose; or if he learns from some other source that the design is dangerous. In such circumstances, I am in no doubt that the architect would be under a duty to review the design.[158]

The case therefore confirms that after the design in question has been constructed, there may be circumstances that reactivate a duty to review the design, and that these could include actual knowledge of a defect, or of a change in the 'state of the art' understanding in the industry regarding that design. The need for a trigger event was subsequently confirmed in *Payne v John Setchell Ltd* by Judge Humphrey LLoyd QC:

> It is now in my view well established that a designer's continuing duty of care only requires a reconsideration of the design if the designer becomes aware or should have been aware of the need to reconsider the design.[159]

This passage touches on an important issue, i.e. whether the trigger event must actually have come to the attention of the architect, or whether it would be enough that it was something the architect ought to have been aware of. The previous edition of this book suggested that the continuing duty probably includes any relevant matters which become known to the construction industry in general, and cited a hypothetical example of a commonly used 1960's brickwork detail where brick slips were stuck to the face of

---

[156] ibid., Dyson J, at para. 15.
[157] Referring to *Jackson and Powell on Professional Negligence*, 4th edn, paras 2–17.
[158] [2001] 1 BLR 74 at para. 16.
[159] [2002] BLR 489, TCC, at para. 21.

concrete slabs. The author considered that 'although it may not have been negligence to specify brick slips without a movement joint prior to the knowledge becoming generally available to the industry, it would be negligent to permit construction to proceed on the basis of such a detail in circumstances where the designer had discovered or ought to have discovered after design, but before construction, that the detail would be likely to fail'.[160] It would seem that the awareness of possible would be even higher where the design was particularly innovative. For example, in *Department of National Heritage v Steensen Varming Mulcahy*,[161] one of the matters asserted was that the lid-down trunking system used for electrical cables was experimental. Although Judge Bowsher QC did not accept this, he nevertheless agreed in principle that 'if a designer adopts an experimental or unusual approach, the duty on him to keep his design under review, is particularly high'.[162]

It would seem logical, given that the standard of care is normally to be assessed objectively, that the duty should arise not at the point when the designer actually becomes aware of the trigger, but when the designer ought to have become aware.[163]

8.7.2 How long does the duty last?

While the design and technical details are being developed, any mistake by a consultant would probably be characterised as simply a design error, rather than a failure to review the design. An example of this can be seen in *Mirant Asia Pacific Construction (Hong Kong) Ltd v Oapil.*[164] Ove Arup was held liable for negligent design of foundations, which included both the original design, and for failing to verify the initial calculation assumptions during the course of construction, when they were engaged as inspecting engineers. As the initial calculations were preliminary, the 'verification' duty was considered part of the normal design finalisation process, not as a separate duty to review, with the court commenting 'In the context of this case, this obligation existed irrespective of the obligation noted in *Brickfield Properties v Newton* . . . where Sachs LJ held that an architect's duty in respect of design continues until the building is constructed.[165]

However, once the design is finalised, a failure to review following an appropriate trigger event would be considered a new breach. An example of this distinction can be seen in *Oxford Architects Partnership v Cheltenham Ladies College*[166] where the court stated:

---

[160] David L Cornes, *Design Liability in the Construction Industry*, 4th edn (Oxford: Blackwell Science Publications, 1994).
[161] (1998) 60 Con LR 33.
[162] at para. 140.
[163] See the very useful discussion of this and other points in Nissen A (2008), 'Designer's Duty – a time for review', Society of Construction Law (Paper 151).
[164] (2004) 97 Con LR 1 (TCC); the point regarding *Brickfield* was not mentioned in the appeal, but the general approach was approved: [2005] EWCA Civ 1585; (2006) 1 BLR 187; 105 Con LR 1.
[165] ibid., at para. 494.
[166] [2007] BLR 293.

If an architect produces a design which is in breach of the terms of engagement and issues it to the contractor who constructs the work to that design, then a breach of contract will occur when, for instance, the architect under stages F to G 'prepares production drawings' or under stage J 'provides production information' as required by the building contract, a cause of action will then accrue based upon that breach of contract.

The continuing duty does not, however, give rise to a single and continually accruing cause of action. Rather, a different cause of action accrues at various stages. Thus, the cause of action for a failure properly to review the design is a different cause of action from a failure to provide a proper design in the first place. The causes of action will therefore accrue on different dates.'[167]

A key question is, therefore, for how long after the design has been finalised must the designer remain vigilant to possible trigger events? Does the duty extend to practical completion, or perhaps beyond, to the final certificate?

In *Equitable Debenture Assets Corporation Ltd v William Moss Group Ltd & Others*[168] Judge Newey, QC, suggested that it might end when the building reached practical completion. However as in that case the defects appeared before practical completion, the duty was expressed in general terms, and the case did not finally decide the point.

The authorities were reviewed by Judge Peter Bowsher QC in *University Court of Glasgow v W. Whitfield and John Laing Construction Ltd.*[169] The case concerned a claim against an architect in the design of the Hunterian Art Gallery adjacent to the University Library of Glasgow University. W. Whitfield was selected as the architect for the project in 1969, having carried out preliminary design work in the 1960s, but due to difficulties in obtaining funds, were not instructed to proceed with design work until March 1971. The contract was let in 1972 on the then current JCT Standard Form of Contract. Work began in 1973 and practical completion took place on 16 June 1978. No final certificate was ever issued. The gallery was formally opened in two stages in 1980 and 1981. From August 1978 onwards, there was water ingress into the building as a result of leaks and condensation. It was only in 1981 that the extent of the problem became apparent, and the architects were subsequently consulted about the cause of the problem. Because the action was brought at some time after the events, it was necessary to consider the point at which the duty to review might cease. Judge Bowsher QC reviewed the various authorities, and concluded:

> [where] an architect has had drawn to his attention that damage has resulted from a design which he knew or ought to have known was bad from the start, he has a particular duty to his client to disclose what he had been under a continuing duty to reveal, namely what he knows of the design defects as possible causes of the problem.[170]

---

[167] ibid., Mr Justice Ramsey at paras 28 and 29.
[168] (1984) 2 Con LR 1.
[169] (1988) 42 BLR 66.
[170] ibid., at 78.

He also said that:

> The judgments of His Honour Judge Newey QC in *Equitable Debenture Assets Corporation Limited v Moss* (1984) 1 CLJ 131 and *Manchester University v Moss* (1984) 1 CLJ 162 are not authorities for the proposition put forward on behalf of the Defendant that the continuing duty extends only until practical completion, and I see no reason in principle why the duty should be so limited in time despite the fact that the architect's right to require work to be done alters at that point. In *EDAC v Moss*, Judge Newey was only concerned with the question whether the duty extended as far as practical completion, and in the *Manchester University* case, the same Judge left open the question whether the duty extended past practical completion.[171]

However, although the Judge found that there was no reason in principle why the duty should be limited to the period up till practical completion, on the issues in this case it was not necessary for the court to decide for how long the duty might continue or indeed what factors might be concerned with an evaluation of that issue.

In the case of *J Sainsbury plc v Broadway Malyan*[172] the court again had to consider whether the duty might continue after completion. It concerned a fire in a Sainsburys' store, which the architects admitted was caused by their negligent design of the fire compartment wall, where inadequate fire protection was specified to encase a steel roof truss to complete a compartment wall between the top of the wall and the underside of the roof. The supermarket was originally constructed in 1985, but in 1991 (before the fire occurred) it was extended to create a new wet fish area. In designing the new area, the architects visited the site and inspected the works from high level scaffolding which had been erected directly adjacent to and in line with the compartment wall, and which meant that they 'had been afforded a bird's eye view of the original error'. In discussing the case the Judge made the following remarks on the duty to review the design:

> BM had later opportunities to pick up its patent mistakes: when the existing design was transmitted to the contractor; but most important of all, in 1991 when its architects literally came face to face with the mistakes. They then devised a correct solution for the modification required to create the wet fish area. Whilst I understand why in human terms BM treated the design as settled, an architect is under a continuing duty as regards design. That duty does not require an architect (or engineer or other professional person) to keep previous work under constant review or to report a mistake that has been discovered, except where third parties may be affected, since the client's interests are protected by the law relating to concealment, but it does come into play when an architect has occasion to look again at the design, e.g. when there is evidence of a possible deficiency or where, as here, the design itself is to be modified. BM's decision not to adopt its original design for the wet fish area ought to have caused it to look again at it and advise Sainsbury that its 1984 design was wrong.[173]

Both of the above cases both involved exceptional circumstances, in that in both the architects had been re-engaged by the client to provide further services. In *New Islington*

---

[171] ibid., at 78.
[172] (1999) 61 Con LR 31.
[173] ibid., Judge Lloyd QC at 54, para. 4.5.

and *Hackney Housing Association Ltd v Pollard Thomas Edwards Ltd*[174] Dyson J distinguished *University of Glasgow v William Whitfield*, where following the occurrence of leaks, the architects had undertaken a fresh duty in 1982 to investigate and reconsider the design, for which they charged a fee. He commented that Judge Bowsher was not 'stating a general principle that an architect is usually under a duty to review his design even after practical completion', but that his finding depended on the special facts. After a careful review of the contractual structure, including the architect's appointment and the construction contract, Dyson J decided that no such duty arose in this case. In reaching this decision he placed particular emphasis on the fact that after practical completion the architect has no power to vary the works. In summary he noted a number of important points:

(1) An Architect on the RIBA standard conditions of engagement would owe a duty until practical completion. There was no implied or express term requiring him to review the design or take action as a result after practical completion

(2) If the employer requests him to investigate a potential design defect after practical completion the Architect may refuse or say he will do so for an extra fee, since work to investigate the effectiveness of the design is not part of his original engagement.[175]

(3) The duty to review only arises (at any stage) if the designer has good reason to reconsider the original design and where the duty arises, it is limited in scope to matters related to the 'good reasons' that gave rise to the duty to review.[176]

This case is therefore good authority for the fact that in a typical RIBA/JCT traditional procurement structure, it is unlikely that the duty to review the design would extend beyond practical completion. However consultants should proceed with caution; depending on the circumstances it could arise in other situations, particularly where the architect is involved in advising on defects.

8.7.3 Contract or tort?

Most of the above cases concern claims made for a breach of contract. The 'duty to review' is likely to be less of an issue in tort, as the limitation period does not run from when the breach occurred, but from when the damage was sustained. However it appears to be at least possible that a parallel duty may be owed to the client. In *Tesco v Norman Hitchcox Partnership*[177] the architect Norman Hitchcox Partnership (NHP) was engaged to design the shell of the shopping centre, but not to supervise its construction. NHP was later engaged by Tesco to provide design services in relation to the fitting out of the supermarket and to supervise this work. Judge Lewis QC said that such latter

---

[174] {2001} 1 BLR 74.
[175] ibid., at para. 22.
[176] ibid., at para. 23.
[177] (1997) 56 Con LR 42.

engagement could not enlarge the contractual duties under the original retainer to design the shell works, and under neither engagement was NHP required to make detailed inspections of the works. Tesco claimed NHP owed it a duty to review its design of the shell works if it noticed or suspected defects in the building. The Judge considered *London Borough of Merton v Lowe* on which Tesco relied, and commented that it was not crystal clear whether that claim was made in contract or in tort, but that given that the case was brought in 1981, it probably had been in tort. He also noted that in *University of Glasgow v William Whitfield* the architects were sued by the plaintiffs both for breach of contract and for breach of an identical duty of care in tort. He stated that:

> I am left in no doubt that an architect has a continuing duty towards his client both in contract and tort to see that his design is appropriate up to the time of completion of a building where he not only designs the building but also administers the construction contract. As I have already said, I also consider that an architect has a duty in contract towards his client for whom he has designed a building to remedy defects in his design even when his duties do not extend to the administration of the construction contract if defects come to his attention before completion of the works. I do not, however, consider that an architect has any duty in tort towards third parties to keep his design under review.[178]

He found that, in this case, there was a sufficiently proximate relationship between NHP and Tesco such that 'if NHP became aware of defects of design or construction in relation to those provisions during the time they were engaged in designing the fit-out works and supervising their construction, they owed a duty of care to Tesco to draw attention to them',[179] however as there was no duty to avoid purely economic loss, the architects were not liable.

In *New Islington and Hackney Housing Association Ltd v Pollard Thomas Edwards Ltd* Dyson J commented:

> The position is quite different where the architect . . . knows, or ought to know, of his earlier negligence. When that occurs, then he may well be under a contractual obligation to review his earlier performance, and advise his client honestly and competently of his opinion. Whether he is in fact under such a duty when he has actual or constructive knowledge of his earlier breach of contract will depend on whether the contract is still being performed. If the contract has been discharged (for whatever reason), *then the professional person may be under a duty in tort to advise his client of his earlier breach of contract*, but it is difficult to see how he can be under any contractual duty to do so.[180]

However any tortious duty to the client to review earlier design decisions would, of course, have to take account of recent developments in the law of tort, including the requirement to demonstrate a close proximity. A designer who gives advice to a former in relation to design undertaken in the past might be an example of a sufficient degree of proximity.

---

[178] ibid., at 170.
[179] ibid., at 170.
[180] [2001] 1 BLR 74 at para. 18, emphasis added.

8.7.4 Summary of duty to review

While the designer is engaged on a project, 'reviewing' the design is part of the normal design development process, and any breach would normally date from the time the design information is finalised and/or handed over for construction. Once the relevant section is constructed, assuming the designer is still engaged, the designer's duty to re-visit the design is normally dependent on a trigger event, which could be the appearance of a defect, or a change in industry knowledge, such as would give a competent designer cause for concern. In either case this would apply to matters of which the architect is actually aware, and of which they ought to have been aware. For limitation purposes, any failure to 'review' at this point would be a further breach, over and above the original design error.

It seems clear that once a designer's contract has been discharged, there is no longer any contractual duty to review the design. This applies whether the services are limited to simply providing a design, or include supervision and certification.

If, following the discharge of their duties, a designer is approached for further advice (e.g. in relation to a defect) then a new contractual or tortious duty may arise (this may well merit consulting with the designer's PI insurers).

Chapter 9
Delegation of Design Duties

9.1 General issues

It frequently happens that during the early stages of project, a consultant may realise that the design is developing in a direction that he or she had not anticipated, and that it is likely that the consultant will not have all the knowledge and skills necessary to complete the design to the agreed level of detail. Faced with this problem, what options are open to the designer?[1]

A starting point is *Moresk Cleaners Ltd v Thomas Henwood Hicks*.[2] In this case Moresk Cleaners employed Thomas Hicks, an architect, to prepare plans and specifications for an extension to their laundry. Although the building was built according to the plans and specifications, the design of the structure had in fact been delegated by the architect to the sub-contractor (the contractor was required to engage a nominated sub-contractor who had prepared the design). Within two years cracks appeared in the structure and the roof purlins sagged. Moresk Cleaners brought a claim against the architect, who argued that it was an implied term of his contract that he should be able to delegate the design to the sub-contractor, or alternatively that he had authority to employ the sub-contractor on behalf of Moresk. The court found that there was no such implied term and that the architect had no such authority, stating:

> ... if a building owner entrusts the task of designing a building to an architect, he is entitled to look to that architect to see that the building is properly designed. The architect has no power whatever to delegate his duty to anybody else, certainly not to a contractor who would in fact have an interest which was entirely opposite to that of the building owner ... If the defendant [the architect] was not able, because this form of reinforced concrete was a comparatively new form of construction, to design it himself, he had three courses open to him. One was to say 'This is not my field'. The second was to go to the building owner and say 'This reinforced concrete is out of my line. I would like you to employ a structural engineer to deal with this aspect of the matter'. Or he can, while retaining responsibility for the design, himself

---

[1] The author is grateful to Jeremy Nicholson QC, for his helpful summary of the relevant case law as presented in his lecture to the Society of Construction Law, 1 November 2011.
[2] (1966) 4 BLR 50.

Cornes and Lupton's Design Liability in the Construction Industry, Fifth Edition. Sarah Lupton.
© 2013 Sarah Lupton and DL Cornes. Published 2013 by Blackwell Publishing Ltd.

seek the advice and assistance of a structural engineer, paying for his services out of his own pocket but having at any rate the satisfaction of knowing that if he acts on that advice and that it turns out to be wrong, the person whom he employed to give the advice will owe the same duty to him as he, the architect owes to the building owner.[3]

Moresk is based on a simple proposition: the architect is responsible for the whole design, and may not unilaterally alter this arrangement without the agreement of the client. In cases where the architect is not able to complete the design, *Moresk* outlines three options: to decline the commission; to ask the client to appoint an additional consultant; or to sub-contract the design to another consultant. To these can be added at least two more options: arrange for a contractor or sub-contractor to undertake the design (i.e. the *Moresk* scenario, increasingly common in modern construction); or simply to consult with others and rely on their advice.

The five options are examined below, with the aim of deriving some principles regarding their legal effect.

9.2 Option 1: Declining the commission

To decline the commission, or agree a reduced scope of services, is hardly likely to find favour with most practices, given the current economic climate! Admitting that some part of the service is beyond the consultant's expertise can also involve a loss of face, as well as a loss of income. However in most of the options considered below, it would be essential to consult with the client before any steps are taken.

9.3 Option 2: Employer engages a specialist consultant direct

This is in effect an extension of the above, i.e. it will require a discussion with the client as to what services are required from the new team member. Most standard terms of appointment will make provision for designers to recommend others to be engaged, and for the consequences. For example, under the RIBA Standard Conditions of Appointment for an Architect 2010 edition (the RIBA Standard Agreement) the architect may suggest a specialist is appointed (cl. 4.3) and is required to notify the client if the architect becomes aware that such appointments may be needed (cl. 2.3.1). The client is obliged to appoint any other consultants identified in the Agreement (cl. 3.8,[4] which states: 'The Client acknowledges that the Architect does not warrant the competence, performance, work, services, products or solvency of any such Other Persons').

If the terms of appointment are silent on the matter, the usual, default position is that the designer is not be warranting the work of other consultants.

---

[3]ibid., at 53–4.

[4]Similar provisions can be found in the Association of Consulting Engineers standard appointment (ACE Agreement 1: Design) recital B6 and cl. F3.3, and the RICS Standard Form of Consultant Appointment 2007 cl. 8.7, although there is no equivalent disclaimer.

An example can be seen in *City of Brantford v Kemp & Wallace-Carruthers Ltd*[5] where the architect (Kemp) proposed to the client that Wallace-Carruthers was engaged as the engineer to design the foundations on a large building project, and the client appointed the engineers direct by a separate appointment. The architect instructed trial boreholes which showed very poor soil conditions on the site. The engineer did not make any further soil tests and relied solely on the results of the trial holes, together with percussion tests, made by a piling company. The architect used the engineers' foundation design but unfortunately the completed building suffered damage due to subsidence. The client brought a claim against both the architects and the engineers, who were found to be negligent. The Judge commented:

> Kemp [the architect] was entitled to rely upon the recommendations of Carruthers and ... there was no negligence on the part of Kemp. He was not advised by Carruthers of the risk involved and according to the evidence, in supervising the work he followed the specification laid down by Carruthers.[6]

Similarly, in *Hill Samuel Bank Ltd v Frederick Brand Partnership,*[7] a dispute concerning glass reinforced cement ('grc') cladding panels, a decision had to be made as to where liability should fall in circumstances where the architects had chosen grc panels but the panels were designed by an engineer. It was held that the architects owed a duty to the original building owners to exercise reasonable skill and care in recommending the use of grc panels and in selecting the consultant to design them.[8] This duty was not affected or reduced by terms in their conditions of engagement which stated they were not responsible for the work of those consultants. It was also held that if architects properly choose a specialist designer, they do not owe a further duty to conduct independent research as to the design produced beyond what would be done by an ordinary competent architect.

In *Investors in Industry Commercial Properties v South Bedfordshire District Council*[9] an architect recommended to the employer that it engaged an engineer to design and supervise the construction of foundations. The developer sued the architect and the engineer, but as in the above case, the claim against the architect failed. The Court commented:

> ...Where a particular part of the work involved in a building contract involves specialist knowledge or skill beyond that which an architect of ordinary competence may reasonably be expected to possess, the architect is at liberty to recommend to his client that a reputable independent consultant, who appears to have the relevant specialist knowledge or skill, shall be appointed by the client to perform this task. If following such recommendation a consultant with these qualifications is appointed, the architect will normally carry no legal responsibility for the work to be done by the expert which is beyond the capability of an architect of ordinary competence; in relation to the work allotted to the expert, the architect's legal responsibility will normally be confined to directing and co-ordinating the expert's work in the whole.

---

[5] (1960) 23 DLR (2d) 640 (Ont. 1960).
[6] ibid., at 655.
[7] (1993) 45 Con LR 141.
[8] ibid., at 152.
[9] (1986) 32 BLR 1 (CA).

However, this is subject to one important qualification. If any danger or problem occurs in connection with the work allotted to the expert, of which an architect of ordinary competence reasonably ought to be aware and reasonably could be expected to warn the client, despite the employment of the expert, and despite what the expert says or does about it, it is in our judgment the duty of the architect to warn the client. In such a contingency, he is not entitled to rely blindly on the expert, with no mind of his own, on matters which must or should have been apparent to him.[10]

The above cases highlight the issue that the designer cannot be entirely detached from the work of the second consultant – a reasonable amount of vigilance is required. In particular, a lead consultant may be responsible for coordinating and reviewing the work of other consultants (see, for example, *Burford NW3 Ltd v Brian Warwicker Partnership plc*[11]). More recently, *Fitzroy Robinson v Mentmore Towers*[12] contains some useful comment on the role of architects as lead consultants. There were some major delay in obtaining planning permission, partly caused by the fact that the plant that was required had been 'strategically' omitted from drawings submitted for planning approval, and once this became apparent the application had to be re-advertised. The architects had raised a query with the planning consultants, and had accepted their response. The Judge commented:

The architect is usually the lead consultant, as FRL were on this project. They have to co-ordinate the work of other consultants. They cannot be expected to turn their mind to every technical consideration arising out of the specialist work of other consultants; if they could, there would be no need to engage those other consultants in the first place. But, by the same token, architects such as FRL must do what they reasonably can to see that the work being done by the other consultants is done on time and in the right form and, to the extent they can sensibly comment on the technical detail of their work, to check that such content is generally suitable for its purpose.[13]

However in this case he found that:

. . . at the time, [the architect] was entitled, so it seems to me, to rely on the advice and expertise of RPS. RPS were involved in this project because of their expertise as planning consultants. They were engaged by the Defendants to fulfil that role . . . I suppose that, in some cases, it might be said that the aspect of the application or strategy in question was so obviously deficient that no reasonable architect should have accepted the explanation given [but] it does not seem to me that the advice – that this could be dealt with by way of a condition to the existing permission rather than an entirely new application – was, of itself, so outlandish that it should have sent alarm bells ringing in the minds of the reasonably competent architect.[14]

It is clear therefore that the architect would not normally be held responsible for the negligence of a separately appointed consultant, subject to reasonable amount of vigilance on the part of the architect, particularly if acting as lead consultant.

---

[10] ibid., Slade LJ at 37.
[11] [2004] All ER (D) 183 (Nov) (TCC); see also section 11.3.2.
[12] [2009] BLR 505.
[13] ibid., para. 240.
[14] ibid., para. 252.

9.4 Option 3: Designer engages specialist designer direct

If a designer sub-contracts the design to another firm, normally the designer will remain responsible for any negligence of the sub-consultant.[15] The court in *Moresk* referred to 'retaining responsibility for the design', and a further example can be seen in *District of Surrey v Carroll-Hatch and Associates Ltd*, a case in the British Columbia Supreme Court[16] (upheld by the British Columbia Court of Appeal[17]). Here the architects Carroll-Hatch and Associates were engaged to design a new police station, and in turn engaged an engineering firm to undertake the structural design. The engineers, who were not soil experts, dug two shallow test pits to examine the ground conditions, but also recommended that further deep soil tests were carried out. The architects rejected the recommendation as they believed the client would not approve the extra costs. Following construction the building settled causing damage, which would have been prevented had the deep soil tests been carried out, and Munroe J found the architects 60 per cent liable for the losses (because they rejected the advice), and the engineers 40 per cent liable (because they should have told the client as well as the architect of their concerns). In reaching his conclusion the Judge stated:

> . . . [the architect's] knowledge of instability in the Cloverdale soils placed upon him a duty to have appropriate investigations made by an expert. He knew that the consulting engineer that he selected was not qualified as a soil specialist. He knew that the plaintiff relied on him to supervise the construction of a useful, safe building on the site which the committee of which he was a member had recommended. He knew that the plaintiff would authorise the engagement by him of whatever competent specialists he needed. He knew that soil testing is a special branch of engineering in which some British Columbia firms specialise. He was not skilled in that specialty. By the contract and by his certificate of responsibility he assumed overall responsibility to design a building that was reasonably fit for the purpose intended and to 'marry' the building to the site.[18]

This passage illustrates two separate bases for a finding of liability. The first is that the architects had overall responsibility 'by the contract' to the client for the design of the building, and the implication is that they would have been liable to the client for any negligence on the engineers' part. The second is that the architects should use reasonable skill and care in selecting and working with the sub-contracted consultant.

It should also be noted that a contract for design work may be personal, in which case the task may not be delegated without the client's agreement.[19] It may even happen (although this would be unusual) that the design task should be undertaken by a

---

[15]The RIBA Standard Agreement provides at cl. 4.2 that the architect may do this with the client's consent, which may not be unreasonably withheld, but that 'any such sub-contracting shall not relieve the Architect of responsibility for carrying out and completing the Services'. Similar provision can be found in the ACE Agreement 1: Design cl. F2.2, and the RICS Standard Form clauses 14.5 and 14.6.

[16](1977) 76 DLR (3d) 721.

[17](1979) 10 DLR (3d) 218.

[18](1977) 76 DLR (3d) 721 at 727.

[19]*Southway Group Ltd v Wolff and Wolff* (1991) 57 BLR 33.

particular individual within a firm, and may not be re-assigned without the client's permission. In *Fitzroy Robinson v Mentmore Towers*[20] Fitzroy Robinson was appointed as architects for the development of three buildings, including the proposed renovation of the In and Out Club in Piccadilly, a project that was estimated to take about three years. The architects were appointed mainly on the basis that the lead designer would be Jeremy Blake, who had acted as leader during the initial negotiations. Mr Blake tendered his resignation before the appointment was concluded, but the architects did not tell the client for several months. The court decided that this amounted to fraudulent misrepresentation.

9.5 *Option 4: Designer arranges for a contractor or sub-contractor to undertake the work*[21]

After *Moresk*, an early case to consider design by a sub-contractor was *London Borough of Merton v Lowe*.[22] Lowe were architects engaged in 1964, on the RIBA standard terms, to design the scheme and supervise construction of a swimming pool. The design included a suspended ceiling with a Pyrok finish throughout the building, including the pool and changing rooms. Pyrok was a proprietary product, supplied only by Pyrok Ltd. Prior to the contract being let, the architects obtained a quotation from Pyrok Ltd for the suspended ceilings. The detailed specification provided with the quote included a base coat of 1:1:4 (mortar:lime:sand) render, a floating coat of 1:1:5, and a final coat of Pyrok (the composition of Pyrok was not specified, as the exact mixture was known only to that firm). The contract was let on JCT63 and Pyrok was then invited to provided an up-to-date price, however this second quotation did not give a detailed specification of the coats. Pyrok was then instructed as nominated sub-contractor.

Unfortunately the plaster cracked throughout. The base coat mix applied was not that indicated in the first quote, but the specified mix would in any case not have worked. It was too weak for the final coat of Pyrok, which it turned out was strong in cement. The court at first instance found that the architects were not liable for the deficiencies in the specification that had been provided by the sub-contractor (but were liable for failing to notice that the specification might be faulty, and in issuing the final certificate without further reviewing the design after cracks appeared). It was recognised, however, that the decision on mix was a design decision, with the court commenting that the 'plane of weakness arose in part from the imposition of the rich finishing coat on a weak undercoat, which was a matter of bad design'.[23]

---

[20] [2009] BLR 505.

[21] The ACE Agreement 1: Design cl. F2.3 expressly provides for delegation to a sub-contractor. The client's permission may not unreasonably be withheld, and the consultant is relieved from liability for the delegated design. Whether the contractor or sub-contractor will assume any design liability will depend on factors such as the main contract terms, see Chapters 7 and 14.

[22] (1981) 18 BLR 130 (CA).

[23] ibid., at 146.

The judgment was challenged in the Court of Appeal. Under a cross-notice, the Borough argued that the architects were responsible for any negligence in the design by Pyrok Ltd. Waller LJ rejected this proposition, and distinguished *Moresk*, saying:

> The argument was that the defendants were responsible, as architects, for the design, and therefore they were responsible for the faulty design used by Pyrok, that is to say, putting the Pyrok mix of cement, lime, and vermiculite onto undercoats of weaker mixes of cement, lime and sand. It was submitted that the fact that Pyrok maintained secrecy was immaterial, and reliance was placed on the case of *Moresk Cleaners v Hicks* [1996] 2 Lloyd's Rep 338; 4 BLR 50. I entirely agree with the judgment in that case. There the architect had virtually handed over to another the whole task of design. The architect could not escape responsibility for the work which he was supposed to do by handing it over to another.
>
> This case was different. Pyrok were nominated sub-contractors employed for a specialised task of making a ceiling with their own proprietary material. It was the defendants' duty to use reasonable care as architects. In view of successful work done elsewhere, they decided that to employ Pyrok was reasonable. No witness called suggested it was not at the beginning.[24]

In fact the cases have much in common. In both, the design was undertaken by a nominated sub-contractor. In neither does the judgement rely on the existence or otherwise of any collateral warranties from the sub-contractor, which might have protected the client, therefore the contractual structure is essentially the same.

The feature that is different is the selection of a proprietary product. The Court felt that using Pyrok was a reasonable decision in the circumstances. It concluded that as this decision had been made responsibly, the architects had discharged their duty of care and were no longer liable for any negligent decisions by the sub-contractor.

However this raises a key issue. The implication of the quoted passage is that unlike *Moresk*, in *Merton* the architect's responsibilities were not 'handed over'. However, as the formula for the Pyrok was a trade secret the architects did not have enough information (at least initially) to specify the other layers. Therefore, by selecting Pyrok, some of the detailing was, in effect, delegated. The decisions are therefore not easy to reconcile.[25]

Following *Merton*, further cases demonstrate a range of approaches. Some, like *Moresk* state that 'in the absence of agreement to the contrary architects cannot escape liability to their clients by delegating their responsibility to others.'[26]

In *Richard Roberts Holdings Ltd v Douglas Smith Stimson Partnership*[27] RRH claimed damages against the architects Douglas Smith Stimson for breach of contract and negligence in recommending or permitting a method of lining an effluent cooling tank, which had been designed and supplied by Erosion and Corrosion Control Ltd (ECC). ECC was engaged directly by RRH. The architects, who charged no fee for this part of their work, asserted that they had no legal responsibility in relation to the lining of the

---

[24] ibid., at 148.

[25] As noted in Jeremy Nicholson QC, *supra*.

[26] *Equitable Debenture Assets Corporation Ltd v William Moss Group Ltd* (1984) CILL 74; 2 Con LR 1; 1 Const LJ 131: see also *Southern Water Authority v Lewis & Duvivier* (1984) 27 BLR 111, and in the context of an employer's duties as to safety, *McDermid v Nash Dredging* [1987] AC 906.

[27] (1988) 46 BLR 50.

tank. RRH, who knew that the architects had no knowledge of linings, had themselves sought independent advice from expert trade associations. The architects also maintained they were acting informally in seeking quotations for the lining in order to be helpful, not as experts or in a professional capacity. RRH argued that they were the architects for the whole dyeworks project, and that if they had wanted to limit their duties in the way they now asserted, they should have done so expressly, which they did not. Judge John Newey QC, Official Referee, found that the architects were responsible for the design of the whole dyeworks and the lining, which was an 'inherent part' of the tanks that had been designed by the architects. He also found that they were negligent in carrying out this design, in that they should have made their own investigations as to possible alternatives for the lining. The architects did not, but should have, sought help from other sources.

A more recent example is *Try Build Ltd v Invicta Leisure Tennis Ltd*[28] where a claim was brought against engineers Buro Happold for failing to specify the edge strip to be used in a roofing material. Here it is quite clear that the court thought that the detailed decisions on specification were part of Buro Happold's duties, despite the involvement of a specialist firm.

The project was for tennis courts near Southampton, and was let to contractors Try Build on a JCT 81 Design Build contract. Buro Happold were novated from Invicta to Try Build at the time the contract was let. Try Build engaged the specialist company Vector as sub-contractors for the design, supply and construction of the roof. The roof was an innovative design with four foil cushions held together by a rope edge detail. Once constructed it leaked, and it was agreed that this was caused by the edge strip which was, at 100 micron, was too thin. Amongst other things the contractor claimed that the engineers failed properly to 'prepare specifications as follows: (a) specifying foil thicknesses that were compatible with the wind forces specified in the structural performance specification; (b) highlighting the need for development by Vector of the edge detail and method of installation'. It was argued that the extent of the design duties of Buro Happold should be determined in the context of Vector's involvement as specialist design sub-contractors, and should not therefore require the provision of such a fine level of detail. The court did not accept this, stating that 'Design duties relating to the roof of the tennis halls (other than steelwork) were sub-contracted to Vector but that does not limit the duties of BH in specification and supervision nor in their duties of general design'.[29]

The court found that Buro Happold were negligent in failing to specify the strip, commenting that they 'specified many other matters relating to the roof, the thickness of the foil, for example, and it is difficult to see how some matters were to be included and some excluded'.[30]

In *Bellefield Computer Services v E Turner & Sons Ltd* (No 2)[31] an architect failed to specify exactly what fire protection measures were needed for a compartment wall in a

---

[28] (1997) 71 Con LR 140.
[29] ibid., at 149 (para. 33).
[30] ibid., at 166 (para. 78).
[31] [2003] Lloyd's Rep PN 53 (CA).

new supermarket. As above, the architects were engaged by a design build contractor, however there were no written terms of engagement and the exact extent of the duties was unclear. The court at first instance determined that these were 'partial' and the arrangement was to produce drawings on demand. The court of Appeal agreed in principle that: 'The architect will not owe a duty of care in respect of defects for which he never had any design or supervisory responsibility in the first place: c.f. the observations of Windeyer J in the Australian High Court in *Voli v Inglewood Shire Council* [1963] ALR 657 at 662'.[32] However it added that an architect may have an obligation to provide more than simply what was asked for, stating:

> if a dangerous defect arises as the result of a negligent omission on the part of the architect, he cannot excuse himself from liability on the grounds that he delegated the duty of design of the relevant part of the building works, unless he obtains the permission of his employer to do so, see *Keating: Building Contracts* (7th edn), paras 13–40 and *Moresk Cleaners Ltd v Hicks . . . .*[33]

Further cases followed a similar approach to *Bellefield*, i.e. the designer was found not liable for the negligence of the subcontractor, but on the basis that the task was not part of its duties. For example, in *Southfield School for Girls v Briggs & Forrester (Electrical) Ltd*[34] the architects were not liable for failing to develop a risk assessment in relation to asbestos removal, but leaving such matters to a specialist company. The court stated 'In *Moresk* there was wholesale delegation to a subcontractor of ordinary architectural duties. Here, B & F could not undertake the work, and neither B & F nor PHP could devise the methodology–those were matters which had to be delegated to a licensed contractor.'[35]

Similarly, in the Scottish case of *Atwal Enterprises v Toner*,[36] architects were appointed to design a football pavilion, and specialist nominated sub-contractors were engaged to design and construct the base to the football pitch. In this case the architects were found not liable for the sub-contractor's negligent design, as it was understood by both parties that the pitch was not their responsibility (the architects were however found liable for failing to take early action when problems became apparent through excessive ponding on the laid base). In reaching this decision the court commented:

> It is also relevant to note that where, as here, specialist sub-contractors are involved, technical matters concerning the sub-contract works or installations may well be outwith the knowledge and expertise of the ordinary architect. The case against the defender must therefore turn on what would or would not reasonably be expected, *in that limited context*, of an architect of ordinary competence exercising reasonable care and skill.[37]

---

[32] ibid., para. 47.
[33] ibid., para. 48.
[34] [2007] EWHC 3403 (TCC).
[35] ibid., para. 210.
[36] 2006 SLT 535.
[37] ibid. para. 38, emphasis added.

The differing approaches were examined in the recent case of *Cooperative Group Ltd v John Allen Associates Ltd*,[38] which also concerned the involvement of specialist sub-contractors. John Allen Associates (JAA), a firm of consulting and structural engineers were engaged by developers Cliveden Estates Ltd, with whom they had worked previously, in relation to the design of a supermarket for the Cooperative Group (CWS). JAA also provided a direct warranty to CWS.

The site had a layer of soft and very soft clay, and a geotechnical report was provided to JAA recommending that 'piling or some form of ground treatment' should be considered. The main building structure and outside walls were designed to be supported by piles with pile caps and ground beams. However at an early stage JAA met and had discussions with Keller, a geotechnical contractor, who advised that the ground floor slab could be ground bearing, if the ground was treated with '*vibro compaction of the subsoils using stone column probes at 2m centres*'. Vibro compaction is a process by which stone columns are placed in the ground and by acting compositely with the soil, improve the load/settlement performance of that ground.

JAA then invited and received tenders from three specialists, including Keller, on tender documents that included a performance specification for soil stabilisation by Vibro compaction based on the recommendations of Kellar.

Cliveden engaged John Mowlem & Company Plc in 1996 on a JCT80 standard building contract. Mowlem also provided a warranty to CWS. The contract sum included a provisional sum of £45,000 relating to the performance specification for vibro compacting ground improvement. Mowlem subcontracted this work, including the detailed design, to Pennine Vibropiling Ltd, as its tender was lower than Keller's. JAA raised various queries with Pennine, but ultimately seems to have accepted its calculations, writing to the architects '*JAA do not intend to pursue the issue on the understanding that the works are underwritten by the Contractor . . .*'.

Following construction, the ground floor slab settled by up to 110mm and because it was supported in places on the pile caps which had not settled, there was significant differential settlement. This caused major damage and remedial works were needed to re-establish a level floor and avoid problems such as rolling shopping trolleys. CWS commenced proceedings against JAA, and Mowlem and Pennine were joined in the action. Cliveden reached a settlement with Mowlem and Pennine who took no further part in the proceedings.

The key argument put forward by CWS was that the engineers were negligent, because vibro replacement 'could never have worked on the site which was highly compressible and therefore was inevitably going to fail and the resulting building was bound to suffer from extensive and unacceptable differential settlement'. The Judge however accepted that vibro replacement, if properly designed and executed, could have limited the long-term settlement to an acceptable extent.

CWS also argued that JAA could not delegate its design liability by relying on the advice of the geotechnical engineers, nor could it delegate its responsibility to the sub-

---

[38] [2010] EWHC 2300 (TCC).

contractor. If JAA had felt it was not capable of undertaking the necessary design work, including checking the calculations of Pennine, it should have made CWS aware of this, in which case it would have commissioned another firm to do the work. CWS relied on *Moresk, Merton* and *Richard Roberts Holdings*, and on leading academic commentaries,[39] and argued that only where the area of design is obviously outside the expertise of any engineer or of the consultants available in the construction industry (e.g. high-speed lifts) may the consultant's duty be limited to the exercise of reasonable skill and care in the selection of the product or specialist services.

JAA argued that the decisions of the Court of Appeal in *London Borough of Merton v Lowe* and *Investors in Industry v South Bedfordshire DC*, provide clear authority that, in general terms, a professional is entitled to rely on specialist contractors or consultants, and there was nothing in the circumstances of this case to suggest that relying on Keller's advice was negligent.

The Judge reviewed all the case law and concluded 'That construction professionals can discharge their duty to take reasonable care by relying on the advice or design of a specialist provided that they act reasonably in doing so.'[40]

When deciding what was reasonable, a court must consider all the circumstances, which include:

(a) Whether the assistance is taken from an appropriate specialist;
(b) Whether it was reasonable to seek assistance from other professionals, research or other associations or other sources;
(c) Whether there was information which should have led the professional to give a warning;
(d) Whether and to what extent the client might have a remedy in respect of the advice from the other specialist;
(e) Whether the construction professional should have advised the client to seek advice elsewhere or should themselves have taken professional advice under a separate retainer.[41]

The Judge decided that in this case the engineers had acted reasonably in relying on the advice of the specialists Keller, and consequently were not negligent. In reaching this conclusion the Judge distinguished *Moresk* by saying that 'It was not argued that if the architect remained liable for the design then it was possible for the architect to discharge a duty to take reasonable care by relying on the advice or design of specialists provided that such reliance was reasonable.'[42]

Essentially, therefore, although the claimant argued that this was a case of delegation, the Judge is saying that this was not delegation, but reliance, which is acceptable if done carefully. It is therefore useful to turn to Option 5.

---

[39] *Hudson's Building and Engineering Contracts* (11th edn), at paras 2-114 to 2-129 and *Keating on Construction Contracts* (8th edn). at para. 13-030.
[40] ibid., Ramsey J at para. 180(2).
[41] ibid., para. 180(3).
[42] ibid., para. 180(1).

9.6 Option 5: Designer relies on outside sources

Relying on outside sources is not only acceptable but is often essential. In *Equitable Debenture Assets Corp Ltd v William Moss Group Ltd* His Honour Judge Newey QC stated:

> modern developments in materials and technologies in the construction industry have been so numerous and so rapid as to exceed the ability of even the most talented and assiduous professional men to master them all. Architects and others must of necessity seek the assistance of specialists when they reach the limits of their knowledge.[43]

Generally the topic of reliance arises in situations where the designer failed to seek assistance, or placed reliance on inappropriate sources. The case of *Greater London Council v Ryarsh Brick Co.,*[44] for example, is a salutary lesson for architects relying on brochures. The case arose out of the construction of boundary walls and stores on the GLC estate at Thamesmead. Some of the walls collapsed and some were demolished. The GLC sued Ryarsh, the manufacturers of the calcium silicate bricks, for breach of warranty and negligent mis-statement and also the main contractor for breach of contract. The essence of the GLC's complaint was that they had specified the bricks to be supplied by Ryarsh after the GLC architect had read the Ryarsh brochure and been in contact with them. The bricks would not adhere properly to the mortar. The evidence in the case was that, at a meeting between Ryarsh's representative and the GLC architect, Ryarsh learned of the intended use of these bricks to build walls and stores, but not about the proposed thickness of the structure nor any other information in relation to the design. Ryarsh did not expect any problems with regard to adhesion. The judge was able to conclude from this that no express warranty or representation as to adhesion of the bricks had ever been given to the GLC and on that basis, he was able to dismiss the GLC's claim against the manufacturer. Similarly, in *Sealand of the Pacific v Robert C. McHaffie Ltd*[45] engineers should not have relied on assurances by a concrete manufacturer. Similarly in *J D Williams & Co Ltd v Michael Hyde and Associates Ltd*[46] architects were found negligent for relying on the oral assurances by a British Gas representative that the flue gasses from an appliance would not cause phenolic yellowing (see section 6.3).

Even relying on sources such as Building Regulations or codes of practice may not be sufficient to avoid liability. In the case of *Holland Hannen and Cubitts (Northern) Ltd v Welsh Health Technical Services Organisation*[47] engineering firm Redpath Dorman Long Ltd, engaged as nominated sub-contractors for two hospital projects, were found liable for designing uneven concrete floors. Robert Goff LJ held that:

---

[43] (1984) 2 Con LR 1 at 25.
[44] (1985) 4 Con LR 85.
[45] (1975) 2 BLR 74.
[46] [2001] BLR 99 (CA).
[47] (1985) 35 Build LR 1 (CA).

The structural engineer will therefore simply consider the profile of the floor as such; and ask himself the question whether there is a significant risk that the floor, with that profile, in the building in question, may be unacceptable. In considering that question he cannot simply rely on the codes of practice. It is plain from the evidence that the code of practice is no more than a guide for use by professional men, who have to exercise their own expertise; this must moreover be especially true in a case such as the present, where the design was a novel one.[48]

More recently, in *Sahib Foods Ltd v Paskin Kyriakides Sands*,[49] a claim was brought against a firm of architects after a fire occurred in a food factory. The experts agreed that there was no evidence that the factory breached the relevant Building Regulations. The premises had a Fire Certificate. However, the court found that the architects' duty was not limited to compliance with Regulations: in designing the project the architects should have also considered insurance company Codes, intended to prevent damage to property. The architects were found negligent in failing to consult these Codes. The Judge did not accept the argument that since the defendants had complied with their statutory requirements and as a result no one was killed or injured they had fully performed their duties.

However none of these cases assert that the designer should not have consulted outside sources, only that this should have been done carefully. Examples of the courts finding it acceptable to rely on the advice of others are cited above in relation to separately appointed consultants. In *BL Holdings v Robert J Wood and Partners*,[50] architects relied on the comments of planning officers regarding the calculation of areas in an application for an office development permit. The Court of Appeal held that it was not negligent of the architect to believe that the characterisation of the areas and hence the exact calculation was a matter of opinion, or that the planning authority had a discretion in the matter, and therefore to rely on their advice was not negligent. In *John Allen*, the relyiance on expert engineering firms was considered reasonable, so that case is instructive on the question of the circumstances where such reliance would be held to be reasonable.

9.7 Is there a difference between delegation and reliance?

In practice, and indeed in some of the above cases, the terms are sometimes used interchangeably, but it is suggested that there is a clear distinction between delegation and reliance, which is important in the context of design liability.

Design is a process of decision-making, often moving from larger, more strategic decisions to smaller, more detailed ones. It would be normal, indeed essential, when making many design decisions, to consult published information, and to ask advice and opinion. The information gathered will be used to inform the decision-maker, and the

---

[48] ibid., at 25–6; note this was a dissenting judgment, but not on the level of care needed.
[49] (2003) 93 Con LR 1.
[50] (1979) 12 BLR 1 (CA).

decision. However, the designer will still make the decision. In delegation it will be 'handed over' and made by someone else.

If the decision is truly delegated, demonstrating that the 'handing over' was done with care, cannot discharge the designer's responsibility for that decision. If it could, as has been recognised, this would create a legal black hole,[51] whereby the client may not be able to claim against either party. In extreme cases, the designer could hand over the entire design, and escape liability for any negligence by the delegee.

Many situations will of course involve both reliance and delegation. *Merton* and *John Allen* are good examples of this. The initial decision to use Pyrok, and the initial decision to use vibro piling, involved placing reliance on the advice of a specialist, which in both cases was considered reasonable. However the selection of vibro piling in *John Allen*, meant that some level of design had to be carried out by the sub-contractor (because this technique was beyond the engineers' expertise, as was Pyrok in *Merton*). Therefore, although the initial reliance may have been reasonable, it inevitably resulted in some delegation. Whether or not it was always anticipated that some level of detailed design would be provided by the sub-contractor is unclear (although the contractual context would not suggest this, as the main contract was not a design-build form, and no warranty was provided by the sub-contractors).

The real difficulty, in the current industry, is in deciding what exactly were the services to be provided. It is so common that matters of detail are left to contractors and specialists, that in many cases it could be argued that it was the intention of both parties that the details in question were not within the remit of the architect or engineer, and that therefore there has, in fact, been no delegation.

9.8 Summary of options

For the client, *Merton* and *John Allen* serve as a warning. In some circumstances they may not be able, as they might have assumed, to hold an appointed consultant responsible for all the decisions necessary to complete the detailed design. They should therefore ensure that the exact scope, level of detail and right to delegate (or otherwise) are carefully defined in the appointment documents. Where it is agreed that the consultant is not to undertake some detailed design aspects the client should, of course, ensure that these aspects are assigned to another party, and not assume that the contractor will become liable for completing the design by default.[52]

It is suggested, however, that consultants should not take *Merton* and *John Allen* as a reassurance that it is acceptable to incorporate design by others, provided it is done carefully: before doing so they should examine their terms of appointment as to whether the client might be expecting them to design that part. If this is the case, only with the client's agreement can they proceed with delegation or sub-contracting. Responsible reliance on external sources in making design decisions is of course essential.

---

[51] Dennis, Joanna, *Limits to Delegation* (2011) 22 3 Cons. Law 20; the point was also argued in *Southfield School for Girls v Briggs & Forrester (Electrical) Ltd* [2007] EWHC 3403 (TCC), at para. 207.
[52] See the discussion of reliance at section 7.2.

To summarise the options:

- *Direct appointment by client*: normally the original consultant will not be liable for the work of other consultants, save for a reasonable amount of vigilance.
- *Sub-contracting the design*: the consultant will remain liable for the sub-contracted work, but should seek the client's agreement, particularly if the appointment is personal.
- *Assigning the design to a contractor/sub-contractor*: despite *John Allen*, there is still the possibility that no matter how reasonable this may appear, the consultant will remain liable for the delegated design. Whether delegation is acceptable will depend on whether it was part of the original scope of services, (express or implied). The client's agreement should therefore be obtained, so that it can take protective measures.
- *Relying on others*: this must be done with care. The advice in *John Allen* is applicable and useful.

Chapter 10
Liability to Third Parties: Procurement Issues

Most projects are designed by a team of people from different firms, including contributions from the construction and manufacturing side. Usually these parties are linked by a network of bi-party contracts, although recently multi-party and team arrangements are becoming increasingly common.

When problems arise, the client may seek to recover losses form any member of this network. If the limitation period has expired, or there is no direct contract, they may try to bring an action in tort; for example a client may try to claim against a sub-contractor, or a contractor against a consultant.

It is clear from Chapter 4 that consultants supplying design services are likely to owe a parallel liability in tort to their clients, but generally unlikely to bear such liability to third parties with whom they have no connection, except where the error causes injury or damage to property not the subject of the design. The position may be different where consultants deal directly with third parties, and provide advice on which they might expect those parties to rely. The liability of contractors providing design is less clear, but it was suggested in Chapter 4 that if sufficient proximity could be established then they too might be liable.

In a team-working environment, it is quite likely discussions will be held, and advice given, between members who have no direct contract with each other. Questions then arise as to what effect the contractual framework has on the likelihood of the courts finding the necessary ingredients for a duty in tort. There are two aspects to this: the general contractual arrangement; and the specific clauses agreed between parties, particularly where these include disclaimers or clauses that seek to limit liability.

10.1. Relationship between contract and tort

10.1.1 Effect of contractual framework on tortious liability

Henderson v Merrett is a useful starting point. As already noted, the claimants were able to establish that the defendant 'names' owed them a duty in tort to avoid causing pure economic loss that bypassed the contractual chain (there was no contract between the names and the indirect investors, see section 4.4). In reaching this decision, however, the House of Lords was keen to emphasise that this was not to be considered a general

Cornes and Lupton's Design Liability in the Construction Industry, Fifth Edition. Sarah Lupton.
© 2013 Sarah Lupton and DL Cornes. Published 2013 by Blackwell Publishing Ltd.

rule, but was due to the particular circumstances of the case. In an important passage Lord Goff said:

> I wish, however, to add that I strongly suspect that the situation which arises in the present case is most unusual; and that in many cases in which a contractual chain comparable to that in the present case is constructed it may well prove to be inconsistent with an assumption of responsibility which has the effect of, so to speak, short-circuiting the contractual structure so put in place by the parties. It cannot therefore be inferred from the present case that other sub-agents will be held directly liable to the agent's principal in tort. Let me take the analogy of the common case of an ordinary building contract, under which main contractors contract with the building owner for the construction of the relevant building, and the main contractor sub-contracts with sub-contractors or suppliers (often nominated by the building owner) for the performance of work or the supply of materials in accordance with standards and subject to terms established in the sub-contract. I put on one side cases in which the sub-contractor causes physical damage to property of the building owner, where the claim does not depend on an assumption of responsibility by the sub-contractor to the building owner; though the sub-contractor may be protected from liability by a contractual exemption clause authorised by the building owner. But if the sub-contracted work or materials do not in the result conform to the required standard, it will not ordinarily be open to the building owner to sue the sub-contractor or supplier direct under the *Hedley Byrne* principle, claiming damages from him on the basis that he has been negligent in relation to the performance of his functions. For there is generally no assumption of responsibility by the sub-contractor or supplier direct to the building owner, the parties having so structured their relationship that it is inconsistent with any such assumption of responsibility. This was the conclusion of the Court of Appeal in *Simaan General Contracting Co v Pilkington Glass Ltd (No 2)*[1988] 1 All ER 791 at 803, [1988] QB 758 at 781. As Bingham LJ put it:

>> 'I do not, however, see any basis on which [the nominated suppliers] could be said to have assumed a direct responsibility for the quality of the goods to [the building owners]; such a responsibility is, I think, inconsistent with the structure of the contract the parties have chosen to make.'[1]

This reluctance to 'short-circuit' the contractual structure has been reflected in many subsequent cases, an example being *Marc Rich & Co AG v Bishop Rock Marine Co Ltd*,[2] which followed soon after *Henderson*. It concerned a cargo ship (the *Nicholas H*) that developed cracks in her hull. A surveyor acting on behalf of her classification society recommended permanent repairs, but after the ship owners expressed reluctance to undertake these, appears to have changed his mind. After temporary repair work was carried he pronounced the vessel fit to sail. Unfortunately the temporary welding repairs cracked almost as soon as the ship embarked on her voyage, and she sank a few days later. The House of Lords found that the classification surveyor did not owe a duty of care to the cargo owners. Although there was sufficient proximity between the parties (the surveyor was aware that his decision would directly affect the safety of the ship, its crew and the cargo, even though the owners were unaware the survey had taken place),

---

[1] [1994] 3 All ER 506 at 521.
[2] [1996] 1 AC 211 (HL).

taking into account various factors, including '*the outflanking of the bargain between ship owners and cargo owners*'[3] it would not be fair or just to find a duty.

In *Architype Projects Ltd v Dewhurst Macfarlane & Partners*[4] Architype was engaged as lead designer in relation to the design and construction of a visitors' centre. Architype had in turn engaged engineers Dewhurst as sub-consultants. Following completion structural defects appeared in the building, and Architype sought to argue, amongst other things, that the engineers owed a duty to Architype's client to avoid causing it economic loss. The court agreed to strike out this part of the claim, as it had no prospect of success, stating that the parties had 'structured their relationship in such a way that it is inconsistent with any such assumption of responsibility' and that 'in these circumstances it is not arguable that it is fair and reasonable that the law should impose a duty in tort on Dewhurst for the benefit of [the client]'.[5]

Nevertheless, the contractual framework is only one factor to be taken into account when deciding whether a duty arises, and (as in *Henderson v Merrett*) would not always prevent it being found. In *Riyad Bank v Ahli United Bank (UK) Plc*[6] the Court of Appeal again had to consider the effect of a contractual chain on the implication of a tortious duty. The defendant Ahli Bank had entered into an agreement with RBE London Ltd ('RBE': the second claimant in the action and a solely-owned subsidiary of the claimant Riyad Bank). The agreement was to provide financial services, including advice, in connection with the development of a Sharia compliant investment fund (the 'Fund': the third claimant). RBE also acted as general investment advisor to the Fund itself, under a second 'advisory agreement'. There was therefore a contractual chain through which the defendant's advice was passed to RBE (who had no expertise in matters covered by the advice), and on to the Fund. The Fund suffered losses and ultimately was suspended.

The Court at first instance held that the defendant owed a duty of care to the Fund to ensure that it gave sound advice, and that it had failed in this duty. The defendant appealed in relation to the question of whether a duty was owed. The Court of Appeal held that the nature and terms of the contracts governing the parties' relationships were not inconsistent with an assumption of responsibility by the bank to the Fund for the quality of the advice it provided, and dismissed the appeal. This was despite the fact that it had clearly been a deliberate decision of the parties not to enter into direct contractual relations:

> Mr Howard then relied on building cases such as *Simaan General Contracting Co v Pilkington Glass Ltd (No 2)* [1988 QB 758] and *Pacific Associate Inc v Baxter* [1990] 1 QB 993 for the proposition that where there is a contractual chain, that chain should not be by-passed by a claim in tort. As Lord Goff said in *Henderson v Merrett* that is, indeed, the usual position. But neither of those authorities considered a case where discussions and representations were made directly to the party who, in the event, suffered loss. There cannot be a general proposition that, just because a chain exists, no responsibility for advice is ever assumed to a non-contractual party.'[7]

---

[3] ibid., Lord Steyn at 27.
[4] [2004] 96 Con LR 3 (TCC)-appealed, but not on this point.
[5] ibid., HH Judge John Toulmin at paras 69 and 70.
[6] [2006] EWCA Civ 780 (CA).
[7] Lord Justice Longman, at para. 32.

Neither *Simaan* nor *Pacific Associates* are cases where advice was given direct (the former concerned the supply of defective glass units by a sub-contractor – see section 3.8, and the latter negligent under-certification – see below). In summary, a formalised contractual structure will weigh against a finding that a duty of care is owed, but will not always preclude it. In all situations the particular circumstances will be assessed, and the exact terms in a contractual chain (the 'links') will need to be examined.

10.1.2 The effect of the contractual terms

As noted in Chapter 3, where a parallel tortious duty is claimed, courts will not normally accept that the duty of care can be more extensive than that assumed under the contract. For example, in *Tai Hing Cotton Mill Ltd v Liu Chong Hing Bank Ltd* the Privy Council stated that 'Their Lordships do not, however, accept that the parties mutual obligations in tort can be any greater than those to be found expressly or by necessary implication in their contract'.[8] There have been exceptions, although these are not common, for example in *Holt v Payne Skillington and De Groot Collis* solicitors were found liable to their clients for negligent advice on planning matters, despite the fact that as their appointment did not include this service, the advice was effectively given free of charge.[9]

The extent of the specified services will be relevant. In *Nordic Holdings Ltd v Mott MacDonald Ltd*[10] an engineer was engaged to investigate the cracking in a newly laid floor, and its client brought a claim in both contract and tort. The court found on the facts that the terms of the contract between the parties required an investigation and report only on the problem, i.e. the physical manifestation of cracking in a newly laid floor, and not to undertake a complete review of the design of the floor, and no wider duty could be found in tort.

This principle has also been applied to claims brought by third parties. In *Bellefield Computer Services v E Turner & Sons Ltd (No 2)*,[11] the court similarly found that the limited duties placed on the architect (to provide drawings to a contractor 'on demand') were relevant to determining the extent of their duty in tort to a subsequent owner.

The existence of disclaimers or express limitations on liability are particularly relevant to whether or not a duty might arise to protect the client against pure economic loss. In *Hedley Byrne v Heller*, although liability was established in principle, the claim was defeated by a disclaimer in the reference (the merchant bankers' reference was headed '*without responsibility on the part of this Bank*'). Lord Devlin said:

> A man cannot be said voluntarily to be undertaking a responsibility if at the very moment when he is said to be accepting it he declares that in fact he is not. The problem of reconciling words of exemption with the existence of a duty arises only where a party is claiming exemption from a responsibility which he has already undertaken or which he is contracting to undertake.[12]

---

[8] [1986] AC 80. See also *William Hill Organisation Ltd v Bernard Sunley & Sons Ltd* (1982) 22 BLR 1.
[9] (1995) 77 BLR 51.
[10] (2001) 77 Const LR 88 (TCC).
[11] [2003] Lloyds Rep PN 53 (CA).
[12] [1964] AV 465 at 497.

As acknowledged by Lord Goff in *Henderson v Merrett Syndicates Ltd* (referring to *Hedley Byrne*) as between consultant and client 'an assumption of responsibility may be negatived by an appropriate disclaimer.'[13]

The interesting New Zealand case of *R M Turton v Kerslake & Partners*[14] dealt with a claim for design negligence by a contractor against an engineer. Kerslake were mechanical engineers who were engaged by a hospital to prepare mechanical service specifications. These were provided to the contractor Turton who constructed the work, using specialist subcontractors for the mechanical services, as required by their contract. Following construction it became clear that the specifications were faulty, and the contractor had to pay to remedy the defective installation. There was no contract between Kerslake and Turton, so it had to bring its claim in tort. The court noted that the contract between Kerslake and the Health Board set out the distribution of risk, and specifically excluded liability for the accuracy of the mechanical specifications. It decided that Kerslake undertook no 'voluntary assumption of responsibility' to Turton, its only assumption of responsibility was to its client. The court concluded that:

> in our view the duty contended for in respect of the alleged representation that the componentry would achieve the required output would cut across and be inconsistent with the overall contractual structure which defines the relationships of the various parties to this work, and in the circumstances of this case it would not be fair, just or reasonable to impose the claimed duty of care.[15]

The court therefore considered that the contractual disclaimer affected not only the liability owed by the engineers to their client, but also the existence of any liability in tort to the contractor. In this case the disclaimer was sufficiently clear to negate any duty of care.[16]

A similar conclusion was reached in *Biffa Waste Services Ltd v Maschinefabrak Ernst Hese GmBH*,[17] which concerned a fire on a PFI project. Biffa Leicester (the second claimant) entered into a PFI arrangement with Leicester County Council for the provision of a waste recycling facility. It then formed a contract with Biffa Waste Services (the first claimant), which in turn entered into a design build contract with Maschinefabrak Ernst Hese (MEH). This contract contained a limitation of liability clause. MEH also entered into a warranty with Biffa Leicester. Under the design build contract MEH undertook to carry out all work with skill and care, and liability for delay was limited by a liquidated damages clause. Clause 2.2 of the direct warranty with Biffa Leicester stated:

---

[13] [1995] 2 AC 145 at 181 (HL).

[14] [2000] 3 NZLR 406.

[15] ibid., para. 32.

[16] See also *Norwich City Council v Harvey* [1989] 1 WLR 828 (CA) and *Ossory Road (Skelmersdale) Ltd v Balfour Beatty Building Ltd* [1993] CILL 882 where subcontractors were able to rely on risk allocation clauses in the main contract to defeat a claim in tort by the employer.

[17] [2009] BLR 1 (CA).

The Contractor shall subject to the terms of this agreement owe no liability, duty or obligation to Biffa Leicester which is greater than would have existed if Biffa Leicester had been named as Provider under the Supply Contract.

Post completion MEH's sub-contractors caused a fire, which resulted in consequential losses due to delay, and a claim was brought against MEH and the subcontractors on the basis of liability in contract and in tort. The court decided that MEH owed a duty of care in tort to the claimants (in addition to its contractual obligations) to prevent consequential loss in respect of physical damage by fire to the plant, but that the duty of care was limited by the combined effect of Clause 2.2 of the warranty and the liquidated damages provisions in the design build contract. In reaching this conclusion it stated:

> The test is whether the parties having so structured their relationship that it is inconsistent with any such assumption of responsibility or with it being fair, just and reasonable to impose liability. In particular, a duty of care should not be permitted to circumvent or escape a contractual exclusion or limitation of liability for the act or omission that would constitute the tort.[18]

The sub-contractor was also held liable in tort, but with no similar limitation.

Recently in *Robinson v Jones*, as already noted (see section 4.6), the terms of the NHBC Buildmark agreement circumscribed the tortious duty, the court concluding that 'The Defendant successfully excluded the concurrent duty of care which I consider that it would otherwise have owed to the Claimant in tort.'[19] In *Arrowhead Capital Finance Limited (in Liquidation) v KPMG LLP*,[20] KPMG were appointed to provide investment advice, under terms that included a clause limiting liability: the existence of the clause helped to defeat a claim in tort by third party investors.

The case law on this point is therefore reasonably consistent: clear disclaimers or limitations will successfully limit any concurrent tortious duty to the other contracting party, and may in some circumstances assist in defeating a claim in tort from a third party.

10.2 Liability in particular situations

Below is outlined how courts have approached liability between parties in particular construction situations, however examples should be read against the developing legal principles, as outlined above and in Chapter 4.

10.2.1 Employer–contractor liability

Whether or not a contractor is entitled to rely on a design as being capable of construction has been considered in a number of cases. One of the leading cases in this field,

---

[18] ibid., Ramsey J at para. 169.
[19] [2010] EWHC 102 (TCC) HHJ Stephen Davies at para 88, see also [2011] 3 BLR 206 (CA) Jackson LJ, para. 84: 'To my mind, however, clauses 8 and 10 of the building conditions put the matter beyond doubt'.
[20] [2012] EWHC 1801.

now more than 100 years old, is authority for the proposition that, by inviting tenders for specified work, an employer does not impliedly warrant to the tenderers that the design is capable of construction.

In *Thorn v Corporation of London*[21] a contractor was engaged by an employer to take down an old bridge and build a new one. Plans and a specification had been prepared by the employer's engineer. The design involved the use of caissons which turned out to be useless and the bridge had to be built in a different manner. The contractor sought compensation for its losses caused by the failure of the caissons on the basis that the employer had warranted that the bridge could be inexpensively built according to the plans and specifications. The House of Lords held that no such warranty could be implied.

Similarly, in the even older case of *Tharsis Sulpher & Copper Company v McElroy & Sons*,[22] a contractor tendered to supply and erect the ironwork for a shed, to the specification of the employer. When the specified thickness of girders resulted in them being impossible to manufacture, the contractor increased the thickness, but was unsuccessful in an action to claim the additional cost.

There is additional case law to support the above relating to the analogous question of problematic ground conditions.[23] The courts would normally hold that an employer does not warrant that a building as designed is capable of being built on a particular site, and that the contractor has taken the risk of unexpected ground conditions. This is based on the underlying rule that construction contracts are 'entire', and the contractor, having agreed to construct the building, must complete the project for the agreed price, despite any difficulties encountered.

Whilst the *Thorn* and *Tharsis* cases provide a general rule on buildability,[24] the position may be different where the contract itself allocates the risk, as it does in standard form design-build contracts (see Chapter 14), or where there is an express warranty that the works are capable of construction in accordance with plans and specification. It would also be different where the employer negligently makes a statement that the contractor relies upon, which could give rise to a claim of negligent misrepresentation.

10.2.2 Consultant–contractor liability

Direct liability from a consultant to a contractor, where there is no contractual relationship, is obviously an area of key interest to consultants. Many of the cases below concern negligent under-certification, but this case law is nevertheless relevant to where the consultant provides design advice to a contractor or sub-contractor, as may arise in design build procurement.

---

[21] (1876) 1 App Cas 120.

[22] (1878) 3 App Cas 1040.

[23] For a full discussion see Julian Bailey, J 'What Lies Beneath' *The International Construction Law Review*, 24(4), (2007), 394.

[24] Note that the position may be different in the United States, see Chapter 18 and *United States v Spearin*, 248 US 132 (1918).

An early example where a designer was found liable to a contractor in tort, as the design provided was in breach of the law, was *Townsend (Builders) Ltd v Cinema News and Property Management Ltd.*[25] This case concerned work to a house at Cheyne Walk, London. The house was owned by Cinema News, which in turn was owned by Mr Harris, who engaged architects David A Wilkie and Partners on an RIBA standard form of appointment for the alterations he wished to be carried out. During construction, it was discovered that the location of a water closet already installed by the contractor contravened London County Council water closet by-laws, as it opened directly off a room which was not a bedroom/dressing room. The architect gave assurance to the contractor that he would clear matters with the council. In particular, in December 1952 he had written to contractor 'you can, therefore, take it that you are safe now in proceeding with the whole of the work as specified and in the course of a post or two we hope to send you further working detailed drawings.' The letter was sent around the time that a notice should have been sent to the local authority, and in response to queries about the notice by the contractor.

The non-compliant work was condemned by the local authority, but allowed to remain subject to certain conditions (because Mrs Harris was an invalid, the work could remain so long as she was in occupation). Mr Harris did not pay the full agreed value of the work, but retained £150 to cover the cost of remedial work. Townsends claimed this amount from Harris, and also brought a claim against Wilkie. The court at first instance found for the contractor. The Court of Appeal upheld these findings, and commented that Townsend was entitled to be indemnified against losses due to the architect's error. Lord Evershed MR stated:

> The responsibility of Wilkie to Townsend rests, it seems to me, quite plainly on the circum-stance that Wilkie, even if there was no consideration as between Wilkie and Townsend, was a professional man acting gratuitously and owing a duty, accordingly, to Townsend. The matter is sufficiently stated in *Halsbury's Laws of England*, 2nd edn, vol. 23 at page 586: 'Where a person skilled in a particular matter gratuitously undertakes to do something involving the exercise of skill he must do it to the best of his skill . . .'. The duty pervaded the whole relation-ship from first to last.[26]

It is interesting to note that this case occurred before that of *Hedley Byrne*,[27] and the emergence of the concept of reliance on a negligent misrepresentation, yet the court had no difficulty in finding that the architect had a duty of care to the contractor.

In relation to certification, before 1974 it was thought that, where a third party has the role of deciding a question between two other parties in circumstances where it has to act fairly between the two parties, the third party could not be held liable in negli-gence for anything done while he was so acting. This was thought to apply, for example, to architects when certifying. It was said that architects, when certifying, were in the

[25] (1958) 20 BLR 118.
[26] ibid., at 146.
[27] *Hedley Byrne & Co. Ltd v Heller & Partners Ltd* [1964] AC 465, see Chapter 3.

position of quasi-arbitrators and were immune from liability. The case of *Sutcliffe v Thackrah & Others*[28] considered that issue.

There the employer engaged architects to act in respect of the design and erection of a house. Eventually, a JCT63 Contract was entered into between the employer and a contractor. The contractor was slow and in due course the building contract was terminated. The architect's interim certificates had been issued without deduction in respect of defective work. The employer could not recover his losses from the contractor, who was now insolvent, and sought damages from the architect. It was held that the architect, in issuing interim certificates, was not acting as a quasi-arbitrator and was not, therefore, immune from liability. An architect issuing interim certificates has a duty to act fairly between the employer and the contractor. The employer can therefore recover his loss from an architect who has negligently issued interim certificates. In *Sutcliffe*, Lord Reid, having described many of the decisions that an architect makes which affect the amount of money a contractor will receive, said:

> ... and, perhaps most important, he has to decide whether work is defective. These decisions will be reflected in the amounts contained in certificates issued by the architect. The building owner and the contractor make their contract on the understanding that in all such matters the architect will act in a fair and unbiased manner and it must, therefore, be implicit in the owner's contract with the architect that he shall not only exercise due care and skill but also reach such decisions fairly holding the balance between his client and the contractor.[29]

Whilst this passage did not go so far as to state unequivocally that the architect owed a duty of care to the contractor in such circumstances, a later case, *Arenson v Casson, Beckman, Rutley & Co*,[30] which concerned negligent valuation of shares by a firm of chartered accountants, made it clear that the architect could owe such a duty. In *Arenson* Lord Salmon said, in the House of Lords, having referred to *Sutcliffe*, that:

> The architect owed a duty to his client, the building owner, arising out of the contract between them to use reasonable care in issuing his certificates. He also, however, owed a similar duty of care to the contractor arising out of their proximity: see *Hedley Byrne Co. Limited v Heller & Partners Limited*. In *Sutcliffe v Thackrah* the architect negligently certified that more money was due than was in fact due, and he was successfully sued for the damage which this had caused his client. He might, however, have negligently certified that less money was payable than was in fact due and thereby starved the contractor of money. In a trade in which cash flow is especially important, this might have caused the contractor serious damage for which the architect could have been successfully sued.[31]

In a case in the Hong Kong Supreme Court, *Shui On Construction Co. Ltd v Shui Kay Co. Ltd*[32] an application was made to the court by defendant architects that the claim

---

[28] (1974) 4 BLR 16 (HL).
[29] ibid., 21; also [1974] AC 727 at 736.
[30] [1975] 3 All ER 901.
[31] ibid., at 924.
[32] (1985) 4 Const LJ 305.

brought against them by the main contractor plaintiffs should be dismissed. The essence of the claim was that the architects owed the main contractors a duty to exercise reasonable skill and care in the performance of their functions pursuant to the contract, and to act fairly and impartially in the performance of those functions. Although of course on this preliminary point the judge did not make a final finding as to a duty or to liability, he refused to strike out the claim against the architects on the basis that there was an arguable claim against them. This decision involved a thorough analysis of the then relevant cases, including *Sutcliffe* and *Arenson*.[33]

In *Lubenham Fidelities and Investment Co. Ltd v South Pembrokeshire District Council & Another*,[34] the Court of Appeal had to consider various matters arising out of a judgment of Judge John Newey QC, Official Referee. Lubenham were bondsmen who had elected to complete certain building contracts in place of the original contractors who had fallen out. The facts are particularly complicated, but in essence, interim certificates that were issued by the architects, who were a party to the proceedings, were not in accordance with the contract and in due course Lubenham terminated their employment under the building contracts. The employer also served termination notices and the parties made a great many claims against each other in the proceedings.

In particular, both Lubenham and the employer made claims against the architects on the basis that their negligence in relation to the certificates was the cause of the loss suffered; further, Lubenham sought to argue that the architects were liable in damages in that they had procured breaches of, or an interference with, the execution of the building contracts by the employer. The judge at first instance, Judge John Newey QC, Official Referee, found that although the architects had been in breach of their duties of care owed to both Lubenham and to the employer, those breaches had not been the cause of the loss, and accordingly he dismissed the claims against the architects. The Court of Appeal subsequently rejected Lubenham's claim that the architects were liable in damages for procuring breaches of, or interfering with, the execution of the building contracts. It appears to have come to this view on the basis that the architects, although entirely misguided, did not act with the express intention of interfering with the performance of the contracts. Lord Justice May put it this way:

> We would not accept the broad contention that an architect, in effecting an interim valuation under this form of building contract, could never in any circumstances expose himself to a claim under this head of tort. It seems to us, for example, quite possible that he could expose himself to an actionable claim that he had interfered with the building contractor's contractual rights if, in effecting a clause 30 valuation, he deliberately misapplied the provisions of the clause with the intention of depriving the contractor of the larger sums to which he would otherwise be entitled.[35]

---

[33] Although *Townsend (Builders) Ltd v Cinema News and Property Management Ltd* [1959] 1 All ER 7 was not considered.
[34] (1986) 33 BLR 39.
[35] ibid., at 74.

In other words, the court regarded the deliberate misapplying of the provisions of the contract as being an essential ingredient to such a cause of action.

10.2.2.1 Michael Salliss

In *Michael Salliss & Co. Ltd v ECA & FB Calil and William F. Newman & Associates*[36] various issues arose between the contractor, an employer and the architects. The contractor was the plaintiff and it made allegations against the architects who were joined in as second defendants in the proceedings. The court reviewed *Thackrah, Arenson* and *Lubenham*, as well as considering *Shui On*. In relation to *Lubenham*, the judge decided that the Court of Appeal in *Lubenham* did not make any finding as to whether or not a duty relationship existed between the architects and the contractor. Having reviewed all the authorities, Judge Fox-Andrews QC, Official Referee, went on to find, amongst other things, that in relation to the JCT63 contract involved in this case:

(1) The architects owed the contractor a duty to use all proper professional skill and care in authorising extensions to the contract period under clause 23.
(2) The architects had breached their duty by certifying an extension of only 12 weeks.
(3) The architects owed to the contractor a duty to act with reasonable expedition in certifying the extension of time, and that compliance with the duty at (1) above would have resulted in a 29-week extension of time for completion.
(4) The architects were in breach of duty to the contractor in failing to certify that the costs, other than the onsite establishment costs, were due from the employer to the contractor pursuant to clause 24(1) (the clause relating to direct loss and/or expense) during the extension of 12 weeks, or alternatively that such other costs during the period of 12 weeks and/ or the period of 29 weeks fell out of the scope of their certificate by clause 24(2) and were therefore recoverable from the employer subject to the general law of contract.

These findings were made in a sub-trial which had been heard on the application of the architects, as to whether the contractor could recover damages for negligence from the architects on the facts pleaded by the contractor, or whether the damages claimed were too remote. In finding that the architects did owe duties to the contractor, the court adopted the reasoning of *Thackrah* and *Arenson* and said that, to the extent that the contractor was able to establish damage resulting from the architects' unfairness in respect of matters in which, under the contract, the architects were required to act impartially, damages were recoverable and were not too remote.

Further, where the architects were acting in their capacity as the employer's agent, for example, ordering a variation, there was no such duty but, for example, once having ordered a variation, they had an obligation to act fairly in pricing the variation. The judge therefore concluded that although the architects might be liable to the contractor for negligent certification, there was no such duty to take all such steps as were necessary to ensure that the contractor would carry out work continuously from the

---

[36] (1988) 4 Const LJ 125.

commencement date, there was no duty owed to the contractor to carry out a full and accurate survey prior to the preparation of the specification and plans and in any event before commencement of the works, and most importantly in terms of design liability, there was no duty owed to the contractor to use all proper professional skill and care in the preparation of the specification and drawings.

10.2.2.2 Pacific Associates

The decision in the *Salliss* case was delivered in the same year as the judgment of another Official Referee, Judge John Davies QC in *Pacific Associates v Baxter*.[37] In this case, the contractor plaintiffs were engaged on the FIDIC contract (the international form of civil engineering contract) to carry out dredging and reclamation works for the Ruler of Dubai, who was the employer. Halcrow were the engineers engaged by the Ruler to administer the contract.

In the construction contract between the contractor and the Ruler of Dubai, there had been an arbitration clause and another provision in the following form:

> Neither . . . the Engineer nor any of his staff, nor the Engineer's Representative shall be in any way personally liable for the acts or obligations under the contract, or answerable for any default or omission on the part of the Employer in the observance or performance of any of the acts, matters or things which are herein contained.

Disputes arose between the contractor and the Ruler which went to arbitration. Those disputes were the subject of an agreed settlement. Thereafter, the contractor started proceedings against the engineers seeking to recover money that they claimed arose from negligent certification by the engineers. The engineers applied to the court to have the claim against them struck out.

The Official Referee came to a very different conclusion from that in *Michael Saliss*: no duty of care was owed by the engineers to the contractor and the judge struck out the claim against the engineers. This case then went to the Court of Appeal which upheld the judge's decision. The basis of the decision in the Court of Appeal was twofold; firstly, they said that the arbitration clause entitled the contractor to challenge, in arbitration with the Ruler, the certification of the engineers. Secondly, the disclaimer of liability of the engineers set out above could not be ignored. These two points taken together prevented the imposition of a duty of care on the engineers.

It is, of course, the case that both the JCT family of contracts and the ICE family of contracts generally contain arbitration clauses, although none of them contain any disclaimer of liability on behalf of the certifier. However, the presence of an arbitration clause in *Michael Salliss* did not prevent the judge there finding a duty of care. In *Pacific Associates*, the Court of Appeal was referred to *Michael Salliss* and the Court did not overrule it: Lord Justice Purchas, however, did say that he doubted the earlier decision.

---

[37] (1989) 44 BLR 33 (CA).

Pacific Associates was followed in the Hong Kong courts.[38] There, a contractor failed to have the architects joined into the proceedings as defendants. They had sought to argue that the architects owed them a duty to give timely, proper and impartial consideration to the claims of the contractor. Mr Justice Bokhary founded his decision on there being machinery in the contract between the contractor and the building owner to deal with such issues. However, this case received some criticism from commentators, as being inconsistent with previous authority. Also, as noted by Cornes in the previous edition of this book, there may be some exceptional situations in which the decision in *Pacific Associates* could be distinguished. For example:

(1) Where there is no arbitration clause in the construction contract or other method of challenging certification by the certifier, and, no disclaimer, or
(2) Where the certifier has under-certified, the employer has become insolvent and the construction contract did not permit the challenging of certificates in arbitration or otherwise until after practical completion.

10.2.2.3 *Developments since* Pacific Associates

The above cases were all primarily concerned with certification, not with design, and were all decided before *Henderson v Merret* extended the potential for liability in tort from negligent misstatement to include the negligent provision of services.[39] Subsequent cases show that courts may now be more likely to find that a designer could take on liability to a contractor.

An example of this is *Cliffe Holdings v Parkman Buck*.[40] Cliffe Holdings was the contractor on a design-build project in Rochester (the Spectrum Business Park). Cliffe Holdings engaged consulting engineers Parkman to undertake engineering and architectural services and it in turn engaged a separate firm of architects for the architectural design element. Towards the end of the project major problems emerged, for example the doors and windows leaked water and the screed on the first floor was cracking and breaking up. The contractor commenced arbitration proceedings against its client to recover withheld payments, but after abandoning the arbitration and settling with the developer, brought a claim instead against the sub-contract engineers and sub-sub-contract architects, including a claim that the architects owed it a duty of care in tort. The architects denied such a duty and argued that 'the position of the professional ought not to be different from ordinary cases where sub-contractors do not owe such duties in tort to the party employing the main contractor'. The Court was clear however that the position of a professional person was quite different as a consequence of the principal established in *Hedley Byrne*. Following *Henderson v Merrett*, the proper test to be applied was 'whether the architect has assumed a responsibility for giving advice

---

[38] *Leon Engineering & Construction Co. Ltd v Ka Duk Investment Co. Ltd* (1990) 47 BLR 139.
[39] *Henderson v Merrett Syndicates Ltd* (1994) 69 BLR 26 (HL), see Chapter 4.
[40] BLISS 9: 1996.

to the contractor in circumstances where he knew that it was likely to be relied upon, and where it was reasonably foreseeable that if it is relied upon, and if it was carelessly given, economic damage would or might result to the contractor.' The judge stated: 'I have no difficulty in concluding that the architect owed a duty of care in tort to the contractor concurrent with the contractual duty of care of the engineer. The position of the professional thus differs from that of the ordinary trade sub-contractor'.[41]

Examples can be found outside the UK. In the Canadian case of *Edgeworth Construction v ND Lea Associates Ltd*[42] a contractor tendered for a project on documents prepared by engineers engaged by the employer. The contractor subsequently lost money because of errors in the drawings, and brought a claim against the engineers based on negligent misrepresentation. The Supreme Court of Canada, determined that in principle the contractor had prima facie case for negligence based on *Hedley Byrne* principles, although in this particular case the drawings in question were not a sufficient basis for a claim, for example they did not contain any affirmation as to the accuracy of their contents. The court accepted, however, that drawings issued for tender by the employer could in principal form the basis for a claim, even though there had been no direct communication between the engineers and the contractor. The court also held that neither the contractual structure nor the terms of the contract between the province and the contractor negated the existence of a duty of care.

The case of *Galliford Try Infrastructure Ltd v Mott MacDonald Lt*[43] is of particular interest to designers, as it concerns the effect of disclaimers on drawings. Engineers Mott McDonald were engaged by Morrison Property in relation to the design of a development on the site of the Birmingham Children's Hospital. Morrison Property also engaged Galliford Try on a design-build and contract. Although it had been intended that the engineers would be novated to the contractor, this did not take place as Mott MacDonald's terms of appointment had not contained any such requirement, and it was not possible to agree terms with Galliford Try. It transpired that the engineers had underestimated the amount of work required, and the contractor brought a claim against them in tort. The contractors argued that the necessary ingredients for negligent misrepresentation were present; there was foreseeability and sufficient proximity (the engineers had been passing information and drawings direct to the contractor). The court disagreed, deciding that there had in fact been no reliance. One important factor was that the specifications and drawings provided to the contractor had contained disclaimers, for example the drawings had stated:

> This document should not be relied on or used in circumstances other than those for which it was originally prepared and for which Mott MacDonald Ltd was commissioned. Mott MacDonald accepts no responsibility for this document to any party other than the person by whom it was commissioned.

---

[41] Transcript, p. 7 of 15.
[42] (1993) 66 Build LR 56.
[43] [2008] 108 Con LR 1.

In reaching its conclusion the court commented:

> (h) So far as disclaimers are concerned, they are simply one factor, albeit possibly an important one, in determining whether a duty of care arises. One can not, usually, voluntarily undertake a responsibility when one tells all concerned that one is not accepting such responsibility.[44]

An example of a contractor claiming against an employer's agent for negligent misrepresentation be seen in *J Jarvis & Sons v Castle Wharf Developments*.[45] This concerned a design-build tender where the tenderers were supplied with Employer's Requirements, which were not kept up to date, and did not show exactly all the details as required by the planning authorities. Jarvis submitted proposals and was told by Gleeds Management Services Ltd, acting as employer's agent, that 15 items in its proposals were unacceptable to the planners. After the meeting Jarvis prepared options relating to the 15 items, which were discussed at a further meeting where revised proposals were agreed, and a letter of intent was issued. Jarvis claimed that it was given the impression that the scheme agreed upon at the meeting would comply with the planning consent that had been obtained, but that this turned out later to be incorrect. The court at first instance found that Gleeds had a duty of care to Jarvis, and that it had breached that duty. Gleeds took the issue to appeal. The Court of Appeal supported the decision at first instance, stating that:

> There is no reason in principle why the professional agent of the employer cannot become liable to a contractor for negligent misstatements made by the agent to a contractor to induce the contractor to tender, if the contractor relies on those misstatements. But whether a duty of care in fact arises in any given situation must depend on all the circumstances, including in particular the terms of what was said to the contractor.[46]

However it found that Jarvis was an experienced design and build contractor, and had not placed reliance on any misrepresentations made, therefore on the facts of this case Gleeds was not liable for the losses suffered by Jarvis.

Although instances are rare, the above cases show that it would be unwise to assume that an architect or engineer could never owe liability in tort to a contractor. If the consultant was to give design advice direct to the contractor in a situation where it might be expected to rely on it, then a court might decide that this fell within the ambit of a *Hedley Byrne* duty.

10.2.3 Sub-contractor liability

These days most work is sub-contracted, and specialist companies form an essential part of the procurement process, frequently providing design services as well as manufacture,

---

[44] ibid., at para. 190.
[45] (2001) 17 Const LJ 430.
[46] ibid., para. 53.

supply and installation and general construction work. Apart from their contractual liability they may also be found liable in tort. As for contractors, in appropriate circumstances they could be liable for injury or damage to property caused by their negligence. The position of a sub-contractor with respect to liability in tort for pure economic loss has largely to be determined by analogy to that of a contractor, as there are few specific examples of claims in tort against sub-contractors, and the outcomes of these are conflicting. Furthermore, all of these cases need to be considered in the light of recent developments such as *Robinson v Jones*.

In *Barclays Bank Plc v Fairclough Building Ltd*[47] a sub-subcontractor was held liable to a subcontractor for negligent specialist roof-cleaning work. The roof was constructed from corrugated asbestos sheets, and the sub-subcontractors failed to follow recommended practice while cleaning off moss, lichens and accumulated dirt using high-pressure hoses, so that asbestos slurry entered the building and contaminated stored files. The sub-subcontractors were found to have a parallel tortious duty to the sub-contractor to avoid causing it economic loss. However it should be noted that this decision was questioned by the editors of the *Building Law Reports*, and was not directly addressed by the Court of Appeal in *Robinson v Jones*.

In *George Fisher Holding Ltd v Multi Design Consultants Ltd*[48] the claimant was the employer under a construction contract with Multi Construction Ltd, which named the defendant Multi Design Consultants Ltd as the designer of the project (at the time the contract was formed MDC was an associated company of MCL but later became independent). The design failed and the employer claimed on the basis of an alleged collateral contract, and in tort. The claim with respect to tort failed as the court declined to find that the sub-contractor owed duty of care in negligence to avoid pure economic loss in respect of design. In reaching this finding it had regard to the contractual context stating '[t]he conclusion must be that the Plaintiff accepted the familiar contractual regime of main contract and sub-contracts, under which it would look to the main contractor alone for redress notwithstanding that the breach complained of might lie at the door of a sub-contractor.'[49]

George Fisher concerned design services, rather than construction work, and is difficult to reconcile with the broader statements in *Henderson v Merrett* at around the same time (see Chapter 4 and above). Also, in other contexts, sub-contractors have been found liable for economic loss, for example in *Bailey v HSS Alarms*[50] sub-contractors to a burglar alarm company failed to monitor an alarm system installed by the company and were found liable to the premises owner for economic loss.

Therefore, although there are few specific examples of a sub-contractor being found liable for pure economic loss, as with contractors such a liability is possible, particularly in situations where advice is given direct to the employer.

---

[47] (1995) 76 BLR 1 (CA).

[48] [1998] CILL 1362.

[49] ibid., at para. 85.

[50] *The Times*, 20 June 2000 (CA), cited in Peter Aeberli, *Tort in Construction* (Aeberli, 2001).

There is also a further possible avenue for a claim in tort. As already noted, *Linklaters Business Services v Sir Robert McAlpine Ltd*[51] examined the question as to whether a subcontractor could become liable for economic loss where its work damages another part of a building. Although the argument was ultimately unsuccessful in that case, the Court did not rule out the possibility that the subcontractor might be liable in different circumstances, for example if it designs and installs an entirely separate element.

10.3 Warranties

Collateral warranties are basically contracts that exist in parallel with another contract, and which enable the party to whom the warranty is given to bring an action against a person providing services under the original contract: for example contractors or consultants are often asked to provide warranties to future tenants, alongside their ongoing contract with the employer. One of their key purposes is to enable parties to avoid the vagaries of bringing a claim in tort as discussed above.

A warranty should be distinguished from the right to assign. Following an assignment the original contracting party has no longer any rights under the contract: the person to whom the contract is assigned takes over all those rights. When a collateral warranty is set up the original parties of course retain all rights under the contract. The employer can make an assignment to only one party, whereas warranties can be set up with any number. Frequently therefore assignment does not suit the original employer, who prefers to set up collateral warranties in favour of future owners, tenants, and financing companies such as banks.

As well as warranties from contractor and consultant to purchaser, tenant and funder, there are other types of warranty, particularly relating to design obligations, for example in design-build procurement warranties may be required from consultants engaged by the contractor to the employer, or from specialist sub-contractors to the employer. Even though the contractor may be liable to the employer for the consultant's or specialist's design, these warranties afford an alternative route for reclaiming losses, which may be essential should the contractor become bankrupt.

10.3.1 Obligation to enter into collateral warranties

Save for commercial pressure, there is no obligation on anyone to enter into a collateral warranty unless there is a binding obligation contained in another contract: for example, the architect's conditions of engagement could contain a clause requiring that architect to give collateral warranties to certain parties 'in accordance with a draft attached'. Provided the obligation and the draft are certain, this is likely to be a binding obligation. Such a well-drafted clause is likely to be effective in law even though the name of the tenant/purchaser is not known at the outset, provided the clause is drafted on the basis that the name of the tenant/purchaser can be fixed by a determination by one party

---

[51] [2010] EWHC 1145 (TCC).

and which determination does not depend upon agreement between the parties.[52] However if the terms are left vague, or subject to further negotiation, this is unlikely to be enforceable.

10.3.2 General considerations

The intention of the collateral warranty is to create a contractual relationship that is collateral to the obligations created by the principal contract. That principal contract can take a great many different forms; for example a consultant's standard terms of engagement, the main construction contract and all the various forms of sub- and trade contracts. The guideline principles should be that *the collateral warranty should not seek to impose any greater or more extensive obligations than those which are created under the principal contract.*

   One exception to this principle is where a subcontract between a contractor and a sub-contractor contains no obligations as to design, whereas the sub-contractor is in fact designing. Clearly, to protect the employer, the design obligation should be the subject of a clause in a collateral warranty so as to create a contractual cause of action in the event of default in the design obligation. An example of this would be where the JCT Intermediate Building Contract is used and a named sub-contractor undertakes design, the sub-contractor should be required to enter into a warranty to the employer (see section 14.1.4).

10.3.3 Terms

There are no universally accepted standard forms of collateral warranty although there are standard forms for particular situations, including the CIC Warranties (Consultant-Employer CIC/ConsWa/D&BE, Consultant-Funder CIC/ConsWa/F and Consultant-Purchaser/Tenant CIC/ConsWa/P&T), the British Property Federation (BPF) forms, and those produced by the JCT for main contractors (e.g. CWa/P&T for purchasers and tenants and CWa/F for funders). These standard form warranties are carefully worded and largely deal with many of the issues raised below.[53] Most of the problems in the agreement of warranties arise because there are a great number of purpose-drafted forms. It is therefore unproductive to look in detail at the precise wording of many of the clauses that appear in practice. However, it is possible to put into categories the types of terms that are commonly found.

10.3.4 Design

An approach sometimes adopted is that the designer gives a warranty to the third party that the designer has and will perform the design agreement with the client in all respects in accordance with that agreement. Although this has the benefit of being truly

---

[52] *May and Butcher Ltd v The King* [1934] 2 KB 17.
[53] for a comparison between the CIC and BPF warranties, see Construction Industry Council, *Liability Briefing: Standard Forms of Collateral Warranty Compared* (London: CIC, 2007).

collateral to the principal contract, it may well have unintended effects. It could result, for example, in a design and build contractor owing all the duties that it owes to the employer under the contract to a tenant including, by way of further example, an obligation to complete on or before the completion date and an obligation to pay liquidated and ascertained damages. The effect of such wholesale incorporation of the principal contract would expand the scope of the warranty to cover far more than merely design duties. It has to be said, however, that some funders may well want more than just a design warranty.

The better way to proceed in relation to design is to repeat in the warranty the clause, or part of the clause, that appears in the principal contract in relation to the particular services that are the subject of the warranty. For example, condition 2.1 of the Architect's Appointment:

> The Architect shall exercise reasonable skill, care and diligence in accordance with the normal standards of the Architect's profession in performing the Services and discharging all the obligations under this clause 2.

Such a clause can easily be transposed into a collateral warranty. A similar approach can be taken to an engineer, a designing main contractor and designing sub-contractors. The CIC warranty refers to the 'services to the Client'; if there is any doubt it may be best to specify exactly which services are warranted and where they are set out.

Difficulties are sometimes perceived where architects and engineers are engaged by contractors in relation to a design and build project of the contractor. In relation to design, a contractor on such a project is in a position to give warranties in relation to the design to the funder, purchasers and tenants. Should the architect and engineer therefore be asked to give warranties as well? Such warranties will usually be needed in relation to a funder and a purchaser where they might wish to protect their position by taking over the project if the contractor/developer fall out of the equation. Usually there will be a chain of contracts, providing a route for a claim but, of course, a chain is only as strong as its weakest link and if a contractor, for example, becomes insolvent, then this chain of contracts will be broken and a tenant would have no right in tort against the contractor's architect.

It is for this reason that warranties are often sought from the design team on a design and build project. As above, architects and engineers should be wary of the wholesale incorporation of standard form condition of engagement obligations into warranties, in case it has unintended results. For example, the architect and the engineer may owe duties in addition to the design obligation, such as inspection duties, to the parties to whom they give such warranties.

10.3.5 Fitness for purpose

Provisions as to fitness for purpose in design are not usually sensible provisions to be incorporated into collateral warranties for the following reasons. First, at least in the case of consultants, this is unlikely to reflect the terms of the principal contract. The basis of the appointment of designers is almost always that of reasonable skill and care – designers do not guarantee that they will produce a particular result (see Chapter 7). Secondly, professional indemnity insurance policies, including those of design and build contractors, are written on the basis of reasonable skill and care. Furthermore, professional indemnity policies usually exclude any liability assumed under a contract which increases the standard of care or measure of liability above that which normally applies under the usual conditions of engagement. It is to the benefit of every party to a collateral warranty that its provisions do not prevent the designer from having recourse to the policy should a claim arise. To put it another way, there is no commercial benefit in drafting and securing harsh provisions if, when liability is established, there is no money available to meet the liability.

Sometimes there is an obligation that a contractor or sub-contractor warrants that materials will be fit for their purpose insofar as they have been or will be selected by the contractor/sub-contractor. Such a clause creates no particular difficulties where it is in relation to a contract for the supply of work and material, and the contract includes no design obligations: it is nothing more nor less than the position at common law (see, e.g. *Young and Marten v McManus Childs*[54]) and under statute (see Supply of Goods and Services Act 1982). Where the term is to be included in a contract where there is design in addition to work and materials, then consideration must be given as to whether or not such an obligation seeks to impose a fitness for purpose obligation in relation to design (see Chapter 7). Where there is any doubt, it may be commercially sensible for all the parties to make such a fitness for purpose obligation in relation to materials subject to a duty to use reasonable skill and care in the selection.

10.3.6 Workmanship

Main contractors are often asked to warrant to third parties that they will carry out and complete the project in accordance with the building contract. However, the words used often seek to impose much greater obligations than are created by the building contract itself. A contractor should not reasonably be asked to give warranties to third parties that go beyond its obligations as to quality contained in the building contract. As with design, this warranty can often be drafted by reference to the wording of the building contract itself in respect of quality. For example, where the main contract is JCT SBC11, the warranty might take the following form:

> The Contractor warrants to the tenant that it has and will use in the construction of the Works (as defined in the Building Contract) materials and workmanship of the quality and standard specified in and/or required under the Building Contract.

Warranties that seek to oblige the contractor to warrant to the tenant that it will carry out and complete the works in accordance with the building contract should be avoided by contractors. (Which of the contractor's duties in the building contract are intended to be owed under such a warranty to the tenant?)

10.3.7 Deleterious materials

Warranties frequently contain a provision that certain materials will not be specified for use and/or used in the construction of the project. It is doubtful whether this is a

---

[54] [1969] 1 AC 454.

sensible and logical way to specify what materials are to be used. The most usual place to specify the quality of the project is in the main contract specification. If certain materials are not to be used, then those materials can easily be incorporated into the specification by way of prohibition. If that were done, then there would be no need for a deleterious materials provision in collateral warranties.

There are other reasons for not having a list of particular deleterious materials in the warranty. First, such a list cannot, by definition, ever be a complete list. Secondly there is the danger that on a particular wording, anything that is not specified as deleterious can be used. Thirdly, and most importantly, there is no reason why the third party should not rely on the general and positive obligations created by warranties as to design and quality of materials and workmanship. For example, could it really be seriously suggested that an engineer would not be in breach of a duty to use reasonable skill and care in circumstances where he or she had specified the use of high alumina cement concrete for the structural beams in the roof of a swimming pool? The same point can be made in relation to all of the seven or eight most commonly stated deleterious materials. There does seem little point in having a definitive list of specific negatives when there is available an overriding positive general duty to exercise reasonable skill and care.

That said, the current convention or perceived wisdom (probably coupled with pressure from tenants and commercial conveyancing solicitors) is to have a deleterious materials provision. If this is done, it may be best to adopt an industry standard such as the one prepared by the British Council for Offices[55] (and is in fact referred to in standard CIC and BPF warranties, and the JCT contracts). There is often a sweep-up provision at the end of the deleterious materials clause, but again it is almost certainly more satisfactory to rely on the positive duty to exercise reasonable skill and care than to have a sweep-up clause as a negative obligation. Some sweep-up clauses are so wide and general that they should not be included in any warranty.

It is important to check that deleterious materials provisions in collateral warranties are not in conflict with the provisions of the contracts to which the warranties are collateral; what is to happen if a material banned in the collateral warranty is specified by the architect to be used in circumstances where the contractor under the building contract has an obligation to comply with architect's instructions?

A designer, who is not also building, can warrant that it will not specify particular materials but cannot properly warrant that it will see that the contractor does not incorporate such materials into construction (even where the designer has not specified them). A similar point arises on the wording of the JCT Contract with Contractor's Design where the employer can require a change.

10.3.8 Copyright

Occasionally, a funder or tenant will seek to have the copyright in drawings and the design assigned. Such a provision is in direct conflict with the provisions of standard

---

[55] British Council for Offices (BCO), *Good Practice in the Selection of Construction Materials* (London: BCO, 2011), formerly published by Ove Arup.

forms of engagement including, for example, the Architect's Appointment 2010 and the ACE Conditions of Engagement. The simplest way to avoid this problem is for the copyright to remain with the designer but for the designer to grant a licence in the warranty in respect of the copyright but limited to the purposes of the development – it would not be sensible for a designer to fully assign away the copyright, or to grant a licence in the absence of such a limitation. A further point is that the Architect's Appointment reserves copyright in documents and drawings and states that they 'may not be used for reproduction of the design for any part of any extension of the Project' (Clause 6.3). It is again important that the warranty should reflect the principal contract. Professional designers may want to see that the granting of the licence in the warranty is conditional upon them having been paid in respect of the work that they have done – this is the position in the Architect's Appointment, and is reflected in the CIC and BPF forms.

10.3.9 Insurance

In warranties given by a party who is carrying out design, there is often a requirement as to the provision of professional indemnity insurance. These provisions vary enormously in their content and effect. A typical term may require the insurance to be in force at the date of the warranty, that the premiums have and will be paid and that the insurance will be maintained into the future, sometimes without limit in time and sometimes with a limit.

These provisions give rise to real practical and legal issues. The professional indemnity market changes from time to time both in the average levels of premium available and in terms of the capacity and, consequently, the amount of the insurance. Professional indemnity insurance is renewable annually and is made on the basis that it covers claims made during the period of insurance (see Chapter 16). Given the vagaries of the professional indemnity insurance market and the annual basis of this type of insurance, it is very difficult for a designer to give warranties in relation to future insurance, even one or two years ahead, let alone for six or twelve years. The CIC warranties, for example, deal with this by allowing the parties to insert a period of years, and including a proviso that the insurance is available at commercially reasonable rates.

This type of provision assumes that the designer's firm or company will continue in business into the future in the same legal form. Where it is a firm, the partners who entered into the warranty (and who are liable for breaches) may cease to be partners and/or may retire or die. Where the designer is a company, it may cease to trade with or without going into liquidation or receivership. These points should be borne in mind by parties seeking onerous insurance provisions in warranties.

There is sometimes a prohibition in policies preventing disclosure of the existence of the insurance to third parties – in such circumstances the insurer's express permission should be obtained on this point prior to discussing the terms of such a warranty with the third party.

Finally, what is to happen if the designer is in breach of an obligation under such a clause? Clearly the designer would be in breach of contract under the warranty and that would give rise to a claim on the part of the other party for damages? Those damages are the sum of money that would put recipients of such a warranty in the position they would have been in but for the breach. That sum of money might be the whole or part of the premium for the professional indemnity insurance – however, it is highly unlikely that a third party would be able to take out professional indemnity insurance on behalf of the designer in any event. It follows that the consequences of breach of a provision of this kind are not terribly helpful to the party in receipt of the benefit.

A fairly unobjectionable provision might be for the designer to warrant that there is insurance in existence at the date of the warranty and that the premium has been paid; designers could further warrant that they will use best endeavours to obtain professional indemnity insurance in succeeding years provided that such insurance is available in the marketplace at commercially reasonable rates; designers could undertake to notify the other party or parties in the event that insurance could not be obtained at commercially reasonable rates.

10.3.10 Novation

Purchasers and funders may wish to have the right to continue with the project, in the event that the employer/developer is unable to, perhaps through receivership or liquidation or a serious breach of the funding agreement, and may seek to include provision for this in the warranty. One method is a novation agreement proper whereby, for example, in the building contract the contractor continues as before and the funder/purchaser, as the case may be, is substituted for the employer/developer in the building contract on the basis that the funder/purchaser takes on all the rights and obligations of the employer/developer. (Note this kind of provision is not appropriate for tenants, nor is it the kind normally used when a consultant switches to work for a contractor in design-build procurement.) That would mean all the rights and obligations both existing and future. It is not unusual for funders and purchasers to try to avoid a commitment as to past liabilities by providing that they shall only be liable on the agreement from the date of the novation.

The consequences for, say, the contractor as in the example above of entering into a fresh agreement with a third party is that such a step is likely to be a repudiatory breach of the principal contract. There must, therefore, be a provision to the effect that the contractor will not be in breach of its principal contract if the funder/purchaser exercises its right to step into the shoes of the developer/employer. The most usual way of dealing with these issues is to have a provision that such novation-type arrangements are contained in a tripartite agreement, that is to say in the case of a contractor, the contractor, the developer/employer and the funder/purchaser should all be parties to the agreement.

The most satisfactory method of dealing with these issues is to provide in the warranty that the contractor and the employer/developer will enter into a novation agreement in the form of a draft attached if the funder so requires. There is much confused drafting around on these issues. Sometimes, draughtsmen seek to amend, in the warranty, the principal contract. This is not sensible. Nor is it sensible to provide in the warranty that the contactor will not exercise its rights to terminate under the building contract without giving 28 days prior notice to the fund, unless this is carefully checked to see that it is not in conflict with the provisions of the principal contract. For example, liquidation of the employer may sometimes create an automatic termination of the employment of the contractor. How is the contractor to give 28 days clear notice to the fund? Convoluted provisions to deal with these kinds of issues are only likely to lead to a lack of clarity and uncertainty. The simplest solution is to provide that, where there is any notice of termination, a copy of that notice is to be given at the same time to the fund.

10.3.11 Assignment

This is one of the most difficult areas of collateral warranties. If there is no provision for assignment in the warranty, then the benefit of a warranty is freely assignable without the consent of the other party. Such an assignment can be either legal or equitable (see section 2.5). Where there is in a contract an express prohibition on assignment, then such prohibition is likely to be effective in law. It follows that, if there is a purported assignment in such cases, it is likely that the assignment will be void.[56]

The most difficult issues arise where there is a purported restriction on assignment in the warranty. It is common to see warranty provisions which seek to impose a limit on the number of assignments that can be made, typically to one or two assignments. This can arise where the draughtsman is attempting to make the provision on assignment and the warranty consistent with the provisions of the professional indemnity insurance policy (where there are restrictions on assignment in the policy). This must be drafted carefully, with a clear prohibition on any further assignments. Any person seeking to bring a claim through an assigned warranty would have to demonstrate that the assignment fell within the limits imposed. The restriction would not prevent, for example, the second assignee purporting to assign the benefit to a third party, but would mean that the third party would have to claim any losses against the second assignee, not direct against the first party. A second method (not likely to be acceptable to the funder or tenant) is to provide in the warranty that assignment is prohibited save where the express consent in writing of the original giver of the warranty has been obtained. The provision could continue to recite that the giver of the warranty shall not withhold consent where the assignment is a first or second assignment. Such a provision puts control in the hands of the original contracting party who needs to have that control, namely, the insured in this example.

Sometimes a provision is inserted into a warranty that the agreement is personal to the parties. This is an attempt to take advantage of the rule of law that the benefits of a personal contract cannot be assigned either by a legal or equitable assignment. However, there is real doubt as to whether a personal contract can be created in law by a provision in the contract that says a contract is personal. The test, which is an objective test, is whether 'it can make no difference to the person on whom the obligation lies to which of two persons he is to discharge it'.[57] It is to be noted that the test is not concerned with

[56] *Linden Gardens Trust Ltd v Lenesta Sludge Disposals Ltd & Others* and *St Martin's Property Corporation Ltd & Another v Sir Robert McAlpine and Sons Ltd* (1993) 63 BLR 1 (HL).
[57] *Tolhurst v Associated Portland Cement Manufacturers (1900) Ltd* [1902] 2 KB 660 (CA).

the personal skill of the debtor so that, for example, if architects give a collateral warranty relating to their design work, whilst the design work will involve personal skill on their part and will not be assignable by the architects to a third party, the benefits of the undertakings arising under the warranty given to a tenant will be assignable to a future tenant because, applying the objective test, it can make no difference to the architects whether their obligations lie to the first tenant or to a future tenant.

10.3.12　Other parties clause

The Civil Liability (Contribution) Act 1978 deals with contribution between people liable in respect of any damage whether tort, breach of contract or otherwise (see section 11.3). Under the provisions of the Act where two or more people are in breach of separate contracts with the same third person producing the same damage, those two or more persons can claim contribution against each other.

Concern is sometimes expressed, particularly among the construction professions, that if they give written warranties and other people do not, they will be liable to the third party for the full amount of the loss and unable to claim contribution from those other parties who did not sign collateral warranties. The other parties may not be liable in respect of the same damage, if there is no remedy in tort against them. The givers of warranties have therefore sought methods to try to ensure they are not liable for the full amount of the loss in circumstances where other parties ought properly to be liable at the same time. But the creation of enforceable provisions to this effect is not easy.

The most effective provision (which is not likely to be acceptable to third parties) is that a warranty does not come into force and effect at all (a condition precedent) unless certain named other parties have entered into collateral warranties with the same third party to the same effect. This is sometimes called the 'three musketeers' clause – all for one, and one for all. Another method is for a developer to give an undertaking in the warranty that it will obtain warranties in the same or very similar form from certain other named parties. What is the effect of this clause in relation to, say, an architect's liability where the developer has failed to obtain those other warranties? Clearly there will be a breach by the developer but does that breach give rise to only nominal damages or something more useful to the architect? This issue will be determined by the rules on remoteness and whether or not those damages are simply too uncertain to be ascertained.

If the client had entered into other warranty agreements, then the firm would be entitled to bring contribution proceedings under the Civil Liability (Contribution) Act 1978 against any other firm who had given a warranty, provided, of course, that the other firm was liable in respect of the same damage. The absence of the warranty would prevent such a claim being brought, there being no liability in tort. It follows that failure by a developer to obtain other warranty agreements will have prevented the architect from seeking contribution from the other firm or firms that would otherwise have been liable in respect of the same damage. Assuming that the architect could satisfy a court that the other firms would have been liable in respect of the same damage had a collateral warranty been entered into, the next issue would be whether the amount of that contribution could be ascertained with any certainty by a court. Courts have entertained such relatively speculative calculations, namely, where assessment is dependent on a contingency (see e.g. *Chaplin v Hicks*[58] and *Cook v Swinfen*[59]). If the court did entertain that calculation, then the architect would recover the amount of the calculated contribution, not from the other firm liable in respect of the same damage, but from the developer as damages for breach of his obligation to obtain collateral warranty agreements from the other firms.

The other type of provision that is being used is the 'net contribution clause' (see section 13.3). Such a clause appears in the Standard Agreement 2010 at clause 7.3 (see section 15.1) and a sample standard clause for use in bespoke appointments is available to download from the CIC website. That agreement is not a collateral warranty but the principles are the same. This limits a designer's liability to the other party to such sum as he or she ought reasonably have to pay, having regard to his or her responsibility for it and also on the basis that the contractor, engineer and so on shall be deemed to have paid their liability in respect of their contribution to the other party. It is an attempt to achieve by contract that which would take place in the courts under the Civil Liability (Contribution) Act 1978 were all the parties liable in respect of the same damage, namely an apportionment of liability between the defendants. It also has the effect of limiting the designer's liability to his or her share even though the other party may not, in fact, have received any contributions from the contractor, engineer and so on.

10.3.13 Limiting liability

The parties to a contract can in English law agree a term excluding liability or limiting the consequences of liability subject only to some statutory regulation, including the Unfair Contract Terms Act 1977. The whole question of consequential loss is a matter that gives rise to great concern amongst the givers of warranties and their professional indemnity insurers (see section 11.2.3). It is one thing, they say, to be liable for the direct costs of remedial works following defective design or workmanship; it is another to have to pay all the other economic consequences that may flow from such a breach of contract. These can include loss of rent, the costs of the tenant moving out of the building whilst repairs are carried out, the costs of disruption/loss of profit and business and the costs of returning after the remedial works. Often, the indirect costs exceed the cost of the remedial works. Various attempts have been made in warranties to try to restrict that potentially wide liability.

One method is to exclude economic and consequential loss. However, those words do not have a precise legal meaning for this purpose and could give rise to difficulty of interpretation on particular facts. There is now a tendency for draughtsmen to provide

---

[58] [1911] 2 KB 786.
[59] [1967] 1 WLR 457 (CA).

expressly for what is covered, rather than seeking to limit the scope of general damages. For example, a firm of architects might seek to limit its liability under the warranty to the direct cost of remedying the defective work, all other costs, losses, damages and expenses being excluded. A further method is to state that the consultant is entitled to rely on any exclusion of liability in its appointment (the method used in the CIC warranties).

Clearly more widely accepted standard forms of collateral warranty would be of great benefit but the drafting and agreement of standard forms is fraught with difficulty. A useful discussion of the clauses in the CIC and BPF standard form warranties is given in the CIC Liability Briefing 'Standard forms of collateral warranty compared'.[60]

10.4 Collaborative working

As outlined in Chapter 1, recent developments in procurement have focussed on systems intended to result in increased collaboration between team members. Part of the motivation for this is to reduce the number of disputes, and consequently the large amount of resources expended on these.

Newer standard forms of contract strive to achieve a higher level of cooperation in several ways: they require the parties to enter a team agreement (such as that in JCT Constructing Excellence and NEC Option X12), or they dispense with bilateral contracts, and engage all parties on a multi-party agreement (such as PPC2000). The design liability clauses within these separate forms are discussed in Chapter 15. In addition, all of these new arrangements, and most long-standing contract forms, now include clauses requiring the parties to behave cooperatively, to treat each other fairly and to generally discharge their duties in a spirit of mutual trust (often termed 'fair dealing' clauses). It is difficult to determine precisely the effect these developments will have on the nature and extent of any design obligations because, perhaps as evidence of their success, there have been few cases to date examining these provisions.

Two cases concerning partnering charters are however of interest. In the Australian case of *P Ward v Civil and Civic*[61] a contractor and subcontractor signed a partnering agreement during period of negotiations before entering a contract. The subcontractor later tried to claim that the extent of its design obligation under the contract was greater than that discussed during negotiations, and that under the fair dealing requirements in the charter the contractor should have pointed this out before the contract was executed; in effect it claimed there had been misrepresentation by the contractor. The court refused to accept this, saying: 'Wards' abrogation of the usual common sense commercial obligation to look at contractual materials prior to executing a contract, cannot in the circumstances here proven, even accepting the "partnering" parameter, sustain this cause of action'.[62]

---

[60] CIC 2007, available at www.cic.org.uk/activities/liability.shtml.
[61] [1999] NSWSC 727.
[62] ibid., para. 658(6).

Birse Construction Ltd v St David Ltd[63] concerned the effect that a non-binding part-nering charter might have determining whether a contract had come into existence. The parties had signed a charter but, because of disagreements over some matters, failed to execute formal contract documents. In the meantime work was undertaken and Birse brought a claim for payment on a *quantum meruit* basis. St David's argued that a con-tract had come into existence, and that Birse should therefore be paid according to its terms. The first instance court decided that a contract had come into existence, based on the course of dealings between the parties, and the fact that the parties had never specifically excluded the formation of a contract unless and until formal documents were prepared and executed. The Court of Appeal reversed this decision, finding that no contract had been formed.

The first instance judge made various comments on the effect of the partnering agreement (not discussed at appeal), including that 'People who have agreed to proceed on the basis of mutual co-operation and trust, are hardly likely at the same time to adopt a rigid attitude as to the formation of a contract'[64] and also that 'The terms of that document, though clearly not legally binding, are important for they were clearly intended to provide the standards by which the parties were to conduct themselves and against which their conduct and attitudes were to be measured'.[65] He evidently felt that even a non-binding charter would have an effect on the manner in which the contract terms might be interpreted. The Court of Appeal made no comment on these views, and unfortunately there has been little case law since on this point.

There have, however, been cases that examined the effect of 'fair dealing' clauses, mostly outside of a construction context. For example, in *Jet2.com v Blackpool Airport Ltd*[66] a contract between the airport (BAL) and an airline contained a clause which stated 'Jet2.com and BAL will co-operate together and use their best endeavours to promote Jet2.com's low cost service from BA and BAL will use all reasonable endeavours to provide a cost base that will facilitate Jet2.com's low cost pricing'. The court consid-ered this would require the airport to act, in effect, against its commercial interests, in this case by allowing the airline to use the airport outside its normal opening hours, at a time when the airport was making substantial operating losses.

Compass Group UK and Ireland Ltd v Mid Essex Hospital Services NHS Trust[67] con-cerned a facilities management contract which contained a clause stating: 'The Trust and the Contractor will co-operate with each other in good faith and will take all rea-sonable action as is necessary for the efficient transmission of information and instruc-tions and to enable the Trust or, as the case may be, any Beneficiary to derive the full benefit of the Contract'. The Trust was very exacting in claiming that breaches had occurred, and in penalising the supplier, to the extent of terminating the contract. The manager, Compass Group, had been in breach, and the Trust was strictly within its rights to take the action it did. However, as the manager had later improved its perform-

---

[63] [2000] BLR 57.
[64] ibid., at 203.
[65] ibid., at 202.
[66] [2012] EWCA Civ 417.
[67] [2012] EWHC 781 (QB).

ance, the judge at first instance felt that the Trust's actions were in breach of the fair dealing clause. He nevertheless noted that there 'is nothing wrong with a challenging approach in managing a contract, even with a contract containing a clause such as 3.5 . . . so long as a party deploys fact and common sense'. The Court of Appeal, after a careful review of the law relating to fair dealing, overturned the first instance decision, stating that 'there is no general doctrine of "good faith" in English contract law, although a duty of good faith is implied by law as an incident of certain categories of contract'.[68] On balance, it seems that the courts are unwilling to accept that such clauses significantly affect or add to obligations undertaken elsewhere under the relevant contract.

Important questions therefore remain for designers, for example whether a duty to cooperate might extend their liability for pointing out the errors of other team members, and to what extent it might impact on any related tortious liability for that advice. Ultimately it may be that only total relief from the threat of claims, which can normally be achieved only through special insurance arrangements such as those discussed below, is likely to achieve a truly 'non-blame' culture.

10.5 BIM

BIM is another tool that has been developed in part to achieve more cooperative working methods (see Chapter 1). It is essentially a technical tool that can be used with any procurement method[69] and its impact on the distribution of design liability amongst the team can therefore only be determined by examining the contractual framework together with any adjustments that have been made to allow for the use of BIM.

At levels 0 and 1[70] BIM is limited to the use of computer aided design (CAD) to generate 2D and 3D graphical representations (hard copy or electronic), which are then distributed to other parties in the normal manner. Its use is therefore purely internal and should have no affect on the liability of parties. Level 2, the approach commonly used in the US and which is being advocated by the government for use in the UK (as a step on the way to Level 3), involves each consultant firm building a separate BIM model that represents its design input. These models may then be linked together to form a project model (sometimes termed a 'federated' approach).[71] In Level 3 all parties work together on the same model. The 'federated' approach will obviously require fewer adaptions that the 'common model' approach, as under the first each party's contribution will be self-contained, whereas the second could involve numerous and continuous interventions from many parties into a constantly changing database. The UK government's BIM working group[72] has concluded:

---

[68] [2013] EWCA Civ 200; Jackson LJ at para. 105.

[69] Building Information Modelling (BIM) Working Group, *BIM: Management for Value, Cost and Carbon Improvement.* A report for the Government Construction Client Group (London: March 2011).

[70] ibid., at 20, and see Chapter 1 of this book.

[71] Note the term is also used to describe how some systems create an holistic 'model' from federated sets of data. This resolves the problem whereby a single model may very quickly outgrow computing capacity.

[72] The working group was set up in 2010 and was supported by the Office of Government Commerce, and by the Department of Business Innovation and Skills.

. . . that little change is required in the fundamental building blocks of copyright law, contracts or insurance to facilitate working at Level 2 of BIM maturity. Some essential investment is required in simple, standard protocols and service schedules to define BIM-specific roles, ways of working and desired outputs.

Looking forward to the achievement of Level 3 integrated working, there are limited actions related to contracts, appointments and insurance that could be taken in advance to facilitate early adoption of integrated working.[73]

10.5.1 Technical issues

However even at Level 2 various matters need careful consideration. The use of this technology will obviously entail new tasks, therefore each consultant may have additional responsibilities. For example, there will be responsibilities with respect to preparation of and accuracy of the files that make up the model, over and above the normal design responsibilities. Matters such as level of detail, file format and data transmission formats will need to be established, to ensure compatibility between models and there will need to be an allocation of risk of technical failures, i.e. data corruption during transmission, software failure, etc. One party will need to take responsibility for management of the federated model (often termed the 'model manager') who may be an existing member of the project team or may be separately appointed.

A benefit of BIM is its ability to highlight conflicts between separate design inputs, so thought needs to be given as to who will monitor and manage this clash detection, and how any clashes are resolved. Although this is no different to normal design integration of consultants, it heightens the importance of achieving clarity as to design roles and responsibility.

10.5.2 Level of liability to the client

A question arises as to the level of design liability when working with BIM, i.e. is it to use reasonable skill and care, or to provide something fit for purpose? One of the key advantages of BIM is that the model can predict environmental performance, durability, maintenance requirements, etc. The UK working group report suggest that it will enable clients 'to set out their requirements in output terms – leaving the supply chain to develop and deliver solutions via a pull model'[74] – so what if it is quite clear after handover that the building is not performing to standard? Clients may well question the purpose of such accuracy if BIM is not used along with a strict liability approach.

---

[73] BIM Working Group, *BIM: Management for Value, Cost and Carbon Improvement*. A report for the Government Construction Client Group (London: March 2011).
[74] ibid., at 20.

10.5.3 Increased possibility of claims?

The BIM database will contain far more information than typical CAD documents, for example it might include design parameters, assumptions, equations or algorithms to calculate changes, and supporting data such as material properties and costs. This information would not normally have been issued to the client or to other team members. There will also be a clear record of which party has contributed to any part of the model, and when this occurred (as all inputs will be traceable). This increased transparency could lead to concern over a higher likelihood of claims from the client or others, as errors may be more easily identified.

On the other hand the model will not necessarily record any 'behind the scenes' decisions, for example if the firm inputting the information to a model took advice from another firm, or delegated a section of the design (with the client's agreement or otherwise).[75] The position could of course get even more difficult at Level 3. The UK BIM Working Group report made the comment that 'the practicalities of identifying contributions may become progressively more complex. In principle, there is no reason why responsibilities should be very different from existing 2D design, providing the extent of each designer's responsibilities are clearly spelt out and understood'.[76] Clearly allocating and delineating design responsibility *and* model responsibility, and avoiding blurring the distinction, will be critical. For example, where a clash results from a *design* incompatibility (not an IT incompatibility), the parties responsible for the conflicting designs will need to resolve the conflict.

In addition, as BIM is intended to be used in a collaborative context, there may be greater potential for cross claims based on *Hedley Byrne* principles, where each party to the process relies on advice provided by the other (either embodied in the model, or advice given behind the scenes). The use of net contribution clauses and provisions that limit liability between team members will therefore be particularly crucial, while any significant risk remains with the team (the alternative would be for the client to accept the risks: see Insurance, below).

10.5.4 Ownership and copyright

The extended content will also raise issues of privacy and copyright. Ownership of the model, and more specifically the right to use the information it contains, is a particularly complex question. With normal 2D and 3D CAD the employer (and contractor) are given a licence to use the graphic outputs for the purposes of the project. With BIM, there are many layers to the copyright of the model: the individual parts, their assembly

---

[75] Monica Chao-Duivas, 'Some Legal Aspects of BIM in establishing a Collaborative Relationship', *The International Construction Law Review*, 28(3), (2011), 264–75.

[76] BIM Working Group, *BIM: Management for Value, Cost and Carbon Improvement*. A report for the Government Construction Client Group (London: March 2011) at 29.

into a complete model, proprietor product information, costing data, etc. This could involve issues of copyright, design rights, data rights, moral rights and privacy.[77]

The general view on copyright is that each would retain ownership of their individual contributions, but that cross-licences would be given to other contributors to use the information for limited purposes (the approach adopted in the CD301 at clause 6.2). For example, the UK report states that 'Ownership and coordination of the model should remain within the supply chain during the currency of the design and construction contracts'.[78] If the contractor is not a contributor, a version would be supplied as a contract document, again with a limited licence for use on the project (this would serve as a benchmark to be used for assessing claims due to subsequent changes). The entire model, or perhaps a reduced version of it tailored specifically for operation purposes, would pass to the client on completion of the project.

For BIM Level 3 the report acknowledges that the model manager, whose contribution will be more significant than at Level 2, may also have copyright in the final model, but the report maintains that this 'will not impact on the ownership of copyright in the individual contributions'.[79] It also acknowledges that at this level joint authorship of parts of the model could arise.

10.5.5 Incorporation of BIM

To date, examples show that the normal approach to incorporating BIM is to adapt the existing contractual set-up, usually by appending a 'BIM protocol' to existing standard form contracts. The protocol is normally common to all those contributing to the model. It should be noted that the term 'protocol' is frequently not being used in the normal sense of 'a set of rules and regulations that determine how data is transmitted in telecommunications and computer networking',[80] but in a wider sense, i.e. the document also sets out roles and obligations of the various parties. It therefore encompasses technical and integrative/team-working aspects of BIM. The protocol could therefore vary the distribution of risk and liabilities (assuming the contract document hierarchy allows for this).

10.5.6 Incorporation of BIM: US

The 'federated' approach has been commonly adopted in the US, where two standard BIM protocols have been developed for use with its standard form contracts, namely the American Institute of Architects (AIA) E202 – 2008 BIM Protocol Exhibit (AIA E202[81]), for use in connection with AIA forms, and the ConsensusDOCS 301: BIM Addendum (CD301), for use with the ConsensusDOCS suite.

---

[77] Martin Roberts, *BIM: Legal and Contractual Implications.* Presentation to the RICS (London: RICS, 2012).
[78] BIM Working Group, *BIM: Management for Value, Cost and Carbon Improvement.* A report for the Government Construction Client Group (London: March 2011) at 21.
[79] ibid., at 25.
[80] en.wikipedia.org/wiki/Protocol.
[81] Note that a proposed new version of this, AIA Document E203–2012, underwent a consultation process in 2012.

CD301 describes a system whereby a 'Full Design Model' comprises coordinated models such structural, architectural, and mechanical engineering, and the 'Project Model' comprises the 'Full Design Model and one or more Construction Models'. The construction models are the equivalent of shop drawings (clause 2.2).

The protocol assumes that the design team will be led by the architect (clause 1.4 states that 'Nothing in this Addendum shall relieve the Architect/Engineer from its obligation, nor diminish the role of the Architect/Engineer, as the person responsible for and in charge of the design of the Project'). It also assumes that there will be no contractor input to design: 'Participation of the Contractor or its subcontractors and suppliers in Contributions to a Model shall not constitute the performance of design services' (clause 1.6). This approach is taken to preserve the position normally assumed in the US under the *Spearin* doctrine.

Points to note about CD301 are as follows:

- It is intended that all contracts include it as an addendum (cl. 1.3).
- The protocol overrides any conflicting provision in the 'governing contract', i.e. the one to which it is appended (cl. 1.11).
- It refers to a BIM Execution Plan, which is agreed after the governing contracts are entered into (cl. 4.1). This sets out 'what Models are to be created, the purpose(s) each Model is intended to serve, and which Project Participant(s) is(are) responsible for creating each Model; ... the level of detail required, procedures for designating which are Design Models' (i.e. complete enough to be incorporated in the full model).
- Each party is responsible for the contribution it makes to a model (cl. 5.1). A contribution is defined as the 'expression, design, data or information that a Project Participant (a) creates or prepares, and (b) incorporates, distributes, transmits, communicates or otherwise shares with other Project Participant(s) for use in or in connection with a Model for the Project'.
- The standard of care is that set out in the governing contract, i.e. the protocol does not affect this aspect (cl. 5.4).
- The governing contract determines any waiver of consequential damages arising out of a contribution to a model (cl. 5.2(b)).
- Each party waives claims against the other parties to the governing contract for consequential damages arising 'out of or relating to the use of or access to a model' (cl. 5.2(b)).

It therefore appears as if the protocol could both enlarge the duties to the client (principally through the BIM Execution Plan) and to a certain extent limit the model provider's liability to other parties to the governing contract (but not to those on an affiliated contract). It is to be noted that clash detection is mentioned only briefly, in relation to the BIM Execution Plan, so it is not clear from the protocol who will undertake this task.

AIA E202 assumes a similar procurement context, i.e. that the architect will lead the design team, and that there will be no design contribution by the contractor. It also assumes that there will be a model manager. A key difference to CD 301 is that it does not envision the execution of a BIM Execution Plan. Although this reduces the scope for inadvertently causing conflict between duties as set out in the primary appointments, and those in the Plan, it may leave some questions regarding model responsibility unanswered. Unlike CD 301, the AIA E202 does contain very detailed provisions concerning reliance on design accuracy. It describes five Levels of Development (LOD), and for each LOD establishes the reliance level and the authorised uses of a model under that LOD. Each element of a model is assigned an LOD, resulting in a table that outlines the author and level of reliance for each element of each model.

10.5.7 Incorporation of BIM – UK

The UK BIM Working Group has recommended that the 'contractual requirements of BIM are incorporated through a BIM protocol', and brought into the professional appointments or any of the standard form contracts using a 'simple additional clause'.[82] It suggests that standard BIM protocols should be agreed at institutional, sector and project level.[83]

However, although it states that 'existing contracts can be used with minimal amendment'[84] the report also states a 'Preference for use of collaborative forms of contract such as NEC, with a collaborative scope of services such as the CIC'.[85] The Working Group report also acknowledges the need for specialist input, stating that the 'construction client should expect the input of specialist manufacturers producing component parts in 3D CAD with data attached for including in the model',[86] although it does not indicate how this will be achieved. Throughout the report, it emphasises that BIM's full benefits cannot be realised unless it is used along with some form of collaborative working, ideally with a 'fully integrated' team.[87] As part of this it recommends that a lead consultant is appointed with overall design responsibility, which is sub-contracted to sub-consultants, and that a separate model manager is appointed with sole responsibility for the building and coordination of the model.[88]

At the time of writing the only UK standard form contract that contains BIM provisions is the recently published CIOB Complex Projects Contract, although the JCT has issued an enabling clause to incorporate a BIM protocol. The CIC has now published a standard BIM protocol (February 2013, available from its web site), intended for use at Level 2.

The UK BIM Working Group's report included a draft (NEC style) BIM Protocol at Appendix 20, intended for Level 2 BIM. This is a much shorter document than CD301, and closer in scope to the AIA E202. Unlike 301, there is no indication of the hierarchy

---

[82] BIM Working Group, *BIM: Management for Value, Cost and Carbon Improvement*. A report for the Government Construction Client Group (London: March 2011), p. 29.
[83] ibid., at 27.
[84] ibid., at 21.
[85] ibid., at 21
[86] ibid., at 27.
[87] This view is supported by many commentators, e.g. see Martin Roberts JCT news April 2012.
[88] BIM Working Group, *BIM: Management for Value, Cost and Carbon Improvement*. A report for the Government Construction Client Group (London: March 2011), 27.

between it and the governing contract, no attempt to set out a matrix of responsibility for development of different parts of the model (termed 'model objects'), and no disclaimer of responsibility for reliance on the model. Instead it focuses on the role of the model manager, setting out who this will be for different phases of the project, and the manager's duties, which include 'defin[ing] interfaces between different Model Developers' deliverables and maintain them under configuration management' and 'Ensur[ing] that model elements received are complete, clash free and conform to Applicable Standards, proactively resolving non-compliances with the relevant Model Element Developer(s).' It also sets out a table of who may use and rely on the information contained in the model. In general its focus is on the technical aspects, and as such is less likely than CD 301 to affect the liability of the parties.

10.6 *Insurance solutions*

There are two principal strategies for insurance. The first is for each contributor to maintain their own insurance as would be normal with most procurement routes.

The working group's view is that existing insurance provisions are adequate for the style of collaboration envisaged at level 2 BIM 'on the assumption that the extent of integration would involve a number of models being brought together in a coordination exercise with audit trails similar to that found at Level 1'.[89]

To date PII companies seem to be prepared to insure consultants up to Level 2, and do not see the use of BIM as a significantly increased risk. However if part of the purpose of using BIM is to increase collaboration and reduce disputes, most believe that an alternative strategy involving umbrella insurance will be needed, which involves a single project insurance with the insurers agreeing to waive rights of claim against all others, thus reducing the 'blame culture'. The incentive to perform is provided with a bonus system or pain/gain mechanism, whereby the losses are shared but capped.

This approach is recognised by the UK BIM Working Group: 'Adoption of Integrated Project Insurance at higher levels of integration will reduce the reliance on these dispute resolution mechanisms.'[90] Two types of insurance are likely to be required: integrated project insurance to cover losses during the construction period, and defects liability insurance to cover losses after completion. However it should be noted that integrated project insurance is not readily available as yet, and that defects liability insurance cover is normally limited to major faults, therefore even this combination my not fully protect the consultant. It is understood that the government is currently running a demonstration project whereby single project insurance and defects liability insurance have been taken out[91] (but possibly only for serious defects). This requires auditing by the insurer's technical team of the developing design, and a requirement to comply with the instructions of the auditors.

---

[89] ibid., at 31; see also the CIC *Best Practice Guide for Professional Indemnity Insurance when using Building Information Models* (London: CIC, 2013)
[90] ibid., at 29.
[91] Stephen Bamforth, Griffiths & Armour, informal talk to the CIC Liability Panel 20 April 2012.

Chapter 11
Damages and Contribution

A person who has suffered loss as a result of a breach of contract or a tort committed by another person will usually be entitled to recover damages from that other person; the object is to provide monetary recompense for the wrong that has been done. It is necessary to look at the general principles relating to damages (e.g. causation, remoteneness, measure of damages and mitigation) before applying those principles to the particular categories of damage that are recoverable from a negligent designer. Some of the more detailed issues relating to damages, such as date of assessment and recovery of interest, are beyond the scope of this book.[1]

11.1 General principles

The most important fundamental principle of damages is that, so far as money is able to do it, the innocent party should be put in the same position that it would have been in had the party at fault not committed the breach of contract or the tort. This is the principle known to lawyers as *restitutio in integrum*. This general principle is subject to particular rules in both contract and tort which may have the effect of limiting the damages that would otherwise be recoverable. Some damage, for example, may be so far removed from the breach of contract or the negligent act that it will not be recoverable. In such cases, the damage is said to be 'too remote'. Another general principle of great importance is that the innocent party must bring its claims in one action for all the damages that result from the same cause of action; it cannot have successive bites at the same cherry.[2] For example, if an employer brings an action for breach of contract against a designer, it must sue in that action for all the breaches of contract.[3]

---

[1] Reference should be made to one of the leading texts on construction law listed in the bibliography.
[2] *Darley Main Colliery Co. v Mitchell* (1986) 11 AC 127.
[3] *Conquer v Boot* [1928] 2 KB 336.

Cornes and Lupton's Design Liability in the Construction Industry, Fifth Edition. Sarah Lupton.
© 2013 Sarah Lupton and DL Cornes. Published 2013 by Blackwell Publishing Ltd.

11.1.1 Causation

Before examining what may be recovered, a claimant must establish a causal link[4] between the breach of contract or breach of duty and the damage it has suffered. In both contract and tort it is necessary to satisfy the 'but for' test,[5] i.e. but for the breach (or negligent act) the damage would not have occurred. In contract satisfying this test may not be sufficient, it may also be necessary to show that the event is the dominant or effective cause of the loss.[6]

If there is a new intervening act (known in law as a *novus actus interveniens*), then the damage will not be recoverable. An example of this arose in *Lubenham Fidelities and Investment Co Ltd v South Pembrokeshire District Council*.[7] In this case, the architects had negligently calculated the amount due on interim certificates and it was alleged against them that this caused the loss suffered by the bondsman (Lubenham), who stepped into the shoes of the contractor. The bondsman had suspended execution of the works, and there were cross allegations from the employer and the contractor in relation to determination. The Court of Appeal found that the claims of the employer and the bondsman (to recover from the architects the amount of the losses suffered as a result of the determination of the contracts) both failed because the architects' breach of duty in issuing the incorrectly calculated interim certificates was not the cause of the losses. The losses were in fact caused by Lubenham's breach of contract in suspending the works without reasonable cause and persisting with the suspension, notwithstanding the service of a preliminary notice of determination. In other words, the loss did not flow from the breach complained of.

A further example can be seen in *Beoco Ltd v Alfa Laval Co Ltd*.[8] There a heat exchanger at the claimant's works exploded causing damage to equipment and economic loss due to the suspension of production. Between its installation and the explosion, repairs had been carried out to the exchanger, but the repair work had not been adequately tested. The Court of Appeal decided that the cost of repairing the exchanger could not be claimed against the original installer, as due to the explosion those repairs were not carried out or were subsumed in the more extensive repairs consequent upon the explosion. The claimant was however entitled to loss of income during the period of the original repairs.

Failure to prevent damage, however, will not normally break the chain of causation. For example, in *Pearson Education Ltd v The Charter Partnership Ltd*,[9] as discussed in section 4.3, the surveyor failed to inform the lessee about the incorrectly designed gutter. Had he done so, this might have prevented the damage occurring. However this did not prevent the claimant from recovering losses from the architect for the negligent design.

Where there are multiple causes of a loss, this will not normally prevent damages being recoverable. In contract, even where a loss is caused only partly by a breach by

---

[4] *South Australian Asset Management Corp. v York Montague Ltd* [1997] AC 191(HL).
[5] *Barnett v Chelsea & Kensington Hospital Management Committee* [1969] 1 QB 428.
[6] *Galoo Ltd v Bright Grahame Murray* [1994] 1 WLR 1361.
[7] (1986) 33 BLR 39 (CA).
[8] [1994] 3 WLR 1179 (CA).
[9] [2007] BLR 324.

the other party, damages may still be recoverable without the court having to assess which cause was most effective (although an assessment will be needed where the party in breach claims contribution from a third party. In tort, where there are a number of possible causes, the test is similar, namely whether the breach of the duty of care materially contributed to the loss or injury.

11.1.2 Contract: remoteness

The kind of damage that can be recovered in respect of a breach of contract is governed by the rule set out in the case of *Hadley v Baxendale*.[10] It has been said that the damage would not be too remote to be recovered if it:

(1) is such as may fairly and reasonably be considered either arising naturally, that is to say according to the usual course of things, from such breach of contract itself, or

(2) arises out of a breach of contract where the parties knew of special circumstances by reason of which that breach might cause a greater loss than might arise in the ordinary course of events.[11]

These principles are known as the two branches of the rule. When considering the first branch the test is based on what is presumed to have been in the contemplation of the parties, whereas in the second branch of the rule, the test is based on the actual knowledge of the parties. This test differs from the test in tort, which is based on foreseeability.

A recent example that considered what losses might fall under the first branch is *Siemens Building Technologies v Supershield Ltd*.[12] Here the court emphasised that the losses may be limited to what the party in breach may reasonably be taken to have assumed responsibility to prevent. The case concerned a sprinkler system where, following installation, water overflowed from the storage tank due to a faulty ball float valve and lever arm. The overflowing water should have drained away safely from the area in which the tank was installed, but unfortunately the drains were blocked. In addition, an alarm system, which should have alerted the occupiers to the overflow, was not properly monitored. The contractor was found liable for the damage. The purpose of installing the ball float valve had been to control the flow of water and the multiple control systems did not reduce the contractor's responsibility. Although neither the blocked drains nor the alarm system were its responsibly, the ensuing flood was 'within the scope of the [contractual] duty' and therefore not too remote.

---

[10](1854) 9 Ex 341; 3 CLR 517; 156 ER 145.
[11]*Victoria Laundry (Windsor) Ltd v Newman Industries Ltd* [1949] 2 KB 528 and *Koufos v Czarnikow Ltd* [1969] 1 AC 350.
[12][2010] BLR 145 (CA).

11.1.3 Tort: remoteness

The question as to whether damage is too remote to be recoverable in claims made in tort is determined by the test of foreseeability. Was the sort of damage that occurred the reasonably foreseeable result of the tortious act?[13] If the damage is in that category, it does not matter whether the damage was most unlikely to occur or even that the risk was very small; the wrongdoer will be liable for the whole loss. It is for this reason that it is often said a person who commits a tort may have to bear a greater portion of the liability than a person who is in breach of contract. However, in many cases the distinction is academic. For example, where a designer is sued by a client in both contract and tort and is found to be liable, the court will not usually be concerned to look at the distinction in the test for remoteness in contract and tort.

Loss which is purely financial, known as economic loss, and which is not caused by some injury to person or property is an area of damages which causes some difficulty. In cases of negligent mis-statement, there is no doubt that economic loss is recoverable.[14] The recovery of economic loss in cases of negligence, however, can be problematic (note that the question of whether losses are too remote to be recovered is a different question to whether there is a duty to take care to avoid economic loss in the first place). The orthodox view is that economic loss which is not due to damage to persons or property is not recoverable. This view was based on two cases. In *SCM (United Kingdom) Ltd v W. J. Whittall & Son Ltd*,[15] Whittall, contractors, cut off the power to SCM's factory by negligently cutting into an underground cable. SCM were typewriter manufacturers and molten metal solidified in their machines, which amounted to physical damage. SCM was successful in their claim for damages limited to the physical damage to the machinery and the loss of profit during the period in which the machinery was being repaired. They were not liable for losses due to the closedown of other plant. The court also considered the position as it would have been had there been no damaged machines and just a loss of production. Lord Denning MR said:

> In actions of negligence, when the plaintiff has suffered no damage to his person or property, but has only sustained economic loss, the law does not usually permit him to recover that loss. Although the defendants owed the plaintiffs a duty of care, that did not mean that additional economic loss which was not consequent on the material damage suffered by the plaintiffs would also be recoverable.[16]

The Court of Appeal adopted the same approach in a subsequent case on similar facts in *Spartan Steel and Alloys SCM (United Kingdom) Limited v W. J. Whittall v Martin & Co. (Contractors) Ltd.*[17] Similarly in *London Waste v Amec Civil Engineering Ltd*,[18] negligently

---

[13]'The Wagon Mound' aka. *Overseas Tankship (UK) v Morts Dock & Engineering Co.* [1961] AC 388.
[14]*Hedley Byrne & Co. Ltd v Heller & Partners Ltd* [1964] AC 465 (HL).
[15][1971] 1 QB 337.
[16]ibid., at 344.
[17][1973] QB 27.
[18](1997) 83 BLR 136.

damaged cables caused an interruption of sales of electricity to a local electricity board. Here losses from the damage to plant were recovered, but not the profits from the sales of electricity. In all these cases the damages, although foreseeable, were considered too remote to be recovered.

11.1.4 Measure of damages

As mentioned above, the amount of damages awarded is always intended to be compensatory, not punitive. The starting point in assessing what amount might be appropriate can be gleaned from well-known principles established by case law (particular issues relating to construction are considered below). With respect to contract, the purpose of a claim for compensatory damages is to return the claimant to the position it would have been in had the breach not occurred, i.e.:

> The rule of common law is, that where a party sustains a loss by reason of a breach of contract, he is, so far as money can do it, to be placed in the same situation, with respect to damages, as if the contract had been performed.[19]

It is not to give the claimant additional profit, nor to award them any profit gained by the defendant as a result of its breach.[20]

In contrast to contract damages, tortious damages are often referred to as 'backward-looking', i.e. the aim of the damages awarded is to place the claimant in the position it would have been in had the tort not have been committed (as opposed to the situation in contract, which is looking forward to what ought to have happened).[21] The measure for tortious damages therefore is:

> That sum of money which will put the party who has been injured, or who has suffered, in the same position as he would have been in if he had not sustained the wrong for which he is now getting his compensation.[22]

In the context of construction, where a designer gives negligent advice, whether under an obligation in contract or a tortious duty, the measure of damages may be very similar (how this is assessed is dicussed further below). This is always assuming that the designer was under a duty not to cause such loss, that causation has been shown, and that the loss in question is not too remote.

11.1.5 Mitigation/reasonable cost

A party who suffers damage cannot necessarily assume that it will recover all the loss from the wrongdoer. As soon as there is a breach of contract or the commission of a

---

[19] *Robinson v Harman* (1848) 1 Ex Rep 850, at 855.
[20] *Surrey CC v Bredero Homes Ltd* [1993] 1 WLR 1361 (CA).
[21] See e.g. the discussion of *Hadley v Baxendale* in Allan C Hutchinson, *Is Eating People Wrong?: Great Legal Cases and How they Shaped the World*, (UK: Cambridge University Press, 2010).
[22] *Livingston v Rawyards Coal Company* (1880) 5 App Cas 25, Lord Blackburn, at p. 39.

tort, injured parties have a duty to mitigate the loss that they suffer. If they do not act reasonably so as to mitigate the loss, the wrongdoer will be able to point to that failure in proceedings and the injured party/ies will not be able to recover damages insofar as they could reasonably and properly have avoided the loss. It may be that the phrase 'duty to mitigate' is a misnomer. Sir John Donaldson MR, in *Sotiros Shipping Inc. & Another v Sameiet Solholt (The Solholt)*,[23] said:

> A plaintiff was under no duty to mitigate his loss, despite the habitual use by lawyers of the phrase 'duty to mitigate'. He was completely free to act as he judged to be in his best interests. On the other hand, a defendant was not liable for all the loss suffered by the plaintiff in consequence of his so acting. A defendant was only liable for such part of the plaintiff's loss as was properly to be regarded as caused by the defendant's breach of duty.[24]

When the appropriate remedial works have been decided on, the damages recoverable are the reasonable cost of carrying them out. The meaning of that general statement was considered in *Richard Roberts Holdings SCM (United Kingdom) Limited v W. J. Whittall v Douglas Smith Stimson Partnership & Others*[25] by Judge John Newey QC Official Referee. He said that the reasonable cost was not necessarily that of the lowest tender which could be obtained. The tenderer's reputation and its willingness to enter into appropriate terms and conditions were relevant. Special circumstances might affect what was reasonable, such as paying what appeared to be an excessive amount in order to have the work done quickly and thereby prevent loss of profit or goodwill. If, however, tenders are received from parties who are otherwise acceptable, then usually the lowest price should be accepted.

Negligent defendants who seek to argue that the claimant has carried out overelaborate or unnecessary repairs do not usually receive much sympathy in court. This will be particularly so where an employer is incapable of deciding for itself what repairs need to be done and relies on the advice of experts (as usually happens). In *Governors of the Hospital for Sick Children & Another v McLaughlin and Harvey plc & Others*,[26] Judge John Newey QC, Official Referee, was confronted with difficult issues because the experts for the defendants took the view strongly that the remedial works scheme of the plaintiff was excessive and very expensive, when compared with their own very much cheaper alternative. The Judge said:

> The plaintiff who carries out either repair or reinstatement of his property must act reasonably. He can only recover as damages the costs which the defendant ought reasonably have foreseen that he would incur and the defendant would not have foreseen unreasonable expenditure. Reasonable costs do not, however, mean the minimum amount which, with hindsight, it could

---

[23] [1983] 1 Lloyd's Rep. 605.
[24] ibid., at 608.
[25] (1988) 46 BLR 50.
[26] (1990) 19 Con LR 25.

be held would have sufficed. When the nature of the repairs is such that the plaintiff can only make them with the assistance of expert advice, the defendant should have foreseen that he would take such advice and be influenced by it.[27]

The Judge then considered the effect that negligence might have in the independent advice received by a plaintiff and the difference between the position where remedial works have been carried out before trial and where they have not. He went on:

> However reasonably the plaintiff acts, he can only recover in respect of loss actually caused by the defendant. If, therefore, part of a plaintiff's claim does not arise out of the defendant's wrongdoing, but is due to some independent cause, the plaintiff cannot recover in respect of that part; *The Liesbosch Dredger v Edison SS* [1933] AC 449 and *Compania Financiera 'Soleada' SA v Hamoor Tanker Corp. Inc., 'The Borag'* [1981] 1 All ER 856 CA. The independent cause may take the form of an event which breaks, that is to say, brings to an end, a chain of causation from the defendant's breach of duty, so that the plaintiff cannot recover damages for any loss which he sustains after the event. The event may take the form of negligent advice upon which the plaintiff has acted. Another way of expressing the matter might be that the defendant could not reasonably have foreseen that the plaintiff would act on negligent advice. Advice which is not negligent will not by itself break the chain. . . . If at the date of trial no remedial works have been carried out by the plaintiff, then the court has, in order to assess damages, to decide what works should be done. The parties are entitled to put forward rival schemes and the court has to choose between them or variants of them. . . . Where works have been carried out, it is not for the court to consider *de novo* what should have been done and what costs should have been incurred either as a check upon the reasonableness of the plaintiff's actions or otherwise.[28]

In *Chancellor, Masters and Scholars of the University of Oxford (t/a Oxford University Press) v John Stedman Design Group (A Firm)*[29] the court had to consider the reasonableness of the cost of remedying defective work against the background of a partial settlement of proceedings. Problems had arisen with a granolithic floor, laid by subcontractors to Norwest Holst Western Ltd, which had developed numerous cracks and extensive surface crazing. After the start of the trial, a settlement took place which left only two parties in the action for the purpose of contribution between Norwest Holst and their sub-contractor. It was argued by the sub-contractor that Norwest Holst's settlement with OUP was unreasonable. The Judge reviewed the authorities on this issue[30] and decided that the settlement, made on legal advice, was reasonable. The judgment is a useful resumé of the matters to be considered in such a situation.

The alleged unreasonable behaviour of a plaintiff had to be considered by Judge Bowsher QC, Official Referee, in *Philip Derek Kremin v Duke Street Investments Ltd &*

---

[27] ibid., at 94.
[28] ibid., at 96 and 98.
[29] (1991) 7 Const LJ 102.
[30] *Biggin & Co. Ltd v Permanite Ltd* [1951] 2 KB 314; *Karpenko v Paroian Courey Cohen and Houston* (1980) 117 DLR (3d) 283, Ontario, Canada; *Radford v De Froberville* [1977] 1 WLR 1262.

Others.[31] Here, it was said that if liability were established, 'the wrongdoer must take the victim as he finds him'.[32] The Judge found that the plaintiff and his wife had:

> ... inflicted their perfectionism on other people to such an extent that dealings with them were difficult and their behaviour described in evidence was found in many respects to have been unreasonable. Their behaviour in relation to the defendants with regard to the subject matter of this action was also in some respects unreasonable. For the plaintiff, it was submitted that that behaviour is not out of character with their behaviour in relation to other people.

The Judge held that if a plaintiff suffers from a mental condition which makes it impossible or difficult for that person to behave in the manner to be expected from the man on top of the Clapham omnibus, the defendant must take him as he finds him in that condition. But if the plaintiff of his own freewill chooses to be a difficult and unreasonable person, that should not be allowed to add to the defendant's burden in damages.

11.2 Damages and designers

Having looked at the basic principles that govern awards of damages, it is necessary to look at the application of those principles to the damages that are likely to be awarded against designers for breach of duty and to set out some further principles which are of importance in that field. Where there are defects in the design or the supervision is negligent, then this is likely to manifest itself by defects in the construction. It is because of this chain leading to the designer that damages will only be recoverable where the damages that are claimed arise from the designer's breach of duty; it does not necessarily follow that because there is a defect in the construction that there is a defect also in the design.

11.2.1 Injunction or damages?

The first thing to clarify is that the normal remedy will be an award of damages, rather than an injunction to re-build the work. For example where a design-build contractor has constructed a building that is defective, it will not usually be possible for a building owner to obtain an order of the court requiring defective construction or design to be put right. An example can be seen in the case of *Taylor Woodrow Construction (Midlands) Ltd v Charcon Structures Ltd & Others*[33] where an injunction was refused by the Court of Appeal in relation to defects which had appeared in pre-cast concrete cladding panels and tiles used in the construction of the Arndale Centre in Manchester. The Court applied the principle in *American Cyanamid Co. v Ethicon Ltd*[34] where it was held, amongst other things, that an injunction will not be granted where a claim for damages

---

[31] unreported, 14 January 1993, 1991 ORB No.1061.
[32] *Bourhill v Young* [1943] AC 92.
[33] (1982) 7 Con LR 1 (CA).
[34] (1975) AC 396.

is an adequate remedy. It was argued for the employer in *Taylor Woodrow* that there was a breach of a statutory obligation in relation to the Building Regulations and that this therefore obliged the contractor to take action to remedy the problem. This argument was also rejected by the Court of Appeal.

11.2.2 Diminution in value or cost of remedial work?

The usual measure of damages is the cost of the remedial work that is reasonably necessary. That cost will include the professional fees that were necessarily expended in arranging for and supervising that remedial work. All the figures put forward by the injured party can be disputed; however, unless any particular aspect of the amount of the claim for damages is disputed on some matter of substance, a defendant is not likely to succeed in reducing the amount of the damages, by nit-picking at every item. On the other hand, the claimant has to prove its loss.

In some cases, it has been argued that the proper measure of damages is not the cost of repair but rather the difference in the value of the property with the defects and the value of the property without the defects, known as the diminution in value. This will usually be the measure of damages in cases where a negligent survey has been carried out for a prospective purchaser of a property.[35]

Whether diminution in value or cost of remedial work is the appropriate measure of damages in any particular case will depend on the facts of the case and, it may be that the choice is an aspect of mitigation. For example, where a car is involved in an accident, it would not be reasonable to spend more on repairs than the value of the car before the accident. This is on the basis that it would be reasonable to replace the damaged car with another car, rather than to spend more on repairing the old car. This principle would not, of course, apply were the damaged car irreplaceable, for example, a vintage car. Some guidance is given on this subject in *Dodd Properties (Kent) Ltd v Canterbury City Council*[36] where it was said:

> The general object underlying the rules for assessment of damages is, so far as is possible by means of a monetary award, to place the plaintiff in the position that he would have occupied if he had not suffered the wrong complained of, be that wrong a tort or a breach of contract. In the case of a tort causing damage to real property, this object is achieved by the application of one or other of two quite different measures of damage, or, occasionally, a combination of the two. The first is to take the capital value of the property in an undamaged state and to compare it with its value in a damaged state. The second is to take the cost of repair or reinstatement. Which is appropriate will depend on a number of factors, such as the plaintiff's future intentions as to the use of the property and the reasonableness of those intentions. If he reasonably intends to sell the property in its damaged state, clearly the diminution in capital value is the true measure of damage. If he reasonably intends to continue to occupy it and to repair the damage, clearly the cost of repair is the true measure.[37]

---

[35] *Phillips v Ward* [1956] 1 WLR 471; *Perry v Sidney Phillips & Son* (1983) 22 BLR 124 (CA).
[36] (1979) 13 BLR 45 (CA).
[37] ibid., Donaldson LJ, at 58–9.

The general rule that the 'cost of cure' is the appropriate measure is therefore subject to a requirement of reasonableness. As an extension of this, it may be that sometimes it is reasonable for the owner to demolish the building and replace it completely. In the Australian case of *Bellgrove v Eldridge*[38] the claimant was considered entitled to the cost of demolition and re-erection when a house was constructed on seriously defective foundations. The Court however emphasised that work undertaken to rectify the premises was necessary to restore the premises to the state that was contracted for and was therefore reasonable.

In the *Maison D'Or* case (*McGlinn v Waltham Contractors Ltd*)[39] the court refused to accept that re-building was reasonable. After reviewing recent authorities, Judge Coulson commented that the court must award damages that are reasonable and objectively fair as between the claimants and the defendants. Therefore he decided that the right measure of loss in this case was the agreed cost of the work necessary to repair the defects for which each defendant was liable. It would be very unlikely that the cost of demolition and rebuilding would be an acceptable measure, unless it could be clearly shown that this was less expensive than making good the damage due to defective design.

The alternative basis of diminution in value was taken in respect of defects in *G. W. Atkins Ltd v Scott*[40] in the Court of Appeal. Here the finding of the judge was upheld. He had considered the defects not to be of a serious character and that that was a good reason in law for using a different basis of assessment than the cost of repair. Diminution is more appropriate where the proportion of defective work is small in relation to the whole property; where the sale of the property is not in prospect and where the damage only affects the 'amenity value' of the property. It was said that the preference of the building owner for reinstatement is only one of the factors the court should consider in deciding what is reasonable.

The proper measure of damages will usually be the cost of the remedial work at least where the injured party wishes to continue to enjoy the property. However, it may be that diminution in value can be claimed in addition to the cost of the remedial work. This situation could arise where remedial works are carried out but, notwithstanding the fact that the defects are remedied, the property is worth less by reason of those remedial works. For example, brickwork subjected to differential settlement and subsequently repaired may detract from the value of the property. In such circumstances, there may be considerable difficulties in proof and evidence from expert valuers would be essential. An example of an award of damages for diminution in value, in addition to the cost of remedial works, is to be found in *Thomas & Others v T. A. Phillips (Builders) Ltd and the Borough Council of Taff Ely*.[41]

Where neither cost of repairs, nor diminution in value are appropriate, then a further measure of 'loss of amenity' may be used. This usually arises in cases concerning purely subjective or aesthetic complaints, and where the court is satisfied that the contract has

---

[38] (1954) 90 CLR 3d 613.
[39] [2007] 111 Con LR 1, for the facts see section 8.6.8.
[40] (1991) 7 Const LJ 215.
[41] (1987) 9 Con LR 72.

been performed to a substantial extent. In such cases the cost of rectification may be wholly disproportionate and, if diminution in value cannot be shown, the court may award damages on a loss of amenity measure. This principle was followed in the House of Lords' case of *Ruxley Electronics and Construction Ltd v Forsyth*.[42] In this case Mr Forsyth employed Ruxley Electronics to build a swimming pool next to his house. The drawings and specification required the pool to be 7ft 6in. deep at its deepest point, but the completed pool was only 6ft 9in. deep. The contractors brought a claim for their unpaid account and Mr Forsyth counterclaimed the cost of rebuilding the pool, which would be £21,560. The trial judge found that the shortfall in depth did not decrease the value of the pool and that Mr Forsyth had no intention of building a new pool. He rejected the counterclaim but awarded £2,500 as general damages for loss of pleasure and amenity. Mr Forsyth appealed and the Court of Appeal allowed the appeal and awarded him £21,500. The contractor appealed and the House of Lords restored the original ruling, confirming that the cost of reinstatement is not the only possible measure of damages where there has been defective performance of a building contract and is not the appropriate measure where the expenditure would be out of all proportion to the benefit to be obtained.

11.2.3 Consequential loss

Consequential losses are losses that a claimant may prove over and above those that arose as a direct result of breaches of contract or negligence (i.e. consequential loss approximates to loss within the second rule in *Hadley v Baxendale* noted above[43]).

The most important items of consequential loss are those caused by delay, loss of use, loss of profit and the costs of vacating premises whilst repairs are carried out. The tests as to whether these are recoverable are the usual tests in contract and tort. For example, where the designer could reasonably have foreseen (tort) or may reasonably have contemplated (contract) that the defective design would necessitate the vacating of the premises and the employer hiring other premises, then the reasonable costs of the removal and the hire of the other premises will be recoverable.

As to the consequences of delay, such as loss of profit, these will be dealt with in different ways according to the circumstances under which the loss is suffered. If the designer by his negligence causes a contractor to be delayed during the course of the works, then under the standard forms of construction contract (e.g. JCT or ICE), the contractor will be able to obtain an extension of time for completion which will prevent the employer from recovering liquidated damages in respect of that delay from the contractor. In such circumstances, the employer would be entitled to claim the value of those liquidated damages from the designer, those damages being a genuine pre-estimate of the employer's loss should delay occur.

Where the loss of use of the property occurs after completion of the project, then the method of calculation of the damages will depend on whether the property is a

---

[42] (1995) 73 BLR 1.
[43] *British Sugar plc v NEI Power Projects Ltd* (1998) 87 BLR 42.

profit-making or non-profit making asset. Where it is a profit-making asset, such as a factory, then the employer will be entitled to recover loss of profits for the reasonable period that the remedial works take.[44] Where the property is non-profit earning, such as a local authority swimming pool, there is no rule of law that damages cannot be recovered. Where a substitute building could be used, then the cost of hire would be appropriate damages. However, in such cases it is likely that no substitute building is available and the proper measure of damages may be interest on the capital value of the property for the period during which the repairs were carried out.[45] These principles as to both profit-earning and non-profit earning property will also apply to cases where there is delay during construction and there are no liquidated damages provisions in the construction contract.

Where a defect in a system designed to reduce fire risk, such as sprinkler systems, causes increased insurance premiums to be paid, then the cost of those increased premiums will be recoverable but only to the extent that the building owner carried out repairs within a reasonable time.[46]

In *Richard Roberts Holdings Ltd v Douglas Smith Stimson Partnership & Others*,[47] it was held that the parent company owner of a dyeworks, let to a subsidiary company, could not recover the consequential losses of its subsidiary from architects who were in breach of contract. However, this case was decided before *St Martin's Property Corporation Ltd v Sir Robert McAlpine*,[48] and it may be doubted that this point would have been decided in the same way if it had been heard after St Martin's.

In *T & S Contractors Ltd v Architectural Design Associates*,[49] a property developer recovered damages in respect of breach of contract by architects, being the reduced value of the development because of a fall in the property market during the period of delay created by the architects.

11.2.4 Distress

Where the defects are serious, damages may also be recoverable for inconvenience and discomfort. Very occasionally there may also be an award for emotional distress, although this is unusual in construction.

Where a design is negligently prepared, or there is negligent supervision, and the designer's client is an individual, rather than a company or corporation, then a great deal of distress and upset can be caused. A court can award damages for such mental distress and frustration in certain circumstances. This arises, for example, where the damage falls within the second branch of the rule of *Hadley v Baxendale*: the parties

---

[44] *The Mediana* [1900] AC 113.

[45] *The Hebridean Coast*, [1961] AC 545; *The Greta Holme*, [1987] AC 596; *Birmingham Corporation v Sowsbery* (1969) 113 Sol J 877.

[46] *Rumbelows v A. M. K. & Another* (1982) 19 BLR 25.

[47] (1988) 46 BLR 50.

[48] [1993] 3 All ER 417.

[49] [1993] CILL 842.

had actual knowledge that a breach of contract might cause greater loss than would ordinarily result. The courts applied this test where a disappointed holidaymaker succeeded in obtaining damages for mental distress from a tour operator.[50] In the case of a designer's breach of duty, such damages will be recoverable by an injured individual provided that the building works were not being carried out for profit as a commercial venture.[51]

In *Franks and Collingwood & Another v Gates*[52] damages were awarded for distress which were less because the construction related to a holiday residence than they would have been had the house been a permanent home. Where there was a negligent survey resulting in a damages award of £4,425, £500 was awarded for distress, worry and vexation[53] and £500 appears to be the sort of modest sum that was awarded for such a claim at that time. For example, in *Haig v London Borough of Hillingdon*[54] the two plaintiffs were jointly awarded £1,000 in respect of the failure of a bedroom floor. However, where there had been two years of very serious discomfort and distress during building works a single plaintiff was awarded £1,500 per annum, a total of £3,000.[55] In a case involving structural damage, with eight plaintiffs who were owners of dwellings in the block, the court awarded £1,250 to the worst affected and £750 each to the rest.[56] Sums awarded have not increased very much over the years: in *AXA Insurance Plc v Cunningham Lindsey United Kingdom*,[57] Mr Justice Akenhead considered what levels of award might be appropriate. He held that (at the end of 2007) the maximum for this type of general damages award, where there had been no physical harm or illness, would not normally exceed £2,500 per person, and in many cases might be less.

11.2.5 Betterment and elaborate repair

Where a building is repaired or replaced as a result of negligence by the designer, the designer will often seek to show that the new building or repairs provide a better building than the employer would have had if there had been no negligence. On this basis, the designer seeks to have the employer's damages reduced on the basis of betterment. It does not always follow that such contentions will be successful.

Where the employer chooses to rebuild rather than repair an old building which was rendered useless by designer's negligence, it does not follow that the damages will be assessed on the basis of the value of the old building before and after the damage caused by the negligent act. In *Harbutts Plasticine Ltd v Wayne Tank & Pump Ltd*[58] it was

---

[50] *Jarvis v Swans Tours Ltd* [1973] 1 QB 233.
[51] *Hutchinson v Harris* (1979) 10 BLR 19; *Perry v Sidney Phillips & Son* (1983) 22 BLR 124 (CA); *Murray v Sturgis* (1981) 260 EG 601.
[52] [1983] CILL 30.
[53] *Bolton v Puley* (1983) 267 EG 1160.
[54] (1980) 19 BLR 14.
[55] *Mattia v Amato* (1983) CLY 963.
[56] *Thomas v T. A. Phillips (Builders) & The Borough Council of Taff Ely* (1987) 9 Con LR 72.
[57] [2007] EWHC 3023 (TCC).
[58] [1970] 1 QB 447.

decided that the employer would recover the cost of rebuilding at least where the new building is merely a replacement for the old building. In such circumstances, the employer will not be obliged to allow anything for betterment. Although this case is overruled, it is submitted that these principles are good law. Indeed, in the Court of Appeal in *Dominion Mosaics and Tile Co. Ltd v Trafalgar Trucking Co. Ltd & Another*[59] it was held, partly on reliance on *Harbutt's Plasticene*, that if business premises is negligently destroyed by fire and the owner reasonably moves to new premises, then prima facie the cost of the new premises is the amount of his loss.

It is the case that damages will usually be assessed without regard to the fact that the old materials, replaced by reason of defective workmanship, were virtually at the end of their working life.[60]

Where the new building does more than replace the old, then there may be an element of betterment for which an allowance should be given. The same will apply where there is an over-elaborate repair of a defective building. There are two aspects to be considered: the first is causation; the question is whether the repair was necessitated by the breach of duty of the designer. If it was not, then a credit should be given. An example of this would be in a claim for hire of scaffolding to repair defectively designed windows where the employer had used the opportunity of having the scaffolding erected to repoint the brickwork, which was its own maintenance responsibility. If the scaffolding is on hire longer by reason of the brickwork repointing, then a credit should be given for the longer period of hire, for which the designer is not liable.

Betterment was considered by Judge Newey QC, Official Referee, in *Richard Roberts Holdings Ltd v Douglas Smith Stimson Partnership*.[61] Here, architects contended that the remedial works carried out by the building owner would give them something better than that which they were entitled to expect under their contract with the architects. Judge Newey said:

> I think the law can be shortly summarised. If the only practicable method of overcoming the consequences of a defendant's breach of contract is to build to a higher standard than the contract had required, the plaintiff may recover the cost of building to that higher standard. If, however, a plaintiff, needing to carry out works because of the defendant's breach of contract, chooses to build to a higher standard than is strictly necessary, the courts will, unless the new works are so different as to break the chain of causation, award him the cost of the works less a credit to the defendant in respect of betterment.[62]

However the defendent would be required to demonstrate a real pecuniary advantage, for example where re-building provides additional lettable floor area.[63]

The second aspect is that of mitigation. The employer should not have over-elaborate repairs carried out. The employer's duty is to act reasonably in both its own and the designer's interest. The question as to whether the employer has been reasonable is a

[59] (1990) 26 Con LR 1.
[60] *Day v O'Leary* (1992) 57 SASR 206, Australia.
[61] (1988) 46 BLR 50.
[62] ibid.
[63] *Voaden v Champion* [2002] 1 Lloyd's Rep 623.

matter of fact to be decided by the court following expert evidence given on behalf of the parties. In circumstances where the employer has taken other professional advice and has carried out their recommendations, it may be very difficult to argue that he did not act reasonably, but each case depends on its particular facts.[64] The designer's prospects of successfully arguing that the employer did not act reasonably will be improved if he or she is able to draw the employer's attention to a less expensive, adequate means of repair before the employer has made his final decision as to which method of repair to adopt; however, the employer is not bound to adopt the solution put forward by the designer. On the other hand, if the employer insists on carrying out repairs which are excessive or unwarranted it will not necessarily be able to recover the cost of so doing from the negligent designer. Recovery will be limited to such part of the loss as is properly to be regarded as being caused by the breach of duty.[65]

In a reported decision where a betterment argument was upheld, the plaintiff was required to give an allowance in respect of the betterment. The argument was in relation to defective tiling on the external elevations of two buildings. Tiling on the first complex had begun in July 1969 and was completed by July 1971; the first serious falls of defective tiles and backing occurred in June 1980. The interval between tiling and falls on Phase II was much shorter. Expert evidence given at the trial put the expected life of the tiles at 10 years. Judge John Newey QC, Official Referee, said that if the employer had starting retiling in July 1980, they would have been doing so when the original tiling on that phase was coming to the end of its life. The tiles on Phase II at that time only had a few years left of their life. The Judge formed the view, in the face of an allegation of betterment, that the plaintiff should give credit for betterment equal to four-fifths of their replacement value on Phase I and one half on Phase II.[66]

Where the proper initial design would have been more expensive than the negligent design that was, in fact, carried out, credit may be given in the claim for damages for a hypothetical additional cost of the proper initial design. In this way, credit will be given for what would otherwise be an element of betterment.[67]

11.3 Contributory negligence and contribution

11.3.1 Contributory negligence

The Law Reform (Contributory Negligence) Act 1945 permits a court to reduce the damages recoverable by parties in circumstances where the damages result partly from their own fault and partly from the fault of another person. However, it has remained, until relatively recently, an open question as to whether or not a party liable under a

---

[64] *Governors of the Hospital for Sick Children v McLaughlin & Harvey plc* (1990) 19 Con LR 25; *Ian McGlinn v Waltham Contractors Ltd* (2007) 111 Con LR 1; *Galliford Try Infrastructure Ltd & Another v Mott MacDonald Ltd* [2008] EWHC 1570 (TCC).

[65] *Sotiros Shipping Inc. & Another v Sameiet Solholt* [1983] 1 Lloyd's Rep 603.

[66] *Victoria University of Manchester v Hugh Wilson & Lewis Womersley (A Firm) and Pochin (Contractors) Ltd* (1984) 2 Con LR 43.

[67] *Bevan Investments v Blackhall & Struthers* (1977) 11 BLR 78; New Zealand Court of Appeal.

contract can have the damages reduced by reason of the partial fault of the claimant where the claim arises in contract. In other words, does the Law Reform (Contributory Negligence) Act 1945 apply to contracts?

In *Basildon District Council v J E Lesser (Properties) Ltd & Others*[68] the Council brought a claim for breach of contract against a contractor in relation to faulty foundations. The court considered whether the job architect's and the clerk of works' conduct in failing to ensure that the foundations were taken to the appropriate depths and failing to detect the lack of support on seeing the contractor's initial drawings was a matter that should be taken into account under the Act. The court was referred to the New Zealand authority of *Rowe v Turner Hopkins & Partners*[69] in which a similar provision in a New Zealand statute was considered. The court adopted the reasoning in *Rowe* and decided that contributory negligence was not applicable to the particular claim. A similar conclusion was reached in *A B Marintrans v Comet Shipping Co Ltd*,[70] i.e. that the defence on contributory negligence was not available in contract.

However in *Forsikringsaktieselskapet Vesta v Butcher & Others*,[71] (both at first instance and in the Court of Appeal) it was held that the court was empowered to apportion blame under the Law Reform (Contributory Negligence) Act 1945 in some circumstances. In *Vesta* the court identified three possible scenarios to consider:

(1) Where the defendant's liability arises from some contractual provision which does not depend on negligence on the part of the defendant.
(2) Where the defendant's liability arises from a contractual obligation which is expressed in terms of taking care (or its equivalent) but does not correspond to a common law duty to take care which would exist in the given case independently of contract.
(3) Where the defendant's liability in contract is the same as his liability in the tort of negligence independently of the existence of any contract.[72]

The approach in the *Marintrans* case was disapproved and the approach in the *Basildon* case was said to be concerned with a different category of case (those cases were considered to fall into categories (1) and (2) respectively). The circumstance in which the *Vesta* case concluded that there can be contribution in contract cases is category (3), i.e. where the defendant's liability in contract is *the same* as its liability would be in the tort of negligence, independent of the existence of any contract.

The approach in *Vesta* has been followed in subsequent cases. For example, in *Barclays Bank Plc v Fairclough Building Ltd*[73] the court confirmed that the 1945 Act could be applied where liability for breach was the same as and co-extensive with a similar liability in tort, independently of the existence of the contract. In that case, however, the claim could *not* be reduced, as under the contract the defendant had a *strict* duty to remove the asbestos, and not simply a duty to take reasonable care (this was therefore

[68] (1987) 8 Con LR 89.
[69] [1980] 2 NZLR 550 (New Zealand High Court).
[70] [1985] 1 WLR 1270.
[71] [1986] 2 All ER 488; [1986] 2 Lloyd's Rep. 179; [1989] 1 Lloyd's Rep 331 (HL) (although in the House of Lords, this issue did not fall to be considered); [1986] 2 All ER 488.
[72] [1986] 2 All ER 488 at 508.
[73] [1994] 3 WLR 1057.

a catgeogry (1) case). In *Raflatac Ltd v Eade*,[74] a contractor was unsuccessful in claiming contributory negligence. Here the contractor was under a contractual duty to use reasonable skill and care in installing a sprinkler system. The employer had insisted the contractor engaged a particular sub-contractor, who negligently caused a flood. However as the contractor would have had no parallel tortious duty to the employer, the defence was not available (a category (2) case).

In *Sahib Foods Ltd v Paskin Kyriakides Sands*[75] damages awarded for a design professional's breach of a contractual duty to use reasonable skill and care were reduced as a result of the negligence of the employer. In this case the architect had failed to specify adequate fire insulation to enclose a food preparation area, so that when a fire broke out it spread throughout the entire factory. The employer had also been negligent, in that an operative had left a pan of oil heating on a burner, which had caused the fire (and therefore fell under the *Vesta* principle as a category (3) case). However, it raised questions as to causation, and by how much the damages could be reduced. At first instance, the trial judge held the architects 100% liable to Sahib (even though Sahib had agreed that it had been 50% contributory negligent) because although the employer's operative started the fire, its spread was entirely due to the architect's error. This followed dicta in *Pride Valley Foods v Hall and Partners*.[76] Although in that case the court found there had been no contributory negligence, it nevertheless considered the alternative position. Sedley LJ stated:

> three questions ... arise. The first is whether the claimant too was materially at fault. The second, if he was, is whether his fault *lay within the very risk which it was the defendant's duty to guard him against*. It is only if his fault was not, or not wholly, within the causative reach of the defendant's own neglect that the question of relative culpability enters into the picture ....

This phrase 'relative culpability' refers to the principle frequently applied to asssessing the amount of reduction, which is essentially a matter for the discretion of the court. In this case the third question did not arise, as the employer's fault 'lay outside the risk' against which the architect had a duty to guard, namely the *spread* of the fire, so the answer to the second question was 'no' and no contribution was required. However, the Court of Appeal in *Sahib* took a different view. Even though the claimant's negligence had not caused the damage outside of the enclosure, it held Sahib two-thirds liable for all damage caused by the spread of the fire, and the architects liable for the remaining one-third, stressing the extreme culpability of the claimant (the operative had been an asylum seeker, and had been required to work 14 hours a day). Similarly, in *Trebor Basset Holdings Ltd v ADT Fire and Security Plc*[77] the court found the claimant 75% responsible, due to its negligent approach to risk assessment, commenting that Cadbury was 'reckless' in its failure to segregate the oil pop production area from the rest of the building and to install sprinklers.

However these cases should perhaps be regarded as exceptions, due to the serious nature of the claimants' errors, rather than as a typical apportionment.

---

[74] [1999] BLR 261.
[75] (2003) 93 Con LR 1.
[76] (2001) 76 CLR 1, at p. 59.
[77] [2012] EWCA Civ 1158 (CA).

11.3.2 Contribution

Rights to contribution are those rights that exist between persons who are liable in respect of the same damage to some innocent party. This is to be contrasted with contributory negligence by which the damages paid to claimants can be reduced by their own contributory negligence. In an action for damages in respect of a building failure it is not unusual for a number of parties to be joined as defendants. In civil proceedings, where more than one party is liable to pay damages for loss suffered, *any one of those parties is liable to the full amount* regardless of their share of the responsibility for the loss. Since the 1930s Parliament has sought to remedy the unfairness which sometimes results from the operation of this rule of law, and legislation has been enacted which enables the party sued to recover contribution from any other person also liable.

The current legislation is contained in the Civil Liability (Contribution) Act 1978. This enables the court to make a just and equitable apportionment of damages between the parties according to their share of responsibility. The Act deals with contribution between persons liable in respect of any damage, whether tort, breach of contract or otherwise (s. 6(1)). It follows that under the provisions of this Act, two parties who are in breach of separate contracts with a third party producing the same damage can claim contribution against each other. For example, where a firm of engineers in breach of its conditions of engagement with its client in respect of supervision can claim contribution from a contractor who is in breach of the JCT Contract, provided the damage to the employer is the same (s. 1(1)).

In order to succeed in a claim for contribution, it must be shown that the party from whom the contribution is sought is liable in respect of the same damage (s. 1(1)). It follows that, if that person is not liable in respect of the same damage, no contribution can be recovered. Examples of this principle being applied can be seen in *Oxford University Fixed Assets Ltd v Architects Design Partnership*[78] where, as a result of the issue of a 'conclusive' final certificate (see section 8.6.2), a contractor was held not to be liable to the employer for outstanding defects, and the architects were therefore unable to claim contribution from the contractor in relation to their negligent certification. Similarly, in *Co-op Retail Services Ltd v Taylor Young Partnership*,[79] consultants were unable to claim contribution from a sub-contractor who was held not liable for losses resulting from a fire it had caused, due to the waiver of subrogation in the JCT clauses covering insurance of the works.

A judgment given in other proceedings is conclusive evidence in the contribution proceedings (s. 1(5)). So that, for example, where an employer has sued an architect and the architect was found not liable, that judgment will be conclusive in proceedings brought by a contractor to recover a contribution from the architect. On the other hand, the fact that there has been judgment in other proceedings does not prevent the recovery of contribution (s. 1(2)).

The Act also deals with the position where one of the wrongdoers settles the proceedings against it by providing that a contribution can be recovered (s. 1(2)). However,

---

[78] (1999) 64 Con LR 12.
[79] (2002) 82 Con LR 1 (HL).

there is no right to contribution from parties who are not liable because the limitation period between them and any person who has suffered damage has expired (s. 1(3)). On the wording of section 1(3) contribution could not be recovered from a party who has settled the action with the person who suffered the damage at a date which is outside the limitation period, unless the contribution proceedings were commenced within the limitation period.

The assessment of the amount of the contribution is also governed by general principles. First, the contribution must be just and equitable having regard to the extent of the person's responsibility for the damage in question (s. 2(1)). Second, where the amount of the damages awarded is subject to a limit in an agreement or by reduction under the Law Reform (Contributory Negligence) Act 1945, the person from whom the contribution is sought cannot be required to make a contribution of a greater amount than the amount of those limited damages (s. 2(3)). An example of this occurs in the JCT with Design Build Contract which provides, by clause 2.17.3, for the limitation of the contractor's liability to the employer in respect of loss of use, loss of profit and other consequential loss arising out of breach by the contractor of its design warranty. Where, for example, such a contractor has sub-let the design to an architect, the contractor will not be able to claim contribution from the architect in excess of the limit of liability set out in the contract between the contractor and the employer, assuming that clause is itself a valid limitation of liability.

When assessing the amount of contribution 'the extent of the person's responsibility for the damage in question' is a key factor. The principle was outlined in *Pride Valley Foods v Hall and Partners*[80] where Sedley LJ stated:

> Contribution starts from a point at which two or more defendants have been held to have contributed by their own fault to the claimant's injury. The remaining task is then to measure their contributions by gauging the relative causative potency of their respective faults and their comparative blameworthiness.

However, the court may take a broader view than strict causative responsibility. An example can be seen in *Brian Warwicker Partnership v HOK International Ltd.*[81] The case concerned the design of doors to a leisure and retail centre (the O2 Centre, Finchley Road, London). Opposite facades of the centre were fitted with automatic opening doors, and when both sets were open simultaneously (which happened quite often as the centre was busy) a north westerly wind rushed straight through the building, resulting in unacceptably cold conditions in the open restaurant areas on the ground floor.

The owners brought a claim against the engineers (Brian Warwicker Partnership), who settled without admitting liability and sought contribution from the architects (HOK). Although the engineers were entirely responsible for the design of the internal environment, the court at first instance decided that competent architects, when reviewing the engineers proposals, ought to have spotted that there could be a problem. It accepted that the architects' lack of due skill and care were not directly causative of the

---

[80] (2001) 76 Con LR 1, at p. 59.
[81] (2005) 103 Con LR 112 (CA), for full account of facts see *Burford NW3 Ltd v Brian Warwicker Partnership plc* [2004] All ER (D) 183 (Nov) (TCC).

loss claimed, but decided that such acts or omission could nevertheless be taken into account in assessing contribution under the 1945 Act, although they should be given less weight. The Court of Appeal upheld this finding. The architects were allocated a 40 per cent liability contribution, which amounted to around £400K.

Some further points bear emphasis in relation to these apportionments carried out by the courts. First, they tend to be a broad assessment in units of 10 per cent, or occasionally 5 per cent. They are not accurately or obsessively examined in great detail. Second, each party found liable in respect of the same damage is liable to the plaintiff for the whole of the damages – the contribution is a matter between the defendants. It follows that, if one defendant cannot pay its share, the other defendants have to pay the claimant. This arises because all the defendants are jointly and severally liable to the claimant for the loss that it has suffered. Third, those who have tried to persuade the Court of Appeal to interfere with contribution percentages decided by the judge have not fared well (see e.g. *Adcock v Norfolk Line Ltd*).[82] The Court of Appeal is clearly loathe to interfere with decisions of judges on these issues – after all, the first instance judge has heard the witnesses and been closer to the issues affecting contribution than the Court of Appeal could ever hope to be. In some cases, however, it may be possible to challenge whether the total amount of damages originally awarded was fair.[83]

11.4 Damages recoverable on assignment

The consequences of an assignment, including its effect on the damages recoverable by those involved, have been considered in a series of cases, commencing with two key decisions in the House of Lord: *Linden Gardens* and *St Martins*.[84] Before turning to those consequences it is necessary to look at the facts in both cases.

11.4.1 The facts of *Linden Gardens*

Linden Gardens concerned the removal of blue asbestos from a building in London then owned by Stock Conversion and Investment Trust Ltd, who entered into a contract with McLaughlin and Harvey plc for that purpose. The contract, which was let in 1979, was a JCT63 contract and clause 17 provided:

> 17(1) The Employer shall not without the written consent of the Contractor assign this Contract.
>
> (2) The Contractor shall not without the written consent of the Employer assign this Contract, and shall not without the written consent of the Architect (which consent shall not be unreasonably withheld to the prejudice of the Contractor) sub-let any portion of the Works.

---

[82] (May 1993), noted at *Building Law Monthly*, 10(9), 6.
[83] *J Sainsbury plc v Broadway Malyan* (1999) 61 Con LR 31 J.
[84] *Linden Gardens Trust Ltd v Lenesta Sludge Disposals Ltd* and *St Martins Property Corporation Ltd v Sir Robert McAlpine and Sons Ltd* (1993) 63 BLR 1 (HL).

Provided that it shall be a condition in any sub-letting which may occur that the employment of the sub-contractor under the sub-contract shall determine immediately upon the determination (for any reason) of the Contractor's employment under this Contract.

In 1987, Stock Conversion transferred its rights in the building to Linden Gardens. The contractor's consent was not obtained under clause 17 or at all. Subsequently, more blue asbestos was found in the building which cost £236,000 to remove.

11.4.2 The facts of *St Martin's*

The facts of *St Martin's* were similar. St Martin's Property Corporation Ltd ('Corporation') developed a site in Hammersmith and Sir Robert McAlpine Ltd were the contractors on a JCT63 contract which contained a prohibition on assignment. That prohibition was for all practical purposes in terms identical to those in Linden Gardens.

During the work on site, at a time before any defects were discovered, Corporation assigned its rights in the development to St Martin's Property Investments Ltd ('Investments'). The contractor's consent was not obtained under clause 17 or at all. In 1980 the project was finished but in 1981 leaks developed in part of the building. Part of the remedial works cost approximately £800,000 and was paid for by Corporation but recovered from Investments. Corporation and Investments claimed against McAlpine.

11.4.3 The *Linden Gardens* and *St Martins* decisions

In *Linden Gardens*, the House of Lords decided that the purported assignment of the benefit of the building contract was ineffective because the contractor's consent was required under the contract and had not been obtained. It referred to the 'unhappily drafted' and 'inelegant phraseology' of clause 17 which referred to the assignment of the 'contract' rather than the 'benefit of the contract' but it had little difficulty coming to the conclusion that the words were not limited to sub-contracting. Linden Gardens' further argument that the clause only prohibited the right to have the contractual obligations carried out and not the right to damages was also rejected by the House. Lord Browne-Wilkinson said:

> The reason for including the contractual prohibition viewed from the contractor's point of view must be that the contractor wishes to ensure that he deals, and deals only, with the particular employer with whom he has chosen to enter into a contract. Building contracts are pregnant with disputes: some employers are much more reasonable than others in dealing with such disputes. The disputes frequently arise in the context of the contractor suing for the price and being met by a claim for abatement of the price or cross-claims founded on an allegation that the performance of the contract has been defective. Say that, before the final instalment of the price has been paid, the employer has assigned the benefits under the contract to a third party, there being at the time existing rights of action for defective work. On the Court of Appeal's view, those rights would have vested in the assignee. Would the original employer be entitled to

an abatement of the price, even though the cross-claims would be vested in the assignee? If so, would the assignee be a necessary party to any settlement or litigation of the claims for defective work, thereby requiring the contractor to deal with two parties (one not of his own choice) in order to recover the price for the works from the employer? I cannot believe that the parties ever intended to permit such a confused position to arise.[85]

Linden Gardens' final argument that the prohibition on assignment was contrary to public policy also failed and Linden Gardens failed to recover any damages.

In consequence of all of that, it was clear that Investments, the purported assignee, could not succeed in the *St Martin's* case. This left to be decided the arguments put forward by Corporation, the original employer and assignor. McAlpine had an apparently formidable defence in law: Investments had suffered the loss but had no cause of action, whereas Corporation had a cause of action but had suffered no loss – either way, they argued, they should have no liability 'a formidable, if unmeritorious, argument'[86] rejected by the House with Lord Browne-Wilkinson borrowing the words of Lord Keith in *GUS Property Management Ltd v Littlewood Mail Order Stores Ltd*:

> . . . the claim for damages would disappear . . . into some legal black hole, so that the wrongdoer escaped Scot-free.[87]

The House of Lords in *St Martins* decided that Corporation was entitled to recover under their contract with McAlpine the loss suffered by Investments. This was said to be a new exception to the general rule that a party can only sue in respect of a loss that it has suffered[88]. In this respect, it was a surprising result to lawyers who held more traditional views. Lord Browne-Wilkinson put it this way:

> The present case falls within the rationale of the exceptions to the general rule that a plaintiff can only recover damages for his own loss. The contract was for a large development of property which, in the knowledge of both Corporation and McAlpine, was going to be occupied, and possibly purchased, by third parties and not by Corporation itself. Therefore it could be foreseen that damage caused by a breach would cause loss to a later owner and not merely to the original contracting party, Corporation. As in contracts for the carriage of goods by land, there would be no automatic vesting in the occupier or owners of the property for the time being who sustained the loss of any right of suit against McAlpine. On the contrary, McAlpine had specifically contracted that the rights of action under the building contract could not without McAlpine's consent be transferred to third parties who became owners or occupiers and might suffer loss. In such a case, it seems to me proper, as in the case of carriage of goods by land, to treat the parties as having entered into the contract on the footing that Corporation would be entitled to enforce contractual rights for the benefit of those who suffered from defective performance but who, under the terms of the contract, could not acquire any right to hold McAlpine liable for breach. It is truly a case in which the rule provides 'a remedy where

---

[85] ibid., para. 48.

[86] ibid., para. 70.

[87] 1982 S L T 533, at p. 538, cited by Browne Wilkinson at para. 65 of *St Martins*.

[88] There was already an exception in relation to carriage of goods: *Albazero, The (Albacruz (Cargo Owners) v Albazero (Owners))* [1976] 3 All ER 129.

no other would be available to a person sustaining loss which under a rational legal system ought to be compensated by the person who has caused it.'[89]

In summary, the House of Lords in the *Linden Gardens* and *St Martins* cases held that the contractual provisions made any attempted assignment of the contract ineffective, which included both the assignees' right to future performance of the contract and the right to pursue any accrued claims. However it also held in the *St Martins* case that the claimants (the assignors) were entitled to claim substantial damages for defective work that had been incurred not by them but by the party to whom they had conveyed the land and the invalid assignment of the building contract. Effectively the employer (who had not suffered a loss) was allowed to claim damages on behalf of the new owner.

The subsequent House of Lords case of *Alfred McAlpine Construction Ltd v Panatown Ltd*[90] brought in an important limitation on this principle. Panatown was part of the Unex Group of companies, which owned a piece of land in Cambridge, England, through another company in the group, Unex Investment Properties Ltd (UIPL). Unex wanted to develop this land and following negotiations Panatown entered into a construction contract (JCT WCD81) with McAlpine to build an office building on UIPL's land. The building contract required that McAlpine executed a duty of care deed (a form of collateral warranty) in favour of UIPL, and this was executed on the same day as the contract between Panatown and McAlpine. Under the duty of care deed, McAlpine undertook to exercise all reasonable care, skill and attention in respect of all matters that lay within the scope of its responsibilities under the building contract. The purpose of the deed was to give UIPL and future purchasers of the building from the Unex Group protection in the event that latent defects to the building appeared.

When major defects later appeared in the completed building, Panatown commenced an arbitration claiming damages for defective work from the contractor for the benefit of UIPL. As a preliminary issue the arbitrator had to decide whether Panatown was entitled to recover substantial damages under the building contract, given that Panatown did not own the building and therefore did not suffer any loss. On the face of it the claim fell within the *St Martins* principle and the arbitrator found in Panatown's favour. McAlpine appealed and the litigation proceeded up to the House of Lords, where the decision was in McAlpine's favour. The court determined that as the duty of care deed was the intended remedy, Panatown was not able to rely on the *St Martins* exception to recover damages. This was the case even though the duty of care deed was not co-extensive with the rights under the building contract (it was less beneficial to UIPL).

11.4.4 Current position

Catlin Estates Ltd, Mr Stephen Catlin v Carter Jonas (A Firm)[91] is a more recent example of the *St Martin's'* principle being applied successfully. Following completion of a

---

[89] (1993) 63 BLR 1, para. 79.
[90] [2000] BLR 331 (HL).
[91] [2006] PNLR 15, see also section 5.1.

hunting lodge Catlin Estates transferred the property to Mr Catlin for its full value. Defects then appeared in the property, and in subsequent legal proceedings Carter Jonas argued that as the first claimant had suffered no loss Mr Caitlin could not recover from the defendant. The first claimant asserted it could recover on the second claimant's behalf on 'St Martin's' principles. The judge accepted the *St Martin's* argument:

> The evidence is clear, namely that Mr Catlin was the controlling shareholder in the private family company. The family company for its domestic purposes contracted to sell the house to Mr Catlin soon after Mr Lindley had certified practical completion. This was a family arrangement which was tax efficient. There is no doubt that if on the evidence I find that Carter Jonas was in breach of its contract with CEL, Mr Catlin would have been the very substantial beneficiary if I had awarded damages to CEL against Carter Jonas. It would be he who suffered the very substantial loss if he or CEL succeeded in the claim, either in his capacity as controlling shareholder in CEL or on his own account.
>
> It seems to me that the law should not tolerate a situation where Carter Jonas can play what Mr Williamson QC calls a 'get out of jail free card' because Mr Catlin has made a family arrangement in relation to the property. This conclusion is of course subject to the requirement which I have yet to consider as to whether Mr Catlin can recover damages on his own behalf. If he cannot do so there is no problem. If he does have a distinct claim under the Defective Premises Act 1972 (although I have concluded to the contrary) I must go on to consider whether that prevents him from making a claim against Carter Jonas for breach of contract as a third party claiming through CEL because he has a direct remedy of his own.[92]

A further example can be seen in *Technotrade Ltd v Larkstore Ltd*,[93] where the developer of a site, which suffered from landslip, was able to claim against the engineer who had negligently prepared a soil report. The engineer had been engaged by the original owner, who had sold the site to the developer. After the damage, the owner assigned the report to the developer (there was no prohibition in the terms of engagement). Although the original owner had suffered no loss (as he had sold for the full value) the developer was nevertheless able to recover. The court confirmed that in principle the developer could recover, but only to the extent that the owner would have done had there been no assignment.

It seems clear from the above that the 'St Martin's principal' survives, subject to the *Panatown* restriction. Where the interest in a property is transferred, the original owner may still be able to bring a claim for breach of contract on behalf of the new owner, even though the original owner has not suffered any economic loss. This only applies where the new owner has no right of action itself, for example through a warranty, or through operation of statute such as the Defective Premises Act 1972, or through some other rule of law.

---

[92] ibid., paras 276–7.
[93] [2006] BLR 345.

Chapter 12
Limitation

If you are thinking of taking legal action against someone, you only have a certain available time-limit in which to do it. This is because the period after which a party is prevented from pursuing a designer for breach of contract and negligence has been determined by statute. The philosophy is that the party who has committed a wrong should not have the possibility of legal proceedings hanging over it like a Sword of Damocles forever and that people injured by a wrong should be encouraged not to delay in bringing their proceedings. The method adopted by statute to achieve these aims is to fix a period after the expiry of which an action cannot be pursued. The period is a matter for Parliament and the present law fixes periods that apply to different circumstances.

The injured party can stop time running against it in proceedings in the High Court by issuing (but not necessarily serving) a writ within the specific period of limitation. However the Court of Appeal has decided that it is an abuse of process to issue a writ without any real intention of serving a statement of claim and in circumstances where there is no evidence or ground upon which a claim could in any case reasonably be served.[1] For an example showing the difficulties that are caused when there is inordinate delay in progressing proceedings see *City of Westminster v Clifford Culpin & Partners and J Jarvis & Sons plc.*[2]

In the case of proceedings brought in arbitration, the injured party stops time running by serving on the other side a notice to concur in the appointment of an arbitrator (Limitation Act 1980, s. 34). The issuing of a writ or the giving of a notice to concur in the appointment of an arbitrator does, therefore, fix the dates on which time stops running for limitation purposes. The question then arises whether these actions were taken within a period specified by statute. To decide that question, the date on which the period of limitation started to run must be fixed. It is in the fixing of that date that case law has become extremely complex, particularly for claims in tort as discussed below. The statutory limitation periods are set out briefly below, and then discussed more fully later in the chapter.

---

[1] *Steamship Mutual Underwriting Association Ltd & Another v Trollope & Colls (City) Ltd & Others* (1986) 33 BLR 77 (CA).
[2] [1987] CILL 356.

Cornes and Lupton's Design Liability in the Construction Industry, Fifth Edition. Sarah Lupton.
© 2013 Sarah Lupton and DL Cornes. Published 2013 by Blackwell Publishing Ltd.

12.1 *Statutory periods*

The Limitation Act 1980, Part 1 states as follows:

2—Time-limit for actions founded on tort
An action founded on tort shall not be brought after the expiration of six years from the date
on which the cause of action accrued. . . .

5—Time-limit for actions founded on simple contract
An action founded on simple contract shall not be brought after the expiration of six years
from the date on which the cause of action accrued. . . .

8—Time-limit for actions on a specialty
(1) An action upon a specialty shall not be brought after the expiration of twelve years from
   the date on which the cause of action accrued.
(2) Subsection (1) above shall not affect any action for which a shorter period of limitation
   is prescribed by any other provision of this Act.

The term 'simple contract' refers to an oral contract and a written contract 'under hand'
(i.e. not a deed but merely signed by the parties) whereas a 'speciality' refers to a contract
under seal or a deed. These periods appear relatively simple, but the real difficulties in law
and in practice concern establishing the date from which the periods start to run.

12.1.1 Latent Damage Act 1986

Under the Limitation Act 1980, in contract the period dates from when the breach
occurred, and in many cases it may be some time after the breach before any damage
is sustained. The position is more complex in tort, as a cause of action in negligence
would not accrue until damage has occurred (damage being an essential ingredient of
this tort). Therefore under the 1980 Act the limitation period applicable for an action
in tort is six years after the damage was first sustained (s. 2), or three years in the case
of personal injury (s. 11), regardless of whether or not it was discovered. The Limitation
Act 1980 was subsequently amended by the Latent Damage Act 1986, partly to deal with
the situation where damage occurs but is not discovered until much later and deals
with latent damage not including personal injuries. The Latent Damage Act 1986
amends the Limitation Act 1980 in certain respects concerning tort actions, discussed
below. These amendments are made by the introduction of sections 14A and 14B into
the Limitation Act 1980. To make matters more complicated, the Latent Damage Act
1986 also contains other sections relating to limitation which are not incorporated into
the Limitation Act 1980, therefore both Acts need to be read together.

The first point to consider is to which types of claim the Latent Damage Act 1986
applies. The main provisions of the Act apply only to 'negligence'. However negligence is
not defined anywhere in the Act. The Act is intended only to apply to tortious negligence
and not to any breach of duty under contract. This point was considered in *The Iron
Trade Mutual Insurance Co & Others v J K Buckenham Ltd*.[3] The commercial court

---

[3] [1990] 1 All ER 808.

decided (in relation to s. 14A of the Limitations Act 1980, inserted by the 1986 Act) that it did not apply to claims in contract because 'any action for damages in negligence' in section 14A meant any action for damages for the tort of negligence and could not be construed as meaning any action for damages, including an action for breach of a contractual duty, founded on an action for negligent or careless conduct. The 1980 Act expressly preserved the distinction between actions in tort and actions in contract and provided that the different forms of action were to be treated separately even though the time-limits specified might be the same. The court said that section 14A could not be construed in isolation from that expressly preserved distinction in the 1980 Act. On that basis, section 14A on limitation will not apply to a claim for breach of a duty under a contract to take reasonable skill and care. This has now been confirmed by the Court of Appeal in *Societé Commerciale de Reassurance v ERAS (International) Ltd.*[4] From the consultant's perspective, an unfortunate consequence of this is that after the contractual limitation period has expired, many clients will attempt to claim on the basis of a parallel tortious duty, in order to benefit from the extended periods.

In relation to a cause of action for damages for negligence (other than personal injury or death) the Limitation Act 1980 states that the action may not be brought after the expiration of the later of two periods (s. 14A(4)):

(a) six years from the date on which the cause of action accrued, or
(b) three years from the starting date as defined by subsection (5) below, if that period expires later than the period mentioned in paragraph (a) above.

For the purposes of that provision, the 'starting date' is 'the earliest date on which the plaintiff, or any person in whom the cause of action was vested before him, first had both the knowledge required for bringing an action for damages in respect of the relevant damage and a right to bring such an action' (s. 14A(5), Limitation Act 1980).

The effect of that provision is to incorporate into the law of negligence a similar test in latent damage cases to that which applies in personal injury cases. As to the knowledge required for bringing an action, that means knowledge of 'the material facts about the damage' that 'would lead a reasonable person who had suffered such damage to consider it sufficiently serious to justify his instituting proceedings' (s. 14A(6) and (7), Limitation Act 1980). In addition this would include other relevant facts as follows:

(1) that the damage was attributable in whole or in part to the act or omission which is alleged to constitute negligence
(2) the identity of the defendant, and
(3) if it is alleged that the act or omission was that of a person other than the defendant, the identity of that person and the additional facts supporting the bringing of an action against the defendants: s. 14A(8), Limitation Act 1980.

There are further qualifications in relation to the definition of knowledge for the purposes of the three-year period of limitation created by the 1986 Act. First, knowledge

---

[4] [1992] 2 All ER 82.

that any acts or omissions did or did not, as a matter of law, involve negligence is irrelevant; further, a claimant's knowledge includes knowledge that a claimant might reasonably be expected to acquire (a) from facts observable or ascertainable by the claimant, or (b) from facts ascertainable by it with the help of appropriate expert advice which it is reasonable for it to seek; but claimants are not to be taken by virtue of these provisions as having knowledge of a fact ascertainable only with the help of expert advice so long as they have taken all reasonable steps to obtain, and where appropriate, to act on that advice (s. 14A(10), Limitation Act 1980).

These qualifications are important, as it means that in practice lack of knowledge will not prolong the period in cases where a claimant might reasonably be expected to have acquired that knowledge. In construction terms, this introduces the concept of 'discoverability', i.e. the starting date runs from the point when the damage was discoverable, not when it may actually have been discovered. The qualifications also deal with situations where the claimant may have needed the assistant of an expert.

An example of the application of this can be seen in *Haward v Fawcetts*,[5] which concerned a claim against a structural engineer regarding negligent design of foundations. Here the court decided that a suspicion of a problem with the foundations would not be enough (in this case some cracks had appeared), and even if the claimant thought there was a real possibility that damage was caused by the foundations, if verification by an expert was necessary to form a more definite view then there was no actual knowledge.

A further illustration is *Renwick v Simon and Michael Brooke Architects*.[6] In late 2000, the Renwicks decided to extend and refurbish their home, including the construction of a large basement room beneath their rear garden. The design was undertaken by Michael Brookes with advice from the engineers Atwells. The basement was to be a concrete structure with external waterproofing. The contractor started work about June 2001, and there was a change in the advice of the Architects and/or Attwell in March 2001 whereby 'the concrete . . . was to be dosed with Sika 1 admixture and the said external waterproofing omitted and replaced by volclay matting on the vertical components and asphalt on the horizontal'. The contractor finished its work by about November 2001, but soon after, substantial quantities of water came into the garden room. The contractor was called in and pumped out the water. At this stage there was clearly a serious problem. The Renwicks terminated their contract with the contractor and Aquarend was called in, inspected the garden room and recommended the use of a waterproof internal render including 'combiflex' jointing over day joints in the floor and upstands. The Renwicks accepted Aquarend's quotation and it completed these works around June 2002. However by the summer of 2008 water started to accumulate under the flooring in the garden room. The Renwicks issued their proceedings on 26 July 2010. Attwell applied for summary judgment against the Renwicks on the basis that the claims in contract and in tort were statute-barred under the Limitation Act 1980. For the purposes of section 14A, it argued that more than enough had occurred and was known about by the Renwicks in 2002 to set the three-year time period allowed by that section to start running. The court agreed with this and the striking out applica-

---

[5] [2008] BLR 229.
[6] [2011] EWHC 874 (TCC); 05 May 2011.

tion relating to the original construction was upheld. However the court decided that any negligent advice relating to the remedial solution adopted could give rise to a different cause of action. It made no findings on when damage resulted from the failure of the remedial solution or when the Renwicks possessed sufficient knowledge about its failure to bring an action (which could have been as late as 2008). The claim relating to the remedial solution was therefore not struck out.

The 1986 Act also creates a 15-year 'long stop'. This is in section 14(B) of the Limitation Act 1980. An action in damages for negligence cannot be brought:

> . . . after the expiration of fifteen years from the date (or, if more than one, from the last of the dates) on which there occurred any act or omission—
> (a) which is alleged to constitute negligence; and
> (b) to which the damage in respect of which damages are claimed is alleged to be attributable (in whole or in part).

It follows from this that an action could be prevented even where injured parties remain unaware that they have the right to bring a claim as section 14B prevents reliance on the other periods at section 14A (namely, six years from the damage occurring or three years from discoverability) if the 15-year period expires first. It is important to remember, however, that the effect of the long stop may be restricted in cases where there is a continuing duty to check and revise design or a duty to warn – see Chapter 8.

In *Perry v Tendring District Council & Others*[7] it was held that by reason of the *Pirelli* decision (see below), where a property was already damaged on sale to a subsequent owner, that subsequent owner had no right of action by reason of the fact that it did not have an interest in the property at the time when the damage occurred. Section 3 of the Latent Damage Act 1986 was intended to correct this mischief. The effect of section 3 is to provide that a fresh cause of action accrues on the date on which the interest in the property is acquired. It should be noted, though, that this section will only be of assistance if there is a pre-existing cause of action in tort in relation to damage in question; where the damage is to the property itself there may be no action (see Chapter 4). It may therefore be of no assistance to purchasers who acquire a defective building.[8]

12.1.2 Contribution

A claim to recover contribution under the Civil Liability (Contribution) Act 1978 (see 11.3.2) will become statute-barred two years from the date on which the right to contribution accrued (Limitation Act 1980, s. 10). The relevant date for the accrual of the right to contribution is defined as either:

> Where there is a judgment in civil proceedings or an award in arbitration the relevant date is the day on which the judgment is given, or the date of the award in the arbitration.
>
> Where (1) does not apply and where the person seeking contribution makes or agrees to make a payment (whether admitting liability or not) the relevant date is the date on which the agreement to make payment is made.

---

[7] (1984) 30 BLR 118.
[8] see *Broster v Galliard Docklands Ltd* [2011] EWHC 1722, approving *Payne v John Setchell Ltd* [2002] BLR 489.

Where an architect claimed contribution from a firm of consulting engineers and the architect subsequently died, the engineers contended that the claim did not pass to the architect's personal representatives. However the Court of Appeal held that the right to a contribution created by the Law Reform (Married Women and Tortfeasors) Act 1935 survived the death and passed to the architect's personal representatives.[9]

12.1.3 Personal injuries

There are special rules when there are personal injuries and none of the other rules apply (Limitation Act 1980, s. 11(2)). The time-limits fixed by the Act for personal injury actions apply to, amongst other things, damages for negligence or breach of duty, whether or not the duty arises under a contract, a statute, or independently of contract (Limitation Act 1980, s. 11(1)). A claim for damages in respect of personal injuries will be statute-barred three years from either the date on which the cause of action accrued or the date of knowledge, if later, of the injured person. Where the injured person dies the cause of action survives the death for the benefit of his or her estate (Law Reform (Miscellaneous Provisions) Act 1934, s. 1) and a claim will be statute-barred three years after the date of death or the date of the personal representative's knowledge, whichever is the later (Limitation Act 1980, s. 11(4) and (5)). There are detailed provisions defining the date of knowledge and the courts are given a discretionary power to allow an action to proceed notwithstanding the periods that are fixed by statue (Limitation Act 1980, s. 33).

12.1.4 Defective Premises Act 1972

A claim for breach of duty under the Defective Premises Act 1972, which only applies to dwellings, is deemed to have accrued at the time that the dwelling was completed or at the time when further work, needed to rectify the original work, is finished (Defective Premises Act 1972, s. 1(15)). The effect of this provision, when read with the Limitation Act 1980, is that a claim for breach of duty under the Defective Premises Act will be statute-barred six years after the completion of the work or the completion of rectification work, whichever is the later. The Latent Damage Act 1986 does not apply to claims under the Defective Premises Act 1972, as these claims are considered a breach of statutory duty, not a tortious liability.

This period set down by statute is to be contrasted with the period during which the NHBC will meet claims for major structural defects, which is ten years. The latter is a period which arises by reason of a contract, not a statute.

12.2 *Limitation and contract*

This section deals in a little more detail with the limitation position in contract. The same principles apply whether the contract is a simple contract with a six-year limitation period or a deed (or under seal) with a 12-year limitation period (see above). The

---

[9] *Ronex Properties Ltd v John Laing Construction Ltd* [1982] 3 All ER 861 (CA).

period runs from the date of accrual of the cause of action. In contract, it is usually accepted that the cause of action accrues when there is a breach of contract or a breach of duty, not from the date of its discovery. In many cases, therefore, the date will not be difficult to find. For example when there is a contractual obligation to pay a fixed sum of money on a fixed date and the money is not paid, the cause of action will arise on that fixed date.

However there are other factors that need to be considered. Where there is any doubt about a cause of action having expired, the courts are not inclined to remove the injured party's remedy and tend to look favourably on an analysis of the position that will give a later date for limitation purposes. For example, in the case of contractors, the relevant date will not necessarily be the date on which the defective work was built; it will usually be the date when the works were completed. This is because the contractor has an overriding obligation to complete the works and it is, therefore, the completion date rather than the date of construction of the defective part that is significant. Furthermore, where there is a provision in the contract for making good defects and a defects liability period, it may be possible to argue that time does not begin to run for limitation purposes until that period has expired. Where the contract requires the contractor to provide a building that performs in a certain manner, or sets out particular requirements as to durability, the breach is normally considered to occur at the completion date, not when the performance failing occurs[10] (although the position may be different under BOT contracts where the supplier also maintains and operates the facility).

A designer's breach of duty in relation to the design will usually arise at the time the defective drawing, specification or instruction is prepared. However, as it is now considered that designers have a continuing duty to check their designs and amend any errors, it will usually be possible to argue for a later date than the date of the drawing, etc. Indeed it has been said that professionals are engaged to see the work through, and if errors emerge they have a duty to correct them such that, where a writ is issued less than six year's after practical completion of a building but more than six years after the breach complained of, an application to strike out the proceedings by reason of limitation failed and the proceedings were permitted to continue.[11]

In the case of supervision, the architect's duties will be spread throughout the construction period but, again, it will usually be possible to argue for a later date by reason of the designer's duties in respect of certification. For example, under JCT SBC11, the payment on interim certificates is in respect of 'work properly executed'; certifying payment in respect of work not properly executed will be negligence and will take place later than the negligent inspection.

12.2.1 Fraud and concealment: contract

However, all this discussion is subject to an extremely important statutory exception. Section 32 of the Limitation Act 1980 provides that the limitation period does not even start to run where the designer or contractor has been guilty of fraud, or has concealed

---

[10] *Crowther v Shannon Motor Co* [1975] 1 All ER 139.
[11] *Chelmsford District Council v T J Evers Ltd & Others* (1984) 25 BLR 99.

any relevant facts from the injured party, or the action arises from a mistake (s. 32, Limitation Act 1980). Furthermore, concealment includes circumstances where there is a deliberate breach of duty which is unlikely to be discovered for some time (Limitation Act 1980, s. 32(2)). Additionally, 'fraud' is not limited to the meaning that it has in the criminal law and includes deliberate concealment of a breach of duty.[12]

The fact that the employer had engaged a clerk of works or inspectors to supervise the work will not prevent the employer relying on section 32.[13] However, it is clear that simply getting on with the building work and covering up shoddy or incompetent work may not be enough to establish deliberate concealment. In *William Hill Organisation Ltd v Bernard Sunley & Sons Ltd*,[14] a case on the Limitation Act 1939, where the words were 'fraudulent concealment' as opposed to deliberate concealment in the 1980 Act, the Court of Appeal found that there ought to be more evidence than simply getting on with the work and that it may be necessary to show concealment from the clerk of works or the architect or the building owner. In that case, Lord Justice Cumming Bruce said:

> [Counsel] submitted that, whenever a builder under contract did shoddy or incompetent work, which was covered up in the due succession of the building construction work, so that when the building was complete the bad work was hidden from view, such facts constituted fraudulent concealment within the well known line of cases on equitable fraud. We do not accept this proposition. Simply getting on with the work after something shoddy or inadequate has been done or omitted does not necessarily give rise to a legal inference of concealment or of equitable fraud. As Edmund-Davies LJ . . . put it in *Applegate v Moss*:[15]
>
> > 'It is a truism that not every breach of contract arising from a defect in the quality of materials or workmanship would justify a finding of fraud. But some breaches can be so fundamental that, if deliberately and knowingly committed, they properly give rise to an inference of fraud by the party in breach. Furthermore, the special relationship between the parties may facilitate such a finding.'[16]

As Lord Evershed MR said in *Kitchen v Royal Air Force Association*,[17] referring to what Lord Hardwicke had said a long time before in relation to equitable fraud:

> . . . it is I think, clear that the phrase covers conduct which, having regard to some special relationship between the two parties concerned, is an unconscionable thing for the one to do towards the other.[18]

In *E. Clarke & Sons (Coaches) Ltd v Axtell Yates Hallet*,[19] Judge Esyr Lewis QC referred to the above passage from *William Hill* and concluded that, although that passage was concerned with the 1939 Act, the observation in that case 'simply getting on with work after something shoddy or inadequate has been done does not necessarily give rise to

---

[12] *King v Victor Parsons & Co* [1973] 1 WLR 29.
[13] *London Borough of Lewisham v Leslie & Co Ltd* (1978) 12 BLR 22 (CA).
[14] (1982) 22 BLR 1.
[15] (1971) 3 BLR 4, at 6.
[16] (1982) 22 BLR 1, at 25 (CA).
[17] [1958] 2 All ER 241.
[18] ibid., at 249.
[19] (1989) 30 Con LR 123.

a legal inference of concealment or equitable fraud' applied also in relation to section 32 of the Limitation Act 1980.

In *Gray & Others (The Special Trustees of the London Hospital) v T. P. Bennett & Son, Oscar Faber & Partners and McLaughlin and Harvey Ltd*,[20] the application of building defects to section 32 of the Limitation Act 1980 was considered by Sir William Stabb QC. A hospital had been built in 1962 and 1963. In 1979 a bulge was noticed in a panel of brickwork. Investigation revealed that inaccuracies in setting out concrete panels had resulted in a lack of fit of the brick cladding and, further, during construction concrete nibs had been severely hacked back to try to fit in the brickwork. The employer brought proceedings against the architect, the engineer and the contractor. Judgment was eventually given for the employer against the contractors but the allegations in negligence against the architect and the consulting engineer were held by the Judge not to have been made out. It is to be noted that approximately 25 years elapsed between the construction of the building and the judgment and tracing of witnesses had proved extremely difficult – indeed, the contractor was unable to call any witnesses at all.

In relation to the assertion by the employer that there was here a clear case of deliberate concealment, under section 32 of the Limitation Act 1980, the Judge said that the facts were very different to those in *William Hill Organisation Ltd v Bernard Sunley & Sons Ltd*.[21] In this case the wrongful and destructive action had been deliberately concealed from the supervisors of the employer and it followed from the Act that the limitation period did not begin to run until the employer had discovered the concealment. That was November 1979 when the bulge in the brickwork was discovered. Further, the Judge held that the effect of the deliberate concealment was to amount to fraudulent concealment and thereby to prevent the contractors from relying on the final certificate as conclusive evidence that the works had been properly carried out – the final certificate was rendered invalid on the principle that fraud unravels all.

In a case on the proper legal construction of section 32, the court has held that a deliberate concealment can have the effect of preventing the limitation period from running even when the deliberate concealment occurred *after* the date on which the claimant's cause of action arose.[22] However, the House of Lords has held that section 32 does not apply if the defendant was not aware that they had committed a breach of duty; in such cases the limitation period would still run from the breach. In order for section 32 to apply, the defendant must have either deliberately committed a breach, or concealed a relevant fact upon discovering later that a breach had been committed.[23]

12.3 Limitation and tort

This section deals with all claims in negligence, excepting those that result in personal injuries for which there are special rules.

---

[20] [1987] CILL 342.
[21] (1982) 22 BLR 1 (CA).
[22] *Sheldon & Others v RHM Outhwaite (Underwriting Agencies) Ltd, The Times* 8 December 1993.
[23] *Cave v Robinson Jarvis and Rolfe* [2003] 1 AC 384.

A claim in negligence will be statute-barred six years after the accrual of the cause of action. Although that definition is the same as for contract, the effect is very different because the general rule in tort is that the cause of action accrues when the damage is caused and not from the date of the breach of duty. It may, of course, happen that in some cases the breach of duty and the damage occur at the same time and that will pose no problem. Difficulties arise where the breach of duty occurs many years before the physical damage which is the consequence of the breach of duty, manifests itself. The breach of duty is unknown and lies dormant until physical damage appears.

The starting point in any analysis is the House of Lords' case *Pirelli General Cable Works Ltd v Oscar Faber & Partners*,[24] which still represents broadly the position of the courts in the UK. However, in order to understand the development to the legal position which that case represents, it is necessary to see how the law has developed since 1983. Three sections follow therefore: the first dealing briefly with the history of the law before *Pirelli* (all now superseded by *Pirelli*); then a second section dealing with the *Pirelli* test itself; and finally the effect of *Murphy* on *Pirelli* and subsequent more recent decisions.

12.3.1 History of development of the law prior to *Pirelli*

In *Cartledge v E. Jopling & Sons Ltd*,[25] a personal injury case, the House of Lords decided that:

> . . . a cause of action has accrued as soon as a wrongful act has caused personal injury beyond what can be regarded as negligible, even when that injury is unknown to and cannot be discovered by the sufferer, and further injury arising from the same act at a later date, does not give rise to a further cause of action.[26]

In other words, whether the injured person knew that he or she had been injured or not, time for limitation purposes began to run from the time that the personal injury was caused whether or not the damage could have been discovered. That case was perceived as creating a mischief and in 1963 Parliament passed a Limitation Act to deal with that mischief. It extended the time-limit, in personal injury actions only, for the bringing of actions where the material facts were outside the knowledge of the plaintiff.

In *Sparham-Souter v Town and Country Development (Essex) Ltd*[27] the owners of two houses which had suffered damage as a result of faulty foundations brought actions against the builders and the local authority. Most of the local authority's breaches of duty (but not all), had occurred more than six years prior to the issue of the writ at a time when the house owners were not the owners of the property. It was held that the

---

[24](1983) 21 BLR 99; [1983] 1 All ER 65.

[25][1963] AC 758.

[26]ibid., Lord Reid at 771.

[27][1976] QB 858.

cause of action accrues when the damage is discovered by the injured party, or when he or she should with reasonable diligence have discovered it. It was said:

> When building work is badly done – and covered up – the cause of action does not accrue, and time does not begin to run, until such time as the plaintiff discovers that it has done damage, or ought, with reasonable diligence, to have discovered it.[28]

This decision was therefore inconsistent with the finding of the House of Lords in *Cartledge* and was subsequently overruled in *Pirelli*.

The next case was *Anns v London Borough of Merton*,[29] since overruled in *Murphy*. This was another claim against a local authority in negligence in relation to inspecting foundations. Limitation was not directly in point in this case but it was considered by the House of Lords. Lord Wilberforce said:

> In my respectful opinion, the Court of Appeal was right when, in *Sparham Souter v Town and Country Developments (Essex) Limited* [1976] QB 858, it abjured the view that the cause of action arose immediately on delivery, i.e. conveyance of the defective house. It can only arise when the state of the building is such that there is present or imminent danger to the health or safety of persons occupying it.[30]

It appeared to follow from this judgment that the *Sparham-Souter* decision was explained by saying that the cause of action is only complete when the damage is such that there is 'present or imminent danger to the health or safety of persons' occupying the building. This view was not accepted in *Pirelli*.

There was, therefore, a conflict between the view that the cause of action in tort accrues when the damage is suffered, whether or not the claimant knows about it, and the view that it only accrues when the claimant discovers the damage or ought, with reasonable diligence, to have discovered it. This was a key issue that the House of Lords had to consider in *Pirelli*.

12.3.2 Limitation in negligence: The *Pirelli* decision

In *Pirelli General Cable Works Ltd v Oscar Faber & Partners*[31] the claimants had had a chimney built which was about 160-feet high. The chimney was made of pre-cast concrete and had four flues. The refractory inner lining was made of a material which was later found to be unsuitable for its purpose. Cracks developed and eventually the chimney had to be partly demolished and replaced. The chimney had been designed by a nominated sub-contractor who was in liquidation but the trial Judge had found that the defendant engineers had accepted responsibility for the design and that finding was not challenged in the House of Lords. The facts were such that the date upon which

---

[28] ibid., Lord Denning MR, at 868.
[29] [1978] AC 728.
[30] ibid., at 760.
[31] [1983] 1 All ER 65.

Pirelli had discovered the cracks was within six years prior to the issue of the writ and on the basis of the decision in *Sparham-Souter* there would be no limitation defence available to Oscar Faber. However, the engineers contended that the cause of action accrued at an earlier date and they suggested three possibilities for that date: (1) when Pirelli decided to act on their advice to install a chimney; (2) the date on which the building of the chimney was completed; or (3) the date on which the cracks occurred. All those dates were more than six years before the issue of the writ and, accordingly, if any of those contentions were successful Pirelli would not be able to pursue their claim by reason of limitation.

Their Lordships found themselves unable to agree with the decision in *Sparham-Souter* and, in particular, Lord Fraser said that he could not agree with the distinction drawn in *Sparham-Souter* between personal injury which was clinically [unobservable and latent damage in a building. He said:

> It seems to me that there is a true analogy between a plaintiff whose body has, unknown to him, suffered injury by inhaling particles of dust, and a plaintiff whose house has unknown to him sustained injury because it was built with inadequate foundations or of unsuitable materials. Just as the owner of the house may sell the house before the damage is discovered, and may suffer no financial loss, so the man with the injured body may die before pneumoconiosis becomes apparent, and he also may suffer no financial loss. But in both cases they have a damaged article when, but for the defendant's negligence, they would have had a sound one.
>
> The plaintiff's cause of action will not accrue until *damage* occurs, which will commonly consist of cracks coming into existence as a result of the defect even though the cracks or the defect may be undiscovered and undiscoverable.[32]

It therefore follows that the House of Lords resolved the inconsistency between *Cartledge* and *Sparham-Souter* in favour of the former i.e. that the cause of action accrues when the damage occurs, not when it is discoverable. The House of Lords found that the apparent approval of *Sparham-Souter* and the date of discoverability in Lord Wilberforce's speech in *Anns* was more apparent than real, and that Lord Wilberforce had not said, and did not imply, that the date of discoverability was the date when the cause of action accrued.[33]

12.3.3 *Pirelli* and 'doomed from the start'

Lord Fraser in *Pirelli*, having set out this test that the cause of action will not accrue until damage occurs, went on to say:

> There may perhaps be cases where the defect is so great that the building is doomed from the start, and where the owner's cause of action will accrue as soon as it is built, but it seems unlikely that such a defect would not be discovered within the limitation period. Such cases, if they exist, would be exceptional.

---

[32] ibid., at 70.
[33] *Brian Morgan v Park Developments Ltd*, (1983), Ireland, 2-CLD-09-14.

It seems to me that, except perhaps where the advice of an architect or consulting engineer leads to the erection of a building which is so *defective* as to be doomed from the start, the cause of action accrues only when physical damage occurs to the building.[34]

The phrase 'doomed from the start' appeared as long ago as 1978 in *Batty v Metropolitan Property Realisations*[35] but there does not appear to be any direct connection between Lord Fraser's remarks in *Pirelli* and the remarks of the Court of Appeal in *Batty*. The effect of Lord Fraser's 'doomed-from-the-start' phraseology appears at first sight to suggest that designers should do their utmost to show that their design was doomed from the start because that is likely to give the earliest possible limitation date and hence the greatest likelihood of defending such an action on a limitation basis. In other words, the more negligent designers are, the better their position for the purposes of limitation. However, unfortunately for those who have sought to rely on this *dictum* of Lord Fraser, the path has proved to be far from smooth.

First, in *Ketteman & Others v Hansel Properties Ltd & Others*[36] (a Court of Appeal case that approved *Pirelli*), Lord Justice Lawton commented that Lord Fraser's reference in *Pirelli* to buildings that were doomed from the start was not necessary for the decision he made (and therefore *obiter*): 'I would regard it as a cautionary dictum so as to leave for future consideration problems which might arise in exceptional cases'. In the *Ketteman* case, the Court of Appeal had found that the facts were broadly similar to those in *Pirelli* and that they were not exceptional – 'if anything, all too common'. When *Ketteman* reached the House of Lords, Their Lordships also rejected the doomed from the start argument.

The courts have also indicated that the type of situation it would consider 'doomed from the start' is very unlikely to occur. The cracks in the *Pirelli* chimney were the product of faulty materials and had developed within a year of construction, and yet even in that case the House of Lords had been unable to regard the design as doomed from the start. If it did not regard those facts as being doomed from the start, then most cases will not be an exception to the general rule.[37] The Court of Appeal in a unanimous judgment took the view that Lord Fraser's dictum was to be limited to extreme cases.[38]

'Doomed from the start' was also argued in *London Congregational Union Inc. v Harriss & Another*.[39] This was a case where there was inadequate drainage to deal with surface water so flooding and dampness had followed. The Court of Appeal said that the concept of 'doomed from the start' had been very frequently invoked but rarely applied and that it would not be wise or useful to attempt to define the kinds of cases which would qualify for inclusion within the dictum.[40]

---

[34] [1983] 1 All ER 65 at 70.

[35] (1977) 7 BLR 1.

[36] [1988] 1 All ER 38; (1987) 85 LGR 409; [1987] 2 WLR 312.

[37] *Kensington and Chelsea and Westminster AHA v Wettern Composites Ltd* [1985] 1 All ER 346; *Ketteman v Hansel Properties Ltd & Others* [1987] 2 WLR 312.

[38] *Jones, Alfred John v Stroud District Council* (1987) 34 BLR 27 (CA).

[39] [1988] 1 All ER 15.

[40] For a rare case where a building was found to be doomed from the start, see *Kaliszewska v John Clague & Partners* (1986) 5 Con LR 63, see section 8.2.1.2.

12.3.4 Developments since *Pirelli*

As has been outlined above, following *Pirelli* the Latent Damage Act 1986 attempted to clarify matters by setting the 'starting point' for time to run as the date when damage was discoverable. However this still left open the question as to what exactly constitutes the actionable 'damage'. Is it the building which is known to embody design errors, and is therefore now worth less, but has not yet developed any physical damage, or is it the appearance of cracks (in either case if rectified, the damage would be purely economic).

Some questions arose regarding the *Pirelli* decision in the light of the decision in *Murphy* in 1990. *Pirelli* was classified in *Murphy* as a case of negligent advice falling under the principle set out in *Hedley Byrne v Heller & Partners Ltd*. Lord Keith, in *Murphy*, said:

> It would seem that in a case such as *Pirelli*, where the tortious liability arose out of a contractual relationship with professional people, the duty extended to take reasonable care not to cause economic loss to the client by the advice given. The plaintiffs built the chimney as they did in reliance on that advice. The case would accordingly fall within the principle of *Hedley Byrne*. . . .[41]

The obvious difficulty with this approach is that it would mean that the decision in *Pirelli* as to the date on which the cause of action accrues is different to that suggested by *Murphy*, namely the date on which Pirelli relied on the advice of Oscar Faber as to how to build the chimney; that is certain to be a date earlier than the date on which 'damage occurs, which will commonly consist of cracks coming into existence . . . even though the cracks . . . may be undiscovered and undiscoverable'.[42] In other words the House of Lords, while approving *Pirelli*, appeared to disagree as to when the cause of action would accrue. *Murphy* however was not a limitation case so care is needed in drawing conclusions from that analysis.

This issue was considered further in *Nitrigin Eireann Teoranta & Another v Inca Alloys Ltd & Another*.[43] This case was concerned with a specialist supplier, not a 'professional man', so it should be considered in that light. A specialist pipe, containing explosive gases, had burst causing damage to the plant around the pipe. Inca had manufactured and supplied the pipe under a contract agreed in about 1981. It was accepted that the claim in contract was statute-barred and the case concerned only a claim in tort. The parties agreed facts for the purposes of the trial on the preliminary issues, one of which was whether, if there was a cause of action in tort, it was statute-barred:

(1) The pipe was manufactured by Inco and supplied in the summer of 1981.
(2) 'Damage' in the form of cracking occurred in the pipe itself in or before July 1983, and was discovered by Nitrigin that month.
(3) Despite reasonable investigation, Nitrigin was unaware of the cause of the cracking, but took steps to repair it by grinding out the crack.

---

[41] [1991] 1 AC 398, at 466.
[42] *Pirelli General Cable Works Ltd v Oscar Faber & Partners* [1983] 1 All ER 65 at 70.
[43] (1991) 60 BLR 65; [1992] 1 All ER 854.

(4) On about 27 June 1984 the pipe again cracked and burst causing damage to the structure of the plant around the pipe.
(5) The writ was issued on 21 June 1990 alleging negligent manufacture and Nitrigin asserted it was issued within the period of limitation in tort.
(6) It was assumed for this hearing (although denied) that the pipe in 1983 and 1984 was defective and cracked by reason of negligence in manufacture, namely inadequate distribution of titanium.

Nitrigin asserted that it did not acquire a cause of action in 1983 when the pipe cracked but that the appropriate date was when the pipe burst on 27 June 1984. Inco, on the other hand, said that the cause of action accrued in 1983 when the pipe cracked and that the claim was statute-barred. Mr Justice May decided that Nitrigin did not acquire a cause of action in 1983 when the pipe cracked. The cracking was damage to the 'thing itself', constituting a defect of quality producing economic loss which was irrecoverable in negligence. He found that the cause of action accrued in June 1984. In coming to this view, he distinguished *Pirelli* on the basis that the relationship between Inco and Nitrigin was not one of a professional and client, that is to say that it did not fall within *Hedley Byrne*. The judge said of *Pirelli*:

> The relevant damage was, however, damage to the chimney itself and *Pirelli* cannot, in my judgment, now be read as a wide general authority that cracking damage to a chimney itself affords a cause of action against anyone concerned with its supply, manufacture or construction. That would be plainly inconsistent with *D & F* and *Murphy*. *Pirelli* remains the leading authority on the limitation point which it decided and it also remains, as Lord Keith explained in *Murphy*, as an example of a case where tortious liability arose from a contractual relationship with professional people. Although . . . it might be possible to argue in the House of Lords that the law as now understood should not afford a cause of action in negligence against a professional man in favour of a client with whom the professional is also in contract, such a conclusion is not open to a court of first instance. [Counsel for Inco] urges me to find that the relationship between Nitrigin and Inco can be equated with that between the plaintiff and defendant in *Pirelli*. I am not so persuaded.
>
> In *Pirelli* the defendants were a firm of professional consulting engineers engaged to advise and design. Here [Counsel] can glean no more from the pleadings than that Inco are alleged to be specialist manufacturers who knew or ought to have known the purpose for which their specialist pipes were needed. In my judgement, that is neither a professional relationship in the sense in which the law treats professional negligence nor a *Hedley Byrne* relationship.[44]

Following *Murphy* the next key case to examine the issue was *Invercargill City Council v Hamlin*,[45] a New Zealand case which came before the Privy Council. The facts here were very similar to those in *Pirelli*. The Privy Council held that, where the claimant was suing for economic loss, and not for physical damage, the problem of when the limitation period begins to run would be resolved if the loss was to be treated as occurring only when the defect is discovered. Although damage in some sense has occurred,

---

[44] [1992] 1 All ER 854 at 859.
[45] [1994] AC 624.

until the defect is discovered, the claimant has suffered no loss (and therefore not all elements necessary to support the claim are yet in existence). Once discovered, the market value of the property would be depreciated, and the measure of damages would be the cost of repair if it would be reasonable to repair it or, if not, the depreciation in market value. The Court stated:

> The plaintiff's loss occurs when the market value of the house is depreciated by reason of the defective foundations, and not before. Since the defects would then be obvious to a potential buyer or his expert, that marks the moment when the market value of the building is depreciated and therefore the moment when economic loss occurs. Their Lordships do not think it is possible to define the moment more accurately. The measure of the loss will then be the cost of repairs if it is reasonable to repair, or the depreciation in the market value if it is not..... .[46]

This is clearly inconsistent with the approach in *Pirelli*, and although it has received some approving comments in academic publishing, has generally not been followed in the UK. For example, in *New Islington and Hackney Housing Association Ltd v Pollard Thomas and Edwards Ltd*,[47] the court declined to follow *Invercargill*. This case concerned inadequate sound insulation between flats, and an action in negligence was brought against the designers. The question here was whether the cause of action in negligence accrued at the date of practical completion, i.e. when the Association took possession of the buildings with their defective sound insulation or when, after a period of occupation by the tenants, the excessive noise transmission became apparent. The court held, following *Pirelli*, that the cause of action in negligence accrued not on knowledge of defect but when the defect existed, which was when the properties were handed over. The court rather reluctantly felt it was bound by *Pirelli*, stating:

> In my judgment, the present state of affairs is hardly satisfactory. If, as Lord Keith said, *Pirelli* falls within the principle of *Hedley Byrne v Heller & Partners* [1964] AC 465 and is an economic loss case, then it is difficult to see why the cause of action in *Pirelli* did not accrue when the plaintiffs relied on the advice of the engineers by instructing them to proceed with the construction of the chimney.[48]

Invercargill was also not followed in *Abbott & Another v Will Gannon & Smith Ltd*[49] where the facts were again very similar to *Pirelli*. The claimants owned a hotel in Torquay where significant cracking had appeared in a large bay window. In May 1995, the claimants engaged a consulting structural and civil engineering firm to investigate and design the necessary remedial work, which was completed in March 1997. Subsequently, in late 1999, the claimants noticed further cracking, and more works were carried out. In September 2003, the claimants commenced proceedings against the engineers in both contract and tort. The contract claim was time-barred, and so the

---

[46] ibid., at 648.
[47] [2001] 1 BLR 74.
[48] ibid., at para. 37.
[49] [2005] BLR 195 (CA).

question of when the cause of action in tort accrued was heard as a preliminary issue, which was then taken to the Court of Appeal. The claimants relied on the decision in *Pirelli* and argued that the cause of action accrued when the physical damage to the building first appeared, namely in late 1999. The engineers argued that the claim against them was for economic loss, which was the loss of market value due to the negligent design, and that this was discoverable before the physical damage occurred. The cause of action therefore accrued when their advice was acted upon by constructing the work, early in 1997. The Court decided it was bound by *Pirelli*. Consequently, the cause of action in negligence against the consulting engineer arose when physical damage to the building first occurred, and therefore the claim was not time-barred.[50]

Abbott & Another v Will Gannon & Smith therefore appears to leave the position much as it was following *Pirelli*, i.e. that time does not start to run until physical damage such as cracks have occurred. This still leaves the *Murphy* dichotomy unresolved, as in many cases it will be possible to identify economic loss at an earlier date. It is therefore likely that there will be further development in this very complex area of the law.

12.3.5 Fraud and concealment – negligence

In addition to all these problems, the provisions of section 32 of the Limitation Act 1980 also apply to claims in negligence so that where there is fraud, concealment or mistake, the limitation period does not begin to run until the injured party has discovered the fraud, concealment or mistake or could with reasonable diligence have discovered it.

---

[50] *Pirelli* was also followed in the Hong Kong case of *Bank of East Asia v Tsien Wui Marble Factory Ltd* [2000] 1 HKC 1, and *Abbot* has been followed in *Oxford Architects Partnership v Cheltenham Ladies College* [2007] BLR 293.

Chapter 13
Measures for Limiting Liability

The preceding chapters have focussed on the liability position that would normally arise where the parties' agreements are silent on the matter, and do not purport to exclude or restrict liability. Obviously, in practice, most will wish to control the extent of their liability in order to reduce their risk (and therefore reduce insurance premiums and avoid attracting uninsured liabilities).

A first step is to limit the extent of liability is to carefully define the roles and duties of both parties. From a practical point of view, most consultants and contractors would prefer not to get the point of facing legal action, and it is surprising how many disputes arise not from failures to perform agreed tasks, but from a lack of clarity as to what the actual tasks were, in particular which areas of design are the responsibility of each of the various consultants and of the contractor. Defining the scope of the services to be provided is discussed in Chapter 15.

A second tactic is to limit liability for design to the use of reasonable skill and care, particularly important as most PII policies will not cover a 'fitness for purpose' obligation. Another adverse effect is the loss of the ability to claim contributory negligence.[1] Other onerous clauses such as a requirement to use 'best endeavours' or 'all reasonable endeavours' should also be avoided.[2] For example, in the case of *Rolls Royce Power Engineering Ltd (1) Allen Engineering Ltd (formerly NEI Allen Ltd) (2) v Ricardo Consulting Engineering Ltd*,[3] the judge commented that an obligation to provide services 'of first class quality' was significantly more onerous than the obligation to exercise reasonable skill and care, stating that 'If services are provided "of first class quality" it seems to me that they are provided to a standard which would not be exceeded by anyone else who might actually have been engaged to provide them'.[4] Any non-standard terms should therefore always be approved by a party's insurers before a contract is agreed.

Other measures used to minimise exposure to liabilities are: to limit the amount of damages by means of a cap; to exclude liability for certain types of losses; to ensure that

---

[1] See e.g. *Trebor Bassett Holdings Ltd v ADT Fire and Security plc* [2012] EWCA Civ 1158 (CA).
[2] See *Jet2.com Ltd v Blackpool Airport Ltd* [2012] EWCA Civ 417.
[3] [2003] EWHC 2871.
[4] ibid., HHJ Richard Seymore, at para. 84.

---

a party is only held liable for the proportion of losses that they are actually responsible for; and to agree shorter limitation periods. These methods are all discussed below.

Limitation clauses will generally be effective against the other contracting party, not only with respect to claims brought in contract, but usually for any claim brought on the basis of a parallel tortious duty. In fact, some forms of limitations on level of liability, such as disclaimers relating to statements or representations, may be effective even with respect to third parties (see section 10.1.2). The case of *Hedley Byrne*, for example, failed on its facts because of a disclaimer within the terms of engagement.

However any clause attempting to limit or exclude liability has to overcome two hurdles; such clauses are likely to be examined carefully and construed 'narrowly' by the courts, plus the clause will be subject to the test of 'reasonableness' under the Unfair Contract Terms Act 1977.

The courts have traditionally taken a 'strict' approach to interpreting exclusion or limitation clauses. The common law rule is that exclusion clauses would be interpreted *contra proferentem*, i.e. if there is any ambiguity the clause would be construed against the person who drew it up. A simple solution to this is to ensure that the clause is clearly worded. The rule also applies to limitation clauses. (A limitation clause can be distinguished from an exclusion clause; the second excludes all liability for the defined risk, the first simply limits the scope of that liability). An example is *Bovis Construction (Scotland) Ltd v Whatlings Ltd*[5] where Lord Jauncey advised that a limitation clause should 'state clearly and unambiguously the extent of the limitation and will be construed with a degree of strictness, albeit not to the same extent as an exclusion or indemnity clause'.[6] This case concerned a clause in a construction sub-contract, which had been executed on a standard form, but where an additional term was incorporated which limited 'time-related' damages to £100K. The sub-contractor's employment was terminated due to its failure to proceed regularly and diligently. However the court decided that the clause, while effective for delay-related losses prior to completion, did not cover losses from non-performance (as opposed to late performance) and the sub-contractor was liable for the losses following termination.

As outlined in Chapter 2, any limitation of liability will have to satisfy the test of 'reasonableness' under the Unfair Contract Terms Act 1977. The requirement of reasonableness in relation to a limiting term is:

> that the term shall have been a fair and reasonable one to be included having regard to the circumstances which were, or ought reasonably to have been, known to or in the contemplation of the parties when the contract was made (s. 11(1)).

Examples of the practical application of this test are discussed below. If a party to the contract is acting as a consumer, then any limitation clause may also be subject to provisions of the Unfair Terms in Consumer Contracts Regulations 1999.

---

[5] (1995) 75 BLR 1 (HL).
[6] [1995] SLT 1339.

13.1 Using financial caps[7]

It is becoming increasingly common to agree a figure (a financial cap), beyond which the consultant will not be liable, and many standard terms of engagement (e.g. RIBA terms) now make provision for inserting an agreed cap. A cap gives both clients and consultants a degree of certainty they would not otherwise have, as for practical purposes recovery is in any event usually limited, for example, in the case of a company, to its insurance cover and assets.

A financial cap on liability in a contract operates to limit the damages payable by the consultant to the client under the appointment to the agreed amount, so that both parties are aware of the exact extent of the risk assumed. The scope of the cap depends on the exact terms used and usually follows one of three alternative models. First, the cap might apply to 'each and every claim' so that each claim could be to the full value of the limit. A second method is for the cap to apply on an aggregated basis, where claims would be 'grouped' according to the particular event that caused the loss/damage, and the limit applies to the total liability for that group of claims. Finally, it could apply as a total limit in which case, regardless of how many claims arose from the event that caused the loss/damage, the consultant's liability would not exceed the figure stated. This option offers the greatest certainty in relation to potential exposure.

It should be noted that although many professional bodies require their members to maintain a minimum level of professional indemnity insurance (PII), it would not normally be a breach of a Code to cap liability at a limit below the required level of insurance, provided the other party had agreed to the cap as a commercial organisation or as a fully advised consumer. The recommended PII levels are to cover the professional's liability as a whole as well as ensuring that each client will be compensated for any negligence.

When considering the limit in any individual contract, the total potential liability under a project needs to be taken into account, together with the total limit of PII held by the consultant. For example, a collateral warranty to a tenant might include a cap of a particular amount in respect of all claims; but if a consultant has given warranties to several tenants, each one would be able to recover up to the value of the cap. If they all brought a claim as a result of the same act of negligence, that might constitute one claim under the consultant's PII policy – and one limit of indemnity would apply.

With respect to the Unfair Contract Terms Act 1977 (UCTA) test of 'reasonableness', where a person seeks to restrict their liability to a specified sum of money, regard shall be had to:

> the resources which he could expect to be available to him for the purpose of meeting the liability . . . and how far it was open to him to cover himself by insurance (s. 11(4)).

---

[7] Part of this text is based on Construction Industry Council, *Liability Briefing: Managing Liability through Financial Caps* (London: CIC, 2008).

A useful example of the test of what is 'reasonable' can be seen in the case of *James Moores v Yakeley Associates Ltd*[8] (a well-known case often cited outside of the field of construction). James Moores employed Yakeley Associates as architects and the contract, which was on the terms of the RIBA Standard Form of Agreement 1992, included a cap of £250,000. A dispute arose between the parties and the client sought a repayment of invoices on the basis of Yakeley's failure to carry out the work with reasonable care and skill. The Judge considered whether the clause as drafted satisfied the requirements of UCTA and concluded that Yakeley Architects proved that the term was reasonable (the burden of proof lying with the architect under the Act). Key factors in reaching the decision were that:

The cap was not an arbitrary figure. The figure of £250,000 had been based upon Yakeley Architects assessment of the likely costs of the work. The Judge commented: 'It would take some quite exceptional circumstance, beyond the reasonable contemplation of the parties, to give rise to a liability for damages in a sum greater than the total estimated cost of the project itself'.[9]

It was also relevant that the limit on damages imposed was more than ten times the amount of the fee in the appointment (The architects' fee was 8.5% of the construction cost, subject to a minimum of £19,125 and assuming a construction cost of £225,000).

Moreover, it was noted that Mr. Moore had a stronger bargaining position than Yakeley Architects when agreeing the contract as Mr. Moore could have appointed any architect. Not only was there a recession and architects were chasing work, but also the client was not in any hurry to enter into the contract and had a solicitor to protect his interests in negotiations.

Both the client and his solicitor were aware of the existence of the clause imposing the cap and both had said that they were happy with the proposed agreement (the client had accepted in giving evidence that if the cap was roughly sufficient to cover the total building cost, that would be 'fair enough').

The architects had in place insurance of £500,000 which was in excess of the cap. However the Judge decided that although relevant this was not determinative.

A contrast can be made with the earlier case of *St Albans City and District Council v International Computers Ltd*[10] where a cap on ICL's liability of £100,000 was not considered reasonable. ICL was engaged to write and operate a computer program to calculate levels of community charge appropriate to each household; due to an error in the system, the council suffered losses estimated at £1.17 million. The Judge at first instance said that the defendant had not shown that it was fair and reasonable to limit liability to the figure of £100,000, which was small in relation to both the potential risk and the actual loss. The court also noted that ICL had liability insurance cover of £50 million worldwide, and that if the loss were to fall on the council it would ultimately be borne by the local population. The court decided it was unreasonable that the party who stood to make the profit, and which had been well able to insure and in this case was insured, should not carry the risk.

---

[8] (1998) 62 Con LR 76.
[9] ibid., para. 31.
[10] [1996] 4 All ER 481.

More recently the case of *Marplace (Number 512) Ltd v Chaffe Street*,[11] concerning the appointment of solicitors, gives some further guidance. The solicitors' retainer letter stated:

> You agree . . . our maximum aggregate liability to you in the event of professional negligence on any matter in relation to which we are instructed shall be £20m.

It added:

> Should you want to vary these limitations we shall be pleased to discuss it with you but we reserve the right to vary our fees accordingly.

Amongst other things, the client argued that the term was unreasonable because the solicitors had a higher level of insurance cover than £20 million; and that the solicitors could not rely on the clause unless the client had had independent advice. The solicitors argued that the clause was reasonable considering that their turnover was £4 million; and that interest and costs would potentially be added to the £20 million so there was 'head-room' between the limit of liability and the insurance cover. The Judge considered carefully the Guidelines in Schedule 2 of the UTCA. He found the clause reasonable, on the grounds that the client was sophisticated and of equal bargaining power to the defendant, the client was familiar with such clauses, the client had discussed the limitation provision with the solicitors and it had not been imposed upon them, the retainer included a provision concerning discussing variation of the cap, and that the limit was struck on 'reasonable commercial principles' taking into account all circumstances of the transaction.

Trustees of Ampleforth Abbey Trust v Turner & Townsend Project Management Ltd[12] is another case where liability was limited to an amount less than the consultants' professional indemnity insurance. The limitation was set out in the terms of appointment which provided that TTPM's liability to the Trust would not exceed the total fees payable to TTPM, which was £111,321. The court decided that even though the limitation clause was plain to read and understand, it nevertheless failed to satisfy the requirement of reasonableness. This was mainly because TTPM's appointment required it at the same time to maintain £10 million professional indemnity insurance. The court decided that the cost of this insurance was essentially being borne by the Trust via the consultant's fees, but that if the cap were enforced 'the greater part of that insurance would be rendered illusory'.[13] In addition, TTPM had already been engaged by the Trust on two previous phases of construction, and had introduced this limitation for the first time under the third appointment, without drawing it to the client's attention. It is generally thought that that does not alter the position as understood following *James Moores v Yakeley*,[14] i.e. it does not suggest that a limit less than the level of cover would

---

[11] [2006] EWHC 1919.
[12] [2012] EWHC 2137 (TCC).
[13] ibid., para. 201.
[14] e.g. see Barnes, Rachel, *Trustees of Ampleforth Abbey Trust v Turner & Townsend Project Management Limited: Implications for monetary limits of liability in appointments* (London: Beale & Co, 2012).

always be considered unseasonable. However it highlights the need to proceed with care when introducing a cap, particularly if this is being done for the first time with a particular client.

13.2 *Limiting liability for loss of profits and consequential losses*

Another possibility is for consultants to limit their liability to the direct losses that result from negligence or breach of contract, and exclude liability for indirect losses, loss of profit and consequential loss (see section 11.2.3). As with all limiting terms, such clauses need to be drafted carefully since where there is doubt courts will always construe such clauses against the person seeking to rely on them. An example is *Ferryways NV v Associated British Ports*,[15] where the Judge held that 'very clear words indeed' would be required to indicate an intention to exclude losses falling outside the established meaning of indirect or consequential loss.

The reasonableness of such limitation clauses was examined in *Regus (UK) Ltd v Epcot Solutions Ltd*.[16] In this case Regus had rented office accommodation to Epcot Solutions, but the air conditioning system had malfunctioned, and Epcot refused to pay the rent. Regus brought a claim for the rent, and Epcot counterclaimed for loss of profit and opportunity to earn profit, and distress, inconvenience and loss of amenity. The contract included a provision which stated 'We will not in any circumstances have any liability for loss of business, loss of profits, loss of anticipated savings, loss of or damage to data, third party claims or any consequential loss. We strongly advise you to insure against all such potential loss, damage, expense or liability'. The contract also provided that liability in any event would be capped at £50,000 or 125% of the fees, whichever was higher. The Court of Appeal decided that the exclusion was reasonable, including the limit on consequential loss. It relied on Epcot's awareness of the clause and the fact that it had contracted on that basis before, and used a similar clause in its own dealings with customers. It was generally more economical for the person by whom the loss would be sustained to take out insurance; this was a sensible measure, and Epcot was in a better position to assess and quantify its insurance requirements. The court also noted that there was no inequality of bargaining power as Epcot could have and did use a local competitor. In summary, the court enforced the limit of £50,000 in the cap, rather than the damages of £626 million that had been claimed.

13.3 *Net contribution clauses*[17]

A third method of introducing a constraint on the amount of damages that may be payable is through the use of a 'net contribution clause'. These are used in situations

---

[15] [2008] EWHC 225 (Comm).
[16] [2008] EWCA Civ 36.
[17] Part of this text is based on Construction Industry Council, *Liability Briefing: Net Contribution Clauses* (London: CIC, 2008).

where many parties are involved in a construction project, as a method of attempting to limit the amount of damages that a consultant may have to pay to the client to a proportion of any total damages payable, that fairly reflects the actual contribution the consultant made to the damage caused.

The net contribution clause is necessary because of the principle of English law whereby if a person suffers loss due to the combined action of several parties, they may pursue any one of those parties to recover 100% of the losses suffered, a principle termed 'joint and several liability'. Under joint and several liability, each party is separately liable to the claimant to the full extent for loss and damage that results from its breach of duty. For example, where a contractor constructs a roof using a material that was not the one specified, but the architect negligently fails to spot the problem prior to issuing a payment certificate, both may be in breach of their contractual obligations, which would cause the client loss should the roof leak as a result. The client would then have two causes of the loss or damage in question; with the architect being liable for one cause (negligent site inspection) and the contractor being liable for the other (the bad workmanship).

Under this principle a consultant might be only 30% responsible for a claimant's loss and yet have to pay 100% of the damages. It should be noted, however, that the claimant is not entitled to recover more than 100% of its damages, so if it succeeds in recovering 100% of the damages from the consultant, it cannot then seek to recover the same or any amount from the contractor.

Frequently in practice the client will sue both the contractor and the consultant. Alternatively, the consultant and contractor can make a claim against each other for contribution under the Civil Liability (Contribution) Act 1978 (see section 11.3.2), so that, if the consultant does pay 100% of the damages to the claimant, it can seek a contribution from the contractor. In both these situations the court apportions liability between them. However, this does not reduce the liability of each party to the claimant, they both remain liable for 100% of the losses. Despite the apportionment it is therefore open to claimants, if they wish, to enforce payment of any amount, up to the full amount, from either party. If either party does not or is unable to pay its apportioned amount (e.g. because of insolvency or anything else), claimants would obviously exercise their rights to enforce payment of the full amount from the other party. Therefore either party may still have to pay 100% of the damages.

Another situation that can arise is where warranties have been required by a third party, but not all parties contributing to the design have provided such warranties. Here consultants and their insurers will be particularly concerned that they may be liable to a third party to whom a warranty has been given, but will not be able to claim contribution form those who have not entered into a warranty with that third party.

This problem can be addressed by including protective clauses known as 'net contribution clauses' in the contract. Under a net contribution clause, a number of assumptions are made, in particular that any third party responsible for the same loss or damage is:

(i) also contractually liable to the other party to the contract, and
(ii) has paid its fair share to the other party – i.e. the share that would be apportioned to it under the 1978 Act.

Thus, in a contract between the consultant and the claimant, the effect of a net contribution clause is that the contractor would be deemed to be contractually liable to the claimant and to have paid to the claimant the proportion of the damages that would be apportioned to the contractor on an apportionment between the consultant and contractor under the 1978 Act, leaving the consultant only having to pay the balance. Similarly, in the warranties situation mentioned above, the clause will assume that the other parties have entered into a warranty and have paid their fair share. These assumptions operate *even if* the others have not in fact entered into contracts or paid their fair share; the clause will nevertheless be effective to protect the party in whose contract it is incorporated. Net contribution clauses are now to be found in most of the standard forms of appointment and collateral warranties. A sample standard clause for use in bespoke appointments is available to download from the CIC website.

Net contribution clauses have not been subject to much litigation, but two Scottish cases give some reassurance that they are effective. In the first, *Glasgow Airport Ltd v Messrs Kirkman & Bradford*,[18] Glasgow Airport claimed damages of £2 million from structural engineers Kirkman & Bradford for a breach of a collateral warranty which contained a net contribution clause. A floor slab designed by the engineers had to be replaced, and the claimant's tenant brought an action against the claimant for the cost of the remedial work, and also their losses due to disruption to business and loss of profit. The claimant subsequently claimed against the defender. The engineer's appointment contained the following clause:

1. The Sub-Consultant warrants that it has exercised and will continue to exercise all reasonable skill, care and diligence in the performance of the services under the appointment. In the event of any breach of this warranty:
   (a) The Sub-Consultant's liability for costs under this Agreement shall be limited to that proportion of such costs which it would be just and equitable to require the Sub-Consultant to pay having regard to the extent of the Sub-Consultant's responsibility for the same. . . .

The dispute centered on whether the term 'costs' meant direct costs only, and not consequential loss. The defendants argued that it did, and that the consequence was that this further limited its liability (over and above the effect of the net contribution clause). The claimant turned this approach on its head and argued 'Even if the defender's construction of the word "costs" is held to be correct the effect of the net contribution clause is to limit the sum recoverable in respect of reinstatement costs and not to limit recovery of other losses'.

The court took a sensible approach and decided that the proper liability of the engineers was, under the warranty, subject to a net apportionment having regard to the responsibility of others, but that 'costs' should be taken to mean any losses for which the engineers would ordinarily be liable, so that the term neither further restricted (as argued by the defender) nor extended (as argued by the claimant) the damages recoverable.

---

[18] [2007] ScotCS CSIH 47.

In *Langstane Housing Association Ltd v Riverside Construction Aberdeen Ltd*[19] the Judge considered whether the net contribution clause in the ACE conditions might be deemed unfair under the Unfair Contract Terms Act 1977 (UCTA). The Judge ruled that the net contribution clause did not purport to exclude or restrict the engineer's liability, it simply 'sought to ensure that the second defenders were only held liable for the consequence of their own breach of duty and were not held liable, by the doctrine of joint and several liability, for breaches of duty by other contractors and consultants', therefore section 16 of UCTA did not apply. However, even if UCTA did apply, the Judge found the net contribution clause was fair and reasonable. It was part of a widely used set of standard conditions drafted by a professional body, and the employer was free to arrange for insurance, which would protect it if the contractor or professional team became insolvent.

It is possible to question the logic of this decision, particularly the claim that the purpose of such clauses is *not* to restrict liability. Other aspects of the reasoning can also be questioned: for example obtaining insurance against workmanship failings would not be easy. It would therefore be sensible for a consultant to assume that a net contribution clause may not always be considered fair by a court, and to highlight any net contribution clauses to its client as it would with any limiting clause in situations where UCTA applies.

13.4 Agreeing shorter periods for limitation of liability

A further option is to specify a shorter period for limitation than would normally apply. The normal limits are six years for breach of contract, dating from the breach, and six years for a negligent act, starting from the date of the loss (see Chapter 12). However an agreement to a shorter period would normally be enforced, provided it is clear.

Such a clause was considered in *Inframatrix Investments Ltd v Dean Construction Ltd.*[20] Here, somewhat unusually, a contractor succeeded in negotiating an amendment to a solicitor-drafted contract, reducing the limitation period to one year. The clause stated:

> No action or proceedings under or in respect of this Agreement shall be brought against the Contractor after:
> a. the expiry of 1 year from the date of Practical Completion of the Services; or
> b. where such date does not occur, the expiry of 1 year from the date the Contractor last performed the Services in relation to the Project.

There were problems with the contractor's workmanship and Practical Completion was never certified. A dispute arose, and during the proceedings the contractor applied to strike out the clause on the basis that it was time barred. The Employer argued that the limitation clause should be construed against the Contractor (as it had negotiated

---

[19] [2009] ScotCS CSOH 52.
[20] [2011] EWHC 1947 (TCC).

the clause amendment), and should only apply where Practical Completion was not going to be achieved because, for example, the owner had abandoned the project (and not where the contractor was in breach). Also, it argued that the clock had been re-set when the contractor attended a site meeting at a much later date than when it ceased work. However Behrens HHJ, rejected this restrictive approach in favour of a more straightforward one, which was upheld by the Court of Appeal; the contractual limitation period expired 12 months after the last date the contractor undertook the services as defined in the contract.

In *Oxford Architects Partnership v Cheltenham Ladies College*[21] a client tried to argue (unsuccessfully) that a contractual clause extended the normal limitation period. The college contracted with the architects for services in relation to a new college building on the RIBA Conditions of Engagement for the Appointment of an Architect (CE/95). Article 5 provided that no action should be commenced after six years from the date of practical completion. Practical completion was certified on 25 November 1998 and subsequently on 24 November 2004 the college served an arbitration notice on the partnership for breach of contract and negligence. The architects argued that the claims were statute-barred. The Court of Appeal considered the effect of the Article and held that there was nothing in the Article that suggested that the parties had agreed to waive their rights under the Limitation Act. The architects were therefore free to argue that causes of action in contract and tort had accrued before practical completion and therefore the claim was indeed statute-barred. If parties intend to prevent reliance upon a statutory limitation defence, then this would have to be clearly stated.

---

[21] [2007] BLR 293.

Chapter 14
Standard Forms of Contract for Design-Build

A primary means of avoiding some of the issues and uncertainties that have been outlined in earlier chapters is to agree specific and detailed provisions regarding design liability. This chapter examines briefly how some of the more widely used standard forms of contract deal with the matters raised in this book.[1] Obviously the overall effect of agreeing to a standard form will depend on the jurisdiction in which it is used. For the purposes of this chapter an English legal framework is assumed, but it should be noted that some local laws in other jurisdictions may restrict the effectiveness of some terms.

Key areas examined are the scope and level of the design responsibility, including exactly what aspects of design each party is responsible for, and whether the level of liability is to use reasonable skill and care or to achieve a result. The chapter also examines whether any limits are placed on the extent of the liability, by means of for example a cap on the amount that can be claimed, and whether insurance is required in relation to the design obligation.

There are also many practical design matters that need to be dealt with during the course of construction, such as the development and finalisation of the detailed design, commenting on or checking of drawings, and the input of specialist sub-contractors. Although initially these can appear procedural, in fact they may affect the design liability of participants so those aspects are touched on also, below.

14.1 Joint Contracts Tribunal (JCT) forms

14.1.1 General considerations

The contracts published by the Joint Contracts Tribunal have the longest heritage of any in the UK construction industry, the first ones being published in the 19th century. The current editions (2011) are the ones on which the main part of this text is based. Having said that, the differences between the 2011 and 2005 editions do not generally relate to design provisions, so many of the following comments are also relevant to earlier forms.

---

[1] Books which cover other aspects of these forms are listed in the Bibliography, including the author's guides to the JCT forms, some parts of which have been adapted for this text.

Cornes and Lupton's Design Liability in the Construction Industry, Fifth Edition. Sarah Lupton.
© 2013 Sarah Lupton and DL Cornes. Published 2013 by Blackwell Publishing Ltd.

The JCT publish a wide range of documents: around 10 key 'main' contracts, most of which have several different versions, a large number of back-to-back sub-contracts and warranties, together with guidance notes and supplements. The contractor's design role varies considerably between forms, as one might expect. The JCT recognises that projects are rarely if ever designed entirely by the consultant team, even where the procurement route is ostensibly 'traditional', therefore almost all forms either incorporate provisions to deal with design, or are published in two versions, one of which has detailed design liability provisions.

In many cases the wording of clauses is standardised across several forms. For example, across all JCT forms, wherever a contractor is required to take on a design liability, this liability is stated to be to use 'reasonable skill and care'. There are no 'fit for purpose' optional clauses as there are in GC Works/1, NEC3 or PPC2000 (see below; these could serve as a useful starting point were such amendments required). In most forms (except for the shorter ones such as MWD11) the contractor is required to provide professional indemnity insurance in relation to the design services. Several of the forms (DB11, SBC11, MP11) use the same drawings submission and approval procedure for the developing design.

14.1.2 JCT Design and Build Contract (DB11)

DB11 is intended for use in connection with a design-build procurement route. It places the obligation for completing the design on the contractor, who is responsible for the production of all further design and/or production information that it requires to complete the project (termed the 'Design Documents'). The main contractor remains responsible for the design whether or not it sub-contracts any design work, either to a domestic or named subcontractor (cl. 3.3.2 and Schedule 2.2.2).

It should be noted that if a two stage tender process was used, the contractor may have been engaged for advice and design services prior to finalisation and award of the main contract. Liability for design undertaken during this phase will be separate to any arising under DB11 as discussed below, and will depend upon the terms used for this appointment. The JCT publishes two 'Pre-construction Services Agreements', PCSA and PCSA/SP (for use with contractor and specialist sub-contractor respectively), intended for use with any of the larger JCT forms. In both cases, under clause 2.8, the contractor is *not* liable to the employer for any design advice given unless appointed to the final contract, in which case the liability is '…the same as if it formed part of the design work undertaken by him under the Main Contract…'.

14.1.2.1 *Extent of design obligation*

In DB11 contractor's obligation to construct the works as described in the contract and to *complete* the design as necessary is stated in Article 1, and amplified in clause 2.1 which states:

The Contractor shall carry out and complete the Works in a proper and workmanlike manner and in compliance with the Contract Documents, the Construction Phase Plan and other Statutory Requirements and for that purpose shall complete the design for the Works including the selection of any specifications for the kinds and standards of the materials, goods and workmanship to be used in the construction of the Works so far as not described or stated in the Employer's Requirements or Contractor's Proposals, and shall give all notices required by the Statutory Requirements.

The Employer's Requirements and Contractor's Proposals are contract documents. The former is sent out with the tender documents, and the latter returned with the tender.

The exact extent of the design role is therefore to be determined from examining these documents. The contract does not stipulate what either should contain, therefore the Requirements could be in the form of a brief of general objectives and requirements for the project, or could include more detailed design requirements in performance or prescriptive terms, or could even include a largely completed design. The Proposals will include a design to the level of development and detail as stipulated in the tender documents.

The contract makes it clear that the contractor is only to *complete* the design, and is not responsible for the contents of the Employer's Requirements, or for verifying the adequacy of any design contained within them (cl. 2.13.2). In this way it differs from some standard forms such as the FIDC Yellow Book (see Section 14.5.2) and many bespoke forms for design-build and turnkey projects, where the contractor assumes responsibly for any pre-designed elements.

Clause 2.13.2 is included to prevent such an obligation being implied, as it was in the case of *Co-Operative Insurance Society* v *Henry Boot*.[2] Here the Co-operative Insurance Society (the Society) engaged the contractor Henry Boot on an amended version of JCT80 incorporating the Designed Portion Supplement, where the relevant terms are similar to those in early editions of the design-build form. During construction, problems arose where soil and water flooded into a basement excavation. An engineer had originally been employed by the Society to prepare a concept design for the structure, and Henry Boot had developed the design and prepared working drawings. The Society brought claims against Henry Boot and the engineers. Henry Boot argued that their liability was limited to the preparation of the working drawings. The judge, however, took the view that completing the design of the contiguous bored pile walls included examining the design at the point that it was taken over, assessing the assumptions on which it was based and forming a view as to whether they were appropriate. Following the case the JCT revised all its forms to include the current Clause 2.13.1 wording.

Although there is clearly no positive duty to check the employer's design, it is likely there would nevertheless be a duty to warn of any errors in fact spotted during the project, particularly if these had a fundamental effect on matters such as safety or structural stability. The contractor is under a general duty to exercise skill and care, and common sense suggests that it would be in breach of this duty if it did not warn of

---

[2] [2002] CILL 1932.

obvious problems in the Requirements.[3] This is in effect an extension of the normal duty to warn, as discussed in Section 7.4.[4] Also, the clause is unlikely to prevent the implication of a 'duty to warn' regarding any other aspects of the project; for example, where the design is varied through an instruction of the employer's agent (for an instance of this see the earlier case of *Plant Construction* v *Clive Adams*[5]).

14.1.2.2 Level of liability

The level of liability is set out in clause 2.17.1 which states that:

> Insofar as his design of the Works is comprised in the Contractor's Proposals and in what the Contractor is to complete in accordance with the Employer's Requirements (including any further design required to be carried out by the contractor as a result of a Change) the Contractor shall in respect of any inadequacy in such design have the like liability to the Employer, whether under statute or otherwise, as would an architect or, as the case may be, other appropriate professional designer holding himself out as competent to take on work for such design who, acting independently under a separate contract with the Employer, has supplied such design for or in connection with works to be carried out and completed by a building contractor who is not the supplier of the design.

In effect, this statement reduces the strict obligation that would normally have been implied to a requirement to use due skill and care (see Chapter 6). It would be clearer if the form simply stated this as, strictly speaking, an architect's liability will depend on the terms of engagement used in each case, but the phrase is intended to mean the normal level assumed by professional consultants. In addition, the standard of expertise to be brought to the design process is that of an architect or other equivalent design professional, therefore it would be no defence for the contractor to argue that its design was as competent as that of other contracting companies, if this is intended to justify a lesser standard. Clause 2.17 also states that, where the contract involves work in connection with a dwelling, 'the reference in clause 2.17.1 to the Contractor's liability includes liability under the Defective Premises Act 1972'. The effect of this is that the contractor is liable to the employer for design in relation to a dwelling to the same extent that an architect would be liable (see Chapter 5).

As well as defining the level of liability, clause 2.17.1 also suggests that the standard the design is to meet is that set out in the Employer's Requirements. However although these might state that any selection of materials should be fit for the purposes set out in the Employer's Requirements, this should not be confused with what is commonly referred to as a 'fitness for purpose' obligation, as by clause 2.17 the contractor's liability is limited to the use of reasonable skill and care in making that selection. Under clause

---

[3] See e.g. Stephen Furst and Vivien Ramsey (eds), *Keating on Building Contracts*, 9th edn (London Sweet & Maxwell, 2012) p. 831 where it states 'it is suggested that a contractor that fails to observe errors that ought to have been obvious to him as Contractor and in the circumstances and exercising such proper skill cannot take advantage of such failure'.

[4] See e.g. *Edward Lindenberg v Joe Canning Jerome Contracting Ltd* (1992) 62 BLR 147.

[5] [2000] BLR 158 (CA).

1.3 provisions in other documents (including the Employer's Requirements) cannot override the printed terms, so any attempt to impose a higher duty in these documents will be unsuccessful. Similarly, any statement in the Requirements to the effect that the contractor's design must meet a particular performance specification, or be reasonably fit for any purpose set out, will only operate to define the *standard* to be met, but will not change the *level of liability* from the use of reasonable skill and care to a strict obligation to meet that standard.

14.1.2.3 *Errors and discrepancies*

As the Requirements and Proposals are key to defining the scope of the design obligation, the resolution of problems with these documents is significant. For example, although the contractor is not liable for design errors in the Requirements, what is the position regarding mistakes in the information embodied in the Proposals? Is the contractor liable for any such errors, or has the employer accepted the risk of these, given that they are now incorporated in the contract?

The form contains detailed clauses to deal with conflicts within the Requirements or Proposals, although it is less clear on conflicts between them. The clauses refer to a 'discrepancy or divergence', which might occur for example where a document gives two different specifications for the same item, or possibly several performance and prescriptive requirements that cannot all be achieved simultaneously. If the problem is within the Proposals, the employer decides how this should be resolved, and any extra cost is absorbed by the contractor (cl. 2.14.1). If it lies in the Requirements, and the Proposals resolve the matter, then the Proposals prevail; in this way if there are two conflicting performance specifications, the employer will have to accept a design solution that meets only one of them, unless it is prepared to meet any additional costs. If the proposals do not resolve the matter, the Employer must issue instructions, which are treated as a 'Change' (cl. 2.14.2). Any discrepancy between either document and statutory requirements must be resolved at the contractor's expense, so that contractors bear the risk of the design meeting statutory requirements, except they are relieved from this liability in situations where there is a change in statutory requirements, or if an approval such as a planning permission is not obtained until after the contract is formed (cl. 2.15).

Where the Requirements are simply silent on a matter (but it is clearly necessary as part of the project), it is suggested that this would not constitute a 'discrepancy'. Instead the contractor should take steps to ascertain what would be appropriate as part of its design obligation, and design and supply it at its own expense.

The contractor is required to notify the employer of any discrepancies once it finds them. Although there is no obligation to search for discrepancies or divergences, nevertheless as noted above the duty to use reasonable skill and care implies that a certain degree of observance can be expected.

It is also possible that there might be conflicts between the Requirements and the Proposals, for example if the design as incorporated in the Proposals does not meet the Requirements. In fact in a large and complex project it may be quite likely that some requirements are not met. The contract does not specifically refer to this type of conflict save to recommend (under footnote 3) that it is resolved by means of an amendment to the Requirements before the contract is entered into. If not resolved, it is generally considered to constitute an inadequacy in the proposals[6], and therefore to be resolved at the expense of the contractor (cl. 2.14.1).

There is some support for suggesting that the Employer's Requirements would prevail. First, the requirement to use skill and care applies to design work already contained in the Proposals, as well as design work yet to be carried out (cl 2.17.1), so that any failure to take account of the Requirements is likely to be a breach of contract. Second, in the case of materials and workmanship, clause 2.2.1 states:

> All material and goods for the Works shall, so far as procurable, be of the kinds and standards described in the Employer's Requirements', or if not there specifically described, as described in the Contractor's Proposals or in [the Contractor's Design Documents]'

This gives the Employer' Requirements precedence. Although it refers only to materials and goods, it seems reasonable to assume that any part of the design should meet any standards in the Employer's requirements, provided that a standard has been set out.

However the third recital states that 'the Employer has examined the Contractor's Proposals and, subject to the Conditions, is satisfied that they appear to meet the Employer's Requirements', which implies that, insofar as the design has been finalised at the time of acceptance of tender, then the employer has accepted the solution. This creates something of a tension. It seems unlikely, in practice, that an employer would be held to have accepted defects in the design which a reasonable inspection would not have revealed. An example might be the design of a roof truss where, without a detailed double-checking of calculations, it would not be possible to ascertain whether the truss would be structurally sound. The contractor would therefore remain responsible for such structural soundness, irrespective of the Proposals. Furthermore, as the article is not a condition of the contract, it cannot override its terms. Nevertheless, the recital is problematic from the point of view of the employer, and is sometimes deleted.

14.1.2.4 *Design Documents*

The contract contains a detailed procedure regarding the submission of the developing design by the contractor (Sched. 1) which sets out time periods for providing comments and affords the contractor an opportunity to answer or dispute any such comments. The employer is entitled to require adjustments if the design does not meet the Requirements, but any further alterations are to be treated as a 'Change'. The details of the type of information to be submitted, and any dates, should be set out in the Employer's Requirements, otherwise the requirement is to submit all information prepared by the contractor 'as and when necessary from time to time' (cl. 2.8) which for practical purposes may not be convenient for the employer, for example if it wishes to have the information checked by its advisors.

---

[6]see Keating Chambers *Keating on Building Contracts* (London: Sweet & Maxwell, loose-leaf, subscription, commentary on JCT DB cl. 2.13.

Schedule 1, paragraph 8.3 states that no comments or any action by the employer will relieve the contractor of its liability to ensure that the document complies with the contract, or that the project complies with the contract. If the contractor incorporates a comment made by the employer without objection, then it effectively accepts that the comment has been properly made (i.e. it identifies some way in which the design document is not in accordance with the contract).

The contractor retains the copyright in all Design Documents, but grants the employer a non-exclusive license to use them for all purposes connected with the carrying out of the works, including subsequent maintenance and refurbishment, and promotion of the project (cl. 2.38).

14.1.2.5 *Limitation on liability*

The contract includes an option to limit the contractor's liability for the consequential losses arising from its failure to meet the design obligations. This limitation does not affect any liability for liquidated damages. This limitation is, in fact, less extensive than it might seem, as it protects the contractor only from claims of certain types of damage (see Section 11.2.3) and not from the losses that would normally be foreseeable as a direct result of a breach of the contractor's design obligations (e.g. cost of repairing defects). The limit also does not apply to work in connection with a dwelling. The limitation of contractor's liability is set up under the Contract Particulars in clause 2.17.3. If no sum is inserted into the Contract Particulars, the contractor's liability in respect of these matters will be unlimited.

Clause 6.12 requires the contractor to take out professional indemnity insurance in respect of design liabilities, to comply with detailed provisions as set out in the contract particulars (note that if the employer omits to set out any requirements, it appears as if there will be no obligation on the contractor). The insurance must be maintained for a period of six years after practical completion, unless another period is stated in the contract particulars. Clause 6.13 states that if 'the insurance referred to in clause 6.12 ceases to be available at commercially reasonable rates, the contractor shall immediately give notice to the employer so that the contractor and the employer can discuss the means of best protecting their respective positions in the absence of such insurance.' This reflects the commercial reality; it would be difficult to predict at the time of entering the contract what insurance products will be available during the required period.

The JCT publishes a sub-contract for use with this form, which mirrors the provisions in DB11, including design obligations, level of liability and insurance provisions. The JCT also publishes warranties for use in various situations, including a warranty between sub-contractor and employer (SCWa/E) which may be a useful safeguard where the employer has agreed that design work may be sub-contracted.

14.1.3 JCT Standard Building Contract 2011 (SBC11)

JCT SBC11 is the benchmark form in the JCT suite. It has evolved from the earlier forms for 'traditional' procurement, where it was expected that the consultant team would provide all information needed, either before or during the construction process. With these forms courts had generally been unwilling to assign any design liability to the contractor, even where the contractor made what were effectively design decisions, on the basis that use of this form meant that no reliance on the contractor's design skill was intended by the parties.[7]

In SBC11 the contractor has a dual obligation: to carry out and complete works described in the contract documents, and also to design the parts of the project identified as being the 'Contractor's Designed Portion' (CDP). This is set out under clause 2.2, which states 'where the Works include a Contractor's Designed Portion the contractor shall ... in accordance with the Contract Drawings and the Contract Bills (to the extent that they are relevant) complete the design for the Contractor's Designed Portion'. The provisions relating to the Contractor's Designed Portion in many ways reflect those of the JCT Design and Build Contract as discussed above. SBC is therefore essentially a hybrid, being a form for traditional procurement, which allows part of the project to be procured on a design-build basis.

The part or parts of the works to be designed are identified in the Articles. The detailed requirements are sent to the contractor, and proposals submitted (eighth and ninth recitals), in the same way that they would be in DB11. The design requirements will have been set out in the Employer's Requirements and sent out with the tender documents. Depending on the information requested in the Requirements, the design may not be fully detailed at the time the contract is entered into.

As with DB11, clause 2.13.2 makes it clear that the contractor is not responsible for the contents of the Employer's Requirements, or for verifying the adequacy of any design contained within them. In addition, the intention of clause 2.2 appears to be that the *only* parts of the project that the contractor is obliged to design are those specifically stated to be within the CDP. It is therefore very important that the delineation between the CDP and the rest of the project is described accurately.[8] This can be quite difficult in practice, especially as the CDP could be several parts or elements, and could also be a system (e.g. services) that is integral to many parts of the building. The contract is clear that the administrator remains responsible for any integration, and this could extend to the physical junctions between the CDP and other parts, but also the combined performance of several systems, or systems with elements. If any of these interfaces (physical or performance) is intended to be the contractor's responsibility to resolve, then the interface would have to be placed firmly within the CDP.

Under clause 2.19.1 of SBC11, the contractor's liability for the Contractor's Designed Portion is limited to using the skill and care of 'an appropriately qualified and competent professional designer'. As with DB11, where the contractor is carrying out work in connection with a dwelling, including design work, this would be subject to the Defective Premises Act 1972 (cl. 2.19.2). In addition, although the contractor's liability is limited to the amount stated in the contract particulars, the limitation does not apply to work in connection with a dwelling (cl. 2.19.3). Similar provisions to those in DB11 apply to the resolving of discrepancies between the Employer's Requirements and Contractor's Proposals (cl. 2.16), as discussed at section 14.1.2.3 above.

---

[7] See e.g. *John Mowlem & Co Ltd v British Insulated Callendars Pension Trust Ltd* (1977) 3 Con LR 64.
[8] An example of the confusion that can arise when the contractor design items are not accurately defined or described can be seen in *Walter Lilly & Company Ltd v Giles MacKay* [2012] EWHC 649 (TCC).

Outside of the CDP, the contract administrator is responsible for supplying any necessary information required to construct the Works (cl. 2.12). The information on drawings and specifications supplied to the contractor should be clear and precise. Use of phrases such as 'or equivalent' in relation to a specified product do not normally present a problem, as they would not result in a material change, but may allow for an alternative make or brand of product. Furthermore, the designer is not obliged to accept any alternatives put forward.[9] On the other hand use of phrases such 'plasterwork to be to the approval of the architect' can create difficulties, as they would be caught by the 'conclusiveness' provisions of clause 1.10. This would have the (probably unintended) result that the employer may be unable to claim against the contractor for any defective plasterwork following issue of the Final Certificate (note this is the only type of claim regarding quality which is barred, the Final Certificate is not generally conclusive on quality).

Complications can arise if any part of the works, not part of the CDP, is specified by performance. Contract administrators sometimes (deliberately or inadvertently) attempt to place a design obligation on the contractor through the inclusion of a performance specification in a description of the works. Another area of difficulty might be if a clause in the specification or Bills specifically requires the contractor to design something, but this has not been identified as part of the CDP. A third might be if the item is simply missed out, i.e. shown in the drawings but not specified, and not made part of the CDP.

Two questions arise from conflicts such as these: who is responsible for designing the item, and is its cost to be treated as a variation? As the form refers to design only in the context of the CDP, and to the architect/administrator supplying all other necessary information (cl. 2.12), there may be a presumption against finding the contractor responsible. However this would depend on the circumstances, and the courts would examine the contract documents as a whole and decide, on balance, whether the parties had intended the contractor to take on any additional design responsibility. The wording of clause 2.3 gives some support to the argument that the contractor, should it make a design decision, would at least be responsible for providing something appropriate to the works. Clause 2.3.3 states:

> To the extent that the quality of materials and goods or standards of workmanship are neither described . . . nor stated to be a matter for such opinion or satisfaction, they shall in the case of the Contractor's Designed Portion be of a standard appropriate to it and shall in any other case be a standard appropriate to the Works.

Something selected by the contractor but not part of the CDP, must therefore be 'appropriate to the Works'. However, although clause 2.3.3 appears to be a strict 'fit for purpose' obligation, it is suggested that in the context of this contract, it would be construed that the contractor is merely obliged to use skill and care in selecting something appropriate, i.e. as noted above, the phrase defines the standard to be met, but not the level of liability.

The JCT has recently introduced provisions for 'Named Specialists' (Amendment 1, February 2012, by means of a new supplemental provision under Schedule 8). This

---

[9] *Leedsford Ltd v The Lord Mayor, Alderman and Citizens of the City of Bradford* (1956) 24 BLR 45 (CA).

gives the employer the right to require the contractor to use a particular firm to undertake part of the works (by naming it in the contract documents or under an instruction relating to a provisional sum). CDP work is specifically excluded from this provision (Schedule 8.7.1) and, unlike the more detailed named sub-contractor provisions in ICD11 (see section 14.1.4), it is not intended that the named specialists undertake a design role. If design input is required, parties would need to revise the provision and to consider many matters, including whether or not the main contractor is to be responsible for that design, the level of liability undertaken, and whether professional indemnity insurance and direct warranties are required.

The form includes an identical procedure to that in DB11 for the submission of the related design information by the contractor, except that in this case comments will be made by the contract administrator, who retains responsibility for integrating the Contractor's Designed Portion with the rest of the design. There are provisions for limiting the extent of contractors' liability, and requiring contractors to carry insurance to cover its design liability, as set above in relation to DB11.

The JCT publish two sub-contracts for use with this form, one of which provides for the contractor to sub-let part of the CDP works. The provisions mirror those in SBC11, including the design obligations, the level of liability and the insurance provisions. The JCT's suite of collateral warranty forms, including SCWa/E, may also be used with this contract.

14.1.4 JCT Intermediate Building Contract with contractor's design 2011 (ICD11)

ICD11 is the version of the JCT intermediate form that allows for the contractor to design a portion of the works (cl.2.2). The provisions regarding the Contractor's Design Portion in ICD11 are largely identical to those in SBC11, therefore the above comments regarding responsibility for design errors in the Requirements or the Proposals, level of liability (cl 2.34.1), limits of liability (cl 2.34.3), and insurance apply equally to this form. The form does not, however, include a detailed procedure for the submission and approval of drawings. Instead, the contractor is required to submit information 'as and when necessary from time to time in accordance with any design submission procedures set out in the Contract Documents' (cl. 2.10.2). The onus is therefore on the employer to set out requirements regarding scope, format and timing of submissions.

There is a facility in this form for the employer to require the contractor to use a particular sub-contractor to undertake part of the works (the named sub-contractor provisions). The provisions allow for the named sub-contractor to undertake design, and in practice are frequently used where a company has been approached by the design team regarding the design and supply of a specialist item (the JCT's guide to the form states at paragraph 126 that 'use of the Named Sub-Contractor procedure is intended primarily for work involving a design input'). This will be during design development stage and before main contract tenders are sought, so that details of the named sub-contractor can be included in the main contract tender documents. The contract states clearly that the main contractor is not responsible for any design carried out by the named sub-contractor, including selection of materials and the satisfaction of any performance requirement (Sched. 2; para. 11.1). The JCT publishes a form of collateral warranty whereby the named sub-contractor warrants to the employer that it will carry out the design with a reasonable level of skill and care, and it would be essential from the employer's point of view that this protection was arranged (ICSub/NAM/E).

A footnote (fn [3]) in the ICD11 contract advises that, if the named sub-contractor is to have design responsibilities, the naming procedure should only be used for discrete parts of the works where the named sub-contractor is solely responsible for design. The naming provisions should not be used for any element of the works within the part or parts for which the contractor has design responsibility. Essentially, a named sub-contractor should not be required to carry out work within the Contractor's Designed Portion. This is because of the conflict that will arise regarding design liability, as the main contractor would be simultaneously liable for such work under the CDP provisions (cl. 2.34.1), but exempt from liability under the named sub-contractor provisions (Sched. 2; para. 11.1).

In theory a named sub-contractor could be required to carry out work which forms part of the Contractor's Designed Portion in cases where the named sub-contractor is not to take on any design liability, but is merely to construct work designed by the contractor. In practice, though, the boundaries may not be that clear, and it may be best to avoid naming sub-contractors for any part of the designed portion work.

The JCT publishes sub-contract documents for use with both domestic sub-contractors (including versions with or without design provisions ICSub/C and ICSub/D/C), and, as noted above, with named sub-contractors (ICSub/NAM/C). ICSub/D/C contains provisions which mirror those in ICD11 regarding design obligations (cl. 2.1), the level of liability (cl. 2.21) and the PII insurance provisions (cl. 6.16). ICSub/NAM/C however, although it includes a requirement to design, does not contain any clauses governing the level of liability, or a requirement for PII. These are instead set out in the warranty with the employer (ICSub/NAM/E), which also includes an obligation to provide information to the contract administrator in accordance with any requirements set out in Schedule 1 of the form. This reinforces the notion that it would be unwise for the contractor to use ICSub/NAM/C to sub-contract any of its CDP work.

14.1.5 JCT Major Project Construction Contract (MPF11)

The JCT Major Project Construction Contract (MPF11) is different in approach, content, format and style from the above forms of contract and in fact at the time it was published it was radically different from any forms previously published by the JCT. It was intended to reflect the reality of modern contracting practice and although not as widely used as the other JCT forms, it is nevertheless an interesting document.

The contract allows for a variable amount of contractor design input, and may therefore be used in both 'traditional' and 'design-build' procurement routes. Unlike the provisions in SBC11, there is no need to identify the part that is to be designed. Under clause 7.1 the contractor is required to complete 'the Project' as described in the contract documents, 'including the completion of the design', in other words, the contractor is required to undertake any necessary design so that the Project will meet the employer's stated Requirements. As with the above contracts, the contractor is specifically stated not to be responsible for the adequacy of the Requirements or any design contained within the Requirements (cl. 11.1).

The contractor warrants that the design of the project will comply with statutory requirements, meet the requirements of any performance specification, and also use materials selected in accordance with the publication *Good Practice in the Selection of Construction Materials* (cl. 11.2)[10]. The contractor also warrants that it will exercise in relation to its design obligations 'the skill and care of a professional designer' (cl. 11.3). It adds that the Contractor does not warrant that the project will be suitable for any particular purpose. Under clause 11.4 the contractor is required to select materials that are fit for purpose.

This is significantly different to the position under SB11, as under clause 11.2 the liability for meeting performance specifications appears to be strict, whereas in SBC11 there is no separate warranty that the design will meet performance requirements. It is unclear what the combined effect of clauses 11.1 to 11.4 would be, but it is suggested that in relation to the clause 11.2 and 11.4 aspects the liability is strict, whereas for all other aspects it is to use reasonable skill and care (it is difficult to see what other purpose the cl. 11.2 warranties serve).[11] If a higher overall level of liability is required, the JCT Guidance Note to MP11 includes a replacement model clause whereby the contractor accepts the more onerous responsibility of ensuring the whole project meets the employer's Requirements.

The contract includes provisions for the contractor to submit the developing design proposals to the employer, which are identical to (in fact they were the forerunner of) those now included in DB11 and SBC11. The employer has the right to review and comment upon these submissions, thus allowing it to monitor the design being prepared by the contractor and satisfy itself that it is in accordance with the contract.

The contractor may be required to take out PII, but this depends on the required policy being described in the contract particulars. Unlike SBC11, there is no reference to a limit for liability for consequential losses for design errors. If this is required it would have to be added.

The contractor may sub-contract the work, including the design of the project, to domestic sub-contractors with the written approval of the employer. There are also provisions whereby the employer may require the contractor to use named 'Specialists' to carry out specific items of work. Unlike the named specialist provisions in SBC11, the work could include a design component, and the provisions could be used in relation to consultants as well as specialist works contractors. This feature therefore provides for the novation of consultants who had up till that point been engaged by the employer. The form does not, however include a document to achieve this novation – this would have to be drawn up separately. If the use of named specialists is required details are to be included in the Requirements, as there is no provision for later naming any specialists. It is notable that the contractor remains fully responsible for the per-

---

[10] British Council for Offices (BCO), *Good Practice in the Selection of Construction Materials*, (London: BCO, 2011), formerly published by Ove Arup.

[11] See also Neil F Jones, *The JCT Major Projects Form* (Oxford: Wiley Blackwell, 2004), which argues that a breach of cl. 11.2 would automatically result in a breach of cl. 11.3.

formance of all named specialists, which would include any design services they were providing (the contract's level of liability for design would not be changed by any previous agreement the employer had had with that specialist). This is to be contrasted with the distribution of risk under ICD11 when using named sub-contractors. Even in the event of termination of a specialist's employment, the contractor bears all of the risk of the additional costs of completing the work.

Under the JCT sub-contract for use with this form, the contractor is responsible for the design and integration of any interfaces between the sub-contract works and other elements of the project unless the sub-contractor has been made responsible for any such design in the Requirements. The sub-contractor must co-operate with the contractor and any others who are required to integrate the design of the sub-contract works and other elements of the project. These provisions would also apply to named specialists, assuming the JCT form was used.

The sub-contract contains equivalent provisions regarding design to those in MP11, namely, a warranty that the design will comply with the Statutory Requirements and satisfy any performance specification contained within the Requirements, and that in the design of the sub-contract works will be carried out with the skill and care to be expected of an appropriately qualified and experienced professional designer. There is no warranty that the sub-contract works, when constructed in accordance with the sub-contractor's designs, will be suitable for any particular purpose. As with MP11, the Guidance Notes suggest alternative wording for a 'fit for purpose' provision.

14.1.6 JCT Constructing Excellence Contract 2011 (CE11)[12]

The Constructing Excellence Contract fills a gap in that it was the first JCT contract to incorporate a partnering ethos.[13] It is a bilateral contract, intended for 'project partnering', i.e. for a single project, rather than for 'strategic partnering'. It could be used in most procurement routes, as instead of the usual obligation to 'carry out and complete the Works' (such as SBC11, cl. 2.1) under CE11 the supplier agrees to 'carry out and complete the Services' in accordance with the contract (cl. 1). 'Services' are defined as 'the services, work and/or goods to be supplied by the Supplier in accordance with this contract' (cl. 1.1). This form of wording is included because the form is intended to be used not only between employer and contractor, but between all other parties to the procurement process, for example employer and consultants, or contractor and sub-contractor. There is also a matching Project Team Agreement, which all the parties involved enter into, and which operates to set out project objectives (in the manner of a partnering agreement). Both CE11 and the Project Team Agreement include pain/gain mechanisms, which relate to target costs for the project. Under these the parties share any excess or shortfall from the targets, subject to an optional cap.

---

[12] For a discussion of other aspects of the form see Lupton, Sarah, 'JCT Standard Forms of Building Contract, 2005–7 Editions: Part 2 – Constructing Excellence', *The International Construction Law Review*, 24(4) (2007), 466–483.

[13] CE is based on the BE Collaborative Contract (BCC), which was published by 'Collaboration in the Built Environment', or BE as it was commonly known.

Under CE the services may well include design services, either alone or in conjunction with manufacture and supply, or with construction work. Clause 4.2 states that the supplier 'shall carry out, or procure the carrying out by his supply chain, the services in accordance with the contract and to the reasonable satisfaction of the Purchaser'.

Where the supplier is providing design or other professional services the contract offers a choice of two levels of liability: the supplier may be required to exercise 'reasonable skill and care' (cl. 4.4), or 'the level of skill and care reasonably to be expected of an appropriately qualified and competent professional designer' (cl. 4.5). The Guidance Notes indicate that the former is intended as a slightly lesser level of care. In the BE Collaborative Contract, on which CE11 was based, there was an optional 'fit for purpose' level of liability to provide services. Although no longer in the form, an appropriate form of wording is suggested in the JCT Guide to CE11, should it be required.

It is not entirely clear within the form itself exactly what standards any design is meant to meet, or where they are defined. The term 'brief' is included in the definitions as 'the requirement that Supplier is to satisfy by the performance of the Services' (cl. 1.1), and information regarding the brief is to be set out in the Contract Particulars. However apart from this instance, the brief is not referred to in any other clauses, for example there is no clause requiring the contractor to meet the brief. The parties should consider clarifying that this represents the standard to be met. It also might be wise to make clear who is responsible for any errors in the information included in the brief. It is also not clear whether meeting a performance specification would be considered part of 'design or other professional services', and would attract the 'reasonable skill and care' or a fit for purpose standard in clause 4.4 and 4.5.

If appointed as the 'Lead Designer', the supplier is responsible for coordinating the design of all suppliers, but would not be liable for their design (other than that provided by its supply chain). The supplier is required to provide 'copies of all designs having, or likely to have, an effect on the appearance, standard or functionality of the Project' (cl. 4.9) and to allow reasonable time for comment, but contains no provisions regarding the procedure to be followed for commenting, and the liability for any comments that require a change to the design. Procedural matters could be covered under the project protocol, but as this is not binding on the parties, issues relating to liability will require an addition to the CE11 terms. Parties could look to the detailed provisions regarding design development in PPC2000, or the useful 'Design Submission Procedure' incorporated in several other JCT forms as discussed above.

There are no provisions concerning insurance, including professional indemnity insurance. These have to be set out in the contract documents.

It should be noted that from the consultant's point of view the Project Team Agreement may have a significant effect on the practical aspects of their involvement, as well as liability. For example, in order to meet the targets the consultant may be tempted to concede to pressure to approve less than wise design decisions; however the consultant's level of liability would not be reduced accordingly. Also, the early warning requirements may lead consultants to admit to errors, which may in some circumstances run counter to their PII requirements. These are issues which are common to collaborative working generally (see section 10.4). However the risk of cross claims between team members is effectively removed. Clause 2.9 of the Project Team Agreement states that any duty of care or liability to each other is excluded, except in respect of the 'risk and reward' sharing scheme (i.e. team members share the risk of not meeting the target cost, but would not be able to claim losses from each other, for example as a result of relying on negligent advice).

14.1.7 JCT Minor Works Building Contract with contractor's design (MWD11)

JCT MWD11 makes provision for the contractor to undertake the design of part or parts of the project. This is in contrast to all earlier versions of the JCT minor works forms, and the current MW11, which make no such provision. It should be noted that whereas these forms had frequently been used in the past in conjunction with contractor design input (possibly conferred through the use of a performance specification) it is unlikely that this would now be successful. *ART Consultancy Ltd v Nevada Training Ltd*[14] is an example of the problems that can be experienced. In this case the claimant contractor was engaged by the defendant client on MW11 to both design and construct works. A dispute arose and was taken to adjudication, but the adjudicator declined to deal with any matters relating to the contractor design, as he decided that unlike other JCT contracts, the MW form is limited to construction. As the Act conferring the right[15] to take disputes to adjudication applied only to written contracts, his jurisdiction was limited to those matters expressly covered by the form. The adjudicator's decision was challenged in court, but the court decided the adjudicator had been correct to strip out of the claim any element relating to design, as design is not covered by the form's provisions.

Under MWD11 the design is included under the second recital, which allows the parties to agree that the 'Works' will include the design and construction of identified parts (the 'Contractor's Designed Portion'). As with SBC11, the contract documents include Employer's Requirements, but there is no reference to contractors proposals, and therefore no assumption that any have been submitted at the time of tender.

The contractor's design obligation is set out under clause 2.1.1, which states that:

> The Contractor shall, using reasonable skill, care and diligence, complete the design for the Contractor's Designed Portion including, so far as not described or stated in the Employer's Requirements, the selection of any specifications for the kinds and standards of the materials, goods and workmanship to be used in the CDP Works.

Although the clause does not state this, it seems reasonable to conclude that the design must be completed in accordance with the Employer's Requirements, given that under Article 1 the contractor must complete the works in accordance with the contract documents. As with the above forms, the contractor is expressly stated not to be responsible for the content of the Employer's Requirements (cl. 2.1.2).

Unlike SBC11, the level of liability is not equated with that of a competent professional, therefore depending on the context, there may be situations where a court would conclude that a lesser standard would be acceptable.

---

[14] [2007] All ER (D) 157 TCC.
[15] Housing Grants, Construction and Regeneration Act 1996.

The procedures for the contractor to submit the developing design are limited. The contractor is required to provide the contract administrator with two copies of 'such drawings or details and specification of materials, goods and workmanship and (if requested) required calculations and information, as are reasonably necessary to explain the Contractor's Designed Portion' (cl. 2.1.5). The contractor may not commence the related work until after seven days from the date the information is supplied (cl. 2.1.6). In practice seven days may not be sufficient to consider the implications of incorporating this design in the project. There is also no system by which the contract administrator may comment or require changes to the design, except that the contract administrator may issue instructions in order to integrate the design works with the rest of the scheme (cl. 2.1.3). If this is not broad enough to cover any alterations required, and if agreement cannot be reached on matters raised, the contract administrator may need to instruct a variation to the CDP under clause 3.6.1. Any changes may, however, result in some ambiguity as to who is responsible for the altered design.

There is no requirement for the contractor to carry professional indemnity insurance. There are also no provisions to cover copyright or that granting of a license to the employer in relation to the contractor's design documents. Taken together with the above, it is clear that additional provisions would be needed if the design element was significant, particularly if it affected the structural or aesthetic integrity of the scheme. In such cases it may be better to consider using one of the other JCT forms.

14.2 GC/Works/1 forms

14.2.1 GC/Works/1: Single Stage Design and Build

The GC/Works suite of forms was prepared by PACE in 1998 for use on government projects, but can also be used in a private context, as unlike earlier versions they no longer refer to the 'authority' but use the term 'employer'. The suite comprises a wide range of forms, for traditional, design-build, prime cost and measured term contracting. They are well-drafted documents, and generally more protective of the employer that other published standard forms. They are, however, surprisingly little used, having fallen behind NEC3 following the support of that form by the Office of Government Commerce.

GC/Works/1 Single Stage Design and Build (1998) Contract for Building and Civil Engineering, was first published in 1993. The following definitions are relevant:

1. 'the Employer's Requirements' means the statement, drawings, and other documents included in the Contract which define the Authority's requirements';
2. 'the Contractor's Proposals' means the statement, drawings and documents included in the Contract which define how the contractor is to implement the Employer's Requirements';
3. 'the Design' means the complete design of the works in accordance with the Employer's Requirements' and shall include (without limitation) the 'Contractor's Proposals' and all design documents for the design and execution of the works in accordance with the contract;

4. '*Design Document*' means any plan, sketch, drawing (including without limitation setting out drawings), calculations, specification or any other document whatsoever in any medium prepared by or on behalf of the contractor in the performance of the contract (or in preparation for the contract) for or in connection with the design (including without limitation, any such document included in the Contractor's Proposals).

The key provisions relating to design are to be found in clauses 10 and 31, in both the design build and the traditional versions. In GC/Works/l Single Stage Design and Build the design obligation states:

10(1) The Contractor has undertaken and shall undertake, and is responsible for the Design. He shall prepare all the Design Documents required for the complete and efficient execution of the Works in accordance with the Contract. The Contractor warrants that the Contractor's Proposals, the Design Documents and the Design have been and shall be prepared with all reasonable skill, care and diligence. The Contractor further warrants that the Design, and the Works meet, and shall continue to meet, the requirements of any relevant Planning Permission and the Building Regulations and comply, and shall continue to comply, with all other relevant statutory requirements. If, after the formation of the contract, there is any change in any such requirements which affect the Works, then such change will be treated as a change in the employer's requirements.

Alternative A
(2) The Contractor's liability to the Employer in respect of any defect or insufficiency in the Design, shall be the same as would have applied in the same circumstances to an architect or other suitably qualified professional designer who had held himself out as competent to undertake the Design and who had acted independently under a separate contract with the Employer and supplied the Design for, or in connection with, works to be carried out and completed by a contractor not being the supplier of the Design.

Alternative B
(2) The Contractor warrants to the employer that the Works will be fit for their purposes as made known to the contractor by the Contract.

Clearly clause (1) together with clause (2) Alternative B results in a strict liability that all aspects of the design will meet both statutory requirements and all other requirements set out by the employer.

The effect of Alternative A is likely to be the same as that arising under JCT DB11, namely, that the contractor's overall level of liability is to use the standard of skill and care applying to a designer. However there is an important exception with respect to statutory requirements, where the obligation is strict.

Under clause 31(2), the contractor warrants that all 'Things' (materials and goods) for incorporation in the works 'shall be fit for their intended purposes . . . and conform to the requirements and standards specified in the Employer's Requirements or, where no such standards are specified, to the appropriate standards and/or standard codes of practice'. The clause states 'with the sole exception of things chosen or selected by the Employer by means of a statement by or on behalf of the Employer in the Contract or in a VI'.

There is therefore a possible tension between clause 10(1) and (2) Alternative A and clause 31, in that under clause 10 the level of liability for design is to use reasonable skill and care, and under clause 31 'Things provided' unless selected by the Employer, must be fit for purpose, suggesting a strict liability. It is suggested that the following is the correct position (reflected in the Guidance Notes to the form):

- in selecting 'Things' the contractor is under a strict duty to select something fit for purpose and/or to comply with requirements of the specification
- in all other aspects of design the contractor is under a duty to use reasonable skill and care.

14.2.1.1 *Discrepancies*

Discrepancies are dealt with in condition 2 and in summary this provides:

(1) The conditions take priority over the other documents forming part of the contract.
(2) The Employer's Requirements take priority over the Contractor's Proposals.
(3) If there is a discrepancy in the Employer's Requirements, or between them and any statutory requirement (including Building Regulations or planning consents), the project manager (PM) resolves the discrepancy and it is treated as a change.
(4) Discrepancies in the Contractor's Proposals have to be resolved by the Contractor, subject to the PM's approval, at the contractor's own expense.
(5) There is an obligation on the contractor to notify the PM immediately if he discovers any of the above discrepancies (but this obligation does not apply to (1) above).

There is a further provision in relation to discrepancies set out in clause 10A(7), over and above those that appear in condition 2. This states that the Employer's Requirements prevail over any design document in the case of discrepancies between them (condition 10A(7)).

The above is similar to the equivalent provisions in the JCT forms, i.e. the effect of condition 2(3) is that any errors within the Employer's Requirements are the employer's risk. However it is notable that a clear priority is stated between the Employer's Requirements and the Contractor's Proposals. This, coupled with the absence of any provision equivalent to JCT DB11 Article 4 discussed above, would give confidence to the employer that any discrepancy between the two documents would be resolved in favour of the Employer's Requirements.

14.2.1.2 *Insurance*

Clause 8A requires professional indemnity insurance for the amount of cover set out in the Abstract of Particulars to be maintained by the contractor for the duration of the contract and six years from certified completion. There is an obligation to provide proof that the insurance premiums have been paid.

14.2.1.3 *Information*

Clause 10A(1) states 'to demonstrate compliance with the Employer's Requirements, the Contractor shall ensure that relevant work will be the subject of a Design Document'. The submission by the contractor of design documents for examination by the PM must be done on such a timescale as reasonably allows the PM time to raise queries and for the contractor to respond – all before the date on which the contractor intends to commence work (condition 10(6)). The PM has the right to raise questions and the contractor must respond 'promptly'. Sub-clause (2) requires the contractor not to commence work in relation to any design document until sure that:

(1) the PM has confirmed in writing that he does not intend to raise any questions, or,
(2) the PM confirms in writing that his questions have been answered to his satisfaction.

In a similar way to DB11 (Schedule 1.8.3), GC/Works/1 makes it clear that the fact that the PM may have seen parts of the design, raised questions on them, and subsequently said that he or she is satisfied with the answers, does not relieve the contractor of any liability under the contract for defects in design, or for inconsistencies or lack of co-ordination in the design documents (condition 10A(5)).

14.2.2 GC/Works/1: With Quantities

The GC/Works/1: With Quantities and Without Quantities forms are intended for use in a traditional procurement route, however the forms make provision for the contractor to be required to carry out design work (cl. 10). The exact wording of the clause is: 'Where the Contractor, either by himself or by means of any employee, agent, subcontractor or supplier, is required under the Contract to undertake the design of any part of the Works, he shall . . .' (cl. 10(1)). Exactly what the contractor 'is required to design' would have to be determined by looking at the contract documents as a whole. There is no requirement under the conditions to actually identify the parts to be designed (in the way JCT forms require identification of the Contractor's Designed Portion, for example in the SBC11 Articles), and there is no reference to Employer's Requirements or Contractor's Proposals. Therefore the contract documents would need to be drafted very carefully to ensure that resulting distribution of design responsibility is exactly as intended by the parties.

Normally anything identified in the Bills/Schedules/Specifications/Drawings as an item to be designed by the contractor, would be its responsibility. For cases of conflict, clause 2(1) sets out a hierarchy of contract documents, including that the specification (whether part of Bills or separate) prevails over drawings. As with JCT contracts, the contractor must inform the PM of discrepancies it discovers (cl. 2(3)). Although there is no express obligation to search for discrepancies, a reasonable degree of observance could be assumed as part of the contractor's general obligations.

It is also likely that anything specified by performance would also become the contractor's responsibility to design. The position is less clear with respect to something which is simply missing (i.e. no information is issued at tender stage) but depending on the circumstances it is likely that a court would conclude that the contractor was responsible for completing the design of those missing items. To avoid confusion, it would be good practice to identify all items to be designed by a contractor or a sub-contractor in the tender documents, possibly using a list or schedule, and as a safeguard adding a general 'catch all' provision requiring the contractor to complete the design of anything necessary to provide the project. It would also be important to state the following:

- requirements for the design (performance, etc.),
- any design information required from the contractor at tender stage,
- any design information required from the contractor during the works (quantity, format, timing etc.).

Where the contractor is responsible for design, as with GC/Works 1: Design and Build discussed above, clause 10 states that the level of liability for design can be either:

- the same as would have applied to an architect or other appropriate professional designer (Alternative A); or
- a warranty that the Works will be fit for their purposes as made known by the contract (Alternative B).

Under clause 31(1) the contractor must carry out the works in accordance with the contract, which would include the drawings and specification and any variation instruction, 'with all reasonable skill and care' and in a workmanlike manner. In addition, under clause 31(2), the contractor warrants that 'Things' (materials and goods) for incorporation in the works 'shall be fit for their intended purposes . . . and comply with the Specification, the Bills of Quantities and the drawings'. The clause states 'with the sole exception of things chosen or selected by the Employer by means of a statement by or on behalf of the Employer in the Contract or in a VI'. As with the design-build version there is therefore a possible tension between clauses 10 and 31 (see section 14.2.1).

There is an express duty to warn under clause 31(3): 'the contractor shall notify the PM before incorporation of any Things that the contractor considers should not be incorporated'. This duty is not qualified, for example by any expression such 'which he notices', so it appears that the contractor has a positive duty to check the specification and quality of 'Things', and then to use 'all reasonable skill and care' in reaching a decision, and warning the PM. This would extend to the possible unsuitability of things selected by the PM, or things selected by the contractor in design proposals submitted at tender stage or shown on information later supplied.

The contractor may be required to engage a sub-contractor nominated by the employer, to carry out work covered by a Prime Cost sum, either in the original contract documents, or in a direction or instruction given under the contract (cl. 63(1)). The contractor can be required to sub-contract design (cl. 10(1)) and remains entirely responsible for any design work sub-let to domestic and nominated sub-contractors (i.e. the position is the same as that in MP11). It may nevertheless be advisable to obtain design warranties.

The contractor is required to provide 'suitable' design information in regard to the completion of design for which the contractor is responsible, either as required in the contract documents, or as instructed by the PM (cl. 10). The related work must not be carried out until the PM has approved it. The clause givens no information regarding: the amount of information, the timing of submissions, or the procedure following comments, therefore these should be set out in the tender documents.

Clause 10 does, however, contain the important statement that 'the approval of the PM shall not relieve the Contractor of any liability which he would otherwise have' although this might not extend to situations where the PM varies the design by requiring, for example, the incorporation of a specific product.

14.3 NEC3 Engineering and Construction Contract (ECC)

The NEC suite of forms, first published in 1993 as the New Engineering Contract, has now reached its third edition (NEC3). The suite has become increasingly popular over the years, through endorsement initially by Sir Michael Latham,[16] and more recently by the Office of Government Commerce. The suite places a strong emphasis on collaborative working and clear management procedures, and it is a testament to its success that it is rarely the subject of litigation.

The NEC3 Engineering and Construction Contract, or ECC, forms part of that suite and is a very flexible document which can be used for a wide range of different procurement routes. It comprises a flexible, 'pick and mix' arrangement of:

- 9 core clauses
- 6 main option clauses
- 18 secondary clauses
- 2 dispute resolution clauses.

14.3.1 Scope of design responsibility

The key relevant Core clauses state:

> 20.1 The *Contractor* provides the *works* in accordance with the Works Information.
> 21.1 The *Contractor* designs the part of the *works* which the Works Information says he is to design.

This is similar to the approach in GC/Works/1 above, i.e. there is no reference to a 'Contractor's Design Portion', so the scope of what is to be designed must be construed from the contract documents, specifically the Works Information (which will comprise a wide range of documents such as drawings, specifications, etc., and may also include contractor design proposals). Any discrepancies within or between documents must be

---

[16] Sir Michael Latham, *Constructing the Team* (London: HMSO, 1994).

resolved by an instruction of the PM (cl. 17.1). Consequential changes are a compensation event, except for changes to the contractor's Works Information 'for his design which is made either at his request, or to comply with Works Information provided by the employer' (cl. 60.1(1)).

The effect of this is that the employer's requirements take precedence over the contractor's proposals, but that other changes will generally be the employer's risk.

As noted in section 14.2.2, GC/Works 1 uses the term 'is required under the Contract' to undertake the design, which might include items which are clearly necessary, but have not been described as design items. In contrast, the ECC term 'says he is to design' is more likely to restrict the obligation to items that are expressly stated to be matters for the contractor to design. This would give clarity to the contractor, but may place more risk on the employer. Work that is specified by performance, but without expressly saying that this is to be designed by the contractor, is unlikely to fall under clause 20.2, although it may fall under clause 20.1 (as work that needs to be provided so as to meet the performance stipulated). Work which has not been described completely, but obviously still needs to be done, (e.g. missing detailed information) does not appear to fall under either part of the clause.

Another complication is that a 'Defect' is defined as:

A part of the works which is not in accordance with the Works information, or
A part of the works which is designed by the contractor which is not in accordance with the applicable law or the contractor's design which the project manager has accepted.

These leaves open several questions, for example what is the position regarding work which accords with the contractor's design, but where that design is faulty? The second part of the definition suggests this would not be a 'Defect'. However this would be in conflict with the first part of the definition, because in all probability the works information will have included a design requirement that the faulty design can be shown not to meet. It is suggested that any work that is not in accordance with the Works Information would be a 'defect', even if it accorded with the contractor's design, but again it might be sensible to clarify this in the tender documents. This is supported by the wording of Option X15, below.

14.3.2 Level of liability

The core clauses do not stipulate a level of liability, but the structure of the main obligation would suggest that it is intended to be strict,[17] and this is supported by the fact that ECC has an option clause (Option X15) for a lesser liability, which states:

Limitation of the contractor's liability to the use of reasonable skill and care. The contractor is not liable for Defects in the Works due to his design so far as he proves that he used reasonable skill and care to ensure that his design complied with Works Information . . .

---

[17] The view taken by other authors such as Frances Forward in *Guide to NEC3* (London: RIBA Publishing, 2011).

This is a different approach to the equivalent JCT clause, in that the onus of proof is on the contractor to show it used reasonable skill and care, otherwise it will remain liable for all defects, whether due to its design or otherwise. In practice this would give assurance to the employer that at least initially the contractor will be liable for all problems, but is more onerous on the contractor than the JCT wording.

A system of approval for the contractor's design is set out in Clause 21.2 which states:

> The *Contractor* submits the particular of his design as the works Information requires to the *Project Manager* for acceptance, and the contractor does not proceed with the relevant work until the Project Manager has accepted the design. A reason for not accepting the *Contractor's* design is that it does not comply with the Works Information or the applicable law.

This leaves an open question as to whether there would be any other reasons for not accepting. For example, what if the particulars comply with the works information and applicable law, but the PM has other concerns about the design, which may not have been anticipated when the works information was prepared? It would seem likely that refusing to accept the design for any other reason may ultimately result in 'Change', as effectively it would be introducing a new requirement into the works information, but as above this would benefit from clarification. It is notable that there is no equivalent disclaimer to that in the JCT and GC/Works forms, i.e. that acceptance or comment would not reduce the contractor's obligations with respect to design.

14.3.3 Partnering option

NEC3 includes a Partnering option X12, the intention being that the contractor, sub-contractors and all consultants engaged on the project (ideally via one of the NEC3 suite of documents) all enter into the Partnering Agreement. This provides for incentivisation through the use of Key Performance Indicators, but without a 'pain' mechanism, i.e. there is no negative adjustment should the targets not be achieved. Under it, the partners are amongst other things required to work collaboratively, and to give advice, information and opinion to the other partners when asked to do so. The advice must be given 'fully, openly and objectively' (cl. X12.3(8)). As with most partnering arrangements, this could considerably widen the liability of any partner, as in addition to being liable to the client, they could now become liable to the other partners should any of this advice be given negligently. Unlike the CE11 Project Team Agreement, there is no clause excluding liability between the partners, although of course such a limitation could be introduced.

14.4 *Project Partnering Contract (PPC2000)*

PPC2000 is published by the Association of Consultant Architects, and was the first multi-party standard form contract, and the first standard form intended for use in a partnering context. It has been amended three times since its original publication, the latest amendments being in 2011.

PPC2000 covers the appointment of the whole team, which includes the client, the contractor (termed 'Constructor'), the client's representative and each consultant or specialist member of the 'Partnering Team'. It covers the entire duration of the project, with works on site being initiated through a commencement agreement, which includes an agreed maximum price and provisions for savings from this to be shared between the parties. After the contract is set up, further Partnering Team members may subsequently join by signing a joining agreement.

PPC2000 comprises a Partnering Team Agreement, Partnering Terms, and a series of Appendixes. It refers to Partnering Documents, which are specially drafted, and include, for example, the project brief, the project proposals, and the consultants' services schedules. The project brief is 'provided by the client' and the proposals are submitted by the contractor, and developed prior to, and possibly during the construction phase. A clear hierarchy is set up in clause 2.6, to be applied if discrepancies cannot be resolved, with the brief taking precedence over the proposals. Clause 2.4 states:

> Each Partnering Team member who prepares or contributes to any one or more Partnering Documents shall be responsible for the consequences of any error or omission in, or any discrepancy between, such Partnering Documents or its contributions to them, except to the extent of its reliance (if stated in such Partnering Documents) on any contribution or information provided by any one or more other Partnering Team member.

The Partnering Terms (Section 8) states that design development is to be undertaken by the Lead Designer and other Design Team members, who are to develop the design with the object of achieving best value for the Client (8.1). Clause 8.2 provides for the agreed design contributions of the Design Team members, and states that design coordination is the responsibility of the Lead Designer. Design Team members would therefore be responsible both for their intended contribution as defined under clause 8.2, and their actual contribution under clause 2.4; i.e. they would be liable for any input, even if not part of their envisaged role. An example might be if the contractor had an input into the Project Brief. Interestingly, they are also each responsible for discrepancies between documents, which would help to avoid gaps in liability for any design interface problems.

The key clause which sets the level of liability is Clause 22 'Duties of Care and Warranties'. Clause 22.1 states:

> In all their activities relating to the design, supply, construction and completion of the project, and all incidental activities governed by the Partnering Documents, each of the Partnering Team Members shall use reasonable skill and care appropriate to their respective roles, expertise and responsibilities as stated in the partnering documents, and shall owe each other such duty of care in respect of their agreed obligations under the Partnering Contract, with only such amendments and restrictions as are as stated in the Project Partnering Agreement.

Under this arrangement, clearly all partnering team members are potentially liable for errors, including any design errors, not only to the client, but also to each other. However the clause contains various options, which if adopted, could have significant effects on the liability of all parties. For example, it is possible for the contractor to accept responsibility for all aspects of the project, i.e. to take on a 'single point responsibility'. If this is required, the obligation under clause 22.1 is amended so that the constructor accepts full responsibility to the client for the design, supply, construction and completion of the project including the selection and standards of all materials, goods, equipment and workmanship. This includes responsibility for any design undertaken before or after the date of the commencement agreement by any other partnering team member. The other partnering team members would remain liable to each other, but not to the client unless they enter into collateral warranties. By a further option the contractor may also be required to warrant that the completed project will be fit for its intended purposes as described in the project brief. This combination would place a high level of liability on the contractor, particularly bearing in mind that the other team members' liability to the contractor would be limited to using reasonable skill and care. The PPC2000 Guide notes that the 'fit for purpose' option should only be adopted if it can be supported by the contractor's professional indemnity policy.

Clause 22.1 has an option whereby all the partnering team members are covered by a net contribution clause. By a further option, the clause can be amended so that each partnering team member's liability is limited to a fixed proportion of any loss or damage suffered by the client, irrespective of their contribution to its cause. Although this is expressed as a limiting clause, it may well result in a member being liable for losses due to errors in which it had no part. The Guide sensibly recommends that this is only used where the client has taken out integrated project insurance.

14.5 FIDIC forms

The International Federation of Consulting Engineers (*Fédération Internationale des Ingénieurs-Conseils*, or 'FIDIC') was founded in 1913 and is based in Geneva. The UK first joined in 1949. It is funded through member fees and through profits from its publications. The organisation represents 30,000 consulting firms worldwide, and runs conferences, publishes contracts, guidance and best practice procedures, runs training programmes, and acts as a centre of knowledge.

FIDIC published its first standard form contract in 1957, which has now developed into a suite of forms, including terms for the appointment of a consultant. The forms are intended for international projects, but have their roots in the common law tradition and UK standard forms, specifically the ACE form which itself evolved from the ICE forms. These origins can still be detected in the wording of some clauses. The key forms are as follows:

- *Conditions of Contract for Construction* for Building and Engineering Works Designed by the Employer (first edition, 1999; 'the Red Book').
- *Conditions of Contract for Construction* for Building and Engineering Works Designed by the Employer (Multilateral Development Bank Harmonised (MDB) ed. version 3: June 2010; 'the Red Book' or sometimes referred to as 'the Pink Book').
- *Conditions of Contract for Plant and Design-Build* for Electrical and Mechanical Plant, and for Building and Engineering Works, Designed by the Contractor (first edition, 1999; 'the Yellow Book').

- *Conditions of Contract for EPC Turnkey Projects* (first edition, 1999; 'the Silver Book').
- *Short Form of Contract* (first edition, 1999; 'the Green Book').
- *Conditions of Contract for Design, Build and Operate Projects* (first edition; 2008; 'the Gold Book').
- *Client/Consultant Model Services Agreement* (fourth edition; 2006; 'the White Book').

14.5.1 The FIDIC Red Book

This form is intended for use in traditional procurement routes, and assumes that the employer will provide the design, although there is provision for the contractor to design part of the works. The form is normally let on a measurement basis, with a bill of quantities, although there is a 'lump sum' option. There is a contract administrator role (the engineer), which includes inspection of the works, and issuing of certificates, variations, extensions of time, etc. The MDB version is essentially the Red Book with amendments required by leading world banks and is for use on projects funded by those banks (the amendments do not affect design liability).

In relation to design, all of the FIDIC forms include a strict obligation for the contractor to provide a design that meets the contract requirements. Clause 4.1 of the Red Book states:

> The Contractor shall design (to the extent specified in the Contract), execute and complete the Works in accordance with the Contract and with the Engineer's instructions, and shall remedy any defects in the Works. . . .
>
> If the Contract specifies that the Contractor shall design any part of the Permanent Works, then unless otherwise stated in the Particular Conditions:
>
> (a) the Contractor shall submit to the Engineer the Contractor's Documents for this part in accordance with the procedures specified in the Contract;
>
> (b) these Contractor's Documents shall be in accordance with the Specification and Drawings, shall be written in the language for communications defined in sub-clause 1.4 [*Law and Language*], and shall include additional information required by the Engineer to add to the Drawings for co-ordination of each Party's designs;
>
> (c) the Contractor shall be responsible for this part and it shall, when the Works are completed, be fit for such purposes for which the part is intended as are specified in the Contract; and
>
> (d) prior to the commencement of the Tests on Completion, the Contractor shall submit to the Engineer the 'as-built' documents and operation and maintenance manuals in accordance with the Specification and in sufficient detail for the Employer to operate, maintain, dismantle, reassemble, adjust and repair this part of the Works …

As with NEC3, it is only the designated part that must be provided to that level (where anything has been specified or otherwise defined in the documents, the contractor will not be warranting its fitness). The FIDIC Guide recommends that the scope of what is to be designed is set out in specification. Any part of the design which has simply been omitted is unlikely to be construed to be the contractor's responsibility.

Section (c) of the clause requires careful consideration and drafting of 'the purposes' within the contract documentation. The 'fit for purpose' definition is narrow, as it is limited to the purposes 'as are specified'. It seems likely that this would include only purposes expressly set out, and not those that could be implied on the basis of the context and other information provided.

Clause 4.1(a) refers to the submission of contract documents, but the requirements and procedure for this submission would need to be detailed in the specification, for example, the number and format of documents, the timing of submissions, and any procedure for approval. The procedures set out in other FIDIC forms could be adapted for the Red Book.

Clause 1.8 states that:

> If a Party becomes aware of an error or defect in a document which was prepared for use in executing the Works, the Party shall promptly give notice to the other Party of such error or defect.

This obligation applies to both parties, therefore it would encompass the contractor's duty to warn regarding information provided, such as information on which the design is to be based, but also the employer's consideration of submitted design documents. The FIDIC guide acknowledges that what constitutes an error will depend on context, for example the laws within the country where the project is sited.

Unlike the JCT forms, there are detailed provisions covering 'Tests on Completion' (clauses 7.4 and 9), which must be successfully undertaken prior to the employer taking over the works (cl. 8.2). The employer may accept the works even if a test is failed, but a reduction is made to the contract sum. The contract also allows for 'Tests after Completion', although, unlike the Yellow and Silver Books, there are no clauses specifically dealing with these tests, so that any details must be set out by the employer in the 'Particular Conditions' section of the form.

14.5.2 FIDIC Yellow Book

This is suitable for all types of projects where the main responsibility for design lies with contractor, although some design may be provided by the employer. Unlike the JCT DB11, the Yellow Book includes a role for a contract administrator. The contractor is required to complete the design to meet the 'Employer's Requirements'. Payment is on a lump sum basis, usually against a schedule of payments.

The Yellow Book, as might be expected, sets out more detail with respect to design responsibility. This is primarily to be found in clause 5.1, which states:

> The Contractor shall carry out, and be responsible for, the design of the works. Design shall be prepared by qualified designers who are engineers or other professionals who comply with the criteria (if any) stated in the Employer's Requirements. Unless otherwise stated in the Contract, the Contractor shall submit to the Engineer for consent the name and particulars of each proposed designer and design Subcontractor.

The Contractor warrants that he, his designers and design Subcontractors have the experience and capability necessary for the design. The Contractor undertakes that the designers shall be available to attend discussions with the Engineer at all reasonable times, until the expiry of the relevant Defects Notification Period.

Upon receiving notice under Sub-Clause 8.1 [Commencement of Works], the Contractor shall scrutinise the Employer's Requirements (including design criteria and calculations, if any), and the items of reference mentioned in Sub-Clause 4.7 [Setting Out]. Within the period stated in the Appendix to Tender, calculated from the Commencement Date, the Contractor shall give notice to the Engineer of any error, fault or other defect found in the Employer's Requirements or these items of reference.

After receiving this notice, the Engineer shall determine whether Clause 13 [Variations and Adjustments] shall be applied, and shall give notice to the Contractor accordingly. If and to the extent that (taking account of cost and time) an experienced contractor exercising due care and skill would have discovered the error, fault or other defect when examining the Site and the Employer's Requirements before submitting the Tender, the Time for Completion shall not be extended and the Contract Price shall not be adjusted.

Under clause 5.2 the contractor is required to prepare drawings necessary for the construction of the works and 'if the Employers Requirements describe the Contractor's Documents which are to be submitted to the Engineer for review and/or approval they shall be submitted accordingly'. The engineer has 21 days to review a drawing, and must then give notice to the contractor that the drawings is approved with or without comments) or that it fails to comply with the contract, and must be re-submitted. Work may not commence on the relevant part until the documents are approved. Any approval or comments by the engineer do not relieve the contractor from its liability for the design (cl. 5.2). If the engineer requires changes beyond those needed simply to meet the requirements, then this might constitute a variation. If the contractor disagrees with the engineer as to whether comments and changes constitute a variation, then the contractor would have to raise this as a claim.

There are significant differences between these arrangements and those under JCT DB11. As with the Red Book, the contractor is strictly liable to ensure the project is fit for purpose. Unlike the JCT form, the contractor is required to provide details of who will actually undertake the design, and to warrant their competence to undertake the task. In contrast to DB11 where the contractors takes no responsibility for errors in the employer's requirements, the contractor is specifically required to search for errors, and is liable for any which a competent contractor should have identified (whether the contractor spots them or not). Equally, the contractor is compensated for costs and delays which a competent contractor could not have identified (cl. 1.9).

As with the Red Book, performance of the project is assessed initially at the time of taking over through detailed testing procedures (clauses 7.4 and 9). However there are also provisions for 'Tests after Completion', which allow the required performance to be checked during normal operating conditions (cl. 12). The tests are undertaken by the employer, and if any shortfalls are identified, the contractor has the option of remedying the problem, or of paying liquidated damages, which are linked to the failure or under-performance. The liquidated damages provisions help to place a limit on the contractor's risk. As with other FIDC forms, there is provision for an overall cap on liability for breach of contract (cl. 17.6), which the under-performance damages would fall within.

14.5.3 FIDIC Silver Book

This is intended for turnkey contracts. In order to provide far greater certainty over price, the contract places additional risk on the contractor to that in the Red or Yellow Books as set out above. Amongst other things, the contractor accepts the risk of unforeseeable ground conditions, and is entirely responsible for the accuracy of the 'employer's requirements'. Clause 5.1 states that:

> the contractor shall be responsible for the design of the works and for the accuracy of the Employer's Requirements (including design criteria and calculations) . . . Any data received by the Contractor from the Employer or otherwise shall not relieve the Contractor from his responsibility for the design and execution of the works.

There is also no equivalent to the Yellow Book clause 1.9, which allows the contractor to claim for delays and costs incurred by errors a competent contractor could not have spotted. It is unusual for the contractor to take responsibility for the Employer's Requirements, and this is the only FIDIC form to take this approach. From the Employer's point of view, this is a simple approach, in that they need not be concerned about the possibility of mistakes in any information provided.

Clause 5.1 sets out some exceptions to the contractor's responsibility for the Employer's Requirements, in that it would not be responsible for:

(a) portions, data and information which are stated in the Contract as being immutable or the responsibly of the Employer
(b) definitions of intended purposes of the works or any parts thereof
(c) criteria for the testing and performance of the competed works, and
(d) portions, data and information which cannot be verified by the contractor, except as otherwise stated in the contract.

Depending on how this is handled, it is possible to adjust the risk on the contractor, for example by extending the list of matters that the employer confirms are correct under sub-section (a).

As with the Yellow Book, there are provisions for tests after completion, however in this case the tests are carried out by the contractor. It is possible to include for liquidated damages for under-performance, and to provide a cap on the total damages that may be claimed.

14.5.4 FIDIC Gold Book

This form is a single contract for the whole of the design, construction, operation and maintenance of a facility, awarded to a single contractor (typically a joint venture or consortium). The contract is split into two distinct phases, the design-build phase and the 'Operation Service Period' (OSP). The intended operation phase is 20 years. As with other DBO projects, by sharing the costs of operation between employer and contractor, this encourages the contractor to design a facility that performs well over time.

The contractor's design obligation under clause 4.1 is similar to that in the Yellow Book, i.e. to provide a completed facility which is fit for purpose; in fact the risk allocation in the design-build phase is similar to that in the Yellow Book. The key difference is the ongoing obligation throughout the operation period.

Clause 4.1 states 'Works are intended as defined in the Contract and the Contractor shall be responsible for ensuring that the Works remain fit for such purposes during the Operation Service Period', and to reinforce this clause 10.1 adds 'During the Operation Service, the Contractor shall be responsible for ensuring that the Works remain fit for the purposes for which they are intended'.

The completed facility's fitness is checked at the time of commissioning the facility, at which point a commissioning certificate is issued. Innovative features of the Gold Book include the provisions for operation and asset replacement. During the OSP the Contractor is required to operate the facility under a license granted by the employer (cl. 1.7) in compliance with the 'Operation Management Requirements' (cl. 10.1, these are set out as part of the Employer's Requirements), and according to a plan for operating and maintaining the facility (Operation Management Plan), submitted by the Contractor at the time of tender, and agreed and included in the Contract.

During the OSP, any assets listed in the 'Asset Schedule' are replaced by the contractor at the dates and for the prices set out in the schedule (cl. 14.5). Any additional costs for replacing these are borne by the contractor, and any savings are shared at the end of the OSP. All other on-going maintenance and repair work costs are borne by the contractor, including the cost of repairing any defects that appear (cl. 12.1) unless these are caused by the Employer (cl. 18).

There are procedures for further inspections towards the end of the OSP, for further tests and for handing back the facility to the employer following the issue of a contract completion certificate (cl. 11.9). Clause 8.8 makes clear that each party remains liable for the fulfilment of any obligations which remain unperformed at the time of that certificate, which is not said to be final and binding. It therefore appears that the OSP would be followed by a liability period according to the applicable law.

Chapter 15
Standard Forms of Appointment

One of the best ways to ensure that the consultant has a reasonable amount of protection in relation to design liability is to make sure that all engagements are on one of the standard terms of appointment published by the professional institutions. These are usually drafted with great care, following consultation with lawyers, insurers, and in many cases with leading clients, to ensure they balance the risks of both parties and are commercially viable. What follows is a brief outline of the key provisions relating to design liability.[1]

15.1 RIBA

The current RIBA Standard Forms of Agreement were introduced in 2010, and comprise a suite of related appointment documents for use in various situations. They are available in versions for use by architects and for use by any other consultant, in hard copy and electronic formats. The consultant version would be particularly suitable for use with a multi-disciplinary consultant team so that all consultants are on the same contract terms. The suite of documents comprises a Standard Agreement (SA10), a Concise Agreement, a Domestic Project Agreement, and a Sub-consultant Agreement. There are also additional Services schedules available for use when the consultant takes on roles such as CDM Co-ordinator, or provides services such as access consultant, design services for a historic building, interior design services, post occupation evaluation, master planning, and project management. The electronic version includes various 'electronic components' that are not available in hard copy, including a draft third party rights schedule, and a sub-consultant warranty, but no consultant warranty or novation agreement.

The guidance notes published with the forms explain that if the architect is dealing with a consumer, the terms (in particular provisions limiting liability, such as the set-off, net contribution, and alternative dispute resolution clauses) would need to be individually negotiated, otherwise some may be deemed void as a result of the Unfair

---

[1] For a full analysis of all the forms' provisions, readers should refer to Rachel Barnes, *Professional Services Agreements: A Guide for Construction Professionals*, 2nd edn (London: ICE Publishing, 2012).

Cornes and Lupton's Design Liability in the Construction Industry, Fifth Edition. Sarah Lupton.
© 2013 Sarah Lupton and DL Cornes. Published 2013 by Blackwell Publishing Ltd.

Terms in Consumer Contract Regulations 1999 (see Chapter 2).[2] Probably because of this the Domestic Project agreement does not include set-off or a net contribution clause, or arbitration.

The Standard Agreement 2010 is published in two versions: for use by an architect, and for use by other consultants. It comprises: conditions of appointment, memorandum of agreement, and schedules (plus an alternative model letter). The conditions of appointment, which apply to all appointments, cover the obligations and authority of the architect and the client, assignment and sub-contracting, payment, copyright and use of information, liabilities and insurance, suspension and termination, and dispute resolution.

The role and services to be performed are described more precisely in the Role Specification and Design Services sections of the Schedule. The role specification differentiates the role of designer, lead designer and lead consultant (as well as contract administrator and CDM coordinator). Whichever ones are selected will affect the degree of responsibility for coordination and integration of the design of others. The role of designer includes design, specification and inspection of works if retained during that phase. The schedule for design services is based on the RIBA Plan of Work, and allows for striking out if not required.

Obviously the consultant will need to ensure that the completed documents define precisely what parts of the project are and are not to be designed, and the proposed level of detail. For example, if certain areas of detail design are to be provided by a specialist sub-contractor, then this should be clarified.

The key clause relating to design liability is clause 2.1 'Duty of care' which states:

> The Architect shall exercise reasonable skill, care and diligence in accordance with the normal standards of the Architect's profession in performing the Services and discharging all the obligations under this clause 2.

The normal Services do not include anything that would amount to a strict obligation, therefore the *Costain v Charles Haswell* issue outlined in Chapter 7, section 7.3 is unlikely to arise unless the form is amended. Should any special services be added, for example that the consultant undertakes that the design will achieve the criteria in the client's brief, then clause 2.1 may not be sufficiently clear to override this separate strict obligation.

With respect to checking the work of others, the Schedule of Services under 'design services' states 'reviewing design information from contractors or specialists to establish whether that information can be coordinated or integrated with other production information'. This is clearly limited to information (rather than design) coordination. However if the role of design leader is undertaken, this requires coordination of all constructional elements, including work by consultants, specialists or suppliers.

Clause 7.2 sets out the limits on liability, clause 7.2.1 stating that liability for loss or damage 'shall not exceed the amount of the Architect's professional indemnity insur-

---

[2] *Munkenbeck & Marshall v Harold* [2005] EWHC 356 (TCC) and *Domsalla v Dyason* [2007] BLR 348 are examples where such terms in standard forms were deemed unfair.

ance specified in the Project Data, provided the Architect has notified the insurers of the relevant claim or claims as required by the terms of such insurance'.

Clause 7.2.2 also adds:

> No employee of the Architect, including any officer or director of a company or a member of a limited liability partnership or any agent of the Architect, shall be personally liable to the Client for any negligence, default or any other liability whatsoever arising from performance of the services.

The RIBA form also includes a net contribution clause as follows:

> 7.3 Without prejudice to the provisions of 7.2, the liability of the Architect shall not exceed such sum as it is just and reasonable for the architect to pay having regard to the extent of the Architect's responsibility for the loss and/or damage in question and on the assumptions that:
> 7.3.1
> all other consultants and contractors providing work or services for the Project have provided to the Client contractual undertakings on terms no less onerous than those of the Architect under this agreement;
> 7.3.2
> there are no exclusions of or limitations of liability nor joint insurance or co-insurance provisions between the Client and any other person referred to in this clause, and
> 7.3.3
> all the persons referred to in this clause have paid to the Client such sums as it would be just and equitable for them to pay having regard to the extent of their responsibility for that loss and/or damage.

This clause appears to be sufficiently clear to achieve the desired aim of limiting the architect's share of any award of damages to a fair proportion, although it has been pointed out that the phrase 'all other consultants and contractors' may not be wide enough to encompass all other persons that might be involved in some projects.[3]

Under the appointment it is possible to indicate which other consultants will be appointed (cl. 3.8, 'Other Persons'), and the architect is required to collaborate with these (cl. 2.3). This includes commenting on information they provide 'where competent to do so'. If, while carrying out the services, the architect thinks that the project will require additional expertise, then he or she may recommend to the client that it appoints an additional consultant to provide this. Clause 4.3 then states 'if the client agrees to make such appointment, it shall be made without undue delay. On such appointment the client shall give written notice to the Architect, who shall be relieved from responsibility for and liability for that element of the Services.' The relief from liability would include any part of the design taken over by the new firm, but only if this has been clarified with all parties. Alternatively, if the architect sub-contracts work then this can only be done with the client's consent, and 'shall not relieve the architect of responsibility for carrying out and completing the Services' (cl. 4.2). In effect the situation in *Cooperative Group v John Allen* should not arise, i.e. that the architect delegates design work without consulting the client (see Chapter 9).

---

[3] See Rachel Barnes *supra*, at 282 and note *West and another v Ian Finlay & Associates (A Firm)* [2013] EWHC 868 (TCC).

Under clause 6.1, the architect owns 'all intellectual property rights including the copyright in the original work produced in the performance of the Services and generally asserts the Architect's moral rights to be identified as the author of such work'. The client has a licence to use information 'for the construction of the project' but not for any extension of the project, or other project (cl. 6.3). This is the normal arrangement in standard forms that include design services. Under the form the client may require the architect to enter into collateral warranties (cl. 7.7.1), or provide rights to a third party (cl. 7.7.2), and/or switch to working for a contractor appointed in a design-build arrangement, but only if this is set out under the agreement (cl. 7.7.3), and the names and terms appended as required. In all cases clause 7.7 states that 'It shall be a condition that any such supplementary agreement gives no greater benefit to the beneficiaries than is given to the Client under this Agreement and that all fees and other amounts properly due to the Architect have been paid at the date when it comes into effect'.

15.2 ACA

The ACA publishes a range of forms for use by consultant architects. ACA SFA has now been updated to ACA SFA, 2008 Edition in both an English law and Scots law versions. It is shorter than the RIBA Standard Appointment, but in terms of design liability it is in many respects very similar. The services to be provided are set out in Schedule 2, which includes 'normal services' (which apply unless struck out) and 'other services', which must be individually selected. The Schedules does not define a role for a lead designer; if this role is needed, the services would need to be set out in a separate document.

The key obligation 'Duty of care' is set out in clause 2.1 as 'The Architect in performing the Services and discharging the obligations under this Agreement shall exercise the reasonable skill and care to be expected of an ordinary, competent architect'. This is similar to that in the RIBA form and to the level that would normally be implied by law.

The architect is required to cooperate with others appointed by the client as identified in a schedule included in the appointment (cl. 2.4) and is required, where appropriate, to provide comment on their services or work (cl. 2.4.2). Clause 3.9 states:

In respect of any work or service in connection with the Project by any person other than the Architect (including by Contractors), the Client shall;

–hold such persons and not the Architect responsible for the competence and performance of such work and services;

–require such persons to co-operate with the Architect, including to provide the Architect with designs and other information necessary for the proper and timely performance of the Services;

–require that such persons shall, when requested by the Architect, consider and provide comments on the work of the Architect such that the Architect can properly integrate his/her own work with that of such persons.

Clause 7.2 allows for the placing of limits on the extent of liability as follows:

The Architect's liability for loss or damage in respect of any one occurrence or series of occurrences arising out of one event (including any liability for costs) shall be limited to the sum stated in Article 8 or the net contribution in accordance with clause 7.4, whichever is the lesser sum.

Article 8 covers both the limit of liability and the level of PII cover, i.e. the figure entered applies to both. The net contribution clause is similar to the format of that in the RIBA forms, and clearly sets out the assumptions in relation to others involved in the design of the project, and upon which the proportion of liability is to be assessed. Those encompassed by the clause, i.e. 'all other Consultants, contractors, sub-contractors, and other persons providing services' (cl. 7.4), could arguably be considered a wider range than those covered by the equivalent RIBA provision. Copyright is covered in clauses 6.1 and 6.2, which grants the client a licence to use materials provided by the consultant for purposes related to the project, but like the RIBA form, excludes their use 'for any extension of the Project and/or for any other project'.

15.3 ACE

The ACE (Association for Consultancy and Engineering) publishes a suite of eight standard forms of agreement, plus a range of schedules of services and versions for use in Scotland. The eight agreements include:

- ACE Agreement 1: Design
- ACE Agreement 2: Advisory, investigatory and reporting services
- ACE Agreement 3: Design and construct
- ACE Agreement 4: Sub-consultancy
- ACE Agreement 5: Homeowner
- ACE Agreement 6: Expert Witness (Sole Practitioner)
- ACE Agreement 7: Expert Witness (Firm)
- ACE Agreement 8: Adjudicator.

The key design liability in Agreement 1 (2009, revised 2011) is expressed as follows: 'The Consultant shall exercise reasonable skill, care and diligence in the performance of the Services' (cl. F2.1). As with the RIBA form, this reflects the normal level of liability that would be implied under common law. The ACE agreement provides for the services to be described by attaching one of the ACE standard schedules. As above, care needs to be taken to ensure the scope and level of detail of design to be undertaken is described precisely. Interestingly, the form expressly provides for delegation of detailed design to a contractor or sub-contractor (cl. F2.3). The client's permission may not unreasonably be withheld. The consultant is required to examine the design and integrate it with the rest of the Services, but is relieved from liability for the delegated design.

There is provision for limiting liability under F7.1: 'the total liability of the Consultant under or in connection with this Agreement whether in contract, in tort, in negligence, for breach of statutory duty or otherwise shall not exceed the sum set out or the amount referred to, as the case may be, in clause B12 of Part B: The Particulars of Agreement'.

There is also a detailed net contribution clause, similar to that under the RIBA form, as follows:

> F7.5   Further and notwithstanding anything to the contrary contained in this Agreement and without prejudice to any provision in this Agreement whereby liability is excluded or limited to a lesser amount, the liability of the Consultant, if any, for any loss or damage . . . in respect of any claim or claims shall not exceed such sum as it would be just and equitable for the Consultant to pay having regard to the extent of the Consultant's responsibility for the loss or damage and on the assumptions that:
>
> (i)   all other consultants and advisers, contractors and sub-contractors involved in the Project shall have provided contractual undertakings to the Client on terms no less onerous than those set out in clause F2.1 in respect of the carrying out of their obligations in connection with the Project.
> (ii)   there are no exclusions of or limitations of liability nor joint insurance or co-insurance provisions between the Client and any other party referred to in clause F7.5 and that any such other party who is responsible to any extent for the loss or damage is contractually liable to the Client for the loss or damage; and
> (iii)   all the parties referred to in clause F7.5 have paid to the Client such proportion of the loss or damage which it would be just and equitable for them to pay having regard to the extent of their responsibility for the loss or damage.

Under the Schedule of Services for civil and structural engineering the duty in relation to approval and checking of drawings supplied by contractors and subcontractors is described as to 'examine detailed designs . . . in respect of conformity with the Consultant's design and in particular in respect of general dimensions, structural adequacy of members and connections and conformity with performance specifications' (a similar item is included in the Schedule for mechanical services). This clearly involves more than the dimensional coordination required in the RIBA equivalent, and therefore an increased responsibility for the consultant. The Client is given a licence to use materials prepared by the consultant for purposes connected with the project (cl. F6.1), and the form states that the 'licence shall enable the Client to use the Consultant's Intellectual Property Rights for the extension of the Project but such use shall not include a licence to reproduce the designs contained therein for any extension of the Project'. This recognises that in practice the information may be needed when extending the property, but still maintains the prohibition on reproducing the design.

15.4 ICE[4]

The ICE publishes the Professional Services Contract (PSC3) as part of its NEC3 suite. Under this the key obligation states that 'the *Consultant* Provides the Services in accord-

---

ance with the Scope' (cl. 21.1). No standard schedules of services are provided, the parties must describe the services as part of the 'Scope' in separate documents identified within the contract data.

'Provides the Services in accordance with the Scope' appears to be a strict obligation. This impression is reinforced by the fact that 'Provides the Services' is defined as 'do the work necessary to complete the services in accordance with this contract and all incidental work, services and actions which this contract requires'. Together this reads as a strict obligation, not an obligation to use reasonable skill and care.

However the subsequent clause 21.2 states: 'the *Consultant's* obligation is to use the skill and care normally used by professionals providing services similar to the *services*'. The relationship between the strict obligation under clause 21.1 and the 'skill and care' one under clause 21.2 is not clear. Strictly speaking, clause 21.2 is simply defining a level of liability, it is not specifying what duties it applies to. However it appears to be that all 'Services' are to be provided with skill and care, but that other obligations in the form, such as a requirement to issue a notice or to meet a 'Key Date', are strict (unlike the RIBA and ACA forms it does not refer to 'performing the Services *and* discharging the obligations'). Care should be taken when drafting the Services, for example any suggestion that some of these are negligence based, and some are strict obligations, could cause confusion (see section 7.3).

Under clause 11.2 a defect is 'a part of the services which is not in accordance with the Scope or the applicable law' and under clause 41.2 the consultant 'corrects Defects within a time which minimises the adverse effect on the Employer or others'. This applies to defects notified by the employer (as well as the consultant), and therefore gives the employer the authority (at least initially) to decide that a 'defect' has occurred and require it to be remedied. If a requirement set out in the Scope has not been achieved, then it may be difficult for consultants to, for example, argue that they have nevertheless exercised the required level of skill and care in undertaking the design, and therefore there is in fact no 'defect'.

Clause 82.1 of PSC3 gives a total liability in an amount to be agreed for all matters other than excluded matters and this cap is said to apply 'in contract, tort or delict and otherwise to the extent allowed under the law of the contract'. The 'excluded matters' are significant, and include such things as loss or damage to third party property. Consultants should therefore check with their PI insurance providers that they are prepared to cover the liability under this form.

Under clause 82.2 the consultant's liability to the employer is limited to 'that proportion of the Employer's losses for which the consultant is responsible under the contract'. As the clause does not include the assumptions set out in the traditional type of net contribution clause such as those set out above for the RIBA and ACE Agreements, (see section 13.3), it is possible that it may be ineffective as a net contribution clause.

15.5 RICS

The RICS publishes a Standard Form of Consultant's Appointment, and a Standard Short Form of Appointment, together with a wide range of services schedules, which are intended to cover the varying roles of its members. The Standard Form of Consultant's Appointment is considered below.

Notably, the form makes it clear that design services would not be part of those offered unless expressly identified. Clause 4.4 states:

> Design Responsibility
> ... The Consultant is only responsible for the design of the Project or any part of it and/or for specifying or approving materials for the Project or any part of it if and to the extent that it is designated as having such responsibility in the Appendix.

Defining the obligation in this way eliminates the need for clauses concerning responsibility for design undertaken by others. If designated Lead Consultant the consultant would be required to coordinate the activities of others and give instructions as necessary (cl. 3.4). The general clause 3.1 covering liability states 'The Consultant exercises in the performance of the Services the Requisite Standard' and 'Requisite Standard' is defined as meaning 'the standard of reasonable skill and care to be expected of an appropriately qualified professional consultant of the discipline specified in the Appendix holding itself out as having the competence and resources to perform the Services and who is experienced in providing services in connection with works of a similar size, scope, nature, complexity and value as the Project'.

It should be noted that the above clause requires consultants to exercise a higher duty of skill and care than that imposed on them by common law, in contrast to the ACE and the RIBA standard forms. The form also contains several of what initially appear to be strict obligations, for example clause 4.3 states 'The Consultant complies with the Statutory Requirements when performing the Services'. The relationship with clause 3.1 above is not clear, i.e. is the obligation to comply with statutory requirements intended to be a separate, strict obligation? It might be wise to clarify that *none* of the obligations, including provision of the Services, is intended to be strict, if this is what the parties intend.

Another point worth noting[5] (in terms of design liability) is that consultants are under an obligation not to put the client in breach of any term in the building contract or third party agreements (cl. 3.6). This could give rise to problems where the employer, for example, has promised that a design will fulfil any specific requirements, for example that it will be buildable, or meet some performance in use requirement. In such cases the consultant may be liable to the client if it suffers losses due to a failure to meet these promises. Consultants should therefore consider including some restrictions on this obligation and ensure they have full knowledge of the terms of all relevant building contracts and third party agreements before accepting this term.

The form sets out clear limitations on liability, including a cap (cl. 5.1) and a net contribution clause (cl. 5.2) of the standard format discussed above. There are detailed copyright clauses granting the employer a licence to use documents for any purpose in relation to the project (cl. 13), with no restriction regarding their use in relation to extensions.

---

[5]For additional points see Rachel Barnes 'RICS Consultancy Form: A False Friend' *Building Magazine* 26 (September 2008).

15.6 CIC

The first edition of the Construction Industry Council Consultants' Contract (CIC/Conditions) was published in 2007, and the second (to take account of the Construction Act changes) in 2011. The Guidance notes state that it:

> ... is intended for use by experienced clients and consultants undertaking major commercial property development projects, primarily in the United Kingdom. It has been drafted with the aim of striking a fair balance between the interests of the Client and the Consultant. The objective is to make available a contract which is acceptable in the institutional market, but with which consultants and their insurers are comfortable.

The document is carefully drafted, and achieves the stated aims. Although some provisions are more onerous that those in, for example, the RIBA terms, they are less onerous than those frequently put forward by clients, and will hopefully be an acceptable compromise in a commercial context.

An interesting feature is that although it could be used with any list of services, it is intended to be used with the CIC Scope of Services,[6] a comprehensive computer-generated spreadsheet of activities assigned to all consultants involved, intended to allow for a fully integrated team to be set up (and conversely, the Scope of Services may be used with any of the above terms of appointment). As it covers the whole team, this will help ensure that all of the separate design tasks are clearly allocated, with no overlaps and no omissions.

The consultant's primary obligation is as follows:

> 3–1.1 The Consultant shall exercise the Standard in performing the Services.

The definition of Standard is:

> the reasonable skill, care and diligence to be expected of a competent consultant of the relevant discipline who is experienced in providing similar services in relation to projects of a similar size, scope and complexity to the Project... .

This a higher duty than that in the RIBA form, and is similar to that of the RICS version, however as the form is intended for use by experienced clients on larger projects, the higher standard is not surprising. It is also intended that all professionals involved in the project use the same terms – this would be important to avoid one consultant being found negligent and others not due to differing contractual standards.

It should also be noted that other obligations, which are not part of the Services, appear to be strict. An example would be the obligation for the consultant to provide information in accordance with the Information Release Schedule (cl. 6–3.2). Although

---

[6] For an outline of these, see Construction Industry Council, *Briefing: Scope of Services Explained* (London: CIC, 2007).

this is 'except to the extent that it is prevented from doing so by any cause beyond its reasonable control', it is nevertheless more onerous than the normal obligation to use due skill and care. There is a separate set of optional provisions for use when the consultant's role includes undertaking design and/or specification:

6–1.1 The Consultant shall use all reasonable endeavours (exercising the Standard) to see that the elements of the Project falling within its discipline are designed so that they can be constructed within the financial limits stated in the Project Brief.

6–1.2 The Consultant shall exercise the Standard to see that, unless authorised by the Client in writing (or, where such authorisation is given orally, confirmed by the Consultant to the Client in writing), it shall not specify or authorise for use in the Project any materials which are generally known within the Consultant's profession at the time of specification or authorisation (as applicable) to be deleterious or hazardous to health or safety or to the durability of the Project in the particular circumstances in which they are proposed to be used.

6–1.3 In complying with §6–1.2 above, the Consultant shall have due regard (where applicable) to the guidelines contained in the edition of the publication *Good practice in the selection of construction materials* (Ove Arup & Partners)[7] current at the time of specification or authorisation (as applicable).

6–1.4 If the Consultant (exercising the Standard) becomes aware of any proposed or actual use of any material which contravenes §6–1.2, it shall notify the Client forthwith.

6–1.5 Unless otherwise agreed by the Client, the Consultant (for itself and on behalf of its employees, agents and any sub-consultant engaged by it on the Project) waives any moral rights which it or they might have under Sections 77 and 80 of the Copyright, Designs and Patents Act 1988 as the 'author' of the Material or the Project.

6–1.6 The Consultant shall be liable for any losses incurred by the Client (and recoverable at law from the Consultant) because the Consultant's design is held to have infringed another person's copyright or other intellectual property rights.

It is not clear why 'all reasonable endeavours' is included for the first obligation, i.e. whether this is intended to add anything to the defined Standard. The phrase 'best endeavours' is generally considered to introduce an onerous obligation, whereas 'reasonable endeavours' is more on a par with the normal level of skill and care, with 'all reasonable endeavours' lying somewhere in between the two.[8] Although the terms 'all reasonable endeavours' and the Standard itself create a higher duty than that normally adopted, they are likely to be acceptable to most insurers.

The obligation regarding work by others is clear; the consultant is said to be not liable for any inadequacies etc., in any designs, work or information prepared by others 'except to the extent that the Services expressly oblige the Consultant to review or inspect such designs, work and/or information'. Where such a review is required, this must be done exercising the contractual Standard (cl. 3–1.4).

---

[7] Note that the current edition is British Council for Offices (BCO), *Good Practice in the Selection of Construction Materials* (London: BCO, 2011).

[8] See Rachel Barnes, *Professional Services Agreements: A Guide for Construction Professionals*, 2nd edn (London: ICE Publishing, 2012), section 4.7 and *Jet2.com v Blackpool Airport Ltd* [2012] EWCA Civ 417.

The consultant is required to exercise the Standard not to cause or contribute to any breach by the client of Third Party Agreements, but unlike the RICS form, this is restricted to agreements that it has been given copies of before the contract date (cl. 3–4.1.2).

There is provision for 'third party rights' as set out in Part 5 – Rights of Interested Parties. Interested Parties are to be identified in the conditions.

There is no net contribution clause as standard in the conditions to the client, except with respect to interested parties. The Guidance Notes explain that such a clause ought to be unnecessary, as the contract is intended for use where all consultants are experienced and holders of appropriate insurance. However the Guidance Notes also set out an appropriate wording should it be needed.

15.7 Novation and Switch Agreements

As explained in Chapter 1, the difference between a 'true' novation, and consultant 'switch' is significant. The first is seldom appropriate where a consultant swaps from working for the employer to working for the contractor in a design-build procurement context (although it may be appropriate in other situations).[9] The services for the employer-client will have been performed with its interests in mind. These interests are very unlikely to coincide with those of the contractor, therefore any attempt to set up an arrangement where it is assumed the contractor was the client from the start will lead to nonsensical results.

The CIC Novation Agreement,[10] published in March 2004, is in effect a 'consultant switch' arrangement. If this is used, the consultant-employer appointment pre-novation, and the consultant-contractor agreement post-novation are treated as separate and distinct. Under the CIC form, the consultant agrees that it will work for the contractor post-novation, and be liable to it for the services undertaken. The contractor agrees that it will step into the shoes of the employer and henceforth act as the consultant's client. The consultant will remain liable to the employer for the services supplied pre-novation.

Under many design-build construction contracts the contractor, as well as accepting responsibility for completing the design, may also accept responsibility for some of the design done pre-novation (i.e. at a time when the consultant was working for the employer).[11] The contractor may therefore want a remedy against the consultant who did the design work to cover it in the event that it suffers loss due to an error in that design. The CIC novation agreement therefore includes a warranty from the consultant to the contractor in respect of services undertaken pre-novation. The consultant warrants to the contractor that, insofar as the contractor is responsible under the main

---

[9] A standard form for *ab initio* novation is published by the City of London Law Society (CLLS).

[10] Part of this text is based on Construction Industry Council, *Novation of Consultants' Appointments on Design and Build* (London: CIC, 2008), which gives further guidance on novation and switch arrangements.

[11] Note that this is not the position under most JCT standard forms.

contract for pre-novation services undertaken by the consultant, such services have been performed *for the employer* in accordance with the terms of the appointment. This means that if the consultant were to have breached the duty owed to the employer, and the contractor suffers loss as a result, the contractor would be able to claim against the consultant.

An important caveat is included in the CIC Agreement: 'save that the Consultant shall not be absolved from liability to the Contractor for such loss merely by virtue of the fact that the loss has not been suffered by the Employer'. The Consultant cannot therefore raise the 'no loss' argument, which defeated the contractor's claim in *Blyth & Blyth v Carillion Construction Ltd.*[12]

In this case consulting engineers Blyth & Blyth Ltd (Blyth) entered into a tripartite agreement, referred to as the 'novation agreement' with Carillion Construction Ltd (Carillion) and THI Leisure (Fountain Park) Ltd (THI) in relation to the design and construction of a leisure development building in Edinburgh (there was a deed of appointment between THI and Blyth, section 6 of which empowered THI to instruct Blyth to enter into the 'novation agreement'). The design and build contract between THI and Carillion was on an amended WCD81. Blyth brought an action against Carillion to claim payment of fees and Carillion counter-claimed in respect of alleged breaches of contract by Blyth. This raised issues about the meaning and effect of the novation agreement, in particular in relation to alleged breaches occurring before the novation. An example would be that as a result of the engineer's inaccurate information regarding reinforcement bars, which was included in the Employer's Requirements, the contractor suffered losses when it eventually had to supply far more bars than it had anticipated. Under the amended terms of the contract the contractor accepted the risk of inaccuracies in the Requirements, and therefore could not claim these losses from the employer. The contractor therefore sought to claim them from the engineers. The court decided that the losses suffered by the contractor were not due a breach of duty *to the contractor* – the consultant's duty was to the employer at that time, but the employer had lost nothing. The engineers were therefore not liable to the contractor for those losses.

Whatever 'novation' arrangement is made, care needs to be taken so that the services to be performed by the consultant for the employer and for the contractor are clearly distinguished and defined. If consultants are required to, for example, inspect work on behalf of the contractor, their obligations will be slightly different from those they would have if inspecting on behalf of the employer (a consultant would not issue certificates when acting for the contractor, for example). There is a schedule attached to the CIC Agreement where any changes in services (and fees) can be recorded.

---

[12] (2001) 79 Con LR 142.

Chapter 16
Professional Indemnity Insurance[1]

16.1 General

A designer faced with a claim for professional negligence is unlikely to be able to make a significant payment in respect of the claim without suffering serious financial consequences or even bankruptcy. There are ways of managing the risk and limiting the liability so that the consequences of a successful professional negligence claim are less severe. One method is by risk transfer through insurance, the principle of which is that insurers collect small contributions (premiums) from the many in order to have the funds available to meet the disasters suffered by the few. In the context of liability for design errors, the type of insurance to cover this risk is known as professional indemnity insurance. Broadly this covers the designer for negligent design, the exact nature of the protection depending on the wording of the insurance contract. In essence, it indemnifies the consultant against claims made by others (if there is no liability to others, there will be no indemnity).

Nowadays almost all design consultants will hold a professional indemnity insurance policy (but see Chapter 17 for some EU national differences). Most professional institutions require their members to take out this type of insurance. The RIBA includes such a requirement under its Code, as does the ARB, the ACE and the RICS. A key reason why institutions make this requirement is for the protection of the profession's clients: should a claim be brought successfully against a designer, but the consultant had insufficient means to meet it and no insurance, the client would suffer a loss, and would rightly question whether there was any benefit in engaging that consultant. Certainty of protection enhances the reputation of that profession. Clients these days will also routinely demand that the firms they engage are adequately insured. Principally, of course, the insurance protects the consultant against severe financial loss, and for this reason all those engaged in design in the construction field should maintain adequate insurance, whether or not their member organisation requires it.

Professional indemnity insurance does not cover every contingency with which the designer may be faced; the usual policy provides cover in respect of any loss from a

[1]With thanks to Melinda Parisotti and Alasdair Niven of Wren Managers, the Wren Insurance Association Ltd, for their helpful comments on a draft of this chapter.

claim made against the designer in respect of any negligent act, error or omission. In other words, the cover is usually limited to professional negligence and would not provide cover where there was a breach of duty but no negligence (see below). Before considering what the contents of a policy should be, it is necessary to look at the principles that govern professional indemnity insurance policies. Before that, however, there is one point to make that cannot be over-emphasised: it is vital that the designer reads the policy to understand the cover (which may involve consideration with brokers), the restrictions on the cover (including the exceptions, the excess and the geographical area covered) and the requirements as to claims notification. There should be one person, with a deputy, responsible for this in every organisation.

In the UK inurance is normally arranged through brokers, who are intermediaries that act as agents for the insurance buyers, and whose job it is to find the most suitable insurance for them. They 'place' the business with insurance companies, of which there are two principal types. The first are the proprietary institutions, whose working capital comes from shareholders, who receive the benefit of any profits earned. The second are the mutual societies which have no shareholders but are instead owned entirely by their policyholders, in a form of self-insurance. The benefits of any profits therefore accrue to the policyholders.

16.2 Principles of professional indemnity insurance

16.2.1 Contract

Arrangements for insurance are made by contract but there are special rules in insurance law, which go beyond that of simple contract law. Unlike most contracts, where the principle of 'caveat emptor' (buyer beware) applies, contracts of insurance are subject to the principle of utmost good faith; This means that the buyer of insurance is obliged to inform the insurer of all facts that could influence the insurer's assessment of the risk. Failure to do so means that the insurer has the right to avoid the policy in the event of a claim.

In addition, policy wordings can be complex, and may contain, for example 'conditions precedent', which are conditions that must be complied with by the insured before the insurers have any liability; and there may be extensive use of 'exceptions' to define the cover provided.

In the general law of contract, a warranty is a term collateral to the main purpose of the contract, breach of which gives the aggrieved party a right to damages but not rescission of the contract. In insurance law, a warranty is a condition of the policy, breach of which discharges the insurers from liability under the contract of insurance from the date of breach. The requirements of a warranty are strict and even an unwitting infringement can have serious consequences for the insured.

The usual procedure is for the designer to complete a proposal form, usually the insurers' standard form; that form will usually refer to the standard conditions of the insurers' policy and by signing the form, the designer is offering to accept insurance on those terms. The terms themselves usually contain a provision that the proposal form is incorporated into and is the basis of the insurance contract. In this way, all the information given by the designer in the proposal form becomes part of the contract. Thus it becomes a warranty, breach of which enables the insurer to avoid the policy or to bring it to an end. It follows that once the proposal form has been given to the insurers and the insurers have accepted the proposal, a contract will exist and the insurers will, and are obliged to, issue a policy in the terms agreed between the parties.

16.2.2 Disclosure and risk

In *Carter v Boehm*[2] a case that retains its seminal importance notwithstanding that it was decided so long ago, Lord Mansfield said:

> Insurance is a contract of speculation. The special facts upon which the contingent chances to be computed lie most commonly in the knowledge of the insured only; the underwriter trusts to his representations and proceeds upon confidence that he does not keep back any circumstances. . . .[3]

Thus we see that the duty of disclosure is based upon the notion of inequality of information and includes at its very heart the obligation on the assured to disclose all material facts or circumstances that it knows (or ought in the ordinarily course of business to know) prior to completion of the contract.

The proposal form that is completed by the designer is a document of the utmost importance. It forms the basis of the contract; the truth of the statements made by the designer in the proposal will often be made a condition precedent to the insurer's liability; that is to say, where the statements are untrue, the insurer can lawfully refuse to make payment in respect of a claim for which it would otherwise be liable. The insurer may also be able to avoid the policy. The information contained in the proposal form enables the insurer to assess the risk so that it can decide whether or not to accept the proposal and on what terms. It follows that the insurer cannot make a proper evaluation unless the designer makes full disclosure of all those matters which are relevant to the risk. That will involve doing more than just answering the questions on the proposal form, if there are other matters of which the insurer should be made aware. It is against this background that the common law developed the principle that a contract of insurance is based on the utmost good faith of the parties (known as the principle of *uberrimae fidei*).

The principle of utmost good faith applies to both parties to the insurance contract.[4] Where the utmost good faith has not been shown by one party, the other party can avoid the contract. In such a case, the contract would be at an end, and the insured

---

[2](1766) 3 Burr 1905.
[3]ibid., at 1909.
[4]*La Banque Keyser Ullman SA v Skandia (UK) Insurance Co. Ltd & Others* [1987] 2 All ER, which was not overruled on this point in either the Court of Appeal or the House of Lords.

would have no insurance cover. The premium will normally be returned except if there has been fraud, when it is not refundable, and a fraudulent claim can result in criminal liability. In any event, the most important aspect of the principle of utmost good faith is the duty imposed upon the designer when making the proposal to the insurer to a) disclose all material facts, and b) not to make a statement that amounts to a misrepresentation of a material fact.

Such non-disclosure or misrepresentation enables the insurer to avoid the policy *ab initio*; existing claims will not be met. Similarly, if the designer fraudulently conceals a material fact, the insurer will equally be able to avoid the policy. Non-disclosure and misrepresentation are now considered separately.

16.2.3 Non-disclosure

A designer has a duty to disclose all facts that are material. Moreover it is the fact, and not the significance of the fact that must be disclosed. If there is a leak through a roof it must be disclosed even though the designer may not know that the whole roof is defective. Where there is a breach of this duty, the insurer has a common law right to avoid the policy. The duty involves consideration of two matters.

First, the designer must disclose all material facts that are actually within the designer's knowledge. However, it should not be assumed that matters not currently within the designer's knowledge are not disclosable. The principle of the utmost good faith probably requires that the designer should include material facts that could be discovered by making reasonable enquiries.

Secondly, the duty is limited to those facts that are 'material'. A designer should be aware that whether or not a fact is material is not to be limited by what the designer thinks is relevant. Section 18(2) of the Marine Insurance Act 1906 states that a fact is material if it would 'influence the judgment of a prudent underwriter in fixing the premium, or determining whether he will take the risk'.

In *Container Transport International v Oceanus Mutual Underwriting (Bermuda) Ltd*[5] the Court of Appeal decided that the prudent insurer test was the sole test, and that the test meant that it was enough that the actual insurer wanted the information, so that it could consider its position, not that it would have acted differently if it had it. The decision was then considered in the leading House of Lords case *Pan Atlantic Insurance Co. v Pine Top Insurance Co. Ltd.*[6] The Court stated clearly that the insurer cannot rely on the mere fact of the non-disclosure, if it wishes to avoid the policy it must demonstrate that it was induced to enter the contract by the non-disclosure.

Where information is known to the insured but discoverable by the insurer on making inquiry this raises difficulties. Does the insurer have a duty to carry out its own investigations? For example, if the insurer is told things *by* the insured that put the insurer in a position where it should make further enquiries of its own, it cannot do

---

[5] [1984] 1 Lloyd's Rep 476.
[6] [1994] 3 WLR 677.

nothing: the insurer must make further enquiries. The insurer also cannot rely on non-disclosure of matters that are public knowledge. This point was canvassed in the Supreme Court of Canada in *Coronation Insurance Co. v Taku Air Transport Ltd, Canada.*[7] The Court decided that an insurer could not rely on a failure on the part of the insured to disclose information that was already held in the insurer's own files. Indeed, in this case, the information was a matter of public record (an air crash) which the Court held the insurer could have discovered on reasonable investigation. Justice Cory said the effort required on the part of the insurer to discover the information was 'light and minimal'. The Canadian Court relied on the English authority of *Carter v Boehm*[8] in coming to its view. This case shows that in certain circumstances an insurer is obliged to undertake its own investigations, although the boundary of that obligation may not be very wide. The designer has a duty to disclose material facts, not only in the proposal form, but also any further material facts which come to the designer's knowledge before the contract of insurance is concluded. For example, where a designer is negotiating with a new insurer and, on having completed a proposal form a claim comes to his attention, there is a continuing duty to inform the proposed insurers of that claim. It should be noted that the date of the contract is unlikely to be the same date as the date of commencement of the insurance cover. The test is when there is a contract.

16.2.4 Misrepresentation

As part of their duty of disclosure, designers must not only make accurate statements as part of the general duty to disclose all material facts, but must also see that any particular questions asked by the insurers are answered accurately. This precludes making statements which are true but by reason of the fact that they are incomplete are misleading.[9] If a statement is untrue, it does not matter that the designer thought that it was true when he or she made it. The insurer will still be able to avoid the policy if the misrepresentation was material. However, where the insured adds a qualification to a statement by saying that it is true to the best of his or her knowledge and belief, then the insured may be afforded some protection provided he or she did believe the statement to be true and that belief was reasonable.[10] That is the position at common law but where the conditions of the insurance provide that the truth of the statements is a condition precedent to the insurer's liability, then honest belief will not assist and the insurer will not be liable.

The test as to whether a misrepresentation is material is the same as that for non-disclosure; the duty to state facts accurately, as with non-disclosure, also continues to the date that the contract is made.

---

[7] (1992) 85 DLR (4th) 609.
[8] (1766) 3 Burr 1905.
[9] *Aarons Reefs v Twiss* [1896] AC 273.
[10] *Wheelton v Hardisty* (1858) 8 E & B 232.

16.2.5 Renewal

Professional indemnity policies are usually written for a period of 12 months. The policy can only, therefore, be renewed where both parties consent. They often do so when the insurer sends out a renewal notice and the designer pays a renewal premium. Even if completion of a new proposal form is not required, the duty of the utmost good faith arises at every renewal because it is, in fact, a new contract of insurance. The basis of the new contract will be the same as the old contract. It follows that the designer has a duty to the insurer to check that the proposal for the old insurance is still applicable and, if not, to notify the insurer before renewal of any additional relevant facts or any other matters which make any of the statements in the original proposal misleading in any way. If a material fact had not been disclosed in the previous year, it is worth considering notifying it on renewal.

It is not uncommon for an insured to change insurer on renewal. The difficulties that can arise where a writ is issued but the extent of the claim was not known until after a new insurer took over the risk were considered by the Court of Appeal in *Thorman & Others v New Hampshire Insurance Co. (UK) Ltd and the Home Insurance Co.*[11] In this case, the architects had been designers on a project that had been completed in 1977. They were covered by New Hampshire (NH) up to 30 September 1983. From 1 October 1983 they were covered by the Home (H). There were terms requiring notification of claims and occurrences which might give rise to a claim in both policies. In 1976, complaints had been made about cracking of brickwork. The owners took possession of the properties between November 1976 and November 1977. In 1978 and 1979 the owners required remedial works to be carried out to the brickwork and the architects informed NH of a claim for the cost of the remedial works. By 1979 NH had filed their papers. In May 1982 the architects were told of further problems and in June 1982 the owners issued a writ endorsed in general terms alleging professional negligence. The statement of claim, which was not served by the owners until January 1984, contained allegations going to a variety of defects beyond the brickwork. NH claimed it was only on risk as to the brickwork and nothing else, saying that the other claims were made only after it had ceased to be the relevant insurer. On this point, the court was heavily influenced by a letter written by the owners' solicitors to the architects in June 1982, which was while NH were on risk and which letter they saw. It said in part:

> Serious problems have arisen in this development, *inter alia*, with regard to cracking and defective brickwork, for which we hold you responsible.

Sir John Donaldson, Master of the Rolls, said of that passage:

> Note the words '*inter alia*'. This is the clearest possible claim in respect of all serious problems which had arisen by that date and is not confined to brickwork. The fact that it was unparticularised and uninformative is nothing to the point. All matters listed in the Scott Schedule [in

---

[11] [1987] 1 Lloyds Rep 7 (CA).

the proceedings] are in this category and it follows that all were the subject matter of a claim before New Hampshire came off risk.[12]

The Court found that the true test was: 'what was the claim being put forward by the claimant?' – not 'what did the proposed defendant think the claim was?'. The writ subsequently issued merely particularised a claim that had been made in general terms before and did not constitute new or different claims.

16.2.6 Waiver

An insurer that discovers a non-disclosure or a misrepresentation that entitles it to avoid the policy does not have to do so. It can elect whether to avoid the policy or not. An insurer can waive its right to avoid the policy by conduct, for example, by taking over the conduct of the defence of the proceedings. Sometimes, insurers who are aware of their right to avoid the policy may proceed on the clear understanding that by so proceeding they are not waiving their rights subsequently to avoid the policy. Insurers who have paid a claim, not knowing at the time that they were entitled to avoid the policy, can subsequently recover sums paid to the designer. The most common waiver by insurers is accepting a premium after they are aware of a non-disclosure or misrepresentation.

16.2.7 Subrogation

Where the insurer pays the amount of the loss to a designer, the insurer has a right to be placed in the position of the designer and avail itself of all the rights and remedies of the designer against third parties. Where there is no condition in the policy dealing with this matter, this right of subrogation is not exercisable until the insurers have paid the loss to the designer.[13] There is much old legal authority on implied terms as to subrogation but the House of Lords has considered the position in *Lord Napier and Ettrick v N. F. Kershaw Ltd.*[14] The implied terms were classified as follows by Lord Templeman:

(1) an obligation on the assured to initiate proceedings in order to reduce his loss;
(2) a promise by the assured to account to the insurer for monies received by him from the third party;
(3) a promise by the assured to allow the insurer to exercise his right of action against the third party wrongdoer in the event that the assured fails to do so himself;
(4) a promise by the assured to act in good faith when proceeding against the third party.

---

[12] ibid., at 12.
[13] *Castellain v Preston* CA (1883) 21 QB 380; *Page v Scottish Insurance Corporation Ltd* (1929) 140 LT 571.
[14] House of Lords, noted in 1992 at *Insurance Law Monthly*, 5(2), (1992), 6.

However, it is likely that the policy will have express provisions dealing with the equivalent of subrogation rights as contractual terms. It will usually be provided that the insurer will be entitled to take over and conduct any proceedings brought in respect of a claim. However, even if the conduct of the proceedings is taken over in this way, the designer will remain the party named in the proceedings.

16.2.8 Premium and duration of policy

The amount of the premium is assessed by insurers on the basis of their experience of claims in the relevant sphere of activity. In any particular case, the average premium based on the claims experience of the insurers may be increased or decreased by reason of a variety of factors including the matters set out in the proposal. The agreement of the premium (or the basis upon which it is to be calculated) is an essential ingredient in the formation of the contract. Once a valid contract has come into being, the insurer may be liable on the policy, notwithstanding the fact that the premium has not been paid. In practice, however, insurers will avoid that position arising by making payment of the premium a condition precedent to their liability under the policy.

The duration of the policy will usually be expressly stated both as to commencement and expiry. The policy will usually contain a condition entitling the insurer to cancel the policy on giving a specified number of days' notice in writing to the insured. The insurer's risk will continue until that period has expired and, where the condition also provides that the designer shall be repaid a proportionate part of the premium, the insurer will remain at risk until that proportionate part of the premium has been repaid: *Bamberger v Commercial Credit Mutual Assurance Society*.[15]

16.2.9 Notifying the insurer of claims made against the insured

The precise wording of this condition is of fundamental importance because observance of the procedure in the policy for giving notice to the insurers is often made a condition precedent to the insurer's liability. However, there are insurers who accept that wording requiring 'immediate' notice or that claims must be notified 'forthwith' are not fair on the insured. It is therefore worthwhile negotiating this part of the policy wording to try to obtain wording that is not a condition precedent. Designers should read the condition setting out the procedure for notification of claims carefully to be certain that they comply with it. The usual wording requires the written notice to be given when the designer becomes aware of *circumstances which may give rise to a claim*. Such wording means that designers cannot wait until a claim is actually made but rather as soon as they know about circumstances which may lead to such a claim, the designer has a duty to inform insurers. If the condition requires the notification to be in writing, then it should be done in writing and to the person specified in the policy, so as to

---

[15](1855) 15 CB 676.

avoid any arguments as to the precise date of notification that might arise if the notification was given at a meeting or in a telephone conversation.

This is generally considered to be an ongoing obligation, so that if the situation develops, a fresh notification may be needed. For example in *Kajima v Underwriter Insurance*,[16] the project was for the design and construction of apartments, involving the novel use of pre-fabricated, stacked accommodation pods. The design-build contractor's insurance policy stated: 'The Insured shall give written notice to the Underwriters as soon as possible after becoming aware of circumstances which might reasonably be expected to produce a claim. . . .' The pods showed problems of settlement, and the design-build contractor notified its insurers. Further problems emerged as a result of an investigation following the expiry of the policy, and the court determined that the earlier notification had not covered these. It commented that in some situations 'it is possible for the insured to give notice of a "hornets' nest" or "can of worms" type of circumstances',[17] but not if it is simply 'guessing'. A fresh notification should be issued as soon as new circumstances come to light.

Generally speaking, experienced consultants ought to be able to make the decision regarding notification themselves. In *John Mowlem Construction plc v Neil F Jones*[18] Mowlem was the main contractor employed on a very large office design and construction project in Bristol. Mowlem employed Commissioning South West Ltd (CSW) as sub-contractors. CSW had PI insurance as required under its sub-contract, and CSW's company secretary was responsible for arranging this cover. CSW believed that Mowlem was withholding payment for the work which it had done, and retained the Solicitors Neil F Jones to 'recover outstanding debt'. An arbitration was commenced and early in the proceedings Mowlem threatened to pursue a counterclaim. Around this time the PII insurance came up for renewal. The form asked if there were any circumstances that might give rise to a claim, to which the company secretary answered 'no', considering that the threat was merely a negotiating tactic. The counterclaim was however pursued and was successful, but as a result of non-disclosure or misrepresentation, the insurers refused to cover the claim. CSW argued that its solicitors should have advised it to notify the insurers at an early stage. The court took the view that the consultant should have been competent to deal with its own insurance policy.

16.2.10 Dealing with the claim

Once a claim has been made, it will be necessary for the proceedings against the designer to be defended. On the usual policy terms, the insurer then has three options; it can:

(1) pay the designer the amount for which the dispute can be settled but not exceeding the limit of the indemnity; or

---

[16] (2008) 122 Con LR 123, relying on *HLB Kidsons v Lloyd's Underwriters* [2007] EWHC 1951 (Comm).
[17] ibid., at para. 99.
[18] [2004] App LR 06/30 JMC.

(2) take over and conduct the defence of the action in the name of the designer, in which case the insurers will probably be unable to dispute that they are liable to indemnify the designer up to the limit of indemnity under the policy;[19] or

(3) permit the designer to conduct its own defence, in which case the policy will usually provide for the designer to be paid his legal costs provided the insurer has so agreed in writing before the costs were incurred.

Where the insurer conducts the proceedings itself in the name of the designer, the insurer owes a duty to the designer to see that the proceedings are properly conducted and, in particular, the insurer should see that the designer agrees with the proposed defence.[20]

Where the policy gives the insurer the right to settle the proceedings, the insurer can settle the proceedings without discussing the matter with the designer and the insurer is entitled to recover from the designer the excess under the policy and any other sums which the designer has to bear under the policy.[21] In practice, the insurer will usually involve the insured in negotiations, particularly where there is a large excess.

Conversely, the consultant should not enter into discussions regarding a possible error without having contacted its insurers. All policies will contain a provision requiring a designer to make no admission or offer of settlement or the like. The observance of such a provision is usually made a condition precedent to the insurer's liability and, accordingly, any such offer to settle made by the designer, without the consent of the insurers, will have the effect of enabling the insurer to repudiate liability under the policy. This can be a particular issue when the consultant is engaged in a 'partnering' or collaborative form of procurement, where all parties may be required to be open about problems that might have emerged, and to give an 'early warning' of any matters that might affect progress on the project[22] (it would be essential to pass all such contracts to the insurers *prior* to tendering for such commissions).

Where the insurer pays in respect of a claim, it will ask for a form of discharge to be signed. The insured should be careful to see that the wording of the form of discharge does not go wider than the matters that are being settled. For example, in *Kitchen Design and Advice Ltd v Lee Valley Water Co.*,[23] a form of discharge signed in respect of a claim for physical damage caused by flooding referred not only to claims advanced but also to any that might be advanced; the discharge prevented recovery of later claims for consequential loss.

It is generally considered that the insured owes a duty of good faith to the insurer when making an insurance claim (as well as when entering into or renewing the policy, as outlined above). For example, in *Black King Shipping v Massie, The Litsion Pride*,[24]

---

[19] *Soole v Royal Insurance Co.* (1971) 2 Lloyd's Rep. 332.

[20] *Groom v Crocker* [1939] 1 KB 194.

[21] *Beacon Insurance Co. Ltd v Langdale* [1939] 4 All ER 204.

[22] Jeffrey Brown, *Do Design and Build Insurance Policy Wordings Fit the Bill?* Society of Construction Law, Paper D120 (London: SCL, 2011).

[23] [1989] 2 Lloyd's Rep 221.

[24] [1985] 1 Lloyd's Rep 437.

Mr Justice Hirst held that the duty of utmost good faith extended to a time after the making of the contract and would be breached by a claim submitted containing fraudulent mis-statements. This reasoning was followed in *The Captain Panagos DP*[25] and approved by Lord Jauncey in *La Banque Financière de la Cité v Westgate Insurance Co. Ltd.*[26]

In *The Litsion Pride* Mr Justice Hirst went further by stating that the duty extended beyond fraudulent statements, and included any mis-statements. He said:

> the continuing duty of utmost good faith requires the insured to make full disclosure of all material facts, whether or not he realises their materiality, and not simply to refrain from dishonest, deliberate or culpable concealment.[27]

Although this aspect is *obiter*, it would be sensible for a consultant to notify the insurers of any material facts that arise.

As to the consequences of fraudulently mis-stating material facts, or fraudulently omitting material facts, it has yet to be decided whether this breach of the duty of good faith entitles the insurer to avoid the policy *ab initio* or not (if it did the assured would lose not just the fraudulent claim but also all previous claims). This issue will be a red herring unless the insurer is also trying to avoid other claims because there will, in any event, be an implied term not to submit fraudulent claims. The issue as to whether fraud is a necessary ingredient, which it is not generally in relation to good faith, has been considered in *Bucks Printing Press Ltd v Prudential Assurance Co.*[28] In that case the insured asserted in its insurance claim that machinery had been properly packed in circumstances where it did not know whether the machinery had been properly packed. Mr Justice Saville found the insured had been reckless, rather than fraudulent, in making the statement and he said:

> ... the making of fraudulent or reckless material misrepresentations by an insured to an insurer in support of a claim under the insurance amounts to a failure to observe the duty of the utmost good faith ... and gives the insurer the right to repudiate liability under the insurance.

Mr Justice Saville was asked whether negligence, as opposed to fraud or recklessness, was enough but he felt it was not (although that part of the judgment was *obiter dicta*). In the Court of Appeal case of *K/S Merc-Skandia XXXXII v Certain Lloyd's Underwriters, The Mercadian Continent*,[29] Aikens J reviewed all previous authorities and rejected the notion that there was any generalised duty of good faith, breach of which would allow the insurer to reject the policy *ab initio*. He confirmed the assured was under a continuing duty to refrain from a deliberate misrepresentation or concealment of material facts

---

[25] [1986] 2 Lloyd's Rep 470.
[26] [1989] 2 All ER 952.
[27] ibid., at 512.
[28] (1991) unreported but noted at *Insurance Law Monthly*, 5(7), (1991), 9.
[29] [2001] 2 Lloyd's Rep 563.

intended to deceive the insurer. However, the remedy of avoidance would not apply unless the fraudulent conduct was such as to justify termination of the contract.

16.2.11 Rights against insurers

A person who brings a claim against designers has no cause of action against the designers' insurers. However, there is one exception to this rule which is provided by statute. Where the designer becomes bankrupt or makes a composition or arrangement with its creditors, or in the case of a company, a winding-up order is made or a resolution for voluntary winding-up is passed, or a receiver or manager is appointed, then the injured party has the right to bring an action against the insurers.

This issue is covered by the Third Parties (Rights against Insurers) Act 2010. This Act, which is being brought into force in stages by Statutory Instrument, takes over from the 80-year old 1930 Act of the same name. The effect of the 1930 Act, s. 1 was to try to put the injured party in the position that the designer would have been *vis-à-vis* the insurer. The insurer is only liable to the injured party to the same extent that it would have been liable to the designer.

Unfortunately case law had limited the effect of that Act. In *Bradley v Eagle Star Insurance Co. Ltd*,[30] Doris Bradley, who had worked at the mill of Dart Mill Ltd for many years on and off, had contracted byssinosis. Dart Mill Ltd had been voluntarily wound up and the company dissolved in 1976. The issue before the court was whether she had a reasonable prospect of making a successful claim against the defendant insurer, who had insured Dart Mill Ltd, under section 1 of the Third Parties (Rights against Insurers) Act 1930. She did not succeed. The Court of Appeal decided that she did not have a right under the Act because that right did not arise unless she had already obtained judgment against Dart Mill Ltd. She could not obtain that judgment because the company no longer existed in law. In these circumstances, she had no claim against the insurer direct. Lord Brandon, agreeing with the decision in an earlier case, put it this way:

> In my opinion the reasoning of Lord Denning MR and Salmon LJ ... on the basis of which they concluded that, under a policy of insurance against liability to third parties, the insured person cannot sue for an indemnity from the insurers unless and until the existence and amount of his liability to a third party has been established by action, arbitration or agreement, is unassailably correct.

It followed that the 1930 Act can only be used where the third party has proven the liability of the insured by way of judgment, arbitration or agreement. Without that, there was little benefit in this Act to third parties. However, it is possible to have a company that has been struck off the Register of Companies reinstated and then pursued to judgment so as to obtain the benefits of the Act.[31]

Under section 2(1) of the 1930 Act, the liquidator of an assured is to 'give at the request of any person claiming that the [assured] is under a liability to him, such information

---

[30] [1989] 1 All ER 961.
[31] ibid. at 965, approving *Post Office v Norwich Union Fire Insurance Society Ltd* [1967] 1 All ER 577.

as may reasonably be required by him for the purpose of ascertaining whether any rights have been transferred to and vested in him by this Act'. The application and effect of this section was tested, following *Bradley*, in *Nigel Upchurch Associates v The Aldridge Estates Investment Co Ltd*.[32] An architect had entered into a voluntary arrangement with his creditors on grounds of insolvency. Proceedings were brought in the architect's name by the administrator of the scheme of arrangement in respect of unpaid fees, breach of contract and remuneration for other work. The defendant denied liability and counter-claimed; he also sought details under the Act of the architect's insurance. As the rights under section 2 could only arise when section 1 was satisfied, the court decided that in the light of *Bradley*, the defendant had no right to see the insurance documents. However the question arose again in the Court of Appeal decision in the *First National Tricity Finance Ltd v OT Computers Ltd*.[33] This time the Court ordered disclosure of information about OT Computers' insurance arrangements. The finance company was entitled to know whether OT Computers was insured for a claim against it.

The 2010 Act, which implements recommendations of the Law Commission, is intended to simplify some of the above problems and complications. It gives a claimant the right to bring a claim against the defendant's insurer without first bringing a claim against the defendant. The right arises when the defendant is subject to an insolvency procedure. This would also apply to claims being brought by companies outside the UK, provided the party they are claiming against has entered insolvency proceedings within the UK.[34] It will therefore allow the third party to claim directly against the insurer without the liability of the insured being established first. It also gives the claimant the right to obtain information about the defendant's insurance, i.e. insurers, and other persons able to provide relevant information would now be obliged to provide it if requested.

16.3 The professional indemnity policy (consultants)

The purpose of this section is to set out some practical considerations that are relevant to the selection of an appropriate policy.

16.3.1 The cover

The usual cover is against the designer's legal liability for damages and costs in respect of claims for breach of professional duty by reason of any negligence, error or omission on the part of the designer. The usual policy wording will not provide indemnity in respect of breach of a fitness for purpose obligation. Generally, terms provide cover solely for 'negligent act, error or omission'. Thus, where designers have given an express or implied warranty that their design will be fit for the purpose required, as this would be a strict obligation there is no cover for breach of that warranty.

---

[32] [1993] 1 Lloyd's Rep 535.
[33] [2004] EWCA Civ 653.
[34] Freshfields Bruckhaus Deringer LLP, *Insurance and Reinsurance News*, May 2010.

Typical policy wording is:

> The Insurer agrees to indemnify the Insured up to the limit specified in the Schedule in respect of any sum or sums which the insured may become legally liable to pay as damages for breach of professional duty as a result of any claim or claims made upon the Insured during the period of insurance arising out of the conduct of the practice described in the Schedule as a direct result of any negligent act, error or omission committed by the Insured in the said practice or business.

The above cover will be limited to liability incurred in connection with the particular business of the designer and the nature of that business will usually be defined in the policy. It is important to see that the description of the business and the work it carries out is properly described either in the policy or in the proposal. The usual legal and insurance interpretation of the words 'negligent act, error or omission' is that, whilst there is cover for breach of a contractual duty as to reasonable skill and care, there has to be negligence and that the words 'error or omission' are to be interpreted only in the context of negligence. However, a different view has been expressed in one case in 1984 where it was said that cases habitually relied upon to support an assertion that the words 'negligent act, error or omission' were apt to cover only negligence did not in fact support that contention. On the other hand, it was said that not every loss caused by an omission or error was recoverable under the policy: it must be one which in principle could create liability and must not be a deliberate error or omission: *Wimpey Construction (UK) Ltd v Poole*.[35] In *Wimpey*, Mr Justice Webster said:

> A professional indemnity policy does not necessarily cover only negligence. In my view I must give effect to the literal meaning of the primary insuring words and construe them as to include any omission or error without negligence. But not every loss caused by an omission or error is recoverable under the policy. In the first place, which is common ground, it must not be a deliberate error or omission.[36]

The precise wording of the liability that is covered will vary from policy to policy and the designer will only be covered for liability that falls within the description of the cover in the policy. Whether the policy only covers claims for negligence (in contract or tort) or is wider and covers breach of professional duty or civil liability depends on the wording.

16.3.2 Exceptions and exclusions

The designer should be aware of the exceptions or exclusions in the policy. These will vary from policy to policy but typical exceptions are:

---

[35] (1984) 27 BLR 58.
[36] ibid., at 92.

(1) the excess/deductible

(2) a claim brought about by any dishonesty, fraud or criminal act on the part of the designer

(3) any claim brought outside a specified geographical area, such as the UK

(4) libel and slander

(5) personal injuries caused to a third party unless they arise out of a breach of professional duty

(6) the usual war and atomic radiation exclusions.

There may also be an exclusion in respect of surveys of existing buildings unless the survey is carried out by someone with a qualification specifically stated in the policy. Another exclusion often found is in the following typical form:

> Any claim arising out of a specific liability assumed under a contract which increases the Insured's standard of care or measure of liability above that normally assumed under the Insured's profession's usual contractual or implied conditions of engagement of service.

This would exclude, for example, any 'fitness for purpose obligation' as discussed above. In addition, the policy may exclude any 'indemnities' or liquidated damages liabilities. Any indemnity (i.e. undertaking by the consultant to indemnify the client against specific claims) may remove from the insurer the ability to handle the claim, may reduce or eliminate the duty to mitigate loss, and will extend the limitation period. With liquidated damages clauses, the concern is that the figure for which the consultant may become liable may greatly exceed the actual loss.

It is essential to check that none of the exclusions contained in the insurer's conditions exclude a liability which the designer wishes to insure. (Some insurers are prepared to read the terms of appointment in detail on an individual project basis, and give specific comments on how to amend the document to bring it within cover). Of those referred to above, three are likely to be more important than the others. The first is the exclusion of claims arising under a contract. It is clear that such an exclusion would be likely to exclude from cover not only fitness for purpose (undertaken either by an implied or an express term in conditions of engagement) but also liability arising out of a collateral warranty. It is vital to agree policy wording to deal expressly with this issue. Typical available policy wording is:

> Notwithstanding Exclusion 'X' above, indemnity provided by this policy shall apply to collateral warranties or similar agreements provided by the Insured but only in so far as the benefits of such warranties are not greater or longer lasting than those given to the party with whom the Insured originally contracted and subject to the following exclusions, unless specifically otherwise agreed by the Company:
>
> (i) acceptance of or guarantee of fitness for purpose where this appears as any express term;
> (ii) any express guarantee including any relating to the period of a project;
> (iii) any express contractual penalty;
> (iv) any acceptance of liability for liquidated damages;
> (v) any assignment of a collateral warranty or similar agreement to:

(a) more than two parties in respect of assignments to funders, financiers and bankers
(b) more than one party in respect of assignments to any other parties.

These exclusions shall not apply to liability which would have attached to the Insured in the absence of such collateral warranties or agreements.

It is to be noted that this wording does not appear to exclude from cover a fitness for purpose obligation as an *implied* term (see (i) above). However, consideration would then have to be given to the meaning of 'not greater or longer lasting' in the opening paragraph.

The second important exclusion is the geographical limit. The wording of this exclusion should be carefully checked, and if the designer is likely to take on work overseas, as is becoming increasingly common, then this matter should be raised. The third (less common) exclusion is in respect of personal injuries. The designer should check that there is adequate cover in respect of death or personal injuries which may be caused to a third party who, in using the building or structure that the designer has designed, is injured as a result of negligent design or breach of duty.[37] Public liability and employer's liability policies will not necessarily provide cover in this respect.

16.3.3 Limit of indemnity

The policy will have a stated limit to the indemnity that is to be provided by the insurer. In some policies, the limit is on the basis of a global maximum in any period of insurance and, more commonly, the indemnity is on the basis that it will apply to each and every claim. In the former case, all claims will be met by the insurers provided they do not in total exceed the limit of indemnity. On an each and every claim basis, the limit of indemnity applies to each claim usually on the basis that the excess is met by the designer on each and every claim. An each and every claim basis will usually be the better proposition for the insured but will be more expensive in premium. What can constitute a single claim can sometimes cause problems, for example where multiple examples of a design are constructed, and each contain the same error, however the courts will usually take a sensible approach. In *Mitsubishi Electric v Royal London Insurance*,[38] where 94 toilet pods were installed with the same defect, the Court of Appeal determined that this amounted to one claim, and hence one deductible.

As to the limit of indemnity, this will be selected by the designer and its level is a matter of balance between cost of premium, the likelihood of claims at any particular value, the value of the construction projects on hand, and the commercial judgement of the designer.

Many professional bodies recommend limits for their members. Although these figures are of interest, every designer must decide the level of the limit of indemnity

---

[37] See e.g. *Clay v A.J. Crump & Sons Ltd* [1964] 1 QB 533 (CA); *Kelly v Frank Mears & Partners* (1981), Ct of Session, Scotland, unreported.
[38] (1994) 74 BLR 87.

which suits their own particular circumstances, and needs to bear in mind that they will have to find the excess of any successful claim brought against them to the extent that it exceeds the level of the limit of indemnity in the policy. It should be observed that the limit applies to the year in which the claim is made and not to either the year in which the work was done or to the year in which the claim is settled.

16.3.4 Employees

Where an employee has been negligent in the firm's business, it is likely that the injured party could, if it so chose, bring an action in tort against the employee directly. It is therefore essential that the policy wording should provide indemnity for any employee in respect of such liability incurred on the firm's business.

Where an employee has been negligent, and the insurer indemnifies the firm, the insurer can recover the full amount of its loss from the employee[39] by using its rights of subrogation to bring an action against the employee in the employer's name (though such procedure has been judicially criticised).[40] To avoid this happening the policy can contain a provision such as that set out in section 16.3.1 or, alternatively, the policy can contain a waiver of the rights of subrogation against employees who have been negligent.

16.3.5 'QC clause'

Professional designers are quite properly jealous of their reputations. Any litigation, particularly litigation with a bad outcome, can be damaging to reputation. Clearly, where an insurer has the right to take over and conduct such proceedings, its interests may be in conflict with the professional interests of the designer. It is for this reason that a QC clause should be included in professional indemnity policies. Such a clause provides that the designer will not be required to contest proceedings brought against the designer except where a Queen's Counsel has advised that the proceedings could be contested with the probability of success. Such a clause is of benefit both to the designer and to the insurer because it is protective of both their interests.

16.4 Avoiding disputes with insurers

Having paid the premiums to secure the benefits of a professional indemnity policy, it clearly makes sense for designers to do everything in their power to ensure they do not lose the benefit of their insurance cover because the insurer has avoided the contract or repudiated liability on the grounds of some inadvertent act or omission by the designer. For this reason, someone in the designer's organisation should be responsible for reading the proposal and the policy conditions and understanding them. A short

---

[39] *Lister v Romford Ice and Cold Storage Co. Ltd* [1957] 2 WLR 158.
[40] *Morris v Ford Motor Co. Ltd* [1973] QB 792.

check list is set out below which should not be considered as covering every matter that needs to be dealt with.

16.4.1 When completing a proposal form

(1) Answer all the questions fully and honestly and, where appropriate, state that they are accurate to the best of the designer's belief.

(2) Consider whether there are any matters which a prudent insurer would wish to take into account in deciding whether to provide cover: if so, disclose them. This should include asking insurers if they want details of collateral warranties entered into.

(3) Ask for a copy of the full policy conditions. Do not rely on advertising brochures. Having obtained the conditions, read them and check that the conditions and the exclusions correspond with what is required. Check, in particular, the items set out in section 16.3.

(4) Keep a clear record of any representations made by the insurer or the broker. The principle of utmost good faith applies to the insurer as well. Brokers can incur liability to the insured.

(5) Insofar as it is possible, satisfy yourself that the proposed insurer has status in the professional indemnity field.

(6) Decide whether extensions are required to the policy: e.g. to cover collateral warranties, the previous business of any partners; persons who are no longer partners – and that such cover extends to their estates should they die; loss of documents; libel and slander; dishonesty of employees.

(7) Make enquiries in writing to senior staff within the firm, and to those to whom design has been sub-contracted (where the firm retains responsibility), requiring answers in writing, as to any matters which they are aware of that should be disclosed to insurers. Check that each addressee responds. It is not necessary to ask every employee, merely those who should be aware of such matters: *Australian and New Zealand Bank Ltd v Colonial and Eagle Wharves Ltd and Boag.*[41]

(8) Decide on the limit of indemnity.

16.4.2 During the currency of the policy

(1) Notify any changes in the partnership, such as new partners/directors/consultants or retiring partners/directors/consultants.

(2) Obtain insurer's agreement to cover any new matters that were not contemplated initially, e.g. a contract outside the geographical limit of the policy.

(3) Ensure not only that any claims received are notified extremely promptly, in accordance with the policy provisions, but also anything that might later develop into a

---

[41] [1960] 2 Lloyd's Rep 241.

claim, e.g. complaints of any kind of defects. Where that provision is to notify on becoming aware of circumstances which might give rise to a claim, it is better to be over cautious and notify all such matters promptly.

(4) Do not in any circumstances agree to compromise or admit liability in respect of any claim or any possible claim.

(5) Do not enter into collateral warranties which have terms that are at variance with the cover provided by the policy.

16.4.3 On renewal of policy

Before paying the premium, read the proposal, if any, the policy and any schedule or schedules, and check every item to see whether insurers should be notified of any changed material facts or changed requirements or any other matters. Make enquiries of staff as set out at (7) above.

16.5 *Professional indemnity insurance for design and build contracts*

This section, which relates to professional indemnity insurance for design and build contracts, should be read in conjunction with the information above for the simple reason that design and build contractors face all the problems of a consultant designer but with many additional difficulties.

Nowadays it is common practice to require design-build contractors to carry professional indemnity insurance (although it would be rare to require them to hold latent defects insurance, this would normally be carried by the employer, if at all, see 16.7.2 below) There is no doubt that contractors and sub-contractors engaged in the design and build field should have professional indemnity insurance, which should be regarded as an essential feature of the design and build process. The design and build contractor is not only constructing the works but also designing them. This is of course a fundamentally different position for the contractor than in the traditional contracting arrangements. A design failure is a potential source of major financial loss and indemnity insurance can help to mitigate financial loss resulting from the failure; however, it should not be regarded as a panacea.

Employers who are not professionally advised may not even consider the insurance aspect of design and build contracts and may, accordingly, fail to take any steps to protect their interests. If they do consider the matter, they will wish to raise the question of professional indemnity insurance with potential contractors, in order to ascertain whether or not their arrangements are satisfactory. For example, the JCT Design and Build Contract 2011 edition requires the contractor to insure the design obligation, although earlier editions did not, nor does the JCT Minor Works Building Contract.

Many contractors believe that their other insurance policies provide them with sufficient protection in respect of design work. This is not so. The usual contractors' all risks policy normally excludes design risks entirely. 'All Risks' does not mean all risks that the contractor undertakes. The usual policy is quite restrictive in its cover. Policies may provide indemnity in respect of damage caused by negligent design but limited to work which is not of itself defective and give no indemnity in respect of the actual defective part itself. Even if the cover does provide that sort of indemnity, the cover often ceases at the end of the construction period or the defects liability period. Design errors do have a habit of showing themselves many years after completion of the building. Furthermore, such a policy usually provides no indemnity in the absence of physical damage or in respect of consequential loss.

Some difficult points of legal construction arose on a contractor's all risks policy in *Cementation Piling and Foundations Ltd v Aegon Insurance Co. Ltd and Commercial Union Insurance Co. Plc.*[42] Cementation sought to recover losses suffered in rectifying gaps and voids in diaphragm walls, forming part of the construction of a series of quays within the existing dock at Barrow-in Furness which they had been contracted to carry out. There were admitted defects in design, materials and workmanship. Commercial Union's policy indemnified Cementation in respect of '. . . physical loss or damage to the property insured'. This was subject to an exception in respect of '. . . the cost of replacing or rectifying defects in design, materials or workmanship unless the property insured suffers actual loss, destruction or damage as a result of such defect'. It was common ground that the costs of removing escaped sand and filling the gap left where the sand had escaped was 'physical damage'. The parties differed as to whether the making good of the gaps between the concrete sections was 'physical damage'. Aegon argued that it was not possible to fill the gaps left by the sand without also making good the gaps between the concrete sections. Commercial Union's position was that the cover was merely property cover and not intended to cover liability. It would follow, CU said, that if the policy was held to cover repairs rendered necessary by negligence, the policy would be extended beyond the scope agreed by the parties at the outset. Whilst the deputy judge accepted that his construction of the policy did involve an element of guarantee, that was consistent with the plain words of the policy. His decision was that Commercial Union was liable to indemnify Cementation.

Nor are contractors' 'public liability' policies usually of any assistance in respect of design failures. The wording of such policies varies considerably from policy to policy and design risks are normally expressly excluded or there is limited cover as described above in relation to contractors' all risks policies. Indeed, by its very nature, such a policy will not generally apply to the contract works themselves but rather to personal injury or damage to property other than the contract works. It follows that the usual contractors' policies are not adequate to provide for indemnity in respect of design liability.

16.5.1 The cover

The principle of professional indemnity insurance for design and build contractors is the same as that for architects and engineers. The cover usually provided will only be

---

[42][1993] 1 Lloyd's Rep 526.

in respect of the 'negligent act, error or omission' of contractors in the performance of their 'professional activities'. The policy wording for the main operative clause for design and build contractors and other parts of the construction industry is often different to the policies of the construction professions. One policy wording, for example, is in the following form:

> We ... agree to indemnify the Assured for any sum or sums which the Assured may become legally liable to pay ... as a direct result of negligence on the part of the Assured in the conduct and execution of the professional activities and duties as herein defined.

An argument sometimes develops as to whether 'negligence' in a clause such as this should properly be construed as meaning claims in tort or for breach of a contract term as to reasonable skill and care or both of these. If it were taken to mean only tortious liability, then the designer would not be insured for breach of a reasonable skill and care obligation in a contract. Normally a court would give this wording a construction that is liberal to the insured, i.e. covering breaches of contract. However, the converse is a possibility: the word 'negligence', in circumstances where a limitation statute was being construed, was said by the court to only apply to tort.[43]

Given these possible difficulties a contractor offered this policy would be well advised to consider whether it should seek to have the wording changed. If that is not possible, then it may seek to have the word 'negligence' defined for the purposes of the policy to include, say, breach of any obligation at common law to use reasonable skill and care and/or breach of any obligation to exercise reasonable skill and care whether arising under a contract (by reason of either an express or implied term) or under statute or otherwise.

Policy wording sometimes found in construction, for example in product liability policies, is as follows:

> ... against all sums which the Insured shall become liable at law to pay as damages and such sums for which liability in tort or under statute shall attach to some party or parties other than the Insured but for which liability is assumed by the Insured under indemnity clauses incorporated in contracts and/or agreements. ...

The words 'liability at law' in this policy were considered in *M/S Aswan Engineering Establishment Co. v Iron Trades Mutual Insurance Co. Ltd*[44] where the court found it was not limited to tort. Mr Justice Hobhouse said:

> A policy of this kind needs to be construed having regard to the ordinary use of language. If the words used have an ordinary and natural meaning that is reasonably clear that is the meaning which should be adopted and the court should not entertain an obscure or contrived

---

[43] *Iron Trades Mutual Insurance Co. Ltd & Others v J. K. Buckenham Ltd* [1990] 1 All ER 808; [1989] 2 Lloyd's Rep 85 at First Instance and in *Société Commerciale de Reassurance v ERAS (International) Ltd* [1992] 2 All ER 82; [1992] 1 Lloyd's Rep. 570 in the Court of Appeal.
[44] [1989] 1 Lloyd's Rep 289.

argument to give these words some different meaning. This principle is reinforced where it is the insurance company that is seeking to reject the ordinary meaning and where the document is, as here, a standard form document produced by the insurance company itself. 'Liable at law' on its ordinary meaning simply means legal liability. This is a commonplace, though to a lawyer tautologous phrase, and is used in the title of the policy itself, 'third party (legal and contractual liability) insurance.'[45]

The court was referred to two Canadian cases, where a different view was formed, but the court declined to follow those decisions.[46]

16.5.2 Terms and fitness for purpose

Two fundamentally important points for design and build contractors arise from the basis of the insurance. First, the contractor's 'professional activities' must be carefully and adequately stated in the policy so that all the contractor's design activities fall within the scope of the policy. If contractors have any doubt as to whether part of their design operation falls within the policy they should clarify the position with their insurers forthwith and, if necessary, a suitable endorsement should be provided to the policy.

Secondly, as discussed in Chapter 7, there is *usually* to be implied into design and build contracts a term that the design will be fit for its purpose. If such an obligation is to be implied or is expressly provided for in the contract, then the professional indemnity policy will not provide an indemnity in respect of a breach of the fitness for purpose obligation unless there is also negligence; the reason for this is that the usual indemnity provided is on the basis of any 'negligent act, error or omission' and not for breach of some absolute obligation undertaken by a contractor under its contract (as discussed in Chapter 14, the JCT contracts avoid the imposition of a fitness for purpose obligation, whereas the FIDIC forms include it, and others such as NEC3 offer alternative clauses). Design and build contractors should always ascertain whether they are adequately insured to cover the liability level in the projects they are undertaking.

The mere fact that a design and build contractor engages independent architects and engineers to provide the whole or part of the design will not affect its liability under the contract to the employer – the contractor's duty is to the employer and the primary liability will fall on the contractor when there is a design defect. Whether or not the contractor can recover from the independent architects or engineers is irrelevant to the contractor's duty to the employer; it follows that, even in circumstances where the contractor sub-lets the design, it should still have professional indemnity insurance cover and should see that the cover provided by the policy extends to sub-letting the design, if necessary, by an appropriate endorsement to the policy. Contractors should

---

[45] ibid., at 293.
[46] *Canadian Indemnity Co. v Andrews and George Co.* [1953] 1 SCR 19; *Dominion Bridge Co. Ltd v Toronto General Insurance Co.* (1964) 1 Lloyd's Rep. 194.

take particular care when involved in a procurement arrangement where they accept liability for the design of a novated consultant.[47] They should check carefully that their policy is drafted widely enough to cover any design for which they become responsible, even if the design work was carried out entirely by the consultant, and before the novation took place.

Particular difficulties can arise for contractors that do not regularly undertake design and build projects. A professional indemnity insurance policy will usually provide indemnity in respect of claims that are notified during the period of the policy, usually 12 months. This does not pose a problem to those contractors who regularly engage in design and build work and renew their professional indemnity policy every year because the indemnity will usually apply irrespective of when the original design error took place.

Those contractors who do not regularly engage in such work have three options. First, do not take out insurance at all. Second, if they take out an annually renewable policy, they should continue to pay the premium for a great many years: actions can be brought against negligent designing contractors very many years after completion of the work and it is not possible to say with any degree of certainty when a contractor could safely cease renewing the policy. Third, although it is not at all common, it is possible to arrange professional indemnity insurance on a single project basis and this could prove to be a more economic course for a contractor who only rarely engaged in design and build projects. However, these policies have a severe handicap in that they will usually have a short life, often only up to a fixed period of time after practical completion. It may be that the insurance market would be prepared to extend that period, but if they did so agree, it would be likely to be a relatively short period. It follows that such a policy would provide no indemnity outside the specified period. However, it might be possible by a combination of such a policy and a limitation of liability clause in the design and build contract to limit the contractor's liability to the employer by agreement; but this is very unlikely to be effective against those with whom it is not in contractual relations.

16.5.3 Proposal form

Insurers will usually ask more questions of design and build contractors in the proposal form than they would of architects and engineers in private practice. Indeed, the amount of the premium can be affected by the professional qualifications and experience of the contractors in-house design team, the insurance cover carried by any firms to whom design is sub-let, the percentage of work value involved in design as opposed to the total project value and, above all, the type of work undertaken to be designed. It is of the utmost importance that these, and all the other questions in the proposal form, are fully and accurately answered in order to prevent the risk of insurers avoiding the policy for nondisclosure or misrepresentation (see section 16.2).

---

[47] See *Blyth and Blyth v Carillion Construction Ltd* (2001) 79 Con LR 142, see section 15.7.

16.5.4 Claims

As with architects and engineers in private practice, there is little point in paying premiums and then losing the benefit of the insurance cover because the insurer has avoided the contract or repudiated liability; design and build contractors should have regard to the suggestions in the procedure for seeking to avoid disputes with their insurers set out at section 16.4. Additionally, they should have in mind the following three points.

First, claims or alleged defects should be notified immediately. It is particularly difficult in a design and build contract to say whether a defect is due to design or workmanship: in many cases it may be a mixture of the two. It is clearly of the utmost importance for the contractor to err on the side of caution and notify insurers immediately of any matter which may involve an allegation of design defects. Second, a design and build contractor must not make good any defects without its insurer's consent. Third, difficult issues can arise as to whether the design defect is the responsibility of the contractor or whether it is in fact the responsibility of the employer by reason of some requirement of the employer. In particular, the JCT Design and Build Contract provides no machinery for resolving discrepancies between the Employer's Requirements and the Contractor's Proposals. Clearly, the contractor's insurers would have to be satisfied that the fault lay with the contractor and not with the employer before agreeing to indemnify the contractor.

16.6 Professional indemnity – changing insurers

There is benefit in continuing to renew cover with the same insurer in the professional indemnity field. Indeed, the consequences of failing to do so can be horrific. It is good advice not to change insurers unless the terms and/or premium are wholly unacceptable. Loyalty and track record do count for something when issues such as nondisclosure or late notification arise. And there may be different policies from insurer to insurer in relation to collateral warranties – the position agreed with one insurer, at the time a warranty is given, will not bind a different insurer at a later date when a claim arises under that policy.

There can also be difficulties in ascertaining under which policy a claim falls. An example is where defects arise. Defects of a minor nature do arise regularly in construction. When do they become a matter to be notified to insurers? Take a situation where minor defects are known about, but not notified to insurers because they are regarded as routine construction defects. The defects then appear to be more serious and are notified, after a new insurer has taken over. There is the risk that the old insurer will seek to avoid liability by reason of late notification and the new insurer will seek to avoid liability by non-disclosure (saying that it should have been told before it took on the risk).

Other difficulties can arise where a specific allegation of negligence is made against say, an architect, by a client and, later, after a new insurer has come on risk, other allegations of negligence are made in relation to other matters on the same or a different project for the same client. This is discussed in section 16.2.5 where the case of *Thorman & Others v New Hampshire Insurance Co. Ltd and the Home Insurance Co.*[48] is considered.

16.7 *Other types of insurance*

16.7.1 Decennial insurance

A system has developed in France and, through France, in many parts of Africa and the Middle East, that provides for there to be a pool of money available immediately a serious construction failure comes to light, so that the building owner can get on with remedial works without delay. In due course the parties can sort out who is liable for what, but at least whilst that is going on the building owner has had the building repaired. This is referred to as 'decennial insurance' of construction works, as it originates form the liability regime established through the French Civil Code (see Chapter 17). The provisions in France are for the works to be insured for 10 years after handover and this is usually provided on the payment of a single premium at the time when the structure is first at risk. The insurance is normally to cover material damages to the structural elements of a building, although it can sometimes be extended to cover the weather shield, and usually only pays a claim when there is actual physical damage to the property caused by latent defects. There is usually no consequential loss coverage and it is a pre-requisite of the insurance policy that the plans are checked, and that there are periodic inspections by the insurer's professional representatives at a cost to be borne by the assured, all of which has to take place prior to the start of the project.

16.7.2 Latent defects insurance

A similar type of insurance is now available in the UK, where it is often termed 'latent defects insurance'. It was initially introduced by a UK-based insurer which was a subsidiary of a French company providing decennial insurance, and the UK version affords a similar scope of cover.

A typical latent defects insurance policy would be taken out by the owner of the building and could optionally extend to the successors in title of the building. It would cover the cost of repairs and certain other costs such as architects' and surveyors' fees. The policy will not cover every repair; it will be limited to major and serious problems such as latent defects in materials, construction or design which result in actual collapse or a threat of collapse or total prevention of the use of the building by some statutory order such as a dangerous structures notice. In other words, this is a major disaster type of insurance and will not usually extend to less severe construction problems.

---

[48] [1988] 1 Lloyd's Rep 7.

The cover extends for 10 or sometimes 12 years following practical completion, and would not cover defects that were already apparent at that stage. As with decennial insurance, it does not normally remove the need for the design consultants to maintain their own PII cover, as once the damage has been rectified, the insurers may try to recover their losses from the design team. Recently it has become more common, however, for insurers to waive these rights of subrogation.[49]

The insurance premium is likely to be a sum of about 1.5% of construction cost (which employers are generally unwilling to pay)[50] but, in addition, it will usually be a condition of the insurance that owners employ at their own expense the services of an inspector approved by the insurer. That inspector will have the duty of examining and verifying the design and the method of work, workmanship and materials used during the construction. This inspection function can of course add enormously to the cost of the construction process and there is a tendency for an over-cautious design in such circumstances, which can also increase cost.

16.7.3 BUILD

The Construction Industry Sector Group of the National Economic Development Council published a report in 1988: *Building Users' Insurance against Latent Defects*, known as BUILD. One major recommendation was that there should be insurance taken out by the developer at an early stage, well before work starts on site. This would be a non-cancelable material damage policy against specified latent defects and damage lasting for 10 years from practical completion. They suggested it should cover at least the structure, the foundations and the weather shield envelope. It should be transferable to successive owners and tenants of the whole building. Where there were multiple tenants, the landlord would indemnify tenants on a back-to-back basis with the policy benefits. It was also suggested that insurers should waive their rights of subrogation against the party liable to the developer, such as the architect or engineer.

This particular form of latent defects insurance was advocated by Latham,[51] and some insurers have taken to providing this type of cover in the UK, although its use is not widespread. There is, generally, no waiver of subrogation rights, leaving it open to the insurer to pursue the negligent designer. In practice, insurers usually require independent verification of the project, not only the design but also the construction, at the expense of the insured. Insurers will consider the giving of cover on completed buildings but because they will not have had the opportunity of that verification process, the premiums will be higher.

---

[49] Vivien Ramsey, *Construction Law Handbook*, 7th edn (London: Thomas Telford, 2007).
[50] Jeffrey Brown, *Do Design and Build Insurance Policy Wordings Fit the Bill?*, Society of Construction Law, Paper D120 (London: SCL, 2011).
[51] Sir Michael Latham, *Constructing the Team* (London: HMSO, 1994).

16.7.4 Single project insurance

A further type of insurance policy is termed 'single project insurance'. This can take many forms, and in fact the term is understood differently in different insurance markets,[52] so the exact cover should always be checked carefully. In some it refers to 'wrap-up' insurance comprising the normal contractor's all-risks insurance, public liability insurance, together with professional indemnity insurance. In other insurance markets it refers only to professional indemnity, i.e. it is similar in approach to taking out a 'professional indemnity' policy on an individual project, and covers failure to provide, or providing incorrect, professional duties. Where the policy covers professional indemnity, it would cover the design consultants and the contractor, but only if it is providing a design service. There need not be an actual physical loss or damage to the building, and consequential and economic loss is covered insofar as it would be covered under a normal annual PI policy. The project insurance usually only provides cover for the project during construction and until the end of the defects liability period, although sometimes it may extend for a few years afterwards (normally not more than five years). The policy is issued in the joint names of the client and the consultants and normally, but not always, rights of subrogation will be waived. However it is normally essential to maintain individual PI insurance policies alongside the project insurance, to cover claims made after this insurance policy comes to an end as well as to cover other projects undertaken by the consultant.

---

[52] Nael G. Bunni, *Risk and Insurance in Construction*, 2nd edn (London: Spon Press, 2003), p. 393.

Chapter 17
Design Liability in the EU

The construction sector plays an important role in the European economy, generating almost 10 per cent of GDP and creating 20 million jobs. In order to strengthen the internal market, the European Commission has issued directives aimed at encouraging the free flow of goods and services in the sector, for example the Public Procurement Directive 2004/18/EC and the Professional Qualifications Directive 2005/36/EC (both currently under review). It has also strived to achieve a level playing field across the member countries by harmonising various aspects of construction regulation, examples being building energy efficiency, construction site health and safety, and construction products.

Contract law and professional liability have, however lagged behind, perhaps due to the difficulty of normalising very different legal systems. There have been many comparative studies of EU law. A key paper that focused on construction liability was that of Claude Mathurin, a French *Ingenieur General des Ponts et Chaussees* (a road and bridge engineer that has attended France's most prestigious engineering school), in 1990.[1] This included an analysis of practice in the Member States, and recommended consideration of three possible directives, including one to harmonise rules on post-construction liability, guarantees and insurance. However that recommendation was never implemented.

Subsequently, an extensive amount of work on European contract law has been undertaken by academic scholars, with the aim of identifying a set of common legal principles,[2] in part funded by the European Commission. In 2005, a network of researchers was established to prepare a Draft Common Frame of Reference (DCFR). This led to a series of publications[3] culminating in 2008 in a DCFR comprising six

---

[1] Claude Mathurin, *Study of Responsibilities, Guarantees and Insurance in the Construction Industry with a View to Harmonisation at Community Level: Final Report (Condensed Version)* (EC Commission, 1990).

[2] See e.g. Ole Lando and Hugh Beale (eds), *The Principles of European Contract Law, Parts I and II* (Kluwer Law International, 2000); Ole Lando, Eric Clive, André Prüm and Reinhard Zimmermann (eds), *Principles of European Contract Law, Part III* (Zuidpoolsingel: Kluwer Law International, 2003).

[3] See e.g. M. Barendrecht, C. Jansen, M. Loos, A. Pinna, R. Cascao and S. van Gulijk, *Principles of European Law, Service Contracts (PELSC)* (Munich: Sellier, 2007), Chapter 2 'Construction'; or Acquis Group, *Principles of European Law. Contracts 1* (Munich: Sellier, 2007).

---

volumes and 6,653 pages (prepared by the Study Group on a European Civil Code and the Research Group on EC Private Law – the Acquis Group).[4]

The European Commission in its 2003 *Action Plan for a European Contract Law*[5] had stated that the DCFR might fulfil two distinct purposes: to act as a legislator's guide or toolbox, setting out 'fundamental principles, definitions and model rules' for revising existing consumer directives; and to provide the basis of a possible 'Optional Instrument' on contract law. Following publication of the DCFR in July 2010 the EU published a Green Paper setting out various options with regard to regularising contract law. These ranged from doing nothing, through creating a CFR toolbox in various forms, a recommendation to Member States on contract law, an Optional Instrument, a harmonising Directive on European contract law, to a full-blown European Civil Code. Following a consultation process in October 2011, the Commission proposed a Common European Sales Law (CESL), comprising a single set of rules for cross-border contracts in all 27 EU countries. The CESL rules are voluntary, apply primarily to sale of goods contracts, and may be adopted in business-to-business, or business-to-consumer transactions. This has now received approval and the European Parliament is expected to pass the CESL early in 2013.

Apart from this voluntary tool, there are some common rules that affect contracts and transactions (examples being Directive 2011/83/EU on Consumer Rights, Directive 2000/31/EC on Certain Legal Aspects of Information Society Services, in particular electronic commerce, Directive 2011/7/EU on combating late payment in commercial transactions, and Directive 93/13/EEC on unfair terms in consumer contracts). However together these cover only limited aspects of contract law and liability. In the meantime significant differences still remain that are directly relevant to design liability.

Below is a brief summary of design liability in several of the member countries. The profiles are presented as an outline comparative analysis only, any party considering working for the first time in an unfamiliar country would of course need to take legal advice as to the exact requirements.

17.1 Belgium[6]

The liability of participants in the construction process is mainly governed by provisions of the Civil Code (*Code Civil Belge*, CCB) and by judicial interpretations of that legislation. The Code is modelled closely on the French civil code as discussed below,

---

[4]C. von Bar, E. Clive and H. Schulte-Nölke (eds), *Principles, Definitions and Model Rules of European Private Law. Draft Common Frame of Reference (DCFR). Interim Outline Edition* (Munich: Sellier, 2008); in particular Book IV, Part C, Chapter 3 'Construction'. An outline of the DCFR is also published, see The Study Group on a European Civil Code and the Research Group on EC Private Law (Acquis Group): *Principles, Definitions and Model Rules of European Private Law, Draft Common Frame of Reference (DCFR)* Outline Edition (Munich: Sellier European Law Publishers GmbH, 2009).

[5]Communication of 12 February 2003, COM (2003) 68 fin., O.J. C 63 of 15 March 2003.

[6]With thanks to Professor Benoît Kohl of the University of Liège (also attorney at the Brussels Bar and invited Professor at the University of Paris II – Pantheon Assas), and to Michel Procès, Université Catholique de Louvain, UCL LOCI, Faculté d'architecture, d'ingénierie architecturale, d'urbanisme, for their helpful comments on drafts of this section.

but there are some significant differences both in the Code itself, and in its interpretation. The liability of the parties can be contractually modified with the exception of some legally binding provisions.

An architect's title and function are protected, in the sense that only architects may use the title, 'architect' and only architects must be employed on certain specialised tasks. Architects have a professional monopoly as only they have the authority to draw up and sign the documents attached to planning permissions. This applies to all construction works requiring a construction permit (with the exception of minor works mentioned on lists defined by the Regional Authorities; and civil works in the Flemish Region, so that bridges, tunnels, etc. do not need the intervention of an architect). For these works, the *maitre d'ouvrage* (public or private client) must work in association with an architect in order to draft plans and control the execution of works (§4,Law of 20 February 1939; and Law of 26 June 1963, which creates the Order of Architects). This protected position is further reinforced by the obligation to decline any work for which they are not retained for supervision, unless assured that another architect will have responsibility for that task. Architects are also required to remain independent of the contractor in all circumstances, i.e. they may not be appointed by, paid by or otherwise linked in any way with the contractor. The responsibilities of an architect are considerable and include the structural stability of the building, even though an engineer may have been involved in the project.

The contractor and architect are of course liable to the client under their contracts. Extra-contractual liability (tort), which covers both liability towards third parties and liability towards clients for so called 'extra-contractual' faults, is governed by Articles 1382 *et seq.* of the Civil Code, whereby a person is responsible for their own (§1384 para. 1) and their employees (§1384 para. 3, 1797) actions. Any third person who has suffered damage arising from the activity of a construction party may claim on the grounds of Article 1382 liability. Parties to a contract may only claim under Article 1382 in exceptional circumstances, for example in relation to activities beyond those the other party was contracted to perform, or where the breach of contract is also a criminal offence.

Parties are jointly and severally liable when several persons are involved in fulfilling the same duty (so-called '*in solidum*' liability) or where it is stipulated by law (§§ 1200–16). This applies whether there are contracts in place or if an extra-contractual obligation arises.

In addition, the Code sets up a particular liability regime with respect to construction projects. Under this, architects and contractors are jointly liable for defects for a period of 10 years as follows:

- 10 years liability for defects which are serious enough to put at risk the solidity of the constructed structure or of an important part of it (§§1792 and 2270). This decennial liability is mandatory, i.e. the parties cannot contractually restrict it. (These defects need to have caused damage such that the solidity of the building is currently in danger, or is certain to be in danger in the future). This liability applies to any such serious defect, even if it was apparent at the time of accepting the works.
- a maximum of 10 years liability for defects called 'venial' or ordinary, which affect the building but are out of the scope of decennial liability. This only applies to defects hidden at the time of accepting the works. The parties are free to agree a shorter period.

After the latent defect appears, the claimant must file a claim within a 'reasonable' time or else claimants will be deemed to have waived their rights regarding this defect.

There is no equivalent under the Belgian Code to the French Code requirements of a two-year warranty for other aspects, i.e. movable/'dissociable' elements (§§1792–3), or the one-year warranty for all defects (§§1792–6), as discussed in the next section. In addition, unlike France, the Article 1792 warranty does not expressly extend to 'inseparable and integral parts of the works', nor to defects which render the works unsuitable for its purpose. However the contract might include such provisions.

The level of liability for errors resulting in serious defects is strict (§1792), otherwise it will depend upon the terms of the relevant contract (§1137 and 1147, CCB). If they are strict (an obligation of result), then the employer will not need to prove negligence, nor will it need to demonstrate causation, for example a contractor or architect would be automatically liable should a defect appear. On the other hand, if the undertaking was to use reasonable skill and care, the employer will need to prove causation and negligence. In practice, outside of the code warranties, the basis of liability is generally negligence. In determining whether it is reasonable to impose a strict obligation the court would look at the terms of contract, the parties' expertise, whether an architect was engaged on the project, and the current state of technology. Liability in contract may therefore be strict in specific situations, e.g. if a turnkey contract is used, or a specialist contractor engaged (e.g. waterproofing, glazing, etc.) and if the contractor is not compelled to construct the project in a particular way.

The legal limitation for bringing an action for breach of contract is 10 years. For extra-contractual liability (tort), claimants purporting to have suffered a damage as a result of fault of the architect must initiate legal action within five years of the date when they had knowledge of the damage (or of its aggravation) and of the identity of the liable person. The claim becomes statute-barred after 20 years following the day when the fault was committed (§2262*bis*).

For architects, insurance companies providing cover will often require them to use standard contracts with employers, otherwise standard terms are not normally used. It is possible by agreement to limit liability to some extent (e.g. for ground conditions, if these are impossible to ascertain), although in practice such limitations are rare. It is also possible to limit liability for certain technical design services, but not for severe hidden defects. As in Italy, architects in Belgium were until recently personally exclusively and solely liable (i.e. could not spread the liability through a partnership). However this changed in 2007 and they may now form partnerships or a private company.

There is generally no legal obligation to carry insurance of construction risks with the exception of professional liability insurance, which must be taken out by architects, health and safety coordinators and expert land surveyors. The architect is obliged to carry insurance covering all professional liabilities, including decennial liability, under Article 5 of the law of 20 February 1939 on the protection of the title and profession of architects. There is currently a proposal to introduce a new statute that will extend this duty to all building contractors, but this has not yet been approved by Parliament.

Belgian architects and insurance companies have established a private technical directorate (*bureaux de controles techniques* as in France), to reduce the risk of building defects. Supervision by one of these organisations is sometimes required if 10-year liability insurance is to be provided. Approval by the technical inspectorate is usually accepted by the insurance companies as evidence of sound practice.

17.2 France[7]

In France a wide variety of procurement routes are used, including traditional and design-build. Management forms of procurement are often used and are more common than in the UK. Architects who are sole practitioners or directors of a practice must be registered with the *Ordre des Architectes* (under Law No. 77-2 of 3 January 1977 and Decree No 77-1481 of 28 December 1977). An architect is required to sign and submit the planning application for all projects whose ground plan area is greater than $170 \, m^2$ (or $800 \, m^2$ if an agricultural building). Use of the title 'engineer' is not regulated, although the title *Ingénieur diplomé* (Diploma Engineer), which is very prestigious, may only be used by those who have completed one of the training programmes listed by the *Commission des titres d'ingénieur* (Commission for Engineer Titles).[8]

France has a codified legal system. General contractual liability is governed by §§1134*ff* of the Civil Code (*Code Civil*, CC),[9] in particular Article 1147, which covers liability for breach of contract. The legal basis of extra-contractual liability (tort) is set out in the five general clauses, Articles 1382–86, which concern damages caused to third parties and damages which are not connected with performance of the contract. Generally, in French law, a person cannot bring a remedy under tort law if they have a contractual relationship with the person causing the harm, even if this would benefit the injured party (under the '*principe de non-cumul*').[10] Under Articles 1383 and 1384 a contractor, for example, would be liable to third parties for damages caused by the building itself or as a result of the construction activities, but not under tort to someone it was contracting with, e.g. an employer on a site visit. The '*action directe*' principle is also important: if a buyer enters into a contract with an intermediate (e.g. a building contractor), it has a contractual claim against any other party in the contracting chain (e.g. the supplier of the materials). Moreover, the unpaid subcontractor has a direct claim against the employer.

Until 2008, the Code stated that liability for breach of contract normally extends for 30 years (§2262) and that tortious claims were subject to a 10-year limitation period (§2270-1). This has been revised, and the general limitation period is 5 years for

---

[7] With thanks to Philip Ridgway of aaPGR – Prat Gigou Ridgway architects, Professor Benoît Kohl of the University of Liège (also attorney at the Brussels Bar and invited Professor at the University of Paris II – Pantheon Assas), and Sam Ross-Gower of RB-Architectes for their helpful comments on drafts of this section.

[8] Centre d'Études d'Assurance (CEA), *Liabilities in Europe* (Belgium: CEA, 2004).

[9] Can be accessed at www.legifrance.gouv.fr (note the English version on this site has not been updated since 2006).

[10] Ulrich Magnus and Hans-W. Micklitz, *Comparative Analysis of National Liability Systems for Remedying Damage Caused by Defective Consumer Services*. Report of study commissioned by the European Commission (Brussels, 2004).

breaches of contract (§2224), and 10 years for tort (§2226). However there are special provisions regarding construction contracts which are outlined below.

The French legal system distinguishes between two different kinds of obligations, *obligation de moyens* (obligation of means) and *obligation de résultat* (obligation of result). For an *obligation de moyens* parties cannot be held liable unless they commit a fault, which the claimant has to prove, whereas for a *obligation de résultat* parties are liable for the non-performance or late-performance of the contract without the need to prove a fault. In France, both contractors and consultants are generally under an obligation of result, at least so far as constructed projects are concerned. For other services (i.e. advice not relating to a realised project) or for errors not covered by the statutory warranties described below, architects would generally be under an *obligation de moyens*.

Contractors, engineers, architects, those selling the completed building, and all those who are linked to the principal by the *contrat de louage d'ouvrage* are subject to a particular liability regime in addition to the normal liabilities under contract and tort. The system originates from the Law No 78-12 of 4 January 1978, also known as the 'Spinetta Law', and applies to any construction, renovation and/or rehabilitation of a structure or building. The liability cannot be excluded or limited, and any clause in a contract attempting to do this will be deemed void (§§1792-5). The duration of the guarantee is:

1. Perfect completion guarantee (*garantie de parfait achevement*; §1792-6) covering all shortcomings, non-compliances as well as apparent and latent defects, which applies for a limited period of time (one year) following approval by the owner (handover). Only building contractors are subject to this liability.
2. Good functioning guarantee (*garantie de bon fonctionnement*; §1792-3). This lasts for minimum of two years, and concerns defective functioning elements of building's equipment, which are not integral to the building structure or fabric. This liability applies to both contractors and architects.
3. Decennial liability (*responsabilité décennale*; §§1792, 1792-2 and 2270).

Decennial liability applies to both contractors and architects. Article 1792 states that 'Any builder of a work is liable as of right, towards the building owner or purchaser, for damages, even resulting from a defect of the ground, which imperil the strength of the building or which, affecting it in one of its constituent parts or one of its elements of equipment, render it unsuitable for its purposes'. Liability is therefore presumed, unless the 'constructor' can show the damage was caused by an extraneous event. An extraneous event would include *force majeure* and other events outside the architect's or contractor's control, except for ground conditions. It would apply if the client, for example, insists that specific materials are used that ultimately are the cause of the defect, but this would be subject to the architect or contractor being able to demonstrate that they had advised the client against doing this.

The liability extends for 10 years (§2270) following approval, and extends to 'all shortcomings indicated by the building owner, either through reservations mentioned in the memorandum of approval, or by way of written notice as to those revealed after the approval' (§1792-6). It concerns defects which:

- compromise the solidity of the structure;
- affect solidity of inseparable elements of equipment, i.e. elements incorporated into the structure in such way that removal, dismantle or replacement of these elements cannot be performed without deterioration of, or removal of material from, the structure;
- affect constituent elements of the works or of its equipment causing the works to be unsuitable for purpose.[11]

The liability is owed to the client, and to any successor acquiring an interest in the property. The overall effect of the above is that before acceptance of the works, architects are liable for any breach of design or other contractual duties (§1147); after acceptance they are under a strict liability for serious defects that appear in the building, and this liability extends for 10 years (§§1792 and 2270-1). As architects and engineers are jointly responsible with the contractor, the client may pursue the designer for any major fault that appears. If there is a claim, all three are normally joined in the action and damages apportioned between them.

The client does not need to prove that the major defect was caused by any fault by a party (i.e. causation), simply that it has occurred. However causation will need to be established when resolving the contribution between the parties. The joint liability would apply to architects even if not involved in supervising the building works, although lack of site involvement would act as a defence to a contribution claim, provided they could show the defect originated during the construction phase and was not due to an inherent flaw in their design.

Construction contracts are made up of general conditions (*cahier des clauses administratives générales,* or CCAG) and special conditions (*cahier des clauses administratives particulières,* or CCAP). The CCAG comprises clauses which are common to any project type and refer to legal codes, French standards, etc. The CCAP includes the parties' details, the particulars of the project, agreed payment dates, fines for late completion, etc. In the public sector, the CCAG are defined by law and are compulsory (CCAG travaux[12]). In the private sector, the main standard form contract is the AFNOR NF P 03.001 (published by the French Standards Agency[13]), which is identical to the public CCAG, but is not compulsory and may be amended. In international contracts FIDIC is often used; ICC turnkey contracts for major projects or industrial plants[14] are also common; alternatively clients will use their own bespoke terms which may in part be modelled on FIDIC or ICC. Contracts for individual houses are known as *contrat de construction de maison individuelle* (CCMI), and can be let using traditional procurement (*contrat de construction avec fourniture de plan*) or design-build (*sans fourniture de plan*). These contracts are regulated through consumer protection legislation that governs (amongst other matters): the contract clauses, the financing of the constructions, and the contractor's performance guarantee.

---

[11] Centre d'Études d'Assurance (CEA), *Liabilities in Europe* (Belgium: CEA, 2004).
[12] www.marche-public.fr/CCAG-travaux-2009.
[13] www.afnor.org.
[14] www.iccbooks.com.

Under the decennial system insurance is compulsory for new construction, renovation works and the restoration of old structures.[15] Insurance requirements are set out in the Code des Assurances (Code of Insurance). The client (*maître d'ouvrage*) is required to insure against decennial responsibility on a project basis, and no limit can be attached to this type of policy, so that if defects or problems develop, the client will obtain the funds necessary to complete essential work prior to apportionment of responsibility (§242.1 of the Code of Insurance). Any defective work is reinstated immediately, and the claim is then settled between the insurance companies of the parties concerned. Contractors and architects must also take out insurance to cover their 10-year warranty (§241.1 of the Code of Insurance). Insurance policies to cover these are of course available commercially, for example in France an architect's PII policy will cover decennial liability, professional negligence and liability to third parties.

17.3 *Germany*[16]

The German construction industry is characterised by an emphasis on very high standards of specification and workmanship. The design and technical information provided to the contractor is likely to be very precise, and decisions on design details are not left to the contractor to resolve. Construction management is the most common form of procurement (client engaging professionals and various specialist contractors separately); traditional, design-build, management contracting and turnkey contracts are unusual. Consultants normally have extensive onsite involvement and play a prominent role in inspecting and monitoring the quality of work.

Plans and drawings submitted to obtain building permission must be signed by an architect or engineer who is a member of a regional professional chamber.[17] The titles 'architect' and 'engineer' are both protected by laws issued by the Länder (states of Germany), and architects must be registered with an *Architektenkammer* and engineers with an *Ingenieurkammer* in order to be eligible to submit planning applications. Fee scales are regulated at Federal level and are compulsory. The chambers impose requirements on registered architects and engineers regarding professional indemnity insurance (see below).

Germany has a codified legal system, and the main provisions governing contract and tort law are contained in the German Civil Code (*Bürgerliches Gesetzbuch*, BGB) of 1900, as currently amended. In addition, as with other codified systems, court judgments should be taken into account since the courts have partly developed rules outside the Code and have also interpreted the Code, which although not binding have weight

---

[15] European Liability Insurance Organisation Schemes (ELIOS), *Liability and Insurance Regimes in the Construction Sector: National Schemes and Guidelines to Stimulate Innovation and Sustainability*. Report for the EU (Brussels, 2010).

[16] With thanks to Alexandra Nicklas and Joachim Jobi of the Federal Chamber of German Architects (*Bundesarchitektenkammer*), and to Katja Timmermann of Capita Symonds.

[17] Alexander Herbert and Markus Eckardt, *Getting the Deal Through: Construction 2011: Germany* (London: Law Business Research Ltd, 2011).

in subsequent interpretations. In general terms parties are free to agree their own contracts, although if they have not done so, the BGB will normally provide a system of basic terms. Liability under both contract and tort is normally fault-based, so that negligence would need to be proved (this is different for construction contracts; see below). The Code requires compliance with the objective standard '*der im Verkehr erforderlichen Sorgfalt*', 'a person acts negligently if he fails to exercise reasonable care' (§276 para. 2). However, fault is presumed if a breach of a contractual duty is established (e.g. a promised outcome is not achieved) and the onus is then on the parties in breach to show that they were 'not reponsible for the breach of duty' (§280 para. 1). The normal limitation period is three years, which applies to claims under contract and under tort (§195), although again this is different for construction contracts.

It should also be noted that in general under German contract law not only can the parties to the contract rely on the contract but often third parties can as well. This depends on the protective scope of the contract (*Vertrag mit Schutzwirkung zugunsten Dritter*). The parties themselves are entitled to choose to extend the protection of the contract to third parties (§328). In construction, in general third party claims would be raised against the client, rather than the contractor, but frequently the architect may also be held liable to third parties.

The BGB includes particular sections that relate to the liability of parties to construction contracts (e.g. architects, engineers, building contractors) for construction defects (§§631 and 633); liability in tort, e.g. for injuries inflicted to third parties as a result of construction operations (§823 (1)); breach of statutory provisions intended to ensure protection of other persons, excluding safety regulations (§823 (2)); and liability for damages caused by agents or subcontractors (§831).[18]

The Code §§631–51 covers 'Contract[s] to produce a work'.[19] Article 631, paragraph 2 states that 'the subject matter of a contract to produce a work may be either the production or alteration of a thing or another result to be achieved by work or by a service'.[20] Therefore the following provisions would cover both construction contracts (works and services), and consultants' engagements with their clients (services only, i.e. a design contract is considered a *Werkvertrag*).[21] The code states that 'the contractor must procure the work for the customer free of material defects and legal defects' (§633 (1)). This is further defined: 'the work is free of material defects if it is of the agreed quality. To the extent that the quality has not been agreed, the work is free from material defects if it is suitable for the use envisaged in the contract, or ... if it is suitable for the customary use and is of a quality that is customary in works of the same type' (§633 (2)).

As with any contract with a promised outcome, liability for a breach of Article 633 would be strict, and would be presumed should a defect appear, although the contractor or architect could as a defence show that the defect was not caused by their error (§280).

---

[18] ELIOS. *Liability and Insurance Regimes in the Construction Sector: National Schemes and Guidelines to Stimulate Innovation and Sustainability.* Report for the EU (Brussels, 2010).

[19] BGB Book 2 Title 9 Subtitle 1.

[20] English translation from www.gesetze-im-internet.de/englisch_bgb.

[21] Stephanie van Gulijk, *European Architect Law: Towards a New Design* (Apeldoorn, The Netherlands: Maklu Publishers, 2009), p. 24.

For example it would be a defence to a claim under Article 633 to show that the defect was caused by *force majeure*, unforeseen ground conditions, or client default. Complying with client requirements may, however, not always be accepted as a reason, and there has been conflicting case law on this point.[22] The contractor would in any event be under a duty to warn of any design error in information provided by the client.

Architects are required to provide a design that is both technically and economically faultless according to the generally accepted standard and state of the art (*Regeln der Technik und Baukunst.*[23]). This is called a *Mindeststandard* and German architects must guarantee (*einstehen*) that the design conforms to this standard. If the design is in breach of the *Regeln der Technik und Baukunst* the design is considered defective. Contractors who design and construct are in the same position.

Specific limitation periods relevant to construction defects are also set out (§634a (1) 2). This is 'five years in the case of a building and in the case of a work whose result consists in the rendering of planning or monitoring services for this purpose'. This applies from acceptance of the building by the client (§634a (2)). It therefore extends the normal three-year limitation period (§195), and is considered to apply to consultants as well, except in very limited circumstances (e.g. for advice unconnected with design or construction, where the normal period would apply). This period starts running at the end of the year in which the liability claim originated, or at the moment the client knew or should have known about the damage.

The client has a range of options if defects appear within the five-year period, including requiring the contractor to correct the work, or correcting it themselves and claiming reimbursement (§634). Contractors and consultants are jointly and severally liable for any losses suffered by the client, who may therefore claim the whole sum against either party, but in practice is likely to bring a claim against both.

Article 823 (1) sets out a general liability that any 'person who, intentionally or negligently, unlawfully injures the life, body, health, freedom, property or another right of another person is liable to make compensation to the other party for the damage arising from this'. Both contractors and consultants therefore may be liable should any negligence result in third-party damage causing injury or damage to property. The same would apply to any breach of statutory duty that gives rise to similar consequences (§823 (2)). If more than one person is responsible for such damage they would be jointly liable (§840).

In addition to their liabilities under contract and tort, Article 319 of the German Penal Code (*Strafgesetzbuch*, StGB), stipulates that architect, engineer and building contractor may be subject to penal liability in cases of structural instability, in particular if a failure to observe generally acknowledged rules during design, supervision or execution of works results in putting life in danger or threatens the physical integrity of persons. For example, all parties must comply with DIN standards (*Deutsches Institut für Normung*). The provisions of Article 319 of the Penal Code together with Article 823 of the BGB therefore provide the legal basis for financial compensation of those persons whose physical integrity or property have been harmed.

---

[22] Jan-Bertram Hillig *The Contractor's Quality Obligations; Different Concepts under English and German Contract Law* (CIB World Building Congress 2007 p. 2169); Axel-Volkmar Jaeger and Götz-Sebastian Hök *FIDIC – A Guide for Practitioners* (Berlin: Springer-Verlag, 2010). p 35.

[23] ibid., p. 51.

There are no private standard forms of contract for the client-contractor contract. Construction works are often carried out under the *Verdingungsordnung für Bauleistungen*, Part B (VOB/B). This set of rules was developed for public contracts (first edition in 1926) and is compulsory in public procurement, but although not compulsory for private contracts it is often adopted there too. They provide a standardised basis of construction contracts and are composed of three main parts: Part A deals with the contract award procedure; Part B with Standard Model Form of Contract, covering execution, handover, payment settlements and guarantee periods. Part C covers mandatory technical construction standards, comprising a set of DIN technical standards. VOB clauses may vary the requirements in the BGB, and the parties may in turn agree amendments to the VOB/B, subject to certain limits, i.e. clause 9, paragraph 2 of the VOB/B stipulates that a clause may be ineffective if it deviates substantially from the BGB or VOB/B.

Generally the VOB provisions are less onerous on the contractor than those under the BGG, for example the VOB introduces a limitation period of four years, which may be extended for a further two years in cases of defects resulting from an incorrect execution of the construction contract.

Architects and contractors are in principle free to reduce the liability created by the Code. For example the parties may contractually define a different liability limitation period, or the amount of a possible indemnity may be limited to a sum set by a professional insurance contract. This can be done through using standard terms of business (e.g. the VOB or architects' standard terms of appointment), or through individually negotiated exclusion clauses, but are in all cases subject to the restrictions set out in Articles 305–10 of the BGB. For example, it is not possible to exclude liability for injury, and any clause limiting the amount of damages for which an architect is liable would only be valid to the extent that it is reasonable considering the design and the anticipated damage. There are in fact very strict conditions for the reduction of liability through using standard terms, and limitation clauses are unlikely to be effective with regard to consumer contracts. In practice most clients may be unwilling to agree a reduction in liability.

As mentioned above, professional indemnity insurance is compulsory for all consultants registered with *Lander*. However registered architects and engineers only need to have valid professional indemnity insurance if they are self-employed and submit planning applications using their own registration number and rubber stamp. Architects employed by an office will usually not have their own indemnity insurance but are covered by that of their employer and the rubber stamp on the submitted documents will then have to be that of their employer. Planning applications will not be registered if a valid indemnity insurance certificate is not supplied as part of the application documents. Contractors can take out insurance on most of their risks, including contractor's all risk insurance, an additional fire carcass insurance (covering damage to the works caused by fires, lightning strikes and explosion) and third-party liability insurance (which is compulsory).[24]

---

[24] Alexander Herbert and Markus Eckardt, *Getting the Deal Through: Construction 2011: Germany* (London: Law Business Research Ltd, 2011).

The main security against construction defects is a system of financial guarantees, frequently incorporated into the financing scheme of the project. Under this system a fraction of the contractor's remuneration is retained by the client as security against post-completion defects. Usually architects will advise their clients on how much money to retain as a 'security' (between 5 and 10%) from every contractor's invoice, after having checked it against tender price and progress of work actually delivered.

The system may be replaced by a financial guarantee provided by an external guarantor such as a bank or an insurance company. The amount of a guarantee is usually 10 per cent of the project value until completion of the project and up to 5 per cent during the period between completion and expiry of the guarantee (which will normally run for the five-year liability period).[25] Such guarantees are generally not compulsory, except in public procurement projects, however they are frequently required under the terms of the contract. If required, the guarantee usually has to be presented as part of the tender submission but in any case prior to the contract being awarded. Insurance solutions developed for construction firms as substitutes for bank guarantees covering construction operations and defects after completion are also available on the market, but not widely used.[26]

17.4 Italy[27]

Most procurement in Italy is done through the traditional route, where the construction of the building works is entrusted by the client to a general contractor, who assumes responsibility for all sub-contractors. All concrete and steel structures must be designed and the construction works supervised by architects or engineers registered with the provincial Chamber (Order). The same applies to constructions in seismic zones. The use of an architect is also compulsory for all buildings that are listed by the *Sovrintendenza ai Monumenti* – part of the Ministry of Culture under Article 52 of Royal Decree No 2537 of 23 October 1925 relating to works of artistic value (e.g. historic monuments).

The architectural profession is regulated, and use of the title 'architect' is controlled by law (Law No. 1395 of 24 June 1923 and Royal Decree No. 2537). Architects and engineers are registered with the provincial Chamber (in the case of architects, the *Consiglio Nazionale Degli Architetti, Pianificatori, Paesaggisti e Conservatori*).

The Italian Civil Code (*Codice civile*, CC of 1942) sets out rules relating to contractual and extra-contractual liability. General contractual liability is governed by Articles §1218–29. The fundamental rule in tort liability is set out in Article 2043 (any deed or delict/tort, that causes others unjust damage, obliges the one who committed the crime to

---

[25] ELIOS, *Liability and Insurance Regimes in the Construction Sector: National Schemes and Guidelines to Stimulate Innovation and Sustainability,* Report for the EU (Brussels, 2010).

[26] ibid.

[27] With thanks to Professor Giovanni Iudica and Roberto Panetta of the Università Bocconi di Milano, and to Luciano Lazzari of Studio Architetti Zelco Lazzari for their helpful comments on a draft of this text.

the damage), which is followed by special rules of liability pursuant to §§2044–59. This liability would be joint and several between all tortfeasors (§2055). The Code distinguishes between *obbligazioni di mezzi* (obligations of means) and *obbligazioni di risultato* (obligations of result). In relation to contract, §1218 CC states that 'the person who does not exactly perform the obligation due must compensate the other with damages, unless he proves that the non-performance or the delay was due to an impossibility of performance, for a cause not imputable to him'. The level of liability under Article 1218 may be strict or negligence, and will depend on the nature of the particular obligation in question. In the case of professional duties, the level of liability will depend on the nature of the specific activity performed (professional diligence: §1176, para. 2). Under Article 2236 CC, whenever the performance of an obligation requires the solution of technical problems of special difficulty, the 'intellectual professional' will be liable only for willful misconduct or serious negligence.

The liability framework relative to construction contracts is mainly defined by the Civil Code (Title III 'individual contracts'). Articles 1655–77 cover contracts for work and materials (contractor) and services (architect), which would include building work, and alterations of buildings (§§1659–1661).

In relation to construction contracts, the warranty periods outlined by §§1667 and 1669 of Civil Code are as follows:

- 2 years from completion, to the client, for any (including minor) defects of the building that are not manifest at the time of the final control by the project manager and/or municipal authorities (§1667 CC);
- 10 years' liability from completion of long-term buildings to the client, subsequent owners and users, for major defects caused by poor ground conditions or construction faults (i.e. total or partial collapse) or defects that deprive the owner of the essential purpose of the building and that weaken structure or functioning of the building (§1669 CC).

The two-year and 10-year periods apply from 'the date of final control' by the project manager and municipal authorities, which is usually taken to be the handover. The Code also specifies the time-limit within which the client is obliged to report such discrepancies or defects:

- 60 days following their detection for Article 1667,
- 1 year following their detection for Article 1669.

Assuming a client reports the fault within the above period, they will be able to bring a claim against the contractor for breach of the above warranties as set out in the Code. This is a strict liability and there is no need for the client to prove causation. However it would be a defence to a claim under Article 1667 and 1669 to show that the defect was caused by *force majeure*, client default or complying with client requirements, provided that contractor had warned the client (this is termed acting as '*nudus minister*', that is, the obligations were performed under specific instructions issued by the employer, and the contractor was unable to autonomously take any decision regarding the works). There is no need for the client to prove that there was a lack of due skill or care. In addition to these warranties, a contractor would also be liable under Article 1218 for any defect up to handover of the work, unless it has been accepted.

The §1669 CC decennial liability would apply where an architect performed the role of a structural engineer or expert and was engaged to undertake calculations relating to a construction made of reinforced concrete or metal, or in supervision (which is unusual). In such cases the architect (or engineer) would bear civil liability jointly and severally with the contractor (§2055 CC). This liability would be strict, but in the case of the architect or engineer the client would need to show causation (there is not the same 'presumption of responsibility' as there is for the contractor). Any party held liable for such damage may subsequently claim contribution from other responsible parties. The architect or engineer might also bear penal liability if a building collapsed and caused personal damage (Law No. 1086 of 5 November 1971). The architect may also be subject to disciplinary measures by the Ordre (§2229).

Where a designer does not perform structural calculations, but prepares technical drawings, for example showing materials and components, and these result in defects, the designer would not be subject to the above special provisions concerning construction contracts, but may be liable to the client for breach of contract (§§1218 and 2229 cc). The client in these cases would have to prove the designer was negligent.

There are no published standard forms of contract which are compulsory for private works, although there are some published by contractors' trade associations that may be used on some projects. In government procurement standard terms such as the Ministry of Public Works 'General Specifications for the Procurement of Civil Works' are used.

In respect of public projects, building contractors are obliged to insure all the risks to third parties which arise from their work (Decree No 163 of 12 April 2006, para 129). Consultants engaged in supervising public works are under a similar obligation (Decree No 163 of 12 April 2006, para 112). In respect of building defects, an insurance obligation was introduced initially by an Act called the 'Merloni law' (*Legge Merloni*, Law No. 109 of 11 February 1994). This law set out an integrated body of rules relating to public procurement, under which the building contractor was required to take out decennial insurance for public construction projects valued over €10 million.

Subsequently, under Law No 210 (2004) the decennial insurance obligation has been widened to cover the private sector as well, but insurance is not compulsory for contractors or consultants undertaking private works. It is however, strongly advisable to be insured and generally contractors will take out extensive insurance. There is a national agreement between the Architects and Engineers Pension Fund (INARCASSA) and Unipol Insurance to provide specific insurance policies at reasonable prices. Insurance is compulsory for architects, designers, etc. for all public works – see *Codice dei Contratti*, Decree No 163 of 12 April 2006, and subsequent rules. Architects are also obliged, in the interim period between approval of working drawings, but before start of work onsite, to arrange for the insurance policy of the *progettisti* (clients), which is specific to that project and not simply a generic insurance policy.

17.5 The Netherlands[28]

In general the construction industry in the Netherlands is highly regulated. It has a codified legal system, and the Dutch Civil Code (*Burgerlijk Wetboek*: BW) includes provisions that cover construction contracts. Design is not covered explicitly in the Code but would fall under its general provisions on liability, discussed below. In addition, standard terms are used extensively: for consultants' appointments, the New Regulations 2011 (*De Nieuwe Regeling*, or DNR 2011) and for construction contracts, the Uniform Administrative Conditions for the Execution of Works 1989 (UAV 1989). In some cases these reduce the liability that would otherwise be imposed by the Code.

The title 'architect' is protected, as only registered architects can use the title of an architect in the Netherlands. This does not apply to other design professions, although all professions are generally members of professional bodies, such as the Dutch Architects Organisation (BNA) and the Dutch Engineers Organisation (*NL Ingenieurs*, or NI).[29] There is no protection of function for these professions, in that there is no requirement to use a qualified person at any stage of the construction process.

Several sections of the Code are relevant to design. Book 3 covers the law of property, and includes general limitation periods on rights of action. Book 6 covers general obligations under contract and tort. In Book 7 ('Particular Agreements'), Chapter 12 ('Contracting for Works'; which came into effect in 2003) covers contracts where 'one of the parties' ('the constructor') undertakes to the other party ('the principal') to make and deliver a tangible construction (on a basis other than an employment agreement), in exchange for a price to be paid in money by the principal (§7:750). It therefore covers contracts for work and materials, or design-build, but does not cover contracts for services only, which would come under Book 6 and other sections of the Code (i.e. §7:400 covering commission contracts; *overeenkomst van opdracht*[30]). Book 7, Chapter 12, Section 1 (§§7:750–64) sets out general provisions for contracting. Section 2 (§§7:765–69) provides for consumer protection in the field of housing construction. Parties can agree different terms to Section 1 (with exceptions), whereas Section 2 is mandatory.

Although there is no specific obligation in the Code to provide a building that is suitable for its purpose, it is generally considered that the contractor has such a duty, subject to the qualifications set out. Article 7:754 places a strict duty to warn on the contractor 'of any inadequacies in the construction or work that is assigned to him as far as these are known to him or reasonably should have been known to him'.[31] This includes 'errors or shortcomings in plans, drawings, designs, calculations, specifications, estimations or

---

[28]With thanks to Professor Monika Chao-Duivis, director of the Dutch Institute of Construction Law and professor of construction law at the Technical University of Delft for her helpful comments on a draft of this section.

[29]Only businesses can be members of NI, whereas the BNA is for individual architects.

[30]Stephanie van Gulijk, *European Architect Law: Towards a New Design* (Apeldoorn, The Netherlands: Maklu Publishers, 2009), p. 21.

[31]Trans. from www.dutchcivillaw.com.

implementing regulations which are supplied by the principal.' Under Article 7:760 the contractor is liable for any defective or unsuitable materials, unless specified or provided by the employer. However, Article 7:760.2 states that the client is only liable for materials or equipment supplied in so far 'as the constructor has not failed to comply with his duty to warn the principal as referred to in Article 7:754 or has not failed otherwise with regard to these defects or this unsuitability in providing the proper expertise or carefulness'.[32] In other words, the contractor will be liable for unsuitable materials, etc unless a) the employer has provided the materials *and* b) the contractor has given a warning. The legislation is written on the assumption that the contractor does not provide the design, or give advice, but if it did, then given the reference to expertise in Article 7:754 it appears that the contractor would be strictly liable to the employer if there were an error in the design or advice.

Once the project is completed, a contractor is relieved of liability, except for problems notified by the employer. Under Article 7:761, a contractor is liable for two years from the moment when the owner has notified the defect to the contractor (but the owner may lose his right to bring an action if he failed to notify within a reasonable time from discovery of the defect). All actions based on latent defects are barred after 20 years following handover of the building. The periods can be reduced by agreement, except that Article 762 states that the liability of the constructor for hidden construction defects of which he was aware and which he has concealed, cannot be excluded or limited by agreement, nor can they be subjected to a shorter prescription period than those set out under the Code. In practice, if bringing an action the employer would need to show that the defect was caused by a default of the contractor, although there would be no need to demonstrate negligence.

Under the Code architects are generally expected to carry out their duties with the skill and care of a competent professional (§7:401). They would also be liable for claims for damages for any failure to perform a contractual obligation (Book 6.1). Generally the level of liability is one of negligence, but for some tasks an 'obligation of result' is assumed, for example, advice on matters that cannot be ascertained precisely must be given with due skill and care, but calculations would have to be correct. Claims for damages or repair must be brought within five years from when 'the injured person has become aware of both the inflicted damage or the fact that the contractual penalty has become due and demandable . . . and in any event 20 years from the day on which the event occurred that caused the damage . . . ' (§§3:306 and 310).

The liabilities under the Civil Code Books 6.1 and 7.12 are owed to the client. If the parties have agreed different provisions which limit the architect or contractor's liability, the client would have to rely on these, and would be unable to take advantage of the provisions in the Code. A third party that suffers a loss due to a design error would be able to claim under the provisions on tortious liability, covered by Book 6.3.

Under most of the standard contracts conditions the liability of the building contractor is strict. The contractor is obliged to deliver the result according to what was defined in the contract, and is only relieved from this liability in exceptional circumstances.

---

[32] ibid.

The Uniform Administrative Conditions for Construction Contracts 2012 (*Uniforme Administratieve Voorwaarden*, UAV 2012, replaces the UAV 1989) is a set of general conditions agreed by contractors, engineers, architects, subcontractors, municipalities and provinces. Although not mandatory, they are very widely used, and are the most common terms for Dutch construction contracts. The conditions are currently being revised, partly to bring them in line with the Civil Code.

UAV 2012 is a traditional form of contract, and the employer must supply all necessary drawings and instructions (cl. 5.1c). Under clause 5, paragraph 2 the employer is responsible for the design it provides (the clause states the employer is liable 'for the constructions and construction methods prescribed by him or on his behalf, including the effect that soil conditions may have on such constructions and construction methods, as well as for the instructions and directions given by him or on his behalf'). It is generally considered that if the contractor provides the design it would be responsible for any errors.[33]

Following completion and acceptance by the employer, the contractor is no longer liable for the works (cl. 12.1), with one exception; the contractor remains liable for any defect which is attributable to the contractor and could not reasonably have been discovered during inspection by the employer's agent, provided that the contractor has been informed thereabout within a reasonable period of time after its discovery (cl. 12.2). This contractual liability continues for five years after acceptance, or 10 years 'if the works have collapsed completely or partially, or threaten to collapse, or have come to be unfit or threaten to be unfit for the purpose for which they were intended as follows from the contract, and this can only be remedied or prevented by taking very costly measures' (cl. 12.4). The periods are additional to any defects liability period specified in the contract.

The more recently developed UAV-GC 2005 (*Uniforme Administratieve Voorwaarden voor Geïntegreerde Contracten*) is an 'integrated contract' that can be used for design and build, or design, build, maintain contracts. Clause 4, paragraph 1 requires the contractor to design and construct to meet the contract requirements. The paragraph 3 requirements includes those 'ensuing from the ordinary use for which the works are intended as well as the requirements resulting from the specific purpose for which the works will be used, yet only insofar as the requirements resulting from the specific purpose are stated in the employer requirements'. The result of this is that the contractor is under a strict obligation to meet any specific requirements set out by the employer, and where these are not set out, to provide works fit for the ordinary use of the building. There is also a duty to warn against faults or defects, similar to that in the UAV 1989 (cl. 4.7).

The combined effect of these clauses is not an absolute guarantee of result; for example the contractor would be relieved from liability if the employer intervenes, and requires specific materials or forms of construction. An example of this can be seen in a court of arbitration case, which concerned the construction of a sauna/pool. The employer instructed pine to be used rather than the contractor's selected type of

---

[33] E.M. Bruggeman, M.A.B. Chao-Duivis and A.Z.R. Koning (eds), *A Practical Guide to Dutch Building Contracts* (The Netherlands: Instituut von Bouwrecht, 2008), p. 62.

meranti. The pine delaminated, but the contractor was relieved from liability for the design, although held partly liable as it failed to warn of the problem.[34]

As with UAV 1989, following completion and acceptance by the employer, the contractor would be liable for any defects that appear and were due to its default, and it was reasonable for the employer not to have noticed the defect at handover (cl. 28.1 and 2). Under the UAV-GC 2005 clause 28 paragraph 3, the contractor's liability is limited to 10% of the contract price, or a maximum of €1.5 million, if this is less.

The most common form of consultant's appointment is DNR 2011 (*De Nieuwe Regeling*, the New Regulations) developed jointly by the BNA and the NI (and which can be downloaded in English)[35]. As an alternative, CR2006 wording (*De Consumentenregeling*) can be used for smaller projects.

Under the DNR 2011 consultants are required to only take on commissions they are able to cope with (cl. 11.1a), and must 'carry out the commission in a proper and careful manner, assist the client independently in a position of trust and conduct [their] services to the best of [their] knowledge and capacity' (cl. 11.2). The consultant is also obliged to take heed of legislation (cl. 11.4) and warn of obvious defects in information provided by the employer (cl. 11.10). PII insurance requirements are set out in clause 11.3.

Under DNR 2011 clause 16.1 a consultant's liability expires five years from the day on which the contract ended due to discharge or termination. Once the client has discovered a shortcoming it must give written notice to the consultant, with 'good reasons', and must bring an action within two years of this notice, otherwise the claim is no longer admissible (cl. 16.3). Under clause 15 liability is limited to either: the value of the fees, up to a maximum of €1 million, or, to three times the fees, up to a maximum of €2.5 million (the former is the default if no choice is made). Also, under clause 14 the type of recoverable loss is restricted to direct loss only (i.e. costs of rectification). Consequential losses such as loss of profits etc. are not claimable, neither are 'costs pertaining to the realization of the object should the commission have been rightly executed from the beginning' (cl. 14.2), which appears to be an exclusion of any betterment. The liability of the consultant is therefore restricted compared with what it would be under the Code.

There is no legal obligation under the Code for construction parties to carry insurance. However BNA members (architects) are bound by professional standards to insure, and consultants are required to have PII under DNR 2011 (cl. 11.3). Contractors must also carry insurance under the UAV conditions. There are a number of warranties available for buyers of dwellings (which may cover new developments and/or refurbishments), e.g. those provided by Bouwfonds, SWK and Woningborg, members of the GIW institute.

---

[34] 4 January 1993, No. 15.975 *Bouwrecht Journal on Construction Law* 1993, p. 480.
[35] www.bna.nl/Architecten/Contractvorming/DNR.

Chapter 18
Design Liability in the Rest of the World

This chapter examines the design liability position in five jurisdictions outside the EU: Australia, China, the Middle East, Russia and the USA. These are included primarily to present an outline comparative analysis which, as in the previous chapter, is restricted to a brief account of the main procurement routes, the role of professionals, their liability under the legal system (contract and tort), and any commonly used standard forms. As with the EU, any party considering working for the first time in an unfamiliar country would of course need to take legal advice.

18.1 Australia[1]

As a Commonwealth country Australia's legal system has much in common with that of England. However Australia has a federal system (a federal constitutional monarchy) whereby each of the six states and two territories has its own parliament, which passes its own laws. The states give power to the Federal government, which also passes laws. The key laws relating to construction are similar in every state but there are local variations, especially in matters such as planning, licensing and occupational health and safety. For example the countrywide Building Code of Australia (BCA) adopted since 1996, includes local (state) variations for climatic and tectonic variance. The Council of Australian Governments (COAG), a co-ordinating body consisting of the federal government, the state and mainland territory governments and the Australian Local Government Association, negotiates harmonising regulations. The Australian Building Codes Board (ABCB) publishes the BCA and is a co-operative arrangement between the states, local governments and building industry representatives. The BCA refers to Australian Standards which are regulated countrywide (and many are also applicable in New Zealand). The BCA permits both 'deemed to satisfy' provisions meeting performance requirements and the alternate option of engineered solutions.

---

[1] With thanks to Tim Browne of Blainey North, and Marlena Lubas of Arup Legal Group for their comments on this section.

Cornes and Lupton's Design Liability in the Construction Industry, Fifth Edition. Sarah Lupton.
© 2013 Sarah Lupton and DL Cornes. Published 2013 by Blackwell Publishing Ltd.

Traditional procurement and design and build are the most common procurement methods for residential projects. Over recent years, newer forms of procurement have been adopted, including 'alliancing contracting' for larger projects (this has similarities with UK partnering contracting).[2] On large government projects PPP (private public partnerships) are used. Government and privately commissioned reports[3] have identified problems within the industry and pointed to innovative and co-operative ways of working which have been employed by other industries, such as manufacturing, similarly to the Egan Report in the UK. Alongside those newer methods there has been an increased use of project managers for all procurement routes, often adopting the role of contract administrator.

Over the past 20 years there has been a significant shift away from use of standard contracts for major projects to 'bespoke' contracts. In many cases this has changed risk allocation embodied within standard contract forms, often to the advantage of the employer.[4] Standard forms of contract are nevertheless still used for smaller projects and by smaller employers, although the available range is not as extensive as in the UK. The 'Australian Building Industry Contracts' (ABIC)[5] are jointly published by the Master Builders Australia (Master Builders) and the Australian Institute of Architects (AIA),[6] and are generally intended for use where architects are to act as contract administrators. The range includes forms for major works (MW-2008, with versions for use for housing and non-housing projects, and a 2011 version for use in Queensland only), simple works (SW-2008, with versions as for MW-2008), demolition and/or groundworks (EW-1 2003) and small commercial works (BW-1 2002). There is also ABP-1 for use where the contract is administrated by the proprietor.

SW-2008 contains no express terms about design. Under clause A2.1b the contractor is required to 'diligently carry out all *necessary work* and complete the *works* to the standard set out in the *contract documents*'. There is no mention of what the level of liability would be if the contract documents attempted to include any design as part of the works.

The most widely used range of standard forms for commercial building work is the Australian Standard (AS) forms, published by Standards Australia Ltd.[7] These include AS 4000-1997 for traditional procurement, AS 4902-2000 for use in design-build (these forms supersede AS 2124-1992 and AS 4300-1995, however the older forms are still available and widely used). There are also AS forms for ancillary services such as equipment supply and installation and asset maintenance/facilities management, as

---

[2] A useful introduction to alliancing can be found at http://www.pcigroup.com.au/publications_pci/.

[3] For recent reviews of procurement see e.g. Blake Dawson, *Scope for Improvement 2011: Project risk – Getting the Right Balance and Outcomes* (Australia: Blake Dawson, 2011).

[4] www.mtecc.com.au/uploads//papers/Shnookal,_Toby.pdf.

[5] www.architecture.com.au/i-cms?page=61.

[6] www.architecture.com.au.

[7] www.standards.org.au.

well as consultant's appointment forms (AS 4122-2010 and AS 4904-2009) and sub-contracts.[8] The suite based upon AS 4000 now includes 16 forms in total.

There are no standard forms to cover partnering in the private sector. Each state may publish its own forms for partnering or co-operative contracting, for example the New South Wales Government GC21 General Conditions of Contract standard form, which is suitable for construction contracts valued at more than $1 million, and may sometimes be used for smaller projects when special circumstances and/or requirements exist (e.g. the use of milestones). This contract is a 'second generation' partnering contract developed from early forms of partnering contracts used in the 1990s in New South Wales. This form allows for a variable amount of contractor design input. Specifically, under the heading 'Design' it states:

> The Contractor has some design, design coordination and design management responsibility. The extent of Design by the Contractor may be as little as shop detailing, as much as the full Design of the Works, or it may be some requirement in between, and Clause 43 applies in all these cases . . . In addition, the Contractor may be required to check, adopt and be responsible for design carried out before the Date of Contract by the Principal. In that case, it is specified in Contract Information item 38, and clause 44 applies.

As with English Law, unless the contract specifies otherwise, terms would normally be implied into a contract to construct works as follows: that the work would be undertaken with reasonable skill and care, that the materials would be of good quality and fit for purpose (unless a particular material is specified), and that the finished works would be fit for purpose.[9] Whether the 'fit for purpose' terms would be implied will depend, as in the UK, on whether there is reliance by the employer.[10]

There is also consumer protection legislation in most states, particularly to protect domestic (homeowner) employers; an example is the Domestic Building Contracts Act 1995 (Victoria), which states at section 8(e):

> the builder warrants that if the work consists of the erection or construction of a home, or is work intended to renovate, alter, extend, improve or repair a home to a stage suitable for occupation, the home will be suitable for occupation at the time the work is completed;

and at (f):

> if the contract states the particular purpose for which the work is required, or the result which the building owner wishes the work to achieve, so as to show that the building owner relies on the builder's skill and judgement, the builder warrants that the work and any material used in carrying out the work will be reasonably fit for that purpose or will be of such a nature and quality that they might reasonably be expected to achieve that result.

---

[8] Bell, M., Legal Research Studies Paper 437: Standard Form Construction Contracts in Australia: Are Our Reinvented Wheels Carrying Us Forward? *Building and Construction Law Journal*, 25(2), (2009).
[9] *Reg Glass Pty Ltd v Rivers Locking Systems Pty Ltd* [1968] HCA 64; (1968) 120 CLR 516 (17 October 1968).
[10] *Timms Contracting Pty Ltd v Pipes International (Qld) Pty Ltd* [2010] QSC 88 (23 March 2010).

Similarly the Domestic Building Contracts Act 2000 (Queensland): states 'the building contractor warrants the detached dwelling or home will be suitable for occupation when the work is finished'. Domestic consumer protection legislation generally requires contractors to hold suitable (domestic project specific) insurance which is a condition of obtaining certification to commence building work.

The Competition and Consumer Act 2010 (CCA) implies terms into consumer contracts, including terms similar to those in the UK Sales of Goods and Supplies of Goods and Services Acts, i.e. that goods should be of 'acceptable' quality, and fit for any specified purpose, and that services should be undertaken with due skill and care.[11] In addition, the CCA implies a 'fit for purpose' warranty into services contracts. These would include contracts to design and build a house for a consumer, but there is a specific exclusion for contracts with engineers and architects,[12] unless they are providing services outside their normal area of expertise.

Contractors and architects may be liable in tort to third parties, a duty which may extend to avoiding 'pure economic loss'. Although Australian courts have not followed the approach taken in *Anns,* and therefore have not developed any over-riding principle or test for establishing such liability, liability for pure economic loss has nevertheless been found in a number of cases. This liability has arisen particularly in relation to dwellings, and has now been embodied in statute in most states and territories. The position is less clear with respect to commercial property, where the court decisions have been affected by a variety of factors, including the extent to which a commercial claimant might be expected to protect itself from a failure to take care.

The architectural profession is regulated at state level by state registration boards. The boards publish a Code of Conduct and facilitate the registration process, comprising three principal components: practical experience log, written exam and interview. A 'nominated' architect must be notified to the relevant registration board for an architectural practice; their registration number must be included on all business stationery and agreements. As in the UK, there is protection of title, but not of function.[13] There are also registration requirements for engineers in some states. In addition to registration, many architects (in the region of 10,000)[14] are also members of the Australian Institute of Architects (AIA), which publishes a Code, standard forms of appointment, and a fees guide to assist with benchmarking fees. Fees are commonly calculated on a percentage, lump sum or time basis. The registration boards' code of conduct notes that architects should have a written agreement with their client and obtain public and professional liability insurance adequate for the nature of work undertaken. A number of the major insurance houses offer insurance products, and in addition the AIA Professional Risk Services offers insurance products to AIA members.

---

[11] CCA, Schedule 2 Part 3-2.
[12] ibid., Subdivision B 61(4).
[13] See Chapters 1 and 17.
[14] www.architecture.com.au/i-cms?page=165.

State registration boards generally allow application for temporary registration of overseas architects for a defined limited period (e.g. with a minimum of seven years practical experience in the case of the NSW registration board). Foreign firms wishing to work in Australia must register under the Corporations Act 2001.[15]

18.2 China[16]

China has a Civil Law system, and the construction industry and construction operations are highly regulated. The relevant laws exist in a series of tiers,[17] from central government laws (the principal ones being the Contract Law and the Construction Law, see below) through to central government regulations and down to local regulations and laws.

Until recently, procurement of projects has normally been through a traditional approach, with design separate from construction, and all design being carried out by a state-owned design institute. Greater openness of the market to foreign companies and influence has resulted in a wider variety of procurement methods, and the laws and regulations have responded to these changes to an extent.

The Contract Law of the People's Republic of China ('Contract Law') was adopted at the second session of the Ninth National People's Congress on 15 March 1999 and came into effect on 1 October 1999. It is a unifying Law that consolidates legislation dealing with all contracts used in business transactions. The Contract Law comprises 428 articles divided into 23 chapters including chapter 16, which deals specifically with contracts for construction projects. Other chapters of the Contract Law deal with general principles such as formation and liability, and other specialist contracts such as contracts for sale and contracts for work.

A separate law, the Construction Law of the People's Republic of China was enacted on 1 November 1997 and put into effect on 1 March 1998, and comprises 85 articles in eight chapters. The Construction Law has been subsequently revised with slight changes in 2011. It covers licenses and permits for construction, qualifications, tendering, design-build and construction-only contracts, construction quality, legal liability, market regulations and procedures in construction projects. The Construction Law consolidated all existing construction-related regulations issued from different sources and governs all activities in the construction industry.

There are also numerous regulations governing the industry, including the Regulations of Construction Quality Administration approved and issued by the State Council

---

[15] www.asic.gov.au/asic/asic.nsf/byheadline/Foreign+Companies?opendocument.
[16] With thanks to Ashley Howlett of Jones Day for his comments on this section, and his helpful guide: Ashley Howlett, *Chinese Construction Law – a Guide for Foreign Companies* (CCH Asia Pte Ltd, 2009).
[17] Zhu Hongliang, Hu Xiangzhen and Wang Ying 'China's Construction Regulatory Systems', *Building Research & Information*, 29(3), (2001), 265–9.

on 10 January 2000. The Regulations specify the responsibilities and duties of all participants in a construction project for project quality. The Regulations contain nine chapters covering the responsibilities and duties of owners, site investigators, designers, construction companies and construction supervisors, as well as liabilities for defects, penalties to be imposed and the government's powers to supervise and inspect.

Parties may contract on any terms, subject to the specific provisions set out in these Laws. Article 62 of the Contract Law states that if the relevant terms of a contract are unclear on quality, that State standards or industry standards should be applied. If there are no State standards or industry standards, generally held standards or specific standards in conformity with the purpose of the contract should apply. Article 56 of the Construction Law requires all design documents to comply with relevant laws, including quality and safety standards.

The provisions regarding construction contracts[18] are quite detailed, and cover both design and surveying services, and construction work. All contracts must be in writing (Art 270), and there are strict limitations on the extent to which the services or work can be sub-let (Art 272). Surveying and design contracts must include:

> clauses dealing with deadlines for the submission of relevant basic information and documents (including budget proposals), quality requirements, fees and expenses, and other conditions of cooperation, etc.[19]

And building contracts must include:

> clauses dealing with the scope of the project, the time-limit for construction work, commencement and completion times for the intermediary stages of the project, project quality and construction costs, the time for the delivery of technical materials, responsibility in relation to the supply of materials and equipment, the appropriation of funds and settlement of accounts, examination and acceptance procedures upon completion of the work, the scope of quality guarantees and the length of quality guaranty periods, and mutual cooperation of the parties, etc.[20]

Article 107 sets out alternative remedies for breach of contract, namely specific performance, rectification, or damages, however specific performance or restoration would normally be the preferred options.[21] Any sub-contractors are jointly and severally liable with the main contractor to the client (§272), and this would apply also to design work. In addition, Article 73 of the Construction Law imposes liability for failure to achieve quality and safety standards.

---

[18] Contract Law, Art 269–87, translation adapted from the above guide (an alternative source is the World Law Guide, www.lexadin.nl/wlg/legis/nofr/oeur/lxwechi.htm).
[19] Contract Law, Art 274.
[20] Contract Law, Art 275.
[21] Howlett *supra*, p. 31.

The Contract Law refers to design 'units' which can be government/quasi government or private entities which have relevant design qualifications. Any construction design unit which does not carry out design work in accordance with construction project quality and safety standards will be ordered to rectify their work and will receive a fine. If an accident arises which relates to the quality of the project, authorities may order the design unit to cease its operations, to be reorganised, or may lower its qualification rating or revoke its credentials certificate. Any illicit gains could be confiscated and fines imposed. The design unit will bear liability for any losses that have been caused. If any crime has been committed, criminal liability will also be pursued.

There are equivalent obligations on the contractor. Under the PRC laws, a designer and a contractor would be liable in tort to third parties such as a future purchase or lessee for any injury or property damage that could be shown to be caused by its negligence, as well as to the client. A party to a contract may not indemnify another party against claims due to such negligence. Although no Articles specifically address the level of liability for design by a contractor or consultant, the overall tenor of the relevant Articles suggest that the liability may be strict.

Various types of sample construction contracts have been issued jointly by the Ministry of Housing and Urban-Rural Development (formerly the Ministry of Construction) and the State Industrial and Commercial Administration Bureau, and are widely used. These include the Model Conditions of Contract for Works of Building Construction (GF-1999-0201). This is a revised version of the Model Conditions (GF-91-0201) originally published in 1991. The revisions took account of user experience, legislation, and other standard forms including the FIDIC forms. There are also forms for general building work (GF-96-0205; GF-96-0206) and for Building and Construction Supervision (GF-2000-0202).

GF-1999-0201 is the most commonly used contract in building construction projects, particularly government projects, and on projects designed primarily by architects. The terms require a high standard of performance from the contractor, for example clause 34.1 requires the contractor to 'warrant to the Owner on the Work [being] in accordance with the current laws, government standards, and related country's warranty policies'.

The Ministry also passed regulations governing construction design contracts in 2000 and included sample agreements for consultants (GF-2000-0203; GF-2000-0204; GF-2000-0209; GF-2000-0210). These contracts of appointment are short in comparison to the RIBA Standard Forms of Agreement, but do provide for standard items such as payment in instalments, interest for late payment, termination of the contract and dispute resolution through arbitration.

FIDIC contracts are also often used, particularly where there is foreign investment involved. The Chinese forms are short in comparison with FIDIC forms, and new editions are likely in the near future.

The architectural profession in China is regulated through the Ordinance of Registered Architect of the PRC 1995 (Registered Architect Regulation), the supervising body being the National Administrative Committee of Registered Architects. Only registered architects are entitled to use the title 'registered architect' (local authorities can check and confirm whether an architect is authorised to practise).

Before the introduction of the Ordinance, design work would always be commissioned through a state-registered 'design institute'. Only the institutes, not individuals, were legally entitled to engage in design activities and issue drawings. Owners would select a design institute either in the same way as when selecting a construction company through competitive tendering, or through a design competition.[22]

The Ordinance now specifies that a building of a certain span and height can only be designed by a registered architect. All registered architects are required to join an 'architectural design unit' in order to practice. These used to be limited to government design institutes but now include private practices. The unit is authorised to accept commissions for work and charges fees accordingly. Should a claim be made for design deficiency resulting in the client's economic loss, the unit would be responsible for compensation. The latter is authorised to demand compensation from the architect responsible for the project.

The Ordinance includes chapters on examination and registration, practice, rights and responsibilities of a registered architect and liabilities. Its scope is wider than that of the Architects Act 1997 in the UK, and covers Codes of Conduct similar to those of the ARB and the RIBA. The Ordinance allows for the creation of the National Administration Board of Architectural Registration (NABAR), closely patterned after the North American National Architectural Accrediting Board's system. The NABAR maintains a register of all Class 1 architects in China, and its sub-committees at various local governments maintain the local Class 2 architects register.

Under the Tendering Law approved by the Standing Committee of the National People's Congress on 30 August 1999, competitive procurement of services such as site and/or ground investigation, design, construction and construction supervision is required for certain types of construction projects. Competitive bidding, however, is optional for all the other construction projects. Two sets of standard documents for tendering of construction projects were published by the authorities in 2007.

Foreign contractors wishing to undertake construction work must establish a Chinese foreign investment enterprise (FIE). All FIEs must obtain the same qualifications and certificates as Chinese firms before undertaking any design or construction works. In the case of design work a foreign company[23] could also collaborate with a Chinese local design company through a cooperative design contract, or set up a design FIE. Foreign investors are often required to partner with a local company.

It is normal practice for consultants to take out professional indemnity insurance, and for contractors to take out all-risks and public liability insurance. Building structure defects insurance is also available.

---

[22] Centre for Cultural Policy Research, *Study on the Relationship between Hong Kong's Cultural & Creative Industries and the Pearl River Delta* (The University of Hong Kong, 2006) (Consultative Report commissioned by the Central Policy Unit, HKSAR Government).

[23] A company registered locally by a foreign investor cannot adopt the cooperative design arrangement, only companies registered outside of China ('foreign design company') may do this.

18.3 The Middle East[24]

The Middle East follows a civil law system, with the majority of countries having adopted a Civil Code which follows the French model, including Algeria, Egypt, Iraq, Jordan, Qatar, and the United Arab Emirates (UAE).[25,26] The civil law systems cover liability in tort, contract and criminal law. Though the codes appear relatively straight-forward on their face, in practice there are often difficulties in their interpretation. This is because the ancient principles of Shar'ia law (the moral code and religious law of Islam) still have a strong influence, both in terms of the drafting of the Codes themselves, and in their interpretation and enforcement by the courts. At the heart of all civil liability in this region is the concept of harm and obligation, and these concepts transcend the traditional Western boundaries of contract, tort and criminal law. For a designer in the region it is important to understand that liability may subject them to prosecution under any or all of these laws simultaneously, as the underlying Shar'ia principles are common to all.

18.3.1 Tort liability

Tort liability in the Middle East stems from a harm suffered. The harm can be to the person (including moral damage)[27] or to physical property, and generally no distinction is made between pure economic loss and physical loss or injury.[28] Design liability stemming from tort will fall almost exclusively into harm to the person or property categories. The most common form of remedy for harm suffered to the person is monetary restitution in the amount of actual loss, however in the case of loss or damage to property, the most common remedy is rectification or specific performance. In general, tort liability is imposed *irrespective of fault* and in common law jurisdictions would be considered strict liability.

---

[24] With thanks to Dr Jay Palmos of the British University in Dubai, for his initial draft of a large section of this text, and also to Jay Palmos and to Eric Teo, of Al Tamimi & Company, for their helpful comments on the text as it developed.

[25] In Egypt the Civil Code (ECC) came into force 1949, that for Iraq in 1953, and that for Algeria (ACC), 1975. The UAE Code for Civil Transactions (ECCT) was issued in December 1985. A new Qatari Civil Code (QCC) came into force on 8 September 2004.

[26] Said M Hanafi, 'Contractor's Liability under the Civil Codes of Algeria, Egypt, Qatar and the UAE,' *The International Construction Law Review* 25(2), (2008), 220–31.

[27] ECCT, Art 293(1) The right to have damage made good shall include moral damage, and an infringement of the liberty, dignity, honour, reputation, social standing or financial condition of another shall be regarded as being moral damage.

[28] e.g. see ECCT, Art. 292 which states that: 'In all cases the compensation shall be assessed on the basis the amount of harm suffered by the victim, together with loss of profit, provided it is a natural result of the harmful act' (trans. from LexGulf- Middle East Business Law series).

Once harm has been suffered due to the actions of another, restitution is required – unless there is an exception under the law. Exceptions within the Code are specific and relate more to particular factual situations than to overriding policy goals such as fairness or deterrence. There is no distinction between intentional and negligent acts, and it is immaterial if tortfeasors suffer from a mental disorder or infirmity, or are too young to understand the consequences of their actions, or that they were intoxicated: personal liability would still apply in all those instances to the individual responsible for the harm.

In situations where design fault causes the death of another human, most Middle Eastern jurisdictions will impose a financial penalty known as Diyya.[29] Diyya (colloquially known as 'blood money') is a non-negotiable payment used in cases of accidental killings. Rather than calculating the value of a lost life, based upon the individual's life expectancy, potential earnings or other criteria, Diyya is pre-established fixed amount (unless the parties agree to another compensation value).[30] In the UAE, a person who causes the death of another person is liable to pay 200,000 AED Dirhams[31] (approximately €38,000) to the heirs of the deceased.

In principle, only the tortfeasor can be held responsible for damage caused to another[32] and liability will fall upon that individual to make restitution. However, there are exceptions to this general rule. Of particular relevance to those practising in the design and construction industries is an exception relating to building collapse.[33] In that situation, any harm suffered as a result of a partial or total building collapse will in the first instance be the responsibility of the legal owner of the structure.[34] However, once the owner is found liable, it may in turn seek restitution from the party responsible for the harm.[35]

18.3.2 Sources of design liability in contract

The law of obligations, or contract law, is perhaps the best defined and most well understood category of civil law in the Middle East since most of the principles stem directly from *hadith*.[36] It is for this reason that most modern construction contracts in the region utilise contractual provisions to define the standards of care which

---

[29] Diyya for homicide and manslaughter stems from the Qur'an IV:92.

[30] ECCT, Article 299.

[31] Federal law No. 3 of 1987, Penal Code for the United Arab Emirates.

[32] ECCT, Article 313(1).

[33] ECCT, Law #5 of 1985, Articles 315(1) and (2).

[34] The principle that the owner of the structure is unconditionally liable for total or partial collapse stems from as early as 1300 AD and is incorporated into the civil codes of Egypt (s. 177), Syria (s. 178), Kuwait (s. 243), Libya (s. 180), Jordan (s. 290) and the UAE (s. 315). All of these codes, to one extent or another, provide that either the owner or a party with power of legal or physical possession over the property will be liable for any and all damages caused by the collapse.

[35] ECCT, Article 313(2) and/or Article 334.

[36] A *hadith* is a reliably transmitted report of what the Prophet Muhammad said, did, or approved.

might ordinarily be implied in English law. An example of a typical contractual provision included in design-only or design and construct contracts in the UAE is as follows:

> GOOD ENGINEERING PRACTICE means, without limiting or prejudicing any higher standards or higher requirements under this AGREEMENT, practices, methods and procedures and that degree of skill, diligence, prudence and foresight which would reasonably be expected to be observed by a skilled and experienced contractor of international repute engaged in carrying out activities the same as or similar to the WORKS under the same or similar circumstances.

This clause demonstrates the expansive nature of the contractual provisions common in the region. Terms of art such as 'reasonable' or 'foresight' are undefined in the UAE and other Codes, as there is no equivalent to the objective test of the ordinary competent practitioner as used in English law. Clauses such as this one will be interpreted *de novo* based upon contractual interpretation of Code provisions which seek to determine the intentions of the parties at the time of signing the contract.[37]

The Code provisions also cover breach of contract, and generally allow an aggrieved party to seek damages for breach and even cancellation of the contract. In certain circumstances the court may require specific performance instead of granting damages.[38]

18.3.3 Muquala

The Muquala provisions of the Code apply to any contracts whereby 'one of the parties undertakes to make a thing or to perform work' for consideration, and specifically address issues relating to the construction industry. Of particular relevance to designers are a number of articles which address liability for 'any total or partial collapse of the building or any defect which threatens the stability or safety of the building'.[39]

The principles established in these articles stem from the French *garantie décennale* whereby owners and successors in interest are afforded a 10-year warranty that a building will be free from hidden defects that either compromise the integrity of the construction or render it unfit for use. However, unlike the French Code which specifies that all successors in interest will be covered by the guarantee, in the UAE liability is limited to those in direct privity of contract. As such, designer liability is not extended to subsequent purchasers of property or unrelated third parties, such as guests or lessors.[40]

---

[37] ECCT, Article 265.
[38] See e.g. ECCT. Articles 338, 380 and 386.
[39] ECCT, Article 880(1), the liability also covers other fixed installations, which includes such as towers and bridges.
[40] Dubai, Court of Cassassion, decision no. 2007/251.

The Muquala sections of the UAE Code impose liability on the 'architect . . . for any total or partial collapse of the building or any defect which threatens the stability or safety of the building'.[41]

The term 'architect' in this clause relates to anyone who performs design functions, specifically including engineers, architects and others who supply drawings. However, the Code differentiates between designers who supervise or inspect the construction work and those who merely supply plans or construction drawings. In the former case, the designer will be held jointly liable with the contractor for all damages, whether created by a failure in design or construction, or, importantly, any other cause including undiscoverable defects in the land.[42] In those cases the parties will need to seek contribution or indemnity amongst themselves (in which case causation will need to be proved). In the case of the latter, liability will only be imposed on the designer for any 'defects in the plans'.[43]

The joint liability under Article 880 is therefore not only strict (i.e. there is no need to prove negligence) but also does not require proof of causation. Although not entirely clear, it appears that the Code also allows an employer to bring an action separately against a design architect/engineer involved in supervision without having to establish negligence or that the cause of the collapse or structural defect was due to a design error.

Only serious defects that threaten the safety or stability of the buildings/installations would attract decennial liability; negligence not affecting the structural integrity of a building is excluded from its scope. The contractor is however liable for defects in materials and workmanship[44] unless obvious and accepted by employer at takeover.[45] These provisions of the codes are additional to the decennial liability under Article 880. Therefore, depending on the type of breach or defects, there are several avenues open to employers: to seek redress for breach of express terms of the contract (under the general contract provisions of the civil code);[46] breach of general statutory codes;[47] breach of building regulations/building license issued by the relevant local authority; violation of trade/customary practice; and/or tort liability (acts causing direct or indirect harm).

Where a contract is silent as to the quality of specification of material or works, customary practice or standards will apply.[48] Contractors will escape liability if they can show that they followed the design and instructions of the engineer. In the case of architects/engineers, they would only be liable for non-serious defects if the contract imposes this liability, and in such cases the employer would need to show causation, i.e. that the defect was caused by a design error, but probably not that the designer failed to use reasonable skill and care (unless the terms are limited in this way).

---

[41] ECCT, Article 880(1).

[42] Joint and several liability of contractor and architect for serious defects in buildings (ECC 651–4; ACC 554–7; QCC 711–15; ECCT 880–83).

[43] ECCT, Article 881; QCC, Article 712.

[44] ECCT, Article 389; ECC, Article 447; ACC, Article 380.

[45] ibid.

[46] e.g. see ECCT Articles 272, 389, 878 and 881.

[47] e.g. see ECCT Articles 272, 389, 878 and 881.

[48] ECCT, Articles 46 and 50, amongst other provisions, provide customary practice with the force of law.

The duration of liability is set by contract, however any provision which seeks to establish a liability period of less than 10 years for structural collapse etc 'from the time of delivery of the work'[49] will be void[50] unless the parties have agreed that the lifespan of the structure is intended to be less than 10 years.[51] Generally a time-limit applies to the bringing of claims for compensation, which is generally three years from the date of collapse or, importantly, 'discovery of the defect'.[52]

In summary, decennial liability in the UAE is a form of strict liability placed on designers for any full or partial collapse of a structure, and any defect which threatens a structure's stability. Further, if designers were involved during the construction phase, they will be held jointly liable for any issues caused by or during construction, including unforeseen ground anomalies. Only those in relationships of privity of contract are subject to this liability; defects which do not threaten the structural integrity of a building are excluded; and designers who do not participate in the construction phase are only liable for defects in the drawings.

18.3.4 Criminal law

Designers may also be subject to criminal prosecution for any of the following: negligence, lack of vigilance, lack of precaution, recklessness, imprudence, or non-compliance with the laws, regulations, rules or orders.[53] In other words, designers can easily face both civil and criminal liabilities in respect of the same acts or omissions.

Specific penalties apply in situations where the offender failed to perform the duties imposed due to the person's role, profession, or craft.[54] In effect, the procedure followed in criminal prosecutions in the UAE is similar to a common law negligence suit. The standard of duty of care is established by reference to the laws, regulations, rules or orders applicable in any particular case. Each municipality has a set of building codes which will specify quality standards to which designers must adhere in order to be granted building permits. These standards are unique to each municipality, but most consist merely of a listing of foreign international standards, such as those published by British Standards or the American Association of State Highways and Transportation. Failure to design to those standards will demonstrate non-compliance with a law and subject designers to criminal penalties.

Criminal penalties are also imposed in the UAE where death or physical injury has occurred as a result of sub-standard design and there is a mandatory sentencing guideline for injury or death caused by design negligence which may involve a prison sentence and/or a fine. For example where physical injury is caused to more than three people, the sentence would be six months–five years' imprisonment plus a fine.

---

[49] ECCT, Article 880(3).
[50] ECCT, Article 882; QCC, Article 715.
[51] ECCT, Article 880(1); QCC Article 715.
[52] ECCT, Article 883; QCC, Article 714.
[53] Penal Code [Fed. Law 3 of 1987], Article 38.
[54] Penal Code [Fed. Law 3 of 1987], Article 342-3.

There are no reported cases (in English) of design negligence causing death or injury in the UAE. However, last year in Turkey a designer was charged and convicted of manslaughter by negligence under a similar penal code.[55] In that case, a primary boarding school collapsed causing the death of 64 students and one teacher after an extremely severe earthquake. The court found that the structure was inadequately designed and that more people died than would normally have been expected from a quake of that magnitude, due to the poor quality of materials specified for construction. In that case, the financial penalty imposed was 343 Turkish Lira (approximately €135) per death and the designer was sentenced to one-year imprisonment.

The combined financial and penal nature of laws relating to personal injury and wrongful death is one of the idiosyncrasies associated with design negligence in the region. While the financial penalties are considerably lower than those found in Western jurisdictions, the imposition of mandatory penal sentences more than compensates from a deterrence perspective.

18.3.5 Other matters

The distinction between the professions of architect and engineer is less pronounced in the Middle East than in other countries, and the word for each is the same in Arabic. Regulation of the professions varies between countries, but generally registration is not required, although there are exceptions. For example in Egypt, the architect/engineer professional is regulated by the Engineering Syndicate, and those practicing must be licensed. Registration is also required in Abu Dhabi. Both title and function are protected, with projects above a certain size in these countries requiring the involvement of an architect/engineer.

No Middle East countries publish standard forms of contract, and generally no particular standard forms are prescribed for use, for example in government contracts. However most employers have their own standardised terms, often based on the FIDIC or other standard models. Although the FIDIC form is widely used, it tends to be significantly modified. The Abu Dhabi Government uses its own standard terms for procuring public works, the 2007 Abu Dhabi Government Conditions of Contract (Laws No 21 of 2006 and No 1 of 2007), which is a modified version of the FIDIC form. The NEC form has also been used in some high-profile projects in the UEA.

18.4 *Russia*[56]

The Russian Federation (RF) is a civil law country. Design and construction activities in Russia are governed by federal legislation (the RF Town Planning Code of 29 December 2004), as well as by regional and municipal legislation. Numerous technical

---

[55] Supreme Court of Appeals, 'Contractor guilty of negligence in earthquake collapse, cays court', *Hurriyet Daily News & Economic Review*, 8 October 2010.
[56] With thanks to Ksenia Bruk of Salens, and to David Lasfargue and Ekaterina Vilenskaya of GIDE for their helpful comments on a draft of this text.

standards and regulations (so-called SNiPs) from soviet times are also still applied – some of them on a voluntary, and some of them on mandatory basis. In the future such standards and regulations will be replaced by the RF federal technical regulations.

The RF Civil Code governs general contract and extra-contractual law. The second part of the Civil Code, which came into force in 1996 and deals with the law of obligations, is the most relevant to construction and design liability. In particular, chapter 37 of the Civil Code regulates the parties' relations under different types of work and labour contracts (including building contracts, and design and survey works contracts).

Article 721 of the Civil Code defines the quality of work as follows:

> The quality of the work performed by the contractor shall correspond to the terms and conditions of the contract and in the absence or in the event of incompleteness of these terms and conditions – to the requirements usually made to the work of appropriate kind. Unless otherwise stipulated by the law, other legal acts or the contract, the result of the fulfilled work shall possess, at the time of its transfer to the customer, the properties, referred to in the contract, or determined by the usually made requirements and shall be suitable within a reasonable period for the use, stipulated by the contract, [or] for the usual use of the result of the work of this kind.[57]

Article 702 explains that these contracts would include 'individual types of work and labour contract (domestic contract, building contract, contract for the performance of design and survey works, contract works for state needs)'. The combined effect appears to create a strict liability for the provisions of works to meet the purpose as defined in the contract, which would apply to both contractor and designer.

Under Article 706 a contractor will be liable to the employer for failures in performance of any sub-contractor. Article 707 also makes all parties jointly and severally liable to the client:

> If two or more persons act simultaneously on the side of the contractor, they shall be recognised in case of indivisibility of the subject-matter of the obligation as joint and several debtors with regard to the customer and accordingly as joint and several creditors.

The period of limitation for claims made in connection with poor quality of work, performed under a work and labour contract, is generally one year (§725) except for 'buildings and structures', where the limitation period is three years (§196). Generally the period starts to run from acceptance of the works, but where the contract itself provides for a guarantee period, the period of limitation starts from the date any defects are notified to the contractor.

Under the RF Town Planning Code, a contractor carrying out design works is liable for the quality of design documentation and its compliance with respective technical regulations. It is interesting to note that the Russian Federation, the RF constituent entity or an organisation which carried out non-state expert appraisal of design works, may be subsidiarily liable for damage caused as a result of those works, where such damages are caused by lack of compliance of the design documentation with the

---

[57] Translation from www.russian-civil-code.com/PartII/.

requirements of technical regulations, and there is a positive state or non-state expert appraisal of such design documentation.

There are no generally accepted Russian standard forms of contract. The construction contracts for major projects are frequently let on the FIDIC forms (red, yellow or silver books) or on terms based on these forms. However, the terms of these forms need to be substantially moderated to suit local conditions and legislative requirements.

Parties can contractually limit their liability in relation to each other (§§15, 400 and 401, Civil Code). Article 400 states that 'By the individual kinds of obligations and by those obligations, which are related to a definite type of activity, the right to full compensation for losses may be limited by the law (limited liability)'. It is generally considered that this allows parties to limit liability to direct losses and to exclude consequential losses, but does not permit parties to agree to remove all liability for an obligation.

Insurance is not generally compulsory under the construction or design contract according to the Civil Code, but is commonly required (e.g. under FIDIC standard terms). Article 705 of the Code states that the contractor bears the risk of an accidental loss or damage of an object under construction, and the cost of all materials and equipment, unless the contract states otherwise. In addition, under Article 741 the risk of 'accidental destruction of, or accidental damage to, the building project, which makes up the subject of the building contract' is borne by the contractor before the project is handed over to the customer. The contractor will therefore normally take out insurance to cover these risks.

In the case of architects, the use of the title is not protected, and registration is not compulsory, but architecture is regulated under Federal Law 'On Architectural Activity in the Russian Federation' No. 169-FZ of 17 November 1995 (as amended).

There is no general requirement for foreign designers or contractors to enter into joint venture arrangements in order to provide services, but under the above Federal Law 'On Architectural Activity in the Russian Federation', architects may only take part in architectural activities in cooperation with a Russian architect. Foreign designers tend to establish subsidiaries in Russia, or are engaged as consultants for owner's development companies.[58]

Since 1 January 2010 operations in the field of construction affecting safety have required a competency certificate provided by self-regulatory organisations ('SRO'). These provisions are set out in Amendments to the Russian Town-Planning Code and Certain Legislative Acts of the Russian Federation (Federal Law No. 148-FZ dated 22 July 2008). The SRO certificate is in the form of a permit to engage in particular types of construction activity in Russia. To obtain one the company must become a member of a SRO (the law applies to both Russian and foreign companies). Currently there are SROs for civil engineers, designers and for builders, and the minimum admittance criteria are established by the SRO. The scope of works covered includes most types of design, engineering, construction, re-construction or repair works (there is an approved list by the Russian Ministry of Regional Development: Decree No. 624 dated 30 December 2009). Conducting work without a SRO is illegal and will result in a fine and suspension of works.

---

[58] Kamil Karibov and Anna Strezhneva, *Getting the Deal Through: Construction 2010: Russia* (London: Law Business Research Ltd, 2010).

18.5 USA[59]

As with Australia, the USA has a common law legal system. As common law jurisdictions, all states (with the exception of Louisiana, which has a French legal tradition) base their contract and tort law mainly on precedents. Each state in addition passes its own laws, therefore the exact position regarding design liability may be different in each state, although the broad principles of contract and tort law are for all practical purposes uniform across all states.

At Federal level the Uniform Commercial Code (UCC) deals with certain aspects of contract (mainly sales transactions). Although a model and not binding, it has been adopted by all states, including Louisiana, although often with some modification. It covers matters such as formation of contract, and implied warranties (§2 of the Uniform Commercial Code and Restatement (2nd) of Contracts). For example, there is an implied warranty of 'fitness for particular purpose' in contracts of sale which states:

> Where the seller at the time of contracting has reason to know any particular purpose for which the goods are required and that the buyer is relying on the seller's skill or judgement to select or furnish suitable goods, there is unless excluded or modified under the next section an implied warranty that the goods shall be fit for such purpose. (§2-315)

There is also a warranty of habitability whereby for new residential structures the contractor owes a duty to build a house (and related fixtures) such that it can be lived in for normal residential purposes. It is possible to exclude the warranty of fitness but not that of habitability. Contractors generally would also be under an implied duty of workmanship, i.e. to make sure that their work is sufficiently free from defects such that it meets the requirements of the contract documents.

As in the UK, the liability of design consultants is on a fault-based system, for example liability for architects and engineers arises out of a failure to perform in accordance with generally accepted standards of professional skill and care:

> Architects, doctors, engineers, attorneys, and others deal in somewhat inexact sciences and are continually called upon to exercise their skilled judgement in order to anticipate and provide for random factors which are incapable of precise measurement. The indeterminable nature of these factors makes it impossible for professional service people to gauge them with complete accuracy in every instance . . . Because of the inescapable possibility of error which inheres in these services, the law has traditionally required, not perfect results, but rather the exercise of that skill and judgement which can reasonably be expected from similarly situated professionals.[60]

An example of a more recent case where this principle was applied is *RCDI Construction Inc. v Spaceplan/Architecture, Planning, & Interiors.*[61]

Although there is normally an implied warranty that material provided by a contractor will be fit for purpose, where the owner describes in detail the materials to be

---

[59] With thanks to Jerry Abeles of Arent Fox LLP for his comments on a draft of this text.
[60] *City of Mounds View v Walijarvi*, 263 NW 2d 420, 424 (Minn. 1978).
[61] PA, 148 F. Supp. 2d 607 (WDNC 2001).

employed and the manner in which the work is to be performed, courts have determined that no warranty of adequacy arises. The contractor in that situation has no discretion to deviate from the specifications and 'is required to follow them as one would follow a road map'.[62]

Of particular note is the 'Spearin doctrine'[63] whereby the US Supreme Court declared that when the government issued detailed plans and specifications to the contractor, it had impliedly warranted the adequacy of the design in those documents. An example of its application can be seen in *Harbor Construction Company, Inc. v Board of Supervisors*.[64] In this project the contract document in several places attempted to place the risk of errors or missing information on the contractor, for example stating: 'All drawings are for reference only. The contractor is responsible for field verification of all dimensions and job site conditions that may affect the cost of the project'. However, the court held that the contract language, however compelling, could not override the doctrine as established by case law, citing Justice Brandeis in *US v Spearin*:

> [I]f the contractor is bound to build according to plans and specifications prepared by the owner, the contractor will not be responsible for the consequences of defects in the plans and specifications. This responsibility of the owner is not overcome by the usual clauses requiring builders to visit the site, to check the plans, and to inform themselves of the requirements of the work . . .

The normal warranty, however, only applies to design specifications, whereby an owner providing plans impliedly warrants that following the design will result in a building acceptable to the owner.[65] There is no equivalent warranty for performance specifications, where the successful contractor is expected to exercise its ingenuity in selecting the means by which the objective is to be achieved.[66] The distinction between the two types of specification can therefore be crucial. In a situation where the drawings and specification of the design provided to the manufacturer are incomplete in some aspect, the manufacturer has been found liable, e.g. in *Penguin Industries Inc. v the United States*,[67] where the exact amount of glue to be applied to bullet casing was left to the manufacturer who was found liable to ensure that the product would be as fit for purpose as possible within the area of discretion allowed. The incomplete specifications were termed 'performance' specifications in order to achieve this result.

When contractors provide a design service in connection with construction, but the contract does not set out the level of liability, it appears that the contractor would be

---

[62] *Blake Constr. Co. v United States*, 987 F 2d 743 (Fed. Cir. 1993).

[63] *United States v Spearin* 248 US 132, 136, 39 S Ct 59, 61 (1918).

[64] 2011 La. App. LEXIS 577 (12 May 2011 in the Court of Appeal of Louisiana, Fourth Circuit).

[65] Justin Sweet and Marc M. Schneier, *Legal Aspects of Architecture, Engineering and the Construction Process* (Stamford: Cengage Learning, 2009), p. 517, citing *Daewoo Engineering and Construction Company v the United States* (2006) 73 Fed Cl 547, at 566–8.

[66] *Norwood Mfg, Inc. v United States*, 21 Cl Ct 300, citing *J. L. Simmons Co. v United States*, 188 Ct Cl 684, 412 F 2d 1360 (1969).

[67] (1976) 530 Fed Rep 2nd Cir 934.

required to provide a building fit for the owner's purposes[68] (i.e. there would be an implied warranty, as was found in the UK case of *Viking Grain v TH White*[69]). Contractors would normally be under an implied duty to warn of design errors they spot in information provided by the employer, and may not be able to rely on the normal warranty regarding plans and specifications when the contractor had reason to suspect a potential problem with the design and failed to warn the owner or take other steps to investigate the adequacy of the design.[70]

Principles of tortious liability also broadly reflect those in the UK. Generally, a consultant may be liable to a third party for errors which cause physical injury. A case-law generated principle termed the 'economic loss doctrine', which is adopted by the common law or legislation in most jurisdictions, restricts the type of damage recoverable by a third party to 'non-economic damages', i.e. personal injury or property damage, and also limits recoverable losses to those resulting from damage to 'other' property. As in the UK, 'harm to the product itself', i.e. the cost to repair any damage to a defective product, including construction work, is not recoverable in a tort claim.

Another principle termed the 'integrated product doctrine' extends the above rule to prohibit tort-based recovery when a defective product is 'incorporated' into a product which the defective product has damaged (equivalent to the 'complex structure' arguments). However, what might be considered 'integrated' is open to argument, e.g. in the case of *Robert R. Dean, et al. v Barrett Homes, Inc., et al.*[71] the New Jersey Supreme Court said an applied stucco product was not 'integrated' and allowed recovery of damages.

Consultants may, however, be liable to third parties for economic loss in the case of negligent misstatement, under the Restatement (Second) of Torts Act 1977, §552(1), which has been adopted in some form by most state courts. An example of this being applied can be seen in the Texas case of *CCE, INC. v PBS & J Construction Services, Inc.*,[72] where significant damage was caused by flooding. The court rejected the designer's argument that its 'professional opinion' as stated in the storm water plans were not misrepresentations of 'fact', and therefore were not within the ambit of §552. The court ruled 'information' (i.e. stabilisation requirements, water quality best management practices) was negligently omitted, and therefore liability existed, whether or not this information was fact or opinion.

The extent of liability for breach of contract and negligence varies from state to state. The most common periods of liability for negligence generally are two, three and six years. In the context of construction the shortest liability period will be four years. Contractors and consultants are therefore likely to be subject to claims if their actions cause personal injury or damage to property. In addition, some states have enacted legislation that gives a direct right of action to homeowners against contractors for defective work.

---

[68] Justin Sweet and Marc M. Schneier, ibid., p. 528, citing *Dobler v Mallory* (1975) 214 NW 2nd Cir 510, at 516.
[69] (1985) 33 BLR 103.
[70] *George B. Gilmore Co. v Garrett*, 582 So. 2d 387 (Miss. 1991); *Parker v Thornton*, 596 So. 2d 854 (Miss. 1992).
[71] 2010 N J Lexis 1219 (15 November 2010).
[72] 2011 Tex. App. LEXIS 809 (28 January 2011).

All forms of procurement are commonly used, and the USA has been a leader in developing more novel methods such as construction management and partnering. The three most common project delivery methods are design-bid-build, design-build, and construction management. It is common for architects to sub-contract to all other consultants such as engineers, and specialist writers of specifications. There is no equivalent to quantity surveyors in the US. It is also normal for contractors to be involved in the detailed technical design, and for them to prepare shop drawings.

The most widely used forms are published by the American Institute of Architects (AIA).[73] In fact these forms are more widely used than their equivalents in the UK, both by private parties and in some cases for public procurement. The AIA publishes over 100 different forms of contract, which are grouped in families for different types of procurement. The A201 family of documents is for traditional procurement, although it makes provision for contractor design input. It includes A201 general conditions, and a range of forms for owner-contractor agreements (A101-2007, A102-2007 and A103-2007), owner-architect (B101-2007 and B103-2007), and for sub-contracting services (A401-2007). There are also families for use in design-build, construction management, integrated project delivery, small projects and international procurement, amongst others.

It is interesting to note that under A201 3-2.2 'the Contractor shall promptly report to the Architect any errors, inconsistencies or omissions discovered by or made known to the Contractor'. This is wider than the equivalent clause in JCT forms, although 3-2.2 makes it clear that the contractor is not required to engage in a professional review of the architect's design.

A warranty of workmanship is in included at clause 3.5.1 which states:

> The Contractor warrants to the Owner and Architect that materials and equipment furnished under the Contract will be of good quality and new unless the Contract Documents require or permit otherwise. The Contractor further warrants that the Work will conform to the requirements of the Contract Documents and that the Work will be free from defects except for those inherent in the quality of the Work the Contract Documents require or permit.

A key clause in relation to design is 3.12.10 which states:

> The Contractor shall not be required to provide professional services which constitute the practice of architecture or engineering unless such services are specifically required by the Contract Documents for a portion of the Work or unless the Contractor needs to provide such services in order to carry out the Contractor's responsibilities for construction means, methods, techniques, sequences and procedures.

The clause then continues to stipulate that where any professional services are required, the architect will specify all performance and design criteria that the services must satisfy, and that the services must be provided by a licensed professional.

Under clause 3.12.4 'shop drawings' are specifically stated not to be contract documents, but to be for the purposes of showing how the contractor proposes to 'conform

---

[73] www.aia.org.

to the information given and the design concept expressed in the Contract Documents'. Where such drawings are provided the contract states that:

> the Owner and the Architect shall be entitled to rely upon the adequacy, accuracy and completeness of the services, certifications and approvals performed or provided by such design professionals, provided the Owner and Architect have specified to the Contractor all performance and design criteria that such services must satisfy.'

The wide terms of clause 3.5.1 suggest that where the work is specified by performance, the contractor is warranting that the work will conform with the requirements in the contract (i.e. a strict liability not dependent on fault, rather than merely exercising skill and care in providing the work to meet those requirements). It is unclear however, should the contract documents require that a professional is used to provide the related design services, whether the level of liability of the contractor for those services would be the lesser one of using reasonable skill and care.

The AIA is not the only body to publish forms. The Engineers Joint Contract Documents Committee (EJCDC, comprising several engineering professional bodies) and the Associated General Contractors (AGC) publish forms which are used for major engineering and civil works, although neither are used as often as the AIA forms. Large projects often use bespoke forms, and the FIDIC forms are also used for major works. A newer suite of forms, 'ConsensusDocs', is intended to result in a more collaborative approach to procurement[74] and is often used in association with projects using BIM. ConsensusDocs has been developed by a pan-industry panel, which includes clients and on which the AGC has prominent representation.

The regulation of professions is state controlled, so that to register as an architect a person must be licensed in the state in which they practice. This requires academic qualifications, training, and sitting a state examination. The licence is not transferable, so architects must sit the state examinations in every state in which they wish to work. Architects register with the relevant State Registration Board and with NCARB (National Council of Architectural Registration Boards), which is regulated by state boards and establishes national standards for certifying architects. A similar system applies to engineers, so that most states protect the title 'engineer', and prohibit its use by those who are not licensed. As well as regulating the practice of the professions in their jurisdiction, each state in addition usually defines qualifications required, and addresses reciprocity of registration with other states. Several states also require contractors to be licensed, for example California requires almost all contracting companies to be licensed whereas others, such as New York, do not.

Contractors are usually required to take out insurance under the terms of individual contracts, but 'works' insurance is not a statutory requirement. Sometimes 'joint names' or 'wrap-up' insurance policies are taken out. Licensed consultants are normally required to have PI insurance, for which a general policy usually suffices (rather than individual cover for each and every claim).

---

[74] www.consensusdocs.org.

Bibliography

3DReid (ed.), *Architect's Job Book*, 8th edn (London: RIBA Publishing, 2008).

Acquis Group, *Principles of European Law. Contracts 1* (Munich: Sellier, 2007).

Aeberli, Peter, *Tort in Construction*. Kings College, London, Centre of Construction Law and Management: Course Papers. (Aeberli, 2001) Available at www.aeberli.com.

American Institute of Architects California Council, *Integrated Project Delivery: A Working Definition*, v2, updated 13 June 2007 (California: McGraw-Hill, 2007).

American Institute of Architects California Council, *Integrated Project Delivery: A Guide* (California: McGraw-Hill, 2007).

Architects Registration Board, *Architects Code: Standards of Conduct and Practice* (London: ARB, 2010).

Atkins Chambers, *Hudson's Building and Engineering Contracts*, 12th edn (London: Sweet & Maxwell, 2010).

Bailey, Julian, 'What Lies Beneath', *The International Construction Law Review*, 24(4), (2007), 394–414.

Barendrecht, M., C. Jansen, M. Loos, A. Pinna, R. Cascao and S. van Gulijk, *Principles of European Law, Service Contracts (PELSC)* (Munich: Sellier, 2007).

Barnes, Rachel, 'RICS Consultancy Form: A False Friend', *Building Magazine* 26 (September 2008).

Barnes, Rachel, *NEC Professional Services Contract (PSC3): A Consultant's Perspective*, Society of Construction Law Paper D127 (London: SCL, 2011).

Barnes, Rachel, *Professional Services Agreements: A Guide for Construction Professionals*, 2nd edn (London: ICE Publishing, 2012).

Barnes, Rachel, *Trustees of Ampleforth Abbey Trust v Turner & Townsend Project Management Limited: Implications for Monetary Limits of Liability in Appointments* (London: Beale & Co, 2012).

Bell, M, Legal Research Studies Paper 437: 'Standard Form Construction Contracts in Australia: Are Our Reinvented Wheels Carrying Us Forward?' *Building and Construction Law Journal*, 25(2), (2009).

Bennett, John and Sarah Jayes, *Trusting the Team* (Reading: Centre for Strategic Studies in Construction, The University of Reading, with the partnering task force of the Reading Construction Forum, 1995).

Bennett, Lawrence, *The Management of Construction: A Project Life Cycle Approach* (Oxford: Butterworth-Heinemann, 2003).

Blake Dawson, *Scope for Improvement 2011: Project Risk – Getting the Right Balance and Outcomes* (Australia: Blake Dawson, 2011).

Cornes and Lupton's Design Liability in the Construction Industry, Fifth Edition. Sarah Lupton.
© 2013 Sarah Lupton and DL Cornes. Published 2013 by Blackwell Publishing Ltd.

British Council for Offices (BCO), *Good Practice in the Selection of Construction Materials* (London: BCO, 2011).

Brown, Jeffrey, *Do Design and Build Insurance Policy Wordings Fit the Bill?* Society of Construction Law, Paper D120 (London: SCL, 2011).

Bruggeman E.M., M.A.B. Chao-Duivis and A.Z.R. Koning (eds), *A Practical Guide to Dutch Building Contracts* (The Netherlands: Instituut von Bouwrecht, 2008).

Building Information Modelling (BIM) Working Group, *BIM: Management for Value, Cost and Carbon Improvement.* A report for the Government Construction Client Group (London: March 2011).

Bunni, Nael G., *Risk and Insurance in Construction*, 2nd edn (London: Spon Press, 2003).

The Cabinet Office, *Government Construction Strategy* (London: HMSO, 2011).

Casson, Sir Hugh, Romanes Lecture delivered in Oxford, 12 November 1979, *The Guardian*, Saturday 24 November 1979.

Centre d'Études d'Assurance (CEA), *Liabilities in Europe* (Belgium: CEA, 2004).

Centre for Cultural Policy Research, *Study on the Relationship between Hong Kong's Cultural & Creative Industries and the Pearl River Delta* (The University of Hong Kong, 2006) (Consultative Report commissioned by the Central Policy Unit, HKSAR Government).

Chao-Duivas, M.A.B., 'An Analysis and Comparison of the Dutch Standard Contract for Integrated Contracts (Turnkey/Design and Build) and the Fidic Yellow Book', *The International Construction Law Review*, 23(4), (2006), 450–78.

Chao-Duivas, M.A.B., 'Some Legal Aspects of BIM in establishing a Collaborative Relationship', *The International Construction Law Review*, 28(3), (2011), 264–75.

Construction Industry Board, *Partnering in the Team* (London: HMSO, 1996).

Construction Industry Council, *Scope of Services* (London: RIBA Publishing, 2007).

Construction Industry Council, *Briefing: Scope of Services Explained* (London: CIC, 2007).

Construction Industry Council, *Liability Briefing: Standard Forms of Consultant Collateral Warranty Compared* (London: CIC, 2007).

Construction Industry Council, *Liability Briefing: Managing Liability through Financial Caps* (London: CIC, 2008).

Construction Industry Council, *Liability Briefing: Net Contribution Clauses* (London: CIC, 2008).

Construction Industry Council, *Liability Briefing: Novation of Consultants' Appointments on Design and Build* (London: CIC, 2008).

Construction Industry Council, *Benefits of Standardised Consultancy Contracts* (London: CIC, 2011).

Construction Industry Council, *Best Practice Guide for Professional Indemnity Insurance when using Building Information Models* (London: CIC, 2013).

Davies, Gillian, *Copyright Law for Artists, Photographers and Designers* (Essential Guides), (London: A&C Black, 2009).

Dennis, Joanna, *Limits to Delegation* 22(3), Cons. Law 20 (2011).

Design Council Committee on the Current Education of Engineering Designers in Britain, *Engineering Design Education* (London: The Design Council, 1976).

Egan, Sir John, *Rethinking Construction: Report of the Construction Task Force* (London: HMSO, 1998).

Eggleston, Brian, *The NEC3 Engineering and Construction Contract – A Commentary*, 2nd edn, (London: Blackwell, 2006).

Elliot, Robert Fenwick and Jeremy Glover, *Building Contract Disputes: Practice and Precedents* (London: Sweet & Maxwell, 1997).

European Liability Insurance Organisation Schemes (ELIOS), *Liability and Insurance Regimes in the Construction Sector: National Schemes and Guidelines to Stimulate Innovation and Sustainability*, Report for the EU (Brussels, 2010).

Fleming, D., 'Design Talk: Constructing the Object in Studio Conversations', *Design Issues*, 13(2), (1998), 41–62.

Forward, Frances, *Guide to NEC3* (London: RIBA Publishing, 2011).

Furst, Stephen and Vivien Ramsey (eds), *Keating on Building Contracts* (London: Sweet & Maxwell, 2006).

Furst, Stephen and Vivien Ramsey (eds), *Keating on Construction Contracts*, 9th edn (London: Sweet & Maxwell, 2012).

Gulijk, Stephanie van, *European Architect Law: Towards a New Design* (Apeldoorn, The Netherlands: Maklu Publishers, 2009).

Hanafi, Said M., 'Contractor's Liability under the Civil Codes of Algeria, Egypt, Qatar and the UAE', *The International Construction Law Review* 25(2), (2008), 22–31.

Hatem, David J., *Design Responsibility in Integrated Project Delivery: Looking Back and Moving Forward,* January 2008, available at www.donovanhatem.com/inthenews/images/Design%20 Resp%20in%20IPD_Jan%2008.pdf.

Herbert, Alexander and Markus Eckardt, *Getting the Deal Through: Construction 2011: Germany* (London: Law Business Research Ltd, 2011).

Hillig, Jan-Bertram, *The Contractor's Quality Obligations; Different Concepts under English and German Contract Law* (CIB World Building Congress, 2007).

House of Commons, *The Private Finance Initiative (PFI); Research Paper 01/117* (London: House of Commons, 2001).

Howlett, Ashley, *Chinese Construction Law – a Guide for Foreign Companies* (CCH Asia Pte Ltd, 2009).

Hutchinson, Allan C., *Is Eating People Wrong?: Great Legal Cases and How they Shaped the World* (Cambridge: Cambridge University Press, 2010).

Jaeger, Axel-Volkmar and Götz-Sebastian Hök, *FIDIC – A Guide for Practitioners* (Berlin: Springer-Verlag, 2010).

Jones, Neil F., *The JCT Major Projects Form* (Oxford:; Wiley Blackwell, 2004).

Karibov, Kamil and Anna Strezhneva, *Getting the Deal Through: Construction 2010: Russia* (London: Law Business Research Ltd, 2010).

Latham, Sir Michael, *Constructing the Team* (London: HMSO, 1994).

Lando, Ole and Hugh Beale (eds), *The Principles of European Contract Law, Parts I and II* (Zuidpoolsingel: Kluwer Law International, 2000).

Lando, Ole, Eric Clive, André Prüm and Reinhard Zimmermann (eds), *Principles of European Contract Law, Part III* (Zuidpoolsingel: Kluwer Law International, 2003).

Law Commission, report No. 242 *Privity of Contract: Contracts for the Benefit of Third Parties.* (London: Law Commission, 1996).

Law Commission Working Paper No. 40: *Civil Liability of Vendors and Lessees for Defective Premises* (London: Law Commission, 1970).

Lupton, Sarah, 'Performance Specification: the legal implications', *The International Construction Law Review* 13(1), (1996), 28–55.

Lupton, Sarah, 'Rotherham M B C v Frank Haslam Milan: a question of policy', *The International Construction Law Review* 14(2), (1997), 234–44.

Lupton, Sarah, Stanley Cox, Hugh Clamp and Koko Udom, *Which Contract?*, 5th edn (London: RIBA Publishing, 2012).

Lupton, Sarah, *Guide to DB11* (*London*: RIBA Publishing, 2011).

Lupton, Sarah, *Guide to IC11* (London: RIBA Publishing, 2011).

Lupton, Sarah, *Guide to MW11* (London: RIBA Publishing, 2011).

Lupton, Sarah, *Guide to SB11* (London: RIBA Publishing, 2011).

Lupton, Sarah and Manos Stellakis, *Performance Specification: A Guide to its Preparation and Use* (London: RIBA Publications, 2000).

Lupton, Sarah and Manos Stellakis, *Performance Specification: Analysis of Trends and Development of a Conceptual Framework* (London: RIBA Publications, 1995).

Lupton S., 'JCT Standard Forms of Building Contract, 2005-7 Editions: Part 2 – Constructing Excellence', *The International Construction Law Review* 24(4), (2007), 466–83. ISSN 0265 1416.

Lupton S., 'Design Liability: delegation and reliance', *The International Construction Law Review* 29(3), (2012), 330–44.

Magnus, Ulrich and Hans-W. Micklitz, *Comparative Analysis of National Liability Systems for Remedying Damage Caused by Defective Consumer Services*. Report of study commissioned by the European Commission (Brussels, 2004).

Mann, Phebe, *Who owns the copyright of architectural works and designs?* Paper for the RICS 2010 COBRA conference (London: RICS, 2010).

Mathurin, Claude, *Study of Responsibilities, Guarantees and Insurance in the Construction Industry with a View to Harmonisation at Community Level: Final Report (Condensed Version)* (EC Commission, 1990).

Merkin, Robert M. and Jack Black, *Copyright and Design Law* (London: Sweet & Maxwell, 2009).

National Building Specification, *National BIM Report 2012* (London: RIBA Enterprises, 2012).

Ndekugri, Issaka and Pauline Corbett, *Supply Chain Integration in Construction by Prime Contracting: Some Research Issues*, COBRA 2004 conference proceedings (London: RICS, 2004).

Nissen, Alexander, *Designer's Duty – a time for review* (Paper 151) (London: Society of Construction Law, 2008).

Phillips, Rolland, *Plan of Work: Multi-Disciplinary Services* (London: RIBA Publishing, 2008).

Pigott, A., 'Economic loss, Transmitted warranties . . . ,' *Construction Law Journal* vol 21(2), (2005), 95.

Ramsey, Vivien, *Construction Law Handbook*, 7th edn (London: Thomas Telford, 2007).

Reid S (ed.) *Architect's Job Book*, 8th edn (London: RIBA Publishing, 2008).

RICS and Davis Langdon, *Contracts in Use; a Survey of Building Contracts in Contracts in Use During 2010* (London: RICS, 2012).

Roberts, Martin, *BIM: Legal and Contractual Implications*, slides of presentation (London: RICS, 2012).

Skeggs, Chris, 'Project partnering in the international construction industry', *International Construction Law Review*, 20(4), (2003), 456–82.

Speaight, Anthony and G. Stone (eds), *Architect's Legal Handbook: The Law for Architects*, 8th edn, (Oxford: BSP Professional Books, 2010).

Study Group on a European Civil Code and the Research Group on EC Private Law (Acquis Group), *Principles, Definitions and Model Rules of European Private Law, Draft Common Frame of Reference (DCFR)* Outline Edition (Munich: Sellier European Law Publishers GmbH, 2009).

Sweet, Justin and Marc M. Schneier, *Legal Aspects of Architecture, Engineering and the Construction Process* (Stamford: Cengage Learning, 2009).

van Gulijk, Stephanie, *European Architect Law: Towards a New Design* (Apeldoorn, The Netherlands: Maklu Publishers, 2009).

von Bar, Christian and Ulrich Drobnig, *Study on Property Law and Non-contractual Liability Law as They Relate to Contract Law* (Munich: Sellier European Law Publishers GmbH, 2004).

von Bar, Christian, E. Clive and H. Schulte-Nölke (eds), *Principles, Definitions and Model Rules of European Private Law. Draft Common Frame of Reference (DCFR). Interim Outline Edition* (Munich: Sellier, 2008).

Zhu Hongliang, Hu Xiangzhen and Wang Ying, 'China's Construction Regulatory Systems', *Building Research & Information*, 29(4), (2001), 265–9.

Cases and Legislation

Cornes and Lupton's Design Liability in the Construction Industry, Fifth Edition. Sarah Lupton.
© 2013 Sarah Lupton and DL Cornes. Published 2013 by Blackwell Publishing Ltd.

LEGISLATION

Australia
Architects Acts
Competition and Consumer Act 2010
Corporations Act 2001

Belgium
Civil Code

EU
Common European Sales Law
Consumer Rights Directive (2011/83/EU)
Certain Legal Aspects of Information Society Services, in particular electronic commerce Directive (2000/31/EC)
Combating Late Payment in Commercial Transactions Directive (2011/7/EU)
Unfair Terms in Consumer Contracts Directive (93/13/EEC)
Professional Qualifications Directive (2005/36/EC)
Public Procurement Directive (2004/18/EC)

France
Civil Code
Law No. 77-2 of 3 January 1977

Germany
Civil Code

Italy
Civil Code
Law No 210 (2004)
'Merloni law' (*Legge Merloni*, Law No. 109 of 11 February 1994)

The Netherlands
Civil Code

PRC/China
Contract Law 1999
Construction Law 1997
Ordinance of Registered Architect of the PRC 1995
Tendering Law 1999

Russia

On Architectural Activity in the Russian Federation' No. 169-FZ of 17 Nove,ber 1995

Russian Town-Planning Code and Certain Legislative Acts of the Russian Federation (Federal Law No. 148-FZ dated 22 July 2008).

UK

Architects Act 1997 1.3.1.1

Building Act 1984 5.2

Building Regulations 2010 5.2

Civil Liability (Contribution) Act 1978 10.3.12, 11.3.2, 12.1.2

Civil Procedure Rules 1995 6.2

Construction (Design and Management) Regulations 1994 5.3.1

Construction (Design and Management) Regulations 2007 5.3.1

Construction (Health, Safety and Welfare) Regulations 1996 5.3.1

Contracts (Rights of Third Parties) Act 1999 2.4.1

Copyright, Designs and Patents Act 1988 5.4.1

Copyright and Rights in Performance Regulations 1995 5.4.1

Defective Premises Act 1972 5.1

Health and Safety at Work etc. Act 1974 5.3

Housing Act 1985 5.1

Housing Grants, Construction and Regeneration Act 1996 2.2.3.2, 14.1.7

Latent Damage Act 1986 12.1.1

Law of Property Act 1925 2.5

Law Reform (Contributory Negligence) Act 1945 11.3.1

Law Reform (Miscellaneous Provisions) Act 1934 12.1.3

Limitation Act 1980 Chapter 12

Local Democracy, Economic Development and Construction Act 2009 2.2.3.2

Marine Insurance Act 1906 16.2.3

Sale of Goods Act 1979 2.2.3.1, 2.3.1

Sale and Supply of Goods Act 1994 2.2.3

Supply of Goods and Services Act 1982 2.2.3.2, 2.3.1

Third Parties (Rights Against Insurers) Act 1930 16.2.11

Third Parties (Rights Against Insurers) Act 2010 16.2.11

Unfair Contract Terms Act 1977 2.3.1

Unfair Terms in Consumer Contracts Regulations 1999 2.3.2

United Arab Emirates

Federal law No. 3 of 1987, Penal Code

USA

Uniform Commercial Code (UCC)

Restatement (Second) of Torts Act 1977

Index

Cornes and Lupton's Design Liability in the Construction Industry, Fifth Edition. Sarah Lupton.
© 2013 Sarah Lupton and DL Cornes. Published 2013 by Blackwell Publishing Ltd.